The 11th Michigan Volunteer
Infantry in the Civil War

The 11th Michigan Volunteer Infantry in the Civil War

A History and Roster

Eric R. Faust

McFarland & Company, Inc., Publishers
Jefferson, North Carolina

LIBRARY OF CONGRESS CATALOGUING-IN-PUBLICATION DATA [new form]

Names: Faust, Eric R., 1971– author.
Title: The 11th Michigan Volunteer Infantry in the Civil War :
a history and roster / Eric R. Faust.
Description: Jefferson, North Carolina : McFarland & Company, Inc.,
Publishers, 2016. | Includes bibliographical references and index.
Identifiers: LCCN 2015039569| ISBN 9781476663166
(softcover : acid free paper) | ISBN 9781476622828 (ebook)
Subjects: LCSH: United States. Army. Michigan Infantry Regiment, 11th
(1861–1864) | United States—History—Civil War, 1861–1865—Regimental
histories. | Michigan—History—Civil War, 1861–1865—Regimental histories. |
United States—History—Civil War, 1861–1865—Campaigns.
Classification: LCC E514.5 11th .F38 2016 | DDC 973.7/474—dc23
LC record available at http://lccn.loc.gov/2015039569

BRITISH LIBRARY CATALOGUING DATA ARE AVAILABLE

© 2016 Eric R. Faust. All rights reserved

*No part of this book may be reproduced or transmitted in any form
or by any means, electronic or mechanical, including photocopying
or recording, or by any information storage and retrieval system,
without permission in writing from the publisher.*

Front cover *inset:* one of the regiment's silk national flags, with battle
honors (courtesy and copyright, Michigan Capitol Committee
and photographer Peter Glendinning); Linus T. Squire (far right)
and his comrades pose on Lookout Mountain sometime after the
Battle of Missionary Ridge (Mollus Mass Civil War Collection, United
States Army Heritage and Education Center, Military History Institute)

Printed in the United States of America

*McFarland & Company, Inc., Publishers
Box 611, Jefferson, North Carolina 28640
www.mcfarlandpub.com*

For

James Wood King
11th Michigan Volunteer Infantry

Darius Ambrose Babcock
6th Michigan Heavy Artillery

Arthur Leo Brazee
48th Wisconsin Volunteer Infantry

all of whom returned from the war disabled.

Acknowledgments

A work such as this can hardly get off the ground but for innumerable acts of kindness and dedication from archivists and librarians. My heartfelt thanks go in particular to Sharon Carlson at Western Michigan University Archives and Regional History Collections, and to Karen Jania of the Bentley Historical Library. The staffs at the Archives of Michigan, Library of Michigan, ABC Library, Zimmerman Library, Clarke Historical Library, University of Minnesota Archives, U.S. Army Military History Institute, and William L. Clements Library all earned my gratitude as well.

James Ogden at Chickamauga and Chattanooga National Military Park kindly lent me precious minutes from a very busy day, shared his immense knowledge, and let me bounce an idea or two off him. (For an encore, he gave me a full copy of the diary of John Bloom.) Anyone who has enjoyed visiting that amazing, monument-dotted wonder of a national park site has benefited from Jim's enthusiasm and energy.

I am again indebted to Hal Jespersen for his incomparable cartography. Four of the maps (the three theater maps, plus the map of Missionary Ridge) are reproduced here with permission, having appeared in my previous book *Conspicuous Gallantry: The Civil War and Reconstruction Letters of James W. King, 11th Michigan Volunteer Infantry* (Kent State University Press, 2015). My deepest gratitude goes to Carol Heller and Will Underwood. The troop positions on the balance of the tactical maps, with the exception of Davis's Crossroads, are based on maps from the cited sources authored by Peter Cozzens, Jim Lewis, David A. Powell, and Mark W. Johnson.

Much to the benefit of this book, researcher Vonnie Zullo reprised her role as my eyes and ears at the National Archives.

Paula Metzner of Kalamazoo Valley Museum, who is no longer with us, was gracious and accommodating in scanning a small mountain of regimental reunion documents. I crossed paths with Paula only briefly in this world, but found her to be as kind as she was enthusiastic. Without her efforts, the epilogue to this book would have amounted to a mere shadow of what it became.

My friends and family again supported me in uncounted ways, big and small, just as they always have. My wife Sandra, and my children Adrian and Nina, serve as perpetual sources of inspiration.

Table of Contents

Acknowledgments	vi
Preface	1
1. "Stars and stripes unfurled": April–November 1861	5
2. "An enemy to be feared": November 1861–April 1862	26
3. "Covered in dust instead of glory": April–December 1862	44
4. "Two huge serpents": December 1862–January 1863	66
5. "Perfectly careless": January–September 1863	78
6. "We fought like tigers": September 1863	96
7. "The enemy fled like a flock of sheep": September 1863–May 1864	113
8. "Sick and tired of fighting": May–October 1864	132
Epilogue	152
Appendix A: A POW Poem	159
Appendix B: The 11th Michigan by the Numbers	160
Appendix C: Unit Roster	164
Chapter Notes	219
Bibliography	233
Index	237

Many people came to the train to welcome home the Old Eleventh. It had left the state three years before with eleven hundred and forty men, and now it was returning with less than three hundred. Many of those who came to the train had seen the regiment drill before it went to the front, preparing for the work that was before it. They remembered that splendid line of eleven hundred and forty men, reaching nearly across the fair-ground; and when they saw less than three hundred men get off the train, some of them asked, "Where are the rest of them?" O, what a question for those men to answer! Where are the rest of them? Ask Stone River's grassy banks, ask Chickamauga's winding stream, ask the slopes of Mission Ridge, ask woods and fields where stood the tented hospital, ask battle fields on hills and plains from Chattanooga to Atlanta, and they give answer, "They rest with us." Forever let them be treasured in the memory of that country for which they gave their lives.

—Private John Florin Downey

Preface

The 11th Michigan Volunteer Infantry was both an extraordinary and a quintessential unit of the Union army. Extraordinary in terms of its under-studied battle record, this regiment has not yet received its due from historians. Yet, outside of those hair-raising moments of combat, the 11th Michigan in many ways typified Federal infantry units as a whole. Its soldiers enlisted primarily to preserve the Union, not to eradicate slavery. They marched off to war confident of a lightning-quick victory, grossly underestimating the threat posed by the Confederacy. They learned to fear disease more than bullets. They struggled at times to respect the rights of enemy civilians. And in terms of morality, their ranks reflected the society from which they came, running the gamut from men who embodied the ideals of Victorian manhood, to the basest of drunkards, cowards, and thieves.

The center of a Civil War infantryman's world was his regiment. Historian Allen C. Guelzo, in enumerating his essential primary sources for *Gettysburg: The Last Invasion*, included "that most peculiar of American literary genres, the regimental history," specifically referring to such works penned by the soldiers themselves.[1] Unfortunately, no such book was authored by the veterans of the 11th Michigan. To be sure, the unit's survivors wrote and spoke publicly about their accomplishments, but none ever prepared an in-depth history of the regiment. In December 1879, Brevet Major General William Lewis Stoughton, the former, beloved colonel of this Wolverine regiment, remarked in a letter that "there are several items in the history of the 11th that ought to be stated with more energy perhaps than has been done before." The recipient of that correspondence, Stoughton's one-time quartermaster sergeant James W. King, was by far the most prolific historian among the unit's survivors. He did his utmost to expound the regiment's virtues and achievements in speeches, as well as in articles he authored for numerous periodicals throughout his lifetime. But with King's passing in 1903, the 11th regiment sank into obscurity. Decades later, others took up their pens to present the unit's history. First, Wayne C. Mann gave the regiment a solid treatment in his 1963 Master's thesis for Western Michigan University. But Mann's study followed these Michiganders' exploits only through the end of their first battle at Stones River. Mann's standard was later taken up by Leland W.

Thornton, who built upon his predecessor's efforts and produced the regiment's first book-length history, *When Gallantry Was Commonplace*, published in 1991.

The 11th Michigan perhaps no longer qualified as obscure, yet the gallant Stoughton's complaint that certain aspects of the regiment's history should be "stated with more energy" still rang true. *When Gallantry Was Commonplace* covered the full three-year service of the regiment, but the embryonic state of Western Theater scholarship at that time precluded the level of detail essential to judge the unit's impact in battle, and that volume omitted maps, an indispensable tool in communicating an active military unit's history. Stoughton, in his aforementioned correspondence, touched upon several acts of great valor committed by his men, but until recently, it was impossible to do these events justice. In this book, the identities and fates of the 11th Michigan's battlefield opponents, immersed in the tactical context of each battle, provide the means to evaluate the unit's prowess and impact on the course of each engagement. For the first time, we fully experience the 11th Michigan's first bloody stand, fielding raw troops against Confederate veterans in the maelstrom at Stones River. Its soldiers' finest hour at Chickamauga, where they executed three successful bayonet charges against superior numbers—and nabbed a Confederate general—is done justice at last, as is the compelling evidence behind their claim to have been the last to leave that greatest battlefield of the war out west. Their astoundingly forgotten role in routing Alexander P. Stewart's division from the summit of Missionary Ridge is asserted for the first time in a modern history. Many additional details are uncovered relating to the regiment's less famous engagements as well, particularly regarding the battles at Davis's Crossroads and Utoy Creek, and the capture of Ferguson's Battery in the aftermath of Missionary Ridge.

Numerous new contributions are made here regarding the regiment's noncombat history as well. Counted among these stories is the attempted impressment into slavery of free black Michigander Tom Steward, who tagged along to Kentucky with the regiment. The 11th Michigan's rough handling of civilians in Kentucky, and the lasting impact of their sacking of Gallatin, Tennessee, is discussed. Accusations of negligence by the regiment's medical staff are brought to light. The unit's roles in separate incidents that endangered each of the 1864 election's vice presidential candidates—not to mention the nation's chief peace advocate—are related in detail (according to the regiment's own lieutenant colonel, the 11th Michigan had to be restrained from murdering George H. Pendleton and Clement L. Vallandigham, yet somehow this anecdote has never made it into any book). Untold accounts of individual soldiers' fates, such as the tragedy of the Seekell family, place the 11th's experience in a more personal context, as do additional accounts of the Michiganders' interactions with Confederate civilians. William Stoughton's involvement in the recruiting of white officers for the U.S. Colored Troops, and Samuel Chadwick's likely meddling in the appointment of Lieutenant Colonel Eldridge, are revealed as well, to name just a few highlights. The regiment's postwar legacy, and the remarkable peacetime biographies of its more prominent members, round out the novel elements of this narrative.

Lastly, the 11th Michigan's narrative is supported here with the elements of a thorough unit history that were omitted from the previous published history: strategic and tactical maps, photographs, statistical analysis, and a full unit roster. The roster is heavily corrected from one published circa 1905, and was generated from a custom-built database into which every soldier's relevant service details were entered. That database, in turn, was queried to provide a statistical analysis of the 11th Michigan, presented here in an appendix for the first time.

More than 1,300 men ultimately joined the 11th Michigan Volunteer Infantry. They put their lives on the line with one unwavering goal: to preserve the Union.

CHAPTER 1

"Stars and stripes unfurled"
April–November 1861

The people of the Great Lakes State were electrified and transfixed by the momentous news coming out of South Carolina. The Confederates had bombarded Fort Sumter; war was thrust upon the Union. The population of Michigan was overcome with indignation at the treason committed by their Southern cousins. On April 16, 1861, telegraph wires delivered to the city of Three Rivers in St. Joseph County the president's call for 75,000 volunteers to put down "combinations too powerful to be suppressed by the ordinary course of judicial proceedings, or by the powers vested in the marshals by law."

A meeting of the citizens of Three Rivers was convened the next evening, and the riled, patriotic crowd adopted two resolutions:

> Whereas, A part of this Union is in a state of open rebellion against our National Government and defy its authority; therefore
> *Resolved*, That we, the citizens of Three Rivers, forgetting all differences of party, and uniting as one body of Union-loving men, will stand by the Administration in its efforts to enforce the laws and preserve the integrity of the Union; and for this purpose we pledge our lives, our fortunes, and our sacred honor.
> *Resolved*, That we will exert ourselves to the utmost in immediately collecting volunteers for the defense of the government and the support of her laws.[1]

Such calls for action, echoing throughout southern Michigan, represented the first step in the conception of the 11th Michigan Volunteer Infantry.

St. Joseph County, home to 20,000 people, had received its first wave of settlers throughout the 1830s—so recently that many of the county's earliest pioneers were still alive and well. Like Michigan as a whole, the county was staunchly Republican, having delivered almost 59 percent of its 1860 vote to Abraham Lincoln. The State of Michigan was but twenty-four years old, and its entire population amounted to less than three-quarters of a million people. The state's militia—1,200 men, badly equipped and worse trained—were dismissed by their own adjutant general as "a burlesque on the military profession." To top it off, the state treasury was broke. It remained to be seen whether Governor Austin Blair had the wherewithal to answer

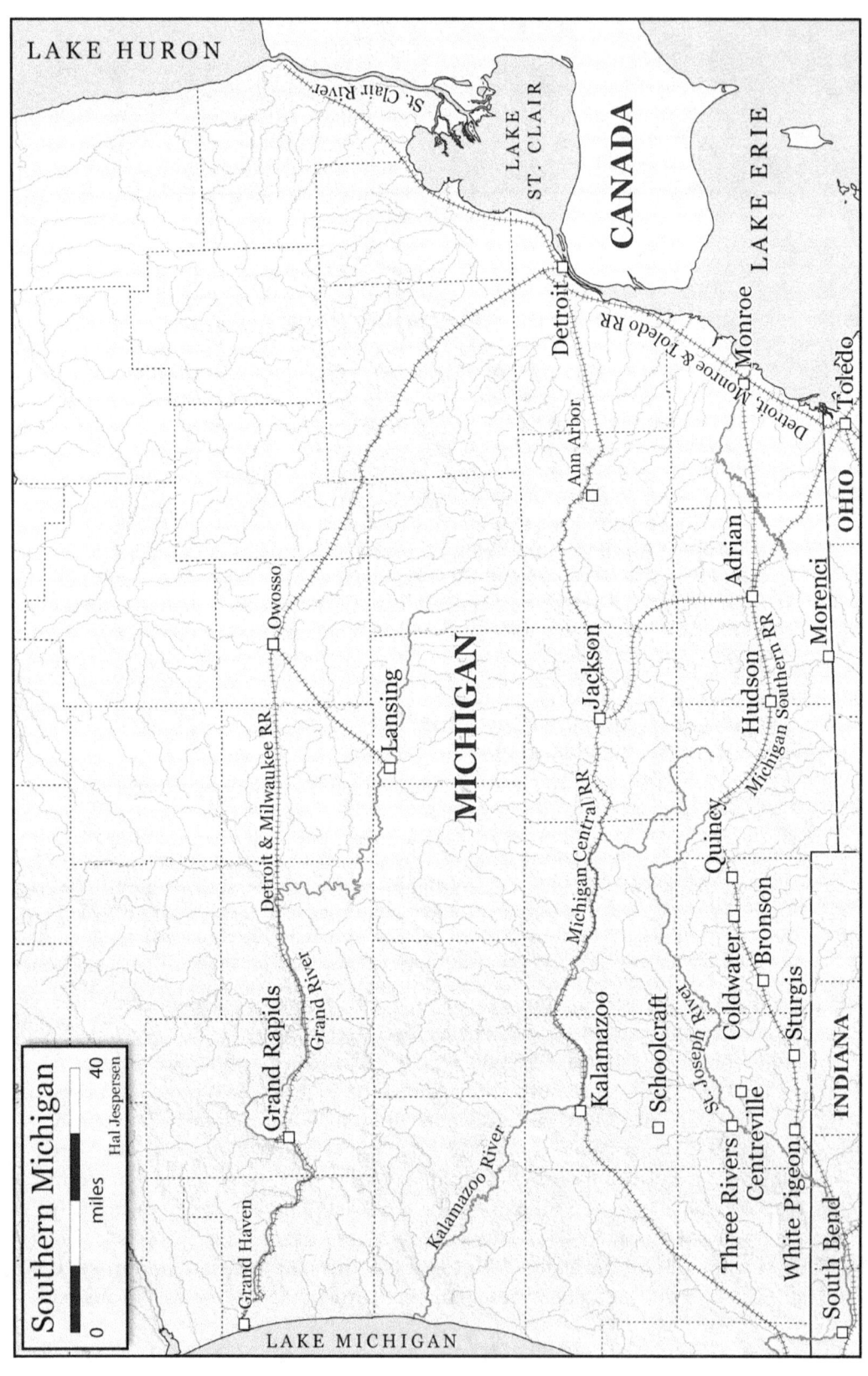

President Lincoln's call for troops at all, let alone to meet the unprecedented emergency about to engulf the Union. Nonetheless, the citizens of both St. Joseph County and the state, undeterred by their modest means, were determined to do their part in putting down the rebellion.[2]

In Three Rivers, forty-three-year-old attorney Samuel Chadwick was the first to act. Chadwick, a former lieutenant of the 1st Michigan Volunteers during the Mexican War, had served as captain of the Three Rivers Wide Awakes (the local branch of a national, quasi-military Republican organization). He promptly hung a recruiting flag outside his office and announced in the local papers his intention to raise a company of volunteers. "Desirous that St. Joseph County shall not be behind her sister counties in her patriotism and devotion to our common country," he declared, "all those persons who are willing to enroll themselves for service, are requested to report their names to me *immediately*. Having marched against the enemy in Mexico, I am now ready to face traitors and rebels on our own soil." Adventure-seeking young patriots flocked to his flag. Just two days after receiving the call for troops, Chadwick marshaled forty eager enlistees. The lawyer-turned-recruiter penned a letter to Governor Blair, boasting that he would command a full company of soldiers in just two more days. When the politician did not reply straightaway, Chadwick followed up with the state's adjutant general, John Robertson. "My Mexican War feeling is up," Chadwick exclaimed. "My men are anxious."[3]

The governor and adjutant general were fairly drowning in offers of troops. Michigan had no problem meeting her quota of a single three-month regiment; the state's dilemma lay rather in choosing who would go, and who would be left behind. Many feared peace would return before they could get into the fight. Robertson broke the news to Samuel Chadwick that Michigan's troop quota was already fulfilled: the attorney had raised his company quickly, but an abundance of pre-existing militia units clambered to muster at once. Things moved fast for Chadwick then. Another company under recruitment, the Union Guard from Constantine, was called into service as soon as authorization was granted to raise a second Michigan regiment. Chadwick was almost simultaneously elected as an assessor of Three Rivers, running on the Union ticket, but his destiny lay elsewhere. He threw in the towel, encouraging his militiamen to go with the troops from Constantine (almost thirty of them did so), and sought a position in Washington with the War Department. While awaiting a reply from the capital, he served as chairman at a Union rally in Centreville, but then the anticipated telegraph came, beckoning him to Washington, D.C. Away he went to accept a clerkship under Secretary of War Simon Cameron.[4]

One of the long-established militia units, the Peninsular Guards, served under thirty-four-year-old New York native William Lewis Stoughton, a resident of Sturgis, St. Joseph County. Stoughton, a loyal Republican who President Lincoln appointed U.S. district attorney for Michigan, offered his company's services to Adjutant General Robertson on April 25. Stoughton's letter did not lack for honesty. "Most of the men are new recruits and are of course not drilled.... The only arms we have are 40 musketoons which are entirely unfit for active service." Stoughton, like Chadwick, was initially passed over, but subsequent to an additional federal call on May 3 for 42,000 three-year volunteers—which obligated Robertson to raise three more infantry regiments—the Peninsular Guards were accepted into the 4th Michigan Volunteer Infantry. On May 27 the company was ordered to its regimental rendezvous point at Adrian, Michigan. Stoughton tagged along to watch his men muster in and rose to the occasion by delivering a speech, but he declined to enter the service himself for the time being, preferring instead to continue serving the president as district attorney.[5]

With additional regiments sanctioned, countless people in southern Michigan enthusiastically joined the recruiting frenzy. Melvin Mudge, a twenty-seven-year-old schoolteacher from Quincy, Branch County, informed Robertson on June 12 that his company, the Quincy Rifles, was nearly filled out. "A better set of men never was brought together," Mudge declared, "tough hardy farmers all of them." He visited the governor's office about three weeks later and was assured that his unit would be mustered in as soon as circumstances allowed. On July 23, two days after the crushing Union defeat at Bull Run, Mudge implored Robertson, "Some of our brothers and neighbors of this place were in the late battle and we must avenge their deaths." But the adjutant general remained silent, and so Mudge found himself penning Robertson again on July 29—by which time Lincoln had authorized 500,000 troops—and this time Mudge struck a sour note. "We think there will not be much chance for us from the fact that we have no Ex Governor or Congressman ... to interceed for us."[6]

Sylvester B. Smith's recruiting efforts in Morenci, Lenawee County, mirrored Mudge's in both timeframe and frustration level. Smith, at twenty-eight years of age, had served the township of Seneca as clerk and justice of the peace. He first offered his Morenci Guards, without success, to Robertson on June 3. On the eighteenth Smith wrote again, expressing hope that his company might help fill out the 7th Michigan Infantry. Six days later Smith heard that the 7th was full, and he danced a fine line with decorum in addressing the adjutant general. His company, he insisted, "certainly made their wishes known earlier than some other companies that now have a place assigned them in some of the Regiments.... If there is ever an 8th Regt formed we shall certainly expect to be 'counted in.'" He then softened the blow by offering the services of a local martial band. "There are but few better in

William Lewis Stoughton, a district attorney and rising star in the Republican party, led the regiment at Stones River and Chickamauga, and commanded its brigade at Missionary Ridge. He lost a leg to amputation at the July 4, 1864, Battle of Ruff's Station. Worshipped by his men, he was brevetted major general, and went on to represent Michigan in Congress after the war (Gracie, *The Truth About Chickamauga*).

the country," he proclaimed. "They are uniformed in good style, Blue Broad Cloth frock coats." Smith followed up by forwarding his company muster roll to Robertson on July 6, and on July 31 mailed a petition to the governor signed by Lenawee County residents, calling for the Morenci Guards' muster into the 8th Michigan Infantry. But the wait continued.[7]

David Oakes Jr., thirty-one-year-old treasurer of St. Joseph County, contacted the adjutant general in the immediate aftermath of Fort Sumter to inquire about raising a company in Centreville. He requested books on military tactics, and by May 2 was forming the Centreville Home Guards. From the start, Oakes was highly visible in the raising of troops. He accompanied Stoughton to Adrian, Michigan, to witness the mustering of the Sturgis company into the 4th Michigan, and a reporter declared that "a generous supply of apples was sent through the ranks by David Oakes, Jr., who for the past few days has been here sharing our soldier's blankets and our soldier's fare, and in various ways making himself a favorite with the boys." Oakes then returned to Centreville, where the townsfolk still maintained a sense of humor about the war, having suffered no casualties yet. Overnight, June 12–13, someone hung Confederate president Jefferson Davis in effigy. Oakes set his coat aside at some point during the following day, and was mortified soon after to discover that it had been commandeered for the cause of clothing Davis's likeness. Oakes's unit, originally designated as home guards, was probably not intended to be anything more than militia at the outset. But on July 30 he spoke at a Union meeting in Three Rivers and offered to form, drill, and lead a volunteer infantry company, and one day later he contacted Robertson to inform him that he had fifty-four men enrolled, with officers already elected, in the St. Joseph County Guard—probably he had simply rechristened his home guard for the occasion. Oakes suggested that he could bring his company's complement up to 100 men within six to ten days. He and his recruits hoped to secure entry into one of the three-year regiments, but they expressed willingness to organize as militia if need be. County Treasurer Oakes appeared at another rally the next day in Constantine, where the crowd was forcibly reminded that the public response to the war was not unanimous: it was announced that a few contrarian locals, emboldened by Bull Run, were outspoken in defense of secession. The *Three Rivers Reporter* staff retaliated in ink with open threats, declaring the Northern secessionists "a dishonor to society ... whose

Sylvester B. Smith, former justice of the peace for Seneca, raised Company F and was soon promoted to major. A bullet wound to the face at Stones River likely prevented him from eventually rising to command of the regiment. Smith served as chairman of Lenawee County's Republican committee after the war (courtesy Archives of Michigan).

language will no longer be tolerated." "Gentlemen," the editorial continued, "you don't seem to understand that we are in the whirl of a revolution when a man's head, especially if he harbor in it your demons of dissolution, is no more thought of than a row of pins."[8]

David Oakes, Jr., treasurer of St. Joseph County, was popular with his peers, and recruited and led Company A. He survived the concussion of a shell at Stones River, only to succumb to typhoid less than one month later (courtesy family of Esther Thompson Hull).

The recent federal authorization for half a million troops made it technically possible to appease everyone clamoring to get into the army, but logistics at the state level constituted a new bottleneck. Robertson in fact was mustering soldiers as quickly as possible with limited resources. Ironically enough, in the cases of Stoughton (who now wished to join the army after all), Mudge, Smith, and Oakes, among others, it was Samuel Chadwick—who had thrown up his hands and gone off to Washington—who succeeded in ensuring their admission into the Union army.

In the panicky aftermath of Bull Run, the federal government was desperate for troops to defend the capital, and Chadwick's efforts were diverted to help facilitate the muster of new regiments into service. He enjoyed his time in Washington, reporting the sights and sounds of the nation's capital in wartime via weekly letters to the *Reporter*. Since the states couldn't act fast enough, permission had been granted in many cases for units to be raised independent of the state governments. A fellow Three Rivers man, Dr. Sydney L. Herrick—who had been elected trustee on the same Union ticket graced with Chadwick's name—journeyed to Washington seeking assignment as a military physician about this time, and upon arrival he alerted Chadwick to the desire of William J. May to raise a regiment. May, a thirty-eight-year-old Pennsylvania native, now a prominent resident of White Pigeon in St. Joseph County, had attained popularity as the past proprietor of the White Pigeon Railroad Dining Hall. Like Stoughton, May offered modest experience as a leader of militia. Chadwick considered May capable, and exerted his influence in the man's favor. May soon received a telegraph from the secretary of war, directing him to proceed with raising a regiment from St. Joseph County. Recruiting began at once, and May's Independent Regiment—the future 11th Michigan Volunteer Infantry—was born.[9]

The raising of men for May's regiment proceeded at several recruiting offices, and maintained a brisk pace throughout August. One such office operated out of Brown's Hotel in Constantine; another at the railroad depot in White Pigeon. Melvin Mudge, Sylvester Smith, and David Oakes all offered their existing companies to bolster May's ranks. More than 500 men were enrolled by August 14. Samuel Chadwick—who rushed back from Washington by August 17 to help recruit—and William Stoughton, having already forfeited their own troops previously, expressed their desires to obtain officers' commissions.[10] The *Three Rivers Reporter* did its part to encourage potential enlistees:

> There are a number of important considerations tending to induce volunteers from this section to join the Three Rivers company Col. May's regiment. They will be in the ranks with those they are best acquainted with; have surgical and medical attendants whose reputations are well established in their own neighborhood, and officers whom they have known for years; while the facility with which communications may be had to and from friends at home will be reliable and direct. No better opportunity to enlist has yet been offered.[11]

Ultimately, more than sixty percent of the regiment's enlistees would hail from St. Joseph County, although seven of May's ten companies based their recruiting efforts outside its borders. "The feeling throughout the county," declared the *Three Rivers Western Chronicle*, "is decidedly in favor of having Col. May's regiment at the disposition of the War Department in as short a time as possible. Meetings are being held all over the county." One such rally took place in Parkville on the nineteenth. Captain Oakes and several members of his St. Joseph County Guards attended; martial music filled the air, and several men were enticed to enroll.[12]

In almost every case, in accordance with custom, the primary figure in each company's creation would be elected its captain. These men came from all different walks of life, and each experienced a recruiting struggle all his own.

Calvin C. Hood, a twenty-eight-year-old merchant from Sturgis, was forming the Sturgis Light Guards by mid–August. Hood was raised in Adrian, Michigan, and had spent the early 1850s trading in Indian goods and furs; on one occasion, all in the name of business, he exhibited his determined spirit by undertaking a 300-mile roundtrip through snow in the dead of winter. Hood's recruits advertised their presence by marching through town and congregating at their recruiting office. One prospective private, twenty-three-year-old Ira Gillaspie, stopped by and asked about the rumored enlistment bonus of $100 and 160 acres of land. Hood's subordinate and brother-in-law, Henry Platt, answered in the affirmative, and thus the company added another soldier to its ranks.[13]

Benjamin Grove Bennett, past editor of the pro-democrat *Western Chronicle*, and former mail agent of the Michigan Southern Railroad, was assembling the Bronson (Branch County) Guards. Bennett had enlisted in his hometown Burr Oak Guards at the outset of the war, and was among the small fraction of willing and able recruits who found their way into the 1st Michigan Infantry in May and rushed off to defend the nation's capital. By mid–June, Bennett was serving as the 1st Michigan's correspondent for his old newspaper back home. As orderly sergeant of Company G, Bennett was in the thick of the fight at Bull Run, where a cannonball struck his musket, inflicting a slight bruise to his arm. As a veteran of the war's first major engagement and a prominent local, Bennett was in a perfect position to attract recruits, and he got to work almost as soon as his three-month enlistment expired. "Everybody knows 'Grove,'" said the *Chronicle*, "and hence it is useless for us to say anything in his favor."[14]

Three Rivers, not to be outdone, enthusiastically swelled the ranks of Henry N. Spencer's Three Rivers Light Guard. Spencer, a forty-three-year-old carpenter, was a past justice of the peace, present sexton of Oakdale Cemetery, and superintendent of the Three Rivers Presbyterian Sunday School. His guard mustered and elected its officers in Three Rivers on August 31, and departed town on September 9 to join May's regiment, marching to the airs of the Three Rivers Brass Band. The company was seen off at the railroad depot by a large crowd.[15]

The initial driving force behind the raising of the Rifle Rangers in Schoolcraft, Kalamazoo County, was Thomas H. Briggs, a native of Illinois only twenty-two years of age. By July 11 Briggs announced that he was raising "a well officered and properly drilled company" with the intent of mustering into a state regiment. Before the month was over, those hopes were dashed by the rapid filling of another regiment's ranks, but Briggs's men were undaunted and elected officers. Although recruiting was based primarily out of Kalamazoo County, more than half the unit would consist of St. Joseph County residents. Briggs stepped aside sometime in late September to concede the captaincy to Charles Moase, a twenty-seven-year-old native of England who had immigrated in 1845. Moase had fought at Bull Run as Benjamin Bennett's superior officer, second lieutenant of Company G. After returning from that whirlwind three-month enlistment, Moase operated a recruiting office for May's regiment at the rail depot in White Pigeon, and the *Chronicle* declared that he would "doubtless get a full company."[16] Since no controversy seems to have ensued over Moase's captaincy, it would seem that Briggs voluntarily deferred to his older and more martially experienced comrade.

The Coldwater (Branch County) Tigers were raised by John L. Hackstaff, a native New Yorker and father to seven children. At age forty-one, Hackstaff, an experienced newspaperman, was co-publisher of the *Coldwater Democratic Union.* His Tigers were mostly Branch County residents.[17]

Mexican War veteran Nelson Chamberlain of Monroe, Monroe County, and his Chandler Guards were latecomers to the regiment, and were the most geographically removed from St. Joseph County. Chamberlain, a thirty-seven-year-old marble cutter originally from Vermont, requested muster rolls on September 23. Eight days later, he wrote again to Robertson to announce that he had between seventy and eighty men lined up, hoped to fill his company within a week, and intended to report to Detroit to muster in. He initially evidenced no desire to join any particular regiment, but four days later he took matters into his owns hands and declared, "I have joined Col. May's regiment."[18]

Master builder William W. Phillips, a thirty-five-year-old New York native and resident of Adrian, Lenawee County—also located a good distance across the state—raised the Lenawee Lions. Phillips was at White Pigeon by September 23 with sixty-four recruits.[19]

In terms of motivation, the 11th Michigan's enlistees seem to have been typical of the Union volunteers of 1861. Slavery had served as kindling for the outbreak of the war, but the institution of bondage alone did not provoke many men to join the army. The surviving writings of May's recruits point instead to a shared, unwavering belief in the necessity of preserving the Union. But it proved far easier for the new soldiers to offer their lives in the name of patriotism than it was for their loved ones at home to accept that decision. Nineteen-year-old James Wood King of Fabius Township, an enlistee in Oakes's company, replied to his sweetheart, who pleaded with him to seek a discharge for his own safety, "You said you did not wish me to let money tempt me. I hope you did not have any such thought.... While your happiness is as dear to me as life, duty prompts me to go. My country first, home and friends next. Jenny, what would friends be to me if I had no country? I hope after this when you think of me, you will remember me as one who is doing his duty." King proclaimed that the Union war effort was "one of the noblest causes that mankind were ever engaged in." Ira Gillaspie, on the other hand, considered money a legitimate part of the equation. But when it came time to persuade his distraught wife of the necessity for him to enlist, he asserted a more honorable inspiration. "I explained to her the state of our country that it is in need of all true patriots to sustain her government." His spouse remained unconvinced, and although Gillapsie's parents agreed with him on principle, they preferred for that principle to be applied to other men, not to their son. Seventeen-year-old Borden Mills Hicks, a member of the Three Rivers Light Guard, offered either the most humorous or the most honest account when he shared his motivations. "My heart was on fire with a desire and longing to be a soldier. All I wanted was a chance to don a uniform, to march and to fight, to do some heroic deed and to come back home and be admired by the girls, as a Hero."[20]

The enlistees and officers alike were instant heroes in their communities. The citizens of Three Rivers provided free room and board to their company, the Three Rivers Light Guard. They gifted a fine saddle to Chadwick, and a sword to Captain Spencer. Sturgis bestowed another blade upon Captain Hood. The St. Joseph County Guard enjoyed gifts of towels and pillowcases from the residents of Centreville and the surrounding communities, and the regiment received 1,001 pin cushions from the women of La Porte, Indiana. Each company, upon departure for the regimental rendezvous, was seen off by an enthusiastic crowd. Contracts were awarded to feed and house the regiment; all that was needed now was to gather the men at their lodging, a 600-foot-long car-house at the White Pigeon rail depot. Seven of May's companies rendezvoused there by September 11. The Michigan Southern Railroad donated its grounds and facilities to the cause, and Colonel May's former dining hall, reestablished under new ownership, was tasked with nourishing the regiment.[21] The *Reporter* boasted of May's fledgling unit:

> The moral and military bearing of its officers, and the quality of the men who have been enlisted, is already looked upon with just hopes, that it is to be the crowning military organization of the state in this mighty struggle.
>
> The few difficulties it has encountered in the process in organization, have served to purge the companies of improper material, so that every man from private up, feels as though his body is already on the sacred altar of his country; and the general expression of every private is, *"I will never return home, except it is to a home over which my country's laws and my government's rights are reestablished."*
>
> Nearly all of those in command have reluctantly left positions of employment; public offices & c., though gladly in view of the cause, and sworn to lead their men to victory.[22]

The same paper was equally effusive about Colonel May, stating that he "has always been known as a military man. He is personally known or familiarly acquainted with every one in the Regiment; and by his habitual friendly bearing and deliberate movements commands the confidence of both officers and soldiers, and will not command his men but with wisdom and discretion."[23]

The job of mustering the volunteers fell to regular army officers. Initially this task fell to Major Goodwin, who towered over the new recruits at the height of six feet seven inches. Goodwin mustered Oakes's company at Centreville on August 24 before proceeding to the encampment at White Pigeon, which was named in his honor. Captain Harvey Tilden, also of the regular army—16th U.S. Infantry—soon arrived to relieve Goodwin, and the facilities

James Wood King, the son of an antislavery man, started out as just another face in the ranks, but his affable demeanor and innate talent for soldiering brought popularity as well as promotions. King earned a nomination for the Medal of Honor at Missionary Ridge, where he fought outside his line of duty and played a key role in the rout of Alexander P. Stewart's division. After the war, he tried raising cotton in the South and butted heads with the Ku Klux Klan. He returned to Michigan and eventually became chief editor of Michigan's premier political newspaper, the *Lansing Republican*. One comrade declared King "as brave and true a man and soldier as ever drew breath" (courtesy Western Michigan University Archives and Regional History Collections).

were promptly re-designated Camp Tilden.[24] The good captain ensured that his stay was memorable for the raw recruits. James King later remembered

> the gay and festive Tilden, who mustered us into service, and the refined speech he made us one evening at the supper table, when some of the boys objected to having their potatoes boiled with the muck of White Pigeon prairie. In that speech he pictured to us the fare of a soldier in the field, which he said, to use his own choice language, consisted of "bull's beef and army crackers, with maggots in them an inch long." This speech was taken with a great deal of allowance, as it was evident to all who heard him that he had either been too close to the six-gallon demijohn of old Bourbon which he kept in his room, or else some of the officers had treated him to a glass of John May's "forty rod."[25]

As an independent regiment, May's unit faced a formidable opponent: Governor Austin Blair. Independent units by their very nature were disagreeable to the state governments. By definition these forces were answerable directly to the War Department, taking the governors out of the equation, and the states received no credit against their troop quotas for independent forces. Blair had already complained to Secretary of War Cameron on August 15 about the chaos accompanying the parallel raising of state and independent regiments:

> SIR: I desire to say a word which is not appropriate for the telegraph. It is to make an earnest appeal to you to recognize no more independent regiments in this State. They are introducing confusion and discord into all our affairs. Companies are divided and officers in unseemly quarrels. I will furnish all the troops you call for much sooner and in better order than these independent regiments can do, and thus avert a great amount of local ill-feeling.[26]

May's was not the only independent infantry regiment forming in Michigan. Thomas B.W. Stockton's independent regiment had three recruiting offices in Detroit alone. Blair seems to have taken greater exception to May's efforts than to Stockton's. Possibly the governor found it easier to forgive Stockton, the former colonel of the 1st Michigan in the Mexican War, for the sin of military independence. When Cameron asked Blair which Michigan regiments could march immediately in the event of an emergency, the governor listed off the major formations available, including Stockton's Independent Regiment, but omitted May's altogether. It is unfathomable that so blatant an omission from such a short and important list could be accidental. And the people of St. Joseph County were fully cognizant of the governor's animosity. On September 11 the *Chronicle* exclaimed that May's regiment was filling up despite the fact that "his *Excellency*, Gov. Blair, has used all his power to crush it."[27] May's regiment did, in fact, face an imminent threat from its own state government.

The War Department was already in the process of ending the entire controversy over independent units—by turning them over to state authority. Blair picked this key moment to order May to transfer 300 of his men away to complete Stockton's regiment. This number represented approximately 40 percent of May's recruits, and would have crippled his efforts to complete the required regimental structure. May took immediate action to save his unit. He telegraphed Blair from White Pigeon on September 15 to ask for a face-to-face meeting in Detroit the very next day, and then promptly departed for an audience with the governor. On the day of that meeting,

Captain Tilden took simultaneous action in White Pigeon to ensure the regiment's survival, telegraphing the War Department in Washington to inform them that the unit had secured the required minimum number of men (it had not), and requesting marching orders. But, almost simultaneously, the War Department issued General Orders No. 78, placing all independent units under the control of their respective governors.[28]

The final result of this high-stakes game was compromise: May would transfer only eighty-three men, the minimum regulation complement of a single company. With recruits still coming in fast, it was an entirely surmountable concession. May returned to White Pigeon at once, called out his regiment, and informed them that the specified number of soldiers must volunteer for transfer to Stockton, or the entire regiment would be disbanded. He additionally announced his intent to offer ten dollars to any man not currently in the regiment who was willing to go to Stockton. If May was bluffing about disbandment, he was never forced to show his hand. There were volunteers enough to end the crisis on the spot, and away they went, cheered by their now ex-comrades. The "83 were not the very best men in May's regiment," the *Mercury* assured its readers. "The men now in camp, are as fine a lot as can be found any where."[29]

Later on that same eventful day, the men elected their captains and lieutenants, who in turn selected the field officers by unanimous vote: May, naturally, was selected as colonel; Stoughton, lieutenant colonel; and Benjamin F. Doughty—a clergyman and officer of the Masonic Society—became major. Brothers-in-law Addison T. Drake and Dr. William N. Elliott were appointed quartermaster and surgeon, respectively. Drake, former supervisor of Sturgis, ran a steam mill and was in the marble business. Elliott, one of the most experienced physicians in St. Joseph County, had immigrated to White Pigeon in 1832, was director of the town's first district schoolhouse, and had held offices in the temperance and medical societies as well as in the township government.[30] Holmes A. Pattison of Colon, a Pennsylvania native, was appointed chaplain. There was only one real surprise: the omission of Samuel Chadwick in favor of William Stoughton. Local journalists had long taken it for granted that Chadwick, who played such a central role in the regiment's organization, was guaranteed the lieutenant colonelcy, and Chadwick and May had publicly indicated that such would be the case. The *Chronicle* on September 11 had chided the

Addison T. Drake, former supervisor of Sturgis, served the regiment capably as its quartermaster, and eventually filled the role of acting corps quartermaster (courtesy Archives of Michigan).

William N. Elliott, ranked among St. Joseph County's foremost physicians, was ultimately remembered with deep affection and respect for the numerous limbs he saved by eschewing unnecessary amputations (courtesy Alyssa Chandler).

Detroit Free Press, among other Michigan papers, for attributing the lieutenant colonelcy to Stoughton—somehow the people of St. Joseph County were the last to learn that things had changed. "To say the least," declared the *Three Rivers Reporter*, "there is something mysterious about it." Presumably May had a change of heart in favor of Stoughton during one of his trips to Detroit, and let the news slip while there. Stoughton, popular and respected, was unmistakably a rising star among Michigan

Holmes A. Pattison, appointed chaplain upon the unit's organization, was considered "just as pleasant a man as ever trod shoe leather." His detachment to minister to convalescent soldiers after Stones River left the regiment without a clergyman for the balance of its service (author's collection).

Republicans. His prominent rank in the regiment could only serve to bolster the unit's prestige and help secure the governor's support. Chadwick demurred and accepted the commission of adjutant in October, after the original appointee, Germain Mason, failed to muster with the regiment.[31]

An artillery battery was assembled at White Pigeon as well, though the infantry and gunners were destined to go their own separate ways after they left camp. All included, there were 718 soldiers gathered at Camp Tilden as of September 23.[32]

Ill feelings still persisted between May's regiment and the governor in early October. Blair by now wished to bury the hatchet, but his efforts got off to a shaky start after he scheduled a visit to Camp Tilden for October 1. The artillerists prepped their lone cannon and fired off a few rounds in anticipation, but Blair failed to show, and the event was rescheduled for two days later. The gunners and regiment turned out for the governor again that day, and the soldiers endeavored to put on the best appearance possible sans uniforms and firearms, which had not arrived yet. The cars again rolled in with no politician aboard, and the dispirited troops dispersed. The overdue pageantry finally came off on October 8. The regiment performed drill and paraded under Stoughton's command, after which Colonel May and the governor reviewed the troops. The soldiers then formed a hollow square around the politician to hear him speak. Blair chose his words well, first apologizing for his prior failures to visit as promised. He assured the troops that the press's claims of his lack of support for the unit were false, and finished off with a skillfully delivered patriotic discourse. The *Reporter* said of the governor, "There had been some impatience betrayed on the part of some who thought they could see neglect on his part, but the cordial good feelings in which he met the volunteers and the citizens, the mild reproof administered to those who had indulged in criticism, and the disinterested patriotism evinced in his remarks has served to inspire all with great confidence in the man as well as to awaken new hope and kindle a warmer fire in the bosom of the loyal."[33]

Another spectacle followed just four days after the governor's visit, when the Michigan Southern Railroad staged the "Grand Picnic Railroad Excursion." Approximately 5,000 spectators, including many of the recruits' family members and sweethearts, piled into—and on top of—crowded passenger cars to visit Camp Tilden. The joy of the occasion was somewhat marred by the increasingly tattered state of the regiment's civilian garb. They did have one new source of pride to boast of, however. Just the previous day, Adjutant General Robertson had formally accepted and designated May's Independent Regiment as the 11th Michigan Volunteer Infantry.[34]

With the regiment under state control and the experiment of independent units a thing of the past, the 11th Michigan's companies were assigned their formal letter designations:

A (St. Joseph County Guards): Centreville, St. Joseph County, Captain David Oakes, Jr.
B (Quincy Wolverines): Quincy, Branch County, Captain Melvin B. Mudge
C (Sturgis Light Guards): Sturgis, St. Joseph County, Captain Calvin C. Hood
D (Bronson Guards): Bronson, Branch County, Captain Benjamin Grove Bennett

E (Three Rivers Light Guard): Three Rivers, St. Joseph County, Captain Henry N. Spencer

F (Hudson Riflemen, combined with Morenci Guards): Hudson, Lenawee County, Captain Sylvester B. Smith

G (Schoolcraft Rifle Rangers): Schoolcraft, Kalamazoo County, Captain Charles Moase

H (Coldwater Tigers): Coldwater, Branch County, Captain John L. Hackstaff

I (Chandler Guards): Monroe, Monroe County, Captain Nelson Chamberlain

K (Lenawee Lions): Adrian, Lenawee County, Captain William W. Phillips[35]

Though Governor Blair had patched things up, the men of the regiment still felt neglected by their government. The federal and state administrations had no experience equipping such large armies, and were utterly overwhelmed with the logistics involved. There were still no uniforms in camp, weapons would not be forthcoming until the regiment's deployment was imminent (per state policy), and there was a limit to just how much the soldiers' imagination and ingenuity could compensate for these deficits when it came time for drill. The *Mercury* insisted that the men were nonetheless "kept actively upon drill and are making commendable progress in the steps and in field movements."[36] But the lack of arms and proper Union blue garb guaranteed that there was no end in sight for the soldiers' stay in White Pigeon. They were afraid the war would end before they headed south. Morale at Camp Tilden ebbed.

Eight hundred good army blankets had arrived on September 23, reassuring May's troops that they were not completely forgotten, but the blankets were too few in number—even with the receipt of additional covers provided by the citizens of Three Rivers—to compensate for the arrival of damp, cool, fall weather in the drafty camp lodgings. Mild sicknesses began to spread. Wishful rumors of uniform shipments had the men anxiously awaiting the inbound trains on a daily basis, but the harsh truth was that the soldiers' clothing was hopelessly snagged in a supply bottleneck in Pittsburg. A small shipment arrived by October 22, but it consisted of just 160 pairs of pants out of 1,000 ordered. "The old R.R. dining house," said one reporter tongue-in-cheek, "presented indeed a lively appearance with its swarms of soldiers partly uniformed." By the twenty-sixth, it was discovered that a government contractor in Philadelphia was responsible for the delays, and a Michigan firm was employed to take over the job. But additional patience would be required while the order was being filled.[37]

In the meantime, the men were gradually adapting to camp life. Typical of Union volunteers, the 11th Michigan had its share of disciplinary issues. Drunkenness, cursing, and gambling were rampant. Addison Drake, a past driving force behind the local temperance movement, was doubtlessly mortified by the prevalence of drunkenness, and James King, mature beyond his nineteen years of age and a model of Victorian etiquette, expressed disquiet with the pandemic camp vices. He helped a superior rein in certain enlisted men who drank to excess and threatened to wreak havoc on the people of White Pigeon. He noted comrades cheating at card games, and frowned at the omnipresent profanity. "I suppose you may think we have rather a hard set here," he wrote home, "and I guess you think right. I think if you would have heard all the oaths I have since I have been writing here, I am afraid you would have a poor opinion of camp life."[38]

With duties and drill growing ever more monotonous with each passing day, the temptation to visit family and friends was strong, and the officers could not always oblige. "If the boys could get their uniforms," said First Sergeant William W. Hoisington of Company E, "and leave for some place 500 or 600 miles from here and finish their drill, they would feel first rate, for while stationed here, so near home, they all want to go home more frequently than can be allowed." Ira Gillaspie's White Pigeon diary entries contain more talk of social visits than of soldiering, and even the generous granting of furloughs did not satisfy. Gillaspie once snuck past the guard to go on leave, and in this he was hardly alone. Hicks discussed the men's fear of getting caught, even despite the lack of firearms for the camp guards: their weapon of choice, "a good heavy hickory club," proved quite sufficient for the task. "We respected those clubs in the hands of a ... soldier of Uncle Sam," joked Hicks, "far more than we did the Springfield Rifle loaded with ball cartridge, after we had been in service a year."[39]

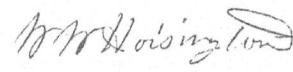

William W. Hoisington exemplified the best young men Michigan had to offer. He was admired as both a scholar and a superior physical specimen. His loss to typhoid served as a stark reminder that even the bravest and boldest soldiers could be struck down by disease at any time (*History of St. Joseph County, Michigan*).

By late October the regiment was nearly full, with about 950 well-drilled infantrymen present in camp. New recruits were still coming in, and they were needed to offset two phenomena that modestly reduced the ranks: first, scattered cases of desertion, and second, parents obtaining discharges for their minor children (below the age of twenty-one).[40]

Most army desertions tended to occur early in enlistment, and in that respect the 11th was typical, with about two-thirds of its cases occurring at White Pigeon. With the unit languishing in camp near home for three months, there were plenty of opportunities for a man with second thoughts about army life to remedy his dilemma. The soldiers had scarcely begun reporting to camp when the first two runaways, Isaac Holland and Orrin Simmons of Company B, took to their heels on August 25. After that, desertions proceeded at a steady trickle through December, with the exception of October 1, when five men from Company K tiptoed away.[41]

A less damaging, but equally bothersome, nuisance came in the form of underage soldiers' parents demanding the discharge of their offspring from army service. Private Edwin J. Hull was first, released from Captain Mudge's company on September 10 as a twenty-year-old who enrolled, allegedly, without his parents' consent. Eugene Barton, eighteen, of Hackstaff's company followed, released by writ of habeas corpus on September 27. October passed without any more incidents. Most of the men fully intended to go south to fight; more typical of their attitudes was that of seventeen-year-old Borden Hicks, who fled from his father—under the threat of being disowned—to join the regiment. Hicks arranged for guards to arrest him at home and whisk him off to camp. But the underage dilemma resurfaced when nineteen-year-old Lynch Gordon of Company C was released by habeas corpus on November 6. When the parents of Private Henry Twiford attempted to follow suit, however, his superior, Captain Bennett, would have none of it. Bennett knew Twiford had enrolled with parental consent. He had spoken amicably with the boy's parents about their son's enlistment, and promised to write letters home for Twiford, who could not write for himself. Bennett accepted the Twifords' verbal consent for their son's enlistment, and did not request anything in writing. Several weeks later, the Twifords presented a writ of habeas corpus to the regiment. But Bennett would not give up so easily. "What is to be done?" he wrote in haste to Adjutant General Robertson. "If we can not hold persons when *over* eighteen, then we may as well give up; for near one half the regiment are under 21." One more young soldier, eighteen-year-old Andrew Hawse of Company B, was released on November 15, but he was the last member of the 11th regiment discharged in this manner. Either Bennett got his way or the Twifords had a change of heart, for their son remained an infantryman.[42]

All things considered, discipline at White Pigeon seems to have been a larger issue for the gun battery than for the infantry. The captain of the artillery appointed an unpopular lieutenant, foregoing the customary election for that officer's position. His men responded by refusing to muster in unless allowed to elect their company officers. "This caused a great deal of excitement in camp," Benjamin Franklin Wells of Oakes's company observed. "Four of the artillery are under arrest and many are the rumors afloat in camp. Capt. Tilden has made many threats.... I think these threats are made merely to frighten the boys but they do not scare worth a cent. I think they are right and they will stand up for their rights. I glory in their spunk." By some means, the tense conflict was ultimately resolved, and the gunners mustered in.[43]

In late November the exasperating absence of uniforms, weapons, and marching orders, all came to a sudden and exhilarating end. The long-promised uniform order finally arrived in bulk, substantially complete, and the men begged for furloughs to go have their pictures taken. Borden Hicks described the uniforms as

> dress coats with brass shoulder scales (frying pans we called them), not only foraging caps, but the tall stiff black hat. As no sheverons were issued to us we bought tape and put them on ourselves, not quite as artistic as the Government issue, but they told the onlookers that we were officers, and did not belong to the common herd. Then we asked for furloughs to go home, and see the girls in our new togery, and when we got there we made a bee line for the photographers, and did not rest till we

had our pictures taken in all the panoply of war. They were distributed not only to our best girl, but to all who asked for them.⁴⁴

A coincidental alignment of good fortune transformed November 26 into a memorable day. First, the muskets arrived in camp, received with great fanfare. Though the troops were delighted, the weapons were woefully obsolete smoothbore muskets purchased from European suppliers. As time passed and the simple novelty of being armed wore off, the Michiganders would recognize the outdated firearms for what they were. Captain Hackstaff soon declared them "not worth the wood and iron of which they are made," and Bennett described the firearms as "miserable things—absolutely good for nothing." King declared that the muskets, with their awful recoil, would "kick a man out of his hat." Hicks more bluntly derided them as "the gun that we feared more, than we did the rebels, as it was sure to hit us every time it was fired," regardless of whether it hit its target (a result that Private Aaron B. White considered doubtful at best). But thanks to the muskets, said Ira Gillaspie, "we began to feel like real soldiers."⁴⁵

Benjamin Franklin Wells, like many Michiganders, was more impressed with the beauty of the South than with its people: he punched a Confederate sympathizer in the face for singing in praise of Jefferson Davis. Wells exhibited the optimism typical of soldiers on both sides, taking it for granted that the war would be over quickly (*History of St. Joseph County, Michigan*).

Later the same day, the regiment was presented with its national flag, financed by local aid societies and private donations, at an elaborate public ceremony. The 11th regiment's new silken banner was bordered with gold tinsel, and its flagstaff was capped with an eagle mounted on a globe of bronze. The flag was revealed to the crowd, and the artillery fired off a salute. "Never before did the stars and stripes unfurled look more beautiful," exclaimed James King, "for as it waved it told of the peril of the country, and of the determined spirit of the loyal men who were willing to lay down life that liberty might live." The presentation address was delivered by Mr. J.W. Frey, speaking on behalf of a local aid society, the Ladies of St. Joseph County. Frey said in part:

> The intrinsic value of the gift is small, but it serves in some degree to show their appreciation of you as gentlemen, and above all, of your patriotic devotion to your country ... in early life sacrificing all the endearments of home and friends, and going forth in battle in her cause, in this her hour of peril.... We now present you this flag in full confidence that you will never suffer it to be trampled in the dust by the feet of traitors.⁴⁶

Lieutenant Colonel Stoughton replied, "I thank you for this beautiful banner.... In presenting us this flag you have nobly done your duty—we will try and do ours.... It

Borden Mills Hicks was just one of many underage soldiers who slipped into the ranks. Enlisting as a sergeant at age seventeen, he rose to the command of Company E just two years later, becoming the regiment's youngest commissioned officer in the process (courtesy Clements Library, University of Michigan).

may be exposed to the winter blast and the battle storm but those who bear it hence will never return with it dishonored."

The flag was handed to the color bearer. The regimental band struck up "The Star-Spangled Banner," and at the tune's conclusion, a newspaper reporter observed, "One vociferous huzza went up from the entire body of citizens and soldiers."[47]

As if this was not enough excitement for the newly uniformed and armed regiment, Brigadier General Don Carlos Buell telegraphed Governor Blair before the day was over, directing the 11th Michigan to deploy to Louisville, Kentucky. Colonel May hurriedly appealed to the War Department in hopes of taking his regiment to South Carolina in order to see action sooner, but without effect, and the regiment began preparations to depart Michigan. It was time for the 11th Michigan Volunteer Infantry to enter the theater of war.[48]

CHAPTER 2

"An enemy to be feared"
November 1861–April 1862

The final days in camp proved eventful. The *Constantine Mercury* sparked controversy with its November 28 issue, wherein it accused May's regiment—freshly uniformed, armed, and ready to march—of being "in a bad way," and suggested that the unit would soon be disbanded. The paper went on to claim that an inordinate amount of money had been spent in recruiting and equipping the 11th. Captain Hackstaff responded forcefully via the *Reporter*, declaring the *Mercury* "as notorious for lying as the god of that name in the mythology of the ancients." He went on to recount the many challenges the regiment had overcome, "not paralleled by that of any other in the state," and meticulously debunked the *Mercury's* claims regarding the unit's cost to the government.[1]

The local merchants, as well as the soldiers, were thrilled when May's troops drew their pay for the first time, on December 4 and 5, to the tune of $37,000 in all. The *Reporter* cheerfully pointed out that "most of this money will be paid out in our county and left with the families of the soldiers, which will add not a little to the circulating medium."[2]

On December 6 the 11th suffered its first gunshot wound. After being excused from drill, Private Charles Leonard of Company C called upon the regiment's sutler, Marshall M. Wells. Wells was a former representative for Oakland County, and had served as a deputy U.S. marshal under James Buchanan. Leonard purchased a pistol from him, and as Wells demonstrated the steps required to load the firearm, as James King reported, "he had placed the cartridge in the barrel, but had neglected to raise the hammer, and in returning the barrel to its place, the hammer came in contact with the cartridge." The bullet bore through Leonard's cheek and lodged in his jawbone. Fortunately, the bloody wound did not prove fatal, and the victim was able to stay with the regiment.[3]

Corporal Joseph Eugene Turner of Company H succumbed to smallpox the next day, triggering panic among his comrades. Rumors asserting that the dreaded disease infected the regiment had been circulating since mid–November, and word of Turner's fatality spread like wildfire among the troops and citizenry alike. Turner's fate spelled the end of prior attempts by the medical staff to allay everyone's fears by identifying the illness as chicken pox. Turner's was not the first death in the 11th: Private George F. Grather of Company A had died of typhoid on October 19, but smallpox, far more than typhoid, struck fear into the hearts of the young soldiers and their families. "It raised an aufull excitement amongst the boys," wrote Ira Gillaspie. "Some was on the point of leaving.... It came very near causing a general mutiny." In death, Turner left behind a seven-month-old daughter, and his wife of just one year.[4]

A perfectly timed distraction came the same day: news that the regiment's departure from Michigan was slated for the ninth. The men had been subjected to rumors of their deployment since almost day one at White Pigeon, but this time they knew it was the real thing. Sure enough, the order to pack up their knapsacks was given first thing on the morning of their departure. "The final leave taking came," wrote James King, "and if the lip quivered when the last goodbye was said, it was the sign of deep affection but not of repining, and each of the 'Boys in Blue' bore to the front with him the impressive influences of friends and loved ones, thoughts of whom strengthened him in the weary march and cheered him on to deeds of valor." The 11th was given a good send off. The Ladies' Aid Society of Centreville gifted a generous list of hospital supplies to the unit, and the *Reporter* exclaimed that "no finer body of troops has gone from the state.... The long time this regiment has spent in camp has perfected them in drill, so they will be ready to take the field immediately."[5]

The 1,004 men of the 11th Michigan Volunteer Infantry embarked railroad cars at White Pigeon at 11:00 p.m. on December 9, 1861. The engineer pulled the train away from the depot just after midnight.[6] Ira Gillaspie described the car trip, which marked the beginning of a momentous new era in the life of every passenger.

> We was all seated in the cars and was soon on our way to Louisville Kentucky. We pased thrue Salem Crossing whare we changed cars. Next day we passed thrue 50 or 60 miles of very low wet marshey land. Today we pased thrue Tippycanoe Laffyett and sevral other smart little places Indianapolis for one. In the night we rode over a very rough oald road tosing us about like an oald lumber wagon. We was a sleepy set of fellows but the road being so rough we could not sleep atall. Just daybrake we arived at Jeffersonville.[7]

"At every station along the route," wrote William Hoisington, "the entire population turned out to greet us with waving hats and handkerchiefs." Captain Hackstaff agreed, stating that "all along we received the most flattering attentions. At Indianapolis a good supper was provided for the officers and coffee for the men." Captain Bennett decried the quality of the refreshments, but many of his comrades were too excited—or too weary—to notice. There was a shortage of coffee, however, and Company C compensated by appropriating a barrel of cider from some unfortunate local. The stiff drink was consumed with gusto during the subsequent thirty-hour ride to Jeffersonville, Indiana.[8]

Upon their arrival at Jeffersonville, the Michiganders detrained and passed a few hours awaiting teams to transport their baggage. "The sun was Just rising in the east in splendor," James King remembered. "The mighty Ohio went swelling on in power

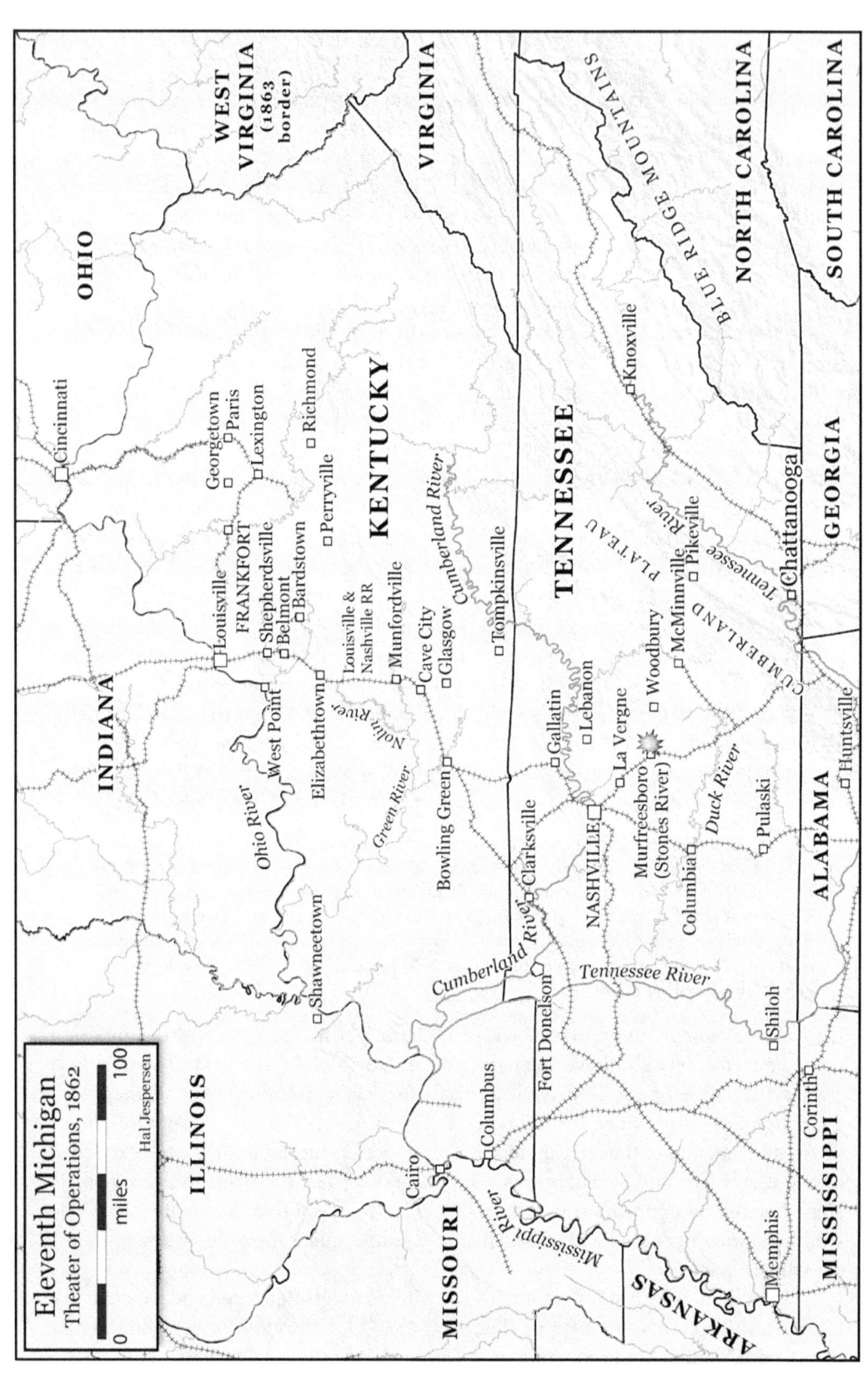

while on its broad bosom were four or five splendid Steamers in sight, on the other shore were the Kentucky hills, and right opposite us was Louisville, a city of about seventy-five Thousand Inhabitants." While the regiment waited to be ferried across the river to Louisville, King continued, "a certain Captain made his company a speech. He could not imitate Napoleon, as he had no pyramids to point to, but drawing his sword he pointed to the Kentucky shore and intimated that rebels over there were as plenty as blackberries in an old clearing.... No cartridges had yet been issued to us, and much discontent was felt after this speech."[9]

It was a raucous ferry ride to the South, with the men cheering themselves hoarse and the band competing with them in volume. After the Federals crossed the grand waterway and touched Southern soil (with many doing so for the first time in their lives), King recorded, "We marched through the main streets of the city. Crowds of people thronged the streets, Ladies with their silks and satins, ribbons flying, men in military dress, Negroes by the wholesale. I saw more colored people yesterday than I ever saw in my life, and most of them slaves. There are some massive and splendid buildings here. They gave us a good welcome. They thought we were the best regiment that had passed through." Henry Platt declared that "our regiment met with a welcome reception from the citizens of Louisville. The windows and balconies along the streets were crowded with fair ladies, welcoming us with the stars and stripes, and waving their handkerchiefs; while men, boys and niggers crowded the walks along the streets as we passed." The *Louisville Journal* proclaimed that the 11th was "a fine body of men, and will doubtless do good service in the Union cause.... The Eleventh is considered as good, if not better, than any regiment yet sent to the war from that State." Not everyone in Louisville was a Unionist, though. Gillaspie noted that "seceshes go around with their heads down with out saying a word." But the Michiganders were instantly taken with the overall friendliness of the locals, and the beauty of their city. They marched to a location behind the railroad depot, and set up camp.[10]

Kentucky had endeavored to remain neutral, but large numbers of troops from both sides occupied the state. Federal troops under the overall commands of Major General Henry W. Halleck and Brigadier General Buell confronted Confederate forces under Albert Sidney Johnston across a wide front stretching from the vicinity of Cairo, Illinois, to the region of Cumberland Gap.

The harsh realities of soldiering began to set in at once. The eager Federals had discovered on the march that their knapsacks, initially no great burden, seemingly grew heavier with every step. "I never was so tired in my life," Corporal James Martin of Company H admitted. Upon reaching camp, the weary soldiers drew rations in the form of hardtack and bacon. One Company A soldier, upon sighting the small mountain of bacon set aside for this purpose, exclaimed, "Good Heavens! Have we got to come to this?" The Michiganders battled furiously to pitch the five spacious Sibley tents issued to each company, and celebrated success only to realize they would hence-

Opposite: **From *Conspicuous Gallantry: The Civil War and Reconstruction Letters of James W. King, 11th Michigan Volunteer Infantry*, © 2015 by The Kent State University Press. Reproduced with permission.**

forth be sleeping on the cold, wet earth. "One old man who had seen service in the Mexican War," recounted Borden Hicks, "assured us that soldiers in the field always slept on the ground." The raw troops grudgingly did as they were told, and awoke the next morning to a cacophony of coughs and sniffles. Desperate to secure bedding, Captain Oakes commanded his company to relieve a local farmer of his haystack. Colonel May stated that he would compensate the owner only if he was a Union man. Though Company A secured its hay, most of the regiment was less fortunate and continued to sleep on (or in) a bed of mud that froze and thawed daily. Daytime temperatures sometimes topped out at a delightful seventy degrees, but at night the mercury seemed to plummet just as precipitously as it did in Michigan.[11]

The 11th did not stay put long, but there was time for some sightseeing. Some of the men saw John Wilkes Booth perform at the theater. The city itself left quite an impression on the Michiganders, including Captain Bennett, who declared Louisville "a much larger and handsomer city than I supposed." Chadwick, who had passed through during the Mexican War, was impressed at how the city had grown.[12] King painted a picture of his own impressions:

> I saw many splendid Buildings. Among them were some private dwellings which were very beautiful. But the most splendid of all was the city post office. It is built of hewn limestone, and [is] a splendid pile. It is situated near the river. The streets are all neatly paved and dry and hard. But their dooryards I admired most of all. They are raised 2 or three feet above the sidewalk. A limestone walk leads up to the mansion steps of Limestone to ascend from the streets. The grass is as green and fresh as in the month of June, and are surrounded by an iron fence resting on a limestone foundation. Standing in one of the main streets, I could see persons of all classes and professions. Here comes some ladies in their carriage who are counted among the upper tens. They are dressed in their silks and ribbons, with a negro driver perched on a box whose business it is to take the ladies wherever they wish to go. You can tell the business man by business airs he puts on. There goes the dandy with his cigar, his hands in his pockets. Here you see the negro with his mule team of four or six mules, riding one and driving the others.[13]

The novel surroundings provided reminders that no amount of drill or marching would turn the young soldiers into veterans; only battle could do that. "We was startled by a heavy fiering of musketry on south of us," Gillaspie wrote on the sixteenth. "It was some Regt. fiering at targots but we was just raw anuff to think evrything was rebils so it caused an excitement in camp." Gillaspie also related that his brother and a friend "shook their heads and grinned like kids" when they were asked what they thought of soldiering, now that they were in the South.[14]

The 11th regiment departed Louisville for Bardstown on December 18. It was the unit's first significant march, covering thirty-five miles as the crow flies, and far lengthier by foot over the winding Kentucky roads. The inexperienced soldiers' overflowing haversacks were described by Corporal Ozro Bowen of Company B as "enormous bundles containing sufficient equipage for a year's tour through Europe, and look[ing] more like a linen peddler's pack than the knapsack of an experienced solder." These encumbrances proved an unbearable nuisance, and Company E put its collective foot down. "We informed the captain," Hicks related, "that we did not enlist to be a government pack mule, and that he must hire a farmer to haul our knapsacks, or we would break our guns around a tree, and go right home." Captain Spencer perceived that he must oblige, and Gillaspie noted with gratitude that Colonel May soon expanded this baggage service to the balance of the regiment. And stragglers on this march had nothing to fear: the wagons brought up the rear and offered a ride to anyone who needed it.[15]

Another attention getter, as the Wolverines saw more of the Kentucky countryside, was the presence of slaves in profuse numbers. Chadwick was impressed that blacks outnumbered whites in rural areas. Hoisington, a man of more democratic leanings, insisted, "I saw slaves yesterday for the first time in my life; there is nothing of the shabbiness and poverty in their appearance that sensation writers are so fond of blowing about, on the contrary, all I saw of the colored population here were well dressed." One of the servants, however, confided in King that the slaves would all run away, given the opportunity. Indeed, during the march numerous slaves offered to serve the regiment in return for protection from their masters.[16]

Chadwick recorded the sights and sounds of the journey to Bardstown.

> On either side of the turnpike over which we marched, far in the fields, were palatial residences; and, as the sound of the fife and drum, or the more enchanting tones of the regimental band, reached the ears of the inhabitants, over fields, and down lanes, might be seen flocks of men, women and children of *all colors*.... Some of these people, from their hearts, would, as they waved the stars and stripes, cry "Three cheers for the Union"; but many held their heads down, and gave a very cool response. Occasionally we would pass bevies of beauties assembled, who waved handkerchiefs when we shouted for the Union. *The sable race was for the Union every time.*[17]

A black Michigander named Tom Steward had accompanied the regiment south from White Pigeon. His experience on this march, communicated to the *Mercury* by a member of the regiment who identified himself only as "Shorty," drove home the fact that Kentucky, though not Confederate, was after all a Southern state:

> Tom ... had quite an adventure on the way, which fully illustrates the beauty of one branch of "the institution." Tom was armed with a gun and revolver, and was walking on ahead of the regiment, in company with one of the men. They drew up at a hotel and halted for the regiment to come up. A knot of men were standing in the bar room, and Tom noticed that they watched him with watery eyes, for Tom might bring a good round price. After eyeing him a few moments, one of the men, who had heard Tom's name spoken by his companion, stepped up to him and said very coolly, "Why, Tom, what did you run away from me for?" This very naturally surprised Tom, and before he had fully recovered the man had him by the collar, and was kindly inviting Tom to walk home with him. Tom jerked away, and by pulling out his revolver and cocking it, gently insinuated that he didn't want to go. The man cowered back, and Tom put up his revolver. His companion urged him to go back and meet the regiment, but Tom thought the chance to rest too good to be lost. In the meantime the one who claimed Tom had got behind him, and was going to secure Tom by jumping on his back. But Tom was wide awake ... swung his gun around and the gentleman found himself at the point of a bayonet. He backed off, muttering something about negroes being allowed to carry guns, got into a carriage and drove away. Tom saw his friend once since in Bardstown, and he (the claimant) swears he will yet have Tom.[18]

Apparently Tom's assailant failed to make good on his threat: Gillaspie would mention on April 7 that "Colored Tom Steward went back to Mich. again."[19]

The regiment spent the first night encamped at a lovely creek, and after the campfires were lit, numerous amiable locals visited. Some ladies presented Company G with a beautiful flag, and other citizens offered pails of milk to the soldiers. But that was not enough for an insatiable minority; certain soldiers further helped themselves to the bounty of rural Kentucky. "That night," King remembered, "the first sheep was sacrificed by the Eleventh Michigan Infantry.... Gates Wheeler of Company 'A' shot it and Bob Renner dressed it. It was nice mutton, and a kettle of it was soon over one of the camp fires, cooking." Foraging was forbidden, and only a cover-up orchestrated by Company A prevented Captain Oakes from apprehending the guilty party. King went on to describe the balance of the march. "After this, it began to grow hilly and rocky, the roughest I ever saw. The roads here are not like ours, they follow the ridges. They go more for the levelness of the thing. The second morning after we started from our camping ground, we traveled about 3 miles when I am sure we were not more than 1 mile from where We started."[20]

The 11th Michigan arrived at Bardstown, Kentucky, late on the afternoon of December 19. Townsfolk cheered the arriving Federals, but Confederate sympathizers were somewhat more in evidence than in Louisville. Gillaspie estimated the Unionists at just one-third of the population, though band member Charles Rice observed a more even split, commenting that "one-half of them are 'secesh' but they have to keep mum." Chaplain Pattison labeled himself unimpressed even with the self-proclaimed Kentucky loyalists: "Most of the so-called Union men here have an 'if' an 'and' a 'but' a 'whereas' a 'howsoever,' & c., at the end of every Union sentiment they utter, which to me, sounds very much like down-right secessionism. Few, indeed, there are ... who are out and out unconditional Union men." Platt offered an intriguing observation about the town's conflicted secessionists. "Although they sympathize with the South," he noted, "they feel safer with Union troops around them." Captain Bennett, after observing the locals for some time, asserted that "the rebel sympathizers have an account to settle with the Union men—and judging from apparent indications, it will, in many instances, be a *final* account. Just as sure as the sun rises and sets, the *Union* men of the South will have full revenge for the wrongs they have suffered. The Kentucky and Tennessee regiments are rampant for revenge—and nothing but the presence of more northern troops prevents them from literally skinning every one of secession proclivities. After the Union troops leave, the rebel abettors had better begin to say their prayers."[21]

Shortly after arriving, Gillaspie reported that "smallpox excitement was grate. Henry Norton was taken with that horable disease." Private George Henry Norton of Company C died two weeks later, and he was just one of the scores of Wolverines doomed to interment at Bardstown. King would remember it as "one of the darkest spots in our soldier life." The 11th was destined to find itself in the thickest of the fight in some of the war's bloodiest battles, yet peaceful little Bardstown would prove the deadliest of the regiment's destinations by far. Smallpox had begun to spread among the Michiganders even before they departed White Pigeon—about thirty men were left behind sick when the unit deployed south, some of them with smallpox—but it was in Bardstown that the feared illness stalked the Wolverines in earnest. "From almost the day that our tents were pitched," said Ozro Bowen, "the work of death commenced. An enemy with softer tread than human footsteps crept through the picket line unheard and marked its victims for the grave. They fell with no ghastly saber cut or shattered limb, but received a thrust from an invisible hand which no physician's skill could parry off. Day after day and night after night we bore them away, until the old orchard just outside the camp was turned into a sepulchre of dead heroes."[22]

The initial Bardstown encampment, Camp May, was situated in an expansive field, traversed by a brook and graced with a bountiful spring. The surroundings were pleasant when dry, but a downpour on the twenty-second converted the heavenly scene into a quagmire. The soldiers were dismayed to spend a dreary day crammed into their Sibley tents, which in retrospect seemed not so large after all. Mail arrived and brought the news that a rumor had spread far and wide back home, stating that the entire unit had been captured or killed. With plenty of time on their hands, the soldiers wrote home to assure their loved ones that reports of the regiment's demise were greatly exaggerated. "We have not seen a live Confederate yet," Private Nathan Adams of Company H remarked.[23]

Company K private Nelson Clifford Bragg complained of "the lonsomest Christmas and New Years I ever spent," but the holidays did not go unobserved in camp. On Christmas Eve, Charles Rice and the regimental band performed what he termed "a Grand Serenade," and the soldiers were invited into the homes of some of the leading local citizens. "I never saw people," Rice declared, "with more cordiality and friendship than they do in Kentucky." The Michiganders drilled on Christmas morning and took target practice, but the rest of the day was free. "Some half dosen darkeys come down to our camp," said Gillaspie, "with fiddles temboreans and banjoes and they had a publick negro show." The weather struck the Wolverines as summer-like. In Company C, the men took up a collection to buy turkeys, and furloughs were freely granted to visit a large cave near town.[24] King described a stroll he took through Bardstown with Aaron Sturges after dinner.

> Every few rods we would meet a negro. Some were riding mules, others mounted on ponies, some were on foot, all as happy as could be, for this is the negroes' holidays. They are all dressed in their best, many of them splendidly. They have nice shirt bosoms, starched collars. Their boots are blacked, and a white handkerchief is almost sure to be seen protruding from some one of their pockets. They go from one plantation to another thus, gathering and feasting and dancing the time away. They do no work from Christmas eve until the day after New Year's. Every little child we met in the street would shout, Christmas gift. They do not wish you a merry Christmas as we at the North do, but it is all Christmas gift. The streets were full of planters and country people purchasing gifts for the holidays.[25]

Later in the day, Brigadier General Thomas John Wood came and inspected the regiment. The locals set off fireworks in the evening, prompting Rice to compare the local festivities with Fourth of July celebrations back home.[26]

The rains came again on the twenty-sixth. On the following morning, Ira Gillap-

Thomas John Wood, a West Pointer, commanded the post at Bardstown and introduced a measure of discipline to the raw troops, but the Michiganders would primarily remember him for unfairly ordering them into isolation for fear of smallpox. Later, amid the chaos of Chickamauga, he would mistakenly pull his troops out of the battle line, precipitating the Union rout and setting the stage for the 11th Michigan's finest moment, its role in the legendary defense of Horseshoe Ridge (Library of Congress).

sie's brother Enoch, another Company C private, failed to show up at roll call. Some of the men had seen him depart camp, and reported hearing a subsequent gunshot. Colonel May sent squads out to scour the countryside, but to no avail. Enoch in fact had deserted and fled to his cousins in Indiana, though Ira would not learn of it until two weeks later (at which time he declared, "I would rather herd of his deth than this"). In the meantime, Ira and some of his comrades took out of their resulting frustration on the locals "by making them furnish us with grub and apples and the like." At dress parade on the twenty-eighth, Chadwick announced orders to be ready to march at 8:30 the next morning. Apparently Company C was still on edge about Enoch's disappearance: That night around midnight, a nervous picket, Samuel Hibberlee, discharged his musket and cried for help, arousing the entire camp. Upon careful examination it was determined that Hibberlee's marksmanship had cost the South its first casualty at the hands of the 11th Michigan Infantry: one mule, wounded in action.[27] It is unrecorded whether Hibberlee's four-legged assailant proved to be of Confederate sympathies, or was rather a victim of friendly fire.

The 11th packed up, marched about five miles and encamped near the rest of the troops serving under Brigadier General Wood—several regiments of Ohio and Indiana troops. The new site was soon designated Camp Stoughton. Almost immediately, Gillaspie reported additional cases of smallpox and measles, and in no time at all, a rumor spread among Wood's Indiana troops that the Michiganders had no less than 300 cases of smallpox in their ranks. The other units panicked—never mind the fact that they were suffering from the same diseases already—and Wood commanded the 11th to move one mile away on January 2 in order to isolate itself. "The night before we moved," Sergeant Benjamin Bordner of Company D related, "the news came that there was six buried out of the hooser reg ... they died with small pox so that shows that they had some thing about them that they did not catch from us." But the brigadier general was not swayed. "Well, adjutant," Wood told Chadwick, "I must say you have the finest set of men I have seen, but it is a matter of precaution, and you have fine quarters where you are going." The general did order a surgeon to inspect the regiment, but the doctor in question nonchalantly declared that the unit had smallpox without examining a single patient. Then the confounded Kentucky rains returned, and matters only worsened when the 11th was ordered to uproot itself again on January 5, this time to Camp Morton. The new grounds were situated on the Bowman farm north of town.[28]

On the way to Camp Morton, the Wolverines passed through the ranks of an Indiana unit afflicted with numerous cases of measles. "Before we came into the city," Bordner recorded, "we stoped a while and we looked back and we saw Baggage wagons coming and when they came up they was loaded with sick and behind these came a string of them. we asked them where they was a going to. they said to the hospital and there was 51 of them all out of one reg."[29] The feared disease soon took the Wolverine soldiers into a deadly embrace.

Including the aforementioned Private Norton, four Michiganders succumbed to smallpox between January 2 and January 8, but by then the disease had mostly run its course, with a total of seven fatalities. Measles, soon to prove a far deadlier enemy, claimed its first victim, Alvin Calhoun, on January 9. "There wasent enough small pox to go around," quipped James Martin, "so we have got to take up with the measles.... It is a hard place to be sick in camp, a sick man isent no more cared for than a sick calf." By the twenty-third, men were coming down sick at an alarming rate. The situation worsened rapidly. Measles alone claimed fourteen of the regiment's twenty-six fatalities in the month of January. "It seems aufull hard," Gillaspie exclaimed, "to lose so many good boys as are dyeing off hear."[30]

Undoubtedly, it was poor sanitary conditions that made the men sick, but the deplorable quality of medical care contributed to the body count.[31] First Sergeant Albert C. Rossiter of Company G penned a telling account of his turn in the hospital for the *Reporter* under the dateline "Small Pox Pest House ... Feb 21, 1862":

> Sergeant [Daniel] Harwood, formerly a resident of Three Rivers, and myself were taken down with small pox on the 23d of December, 1861, and on the 25th we were both taken to the pest house; consequently we did not have a merry Christmas or a happy New Year. During our stay there our diet was chiefly corn meal gruel, seasoned only with the fair promises of Doctor Elliott of better fare soon, for we had neither sugar nor salt half the time. Sometimes we got bread by sending out and buying of the citizens, but the money to pay for it had to come out of our own pockets.
>
> We remained in this place until the 12th of January, and on the eve of the 12th, just as the straw had been shaken, and the blankets spread for the night, three baggage wagons arrived with an order for our removal to another pest house about two and a half miles distant, near the camp. The night was dark and stormy, the rain and

sleet fell thick and fast, but with a little assistance, and a great deal of pain, we were finally ready. Our feet were swollen so much we could not get on our boots; but with the assistance of two men I could walk to the wagon. The wagons were without springs, and it was the roughest road that I ever had the misfortune to travel, and the groans of the poor sick men may be better imagined than described; covered, as we were, like Job of old, with bruises and running sores, thrown from one side of the wagon to the other, and jolted from rock to rock.... Reaching our place of abode we entered, and of all the places I ever beheld for sick men this was the worst. The window sashes had been broken out, and the places where they had been were partly filled by nailing up boards ... through which cold air came in decidedly fresh, if not health giving currents, while a large rent in the roof let in the rain, which gave us an excellent opportunity for enjoying a shower bath....

...We had two waiters and one cook, and they were all left behind with one sick man, and our situation reminded me very forcibly of the blind leading the blind, for the sick waited upon the sick.... We had only one cup, one plate, one knife, one spoon and one kettle in which to cook gruel, providing we had it. Unfortunately our plates, cups and cooking utensils were all left with the cook and waiters, so we had to cultivate patience and wait for each other to eat, and by the time we all got through the first was ready to eat again.[32]

People back home sought to place blame for the calamitous state of the regiment's health, and inevitably the unit's officers and medical staff came under scrutiny. "The boys," Adams said, "are all down on the old doctor they think that he killed more than he cures." Rossiter reported that his pest house complaints were resolved after Colonel May learned of the patients' sufferings. But the evidence suggests there was some truth—at the company level, at least—to the claim that certain officers bore more direct responsibility for the spread of the illnesses. For the months of December through February, companies B and K lost only three men each, while companies C, G, and H each recorded nine deaths.[33]

The officers faced criticism from another worrisome direction that month: General Buell's Special Orders No. 12 declared that "a Board of officers is hereby appointed in conformity with Section X of the Act of Congress approved July 22 1861 to meet at Bardstown Ky on the 18th Inst or as soon thereafter as practicable for the purpose of Examining in the 'Capacity, Qualifications, Propriety of Conduct &c' of such officers of the volunteer service as may be brought before us." The board, established by mid-January, included among its members Colonel William Ward Duffield of the 9th Michigan Infantry, and Lieutenant Colonel Charles Norris of the 2nd Indiana Cavalry. The officers of the 11th Michigan all passed the examination with one exception: the board found Company K's Captain William W. Phillips "entirely deficient," and recommended his discharge. It was not the first sign of trouble for Phillips. Nelson Bragg had claimed back in mid-October that the "dishonerbel" Phillips was placed under arrest at Adrian, Michigan (without naming Phillips's offense). The censured officer resigned in mid-February to escape the humiliation of having his commission revoked. His place would be filled by Second Lieutenant Lewis Wadsworth Heath of Company F, another veteran of the 1st Michigan Infantry, who would be raised to captain effective April 1. Heath was promoted over Company K's First Lieutenant Ephraim French, much to the chagrin of the popular French's subordinates.[34]

February's disease toll was even worse than January's, with death visiting the regiment more than once a day on average. Captain Bennett had regularly written to the newspapers back home, reassuring everyone that the reports of sickness were exaggerated (on one occasion joking, "From this you will see that there is at least one man yet alive in the Michigan 11th"). As late as January 27 he declared the measles "under perfect control." But now he could no longer conceal the truth. "There is an enemy to be feared and which is more fatal than any to be found on the battle-field," he admitted via newspaper to the audience back home on February 3. "At least such has been the experience of the Michigan Eleventh." The fatalities peaked on February 5, when a single day saw four young lives cut short, including the most prominent casualty to date, First Lieutenant Christopher Haight of Company A. About two hundred men were in the regimental hospital. Company D's Irving Metcalf wondered "why my life & health is spared whilst my companions are suffering and dieing. God grant this fearful mortality amongst us may soon cease.... It seems as if a curse had followed us when it will end God only knows." Jacob Bowers of Company E perished from pneumonia on February 22, just as the regiment's death rate finally showed signs of declining markedly. When Benjamin Wells's wife Melissa heard of Bowers's fate, she might have been speaking for any of the sixty-six Michiganders who had been struck down in their prime by the end of February 1862—without having even met the enemy they enlisted to fight.[35]

> I guess he little thought when he enlisted in that company last summer that his days were numbered and that he would meet with such a fate and what sad news it will be for his friends at home. O how many hearts have been made sad and how many homes desolate since the commencement of this awful rebellion. it seems as though the whole world would be clothed in the habiliments of mourning. I hope that I may not be called to wear the garb of mourning caused by this horrible strife yet no one knows how much sorrow is in store for them or what one day will bring round for this is a world of chance.[36]

Melissa's own turn in the "garb of mourning" would come six months later, when her brother William Hoisington died of typhoid.

In addition to disease, there was another disagreeable constant for the Michiganders at Bardstown: the never-ending, mud-spawning, precipitation. After one cloudburst, Gillaspie declared the camp "a perfect lake," and such became a normal state of affairs. Mother Nature delivered snow on occasion as well. "This looked like home," King said of the first snowfall. "But we did not behold this sight long. Before evening it had nearly disappeared, and instead of the beautiful mantle of white which we beheld in the morning covering the bosom of the earth, this vile Kentucky mud met our gaze. Oh Jenny you know nothing of mud."[37]

Sickness, inactivity, and awful weather dragged down the men's spirits, yet they hung in there, and their officers remained impressively harmonious in their efforts to maintain morale—with one exception. It became painfully evident via the Three Rivers papers that one individual was beginning to crack. It all began when a letter from Captain Oakes (a former Republican officeholder), presenting an unflattering opinion of Kentucky and its residents, was published without his permission in the

February 1 *Reporter*. Company H's Captain Hackstaff (a former Democratic newspaper editor) responded with a scathing, acidic rant against Oakes that was printed in the February 26 *Chronicle*, attributing Oakes's low opinion of the Bluegrass State to his abolitionism, as Hackstaff termed it, and further implying that there were poor relations among the regiment's officers. Hackstaff claimed to speak for all his comrades, yet others jumped to Oakes's defense, including Chadwick, who publicly rebutted Hackstaff's claims. Chadwick and Oakes independently asserted essentially the same counterargument: Hackstaff had been sick and out of command so long that he had little knowledge of the regiment's affairs, and as Oakes put it, "Hackstaff excepted, there is, generally, the best of feeling manifested among the officers of the 11th." Hackstaff had indeed been ill, and admitted as much in a letter to the *Sturgis Journal*. He would resign effective March 11 and return home, only to die from a relapse of camp fever on May 22. He left behind a wife and five minor children.[38]

It should not be construed from this that Hackstaff was the only man in the regiment who was not on his best behavior in Kentucky. Gillaspie's diary relates stories of men in Company C who harassed slaves for the sake of amusement, and hints at overly friendly relations with the local girls (with money probably trading hands, in at least some cases). Perhaps the most notable theme in Gillaspie's accounts is the anti-whiskey capers of his company, in most cases led by a man of no less stature than Captain Hood himself, who championed a decidedly hands-on approach to temperance. Even back in White Pigeon, Hood had led his men on at least one expedition to obliterate the whiskey stock from local establishments. Now that he was in the South, the gloves were off and Hood led his men through the countryside, ransacking and foraging through private residences suspected of offering the strong drink for sale. Though nobody seems to have been injured in these outings, intimidation was readily brought to bear against anyone who failed to point out their stores of alcohol—whether they actually possessed any or not.[39]

Simple boredom impaired morale as much as sickness, and probably accounted for the lion's share of the disciplinary issues. Benjamin Bordner summed up the doldrums of camp life for the rank and file at Bardstown: "We dont have much to do except to eat a little mush & drill a little." Life was not completely miserable, though. The regiment established a bread oven that could produce four hundred loaves in a single batch, and the men took pride in the appearance of their camp. "We tore the fences down and made roads of them," King related. "This is quite an improvement, only think railroads all around our camp. You may think that our camp must be woeful looking by my speaking of mud, but you would think different if you would see it." James Martin wrote that he and "some other boys went to get some cedar boughs to make our streets look like park lanes." Benjamin Wells, Daniel Rose, and James King enjoyed wandering the countryside and marveling at the strange sights and mild climate. Irving Metcalf raved about his sightseeing excursion to unforgettable Mammoth Cave. And social life, though reduced, had not ground to a complete halt. "We are not without our enjoyment altogether," noted Chadwick, "as we are occasionally invited out to dinner. Col. Stoughton and myself took dinner at a regular secessionist's house…. Such style I have not seen for many a day." Platt noted that the hosts of such dinners were deeply gracious, but if the war came up in conversation, the host would bluntly state their desire for the Federals to be whipped—even while hastening to disavow any personal animosity.[40]

Samuel Chadwick discussed Kentuckian hospitality at greater length in a letter to the *Reporter*:

> The citizens of the South are proverbial for their hospitality. They seem to vie with each other in this respect. It is not put on for the occasion, but wherever you go you meet with the warmest reception. It seems as if they could not do enough for you. They never tire in their entertainments, and think it very impolite if you do not accept their invitations. It is a common custom among the inhabitants, wherever you go, to first offer you a glass of whiskey.... If you are an invited guest to dinner you will have placed before you, about half an hour before the meal, a large vase of eggnogg, another of apple toddy, and then decanters filled with the finest of liquors, generally ten years old or thereabouts. The readers of your paper will be loth to believe that this is the case, not only with professors of religion, but *pastors of churches*.[41]

Despite the occasional pleasantry, it must initially have seemed like a welcome distraction when, on February 5, the regiment was ordered on a march out of isolation and toward town. With smallpox tapered off, the regiment's quarantine was loosened. To the Wolverines' surprise, they proceeded past Bardstown and trekked five miles south of the settlement. Upon arrival, the soldiers found a mass of other Union troops present—Chadwick counted nine regiments—and learned that they were brought to witness the execution of a serial killer, Samuel H. Calhoun of the Union 2nd Kentucky Infantry. Calhoun was convicted of murdering local civilian William Sutherland, and confessed to additional past killings. The convict had stolen a hog from Sutherland; the civilian then reported the theft to Calhoun's colonel, who punished his subordinate. Calhoun later took revenge, shooting Sutherland down in cold blood. "There he stood," Metcalf described the scene at the scaffold, "just entering manhood endowed by God with a liberal share of God's Gifts, the life flowing through his veins in healthful currents, and to soon to be launched into that unknown space. I never felt more solemn in my life and I presume the same feeling pervaded the whole assembly." The indifferent manner in which the young killer accepted his fate seems to have unnerved the onlookers. "He seemed to take it as coolly as if he were a spectator," Platt recorded. Daniel Rose, just arrived from treating the sick left behind at White Pigeon, reported the climax. "He rode down there on his coffin and mounted the scaffold ... then he turned around and helped fix the rope for his own neck, when the chaplain prayed he knelt down but did not seem affected in the least. then he turned around waved his hand and said 'farewell boys' then took the cap and drew it over his face and placed his hands behind to be tied. after the noose was put around his neck he stepped back on the trap. when the word ready was given he said 'bully.'"[42]

The regiment took another small step toward active operations on February 9 when Companies D and E were ordered to pack up and prepare for duty as the provost guard for Bardstown. This promising change of affairs was courtesy of Colonel William Haines Lytle, who succeeded General Wood at Bardstown. Soon after taking command, Lytle had visited the 11th Michigan and declared in strong terms his high regard for the Wolverine regiment. Two days after the news of the provost assignment came, Captains Bennett and Spencer marched their men to town through a snowstorm. Two weeks later, the balance of the regiment shifted camp one mile closer to town amid rumors that they would soon deploy to Bowling Green. The new campsite occupied a farm owned by Dr. John Jackson, brother of Elmer Ellsworth's infamous murderer, James W. Jackson. (Dr. Jackson's land was conveniently vacant because he had been charged in November with killing a Union soldier trespassing on his ground.) Platt described Jackson's house as "a plain story and a half building, with the usual number of negro huts surrounding it, and but for its associations would attract but little attention." The regimental band moved into town and made quite an impression on the residents, according to the *Bardstown Gazette*. "Every evening at sun set the band of the 11th Mich. Reg. attracts a large crowd of our music loving citizens to the public square to listen to its soul stirring martial airs. This is one of the best bands we have ever heard discourse a sweet concord of harmonious sounds."[43]

The camp was located just across a ravine from the home of former Kentucky governor Charles Anderson Wickliffe, who was presently serving his state in the U.S. House of Representatives. The Michiganders admired the governor's mansion, Wickland. "This is the most tasty residence I have seen since we left Louisville," King declared. "The house is large, two stories and a half high, and built of brick. The grounds around the house are set with Evergreens and trees of Every description. I have seen many splendid groves, but none that will compare with this. I visited the grounds yesterday but did not see any of the inmates, only a couple of negroes who were plowing in the field adjoining the house."[44]

On February 24, with the regiment over the hump health-wise, it finally occurred to someone that the 11th Michigan might be put to good use. Colonel John C. Walker of the 35th Indiana wrote from Munfordville to department headquarters stating that "the Medical Director at Bardstown informed me a few days ago that there was no small pox in the 11th Michigan Regiment Col May, and that it would inspirit the men and improve their health to assign them some light duty." Walker suggested forwarding the Michiganders to perform guard duty at Munfordville. Buell took his advice and dispatched the necessary orders on the twenty-seventh. On Monday, March 3, the marching orders were countermanded, but the resulting disappointment was mixed with relief. "I am glad of it," Captain Bennett insisted the next day, "for the roads are in a most horrid state. Friday last, Feb. 28th, was a beautiful spring day—the sun shone out bright and warm, and the birds were singing blithely, but on Saturday morning the ground was covered with snow. Saturday night we had a heavy thunder storm, and the rain came down in torrents until midnight on Sunday. Monday was a cold, cloudy, drizzling day." Any remaining sorrows were dispelled by the receipt of two months' pay on March 5.[45]

Ira Gillaspie had reported "grate joy and excitement amongst our boys" when news came of the February 16 fall of Fort Donelson. That spectacular triumph of Halleck's subordinate, Ulysses S. Grant, soon presented the regiment further cause for celebration. With the Union army set to advance deep into Tennessee, the Wolverines were needed for active service. Their first assignment was mere railroad guard duty, but after nearly three disease-ridden months of doing nothing but sickening and dying near Bardstown, the Michiganders were ecstatic for the opportunity. The 11th Michigan finally left on the morning of March 6. "We gladly turned our backs on Bardstown," Ozro Bowen exclaimed. Chadwick wrote to the *Reporter*, "Alas! how many who, two months ago, at Camp Stoughton, stood in the ranks and answered to their names, as full and as buoyant as any of those now present, have gone to their long homes! How many friends at home mourn their loss, as well as their comrades here!"[46]

Bardstown had one last curse in store for the 11th, as a last-gasp winter storm dumped three or four inches of snow on the marching troops, burying roads already muddied by the rains. "The road was nothing but mud with hills looming out of it," Shorty declared in a letter to the *Mercury*. The determined troops trudged close to ten miles, yet the meandering lanes of the Kentucky hills edged them only four or five miles closer to their destination of Belmont Furnace, located less than twenty straight-line miles northwest of Camp Morton. "At night we had to stick our tents in two inches of snow," remarked Benjamin Bordner. "I tell you it was fun." The wagons kept getting stuck in the mud, and the last of the exhausted teams did not reach camp until 10:00 p.m. The second day offered up similar challenges, with mud knee deep for the first two miles, and at times the tired Federals endured single-file crawls up hillside ravines.[47] The rural population delivered some comic relief to blunt the strain of the journey, as related by Shorty:

> The [second] day the road was worse, if anything, winding around hills, crossing creeks and ravines, and at times directly in a small stream. The people along the route stared at us as though we were some of Barnum's curiosities escaping.... Their ideas of the war are very meager, if they have any at all. Indeed we found some who actually did not know there was a war, and wanted to know "what them men were all dressed alike fur?" We of the North have always heard a great deal of the superior intelligence and cultivated intellectual faculties of the Southern people, but taking the country and city inhabitants in general I cannot see as they are far ahead of us.[48]

Dawn of day three saw the regiment situated four or five miles short of Belmont Furnace, where the Wolverines were due to relieve the 3rd Minnesota Infantry. The Minnesotans lent their teams out to ease the burden, and the 11th Michigan finally arrived later that day, March 8.[49] Belmont occupied an idyllic setting. King described the village as

> a place of about 50 houses, situated in a valley of about 200 acres, surrounded by mountains which raised their lofty heads far above us. These mountains are covered with a fine growth of timber. A few of their tops are covered with evergreens, which give them a very beautiful appearance. There is something of awe and grandeur in one of these huge piles [that] one feels which I cannot describe.... Tis a sight worth beholding. The principal buildings in Belmont is a large iron foundry, a large frame dwelling, and a large brick building.[50]

About half the town's structures had been commandeered to serve as a hospital complex, and the aforementioned brick building served as Colonel May's headquarters.[51]

The desolate winter suddenly gave way to a captivating spring, reinforcing the perception that the regiment had awakened from a nightmare when it departed Bardstown. Or perhaps more accurately, the soldiers now felt like they were dreaming. "We have got the best camping ground that we ever had," a jubilant James Martin declared. "We can ride on the cars from here to Bowling Green free of charge, and we have bully good times.... The peach trees are in bloom and every thing shows summer is nigh." Shorty reported that the regiment was "daily thronged by the denizens of the surrounding hills" who descended upon the settlement to sell butter, eggs, pies, and assorted farm goods. It was great news for everyone except the sutler. The plentiful fresh food and good weather worked wonders for the Michiganders' constitutions. "Applejack and chickens were plenty in that portion of the state," wrote Shorty, "and the health of the regiment improved rapidly." "We have but little to do & pretty good fare for soldiers," Wells added. "We are fleshing up. If we were to be put on a forced march & be on the battle field (of which there is not much danger) a few days without anything to eat I think it would take some of the fat off. I heard from Wall [William "Wallace" Hoisington, Wells's aforementioned brother-in-law] yesterday he is getting as fat & lazy as there is any need of being."[52]

The regiment was scattered on guard duty along the Louisville and Nashville Railroad, a vital supply line for the advancing Union forces. It was easy, safe, pleasant work. Regimental headquarters remained at Belmont, as did the band and two companies. Company A was stationed at Elizabethtown, D at the Nolin River railroad crossing, E at Shepherdsville, and the balance at various points between Shepherdsville and Nolin River. The closest any member of the regiment came to harm in this period was when a guardhouse caught fire while Private Coe Holly of Company C was sleeping inside. Holly narrowly escaped, but the guards' equipment and clothes were consumed in the conflagration. "We had lots of fun with them about the fier," Gillaspie remarked, "for they was consiterable in want of clothing. Some of them had no caps and some had lost one thing and some another. They looked motly and like some renegades."[53]

But the only real drama during the regiment's weeks of guard duty involved the colonel. On March 12, James King, who had been left behind to treat the sick at Bardstown, arrived in Belmont and reported to Colonel May. "He wished me good morning," King remembered, and "asked me how the sick were getting along up at Bardstown. I told him four of them had died since the regiment left. 'My God,' said he, 'how many of our boys are going to die? Would to God I had never seen a regiment.' A great many blame Colonel May, but I believe if there ever was a kind hearted man and one who tries to do right, Col. May is one. I have seen better managers than him, but he has a heart." May, like the rest of the officers, had come under fire for the sickness and mortality suffered by his men at Bardstown, and undoubtedly the stress took a steep toll on him, both emotionally and physically. Although the colonel was generally liked and respected by his men, he had been the subject of cruel rumors since day one. In January an astonishing claim had been repeated in the *Chronicle*, proclaiming that May had attempted to arrange for the capture of the 11th Michigan by sending a subordinate disguised in women's clothing to coordinate the treachery with the Rebels. The soldier in this fiction was shot in the act; May was caught red-handed and supposedly scheduled for execution. Captain Spencer revealed the falsity of this tall tale to the newspaper and tried to deflect any tension with humor: "Served [Colonel May] right enough, if he had been guilty." But the false rumors did not stop there. The *Reporter* published an equally base tale in February under the sensational headline "Col. May arrested! Is to Be Tried by Court Martial!" asserting that "a reliable gentleman now at the camp of the Eleventh Regiment" passed along this shocking news—without any further explanation from the newspaper. The *Reporter* further tarnished its reputation by accepting this story at face value and stating that such bold action as a court-martial, pursued sooner, would have saved many lives and much treasure. May had been physically ill even back in White Pigeon, and the hard times in Kentucky did nothing to improve his health. By mid–March it was common knowledge that his fitness had declined to the point where not only his command, but also his life, were in danger. By March 22 the colonel was transported to Louisville for medical care and was bedridden. One week later he was able to stand on his own two feet again, but he was still in no condition to leave his room. By then he realized that his constitution was inadequate for further military service. May resigned as colonel of the 11th Michigan Infantry, effective April 1, 1862.[54]

It was an exciting time. May had been popular enough, but his bond with the men had never been cemented by the shared trauma of battle. Stoughton was every bit as likeable, and more highly respected. "There is not much doubt that the Lieutenant Colonel will take [May's] place," King wrote. "I think Lieut. Colonel Stoughton a better military man than May, and the regiment will probably do better under his management than May's." The men credited Stoughton when they were at last issued Springfield rifles on April 9, a vast improvement over their decrepit smoothbore muskets. The rumor mill declared that the regiment would be sent south of Nashville and brigaded in the wake of Grant and Buell's April 6–7 victory at Shiloh. Glorious spring was in full swing; the deadly past winter was sinking into memory. Union soldiers were advancing through Tennessee, and with Stoughton as colonel, the 11th's future was looking brighter. And then, the anxiously awaited word came: on April 23, Chadwick announced that the regiment had been ordered to Nashville, Tennessee. "The news was what we all wanted to hear," Gillaspie commented. At last, the 11th Michigan Volunteer Infantry would occupy Confederate soil.[55]

CHAPTER 3

"Covered in dust instead of glory"
April–December 1862

Following the Union victory at Shiloh, the Confederates, now led by P.G.T. Beauregard, fell back to Corinth, Mississippi. Grant's and Buell's forces, now under the overall command of Henry Halleck, advanced timidly. In the meantime, Buell's subordinate Ormsby M. Mitchel occupied Huntsville, Alabama.

On Friday April 25 Colonel Stoughton received follow-up orders to prepare his regiment for deployment to Nashville in three days. This time there was no mistake and no delay; the Michiganders spent all day Sunday packing and were roused for departure early in the morning of Monday April 28. Deployment to Tennessee would have been swiftest by southbound train, but Confederate harassment of the railway dictated a combined approach, first by train to Louisville and then by river boat to Nashville. The soldiers were rushing for the depot by 6:00 a.m., only to wait impatiently until late afternoon for their ride to show. Then it took the cars twenty-four hours to traverse just twenty-five miles. Wells blamed the maddening pace on the "length and weight of the train," but Gillaspie recorded a more specific explanation. "We run off the track a cople of times," he explained, "and broke up one car so as to have to leave it on the side of the road on its side. The engineer was drunk and then some. He would run like all possessed and then the train would barely move along."[1]

The Wolverines disembarked around 4:00 or 5:00 a.m., relaxed for a couple of hours, and then tramped through Louisville to the wharf. There the *E.H. Fairchild* awaited, a fine steamer that provoked comments of admiration from the Michiganders. By 5:00 p.m. the boat was underway down the Ohio River under a perfect blue sky. The state of the waterway imparted a strong impression: it was severely flooded, in many cases forcing the occupants of riverside dwellings to the second floor—for those lucky enough to have an upper story. King described the Ohio River as looking "more like a vast lake than a river," and Bennett noted that Shawneetown, Illinois, was submerged, with "small boats plying about the streets." Private Henry Hall of Company A was intrigued at the how the locals along the Ohio coped with such adversity. "Some of their grain they have managed to save by placing it on rafts," he noted, "and they have platforms built for their cattle and horses, some standing in the water and perish[ing]. Yet, notwithstanding their gloomy condition, they cheered us heartily. One instance that came under notice, was a horse hitched to a canoe, one man riding the horse while another man was sitting in the stern, steering the canoe. The man on horse-back waved his hat and cheered us, but as the boat passed, the waves took him and knocked him off his horse." With a long trip ahead, the men sought ways to amuse themselves, and inevitably it occurred to someone to test their marksmanship with the Springfield rifle on the buzzards infesting the river banks. Around sunset the *Fairchild* approached West Point, Kentucky, where Battery F of the 1st Michigan Light Artillery was stationed. The gunners and infantry had heard that they might enjoy a fleeting opportunity to greet each other in passing, and they made the most of it. The *Fairchild's* passengers were especially keen on greeting the artillerists' first lieutenant, Norman S. Andrews of Three Rivers. "As the flag bearer stood on deck and waved *our* flag," wrote Chadwick, "and the whistle sounded, flash went one of Norm's guns, and the roar of the welcome from its mouth incited our boys to cheer after cheer as we neared the bank.... [We] gave them in return music from the band and cheers without number."[2]

Twenty-four hours later, the steamer navigated into the Cumberland River, where the scenery elicited gasps of awe. Benjamin Wells called it "the most beautiful river I ever saw it still waters gliding gently down to the mighty deep at some places the banks are several hundred feet high with rocks & trees & the scenery is magnificent." During the next morning, May 1, the now famous Fort Donelson came into view. The men were fascinated, and pleaded with the boat captain to stop for a better look, but he declined. "Close to the water's edge," King observed, "was a breastwork where they had several batteries of the heaviest caliber. These were the batteries which done so much damage to our gunboats. Farther up the bank, where the battle raged with the greatest fury, was another breastwork. I noticed some trees which looked as though Ten thousand lightnings had played among their branches. Twas through these trees our gallant boys poured their shot and shell, sending death and destruction into the enemy's camp." The ship stopped for wood and coal at Clarksville, Tennessee, a settlement already run down by the one-two punch of a stagnating economy and war damage. Metcalf eyed a majestic railroad bridge over the river that had narrowly survived being put to the torch. The *Fairchild* was soon under steam again, and farther downriver the men spotted Fort Zollicoffer, which had been abandoned upon the approach of Federal forces. King spotted one cannon partially submerged near the stronghold, and Wells noted several others on high ground that had been spiked.[3]

The *E.H. Fairchild* anchored at Nashville around 9:00 p.m., and the regiment slept onboard. After sunrise, May 2, the unit reunited itself with terra firma and entered Nashville. Unlike Kentucky, this was occupied enemy territory. The Wolverines found neither the citizens nor the settlement pleasing. "The people here are nearly all secessionists," King remarked, "and look upon us with a coldness." Bennett joked that Union men were "as scarce as honest men" in President Buchanan's cabinet, and he was shocked at the condition of the city. He considered Nashville's economy "literally ruined by Secession. Trade of all kinds was at a perfect stand-still.... I don't believe there was ten dollars in good money in the whole town. The currency was composed of shinplasters of all kinds. The Banks issued bills as low as five cents.... 'Confed. Scrip' made up the currency above $5, and any one who refused to take this trash was deemed a traitor and punished accordingly." The Michiganders used the opportunity to unload broken bank notes from their home state upon the desperate locals. Daniel Rose went so far as to write home for the otherwise worthless paper to be forwarded for him to spend. Chadwick dismissively declared Nashville "not so fine a city as I expected to see." The Wolverines came to a halt at the headquarters of Brigadier General Ebenezer Dumont, who was engaged in a public harangue against the rebellion. The general acknowledged the newcomers with a short speech and complimented their military bearing. The 11th then continued two miles outside of town and bivouacked.[4]

Everyone had high hopes that the 1862 military campaign would prove decisive, and Stoughton's troops continued to fret that they would not get into the action before the war was over. New Orleans had succumbed to David Glasgow Farragut's naval assault. Shiloh had knocked the western Confederates back on their heels, and George Brinton McClellan's Peninsula Campaign was widely expected by Northerners to culminate in the capture of Richmond. "Our troops are continually advancing and the rebels are falling back," Daniel Rose commented. Wells further proclaimed, "I think we have got as far South as we will get during the war; we will not move many more times ere we move for home. I think the war will soon close: For the two armies are now in close contact, there will be but a few more forced marches ere the decisive blow will have been struck." Company A private Rollin Eaton predicted that "most likely we shall march for Mississippi and be there when our troops atact Richmond."[5]

On the morning of May 3, the unit shifted a short distance and set up camp on the farm of former Tennessee congressman Andrew Ewing. King noted that Ewing's wife had not yet evacuated, and one of their slaves said that he "guessed his missus would go crazy." "This was one of the loveliest spots in nature," Chadwick declared, "and the boys remarked—'This is too fine a spot to stay in long.' The trees were all clothed in their Summer garb, and the cool shade was refreshing." Although wartime Nashville failed to impress, its surroundings elicited quite the opposite response. King added that "the nicest country I ever saw is here. Our camp is in a grove of trees of the richest foliage," and he went on to describe Ewing's nearby residence as "a perfect palace situated in a fine grove of trees. The yard is filled with flowers of every description." Bennett raved that "this is the most lovely and delightful country that I ever saw. We are wont to praise the beauties of our own prairies and openings, but if you wish to see the very 'poetry of Nature,' you must come to middle Tennessee. Such scenery—such a soil—such a climate—why, it would seem that in its creation the hand of Divine Providence had tried its best to see what blessings could be provided for man's enjoyment on earth."[6]

Chadwick's prediction about the camp being "too fine a spot to stay in long" proved all too prophetic. The very next night, Colonel Stoughton—whose widely anticipated promotion to colonel had been confirmed just days before—was awakened with urgent orders to prepare for departure to the train depot at 10:00 p.m. The weary men of the 11th, who had just nodded off, were allowed all of ten or fifteen minutes to arise and prepare for the march. Leaving their tents and camp equipment behind, the Wolverines hurried along and reached the depot at midnight. They caught some shuteye there, having rushed only to languish idle for seventeen hours while awaiting further orders. At 5:00 p.m. word finally came that they must proceed to Columbia. Brigadier General James Scott Negley was convinced that significant Rebel forces were threatening his position from both east and west, and was frantically calling for reinforcements. Rumor had it that the Confederates were led by none other than the famed raider, cavalryman John Hunt Morgan. The Michiganders, anxious to see action for the first time, pulled into a disappointingly tranquil Columbia between midnight and 1:00 a.m. on May 6. They crossed the Duck River on a pontoon bridge constructed by the 1st Michigan Engineers—the main bridge was burned out—and rested up in the courthouse (with Captain Spencer, at least, finding enough time for a nap) before taking up a defensive position two miles south of town.[7]

At about the same time of night that the main body of the regiment arrived in Columbia, the fifty soldiers left behind ill at the Nashville camp experienced their own share of exhilaration. Rebels—probably guerrillas—approached the scarcely defended encampment, and Quartermaster Addison T. Drake desperately formed his convalescents into line of battle (such as he knew how). "Fall in, boys, in two rows," he shouted. "Some on one end and some on the other!" Mercifully, the enemy—if an actual enemy was indeed present—backed off and left Drake's grasp of tactics and command untested.[8]

The assault that General Negley dreaded at Columbia failed to materialize, but the Federals there remained on constant alert. Morgan's stealthy hit and run tactics had everyone on edge, from General Negley down to the lowliest private. But the Michiganders enjoyed experiencing some commotion for a change. "We feel as though we were doing the country some service," said Chadwick. "Orders reach us at all hours, and we are sent out on this expedition or that; sometimes the whole regiment, then again in companies and detachments. Picket duty of companies every night." On May 7, Companies A, D, F, H, and I were dis-

John Hunt Morgan was a brilliant Confederate cavalryman with a talent for conducting stunningly successful raids behind Union lines. He triggered the introduction of the 11th Michigan to active military operations, which instilled confidence in the green regiment's soldiers. His bogeyman reputation intimidated Federal commanders and prevented his capture at Paris, Kentucky, by a Union force that included the 11th Michigan. The subsequent sacking of the town of Gallatin, executed in part by Stoughton's Wolverines, hardened Morgan's attitude toward Union civilians (Library of Congress).

patched to escort more than 100 provision-laden wagons earmarked to supply Brigadier General Mitchel at Huntsville. After traveling most of the distance to Pulaski, marching quick time part of the way and living off hardtack, the escort was relieved by a rendezvousing cavalry regiment from Huntsville. The Wolverines returned to camp on May 9 all worn out. "We had all the geese and turkeys we wanted to eat," remarked Daniel Rose, "but I never had sorer feet in my life." It was a virtually empty encampment that greeted them upon return. The other half of the regiment had set out on a fruitless attempt to bag a Rebel force—again said to be Morgan—supposedly assembling in swampland nearly ten miles away. The pickets had captured some Confederates believed to be Morgan's that morning, and this little adventure in the marsh was probably the result of the prisoners' ensuing interrogation at Negley's headquarters. "We traveled all day thrue a large thick and wet swamp," Gillaspie complained, "cutting our way thrue the brush and wading in water to our brests." These Confederates, like their predecessors, proved either elusive or imaginary, and the fatigued Michigan unit was reunited just in time to relocate camp that night to a hill overlooking town, where they were stationed in support of an artillery battery.[9]

On the night of May 12 the regiment suffered its first friendly fire casualty. Company B, out scouting after dark, lost its way and wandered into the line of fire of Company I's pickets. Sergeant John McGuire and Private Henry Jubenville discharged their rifles, slightly wounding a member of Company B. "I tell you," Gillaspie wrote of McGuire and Jubenville, "they was 2 mity shaky boys never haveing shot a body before they was really week in the knees and sick of heart."[10]

Another supply train was dispatched for Pulaski on the sixteenth, and the entire 11th Michigan was assigned to guard the wagons this time. Apparently the tediousness of the previous escort duty was still fresh on everyone's minds. Chadwick was left behind in charge of camp with 200 sick, vexed in his belief that "many of these men 'played possum'" to avoid the strenuous ordeal—a suspicion James Martin shared, given that only thirty-two men from his company reported fit for duty. The adjutant was thus entrusted with maintaining a proper camp guard with limited resources, and under his watch Privates Kneeland Latham of Company E and Jonathan Ferguson of Company I, dispatched in hot pursuit of some stray mules, were taken prisoner by seven guerrillas who rushed them from a thicket. The frightened Federals were stripped of their weapons and accouterments, marched six miles, forced to take the Confederate oath, and released on parole.[11]

Also during the brief period of Chadwick's camp command, the 11th's newly appointed lieutenant colonel, forty-nine-year-old Nathaniel Buel Eldridge, arrived from Michigan. On the surface, Eldridge was seemingly unconnected with the 11th regiment, and his appointment was therefore unexpected, even though he was a qualified officer. Fifteen of the regiment's commissioned officers had signed an April 10 petition pressing for Stoughton to be promoted to colonel, and for Captain Chamberlain to be raised into the resulting vacancy at lieutenant colonel. But Governor Blair had already acted by the time the petition reached his office. Eldridge, a prominent citizen of Lapeer, Michigan, was a past representative in the state legislature and had served as major of the 7th Michigan Infantry at the outset of the war. After suffering through the Federal calamity at Ball's Bluff, Eldridge penned a private letter, deeply critical of Brigadier General Charles P. Stone. This correspondence somehow found its way into print, and Stone had his detractor arrested. Eldridge resigned in response, and accepted an offer from Governor Blair to serve on the State Military Board. By April 17 Eldridge received an offer for the 11th Michigan's lieutenant colonelcy, and he responded to accept the commission (nonchalantly commenting that he'd prefer a command of his own) from Adjutant General Robertson. Eldridge followed up with another letter written from Lapeer on May 7 to ask for his commission to be forwarded, and to request the helpful information of where the regiment was actually located, so that he might report for duty.[12]

The selection of Eldridge, an outsider to the regiment, is particularly of interest since he was, in fact, an old friend of Chadwick's—both had grown up in Cayuga County, New York. Chadwick had been back in Michigan on recruiting business at the same time May decided to resign, and returned to Kentucky too late for any involvement in the petition favoring Chamberlain for lieutenant colonel. It seems likely that Chadwick, while in Michigan, seized the opportunity to recommend his friend for the vacancy. "He is a guest of the adjutant," Chadwick informed the *Reporter* when Eldridge arrived at Columbia, and "not an unwelcome one I assure you.... He is a fine good looking man, and, for a civilian, a good officer. He will be popular in the Regiment, I have no doubt. But for a clique in the regiment one of our own number would have been appointed." The historical record offers no further evidence of this clique, but this comment suggests all the more motivation for Chadwick to have exerted his influence in favor of Eldridge. There is, however, no indication of hard feelings over the new lieutenant colonel's appointment. On the contrary, Wells remarked several days after the newcomer's arrival that he was already popular with the regiment.[13]

The situation at Columbia was calmer for the balance of May, and the 11th was told to settle in. Companies B and G were detailed as provost guard under Captain Mudge, policing the town's "self-willed, bull-necked secessionists," as Aaron Sturges put it.[14] "You see we are still at this place, as usual," Chadwick told the *Reporter* in early June.

> We have always been doing what some of us call the dirty work of the Post....
> ...The General commanding a post is instructed to keep the best disciplined troops in his brigade, and the best and most orderly men for guard and fatigue duty, while he pushes forward the remaining. The Eleventh having, in every place borne the character of the *best*, we are constantly kept at such work....
> ...We were called here *in an emergency*. We have been here three weeks and the *emergency* has been, to load and unload cars and wagons.[15]

Between illness and furloughs, the regiment's rank and file present for duty had dropped below 600 men. Each soldier was standing guard every other day, leaving no time for regular drill. Stoughton and Oakes were detailed on general court-martial duty.[16]

Finally there was some genuine excitement on June 2. Tennessee's military governor Andrew Johnson and ex-governor Neill S. Brown were scheduled to arrive at

Nathaniel Buel Eldridge was prompted to resign his position as major of the 7th Michigan after denouncing a superior officer for the Federal disaster at Ball's Bluff. He may have owed his unexpected appointment as lieutenant colonel of the 11th Michigan to the support of his childhood friend, Adjutant Samuel Chadwick (courtesy Archives of Michigan).

11:00 a.m. via rail from Nashville to give public speeches. The 69th Ohio—destined to be brigaded with the 11th Michigan in time for a future fight near Murfreesboro—escorted the governors from Nashville. Chadwick detailed 150 of the finest men in the 11th to polish their guns, boots, and equipment, and marched them to the depot to greet the dignitaries. Accounts of the scene at the rail station vary wildly; Chadwick bitterly exclaimed that "*not a single citizen was there, at the depot, to receive*" Johnson, whereas King reported that "at an Early hour the people began to flock in. Men who had not been in town since our troops gained possession of it. I could tell every one of them by their shy looks." Similarly, a reporter from the *New York Times*, although apparently not present at the depot, reported a large mass of citizens present for the governors' speeches across town later in the day (as did Aaron Sturges and Nathan Adams), while Chadwick asserted in disgust that less than 100 locals were present then. Perhaps his claims of poor turnout spoke more of his opinion of the character of the citizenry than anything else. Captain Mudge, as provost marshal, furnished a carriage for the speakers, and Captain Spencer led Company E, the regimental band, and two companies of Ohioans escorting Johnson and Brown to the Nelson House. Johnson, as the most prominent of Tennessee Unionists, was a high-value target for the Rebels, so there was ample cause for the escort to remain wary.[17] The carriage, furnished and escorted by the 11th Michigan, rolled along, conveying the future vice president (and later president) of the United States. Suddenly, as Johnson's fellow passenger Samuel Glenn of the *New York Herald* related,

> the horses, from some cause or other, took fright as the carriage

was passing up the hill at the edge of a steep embankment, and suddenly turned nearly around. Governor Johnson's quick eye discovered the movement, and in a moment he opened the carriage door and landed upon terra firma, followed by the other occupants of the vehicle. Had the carriage overturned at the spot, there is no knowing what damage might have ensued. As it was, the Governor concluded not to try a similar experiment; for there was no calculating what mischievous or dastardly tricks the secessionists of the vicinity might undertake in order to wreak their vengeance upon him.[18]

The unnerved politicians elected to walk the remainder of the route. Brown, an ex–Confederate, had experienced a change of heart and swore allegiance to the Union after being captured and brought up on charges of treason. He spoke to the assembled crowd first, and by all accounts he and Johnson, with the stump of an enormous oak tree for a platform, presented powerfully stated cases against the continuation of the rebellion. Chadwick had heard Johnson speak "several times, once when he made the southern senators tremble, in the Senate Chamber, at Washington, but his speech at this meeting was a masterly effort. Strange that people will not regard his teachings." The meeting broke up at 5:00 p.m., the politicians departed by rail, and the 11th Michigan was swiftly deployed to a defensive position on the outskirts of the city amid rumors that Morgan was scheming to capture or kill Governor Johnson.[19] But once again, the wait for the Rebel Raider amounted to nothing more than an unrewarded exercise in patience.

Early on June 9, the 11th was ordered to head for the train depot on a moment's notice, leaving the camp equipment behind again. At 1:00 p.m. marching orders were announced, and unprecedentedly, a train was ready and waiting at the station. The cars whisked the Michiganders to Murfreesboro, where they arrived about nightfall and bivouacked in a grove half a mile outside of town. The next day was spent in tense anticipation, with the regiment, as Sturges described it, "fogged in the mist of rumors." The rumor mill was hit and miss as usual: word spread that there was to be an eastbound expedition under General Dumont—true enough—but this was appended with the traditional exaggeration of military gossip. No less than 12,000 troops were said to be gathering for that purpose, and for good measure, someone added the outright falsehood that the Michiganders would be left behind on provost duty. Dumont in fact planned

Andrew Johnson was counted among the few prominent Southerners to remain loyal to the Union, and was appointed military governor of Tennessee. The 11th Michigan escorted Johnson to his speech in Nashville on June 2, 1862, and furnished him with a carriage that violently overturned. The future U.S. president narrowly escaped harm (Library of Congress).

a reconnaissance beyond McMinnville, intended to drive off a Rebel cavalry force in that vicinity. That evening, the 11th was ordered to prepare rations for six days and be ready to march at 7:00 a.m. The balance of Dumont's force initially consisted of three full infantry regiments and part of a fourth (the 3rd Minnesota and the 69th and 74th Ohio, joined by two companies of the 28th Kentucky), two battalions of the 7th Pennsylvania Cavalry, and two gun batteries.[20]

The Union brigadier pressed his troops forward into the June heat. They reached Woodbury at 5:00 p.m. and encamped, but were soon ordered to pack up, and were underway again at 11:00 p.m. A full moon lit the way until it surrendered to Earth's shadow, and the soldiers enjoyed a total lunar eclipse on the march. They entered McMinnville, a rest stop, at 10:00 a.m., completing the arduous, foot-borne voyage of forty miles from Murfreesboro in just over twenty-four hours. The horsemen took possession of town, permitted no one to leave, and detained anyone who entered. The oath of allegiance was administered to 250 citizens. Dumont stayed put the following day but resumed the march at 3:00 a.m. on Saturday the fourteenth, again shunning the daytime heat. The 8th and 21st Kentucky Infantry, and the 4th Kentucky Cavalry, rendezvoused to inflate the blue ranks to some 5,000 men. Later that morning, Gillaspie reported, the 11th incurred its first casualty of the expedition when Francis Jerome of Company E "went to ride acrost the river on a pease of artilery. He slipt off over the front sight of the gun wounding himself very bad in the secrets." Dumont learned that the Rebels were presently near Pikeville, and tested the mettle of his troops with another forced march—this time with the added challenge of clambering over mountainous terrain. Wells exclaimed that at one point the blue column "had to climb about three miles over the roughest road I ever saw many of the men were entirely worn out & the side of the road was strewn with men that could go no further." This time the voyage terminated in the evening at a patch of woods shy of Pikeville, more than forty miles from the point of origin. There was nothing to eat since the wagon teams had fallen behind, struggling with the terrain. An unlucky flock of sheep, caught in the wrong place at the wrong time, paid the ultimate price for the soldiers' hunger. But there was not enough meat to go around, and with no salt or cookery on hand, the repast impressed no one. The sleeping arrangements were equally uncomfortable, since the blankets were left behind on the wagons as well.[21]

On Sunday morning, with supplies running low (the Wolverines had just one day of rations remaining) and with word arriving that the Rebel horsemen had fled before the Pennsylvanian and Kentuckian troopers, the expedition about faced and headed back whence it came. Dumont solved his logistical dilemma by sending advance word to McMinnville that he would torch the town unless the occupants provided a generous supply of bread (Wells said 5,000 pounds; Gillaspie, 3,200). The citizens in response discovered hidden reserves of motivation, and punctually provided the quantity demanded, if not the quality desired. The Federals arrived on Monday, picked up their bread order, and set out again the next morning at 5:00 a.m. The stars and stripes were left flying high over the town, with another promise from Dumont to burn the place to the ground if any harm came to the flag. The Union soldiers finally returned to Murfreesboro very early on June 20, and they did so in fine fashion, according to Benjamin Wells. Despite a steady downpour, "the boys seemed to feel first rate for they were singing and hurrahing all the time it rained: We got here into camp about ½ past four yesterday morning & a more tired & worse used up set of boys I never saw. There were but a few men in the Reg. that would have gone 3 miles further.... But few troops in the service would have made better time under similar circumstances than we made on this march." Colonel Henry C. Lester of the 3rd Minnesota provided a succinct and honest summary of Dumont's trek to Pikeville, saying, "The expedition was worthy remark only for the rapidity of the march and its fatigues." Nathan Adams put it more bluntly: "Our regiment has gone off on a wild goos chase."[22]

The return to Murfreesboro was doubly sweet as the soldiers had a pile of letters from home waiting for them. "It is an interesting spectacle," Sturges noted, "to see a regiment of soldiers all seated upon the ground each man with an open letter in his hands, silently and intently perusing its contents. How varied the character of these missives; and what volumes do they express of love, friendship and anxious solicitude. To the soldier, letters from those he has left behind, are sweet sprinklings of poetry in the hard, dull prose of his life."[23]

The 11th returned to Nashville by rail, where the soldiers were detailed on what Wells described as "a heavy Guard duty." Gillaspie was grateful to have "a hansome camping ground and a noble spring and a nice litle brook." The weather was uncomfortable—rainy and warm—but Wells cheerfully reported an abundance of ripe fruit on the local market and declared the regiment to be in good health, excepting some minor physical complaints that resulted from Dumont's pursuit of the Confederates. The stay in Nashville was a welcome respite, generally peaceful and uneventful. There was a scare during drill on June 25, however, when Daniel Shippy of Company D accidentally discharged what he thought to be an unloaded rifle. The unexpected bullet killed Stoughton's horse instantly; luckily the colonel escaped injury despite having one foot pinned under the dead weight of his fallen mount. On June 30, two detachments of twenty men each were dispatched separately by train under Captain Hood and First Lieutenant Ephraim Gaylord Hall to help transport Confederate prisoners north. Gillaspie placed the prisoner count at 1,400 and believed they were from Shiloh, but either his count was exaggerated, or the captives originated from multiple sources. Hood and Hall escorted the prisoners to Louisville, and then via the steamer *Autocrat* to Cairo, Illinois, where Gillaspie noted that "we did not land until next morning for we was afraid of losing some in the dark." The Confederates were delivered without incident to the barracks, and the Federals backtracked to Nashville, arriving at 5:00 p.m. on July 8—reuniting with the regiment just in time to partake in another hunt for John Morgan.[24]

The Confederates had evacuated Corinth on the night of May 29. With Halleck's objective secured, he sent Buell east to link with Mitchel and threaten the strategic rail hub of Chattanooga. Like Halleck, Buell advanced at a leisurely pace, and the Rebels soon unleashed two of their most capable cavalry commanders, Nathan Bedford Forrest and John Hunt Morgan, to raise hell in Buell's rear and tear up his supply line.

Morgan struck on the morning of July 9 with a surprise attack that routed a three-company detachment of the 9th Pennsylvania Cavalry at Tompkinsville, Kentucky. At 10:00 that night, the 11th Michigan startled awake to the bugle's call. Under the orders of Nashville's post commander, Colonel John Franklin Miller, the 11th formed up and repeated the now familiar ordeal of hastening to the depot only to spend hours awaiting a train. The cars eventually showed up and whisked the Federals off to Bowling Green.[25]

The Wolverines arrived in Bowling Green early the next day but were rolling along the rails again a couple hours later, this time bound for Cave City, where an optimistic soldiers' rumor promised that they would intercept their quarry. Upon arrival, the regiment learned that Morgan was actually at Glasgow. Henry Platt and another lieutenant scouted on horseback in the direction of Glasgow until they were convinced by the citizens along their route that they had heard right about Morgan's whereabouts. Around 11:00 p.m. Stoughton pressed his men forward on an overnight march through what Martin termed "a drenching rain" in hopes of bagging the Rebels. At 7:00 a.m. on July 11 the weary, soaked soldiers plodded into Glasgow to the sight of a torched supply depot. Morgan had skipped town ahead of them. The crestfallen Federals rested a bit and then received new orders through Buell's chief of staff, James B. Fry. The regiment doubled back to Cave City and was conveyed over the tracks again. A detachment was diverted to bolster the garrison at Bowling Green while the bulk of the regiment continued to Munfordville, where they protected the Green River bridge against an expected attempt by Morgan to destroy the span.[26]

John Franklin Miller led the expedition that engaged Morgan's men at Gallatin and sacked the town. Shortly thereafter, he was placed in command of a secretive, but short-lived, light brigade that included the hard-marching 11th Michigan (Library of Congress).

Accurate intelligence of the Rebels' movements led the 11th to embark a train again on July 13, this time bound for Lebanon, but a burned out bridge at New Haven brought their excursion to an unanticipated halt. The Michiganders visited Shepherdsville the next day, and then coasted into the station at Louisville on the morning of July 15. "There was an aufull excitement amongst the people hear fearing an atackt from Morgan," Gillaspie observed, and sure enough the regiment was quickly deployed two miles out of the city on a false alarm. They encamped in an oak grove, boarded the cars for Frankfort on the seventeenth, arrived there at nightfall, and bedded down in a hotel ballroom—surely their most pleasant accommodations since the chase inaugurated. "I have not even had a blanket with me since we left Nashville," Platt complained, "and have slept on the ground, in the cars, and almost every posture imaginable but an easy one."[27]

The 11th Michigan had yet to catch even a glimpse of Morgan's raiders, let alone bring them to battle, yet their role in harassing the Confederate cavalrymen garnered public recognition. The *Chronicle* in its July 23 issue reported that "the 11th has been crowding the guerrilla Morgan pretty hard of late," and printed a letter from Lieutenant French enumerating the long line of pursuit. The *Louisville Journal*, in the wake of the 11th's return, expounded the unit's virtues. "This fine regiment, under the command of Col. Stoughton, has for several months performed most efficient service in Kentucky, and has lately been distinguished for its alacrity and zeal in the defence of various points of the State against the marauding bands under Morgan.... Their evening dress parade, which we attended last evening, was distinguished by the solidity of movement and soldierly bearing of the troops, and the precision with which the officers gave their commands. Kentucky owes a debt of gratitude to this gallant regiment for all the privations it has undergone in defending it against invasion." The Michiganders received recognition of a more official nature when Assistant Adjutant General Oliver Green wrote to Buell's chief of staff, crediting Stoughton's regiment with saving the bridges at Bowling Green and Munfordville from Morgan. But additional journalistic coverage gave the people back in Michigan a scare. Nathan Bedford Forrest bagged Murfreesboro with its garrison on July 13, and the *New York Times*, among other papers, erroneously listed the 11th Michigan among the units captured (in fact, the 9th Michigan had been taken as prisoners). This error may have been triggered by Buell's Special Orders No. 92 of July 1, which included an order, promptly countermanded, for the 11th to report to Murfreesboro. The gaffe was corrected in the July 19 *Reporter*, but the panic back home became common knowledge to the soldiers, who hastily penned letters home to reassure their loved ones. Platt further took the time to inform the *Journal* that "this is a mistake, the Michigan 11th *never surrenders*."[28]

The Wolverines' slumbers in the Frankfort ballroom were fleeting, for the now despised bugle blared out at 1:00 a.m., and one hour later the soldiers were on their way to Morgan's last known location, Georgetown. This foray out of Frankfort for the first time involved the 11th in a well-orchestrated attempt to engage Morgan's Rebels, and to the credit of the cavalry-starved (and thus intelligence-deprived) Federal commanders, against all odds it very nearly succeeded. Colonel Cicero Maxwell of the 26th Kentucky Infantry had taken command at Frankfort, and it was Maxwell who ordered the regiment on this bleary-eyed voyage. Maxwell was charged with coordinating his force—the 11th Michigan, the 55th Indiana, two sections of the 13th Indiana Light Artillery, and modest detachments from the 16th U.S. Infantry and 9th Pennsylvania Cavalry, totaling some 1,200 soldiers—with General Green Clay Smith, who was already on his way from Frankfort to Lexington. Upon arrival at Georgetown at 11:00 a.m., the Wolverines heard the usual refrain from the occupants: Morgan had just left. "We began to see the affect of such a rebil passing thrue the country," Gillaspie said with disgust. "He took and alowed his men to take all that he wanted that belonged to a union man without recompence of any kind save curses from him and his men." Orders from Smith came at midnight for Maxwell to set out for the town of Paris. Around 2:30 a.m. the 11th Michigan found itself on yet another overnight tramp after Morgan. "We moved toward Paris," Maxwell reported, "though slowly at first, owing to the fact that the men ... had slept but little, the officers urging them forward as fast as possible." About midway through the trek, Maxwell received another order from Smith, urging him to come quickly before Morgan bolted.[29]

Four miles short of town, around 8:30 a.m., Maxwell learned that Morgan was still at Paris, drawn up for battle on the estate of wealthy attorney Garrett Davis. Amazingly, the escape artist Morgan, despite his force's profound advantage of hooves over feet, was on the verge of being snared by a conglomeration of Federals consisting primarily of infantry. Smith was in position already and soon began skirmishing, so Maxwell needed only to close the trap. It could have been the endgame for Morgan, but his bogeyman reputation came to his rescue. Maxwell advanced a short distance, halted, formed in line of battle, sent out scouts, and then stood inanimate for two hours. Colonel Stoughton was livid at the timidity displayed, and declared his intent to engage Morgan with the 11th, but was denied permission. Wells quoted his colonel as vehemently insisting that "there was no use marching men to death to get in sight of the enemy & then fold their arms and let the traiters get away unmolested & he for one would do it no more." Stoughton's protest was too little too late, and the Rebels slipped through Federal fingers again. Morgan's subordinate Basil Duke declared, regarding the nonevent at Paris, that the Union troops "came on very slowly, and there was at no time any determined effort made to engage us. If a dash had been made at us when we prepared to leave, we could have been compelled to fight, for ... we were very much incumbered with carriages containing wounded men."[30]

Smith was by no means ready to give up his prey, but by the time the Federals and their steeds had their fill of rations and feed, a thunderstorm rolled in and persisted most of the night. The Union contingent marched to Winchester early the next day. After arriving at 5:00 p.m.—just after Morgan skipped town, of course—Smith determined to focus on mobility and ordered Maxwell to load most of the infantry, 11th Michigan included, into wagons. By 11:00 p.m. they were on the Rebels' heels again, bound for Richmond, Kentucky, in defiance of the darkness and yet another rainfall. They arrived on July 21. The Southerners remained one step ahead. Morgan had initially thought to make a stand at Richmond, but concluded that the numbers too strongly favored the Federals. In the end, the Michiganders vented their annoyance equally at Smith and Morgan: Smith, because he was the ranking officer of the debacle at Paris, and Morgan, as Martin explained, because "he is an almighty coward or he would stood a fight." In frustration, tempers flared: Gillaspie reported that a company of regulars was tagging along and its captain drew his revolver on a Company F Wolverine. "In an instant," Gillaspie exclaimed, "some half dosen of us boys was at a ready for the Capt. Had he of shot it probley would have bin his very last shot. On that you can depend. Gen. Smith huried him of fast." Smith and Maxwell parted ways, with Smith continuing his fruitless quest while Maxwell's command piled into wagons and diverted for Lexington. At Lexington the next evening, Gillaspie recorded another near fracas when the sergeant major of a three-month regiment, the 55th Indiana, tried to seize horses and feed from Stoughton's unit. "We stood our post and told him and his major of that Reg. that he had not anuff men at all in his Reg. to take the horses but that he was very welcom to just try it. He backed of in a hury."[31]

Stoughton and his aggravated troops arrived in Frankfort by train at dawn on the twenty-fourth, and reached Louisville late the following afternoon. The gradually diminishing regiment finished July with 559 officers and enlisted men present for duty. Captains Bennett and Mudge were shipped back to Michigan to recruit. Kentucky military governor Jeremiah T. Boyle wished to dispatch the hard-marching Wolverines southwest to Russellville to suppress guerrillas in Logan, Christian, Todd, and Trigg counties, but he was overridden by Buell on the twenty-seventh with a dictate to send Stoughton's Federals back to Nashville. They returned on the twenty-ninth and slept without their tents, which showed up the next day with the arrival of the 11th's aforementioned garrison detachment from Bowling Green. "Our Regiment is doing a great deal of hard service," Sergeant Edward M. Frost of Company E wrote during this period, "not more than two or three companies in camp at a time, and they are on guard about all the time, laying on their arms every night, or else marching double-quick down town to find out what some fool of a guard has got scared at." A detail of sixty men, under First Lieutenant Patrick H. Keegan of Company K and Henry Platt, were directed to assist the 28th Kentucky in the construction of fortifications (probably Fort Negley). Platt and Keegan took turns scouring the hostile countryside for axes, but most of the locals predictably claimed not to possess such tools. Only a few implements were obtained, and even these proved to be in various states of disrepair."[32]

On August 12 John Hunt Morgan struck again, this time at Gallatin, twenty-five miles northeast of Nashville. The Confederate cavalryman was now operating under instructions to break up the Louisville and Nashville Railroad to immobilize Buell in advance of Bragg's planned invasion of Kentucky. Morgan captured Gallatin along with Colonel Boone's 28th Kentucky, and then collapsed an 800-foot railroad tunnel outside of town, instantly crippling Buell's line of supply. The soldiers of the 11th may not have been veterans of the battlefield, but they were by now a crack regiment when it came to late night alarms and hurried marches in pitch darkness. They exited camp at 11:00 p.m. and joined the 69th Ohio with two sections of the 4th Indiana Light Artillery to comprise the Union response out of Nashville under Colonel Miller. By about midnight they were rolling down the tracks. The train—necessarily traveling slowly for fear of sabotage to the tracks—screeched to a halt shy of a burned-out railroad bridge a couple miles short of town, and Miller's troops disembarked and continued inbound on foot, with the sun now rising. Edward Frost observed cut telegraph wires and smoke rising from Gallatin. After wading the now bridgeless creek, the Union troops surged forward along the pike on the double quick, with the 69th Ohio in the lead. Without warning, the Ohioans stumbled upon Morgan's pickets at a cornfield and traded fire with them. The Federals were unharmed, but three of Morgan's raiders were killed, including two officers. "Col. Stoughton saw the men fall," said Frost, "when he turned in his saddle, took of his hat and waved it to us; at the same time saying 'Come on boys—double quick!' and then if you ever heard loud cheering, you can just imagine what a noise our little regiment made.... The way the canteens, haversacks and blankets flew was a caution. The road was completely covered with them." Frost tripped over a dead Confederate officer and scrambled to regain his footing: the Federal cannon were bringing up the rear, and nearly ran him down.[33]

The chase continued for more than a mile before the infantry conceded, panting and drenched in sweat. They had encountered a force Morgan left behind to torch the same amphitheater that had served as the 28th Kentucky's encampment. Morgan's main body had skipped town about the same time the Federals left Nashville. Though the Michiganders witnessed the Confederates being put to flight by the Ohioans, they were once again too late to join in battle, and again their frustration boiled over. Martin looked upon the Confederate dead and told his parents, "I never looked at dead men when I cared as little as I did about them I didn't feel half so bad to see them lay there as I did when our little dog died." The Wolverines entered Gallatin under orders to search the entire town. They did so and confiscated several firearms, but they also looted the stores. In so doing, they trod a well-worn path in the evolution of wartime attitudes toward the enemy. Units that had shown restraint in the past increasingly committed depredations against enemy civilians. Less than six months before, Colonel Lytle had declared that "no wanton outrages have ever been laid to the Michigan 11th. The property of the citizen has not been taken away by you without orders, and I am fully satisfied that if the opportunity ever offers you will fully sustain the reputation of the army of the Union." The Michiganders' actions in Gallatin revealed a retrospective irony in Lytle's words, for the 11th in this instance was indeed sustaining the Union army's growing reputation—for plunder.[34]

At 4:00 p.m. Miller's expedition departed town and began to embark the cars for the return to Nashville. The Michiganders had just finished entraining when, Frost recalled, "all at once we were fired into, and such a snapping and cracking, the like of which I never before heard." The artillery was not yet loaded, and the 69th Ohio was still crowded at the rear of the cars, waiting to board. Two Ohioans and one railroad hand fell. The Wolverines scrambled and set the all-time regimental speed record for disembarking passenger cars. Company E, having served as rear guard during the march, was last to board the train and first off. With Captain Spencer home on furlough, Lieutenant Charles W. Newberry was in charge. His Three Rivers boys deployed to the right as skirmishers, obtained a fleeting glance of their assailants in an adjacent cornfield, and advanced on the double quick, pausing to fire the first volleys in their regiment's history. The rest of the 11th pitched in, and the Hoosier battery unlimbered and opened with canister. King witnessed one burst taking out four Rebels. "We gave them grape and canister and musketry," exclaimed Martin, "untill they were glad to hunt their holes.... We know that we killed a number." The Michiganders in their letters and diaries consistently proclaimed that the Federals had hit between twenty-five and forty Rebels, but the brush and cornfield made an accurate count impossible. Frost summarized the Confederate ambush as "a complete surprise, but they could not back what they had commenced." The 69th Ohio had one dead and one wounded. Although the short, sharp fight was bloodless for Stoughton's men, two of them straggled from the regiment and were captured. Privates Leonard F. Carkenard of Company A and Byron Liddle of Company D would ultimately be released in prisoner exchanges.[35]

The clash at Gallatin had one lasting legacy: Morgan, incensed at the treatment of the town's citizens and by a rumor (false, judging by Federal accounts) that his men were given no quarter by Miller's troops, soon published a proclamation declaring a policy of retribution against Union civilians. But for the 11th Michigan, the clash with Morgan's men was a confidence builder. Aaron Sturges, for one, considered it "a right smart little victory."[36]

Stoughton and his soldiers were back in Nashville right about dawn on the fourteenth. They were dispatched for Gallatin all over again the next afternoon, awaited cars at the depot for hours, and then traveled overnight. "It seames," complained Gillaspie, "that we always run by night when we could sleep and at day we do some thing else. I have not had a good nights sleep in so long I can not remember how it feels." The soldiers had scarcely stepped off the cars at Gallatin the next morning when they were commanded to go right back to Nashville, "covered in dust instead of glory," in Ozro Bowen's words. The ensuing days saw the poorly supplied Union garrison at Nashville put on short rations, and the 11th was called out almost nightly to take up a defensive position and sleep on their arms in case of an assault on the city. Companies were routinely detached to guard various locations. Perhaps worst of all from the soldiers' point of view, the severed railroad line meant no mail to or from home. "You dont know how lonesome it is," Martin griped, "when we dont hear from home as often as once a week."[37]

With Buell's supply line beset by cavalry and guerrilla raids, the general on August 27 sought to remedy the nuisance with the secretive creation of a light brigade. This unit was intended to balance sufficient punch with the mobility required to overtake and overwhelm Morgan and Forrest. The hard-marching 11th Michigan was teamed up with the 19th Illinois Infantry, artillery support, and a sizeable cavalry contingent encompassing the 2nd Indiana, 5th Tennessee, 1st Kentucky, and a detachment of the 4th Kentucky. Colonel Miller was placed in overall command, with Stoughton in charge of the infantry, which would be wagon-borne to keep pace with the horsemen. The cavalry was entrusted to the 1st Kentucky's Colonel Frank Wolford. Buell expected Miller's lean force to live off the land, limiting baggage to just one blanket per man, and to stay on the move, patrolling "especially the region along [a] line through Carthage, Lebanon, and Woodbury, Liberty, and Smithville." The 11th regiment departed Nashville about 5:00 a.m. on the thirty-first and endured heavy rains on the march, arriving at the light brigade's rendezvous point of Murfreesboro about 3:00 the next afternoon. There, the Wolverines encamped on the same ground occupied by the 9th Michigan at the time of its capture by Forrest.[38]

The stay at Murfreesboro was short-lived. At 3:00 a.m. on September 4 the Michiganders struck their tents and doubled back the way they came, prompting Martin to label the expedition "some fool's errand." A sad incident occurred on the march when some stray horses galloped past the formation, driving one of the mule teams into a frenzied panic. Private Charles B. Purchase of Company A was struck down by the mules' wagon and soon perished. That evening, the regiment bivouacked at

La Vergne, where Gillaspie reported good eating. "Some of our boys went out and pressed some fowls into the cirvus of the 11th Mich. Reg. They was good companyons at supper but I tell you hunger and half rations will caus a soldier to do many things he would not do was he at home in a land of freedom and plenty. The boys allso brought in a young beef or veal.... We had plenty for the whole Co. C for the first time for a long while."[39]

The light brigade was disbanded just days after its inception. With Confederate general Braxton Bragg launching an invasion of Kentucky, Buell withdrew north in pursuit, passing through Nashville on the way. Negley's garrison found itself in utter isolation. Chasing cavalry across the countryside was the least of Negley's worries now, as foraging, guarding, and constructing fortifications took priority. The 11th Michigan was integrated into Negley's division in a new brigade encompassing the

James Scott Negley led the 11th Michigan's division through the siege conditions at Nashville, and during the battles of Stones River and Chickamauga. His decision to flee the battlefield at Chickamauga resulted in his removal from command, though he was later exonerated (Library of Congress).

19th Illinois and the 18th and 69th Ohio regiments, all under the command of Colonel Timothy Robbins Stanley, former commander of the 18th Ohio. Stanley's unit was formally designated as the Army of the Ohio's 29th Brigade, 8th Division.[40]

The 11th Michigan underwent changes in personnel about this time too, due in part to the actions of the War Department. In July 1862 regimental bands had been ordered to be disbanded within thirty days. With regiment sizes contracting as the war progressed, these bands represented a proportionally growing drain on manpower and resources. The thirteen members of the 11th's band mustered out August 22. (At least two of these musicians, Charles Rice and John Ludwig, later enlisted in brigade bands.) More significantly, Major Doughty resigned his commission for health reasons, effective August 18. His vacancy was soon filled through the promotion of Sylvester Smith. Other absences, temporary in nature, included the aforementioned recruiting assignments for Captains Mudge and Bennett, as well as the detailing of Quartermaster Drake as acting assistant brigade quartermaster on September 10.[41]

Then there was the more complicated story of Samuel Chadwick. The adjutant had taken a twenty-day furlough starting on July 25, and returned to Michigan. On the last day of the month, the War Department issued an order declaring that anyone fit for duty, but absent from their post on August 18 at 10:00 a.m., would "be regarded as absent without cause, their pay will be stopped, and they dismissed from the service, or treated as deserters." Chadwick, fully cognizant of the order, departed Three Rivers on August 11 and reached Bowling Green on the fourteenth. He had two days left in his furlough, and four days before the mandated muster, normally more than enough time to reach Nashville by train. More to the point, there would have been plenty of time if Morgan hadn't demolished the railroad tunnel near Gallatin. The adjutant therefore didn't reach Nashville until the twentieth, at which time Stoughton informed the man that he was considered dismissed from the service. Chadwick demanded a court of inquiry to prove his absence was for good cause—a valid defense, provided for in the associated War Department order—but Buell's headquarters was uncertain whether to hold the inquiry at the regimental or brigade court. With communications cut off between headquarters and Washington, Chadwick feared an answer would be a long time coming. He returned to Michigan and then proceeded with haste to Washington, where he successfully obtained an order requiring Stoughton to return his adjutant to duty. Chadwick was reinstated on September 4, and Captain Ephraim Hall, who had been assigned as acting adjutant in the meantime, was restored to his captaincy.[42]

By September 8 the brigade was encamped about six miles outside of Nashville. Colonel Stanley and the 18th Ohio had not yet rendezvoused, and Stoughton, as the senior officer present for the brigade, was subjected to an unexpected test of his leadership qualities. The 19th Illinois was a spirited Zouave regiment that, along with the 18th Ohio, had pillaged Athens, Alabama, in May under the command of the 19th's colonel, John Basil Turchin. Turchin faced court-martial, but was rescued by his wife, who rushed to Washington on his behalf. Turchin as a result not only escaped dismissal from service, but enjoyed promotion to brigadier general as well. It is not clear whether Turchin's old regiment knew of his reinstatement when they mutinied around

September 8. "I heard an awful uproar at the guard lines," Gillaspie remembered. "Presently whang whang whang went some seven or eight guns. In the direction of the uprore the sound of the 19th Ill. Reg. could be planely heard shouting Zouave Zouave Turchin Turchin Turchin at the top of their voices." The Wolverines' response was resolute, and escalated rapidly. Captain Hood turned out Company C, and Lieutenant Colonel Eldridge ordered the Michiganders to load their rifles, and marched them into place behind the Illinoisans. When he commanded the Zouaves to disperse, they responded only with the protesting cry, "Give us Turchin Zouave!" Stoughton formed the balance of the brigade, also with rifles loaded, into a square surrounding the mutineers. The colonel then placed himself in the middle of the Illinoisans, Gillaspie recorded, and "adresed them for about a half hour giveing them to understand that it was Wm. Stoughton that they was dealing with and that oders they must obey. They gave him 3 hearty cheers when they found that they had found an officer that they could not rule nor scare and then said that they would gladly dy for him if that was his orders. He thanked them and dismissed them."[43] Thus an intense situation was defused, and Stoughton importantly earned the respect of a regiment of brave soldiers, more than a few of whom were indeed destined to lay down their lives executing his orders.

But the situation at Nashville grew desperate. "We were as completely shut in from the outside world," declared Ozro Bowen, "as though we had been left on an island in mid-ocean. All telegraphic and railroad communications were severed, and we were left to our own resources and defense." Martin explained the key to survival: "We go out and draw fat cattle, sheep, and chickens and potatoes and everything else that we want, it makes some of the secesh mighty mad; we tell them that they must not alow our bridges to be burnt so that our provisions cant come through; for we dident come down here to starve." The short rations were wholly insufficient, and had to be supplemented with harrowing foraging expeditions into the hostile countryside. The picket lines were constantly harassed by Confederate cavalry and guerrillas, and the Federals were left in complete ignorance of not only the status of Buell's army—upon which their own survival depended—but also of the well-being of their loved ones. "I feel so ancious," Gillaspie confided, "to git a leter from home but I cannot at present so I must content myself." King, after hearing of the narrow escape of one of the 11th's foraging parties from a guerrilla ambush, expressed an opinion of Buell that was shared by many of his comrades. "General Buell has been lying before Chattanooga in a state of inactivity, letting a large force invade Kentucky and cut off his supplies.... If the truth was only known, General Buell is a rebel at heart and has done all in his power to aid the rebel cause. His very acts show him to be one. But I will say no more of him at present, but it will someday be shown to the world that Maj. General Buell was not a man to be trusted." Another member of the regiment wrote anonymously to the *Reporter*, blasting Buell's "most disgraceful act" and "criminal inactivity." Benjamin Wells concluded that "there seems to be a deep gloom resting over our army & Nation."[44]

"There is no news or nothing new to us," King wrote of the imposed isolation. "'Tis one thing over & over. Every day. Here we have been since Buell passed through here, in the same camp, nothing going on Except building fortifications & Foraging." Such monotony only compounded the stress of eking out a tenuous day-to-day existence. The Wolverines' most significant operation during the siege of Nashville occurred on October 5, when Colonel Stoughton led the 11th Michigan, 37th Indiana, 74th Ohio, and a section of the 5th Michigan Light Artillery on a mission of foraging and reconnaissance, escorting 250 wagons along the Cumberland River. Guerrillas attacked the column near Fort Riley but were brushed off with ease. Farther down the riverside trail, the path was obstructed with felled trees. After clearing the way and rebuilding the road, the Federals were again subjected to some ineffective fire. They forged ahead and gathered corn, wheat, and pork before turning back. A third assault occurred when guerrillas opened fire from across Neely's Bend in the river during the march back to Nashville. The Union artillerists unlimbered a gun, and their infantry support volleyed. The Federals claimed to have inflicted sixteen casualties on their assailants.[45]

Bragg's campaign in Kentucky was checked at Perryville on October 8—a marginal, uncoordinated Federal success, achieved rather despite Buell than because of him—and lead elements of the Union army reentered Nashville by November 7. The army was "greeted as friends & deliverers" according to Wells. Five days later, Stoughton's men were overjoyed to receive a pile of long overdue correspondence from home.[46]

Despite the happy ending, the short rations and stress had taken their toll. During the month of October, the regiment was forced to grant seventeen discharges to ill soldiers, and suffered three fatalities from disease. Among the latter number was a victim of typhoid fever, Musician William H. Seekell. Seekell had enlisted in August 1861 along with his twin fourteen-year-old sons, James Wesley and Charles Leslie. James joined the service as a drummer and Charles, as a fifer. In the wake of William's death on October 20, the citizens of Three Rivers petitioned Colonel Stoughton to secure the boys' release home as "the only remaining consolation to their afflicted mother." Stoughton forwarded the letter up the chain of command with his endorsement, stating that the boys were "too young in my opinion to endure the hardships of a winter campaign. Their father has lately died in the service leaving them without his protection and care—I respectfully recommend the discharge." The fatherless boys were ultimately released on February 4, 1863, to return home.[47]

Although Buell's army had returned, its general had not: his lackluster performance had not impressed Washington any more than it had James King. Buell's replacement was Major General William Starke Rosecrans, a talented West Pointer who had achieved a victory at Corinth on October 4 and was popular with the troops. "News has reached us today of the removal of Maj. General Buell," King recorded on October 29, "and the gallant Rosecrans appointed in his stead. This is hailed with Joy by all the Officers & Soldiers in this Division…. We have tried such Generals too long." Rosecrans went to work at once for his new command, focused on resolving supply, organizational, and morale issues. He ingratiated himself to the men by walking among them often, and by exhibiting genuine concern for their well-being. "I have great confidence in Major General Rosecrans as a commander," King continued, "he

Left: George Henry Thomas led the Center Wing at Stones River and was in overall command of the Union defense of Horseshoe Ridge, which earned him the nickname, "the Rock of Chickamauga"—along with the undying respect of Stoughton's troops. Thomas went on to replace Rosecrans as commanding general of the Army of the Cumberland (Library of Congress). *Right:* William Starke Rosecrans was popular with his troops, and proved himself a capable commanding general. He led the Army of the Cumberland to victory at Stones River and brilliantly outmaneuvered Braxton Bragg in the Tullahoma Campaign. But his subsequent, overzealous pursuit of the Army of Tennessee triggered the calamity at Chickamauga (Library of Congress).

has shown himself one. He passes through our camp nearly every day. Day before yesterday was Division Review. It was a grand sight. But what was the best of all, The General said as the 11th Mich. Vols. passed him, that it was the finest Regiment he had seen."[48]

Rosecrans steadfastly resisted pressure from Washington to strike before his army had recovered sufficiently for active campaigning. Railroad repairs were completed on November 26, and desperately needed supplies started rolling in. The general restructured his army into three wings: the left under Thomas Crittenden, the center under George H. Thomas, and the right under Alexander McCook. Negley, promoted effective November 29 to major general, led the 2nd Division of Thomas's Center Wing. His unit was comprised of three brigades, including Stanley's, with a total of thirteen infantry regiments and three artillery batteries. The other two brigades were commanded by Colonels Miller and James G. Spears.

Rosecrans had issued orders declaring that each infantry company would detail two carefully selected men to serve in a newly formed Pioneer Brigade, with half of these men from each regiment consisting of laborers, and the other half, mechanics.

Each pioneer detachment would nominally be attached to its regiment, but with the understanding that army engineering needs may dictate that the entire pioneer contingent be massed together at times. "The most intelligent and energetic lieutenant in the regiment, with the best knowledge of civil engineering" was to command the detachment. The ranking pioneer corps officer from the 11th Michigan was Captain Hood, who was granted command of one of Rosecrans's three pioneer battalions.[49]

The 11th regiment departed Nashville on December 11, marched five miles down the Franklin Pike, and set up camp on the plantation of John Overton. "Our line of Battle is several miles in length," King noted on the fourteenth. "As far as the Eye can reach, Camps of men can be seen. Every piece of ground suitable for a Camp is occupied. There is a probability that a battle will take place near here at no distant period." But then things calmed down. Daniel Rose saw no hint of impending hostilities on the twenty-second, and two days later King reported that "there has been no change of any importance, since I last wrote you." Everyone believed that they had settled in for the winter—everyone, that is, except William Rosecrans. Just one week later, the 11th Michigan Volunteer Infantry would battle through its bloodiest day of the war.[50]

CHAPTER 4

"Two huge serpents"
December 1862–January 1863

Private Daniel Rose and Corporal James King were hardly alone in anticipating a quiet winter. Confederate president Jefferson Davis had ordered the detachment of an entire division from Bragg's Army of Tennessee at Murfreesboro on December 12. Bragg scattered much of his force into winter quarters, and Morgan and Forrest departed to strike the Federals elsewhere. With Bragg thus weakened and Halleck (now serving as general in chief) demanding action, General Rosecrans determined to hit the Rebels. On the morning of December 26, 1862, the 14th Corps, now known as the Army of the Cumberland, streamed southeast from Nashville.[1] Bragg's army would sorely miss its detachments in the days to come, but Rosecrans was compelled to leave behind a very substantial force to guard Nashville and the vulnerable rail lines that delivered materiel and sustenance to his army.

Even so numerous a rear guard proved insufficient. Morgan severed the tracks far in the Federal rear the same day Rosecrans advanced. This time, however, the Union troops and their general were not so easily discouraged. The extensive preparations at Nashville—perceived in Washington as needless delay—ensured a sufficient supply stockpile for the Federals to shrug off Morgan's mischief. The blue legions advanced in their three separate wings: Crittenden's on the left, Thomas's in the center, and McCook's on the right. At the vanguard of the center marched Negley's division. One of his brigades, under Colonel Spears, remained behind to garrison Nashville, while Stanley's and Miller's brigades moved forward. They followed the Franklin Pike to Brentwood, and then proceeded down the Wilson Pike to Owen's Store. After two weeks of beautiful weather, the skies deluged the soldiers that night, reducing the roads to a quagmire, yet Rosecrans's army plodded onward through the mud the next day undeterred. Negley departed Nolensville at 10:00 a.m. and marched east to Stewartsboro to cover Crittenden's right.[2]

All eyes across the Union and Confederacy—and many overseas—gazed intently on southern Tennessee. The Union had recovered from McClellan's defeat in the Seven Days Battles with his strategic victory at Antietam in September—the trigger for Lincoln's Emancipation Proclamation—but Burnside's December 13 debacle at Fredericksburg ended the campaign of 1862 in the East in disaster, and Grant's advance against Vicksburg was stalling out in the West. With the Confederate star ascendant, there existed an increasing likelihood that England and France would recognize Southern independence and help propel the Confederacy to victory. Domestically, antiwar sentiment was swelling in the North. Perhaps the very fate of the Union cause rested squarely on the shoulders of Rosecrans and his shivering, exhausted troops as they trudged through incessant rain and thickening mire toward Murfreesboro.

Bragg regrouped his scattered army in a defensive stance. The Army of Tennessee counted several thousand less infantry than the Army of the Cumberland, but compensated for that disparity with a superior cavalry arm. The Rebel horsemen under Joseph Wheeler delayed the Federal advance with help from the ongoing precipitation. Rosecrans showed his customary respect for the Sabbath on Sunday the twenty-eighth, remaining largely inactive and resting his weary troops. The 11th Michigan enjoyed a lazy day, gratefully feasting on fresh beef and waiting for the regimental wagon train to fight its way through the mud and catch up with the unit. That evening, the soldiers congregated around comforting fires and conversed about the imminent clash. "As I lay thare," Gillaspie confided in his diary, "I could not help but think that some who was in the talking tonight would not be able to talk ever agane maby in a few hours or days."[3]

To everyone's relief, the following day brought pleasant, if chilly, weather. By nighttime, Negley's division was confronting Confederate positions before Murfreesboro. "The armies of Rosecrans and Bragg gathered themselves," said King, "like two huge serpents, for the conflict." McCook's Right Wing, however, finished the evening well short of its intended position astride Thomas's wing. Considerably less than half of the Army of the Cumberland was present, and Stanley's brigade sat unanchored on the extreme right, frightfully exposed. Ozro Bowen remembered that "a cold, drenching rain, without fire or shelter, and the realizing fact that we were just on the verge of a bloody struggle, did not tend to make our slumbers peaceful on that dark, foreboding night. Many eyes that were wakeful, eagerly watching for the first dawn of morning, were soon closed in that eternal sleep that knows no waking."[4]

December 30 saw heavy, widespread skirmishing as the opposing armies felt each other out and unit commanders linked up with their neighbors to safeguard their flanks. With McCook's arrival, Negley represented the center of the Union battle line. The 19th Illinois fanned out and advanced as skirmishers for Stanley's brigade in the morning. A Rebel sharpshooter with a telescoped rifle dropped four of the advancing Federals before a sharp-eyed Illinoisan beat the marksman at his own game. The 69th Ohio took over early in the afternoon. At 3:00 p.m. Companies A, D, F, and I of the 11th Michigan joined the fight. "They did not shoot as much as the 19th Ill. 18th and 69th Ohio had," Gillaspie said of his comrades, but "they made every shot count." All too soon, though, the 11th suffered its first loss in battle. A stretcher came back from the strife carrying the remains of First Lieutenant Joseph Wilson of Company F. "As we looked on his still form," Second Lieutenant Borden Hicks recorded, "we realized what war meant, our cheeks paled as we viewed our first sacrifice for our country." Wilson, who Gillaspie remembered as "a much loved and respected officer," had been shot in the head. His fate left two young children fatherless.⁵

After nightfall, the bands of the two armies competed with each other in the dark, belting out their respective patriotic tunes. At one moment, a band struck up "Home Sweet Home," and the melody was taken up by musicians on both sides, with thousands of soldiers singing in unison. Hours later, they would be slaughtering each other by the thousand. Generals Rosecrans and Bragg settled on equivalent tactical plans for the morning to come, each preparing an assault on the enemy's right. Rosecrans ordered his Left Wing to attack after breakfast, but Bragg ordered his left corps to strike at dawn.

The Wolverines passed another damp, chilly, wakeful night on the picket line. Colonel Stoughton apologetically forbade fires, which would reveal troop dispositions to the enemy. "He showed much anciety about our comfort," Ira Gillaspie commented, but the corporal awoke in the morning "allmost froze to death and wet with the heavy dew." The bleary-eyed Michiganders were relieved by the 18th Ohio and went to the rear to grab breakfast. Coffee, bacon, and hardtack were prepared in short order, but the welcome repast was dramatically interrupted. The soldiers were startled by a crescendo of musketry to the west, which rapidly escalated to the unmistakable din of a general engagement. The rank and file stumbled to their feet and sprinted in response to tense, insistent orders to fall in. "Now my brave boys," Stoughton's voice rang out, "be cool and calm, take good aim, shoot low and be sure of your man." The 11th Michigan, so long drilled in preparation for this moment, filed into line of battle.⁶

McCook's Right Wing was crumbling away. A long, eerily quiet line of Rebels had emerged from a twilight mist and swarmed the Union flank. Some Federals were caught breakfasting or seeking water, while others were busy sipping their morning coffee. Richard Johnson's entire division was smashed in short order and flooded to the rear. The adjacent division of Jefferson C. Davis put up more of a fight, but before long, two of his three brigades were hot on the heels of Johnson's panicked troops. In the space of just one hour, five brigades were completely routed. The soldiers of Negley's division watched and listened to the calamity unfolding in the distance and creeping ever closer. Chadwick compared the sound of the advancing Rebels with "the yell of demons." J. Henry Haynie of the 19th Illinois declared that "we began to choke in the throat, so to speak, to think of home, and ... wondering if our own turn would come soon.... Our comrades were falling as the wheat falls before cradling machines at harvest time. We could hear the hoarse shriek of shell, the swift rattle of musketry, the sound of buzzing bullets, the impact of solid shot, the chug when human forms were hit hard, the yells of pain, the cries of agony, the fearful groans, the encouraging words of man to man, and the death gasps which told of those who reported to the God of Battles."⁷

The rapidity of the Right Wing's collapse was breathtaking. There was a real and growing possibility that the entire Federal army would be rolled up from its right. But next in line stood the third and last of McCook's division commanders: Phil Sheridan. Sheridan had anticipated the assault, and his men were ready—had been ready for hours—and no longer would the Rebels enjoy a lopsided contest. Sheridan drove his attackers back with heavy loss, holding against superior numbers. But the Federal line had bent back so sharply as to form a V-shaped formation, with Sheridan's men comprising the left leg. The 11th Michigan waited apprehensively near the exposed apex of the battle line.

Some of Stoughton's men had been detailed for duties in the Federal rear and presently experienced firsthand the utter panic of the conquered divisions. King, Martin, and Private Billy Davis of Company A had escorted the regimental wagons to safety and found themselves swept up in a churning sea of retreating Federals. King and Davis borrowed rifles and attempted to find the 11th, but their efforts were fruitless. Private William E. Raymond of Company F, charged with driving an ambulance wagon, was kept occupied dodging Wheeler's horsemen. "The Rebel cavalry wold charge up on us," he wrote, "and then we had to skeedaddle."[8]

As the Wolverine regiment awaited the Rebel assault, Rosecrans, who was seemingly everywhere at once, approached Negley. "Sir," Rosecrans implored, "they have turned me back, and all depends on you. The day must be ours." Negley answered resolutely, "Let them come, my boys are ready." The 11th, held in reserve, initially faced west but was ordered to change front under heavy artillery fire as the Rebels approached from the south. The Michiganders entered the fray in an unusual manner when Major General Lovell Rousseau, who was in reserve, stuck his nose into Sheridan's and Negley's business and ordered Stoughton to relieve a regiment of Sheridan's neighboring brigade under Colonel George W. Roberts. The Michiganders deployed 100 yards to their right and into the line of battle. "They looked rather tierd out and bloody," said Ira Gillaspie of Roberts's men, "as they went to fill their cartridge boxes and we took their places." Hicks observed with concern that "we lay in the open field, on the side sloping towards the enemy, when we could have been protected by moving back a couple rods, and getting below the crest or rise in the ground."[9]

For the Wolverines, the battle began in earnest. "Now," Stoughton called out above the commotion, "we can try and see what the Michigan 11th can do." Three Federal gun batteries were amassed atop a knoll to Stanley's left, and these cannon had already done good work firing over Stanley's brigade into Sheridan's assailants. The Confederates would have to seize or disable this artillery in order to break the Union defenses. Patton Anderson's Rebel brigade made a beeline for the Federal batteries, which belched grape and canister in response. In conjunction with the neighboring regiments, the Springfield rifles of the 11th Michigan unleashed a full volley in the face of the enemy. The lieutenant colonel of the 30th Mississippi looked on in horror as dozens of his subordinates, advancing in fine order just moments before, sunk to the ground with a moan. The Mississippians' corps commander, Leonidas Polk, exclaimed that "such evidences of destructive firing as were left on the forest ... have rarely, if ever been seen." Anderson's battered troops fled, and Stanley's and Roberts's men cheered and caught their breath while the Rebels rallied for another charge. Second Lieutenant Loren Howard was amazed to realize the 11th had suffered just one death and several wounded in the initial exchange. "It does not seem possible," he related, "that half of us could have escaped; I think they fired over us."[10]

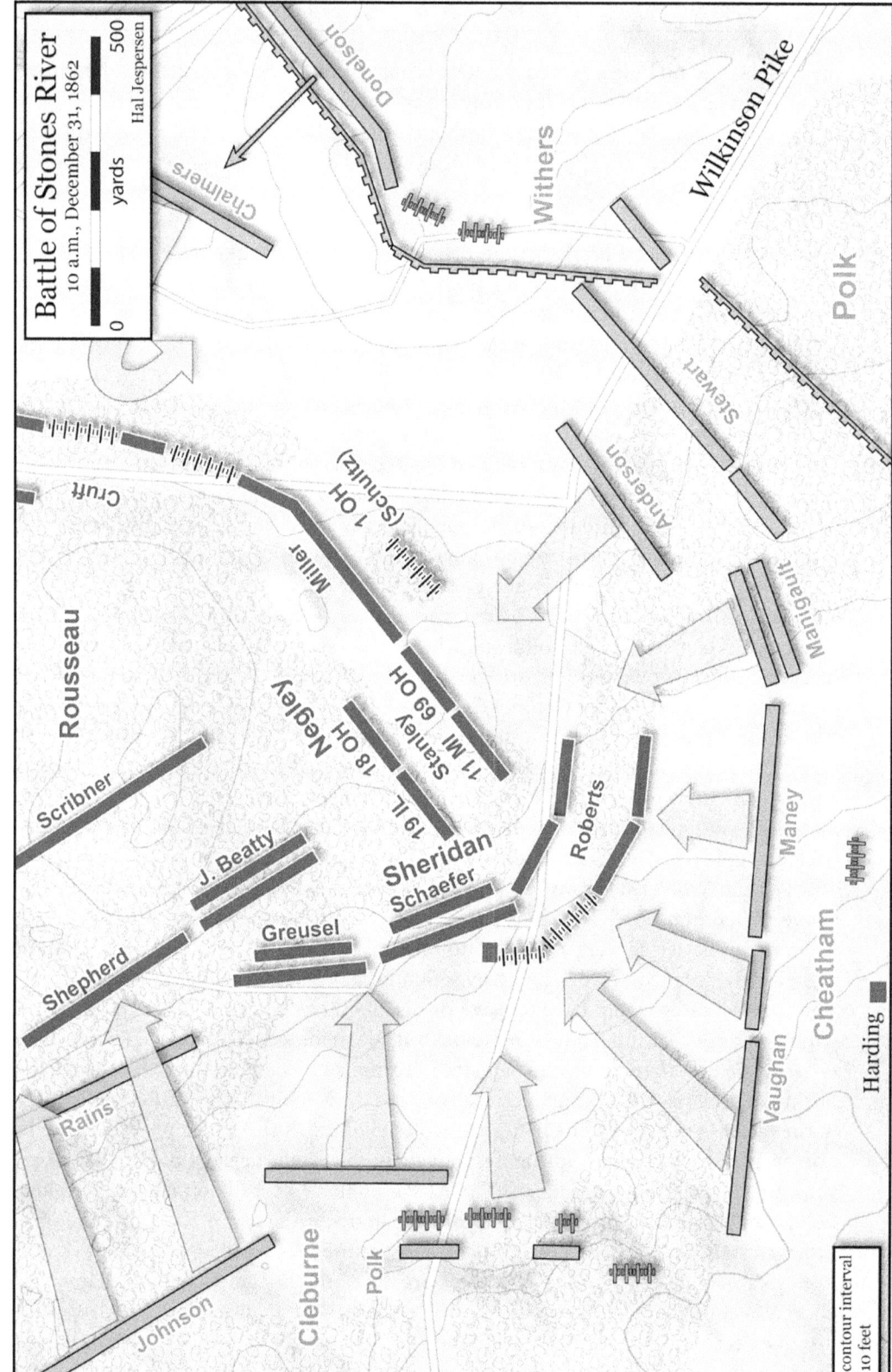

"A moment longer," Ozro Bowen recalled, "and line after line of butternut and gray, exultant over the triumphs they had already achieved, came sweeping down upon our division like an Alpine avalanche.... The crimson billows of death surged back and forward over that field of carnage." The Confederates were determined to seize the Union batteries. This time, Anderson coordinated his assault with Alexander P. Stewart's brigade and marshaled overwhelming artillery support. The Federal gunners were in grave danger of being overrun. The 19th Illinois and 11th Michigan were ordered to redeploy a short distance east under fire in support of the artillerists. To do so directly would have exposed the Wolverines to a murderous raking fire. Stoughton astutely about faced his men, backpedaled them just beyond the modest rise for cover, and then marched the regiment on the double quick by its right flank into position amidst a series of remarkable rock outcroppings that came to be known as the slaughter pen. Stoughton would remember this as one of his regiment's finest moments. With the Confederate infantry closing to within 100 yards, Howard recorded, the Michiganders "poured a volley into them that made them drop like leaves from the trees." Stoughton watched as his men "continued to load and fire with great coolness and bravery." According to Howard, a Confederate prisoner stated that one volley from the 11th dropped sixteen men in a single Rebel company. The outnumbered Michiganders and Illinoisans exalted as the two enemy brigades faltered and fell back before them.[11]

But the Confederates soon returned. Two of Anderson's Mississippi regiments each had 200 men down, yet on they came. "The enemy was so close," Haynie declared, "that we could smell their burning powder and see into their exulting eyes." Colonel Stoughton exclaimed that "the fire of the enemy was apparently concentrated on this point, and was terrific. The slaughter was great, and men and officers fell on every side." Howard related that he and his comrades "laid down as much between the rocks as we could to shelter us from the enemy's fire of musketry, shot and shell. Trees and limbs and rocks were flying over our heads and all around us." A bullet tore through Major Smith's face. First Lieutenant Mathias Faulknor escorted Smith away, but then lost his way in the smoke and chaos, and wandered into the Rebel lines. Stoughton remained on horseback near the colors to inspire his men until his mount was struck down. Chadwick's horse absorbed multiple hits, and a solid shot knocked his sword from his hand. He acquired another steed, only to have that one shot up as well. Then a Minie ball severed his belt. "The ground," Haynie recalled, "was thick strewn with dead and wounded; struck horses, no longer neighing or whinnying, were agonizing in their frantic cries. Cannon balls cut down trees around and over us, which, falling, crushed living and dead alike." Stanley's brigade, in addition to being woefully outnumbered, was now subject to a deadly crossfire from four Rebel gun batteries. The 69th Ohio, whose colonel had just been relieved for drunkenness, struggled to hold its ground. The blue line wavered. The 74th Ohio of Miller's adjacent brigade provided a brief glimmer of hope, marching up as though on the parade ground and giving the Confederates a volley. But it was too little too late.[12]

Without warning, Stanley's flank was suddenly hanging in the air as the extreme right of the Union battle line. Phil Sheridan's division was gone. Sheridan's men had heroically blunted the Rebel assault's fearful momentum, but their ammunition had finally given out, and now the Confederate brigades of George Maney and Arthur Manigault were flooding into the resulting gap. McCook's entire wing of the Union army had been driven from the field, and Negley's division was on the verge of being surrounded and swallowed whole. "Now men," Negley shouted over the din, "we are in a tight place and must retreat, but if you will follow me I will take you out. We are almost surrounded and must cut our way out with fire if necessary." A bugle blared the call for retreat.[13]

The 11th pulled back 100 yards, turned, and fired into their pursuers. The Wolverines then performed a fighting withdrawal through a thick patch of cedars already flooded with fleeing Federals. Stewart's and Daniel Donelson's Rebel brigades pressed from behind, and shells soared into the swarming blue masses. Stoughton's casualties continued to mount in the converging crossfire. First Lieutenant Ephraim Hall was shot through the neck and captured, and First Lieutenant Thomas Flynn, commanding Company E, was shot dead through the forehead as he waved his sword and shouted for his company to stand firm. Yet the inexperienced Wolverines, as Stanley witnessed, despite suffering through a nightmarish carnage and being engulfed in a demoralizing wave of skedaddling Federals, kept up their fire, maintained their formation, and remained responsive to the colonel's orders: "Halt! About face!" While neighboring units disintegrated in rout, the 11th Michigan Infantry confronted the oncoming avalanche of Rebels, leveling 300 rifles at their elated enemy. Ira Gillaspie sighted his Springfield and squeezed the trigger, swelling with pride as he and his comrades, under gut-wrenching duress, "pored a very destruktive fier sending many of the traitors to their mother earth and puting the rest to a halt." It was a moment that the survivors—angry, scared, excited, or numb with emotional shock—would never forget. Their raw regiment had absorbed severe punishment, but they had dealt out death in return. Still they were standing, still they were following orders, and their retribution was not over yet.[14]

Stoughton's troops resumed their retreat and emerged into a sprawling, open field. They immediately realized they must traverse the expansive distance without cover, and still under severe fire from behind. But there was help ahead: Rosecrans had cobbled together a new defensive line. Thomas launched his brigade of regulars forward, and they plunged into the woods in a costly bayonet charge that stalemated Stewart's troops. And then there was Lovell Rousseau, who again inserted himself into Negley's affairs, ordering the 18th Ohio back into the cedars to support the regulars. Stanley responded by charging the 11th Michigan back into the teeth of the Rebel advance as well. The brigade commander was awed at how the tattered Wolverines rushed back into the fray "most gallantly." The Ohioans and Michiganders traded volleys with George Maney's brigade for several minutes, stifling the Confederates' attempt to further exploit the breech in the Union line. The Federals were then ordered to fall back. The regulars and the 18th Ohio headed out first, with Stoughton's soldiers the last to concede the bitterly contested woods. At first, the orders for the 11th to pull out were lost in the din of the firefight. Half the unit withdrew while Stoughton and the other half went on fighting. Howard realized the mistake and alerted the colonel promptly. Donelson's Rebel Tennesseans attempted a hapless pursuit into the open field, but the Union artillery made short work of them. Forty-five years later, Hicks would remember that "the concussion from twelve guns just back of us and over our heads was terrific, and affected our ears, it caused mine to ring, and they have been ringing ever since."[15]

The contest rumbled and roared as long as daylight continued, but the long, brave stand by Sheridan, extended by Negley and backed by Rosecrans's fallback point, had thus far held the Confederates shy of a decisive victory at the Nashville Pike, Rosecrans's critical line of supply and retreat. Though the 11th was not engaged in the balance of the afternoon fighting, twenty familiar faces recently detached from the regiment's ranks were very much in the thick of it. In desperation, the Pioneer Brigade, including 11th Michigan captain Calvin Hood's 2nd Battalion, was thrown into the last-ditch defense of the pike. The Pioneer Brigade was never intended to join in battle, but desperation forced Rosecrans's hand, and in they went. The pioneers, who had never drilled—let alone fought—together, stood their ground, discharging volleys into successive doomed assaults by Mathew Ector's and Evander McNair's brigades of John P. McCown's Confederate division. Hood at one point was forced to change front to meet a flanking attack by Ector's dismounted Texas cavalry. Hood's Federals lay in wait, then arose, fired, and charged in conjunction with the 79th Indiana to eliminate the threat. The pioneers counted among their death toll the 11th's Private Bennett Smetts, who was shot from his horse while serving as Hood's orderly.[16]

It was a self-serving custom for commanders to praise their own troops in their official reports, but the 11th regiment earned the additional commendation of Major General Rousseau, who gratefully held up the example of "the Eleventh Michigan and its gallant little colonel" in his report. "How proud we felt," said Chadwick, "of our noble commander of the Eleventh." Gillaspie added that the "allmost worshipped" Colonel Stoughton "won from his men that esteem that will last while life lasts." Stanley would later write to Governor Blair, beseeching the Michigan politician to exert his influence in Washington to obtain a brigadier generalship for Stoughton.[17]

The 11th Michigan counted itself among a happy minority of Federal troops supplied with something to eat that night. King and Private Davis loaded up wagons with food and ammunition and "found our regiment," said King, "or what was left of it." Gillaspie noted that Company C had no commissioned officers left standing, but consoled himself that "all of the officers that is nessary in a fight is a good colonel and a good color barer and a Sargt. If you have these and the right kind of boys you are all right." The Wolverines had gone into battle with 440 men and officers, and their first ever day of full-blown engagement had cost them nearly 30 percent casualties—and that count excluded the numerous walking wounded. Many had been bruised, cut, or scraped by falling tree limbs, and entire trees, that came crashing down in the Confederate bombardment. Others walked away from direct hits that could easily have proven fatal, as in the case of Daniel Rose, who had a bullet penetrate his canteen, haversack, and uniform before barely breaking his skin. Howard had been struck with spent grapeshot during the retrograde through the cedars, and Captain Oakes was knocked down by the concussion of a shell. "The old year died out," said Ozro Bowen, "and the new year was ushered in amid ... the groans of the dying. There has been but few watch-meetings on earth as we kept that night among the dead." The temperature plummeted toward freezing, compounding the suffering of the thousands of wounded men trapped between the lines. Bragg wired Richmond that night, announcing a great victory. But he awoke in the morning stunned to find the Army of the Cumberland still drawn up before him, offering battle. The Federals had come to fight it out.[18]

The shooting picked up again temporarily on the morning of New Year's Day 1863, and the vulnerable Union wagon train departed for safety again, leaving the Michiganders to go hungry. King and Davis were initially part of a planned six-mile retreat for Rosecrans's supply convoy, but ultimately found themselves all the way back in Nashville after the train was assaulted by Confederate cavalry near La Vergne. The 11th's wagons and escort were mercifully unscathed, but a hasty retreat ensued. The balance of New Year's Day passed without a general engagement at Murfreesboro, but Negley's division was hurried to the far right of Rosecrans's line on a false alarm. "We were a galloping around from one place to another," remembered James Martin, "through the mud about knee deep, without any thing to eat whatever; so we spent our holly day."[19] After driving the enemy the day before, Bragg failed to act, and the initiative slipped through his fingers. Rosecrans, on the other hand, seized vital high ground on his own left flank.

On the morning of January 2, Gillaspie recounted, "our boys arose very lame sick and stiff from the affect of laying on the wet ground in the rain without any blankets or anything else." But the forenoon again passed in relative peace. In the afternoon, Bragg commanded John C. Breckinridge's Rebel division, against its commander's better judgment, to strike the Union left. The line of assault would necessarily cross Stones River under Rosecrans's artillery massed on the newly occupied high ground. Active skirmishing and occasional Confederate shelling tipped Bragg's hand, and Negley's division was ordered clear across the field to bolster the threatened blue flank. "We marched in quick time," Martin recorded, "untill we got to the banks of stone river, when we were orderd to lay down.... We had just got nicely settled down when the 'rebs' opened fire."[20]

Breckinridge's troops stepped off at 4:00 p.m. and looked unstoppable. Van Cleve's Union division under the command of Colonel Samuel Beatty scattered before the Confederate advance, but then the fifty-seven Federal cannon arrayed in support opened up a thunderous reply, firing over Negley's prone soldiers and tearing holes through the Rebel ranks. The brave Confederates forged ahead, staggering but undeterred, and began to splash across the shallow waterway. Just ahead of them, Negley's division lay flat on the ground, unseen. "We could tell by the fireing that the 'rebs' were driving [our men] back," declared Martin. "There we lay as quiet as could be untill they drove Vancleaves division over us." As the Confederates traversed the river and closed in—just a few yards distant now, Gillaspie noted—the 11th Michigan and the rest of Negley's division arose and pummeled the enemy with a devastating hail of two thousand Minie balls. Breckinridge's soldiers collapsed in windrows. The 11th

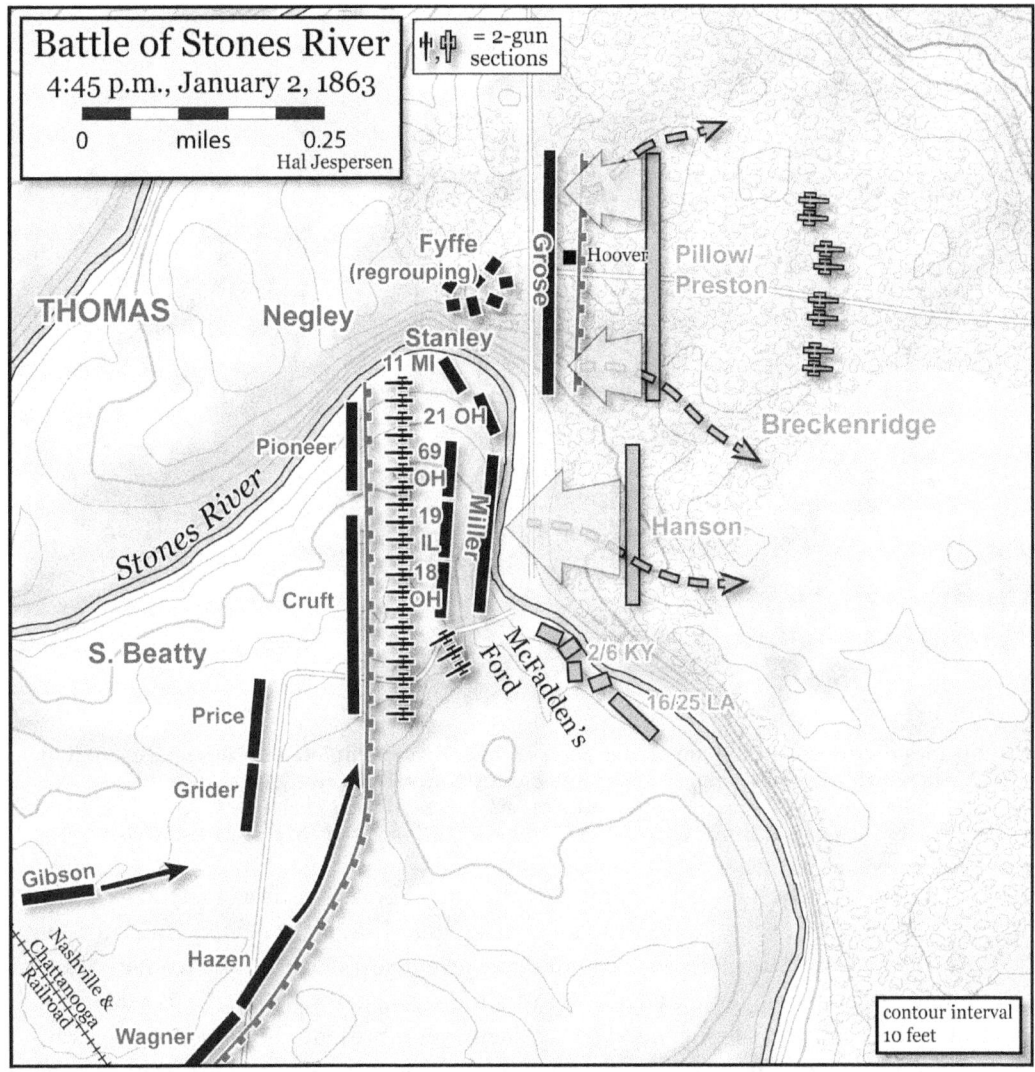

regiment and the surrounding units, shouting in elation, charged across the river in pursuit of the now stampeding Rebels. "We pourd volley after volley into them," exclaimed Martin, "till the ground was coverd with their bloody forms. I gave them the best turn I had in the wheel house. I fired twenty five rounds at their gray jackets and I know some of them must of taken effect." The chase continued up the slope from the river bank. The Rebels attempted in vain to rally. Stanley proudly observed Stoughton's Michiganders "charging and driving the foe in terrible confusion" as the division swarmed over a Confederate battery and seized the colors of the 26th Tennessee. Hundreds of Rebels surrendered. The 11th Michigan Infantry let out "a shout of triumph," Ozro Bowen declared. "The great battle of Stone River was won."[21]

When Breckinridge's devastated division regrouped that evening, they found their ranks short 1,800 veteran troops. With the contest decided, at least for the time being, Gillaspie boasted in his diary that the 11th was "more determined than ever

Negley's division's triumphant charge across Stones River completed the devastation of John C. Breckinridge's division, and ended the bloody contest in a sudden, stunning Union victory. "We pourd volley after volley into them," James Martin exclaimed, "till the ground was coverd with their bloody forms" (*Frank Leslie's Illustrated History of the Civil War*).

seeking revenge for their fallen comrades." But these brave words were tempered with the harsh reality of the battle's appalling slaughter. The final casualty count for the 11th Michigan at Stones River came to thirty-two dead, seventy-nine wounded, and twenty-nine missing, for a total of 140 casualties—a 32 percent loss. It was a daunting toll for the regiment's first general engagement, yet represented a merely average rate of loss across both armies in this momentous encounter. Gillaspie exclaimed in the nighttime aftermath of the combat, "O how horable to hear the sound of booming cannon and the sharp cracking of the rifles in the night when you no that nearly evry shot is sending death or ruin to some poor human being." "Stern war," Chadwick added, "with all its realities and horrors have been ours. The boys have always expressed great anxiety to be in a battle. To-day, none wish to see another." Martin insisted that "no tongue can tell the horrors of a battle; to hear the groans of the dying, to see men fall all around you to hear shot and shell screeching and bursting in the air; its enough to make a mans blood run cold."[22]

Bragg held his ground on January 3 before undertaking a demoralizing retreat that night. On the morning of the fourth, Stanley's brigade was the first Union force to march into Murfreesboro. Chadwick toured the battlefield with some of his comrades and wrote back to Three Rivers, "Oh! what awful sights we beheld. I had thought the reports of robbing the dead was exaggerated heretofore. But the sight of one's own eyes is proof. Our dead were stripped to the skin of all clothing—boots, shoes and stockings, that were of any service.... Language is too feeble to picture this awful scene." Two days later, King, just returned from Nashville, viewed the horrors of the battleground and was moved to quote a passage about war from Sanders' Fourth Reader. "They have rushed through like a hurricane, like an army of locusts they have devoured the earth. They have deluged the Land with Blood. The smoke rises not through the trees; the honors of the grove are fallen. The hearth of the cottages is cold: But it rises from the villages Burned with fire and from warm ruins spread over the Land. The groans of the wounded are in the hospitals, and by the road side, and in every thicket." "Ah Jenny," King continued in his own words, "you at home know little of this war. You cannot have the faintest idea. I have seen sights which would make the blood curdle in one's veins. And who will be accountable at the 'Bar of Justice' for these unholy scenes? The leaders of this unholy rebellion are alone accountable. Tis the vile traitors who plunged our peaceful land in civil war, the worst scourge that can befall a nation."[23]

Ten months prior, Charles Rice had declared at Bardstown "without hesitation that we have got the best set of officers, the best set of men, and the best drilled regiment in Kentucky, and if they will let us loose, we will prove it."[24] If the 11th Michigan had not yet completely proven Rice's assertion, they had certainly taken a long stride in that direction by showing their mettle at Stones River. When they met the Rebels in all-out battle again, they would do so as a veteran regiment, and for Bragg's Confederates, the result would be a bloodbath.

CHAPTER 5

"Perfectly careless"
January–September 1863

Northern war spirit ebbed. Stones River may have helped prevent the collapse of the Union war effort, but it could not erase the anguish of Burnside's folly at Fredericksburg, or the disappointment of Grant's sputtering drive toward Vicksburg.

Rosecrans and Bragg hunkered down to rebuild their devastated armies. The Federals settled in at Murfreesboro; the Confederates, primarily between Shelbyville and Wartrace, with headquarters at Tullahoma. "There is no prospect," Rose rightly said, "of another battle in this region very soon." The men of the 11th Michigan were grateful in the aftermath of Stones River to land the plum assignment of provost guard. Stoughton was appointed provost marshal by January 8, and promptly secured the post of guard for his regiment. The Wolverines were comfortably quartered in town, and viewed their lodgings as a godsend compared with the little shelter tents they were issued on January 5 and 6. Rose described the tents as dog kennels, "the poorest things that ever soldiers stayed in." The men suddenly acquired a complete admiration for the same Sibley tents they had looked upon with contempt a year before—tents which were lost in the chaos of the Stones River campaign. Companies C and H succeeded in obtaining Sibleys no longer needed by the 69th Ohio. Many weeks of miserable weather lay ahead, with rains that summoned up distasteful recollections of wallowing in the mud of Kentucky. Martin communicated this misery tongue-in-cheek when he described to his parents the army wagon teams, locatable now only by "the mules ears sticking out of the mud." King enjoyed a nice, dry office across from the courthouse, where he had a front row seat for the daily spectacle of the arrival of captured Confederates, "the worst looking set I ever saw. They look as though they had got all the *Southern Rights* they ever asked for, and were now willing to go home." One private noted that Stoughton was required to strip from the prisoners anything resembling a Union uniform. "There was a major brought in the other day," the private wrote, "who had a pair of Federal pants on. The order was carried into effect, and left the major in delicate circumstances."[1]

Others agonized through the loathsome duties of hauling debris and interring corpses from the battlefield and hospitals. "I was detaled Corp. of the buryal guard," Gillaspie sighed on January 31. "We buryed 27 dead bodeys and one extra leg and three arms. The wounded men are dieing off very very fast now." Sixteen of the 11th's wounded from the recent battle succumbed to their wounds in January, and two more followed after languishing into February. Gillaspie was on burial duty again on February 10, when he laid another forty-eight deceased soldiers to rest and casually noted of the hospital system that "it seems thare is more of the rebils that dies than of our men." Even his luckier comrades, who settled down among the urban comforts, eventually felt an inevitable, gnawing discontent—that of idle soldiers. "All I have to do," reported Martin, "is to draw rations for the Co and that is only once in five days. The rest of the time I lay around and do nothing.... There is nothing going on in town whatever; the inhabitants all left with old Brag. All you can see and hear is the rumble of wagons and the marching of troops." Though freshly informed about the horrors of battle, the Michiganders still detested prolonged, static military affairs, and much preferred active campaigning. "A soldier's life is nearly a sameness while in camp," King wrote his sweetheart, "and one letter tells all." The example of Benjamin Bordner was typical. He initially said with cheer that "we are having some tall times since we came to this place," but less than one month later his tone changed. "Well I will tell you [what] we are doing. Nothing at present but guarding." Provost duty kept the soldiers occupied only every other day, and the men had too much time on their hands. Bordner took up making and selling apple pies as a lucrative pastime.[2]

The weather was reminiscent of Bardstown not only in terms of the sheer volume of mud generated, but in the weather's apparent role in spreading deadly illnesses. "Evry man in our Reg.," Gillaspie remarked, "and all the others hear is sick with some thing or other. I dont know when they all will git well or how." Captain Oakes came down sick by January 8 and died of typhoid on the thirtieth, and twelve other Wolverines capitulated to disease during January and February. Eleven more were discharged for disability. Among the former, Clifford Bragg succumbed on January 16, just two weeks after his brother Myron was wounded at Stones River. Frederick Marsh, a new Company C recruit who Gillaspie remembered as "a noble boy and much too young to die," perished of illness on February 12, only thirty-three days after joining the regiment. Sturges, newly promoted to second lieutenant, resigned due to disability on February 13 only to die on March 1. Captain Chamberlain came down ill as well, and resigned on February 19.[3]

Several other prominent figures chose to leave the regiment in the wake of Stones River, and this phenomenon combined with illnesses and recent battle casualties to trigger a flurry of void-filling promotions that significantly altered the regiment's makeup. Lieutenant Colonel Eldridge elected to resign his commission on January 7. With Stoughton on duty as provost marshal, the regiment was left without a field officer, and Lewis Childs, who had entered the recent battle as a mere first lieutenant, suddenly found himself raised to captain and in temporary command of the entire regiment in mid–January. The colonel responded by requesting promotion for the recuperating Major Smith, and for Captain Hood, who was still detailed with the Pioneer Brigade. Both commissions were forthcoming, but Hood determined on

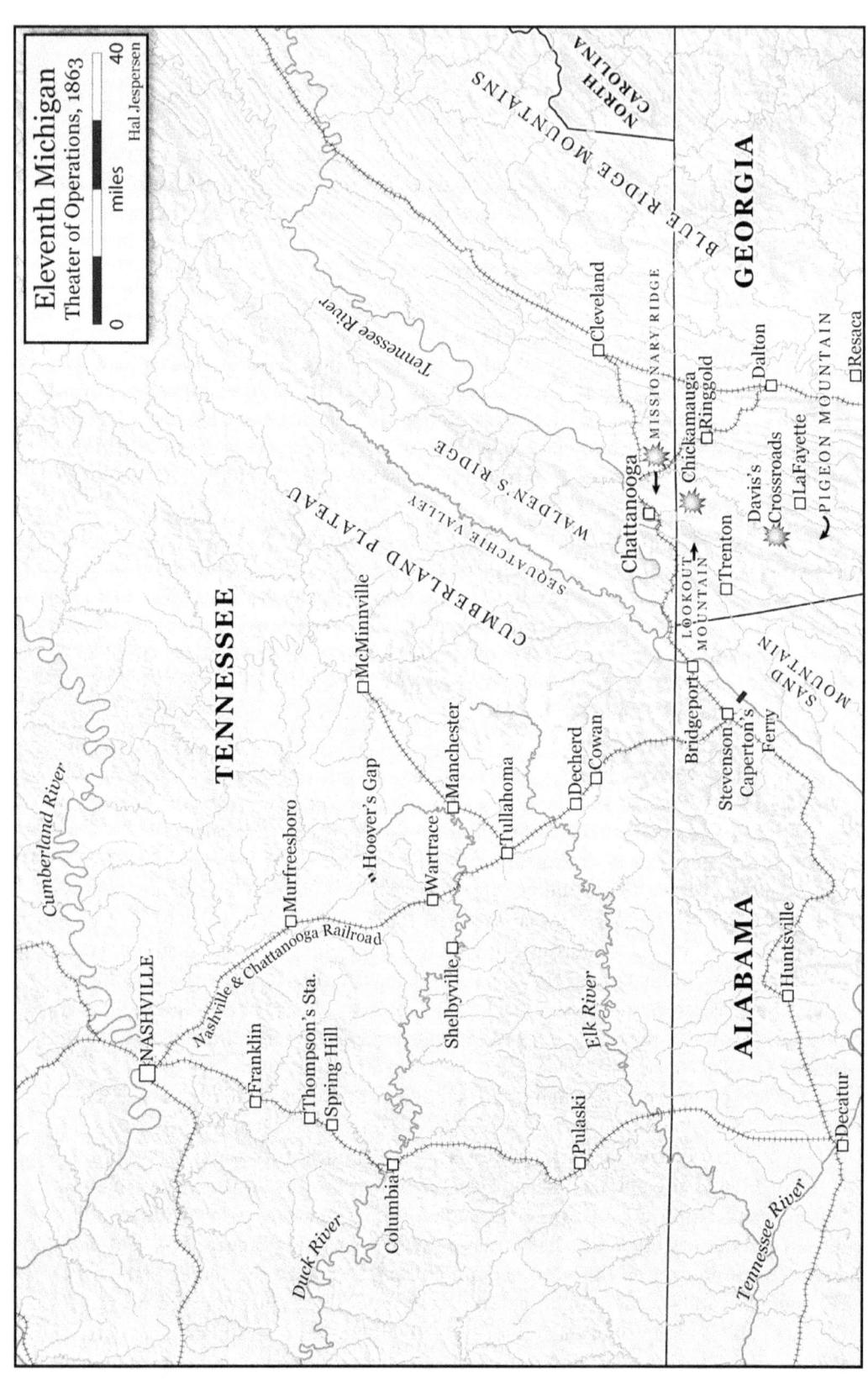

March 17 to retreat to civilian life, and Smith declined his commission and resigned two days later due to disability caused by his Stones River bullet wound, which had shattered both sides of his jaw. Stoughton, supported by a petition from his officers, raised the popular Captain Mudge—who had missed Stones River along with Captain Bennett on recruiting duty in Michigan—to the lieutenant colonelcy by April 25. The position of major would remain vacant until granted to Bennett in August. Last but not least of the personnel changes, Chadwick departed on sick furlough in January, never to return. He headed back to Three Rivers and resigned his commission on February 13. First Lieutenant Linus Truman Squire became acting adjutant, an assignment that would be made permanent in August.[4]

Among the regiment's newer officers was Borden Hicks, commissioned second lieutenant of Company E in November. Hicks, it will be remembered, had enlisted against the wishes of his father, who in turn had informed his son that he should consider himself disowned. Yet the senior Hicks was so proud upon hearing of his son's lieutenancy that the two reconciled, and the soldier's father paid him a visit in Tennessee. The otherwise happy reunion that ensued in Murfreesboro concluded in the termination of Lieutenant Hicks's short-lived equestrian career.

Linus Truman Squire enlisted as a sergeant in Company H and rose to the rank of adjutant. At Missionary Ridge, he charged most of the way up the heights side by side with James King before becoming disabled under fire. After the war, he served in the Freedmen's Bureau, earned a medical degree, and was employed in the federal government's post office and pension departments (Mollus Mass Civil War Collection, United States Army Heritage and Education Center, Military History Institute).

> My father came down to visit us. I made up a party to visit the battle field of Stone River, getting horses to ride, I had just blossomed out in a new uniform, with Lieutenants shoulder straps as large and gaudy as could be bought, I had never been noted for my horsemanship, and the farther we rode the more my pants insisted on crawling up my legs, and reach high water mark. As we rode through the camp of a cavalry regiment, they commenced to guy me, by calling out "pull down your pants, Lieutenant, pull down your pants." Whenever I had occasion after that to ride a horse, I went afoot.[5]

Opposite: **From** *Conspicuous Gallantry: The Civil War and Reconstruction Letters of James W. King, 11th Michigan Volunteer Infantry,* **© 2015 by The Kent State University Press. Reproduced with permission.**

Ira Gillaspie was not alone in observing February 24, the midway point through the regiment's earliest three-year enlistments. "Our first eighteen monthes are most gone," he wrote, "and the war is not over yet. I begin to think for the first time may be we will have to stay our three years out yet.... I am willing to quit soldiering as soon as our Union is restored but should ... the south continue to defy the athoratys of the United States I am willing to remain in the armey for years yet. Thus endeth the first year and a half of my life as a soldier. My energy is with my country heart with my friends." Corporal Gillaspie would serve out his three years and live another thirty-two after the war's end, but his voice goes silent beyond this point. He had filled the last page of his diary, and if he continued his writings in a successive volume, its whereabouts are a mystery.[6]

The regiment received four months' pay on February 25. "You know how good it makes a man feel to have a 'green back' or two in his pocket," Rose remarked, "even if it is at about sixty per cent discount for gold, but alas how soon it vanishes." As usual, most of the soldiers sent at least some of their pay to loved ones back home, while others loaned it out, or did both.[7]

King and Rose both conversed with Confederate prisoners in Murfreesboro who claimed to have been coerced into military service. "There is a Rebel Hospital, the next room to ours," King wrote. "They have as good care as our men. The Government provides them Rations and medicines, and the women in the Town bring them many delicacies. I have talked with many of them who say they were forced to go into the army or be hung, and of course they went in. They tell about the suffering of the South. That is, the people. Men who never knew what it was to want, Are now suffering for the necessaries of life." Rose noted that "there is a rebel soldier staying with our Co waiting for his papers to go to his home in New York. he was in Florida at the breaking out of the rebelion and they made him enlist, he is quite a good fellow." Stoughton saw to it that the man was taken care of.[8]

Though most civilians had evacuated the Murfreesboro area, there were of course some holdouts, and inevitably the soldiers socialized with the remaining locals. King, along with Sergeant Cuthbert Dixon of Company A, visited with one Southern belle of open Confederate sympathies who had a surprisingly open mind and was considering moving north with her daughter, who she thought would prefer Northern culture. On another occasion, King and several of his comrades visited a plantation on the battlefield, belonging to Giles and Mary Harding, near the site of the 11th's skirmish of December 30. The soldiers were invited in and shown the family piano, which had suffered one leg splintered by a Federal cannonball that crashed through the house. The soldiers called upon one of the ladies, likely Mary Harding, to play the instrument for them, but after initially demurring, she slyly treated them to secessionist melodies. (Mary's lack of hospitality must be placed in the context that Federal soldiers had stolen some of her livestock and threatened to hang her husband from a tree.) Ephraim Hall, just returned from Libby Prison following his wounding and capture at Stones River, traded barbs with this spirited lady, and the guests took their leave.[9]

In politics, the opening months of 1863 were dominated by two great controversies: the implementation of the Emancipation Proclamation in January, and the institution of the draft in March. Adherents of the North's antiwar movement, the Copperheads, were emboldened by the instituting of these policies during a time of war weariness. The Copperheads' actions naturally struck a nerve with Federal soldiers, who responded bitterly in their letters home. One Wolverine wrote anonymously to the *Reporter* to assure its readers that Copperhead claims of growing discontent among Union soldiers were false. And Private Latham penned a diatribe, printed in the same issue, against "the infernal machinations of that unholy crew at home, who write, and speak, and print treason, curse the Administration and upbraid the soldiers for 'fighting for the nigger' and curse him for engaging in a 'damned abolition war.'... Will our neighbors at home stand by us in our death struggles for their own safety? We ARE in the right, and why should we draw back?" Myron Bragg expressed his opinion regarding these prominent subjects of public debate by declaring one black man "worth five of your blame copperheads."[10] King, Rose, Bordner, and Martin all railed against the peace democrats in private letters during early March 1863. King decried

> the Sympathy Shown these black hearted traitors by a few, No I will not say a few. But by some of the Northern Peace Men. While we are here undergoing the dangers and privations of a soldiers life and attempting to put down the vile miscreants who are aiming at the life blood of our Beloved Country! Many of our brave men pouring out their life's blood in the cause of the Union, There is a party at Home who sympathize with the traitors and are doing all in their power to Clog the wheels of Government and stop the prosecution of the war. They find fault with the Proclamation of the President and in Every act of the Administration. The Detroit Free Press says if the President had not issued the proclamation there would have been Volunteers Enough to fill all demand. Now Jenny I do not think this issuing of the Proclamation has made the difference of one man. Why don't they find fault with the Southern Confederacy who have trampled all rights and Liberties under foot? Oh no, not a word to say, they are a much abused people and the North was the aggressors.[11]

Rose considered the antiwar crowd a dire threat, calling the Copperheads "a regular stimulant (so to speak) to the rebels.... It is my opinion that the Confederacy will be recognized before two more years passed by." He continued in a subsequent letter, "I would as soon fight traitors at home as here. I think I would flatten out a few copperheads." The same act of conscription that fanned the fires of the peace movement was popular with the soldiers. Martin looked for the draft to "make some of those fellows open their eyes that loves their freedom so well, but are not willing to fight for it," while Bordner was concerned that without the draft, the less patriotic men at home would "all get married and not let a woman for the soldier."[12]

The marked unrest in the Army of the Cumberland regarding the Copperheads did not go unnoticed, and at least one Union meeting was convened in the upper story of the Murfreesboro courthouse around the end of the first week of March. King and Rose attended one such meeting, and the bulk of the regiment was likely present as provost guard. King noted that the courthouse, decorated for the occasion and graced with the airs of the Army of the Cumberland's regular army brigade band, was overflowing with attendees. Rosecrans originally intended to speak but could not make it, so his chief of staff (and future president of the United States) James Abram Garfield spoke in his stead. "He said this was a peculiar kind of meeting," King recorded, "but the Army of the Cumberland would never flinch from its duty, even if the whole North turned against us. There were peace men in the north who were doing all in their power to aid the Rebels. But he was satisfied that the masses at Home were with us." Garfield then introduced the main speaker, Thomas Buchanan Read, noted painter and poet. Read addressed the soldiers' fears about the peace movement, relating his heartwarming experiences at a large Union meeting in Cincinnati and ensuring the soldiers that the Copperheads were doomed to fail. He then recited his poem "The Oath," which had been read before Congress and deeply affected President Lincoln. It was a morose piece, chiding the peace movement while simultaneously bemoaning the human cost of the war—and then espousing revenge. King considered it "thrilling and beautiful."[13]

On April 6 Captain Bennett, enjoying temporary command of the regiment, formed the 11th up on the parade grounds. The entire division, including General Negley and Colonel Stanley, gathered around. Colonel Stoughton was summoned, ostensibly to drill his regiment, and was stunned to discover upon arrival that he was the center of attention for a huge throng of soldiers. Captain Mudge presented Stoughton with an ornate sword with an engraved hilt, purchased in Nashville by Captain Heath with $600 donated by the regiment, along with what King described as "trappings which would do honor to the Uniform of a Major General"—silver and steel sheaths with gold trim, a belt, a pistol, a cartridge box, a sash, gloves, and spurs. Negley remarked to Stoughton that the gifts represented a great honor, but not so great an honor as "to be the leader of such men as the noble Eleventh." King observed that "there was a feeling Expressed on the countenances of all which cannot be described. Nineteen long months, months of darkness and danger, have we been with him, always at our head and never from his post in time of danger."[14] A reporter from the *Nashville Union* recorded the speeches that followed. Mudge stood and spoke at some length.

> Col. Stoughton—you were invited inside this square to receive a testimonial of the affections of the officers and men of the 11th Michigan Infantry.
> Allow me to present you with this package, which contains the names and amount contributed by each, to purchase for you these presents, as a token of our appreciation of your merit as a friend and a soldier, and the confidence reposed in you as our commanding officer. You will see by this document that the privates and non-commissioned officers donated by far the larger amount. For the honor, reputation and praises awarded the regiment for its part in the bloody battle of Stone River, we are indebted to you for your bravery, coolness, and military skill, which directed and led us on to victory and glory.
> We ask you to accept this sword and accompanying articles. Its donation is but the promptings of a soldier's heart who loves the brave and appreciates merit. We know that in your hands traitors will cower before its glittering blade, for a patriot wields it in defense of a nation and freedom.
> It is with sadness that we look upon the present state of the country. By peace it had grown great and prosperous. The government, generous and munificent, had showered upon her people liberty and plenty. No class but what had received rich

benefits from its wise legislators—and yet, without cause, ungrateful men have taken up arms for its destruction. Yonder flag, upon whose beautiful folds the sons of liberty never tire in gaze, has been torn from its staff and roiled in the dust. These vile traitors with the bloody implements of war, have sought to destroy our government and liberties, and build upon its ruins a despotism, having in tyranny not its parallel in history.

It is in the valor displayed in fighting this enemy that you have won our confidence and love. The Eleventh, with you as its commander, will strike deeper blows, if possible, with the brave army of the Cumberland, will free our land of its foes, and again shall our father's flag float, as of yore over every foot of freedom's soil.

A deeply affected Stoughton replied in part,

I accept at your hands this magnificent and unexpected gift with emotions of heartfelt gratitude. Its rare beauty and intrinsic worth are all that can be desired, but I shall prize it still more highly for its history and associations. We are no strangers; the camp, the march, the bivouac and the battle-field have created those ties and memories that can only cease with death.

Many of our gallant comrades now "sleep the sleep that knows no waking," but we are reminded of the past and look to the future with a calm assurance of victory.

There is no faltering in the hearts of those, who, after the scenes in which you have borne an honored part, voluntarily bestow on your commanding officer a sword like this "Damascus blade" at once the emblem of your unwavering devotion to your country, and of that command and power which can only be maintained by your bravery and courage.[15]

"Taking it all in consideration," Martin summarized the ceremony, "it was quite a magnificent affair."[16]

With the arrival of warmer weather, the 1863 campaign season was soon underway. Back east, the Army of the Potomac had changed commanders yet again. Joseph Hooker prepared to advance an enormous host against Lee and the Confederate capital. Out west, Grant had expended February and March on abortive attempts to engineer an approach to Vicksburg through the morass of surrounding bayous and river delta, but as the weather grew fair, new options opened up before him, and his troops resumed operations in earnest. Rosecrans's army slowly began to stir as well. Supplies were certainly no issue. Martin declared that "if you could see the pile of provisions that we have got piled up here you would think that we were agoing to do something. We have got two or three piles of hard crackers twice as large as John Reynolds barn and every thing else in proportion," although he noted that some of his comrades expected to stay put until Vicksburg fell (which was Rosecrans's preference, but not Halleck's or Lincoln's). King and Martin both communicated hopes that Bragg would come and attack the Federals behind their fortifications at Murfreesboro. By May 21 the Michiganders were alerted to be ready to move on short notice, although Stoughton warned his men that the 11th, as provost guard, may be left behind when the army advanced. Word reached Murfreesboro of Grant's victory at Jackson, Mississippi, and of Hooker's devastating defeat at Chancellorsville in Virginia. News of prodigious battles elsewhere only made the Wolverines all the more anxious for action.[17]

The reassurances of Thomas Buchanan Read at the recent Union meeting seem to have allayed the Wolverines' fears regarding the peace movement. On May 24, as provost guard of Murfreesboro, they had an opportunity to see the best known (and among Unionists, the most reviled) of the Copperheads up close. Chief among the North's antiwar faction stood former Ohio representative Clement Laird Vallandigham. After tasting defeat in the 1862 election, Vallandigham's rhetoric had grown desperate as he pursued the governorship and grasped for some means to undermine the Union war effort. The Ohioan bitterly asserted that secession was a right, and that the war against it was unconstitutional. He referred to the president as a despot: King Lincoln. His oratory danced a fine line with treason, and his speech in Mount Vernon, Ohio, on May 1, crossed that line. Vallandigham was arrested, and there was an immediate outburst over the constitutionality of the candidate's detention and ensuing military trial. Lincoln astutely headed off the controversy by ordering the Copperhead's banishment to the Confederacy. It just so happened that the peace advocate was conveyed to the Rebels via Murfreesboro, where Hicks noted that the 11th regiment was among the units that "had the pleasure, as well as the duty, of escorting Vallandigham through our lines, and turning him over to his avowed friends, our enemy." Company E, in conjunction with Rosecrans's provost marshal general, William M. Wiles, escorted Vallandigham from his nighttime arrival at the train depot to Wiles's headquarters, the home of John Hunt Morgan's father-in-law, former congressman Charles Ready, Jr. Rosecrans conversed with the unwelcome guest while the Michiganders stood guard outside. The general purportedly commented to Vallandigham, "Why, sir, do you know that unless I protect you with a guard my soldiers will tear you to pieces in an instant?" The Copperhead departed with a cavalry escort at 2:00 a.m., bound for transfer to the Rebel lines, but he was destined to cross paths with the 11th Michigan again—and with harrowing results.[18]

Clement Laird Vallandigham was the best known, and most reviled, of the Northern peace activists, known as the Copperheads. The 11th Michigan resented being ordered to escort Vallandigham safely through the Union lines upon his banishment to the Confederacy, and dangerously took their frustration out on him when they chanced across him again in Sidney, Ohio, on their way home to Michigan in September 1864 (Library of Congress).

Provost duty provided some additional, albeit macabre, excitement on June 5 when Colonel Stoughton was required to arrange for the hanging of accused murderer William A. Selkirk. Selkirk, despite proclaiming his innocence in highly detailed testimony—which was transcribed by James King—was convicted of killing another citizen, Adam Weaver of Wilson County.[19] About 10,000 people gathered to witness the spectacle, most of them Federal soldiers. A witness recorded the scene on behalf of the *Nashville Daily Press*:

As the prisoner gazed upon the vast multitude, his whole appearance changed from an almost rose color to an ashy paleness. The recollections of the dreams of happiness he once found all seemed to vanish when he gazed intently on the assemblage and the rope which hung carelessly over his head. He gave but one solemn, melancholy, dejected look of acute anguish at the rope and the scaffold, and then turned and looked abstractedly towards the guard which escorted him.... Rev. Mr. Patterson [Holmes A. Pattison] of the 11th Michigan made a most fervent and eloquent prayer, the prisoner on his knees with eyes uplifted to heaven and seemingly praying with all the fervor of his soul. After Mr. [Pattison] had finished praying the Adjutant of the 11th Michigan [Linus Squire] stood up in the wagon and read the "General Order" ... and then told the prisoner that he had five minutes to live and make any remarks he wished.[20]

Selkirk desperately asserted his innocence and prayed for eternal life. The murder victim's seventeen-year-old daughter asked Wiles for permission to place the noose around the convict's neck, but her request was denied. She watched numbly as Selkirk's life was snuffed out. "I will not give you a description of the scene," King remarked. "Such things are too gloomy to relate."[21]

Five days later, the regiment lost its chaplain. Holmes Pattison was popular, at least with Myron Bragg, who declared the chaplain "such a common man not proud but just as pleasant a man as ever trod shoe leather." Pattison was detached to minister to convalescent soldiers in Murfreesboro, a role he would remain in for the balance of his military service. He also took the opportunity to run a Sabbath school with two of his counterparts, and brought his wife south to keep him company. In a bizarre side story, Pattison became attached to an affable drummer boy of the 33rd New Jersey, William Henry McGee. McGee nearly succumbed to typhoid at the hospital but recovered with Pattison's help, and the chaplain legally adopted the young soldier, who was fatherless but had a mother alive and well in New Jersey. After the war ended, McGee came to Michigan. He described to Pattison an impressive claim of his supposed heroics in a charge against Nathan Bedford Forrest's troops at Murfreesboro on December 7, 1864—likely a complete fiction, as no evidence exists that McGee even participated in the battle in question. Pattison responded by asking General (and now congressman) Lovell Rousseau to recommend McGee for the Medal of Honor. Remarkably, Rousseau, who was not present at the battle, added his endorsement to Pattison's letter and forwarded it to the War Department. Even more stunningly, the medal was promptly forthcoming, based on nothing more than the correspondence of Pattison and Rousseau—without a single eyewitness account. McGee went on to prove himself a con man, an alcoholic, and worse. He leveraged his medal to secure an appointment to the regular army, and then shot dead his regiment's assistant surgeon in revenge for being accused of petty theft. McGee was court-martialed and sentenced to prison, but Pattison again stuck his neck out for the young man, successfully enlisting the help of former New Jersey governor Marcus Ward to obtain for McGee an executive pardon from President Ulysses S. Grant. The relationship between Pattison and McGee soured in the wake of his crime, however, and the two parted ways soon after.[22]

Rosecrans had been subjected to prolonged pressure from Washington to strike at Bragg again. On June 23 the Army of the Cumberland finally moved to engage the enemy. Benjamin Wells, recuperating from chronic illness at the general hospital in Murfreesboro, did not need to be told what was happening when he witnessed hundreds of soldiers, unfit to march with the army, flooding into the hospital. "There will be a Battle ere many weeks," he wrote. "There are a thousand vague rumors afloat in camp about the anticipated move." Myron Bragg, who had been chronically ill, was forced to choose between joining the Invalid Corps or advancing with the 11th Michigan. He adamantly chose the latter. Elements of Rosecrans's army advanced in a feint against Bragg's left at Shelbyville, with the bulk of the Federal infantry getting underway early the next morning in hopes of turning the Rebel right in order to avoid a costly battle amid rough terrain. McCook's 20th Corps was to make for Liberty Gap. Thomas's 14th Corps would head for Hoover's Gap, and Crittenden's 21st Corps would march clear around Bragg's flank and push south to Manchester. The foot soldiers were commanded to travel light, dispensing with all unnecessary encumbrances and stowing three days' rations in their haversacks.[23]

Negley's division—now designated the 2nd Division of the 14th Corps—encompassed the brigades of Stanley, Brigadier General John Beatty, and Colonel William Sirwell. They were underway at 11:30 a.m., following the Winchester Pike toward Manchester in a downpour, and slogging through mud churned up by Rousseau's train ahead of them. The division resumed its advance at 10:00 the next morning, and with Stanley's brigade—under the temporary command of Colonel Stoughton, with Stanley absent—guarding the train, they struck out for Hoover's Gap and arrived about 1:00 p.m. A mounted Federal brigade under John T. Wilder, armed with Spencer repeating rifles, had seized the gap with lightning speed the day before, but Confederate resistance beyond the pass caused a blue traffic jam to form in the rear. Negley's men bivouacked near Jacob's Store and set out again toward Fairfield at 7:30 a.m. on the twenty-sixth. On the way, the men passed through Hoover's Gap. Rosecrans had originally looked to Crittenden on the left to turn Bragg out of his position, but Thomas's rapid exploitation of the gap—a natural defensive position manned only by a token Confederate force—became the key to the campaign's success. King described the pass as "a narrow valley about 3 miles long, surrounded by high hills covered with a dense, heavy growth of timber.... Had this gap been properly fortified, It would have been a second Thermopylae." Martin complained that passing through the gap required wading across the same winding creek ten times.[24]

That evening, the 11th Michigan joined in a modest skirmish, with the enemy readily giving way. The division continued forward, arrived at Manchester on the evening of the twenty-seventh, and took up a defensive position on the Hillsborough Pike. The advance resumed on June 29, again slowed to a crawl by nonstop rains. Half of Stoughton's regiment was detailed to the backbreaking duty of hauling artillery through the muck. King described this portion of the countryside as "the poorest I ever saw, and an unbroken wilderness. I do not remember of seeing a single habitation." Martin agreed, referring bitterly to "the worst places that men ever marched," and adding that "it dont do nothing but rain rain all the time. I am sick and tired of such weather." The disagreeable trek terminated at Bobo's Crossroads by 9:00 p.m. The following day was devoted to an uneventful reconnaissance.[25]

On July 1 Thomas rushed his corps forward in an attempt to head Bragg's retreat off at the bridges traversing Elk River. The Rebels had been caught off guard by the speed of Rosecrans's turning movement, combined with the feint at Shelbyville, and the result was a tantalizing opportunity to entrap the fleeing Confederates. Negley's division hurried toward Hale's Mill at 11:00 a.m. despite oppressive heat, with Beatty's brigade taking the lead. A spirited skirmish broke out three miles into the march. Bragg, however, narrowly won the race to the river. Negley's exhausted troops arrived near nightfall to find the Rebels drawn up just shy of a bend in the waterway, situated on a ridge with strong artillery support.[26]

Stoughton deployed the 18th Ohio and 19th Illinois with a battalion of cavalry to test the enemy defenses, but this reconnaissance-in-force was stymied by a large contingent of Rebel horsemen. Negley decided to up the stakes, and the 11th Michigan launched into the fray after 7:00 p.m., followed by two of Beatty's regiments. The Confederate cavalry were driven half a mile back, onto their infantry support, which Negley identified as troops belonging to the divisions of Cleburne and Stewart, plus Archibald Gracie's brigade. The Michiganders and their comrades forced a hot skirmish for some time before assuming a strong defensive position for the night. Stoughton reported just one casualty: First Lieutenant Henry Platt, serving as aide de camp and acting brigade ordnance officer, was captured.[27]

On July 2 Negley tried to seize the Elk River bridge after the Rebels crossed, but the Confederates torched the span just soon enough to render it unusable before the Federals could douse the flames. Negley in turn disputed Rebel possession of a nearby ford—which proved temporarily impassable due to the rains—and succeeded in shoving the Confederates away after getting the upper hand in an artillery duel. The blue division's efforts in this vein amounted to a diversion that enabled the balance of Thomas's corps to cross the water elsewhere. At 10:00 the next morning, the division traversed the Elk, and King reported that the soldiers were afterward treated to an extraordinary sight. "Our road led up the side of a very high hill; when I reached the top I stopped to gaze on the scene that lay spread out as a picture below me. To the north, on the same road we had come, could be seen long white trains. Two or 3 Divisions of Union soldiers were making their way across the fields. To the East and West, as far as the eye could reach stretched the green Valley, while Elk River in its Serpentine course ran through the center." The troops marched three miles and encamped near Decherd on the Nashville and Chattanooga Railroad that evening. Stark logistical realities indicated an extended stay. "For the last three days," Martin reported, "we have lived on corn and blackberries. Once in a while we get a little fresh meat and that we have to eat with out salt. What corn the boys have had to stew they have stole it away from the mules while they were eating and the poor mules are howling around about as near starved as we are.... There is one thing certain that we cant march much farther untill we get some provisions on hand." Martin's mood picked up ten days later when the train cars started rolling in. "We have got a good camping ground and are having tolable easy times," he remarked.[28]

Rosecrans had brilliantly turned Bragg out of his position, with little bloodshed, in what would be remembered as the Tullahoma Campaign. Negley's entire division tallied merely nine casualties while taking sixty-two prisoners. These loss rates were fairly indicative of the overall results. The Army of the Cumberland had lost less than 600 men, and captured more than 1,600 Confederates while driving Bragg all the way back to Chattanooga. The Confederates had conceded scores of miles of terrain that could have proven eminently defensible. A huge swath of Tennessee changed hands in a matter of days. "This army," Bennett declared, "is penetrating the bowels of Dixie by degrees."[29]

At Decherd, with the Cumberlanders already riding a morale high, news came of a series of disasters to Confederate arms that occurred in the brief span from July 3 to 9: Lee's resounding defeat at Gettysburg, Grant's seizing of Vicksburg with 30,000 prisoners, and the subsequent fall of Port Hudson. A false rumor of Charleston's capture was thrown in for good measure. "I think that everything looks promising," Martin wrote, "to crush this rebellion and restore peace to our once happy country." Many days passed by as Rosecrans stockpiled supplies and considered his next move. The 11th regiment, primarily occupied with railroad repairs and picket duty, shifted five miles to Cowan, at the foot of the Cumberland Mountains, on August 9. "The natural scenery of the place is magnificent," King commented. "We are camped in a pleasant grove near the Bank of a creek that goes dancing o'er its rocky bed, seeming perfectly happy in its winding course. In front on the left and right rise the Cumberland Mountains in all their grandeur."[30] Bennett described Cowan as

> a regular Tennessee city; consisting principally of a Rail Bridge, a turn-table, a cornfield, a garden without a fence, two chimneys with a house between them, a few negro huts, and a hotel....
> The inhabitants hereabouts are of the same stripe as those I have seen elsewhere in the State—lean, lank and cadaverous, and using a language which I should term "broken African." It is evident that if the country ever contained any of the genuine *chivalry*—that class whom Artemas Ward would term "gay and festive cusses,"—they have all gone farther south. The inhabitants from all points are flocking into our camps, begging for provisions. We behold many sad spectacles—They all tell the same story of want and suffering. At present we can furnish them but little assistance.[31]

By August 12, the Michiganders—back under Stoughton's command now that Stanley had returned to the brigade—were sharing rumors of a resumed advance, directed toward Atlanta and to be inaugurated the following day. Mudge led most of the regiment on a labor detail to help clear a path over the mountain. "In a short time," a confident Bennett predicted, "Thomas' and McCook's entire corps will be in Alabama; then you may look out for a big fight or a rebel skedaddle." Negley's division departed on the sixteenth, which represented a surprise to at least one of Stoughton's men: to King's recollection, it was the 11th's first march on the Sabbath since Rosecrans took command.[32]

True to form, Mother Nature synchronized torrential downpours with the Army of the Cumberland's advance. Bragg was still holed up in Chattanooga, and Rosecrans's strategy called for a demonstration against the city while the balance of the Union army penetrated the gaps through the mountainous region to the south, turning the Confederates out of their stronghold. The Michiganders trudged over the mountains, prompting Rose to complain that "we marched slow but our load and hot weather gave us considerable fatigue." King declared that he "could not tell or convey to you half of the roughness that we had to pass over." The hike then crossed what he described as "a narrow valley, which wound for miles among the mountains. I do not know when I have enjoyed a trip as well as I did this. The road led through the Valley which seemed, or in fact is, walled in from all the rest [of] the world beside. This Valley is one vast cornfield. You seldom see any other article raised. Once in a while a small Field of Tobacco, but seldom." The Wolverines tramped sixteen miles in all before bivouacking. The next day they made twenty miles, coming to a halt at a grove near a creek just outside of Stevenson, Alabama, where they settled down to await the laying of pontoon bridges across the Tennessee River. Rose described the new encampment "between two ranges of mountains in a fertile valley averaging in width from 80 rods to two miles." Supplies continued to flood in by rail, and the regiment enjoyed ample rations and relaxation.[33]

The Michiganders were beaming with confidence. Rose noted that "it is reported that the rebs and our pickets go in swimming and play cards together nearly every day. I think the rebelion is about played out our prospects are the best they ever was at present." King was "in hopes that in a few short months, this land will be freed from the wicked war which has so long threatened to swallow everything. Already in the distance can I see the light breaking. If our successes for the next three months are as great as they have been in the past, there will be no Confederacy. The armies of Grant and Rosecrans will sweep from here to the gulf, and no power on earth can stay them. In the meantime, Charleston must fall. When this is done, then may we look for Peace."[34]

Everyone appreciated the serene stopover at Stevenson. Diarist Private John J. Bloom of Company E jotted in his August 24 entry, "Got [a] Barell of Beer & Treeted the Reg." When the rejuvenated, self-assured Wolverines departed camp late in the afternoon of September 1, they did so without any inkling that they were embarking on a three-week whirlwind that would alter the entire complexion of the war—and of the regiment. Their division arrived at the Tennessee River after dark and crossed at Caperton's Ferry, footing another four miles before they lost their way in the pitch dark. Stoughton barked the order, "In place, rest," and his soldiers bedded down where they stood. The supply train had necessarily split from the infantry and awaited moonrise before spanning a pontoon bridge constructed by the 1st Michigan Engineers at Bridgeport. The regiment was underway again the next morning, struggling along a narrow trail—scarcely wide enough to accommodate a wagon—that was bordered on one side by a precipitous drop to the river, and on the other side by Sand Mountain. As evening approached, the Michiganders began to ascend the incline, and halted for the evening at a recently abandoned Rebel camp. "I am almost Tyred Out," Bloom complained that night. The balance of the division remained behind at Moore's Spring, near Taylor's Store, to take advantage of the fresh water supply. The wagon train caught up the next morning, and the entire division was gainfully employed in repairing the road and dragging their supplies up the mountainside before encamping on the summit near Warren's Mill that night. Negley boasted to Thomas that the demanding ascent was accomplished "without the loss of a wheel."[35]

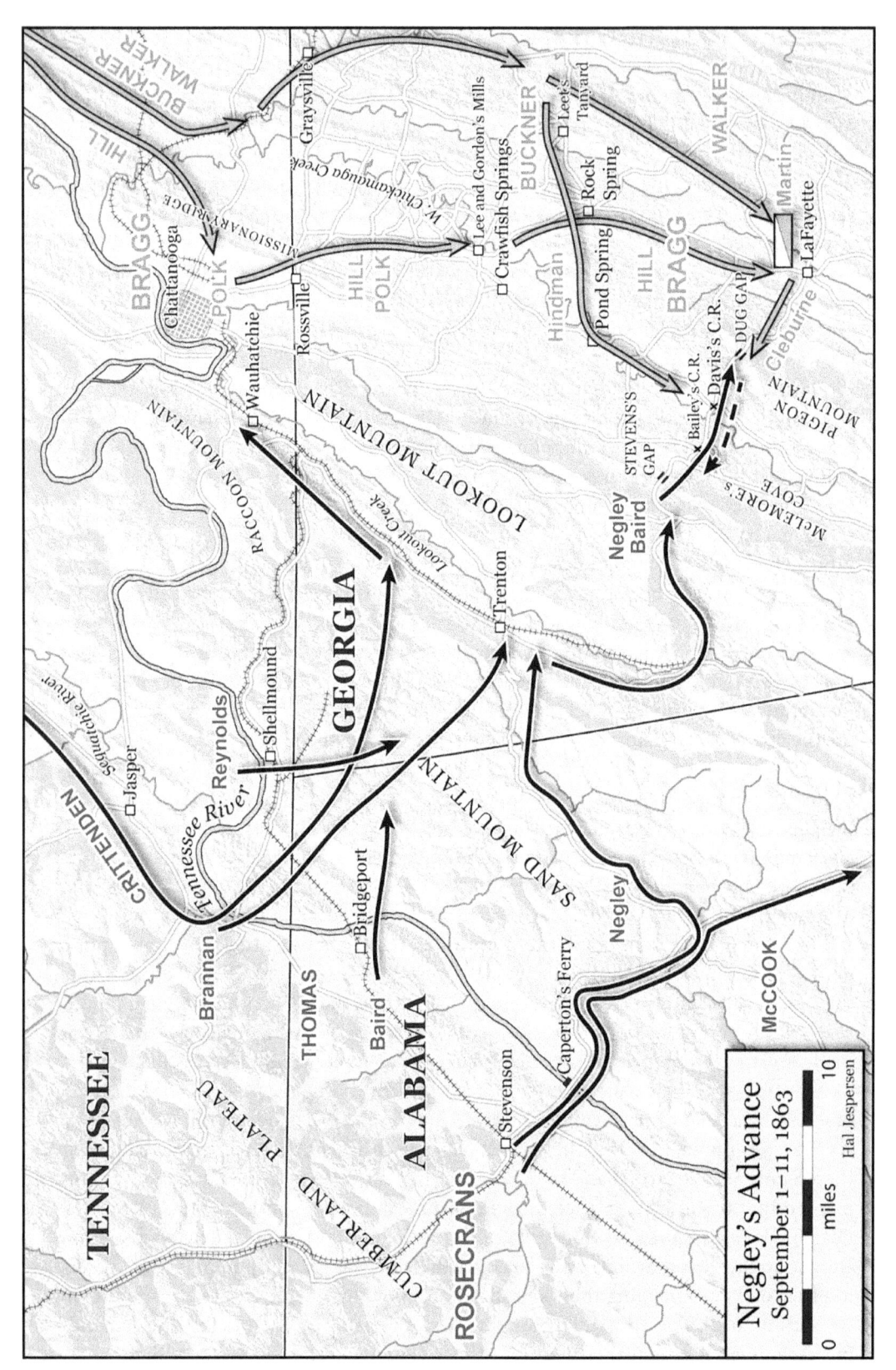

The 11th Michigan's supply train crossed this Tennessee River pontoon bridge, constructed by the 1st Michigan Engineers, at the outset of the advance that led to the Battle of Davis's Crossroads (Belknap, *History of the Michigan Organizations at Chickamauga, Chattanooga, and Missionary Ridge*).

The next morning, September 4, the regiment marched four miles before being delegated to reinforce a replacement bridge constructed by the 78th Pennsylvania the night before. The Wolverines reinforced the span sufficiently to support the passing of the corps artillery. The 11th Michigan, assigned as the vanguard of the entire 14th Corps's advance, descended to the foot of the mountain near Trenton, Georgia, and captured some Confederates at the Macon Iron Works. There, they set up camp and slaked their thirst at Brown's Spring. Negley's force rested the next day (with the exception of some scouting performed by Sirwell's brigade), and King and Rose, both enjoying lively correspondence during this campaign, took the opportunity to pen letters home. "On our march," King remarked, "there has been nothing exciting. No Rebels have appeared to Stop our progress. The Country is very mountainous, and but few inhabitants." Rose reported that "the boys are all quite well we stood the march good. there has about ten reb soldiers reported here since we arrived." Ongoing defections from Bragg's army increasingly convinced Rosecrans's troops that the end of the war was in sight.[36]

Negley's advance through lush Lookout Valley resumed at 10:00 a.m. on September 6, when the Union troops trudged six miles down the road toward Stevens's Gap, a key pass through the looming Lookout Mountain. This dale was unspoiled by war, and the soldiers feasted on plentiful peaches, potatoes, chickens, and hogs. Beatty's brigade scouted ahead to the entrance of the gap, and backed off after exchanging fire with Rebel pickets—a hint of things to come. The next morning, Stanley's brigade, weakened by the recent detachment of the 69th Ohio for other duties, led the advance to the gap. Skirmishers from the 11th Michigan, 18th Ohio, and 19th Illinois sent an overmatched line of dismounted Rebel cavalry scurrying back through the mountain pass. The Confederates left a tangled mass of hewn trees obstructing the entrance, and the Federals painstakingly cut their way up the rising path, dripping sweat in the late summer heat, before encamping at the gap's highest point for the night.[37]

The orders for September 8 called for the 11th Michigan to advance—again as the lead element of the entire corps—and to enter McLemore's Cove to secure the foot of the pass. They discovered fallen trees barring the way again, and Second Lieutenant Stephen Marsh of Company A led a detachment to clear a path. The regiment navigated the plunging, rocky trail, and at 2:00 p.m. became the first Federal unit to enter McLemore's Cove. The Confederate horsemen threw out skirmishers again, but Stoughton responded with a heavy skirmish line of his own, followed by the regiment in line of battle. The Michiganders forced their opponents back a considerable distance before falling back to the gap, where they deployed pickets. The sentries were assaulted, and the entire sequence of events repeated. Stoughton this time assumed a defensive position in a semicircle at the base of the gap, with half the regiment told to sleep on their arms and the other half assigned to picket duty. Negley was unnerved by a local Unionist's claim that the Confederates planned to ambush the Michiganders overnight, and at 8:00 p.m. he ordered the 11th to pull back to the security of the main body of Stanley's brigade. "Both officers and men protested," King later remembered. The colonel, after holding counsel with Mudge and Bennett, remonstrated with Negley, hesitating to surrender the ground they had won. The general conceded that one wing of the 11th could hold position while the other would withdraw as ordered. Mudge remained in charge of the force that was left behind, but it soon dawned on him that he lacked the manpower to maintain a proper picket line all night. He pulled his men back to higher ground. In the morning, when he deployed Company B forward as skirmishers, they discovered that the Confederates had indeed invaded the abandoned Wolverine camp overnight. Stanley's skirmishers subsequently advanced about two miles into the cove that day, halting at Bailey's Crossroads.[38]

Bragg realized what Rosecrans had up his sleeve, and evacuated Chattanooga. Rosecrans believed the Rebels were on the run and offered little threat to the Federal army, so he pressured his corps commanders to pursue with abandon. Thomas, lacking cavalry support and blind to the whereabouts of the enemy, preferred to consolidate the army before proceeding. But the commanding general would countenance nothing short of a vigorous chase. Bragg in fact would regroup his army toward the vicinity of La Fayette, seeking an opportunity to seize the offensive. On September 9, once again, Stanley's brigade acted as the spearhead of the 14th Corps. The Federals, preceded with a protective blanket of skirmishers, edged forward amid unverified rumors of massed Rebel troops approaching, and engaged the enemy throughout the day. The 11th Michigan took several prisoners, including a lieutenant. That night, Bragg learned from his cavalry that four or five thousand Federals had invaded McLemore's Cove, and promptly dispatched orders designed to bag Negley's isolated unit whole. Thomas had ordered another Union division, under Absalom Baird, to close up on Negley, but those troops would need more than a full day to catch up. Negley, meanwhile, reported that his newest intelligence now indicated "no considerable rebel force this side of Dalton."[39]

On September 10 Negley pressed ahead in earnest under a new dictate from Thomas to drive forward through Dug Gap and on to La Fayette. And so Negley did—still unsupported, and obliviously marching right into the waiting maw of Bragg's army. A stunned Confederate scout eyed the Union advance and reported "the enemy perfectly careless.... I am sure the whole division can be captured in three hours, wagons & all." Sirwell's brigade took the lead, and his skirmish line came under fire as they marched through Bailey's Crossroads and then Davis's Crossroads on a beeline toward Dug Gap. Negley, increasingly concerned by the growing resistance to his advance, and by accumulating reports suggesting that the Confederates were eagerly awaiting his arrival, halted to assess the situation, and sent a courier to hurry Baird forward to his aid. At 1:30 p.m. a Unionist civilian warned Negley of a massive Rebel formation only three miles off his left flank. Soon after, a prisoner and additional locals informed Negley that he "was confronted by Hill's corps of three divisions (twelve brigades) ... and Buckner's corps of two divisions (eight brigades).... Polk's and Breckinridge's commands were in supporting distance." This intelligence, in fact, was fairly accurate: Bragg was now perfectly positioned to envelop the entire Federal division. Less than 5,500 Union soldiers had blundered within easy striking distance of 17,000 Confederates, and thousands more Rebels were on the way.[40]

CHAPTER 6

"We fought like tigers"
September 1863

Much to the relief of Negley, Stanley, Stoughton, and every soldier in their commands, the waning hours of September 10 slipped by in a relative, inexplicable calm. Around sunset, the Federals drove the Rebel skirmishers of Sterling A.M. Wood's brigade, of Cleburne's division, all the way back to Dug Gap before disengaging and falling back. The three Confederate divisions to the Union left—Patton Anderson's, Alexander P. Stewart's, and Thomas C. Hindman's, all under Hindman's overall command—failed to pounce on their badly outnumbered prey. Scouting reports had persuaded Hindman that a much greater mass of Federal troops was approaching, and his promised support from Daniel Harvey Hill, with whom he was supposed to coordinate his attack, had not yet materialized. Evidently, neither Hindman nor Hill were sanguine about taking the offensive so soon after abandoning Chattanooga.[1]

Negley reeled in Stanley's and Sirwell's pickets at 3:00 a.m. on September 11, fearing their capture in the face of superior numbers, and arrayed their two brigades in a semicircle just east of Davis's Crossroads. Beatty remained to the rear, guarding the vulnerable division train. Hill's subordinate Patrick Cleburne had two Rebel brigades in place at Dug Gap now, bolstering the Confederate forces present to 20,000 troops and compelling Negley to retract his skirmishers from the pass. Help arrived for the Federals around 8:00 a.m. in the form of Absalom Baird's division. But Baird was shorthanded, with one brigade left behind at Bridgeport, and his two brigades onhand, under Benjamin Scribner and John Starkweather, were each short one detached regiment. The addition of 2,800 soldiers still left the Union force woefully overmatched. Hindman's division alone nearly equaled in numbers all of the Federals present—and this stark fact grew all the more apparent as brisk skirmishing broke out clear across the Union line. Yet the situation remained virtually static for the balance of the morning.[2]

Around 1:30 p.m. Lieutenant Marsh climbed a tree, braving the threat of Southern sharpshooters, while Negley's staff watched anxiously from below. Marsh took in the martial and geological wonders of the scene from that better vantage point, and soon returned to Earth to confirm the presence of a vast formation of Rebels little more than one mile, now, from the Federal left. This report, combined with pressure from Cleburne's skirmishers and a reappraisal of the local terrain, was enough to shake Negley's confidence in his position. "The preservation of the trains," he concluded, "perhaps the safety of the entire command, demanded that I should retire ... where we could get our trains under cover and fight the enemy to a better advantage. I therefore directed that the trains should commence moving back slowly and in good order." He ordered Baird to deploy Scribner to relieve Stanley, and Starkweather to replace Sirwell. It was a risky move, relieving a battle line in the immediate presence of an active enemy. The threat from Cleburne providentially slackened at just the right moment, and the redeployment came off flawlessly. Another flurry of activity ensued as Negley dispatched Beatty to escort the wagon train back to the relative safety of Bailey's Crossroads, more than two miles back. Then Stanley withdrew his men, marching in quick time, to a more defensible rise west of Chickamauga Creek, where his soldiers frenziedly threw up breastworks. Sirwell's brigade took up a position behind Stanley. These events were set in motion about 2:00 p.m. Almost two hours later, with Hindman still petrified with indecision, Scribner and Starkweather were ordered to fall back behind Stanley. Ultimately, Negley and Baird would continue to withdraw in this manner, inaugurating a series of alternating retrogrades, with each division taking turns falling back and digging in to cover the other's retreat.[3]

Scribner pulled out of the front line first, obeying orders to rendezvous with Beatty and the division train, and was followed by Starkweather under duress. Cleburne's third brigade, under Lucius Polk, had arrived, tilting the scales even further in the Rebels' favor. Polk was on the verge of overlapping Starkweather's flank as he took flight, and Stanley's position was threatened as well. A detachment of the 19th Illinois, reinforced by one company of the 24th Illinois, rose up from behind a stone wall at the edge of the creek, well in advance of Stanley's works, and volleyed with lethal accuracy into Confederate cavalry pursuing Baird's troops. The Illinoisans then hastily returned to their works. Hindman, detecting Baird's retreat, had finally unleashed his three divisions—quite a startling turn of events, given that he had just been on the cusp of ordering a Rebel withdrawal.[4]

The massive Southern host ponderously deployed and wheeled right to cross the creek and swallow Stanley's little brigade, and Semple's Battery of Cleburne's division rolled forward in support. Stanley's troops looked aghast upon the equivalent of an entire Confederate corps, roughly fifteen times their own number, bearing down on them. "In front of the right wing," King noted, "was an extensive cornfield.... When the breastwork was completed the men lay down waiting the approach of an overwhelming force of the enemy. Soon the glint of their gun barrels could be seen in the standing corn.... A number of pieces of Confederate artillery were pushed by hand through the cornfield, followed by several lines of infantry closed en masse." The reinforced skirmish lines traded fire, and the artillery on both sides opened with good effect. Myron Bragg called the exchange "murderous." Stanley had placed the 19th Illinois on the left, the 11th Michigan on the right, and deployed the 18th Ohio from his reserve to extend his right, which remained hopelessly overlapped by the Con-

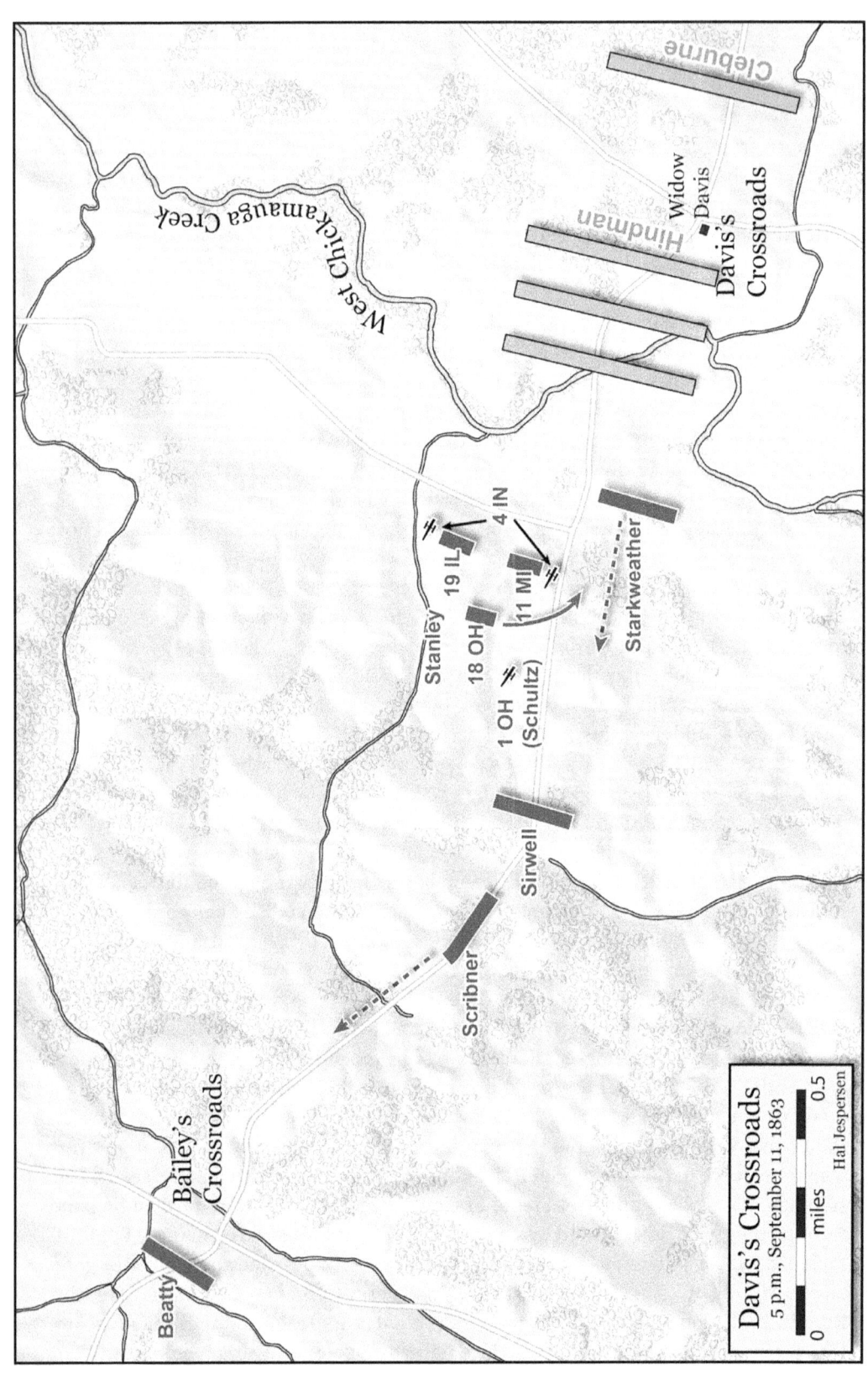

federate advance. To worsen matters, the Ohioans, who hadn't time to dig in properly, started to break under a skillfully directed shelling, and two sections of the Indiana artillerists were observed briefly abandoning their guns whenever the incoming fire grew hot.[5]

With fortuitous timing, a courier alerted Negley that the division train had reached Bailey's Crossroads. Stanley was permitted to pull out just as his unit's circumstances grew critical. The jittery Ohioans retreated first, followed by the Indiana artillerists and Illinois infantry. The 11th Michigan moved out last, with the Rebels right on their heels. "We came off the field in good order," Martin proudly declared, "every man in Co. H was right to his post." Starkweather's and Sirwell's brigades confronted the Confederates when they crested the vacated high ground, and that was all the discouragement necessary to terminate Hindman's halfhearted pursuit. "They dident make us run," Martin insisted, "but we done some tall walking."[6]

"Worst of all," in Bloom's estimation, the Wolverines had tossed aside their haversacks and blankets in their haste to construct breastworks, and in the frantic rush to withdraw, these precious articles were regrettably left behind—by most. Hicks later remembered that "I had hung my haversack on the limb of a tree.... I had gotten back about two or three rods, when I realized that I had deserted my base of supplies, so back I charged in the teeth of the enemy. This was a very brave and heroic deed, and yet it was not reported to the General Commanding, neither has Congress ever voted me a Medal of Honor, and no song has ever been dedicated entitled, 'Oh save my knapsack.'" But those who had forfeited their possessions were not in such good humor. "I lost nearly everything I had," Rose moaned, "paper, envelops and stamps and my pictures."[7]

"The battle of Davis' Cross Roads," King summarized, "may be called the prelude to Chickamauga and was one of the sharpest and most stubbornly contested fights in which the 11th was ever engaged." Though the number of casualties was relatively minor on both sides—sixty Federals, and probably fewer Rebels—it was evident to the Union rank and file throughout the skirmish that the capture of the entire Union force was an entirely conceivable outcome. Baird declared that the encounter, "while too unimportant a character to be dignified by the name of a battle ... still presented occasions of as severe trial to the parties involved as a general engagement." Stanley's brigade bore the brunt of the conflict with its final stand against Hindman, taking thirty-eight casualties in all. The 11th Michigan was the most heavily engaged of all the blue-clad regiments, being the last to leave the field in the face of Hindman's immense numbers. Three Wolverines gave their lives: Sergeant James T. Lovett of Company A and Private Hiram L. Hoxie of Company D were killed outright, and Sergeant David Edwards of Company F, severely wounded in the cheek and neck, would expire ten days later. Ozro Bowen memorialized the deceased as "some noble men as ever shouldered a musket." Thirteen more were wounded, and three were captured: Private James H. Ensign of Company A, along with First Sergeant Elmer Bradley and Corporal Oliver W. Brockway of Company K, were all doomed to perish in captivity at the reviled Andersonville Prison.[8]

Thomas's corps regrouped on September 12, with headquarters at Stevens's Gap.

Company E advanced as skirmishers, and Bloom noted "not a Rebel to be Sen." The Michiganders that day received confirmation of Bragg's abandonment of Chattanooga. Negley selected strong defensive ground in the vicinity of Bailey's Crossroads, where his division would encamp through the sixteenth. Stoughton's troops enjoyed all the bounty the heretofore unspoiled valley had to offer—particularly chickens, hogs, and sheep. But the men were cognizant that the Confederate army was in close proximity. "There is so many rumors afloat," declared Martin, "that it is hard telling anything about it. I think that before many days we will have a general engagement.... [The Rebels] will fight with desperation.... I suppose they feel mighty nice because they drove us." Rose offered a somewhat more optimistic perspective. "It is reported that the rebs are retreating," he wrote, "but we may have a heavy battle near hear yet for the rebs are nearly surrounded and they will either fight or surrender." The Michiganders, still in disbelief that Bragg had not immediately followed up on the action of September 11, performed tense picket duty on the thirteenth and fourteenth, with the main body of the regiment drawn up in line of battle at times. Bloom observed "not a Gun Herd to Day" on the thirteenth, but "canonading on Our Left" the next day. On the afternoon of the fourteenth, the Wolverines discovered their dead, still unburied near Davis's Crossroads. Martin noted with disgust that "some of our boys helped bury them they said they were bloated so that they had bursted open their clothes, and that they were full of magots." Skirmishing intensity continued to alternate from day to day, with Bloom terming it "very Hot" on the fifteenth and "all Quiett in Front" the following day.[9]

The corps was on the move again on September 17, when Negley shifted left to Owen's Ford. That morning, King recorded, "the pickets captured two Confederate officers, who told us that Bragg had been heavily re-inforced, and that it would be impossible for Rosecrans to save his army from destruction." Stanley's brigade brought up the rear that day, and was shadowed and harassed by Confederate horsemen. The following day saw Thomas's divisions rushing northeast for Crawfish Spring, with Negley directed to relieve John Palmer's division upon arrival. There was a palpable urgency to the march, owing to a heightened sense in the ranks that the armies were on the verge of an extraordinary collision. As Stoughton's soldiers trudged up the road, they observed the initial clashes of the opposing forces miles ahead. "The whole country in that direction," King commented, "was enveloped in smoke and dust. The boom of cannon and the rattle and roll of musketry, and the cheers and yells of the contending hosts in their charges and countercharges, produced an impression never to be forgotten." Bowen added that "we needed no interpretation to tell us that the enemy were being reinforced and that the capture of Chattanooga was to be no bloodless contest.... Two great armies were hurled against each other in mortal combat." Upon Negley's arrival, Palmer's brigadier William Hazen confessed ignorance of any orders for his unit to give way to Negley, and this mix-up resulted in Negley's men damming the road for hours. Stanley's brigade was mercifully permitted to bivouac at Crawfish Spring and get some rest, but Beatty and Sirwell were ultimately directed, late at night, to relieve Palmer after all. The balance of the 14th Corps experienced an even more trying night. Rosecrans realized that he was in grave danger of being cut off from Chattanooga, and rushed Thomas, minus Negley, on an overnight forced march to leapfrog Crittenden and extend the Union left farther north.[10]

Bragg's Army of Tennessee had been reinforced from Mississippi, Tennessee, and Virginia, and presently enjoyed an advantage rarely secured by Confederate generals: superior numbers. The Battle of Chickamauga began in earnest on the morning of September 19. The shooting gained intensity in the distance to the Union left, with the 14th Corps generating much of the racket. "It was plain to be seen," said Martin, "that Bragg was trying to turn our left flank and cut off our communications with Chattanooga." Negley dispatched his division train, with the exception of the ambulance and ammunition wagons, to seek safety at the city. "We could feel the throb of canon and hear the roar of musketry as we left," King recalled. He went on to describe the buoyant confidence of the soldiers of Stanley's brigade, "veterans of two years of active service in the field. They had been thoroughly tried in the crucible of battle. The Eleventh Michigan knew it could rely upon the Nineteenth Illinois and the Eighteenth Ohio to do their full share of the terrible and difficult work before them, and each soldier had perfect confidence in his file companion.... It would have been hard to have found a brigade in the army of the Cumberland, or in any other army, that ever marched into battle with more confidence than did this little brigade on this historic field of Chickamauga." The brigade was indeed "little," as King put it, with the 69th Ohio still detached and the attrition of active campaigning taking its toll. Stanley's three regiments went into battle with perhaps 800 officers and men present for duty.[11]

Thomas described the battlefield as "undulating and covered with original forest timber, interspersed with undergrowth, in many places so dense that it is difficult to see 50 paces ahead."[12] Coordination even at the division level would often prove impossible, so the ebb and flow of the battle would frequently be dictated by decisions made in isolation at the brigade, or even the regimental, level. The strife of September 19 thus consisted of a series of disjointed strokes and counterstrokes. Both sides claimed their share of tactical victories as the body count skyrocketed, yet the coordination required for the knockout blow proved elusive. The weight of the Union army shifted inexorably toward its left, where Thomas, bearing the brunt of the Rebel attempt to turn Rosecrans's flank, was frantically calling for reinforcements.

Beatty's brigade was engaged in a sharp morning skirmish, reinforced by Stanley with the 18th Ohio and Schultz's Battery. Otherwise, Negley's soldiers spent most of the day waiting and listening anxiously to the rising crescendo of the war's largest battle in the West. At 3:30 p.m., the division was finally called on, ordered to make haste for Rosecrans's headquarters at the Widow Glenn's house. As the Wolverines got underway, their brigade band belted out the tune "Red, White, and Blue." When they reached their destination, Rosecrans himself pointed them in the direction of a Confederate breakthrough. Stewart's troops had penetrated so deeply as to threaten the crucial roads to Chattanooga. "You will find the enemy right in there," Rosecrans declared. He dismounted and watched his soldiers pass. As the 11th Michigan strode by the commanding general, each company was ordered to carry or shoulder its arms in salute, and the colors were dipped in the general's honor. Rosecrans responded,

"Make it warm for them, Michigan boys." The Wolverines cheered raucously, and their army commander added, "I know you will."[13]

Stanley's and Sirwell's brigades advanced through the woods and proceeded toward Brotherton Field. The Rebel assault was already played out, and Henry Clayton's Alabamian skirmishers sullenly gave way. Negley pushed his brigades forward again at 6:00 p.m., triggering a sharper skirmish and pushing the Confederates back a good distance, and then retired after nightfall to the woods at the edge of the field. Each regiment detailed one company on picket (Companies C and E took turns for the Michiganders), and the Federals cobbled together log and rail breastworks. The thousands of wounded men scattered across the battlefield faced a suffering reminiscent of that after sundown the first day at Stones River. The conditions were trying even for those who still enjoyed good health. "It was so cold," Hicks exclaimed, "that it was impossible to sleep.... I was informed by one of the residents of the battle field, that ice formed that night ... it certainly was very cold especially for men who had just loaned their blankets" to the enemy at Davis's Crossroads. Martin complained that even the lucky few who still possessed their covers "werent allowed to undo them for we were liable to have a fight at any moment and I tell you we almost froze."[14]

The lucky minority of Michiganders who eventually nodded off were awakened at 3:00 a.m. The regiment breakfasted on hardtack and raw bacon while standing at the ready in line of battle. Thomas, stretched perilously thin on the left, again called for reinforcements, and around 8:00 a.m. Negley received orders for his division to reunite with its corps, but only after awaiting his unit's relief from the front line by other troops. Beatty's brigade was uncommitted and departed at once, but Stanley and Sirwell were locked in place, actively skirmishing, and per orders it was imperative for them to stay put. Yet Negley was so anxious to support his corps commander that he ordered Stanley and Sirwell to pull out. The 11th Michigan had marched just 500 feet when Stoughton observed that the Rebels were about to overrun his vacated breastworks, establishing a dangerous breach in the Union line. The Wolverines about faced and charged their own works. "Whether we were nearest or the swiftest sprinters," Hicks remarked, "I do not know, but we got there." The 11th fired into the outraced Southerners at short range, and the 19th Illinois and 18th Ohio contributed their weight to the repulse. The bloodied Confederates backed off, but Rosecrans himself had witnessed Negley's poor judgment, and the distraught division commander was vehemently upbraided.[15]

Between 9:30 and 10:00 a.m., Negley's position was finally filled by troops from Thomas J. Wood's adjacent division. Stanley was relieved first and dashed his brigade north. The day's Confederate onslaught against Thomas was already well underway. Beatty's attempt to reinforce the 14th Corps had terminated in the scattering of most of his troops, and the Rebel brigades of Daniel Weisiger Adams and Marcellus Stovall were in the process of flanking Thomas's left. The Army of the Cumberland was teetering on the edge of ruin. Beatty knew the remnants of his unit were about to be overrun. He mounted his horse and galloped south, frantically seeking Thomas or Negley. Before long, he sighted a rising cloud of dust ahead. It was Stanley's troops, winded, but determinedly making their way north on the double quick. A grateful Beatty hurried his reinforcements to the point of attack, and placed his own brigade fragment in support. The immediate fate of the corps, and perhaps of the army, now rested in part with Stanley's brigade, and his troops could hear the Rebels coming.[16]

Stanley formed up in the rear of Thomas, facing north at a right angle to the corps's predominantly east-facing battle line. The 11th Michigan took the right and the 18th Ohio anchored the left, with the 19th Illinois in reserve, bringing to bear a combined 700 muskets. The woods offered poor visibility, hardly an ideal site for a last ditch defense. Stoughton hurriedly surveyed the ground his men occupied. Few colonels would have thought to do more at this moment than to instruct their regiment to prepare to fire, but Stoughton was no ordinary officer. While Stanley looked on, Stoughton seized the initiative, ordering the Michiganders and Ohioans to tear the dense underbrush from their front, pile it in a wall in advance of their line, and lie low behind. By this course of action, his men enjoyed concealment as well as an enhanced field of fire. Stoughton rushed up and down the brigade line, ordering the colors dropped to the ground. "Boys," he said emphatically, "we have got them; take aim at their legs, as if you were shooting at a target, and you will bring down their front rank. No troops in the world can stand to have their front rank shot down, and we will capture the balance. Don't waste a bullet; pay strict attention to orders, and we will make those fellows sing a different song."[17]

Brigadier General Adams led 900 exultant Southern soldiers through the woods, driving into the rear of Thomas's corps. The Confederates charged ahead fearlessly, driving Stanley's and Beatty's skirmishers in before them. "On came the rebels yelling like mad men," remembered James Martin, "we laid still and said nothing." Stoughton bided his time to let the distance close, then arose at the last possible moment and shouted, "Aim, fire, and charge!" The Michiganders and Ohioans arose en masse with their rifles leveled at the onrushing Rebels. A rolling clap of thunder announced the decimation of Adams's front rank. The combined 16th and 25th Louisiana was shredded by the Wolverines' volley, and General Adams himself, situated at the rear of that formation, was wounded and went down. The Illinoisans advanced from Stanley's reserve, and the entire brigade launched a bayonet charge that bagged a herd of prisoners. Second Lieutenant James M. Whallon of Company C said of Adams, "As the line passed over him, he was reclining on his right side.... On being asked if he was seriously hurt, General Adams replied: 'I am wounded in the side and am bleeding profusely.'" Stanley observed that "quite a number of other officers were near him, dead and wounded." Sergeant Major Irving Snyder of Three Rivers accepted the surrender of the general's sword and handed the blade to Borden Hicks, who "carried his sword on the charge we now made to the McDonald field, going into this charge with a sword in each hand, and looking savage as a meat ax." The triumphant Federals drove the Confederates back pell-mell, nearly half a mile.[18]

But Stanley's soldiers proved all too eager in their pursuit of the Rebels. They charged headlong into tactical isolation and fell under punishing artillery fire from Slocomb's Battery at McDonald field. Stanley ordered a retreat, but after about-facing, his soldiers found themselves subject to a deadly flanking fire from the advancing brigade of Daniel Govan. The Wolverines and their sister regiments returned fire,

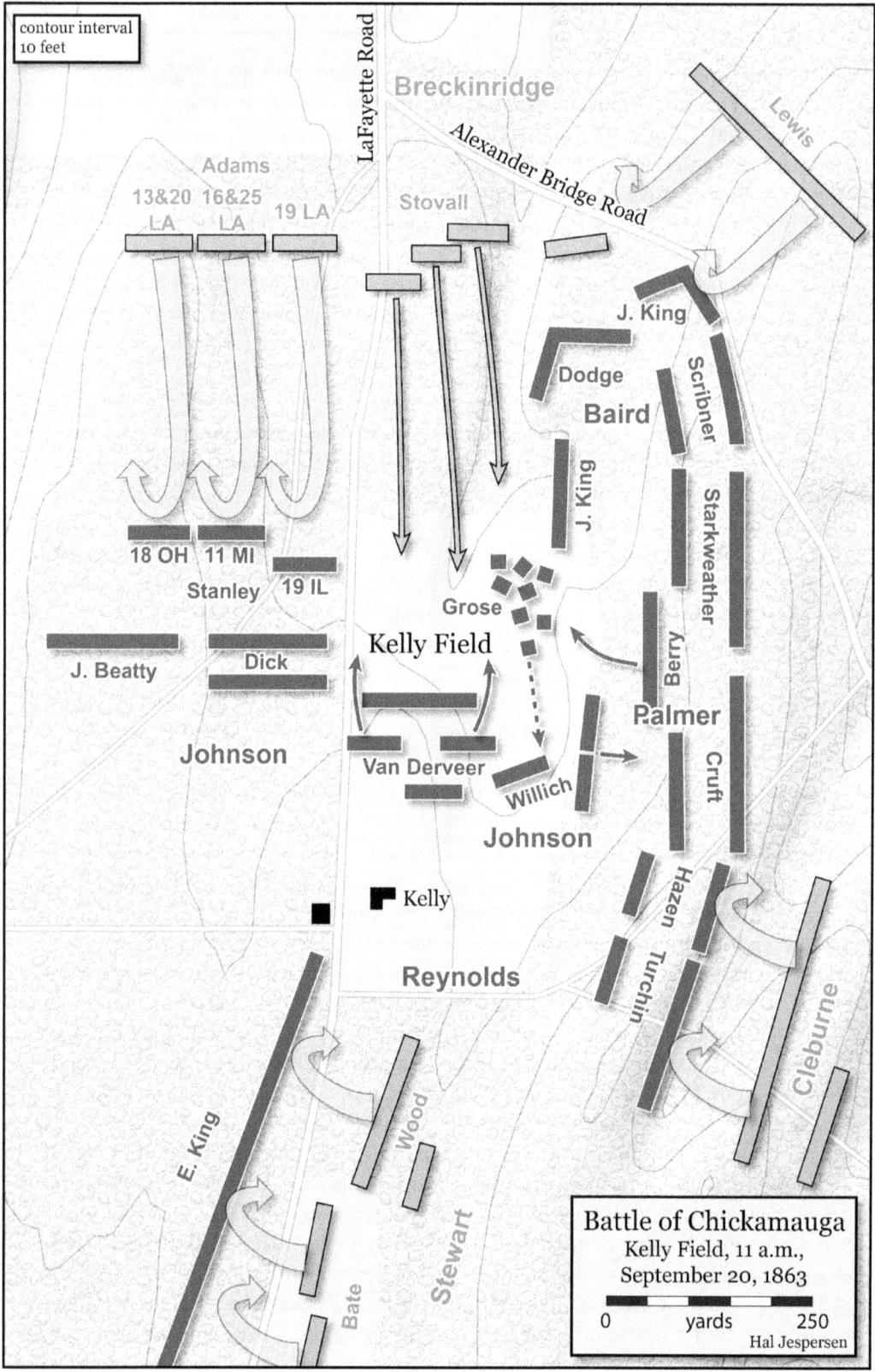

maintained their order, and executed a fighting withdrawal, but casualties were mounting fast. Captain Childs was shot through the body and left for dead—he would survive only to suffer capture—and Captain Briggs took a ball through his right leg. Beatty and Stanley, so focused on rescuing Thomas, had temporarily pocketed an order from Negley to divert their troops west for a rendezvous with Sirwell on high ground, but now, under a withering fire, this course of action proved to be their only viable option.[19]

In the meantime, the ultimate course of the battle had been decided by a fluke that transpired a short distance to the south. Miscommunication between Rosecrans and Wood caused the latter to vacate his position in the Union line just as James Longstreet, recently arrived from Lee's Army of Northern Virginia, launched a powerful assault into that very section of the Union line. Exuberant Confederate

This stone monument, nestled in the woods west of Kelly Field, marks the location of the 11th Michigan's capture of Brigadier General Daniel Weisiger Adams (photograph by the author).

troops poured into the resulting gap, and the southern third of the Union army—along with Rosecrans, McCook, and Crittenden—was swept away in a complete rout. The destiny of the Army of the Cumberland now lay in the hands of Thomas and his severely outnumbered soldiers.

Stanley's troops scaled Horseshoe Ridge, a spur of Missionary Ridge also known as Snodgrass Hill. Stanley met with a rude welcome there. First, he discovered that Negley and Sirwell were nowhere to be found. Negley had been diverted by Thomas to gather all available artillery on the ridge, and subsequently witnessed the stream of routed Federals fleeing from Longstreet's breakthrough. He determined to retreat as well, taking Sirwell's brigade and several desperately needed gun batteries out of action. To make matters worse, Stanley was greeted on the high ground with a shell fragment hit to his shoulder that toppled him from his mount. He stayed on the field, but relinquished command. On the brink of this most desperate stand, Stoughton was thrust into the weighty responsibility of brigade command. "I never shall forget how his eyes sparkled," Myron Bragg remarked. There was no time for Stoughton to contemplate his dilemma, for some of Longstreet's Rebels—Kershaw's South Carolina brigade, veterans of Gettysburg—were close at hand. "Battalion forward," the colonel barked, "double quick, guide center march." His brigade rushed to check the Confederates, who had already fought their way to the contested ridge crest.[20]

Stoughton's Federals stood up to the seasoned Rebels. It was a brief but sharp struggle, fought at close range. The 11th released a volley of bullets, promptly followed

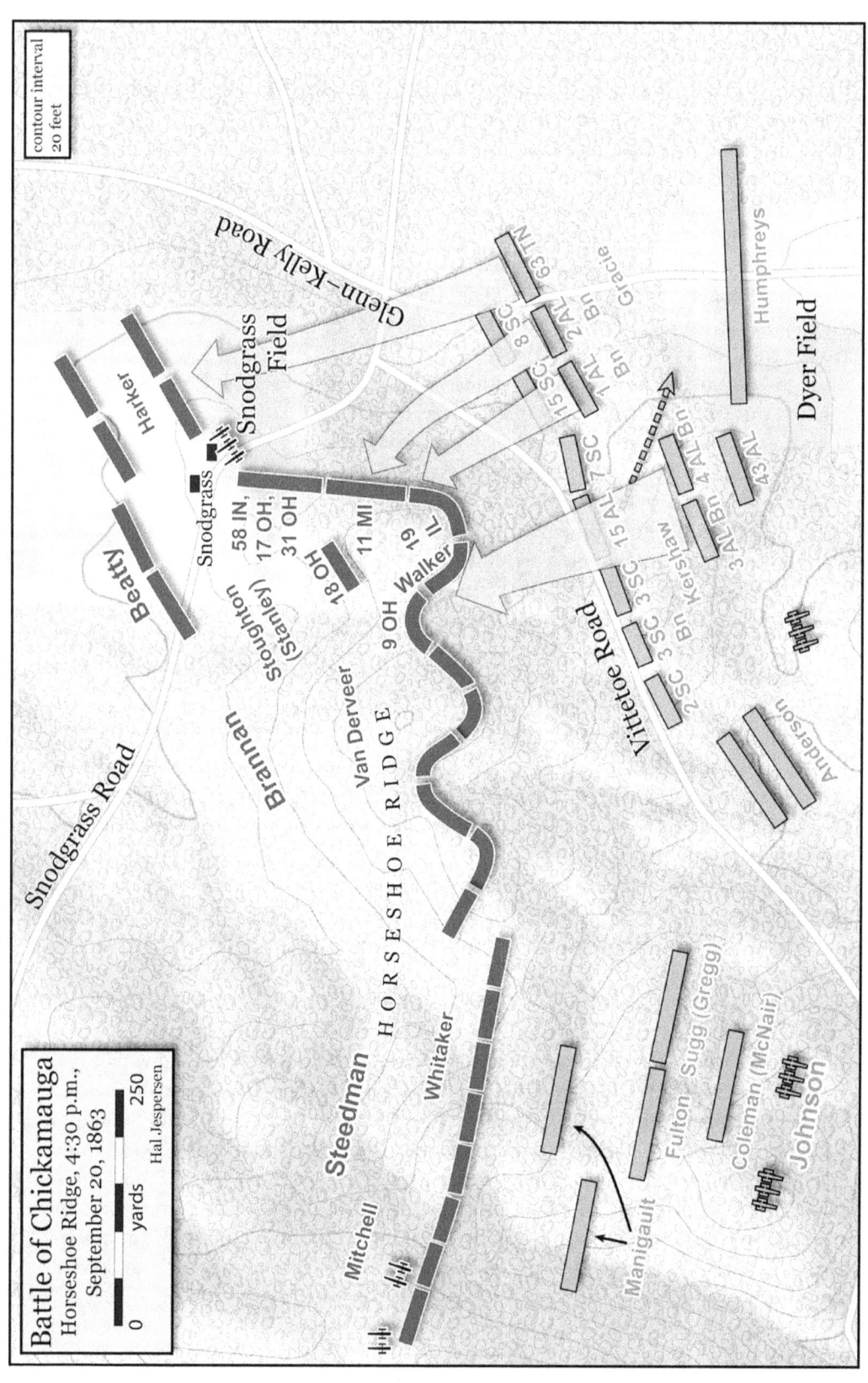

with a volley of curses: the barrels of their heavily-worked Springfield rifles were so fouled with gunpowder that reloading became a battle in of itself, and furthermore, ammunition was growing scarce. Nonetheless, the Michiganders overpowered the 7th South Carolina, which spilled back down the hill. "Immediately after this charge," Stoughton recorded, "I was informed by Genl. John Beatty that our position on this hill must be maintained." Stoughton arranged his defensive line on the ridge summit, aligning with a hodgepodge of rallied Union unit fragments, with the 11th Michigan on the left, the 19th Illinois on the right, and the 18th Ohio in reserve. Casualties, combined with the dispatch of a large detail to escort prisoners to Chattanooga, reduced Stoughton's brigade to about 600 men—far closer to the complement of a typical Federal regiment than a brigade. The clash with Kershaw had contributed to the mounting losses. Captain Newberry was killed instantly, raising Hicks to command of Company E, and Sergeant Major Snyder, captor of General Adams, fell mortally wounded. In the long, trying hours ahead, every rifle and bayonet would count. The time was approaching 2:00 p.m. The Confederates had only just began their assault on Horseshoe Ridge, and the only question was how long Thomas's smaller forces there, and at Kelly Field, could possibly hold out.[21]

Attacks off to Stoughton's right were repulsed by timely Union reinforcements, but his brigade was soon targeted with rare ferocity. William Preston's division was ordered into the fracas by Longstreet, and came into range around 4:30 p.m. Leading the way was Archibald Gracie's brigade, marching in the general direction of Stoughton's defenders. Gracie's troops were raw, but their untested ranks swelled with nearly 2,000 men. Fortune intervened to mitigate the odds as Gracie attempted to advance his troops in one long battle line through the broken terrain. The left side of his brigade entangled upon the ranks of its comrades positioned along the line of march, and his rightmost regiment veered off to the right, where it was promptly met with a destructive crossfire.[22]

Gracie's 1st and 2nd Alabama Battalions, however, advanced on a beeline for Stoughton's light breastworks. Under fire, the Southerners exhibited not one hint of their inexperience. "The first volley of the enemy," declared Alabama private Lewellyn A. Shaver, "who were lying in wait behind a fortification of logs in an excellent position, bore with fatal precision upon our line, and created many a gap in our heretofore intact ranks; but it was responded to by an answering volley and a rousing cheer, which rose high above the din of the conflict. I shall attempt no recital of what followed—the heart grows sick at the memory!" Gracie's Rebels marched fearlessly up the slope, right into the muzzles of the awaiting 11th Michigan and 19th Illinois. Stoughton's voice, ever clear and confident, repeated the orders he had issued to such effect against Adams: "Aim, fire, charge!" His brigade delivered a crushing volley at close range, followed straightaway with a bayonet charge that scattered the Rebel ranks down the incline. "There was never another brigade," J. Henry Haynie of the 19th Illinois wrote of this feat, "that could do the volley and charge so well as ours." The Federals returned to their works, and the enemy traded fire with them from below for a time. Then they came right back up the incline again. "A contest ensued," Stoughton exclaimed, "which in its fierceness and duration has few parallels."[23]

The blue brigade had less than 400 rifles left in its front line, but the soldiers aimed with the kind of accuracy under pressure that is obtained only through battle experience. Time and again the Confederates charged, and time and again they were driven back. Both of the Southern unit commanders went down, and their broken subordinates littered the hillside. The Alabamians, Stoughton observed, "fought with the most determined obstinacy. As fast as their ranks were thinned by our fire they were filled up by fresh troops.... A dense cloud of smoke enveloped our lines, and in some places the position of the foe could only be known by the flash of his guns." The courageous Rebels' casualties climbed disastrously. "Their dead and wounded," said Lieutenant William G. Whitney of Company B, "lay in great numbers, right up to our works." Confederate generals witnessing the assault from below stood in awe of the stouthearted defenders. Kershaw, who had been in the thick of it at Gettysburg less than three months prior, proclaimed this "one of the heaviest attacks of the war on a single point," while Hindman insisted that he had "never known Federal troops to fight so well." With the Union troops desperate for ammunition, Whitney leapt over the works between charges and cut cartridge boxes from fallen Southerners between the battle lines, an act that was performed under fire and would earn him the Medal of Honor.[24]

By all rights the Alabamians should have retreated, yet they kept coming. The battle raged on at close range, and with Gracie's 43rd Alabama Infantry now piling into the 11th Michigan's front too—close to 400 additional Confederates, raising Gracie's numerical advantage over the Wolverines to three-to-one—the fighting briefly evolved into clashes between bayonets, clubbed rifles, and fists. "They rushed on us," James Martin exclaimed, "and drove us back a bout five rods from our rail piles and planted their colors on top of them, we fought at the distance of five rods for an hour, we shot down their colors time and time again and they hoist them right up again in our faces." The dent in the Union line occurred at the junction of the Michigan and Illinois regiments. The Federals afterwards insisted that they gave up the ground deliberately and in an orderly fashion—and the casualty figures tend to back them up.[25]

The part of Stoughton's line that had conceded their breastworks regrouped after watching the Rebels plant their colors over the rails. It was an amazing feat of bravery for Gracie's previously untried troops, but it was also accomplished at an abhorrent price, and for no lasting gain. The color bearer of the 2nd Alabama, Robert Hiett, received three wounds. His battle flag drew the ire of the Michiganders and was riddled with eighty-three holes. (Jefferson Davis himself would later promote Hiett and ask to see the ragged colors.) The Union and Confederate casualties both mounted—in part due to hellish, scattered brushfires, sparked by gunfire, that engulfed the dead and wounded alike—but the battle losses climbed in grossly unequal terms. The terrible bloodletting that Stanley's troops endured at Stones River paid off in the form of admirable steadiness under fire. Gracie's two battalions, combined, counted 259 men killed or wounded out of 467 engaged—55 percent casualties. Their latecomer comrades of the 43rd Alabama had an additional ninety-nine men hit out of 400. Stoughton's line, in comparison, tallied its casualties on the ridge at only a few dozen.

The 11th Michigan and the 2nd Alabama Battalion vie for control of Horseshoe Ridge. The 11th Michigan, outnumbered three-to-one and running out of ammunition, performed one of the great feats of the war, fighting hand-to-hand at times and inflicting six casualties for each one it suffered. "The slope in our front," Borden Hicks remembered, "was strewn with the enemy's dead, so thick you could almost walk on them, our men's faces were black with powder smoke, their tongues fairly hung out for want of water." Confederate generals declared it "one of the heaviest attacks of the war on a single point," and had "never known Federal troops to fight so well" (from *This Terrible Sound: The Battle of Chickamauga.* © 1992 by the Board of Trustees of the University of Illinois. Used with permission of the University of Illinois Press).

Tightening the focus on the 11th Michigan, the Wolverine regiment suffered perhaps twenty-five men hit on the ridge while inflicting approximately 150 casualties on Gracie's troops—a loss ratio of six-to-one, inflicted by troops who were outnumbered three-to-one. Among the Michigan wounded, however, was Lieutenant Colonel Mudge. Command of the regiment devolved to Major Bennett, the regiment's third commanding officer of the day.[26]

The final act of this murderous drama transpired about 6:00 p.m., as the sun approached the horizon. By this time, even those lucky enough to remain uninjured were fast approaching the limits of human endurance. "The slope in our front," exclaimed Hicks, "was strewn with the enemy's dead, so thick you could almost walk on them, our mens faces were black with powder smoke, their tongues fairly hung out for want of water." Stoughton, peering through the smoke and perceiving a wavering in the thinning enemy ranks, commanded his uncommitted reserve, the tiny remnant of the 18th Ohio, to fix bayonets, and then led the brigade forward in its third bayonet charge of the day. Gracie's survivors, who were already preparing to withdraw, had little fight left. "Finily," an exhilarated James Martin declared, "we rushed on them again and drove them down the hill." After repairing to their breastworks, the victorious Federals celebrated with abandon a feat they would never forget. Martin recorded "such cheering you never heard, as there were the whole length of the line. The boys sang 'rally round the flag' and national airs right in the rebels faces." Myron Bragg summarized the fight in plain terms: "We fought like tigers."[27]

For Stoughton's exhausted men, the day ended in a frightful fashion that has gotten lost in modern accounts of Chickamauga. It is commonly accepted that the Federals on Horseshoe Ridge were retreating en masse by sunset, with the only exception consisting of five regiments remaining on the rise: the 22nd Michigan and the 21st and 89th Ohio representing the Union right, and the 9th Indiana and 35th Ohio on the left. The Rebels, under cover of darkness, encircled and captured the three rightmost regiments. The remaining Indianans and Ohioans then pulled out, narrowly avoiding encirclement, and were credited as the last Federal units to leave the battlefield (Thomas's other position at Kelly Field having already been evacuated). But surviving accounts from Stoughton's brigade consistently state that his unit stayed on the field much later than intimated in the above chronology—with their departure from Horseshoe taking place around 8:00 p.m. (Hicks alone asserted 10:00 p.m.) Wolverine sources indicate that gunfire rang out to Stoughton's right sometime around 7:00 p.m.—consistently timed with shots that were fired as the 9th Indiana and 35th Ohio, located to his right, contended with Rebels in the dark just before retiring. The Michiganders' accounts go on to state that Stoughton then sent a scout to the right, who returned to report the capture of the aforementioned Michigan and Ohio troops on the far right. Lastly, they assert that Stoughton's troops were astonished another half hour after that, when two more scouts braved the darkness to discover that the troops to their right (the 9th Indiana and 35th Ohio) had entirely pulled out, leaving them in utter isolation. The timing and observations of these scouts are consistent with events taking place on the ridge long after Stoughton is generally assumed to have departed the field. The 11th's story on Horseshoe Ridge ends with an order finally arriving from Brigadier General John M. Brannan—who had commanded those troops on the right to withdraw—directing Stoughton to retreat in silence. "This," Hicks remarked, "was the first intimation that we had received that the battle had gone against us." Stoughton's diminutive brigade was facing Bragg's army in the dark virtually alone and without ammunition, and may in fact have represented the last Federals to retreat from the Battle of Chickamauga. This is exactly what the Wolverines asserted afterwards: that the 11th Michigan Infantry was both the first regiment to enter the Chickamauga Valley (at McLemore's Cove), and the last to leave. In the end, the brigade departed the ridge so silently that the Confederates had no inkling that they had the field all to themselves, until well after sunrise.[28]

Stoughton's retreat ended in the vicinity of Rossville around 11:00 p.m., where his troops met Quartermaster Sergeant King carting desperately needed rations from Chattanooga, along with what Hicks described as "better than even something to eat, letters from the loved ones at home, for we had not received any mail from home since the commencement of the campaign." The Michiganders broke their fast and slaked their thirst with cold creek water. The soldiers then lay in line of battle and rested as best they could until 3:00 a.m. Stoughton was selected to bar the Confederates from Rossville Gap (indelicately nicknamed "Skidattle Gap" by John Bloom) in order to provide a rear guard and buy time for the Army of the Cumberland to rally and dig in at Chattanooga. By daybreak, the 11th Michigan blocked the entrance to the east end of the gap and felled trees to fashion breastworks while the balance of Negley's division arrived and deployed to support Stoughton and extend the defensive line onto Missionary Ridge to cover the Wolverines' flanks. Other units gradually lengthened the defenses on the heights in either direction.[29]

Though Bragg's army as a whole did not press the pursuit of Rosecrans's demoralized troops, Nathan Bedford Forrest probed Stoughton's defenses that day enough to impress upon the Union force the precariousness of their situation. Artillery duels in particular occupied a good fraction of the day. Attempts by Forrest to approach the gap were fended off by Stoughton's skirmishers, although on one occasion, as Bloom put it, "the Rebels Got There Jackass Battery on The Mountain & Give us Grape & Canister," causing Company E to break and run. (More than forty years later, Hicks could look back at this and laugh: "It was my duty as Company Commander, to run as fast as possible, and get ahead of the men, so as to allay their fears, I overtook one of my men and chided him for running from the enemy, he looked up at me very innocently, and says 'Captain what are you running for?'") Fortunately, Forrest's gunners were promptly driven from their lodgment on the high ground by the 15th Kentucky. Toward midnight, Stoughton ordered his battle line to retire quietly, and the troops headed out, lugging the artillery, with its wheels muffled, off by hand.[30]

About this time, Beatty was nearby, enjoying a happy reunion with some of his troops that had been scattered on September 20, and recorded an observation that elucidated the magnitude of Stoughton's duties that night. "The army is simply a mob," he exclaimed. "There appears to be neither organization or discipline. The various commands are mixed up in what seems to be inextricable confusion. Were a division of the enemy to pounce down upon us between this and morning, I fear the

Army of the Cumberland would be blotted out." Forrest thought the same—except that he suggested to Bragg that a mere brigade would do the trick. Stoughton remained in charge of the remaining picket line, which he withdrew in silence slightly after 4:00 a.m. the next morning. He later told King of the rearguard action, "I received my final orders from Gen. George H. Thomas, and I know he regarded it as a dangerous and important duty, and he complimented me personally on my success."[31]

This was hardly the only recognition Stoughton received for his actions of September 20–21, 1863. Division commander John M. Brannan gave a nod to Stoughton's "great gallantry," and Thomas remarked on the bravery shown by the brigade in defending Horseshoe. All three of Negley's brigade commanders chimed in as well. Stanley declared that his subordinate "sustained himself well and, with the brigade, made such a fight as is seldom made by so small a number of men." This statement was accompanied with an observation that Stoughton overly exposed himself to enemy fire, even after Stanley advised him against doing so. Sirwell also showered praise on the colonel, but John Beatty, who stood with Stoughton on Horseshoe Ridge, put it in the strongest terms. "I never witnessed a higher order of heroism than was displayed on this part of the field, and, though not strictly within the province of this report, I cannot refrain from especially mentioning Colonel Stoughton ... and others as deserving the gratitude of the Nation for an exhibition on this occasion of determined courage, which I believe unsurpassed in the history of the rebellion."[32]

Upon arrival in Chattanooga, the brigade, now back under the recuperating Stanley's command, settled in at a site that would come to be known as Fort Negley. Long days of fortifying and living on short rations lay ahead, for the Federals found themselves reduced to siege conditions. Yet spirits remained unbroken in the 11th Michigan. Incredibly, after helping to repulse Adams's, Kershaw's, and Gracie's brigades, the Wolverine regiment counted only five of its number among the dead. Forty-two were wounded, and nineteen missing. General Thomas had saved the army, and fairly won the sobriquet "Rock of Chickamauga," but it must be remembered that he owed his reputation as much to his subordinates' bulldog determination as to his own. It was Daniel Rose who most succinctly described the Army of the Cumberland's misfortune at the Battle of Chickamauga: "We was a little worsted." For the individual soldiers of the 11th Michigan, Martin most capably summed it up. "Well, dear parents," he wrote, "take it all together we have had a rough time.... I have seen fighting enough to last me forever."[33]

CHAPTER 7

"The enemy fled like a flock of sheep"
September 1863–May 1864

Despite the heroics, the 11th Michigan Infantry was fated to share in the Army of the Cumberland's humiliation, bottled up and gradually starving under siege in the dearly won city of Chattanooga. With Stanley back in command of the brigade, Colonel Stoughton was heartily welcomed back to his regiment.

For most of the Army of the Cumberland, the Battle of Chickamauga had ended in a demoralizing retreat. The act of hunkering down in Chattanooga, deprived of sustenance and supplies, only compounded the disgrace. "The enemy," Ozro Bowen remarked, "from Lookout Mountain and Missionary Ridge looked down upon us in exultant glee to see the starving process go on." Yet the 11th Michigan and its sister regiments continued to enjoy high morale. They had routed Adams's brigade and nabbed its general, had scattered Kershaw's fresh arrivals from Virginia down the slope of Horseshoe Ridge, and finally carpeted that bloodstained incline with about 150 of Gracie's troops. In short, these Wolverines withdrew from Chickamauga buoyed with the knowledge that their little brigade had soundly thrashed three of its Confederate counterparts. King spoke in a tone typical of his comrades when he boasted that the Army of the Cumberland remained in possession of Chattanooga, "the place which, of all others, the Confederacy desired to hold. The Land which his Majesty Jefferson [Davis] said nearly a month ago must be wrested from the hands of the invaders, as the glorious victory which they won in Georgia would amount to nothing. They have not wrested from us the coveted treasure, and his saying has wisely come to pass. We have gained all that we worked for, and they have lost." Martin concurred, predicting that "some of the northern doughheads will [say] that Rosecrans got out generaled but I dont think so, he started to take Chatanooga, and we are here and I think that we are able to stay." Rose insisted, "I *never* will own that they have whipped us.... I think we never will fall back from here." Captain David Bremner of the 19th Illinois agreed that Rosecrans's success ought to be measured not by the recent battle's outcome, but rather by his accomplishment in taking and holding the city, his strategic objective. Without exception, these men considered the retreat from Chickamauga the natural result of Bragg having received overwhelming reinforcements, and thus nothing to be ashamed of.[1]

In their initial days at Chattanooga, most of the Michiganders were detailed as laborers to help construct Fort Negley. Bloom, engaged in this back-breaking labor and expecting a Rebel assault at any time, considered the highlight of this period to be the delivery of several barrels of whiskey to the regiment (predictably, "some of the Boys Got Tite"). "The whole army," Martin reported on September 24, "have been to work for two days and nights in throwing up rifle pits and fortifying. Day before yesterday our Reg. worked all day on the fort and makeing us a rifle pit and at night and all day yesterday we worked evry three hours…. They tried to shell us away from the fort when we were at work and evry shot they fired the boys would cheer as loud as their lungs would let them." Three days later Rose declared that "we have been fortifying day and night incessantly we have things nearly completed." Those spared from the labor details (which soon involved additional forts) and ongoing skirmishes were sucked into desperate efforts to keep the army supplied. Quartermaster Drake, who had been serving as acting division quartermaster, was placed in charge of the supply train, and Corporal Lemuel Pierce of Company A, among others, was dispatched to the supply depot at Bridgeport almost immediately after arriving in Chattanooga. On October 15 King reported Pierce "nearly worn out with exposure, not having had any rest since we occupied" the city. Heavy rains exacerbated the burden of attempting to supply the entrapped army.[2]

"Now and then," King recorded, "rumors came from the outside world that reinforcements were coming from the Potomac and the Mississippi." The essence of these hopeful claims was soon confirmed. Martin stated that Rosecrans informed his soldiers on the night of September 23 that Lincoln had ordered Ulysses S. Grant to come to their aid.[3] Grant dispatched parts of two corps from Vicksburg under William Tecumseh Sherman, but Sherman's men were to repair the railroad along their line of march, significantly hampering their progress. Ultimately, Joseph Hooker would bring two corps from the Army of the Potomac, but for weeks to come, the Army of the Cumberland would be left to its own devices to survive.

The siege conditions worsened on October 2 when Joseph Wheeler's Confederate cavalry intercepted an 800-wagon supply train between Chattanooga and Bridgeport. King called it "the worst Blow which we have received…. Our Regimental Teams were among them. Billy Davis was in charge of our train, but made his escape. I should have went with them, but it being the end of the month, the Q Mas. said I had better remain and make out the reports. Many of the teamsters were taken prisoners, and some of them killed. Billy was back today at the spot where they were captured, and everything is a perfect mass of ruins." Private Solomon Shirey of Company E was counted among the captured Federals. Martin reported in the aftermath that "we are mighty hard up for eatables." Indeed, the Wolverines hadn't secured a bite to eat for two days. The 11th Michigan was dispatched on a desperate foraging expedition on October 9. "We crossed the mountains," Martin said, "and went 40 miles up in [Sequatchie] Valley and loaded 400 wagons with corn and done it all in four days on nine crackers and got back in camp allright." But there were simply too many men and animals in Chattanooga to sustain by foraging alone. Hicks declared that "we were reduced to quarter rations, which meant go hungry, even a dog straying through our camps, stood little show of escaping the soup kettle." On October 26 Martin reported that "there isent half of the time that we have anything to eat whatever. The boys goes to the slaughter yard and pays thirty and forty cents for a beefs head, and some of them has even went so far as to eat their tails.... The horses and mules are so poor that they cant wiggle; unless there is more feed for the horses than they have had lately, there wont be a team in the department able to draw an emty wagon ... [but] good pluck is half of the battle and it isn't best to grumble to much for it will do know good."[4]

Although the main bodies of the opposing armies remained largely inactive, occasional artillery exchanges punctuated the deceptive calm and kept the soldiers alert. On October 5, when the guns at Fort Negley opened on the Rebels, King noted that the Confederates did not respond. But later the same day, Martin said, the Rebels "threw shell and shot over us, and under us, and right in amongst us.... Seth [Dusenberry of Company H] and I was standing together talking, when a thirty-two pound solid shot just missed our heads and struck about ten feet in front of us. I tell you, it makes a fellows hair stand up to have as large a ball as that just miss his old head." The picket lines, however, enjoyed a truce. When the Michiganders went on picket for the first time on October 3, Rose remarked that "one of the 'Co. E' boys of our reg. held up a paper and then he saw the 'reb' do the same, they both advanced and met about half way between the lines, shook hands, talked a short time, exchanged papers then each returned to his respective post, so you can see how much the 'reb' soldiers and ours hate each other." He estimated the initial distance between the picket lines at eighty rods. Eleven days later Martin related that the opposing sentries "stand about 40 rods apart in plain sight of each other.... We exchanged papers with them and talked with them about the battle and had a regular old conflab." On October 26, he noted that the lines were separated by just ten rods. The opposing soldiers shared a spring for their fresh water, traded knives and tobacco, and developed a genuine camaraderie.[5]

The passing weeks witnessed the gains and losses in personnel that inevitably follow in the wake of a major battle. Sergeant Major Snyder succumbed on October 5 to the wound he received fighting the 7th South Carolina on Horseshoe Ridge, and was buried the next day. Surrounded by death and desensitized to the loss of one man, Corporal William Frankish of Company E (who was quickly promoted to fill Snyder's vacancy) penned an impersonal letter of notification to Snyder's father.[6]

> Your son W Irving Snyder Died at five o clock this P.M. of wounds recd in the Battle of Chickamauga. I did not know that his situation was so critical until this P.M., started for the hospital forthwith but was to late to see him alive. The following is his list of his effects.... I have his remains with me and will give them as decent a burial as possible under existing circumstances, this consolation for you, he died a brave Soldier. Please answer this as soon as possible. My respects to ... your family.[7]

The sword Snyder seized as a prize from General Adams was ultimately returned to Snyder's family in Three Rivers (Snyder's brother and James King would return the blade to Adams's sons in New Orleans around 1897, and it now resides at Confederate

Memorial Hall Museum). On September 29 Bloom witnessed the arrival of Union ambulances retrieving the wounded from the battlefield, and declared it "an awfull Sight." Wounds from the strife of September 20 continued to claim victims throughout October. Private Perry Richardson of Company D died on October 11. Five days later, Corporal David Clase of Company E perished from a gunshot wound to his femur, leaving his sons, ages four and nine, orphans in the care of their stepmother. Another eventual fatality was that of Private Abner Wilcox of Company A, who was wounded, captured, and then paroled, only to expire on October 29. "He was a noble young man and a good soldier," Rose mourned, "his loss is felt by all of his fellow soldiers." Wilcox's father rushed south hoping to see his son alive one last time, but arrived one day too late. There was, however, the occasional happy ending. Captain Childs, who was shot through the body, left for dead, and captured after the charge against Adams's brigade, was paroled and recuperating in the division hospital by October 15. He was granted a medical furlough before the month was out, returned to Michigan until he was finally exchanged in June 1864, and returned south to see out the balance of his enlistment. Childs's sturdy constitution and will to survive would extend his life by twenty-five years.[8]

The regimental command structure went through its own share of convulsions, with the entire unit devolving to the command of Company H's Captain Keegan on October 17, when Stoughton was detailed to a board of examination. Lieutenant Colonel Mudge's wound from September 20 culminated in medical furlough, and he would be out of action for several months. Major Bennett was detailed for duty in Nashville on October 7 and would not rejoin the regiment until mid–November. Hicks's promotion to captain, dating from the death of Captain Newberry at Chickamauga, wouldn't be made official until February.[9]

Grant was assigned command of the newly created Military Division of the Mississippi, which merged his department with those of Rosecrans and Burnside. One of Grant's first acts in his new role was to supplant Rosecrans with Thomas. The Michiganders took the news in stride. "We have lost old 'Rose' and we dont like it much," Martin commented, "but then Gen. Thomas is good…. I guess we are alright yet." King, somewhat misinformed, bemoaned "the authorities at Washington making Gen. Rosecrans the scape goat for Halleck's and the War Department's blunders," though at the same time he reveled that "that grand hero and superb man, Geo. H. Thomas, was placed in command." Grant reached Chattanooga on October 23 and ascended Cameron Hill, site of the Wolverines' encampment, two days later with Thomas.[10] King chronicled the event:

> Gen. Thomas spent nearly an hour in pointing out the exact situation of the two armies. The writer of this remembers the great commander, Grant, at that time as a man of medium size, light complexion, full beard closely trimmed and clean-cut features as were ever placed on the face of mortals. He was dressed in citizen's clothes of a brownish hue, a slouch hat, cavalry boots well bespattered with Tennessee mud, and nothing on by which you could designate his rank. He had ridden eight miles on horseback that morning from Brown Ferry over roads not much better than a mortar bed, and that accounted somewhat for the dilapidated appearance which he presented alongside of that beau-ideal soldier, Geo. H. Thomas.

The presence of these two noted generals attracted the attention of all the men in camp, and they gathered around as closely as they dared in order to see and hear what was going on. It may have been the looks of the veterans of the 19th and the 11th, or that in part, which [later] caused Gen. Grant to say to Sherman that "Thomas' army were so starved that the men in hunger stole the few grains of corn that were given to the favorite horses; that the men of that army had been so demoralized by the battle of Chickamauga that he feared they could not be gotten out of the trenches to take the offensive, and he wanted Sherman's troops to hurry up and take the offensive *first*, after which he had no doubt the army of the Cumberland would fight well." Right there before him, however, were the veterans who had stood with Thomas on Snodgrass Hill in the fiercest tempest of bullets ever encountered by mortal man since the use of firearms began.[11]

With Grant in command, the Federals wasted no time. Hooker had already arrived in the theater, but had not yet linked up with Thomas. The two generals coordinated to break open a line of supply, dubbed the Cracker Line, and secured that route for good by repelling a Confederate counterpunch in a rare night battle at Wauhatchie on October 28–29. The worst of the supply and communication nuisances were now in the past (and critically so—Bloom had just jotted "nothing to eat" in his diary for the third consecutive day, not to mention "almost Starved"). Grant still needed time to consolidate his gains, and to await Sherman's arrival, which would secure a sufficient numerical edge to offset Bragg's advantage in possessing the commanding heights of Lookout Mountain and Missionary Ridge. Inclement weather continued to slow the pace of operations: King on October 30 reported "not one of those gentle pattering showers which is spoken of in the song, but a shower such as they had in the days of Noah, a regular deluge, though I do not think it will continue forty days and nights."[12]

Much of November passed in the now established routine of social gatherings among the opposing pickets, contrasting starkly with the occasional storm of shells. Bloom noted the receipt of four months' pay on November 19 with the usual results ("The Boys Got Big Times & So Forth"), but rations and other supplies remained tight. "There is nothing new," King wrote home on November 20, "but in a few days the army must again fight or fall back."[13] With Sherman's arrival imminent, Grant entertained no intention of doing the latter. He was determined to drive Bragg from the heights and break out of Chattanooga. In the meantime, Bragg in tandem with Jefferson Davis had done the Federals a tremendous favor. The Confederate general was in the habit of arguing and trading recriminations with his subordinates after each battle, and Chickamauga was no exception. Bragg and Davis addressed that rancor by detaching Longstreet, one of Bragg's chief contenders, with troops to assail Burnside's inanimate host at Knoxville. In a matter of weeks, the Confederate Army of Tennessee went from besieging an inferior force under a cowed general to instead holding a tiger by the tail: the aggressive Grant now confronted the Confederates with a potentially decisive numerical advantage.

The 11th Michigan and its brigade were arrayed for picket duty at their accustomed location (a rolling mill near the base of Lookout Mountain) on November 22, an assignment that would drag on for three days and nights, depriving the Wolverines of sleep on the eve of battle. Grant's breakout attempt inaugurated the next day when he ordered Thomas to make a demonstration toward Missionary Ridge. While the enthusiastic Wolverines looked on, Thomas J. Wood's division advanced and swarmed the Rebels on Orchard Knob, a key rise between the city and the heights. "There has been some heavy fighting today," King wrote. "We are confident of success. The Enemy's Batteries on Lookout mountain and Missionary Ridge were handsomely worked. Our artillery firing, splendid. Moccasin Point battery [has] complete range of the Enemy's camps and Lookout, while the guns from Forts Wood and Negley caused much commotion among them to the East." On November 24, picket duty at the rolling mill offered the Michiganders front row seats as Joseph Hooker's troops, reinforced with two brigades from Thomas, charged up Lookout Mountain and clashed almost blindly with the Confederates amid a dense blanket of fog. "The north end of Lookout," Martin related, "is cleard of all the trees and we could see the whole maneuver of both armies. Hookers men fought splendid; they drove the 'rebs' from one breastwork to another and the rebels would rally as often, and again Hookers men would charge them untill they drove them entirely from the mountain. It was the most splendid sight in the world." Bordner labeled it "one of the greatest sights ever was witnessed." King, whose brother took part in the assault with the 96th Illinois and received a minor head wound, described the scene as the battle continued deep into the night. "The flashes of Hooker's and the enemy's musketry on the mountain side, had the appearance of ten thousand fireflies." Hicks concurred, calling it "a most wonderful display of fireworks."[14]

Every night for weeks, the Wolverines had gazed upon the nightly spectacle of Confederate campfires stretching along a miles-long crescent running up and down Missionary Ridge, then across the valley and up Lookout Mountain. The towering rise of Lookout, in the midst of changing hands, had gone dark now, a powerful visual cue that the military situation was again fluid. The sleepless Michiganders were treated around 2:00 a.m. to the beginning of a lunar eclipse. The moon had almost completely disappeared by 4:00 a.m., leaving soldiers on both sides to wonder if they were witnessing an omen for the day to come. The rumor mill in the 11th Michigan asserted that the Army of the Cumberland was poised to charge the ominous-looking Rebel works on Missionary Ridge when daylight returned.[15]

On the morning of November 25, 1863, the Michiganders—exhausted from lack of sleep, and still going hungry on short rations, since the supply situation remained less than ideal—scarfed down their small breakfasts and noted the absence of the Rebel pickets from their front. "Our friends the enemy," said Hicks, "who had occupied the other side of the creek, and with whom we had been chummy all the day before, while our brothers were fighting for the possession of Lookout Mountain, were not to be seen." Shortly after dawn, a Union flag was raised in triumph atop Lookout. "Such loud and joyous cheering was never heard before," Sergeant Edward Frost of Company E remembered. Hicks led a detail to reconnoiter the valley, and verified that the Confederates had fallen back on Missionary Ridge. Soon after, the Cumberlanders were assembled in line of battle facing the ridge, confirming the essence of the rumors from the night before.[16]

The army had seen some restructuring after Chickamauga. Negley had been removed from active duty for leaving the field of battle on September 20 (he would be cleared of wrongdoing, but would never again lead troops in battle). His place as division commander was filled by Brigadier General Richard W. Johnson. Stanley had resumed command of his old regiment, the 18th Ohio, and transferred out of the brigade with that unit. The balance of Stanley's old command—the 11th Michigan, 19th Illinois, and 69th Ohio—was merged with the brigade of Brigadier General John Haskell King, and formally designated the 1st Division, 2nd Brigade, including the 15th, 16th, 18th, and 19th U.S. Regulars. General King had been ill, leaving Colonel Marshall Moore of the 69th Ohio temporarily in command, but Stoughton returned that morning to lead the unit, which amounted to three times the force he had wielded at Chickamauga. The brigade was divvied into two demi-brigades, with Major John R. Edie in charge of the regulars and Moore assuming overall command of the volunteers. Major Bennett had returned from Nashville, and resumed the role of commanding officer for the Wolverines. Stoughton's line of battle consisted of 1,541 men and officers, but Bennett's ranks, diminished by two years of hard service, contributed a mere 255 Michiganders to the line.[17]

The Federals stood anxiously in line of battle, hour after hour—a seeming eternity for soldiers anticipating a fight—listening to Sherman's assault foundering on Bragg's right. Martin remembered that he and his comrades "could see the artillery fight there, we

Richard W. Johnson replaced James Scott Negley after Negley was removed from command for his unsatisfactory performance at Chickamauga. Johnson led the 11th Michigan's division at Missionary Ridge, and was elevated to corps command during the Atlanta Campaign (Library of Congress).

could hear the musketry and tell that the fight was raging heavy." James King recalled seeing "the glint of the enemy's rifles in the sunlight, as the troops were moved from one position on the Ridge to another." Around 1:00 p.m., Stoughton executed orders to shift the brigade left to close up on the right of Francis Sherman's brigade of Sheridan's division. The regulars comprised Stoughton's right. Moore deployed his volunteers to the left with the Ohioans on his right, the Illinoisans on the left—representing the extreme left of the division—and the Michiganders forming his reserve. A nearby clump of trees obscured Stoughton's line of sight to the ridge, but his soldiers knew what awaited them beyond the woods. The first half mile, consisting of open field, would witness a cannon barrage. A line of rifle pits protected the base of the ridge, another marred the slope partway up, and atop the crest, gun batteries were tucked in a final line of entrenched Rebels. "It was hard work," Bordner remarked, "but we must do it." The Confederates opposite Stoughton consisted of Otho Strahl's brigade: 947 entrenched veteran Tennesseans, supported with eight cannon. To Strahl's right, another potential menace for Stoughton existed in the form of the Wolverines' old nemeses from Daniel Adams's brigade, now under the command of Randall Gibson. In all, about 23,000 Federals under Thomas faced 16,000 Confederates. With the Rebels dug in on imposing high ground and the Federals facing a half-mile initial charge—under cannon fire and without cover—just to reach the base of the ridge, the odds superficially appeared to favor Bragg. In Stoughton's section of the line, the approach from the base to the summit represented something approaching a 500-foot climb over extremely difficult terrain, traversing half a mile of slope that at times approached a forty-five degree incline. It would be an exhausting ascent on a calm day, even without the weight and bulk of soldiers' gear combined with the threat of bullets and shells flying overhead. And it represented a challenging enough climb for a rested man in perfect health—but Stoughton's men remained undernourished, and had been awake almost nonstop for three days and nights on the picket line.[18]

It was fast approaching 4:00 p.m. when six cannon on Orchard Knob boomed in rapid succession, announcing that the time had come. The apprehensive Wolverines spied an aide galloping their way. The courier pulled to a halt before Colonel Stoughton and announced, "The general commanding sends his compliments and directs you to charge the hill." The colonel turned to address his brigade and ordered the blue ranks to advance through the woods. Fifteen hundred Union soldiers stepped off in unison with their neighboring units, pausing only to fix bayonets.[19]

Grant had ordered Thomas to take only the rifle pits at the base of the ridge—his goal was merely to relieve some of the pressure on Sherman—but the veterans of the 11th Michigan Infantry marched with their eyes transfixed on the summit, in full expectation that they would sweep the Rebels from the heights or die trying. Even the night before, the talk in camp had been of an imminent, all-or-nothing death struggle to break the siege. There had been a widely discussed bit of drama in camp that evening. King, as quartermaster sergeant, should have been with the supply train and not standing in the ranks with a gun, but he had persuaded Stoughton to let him into the battle, which King expected to be decisive. Bennett, upon hearing of this, became visibly upset, predicting a bloodbath and sharing a premonition of his own

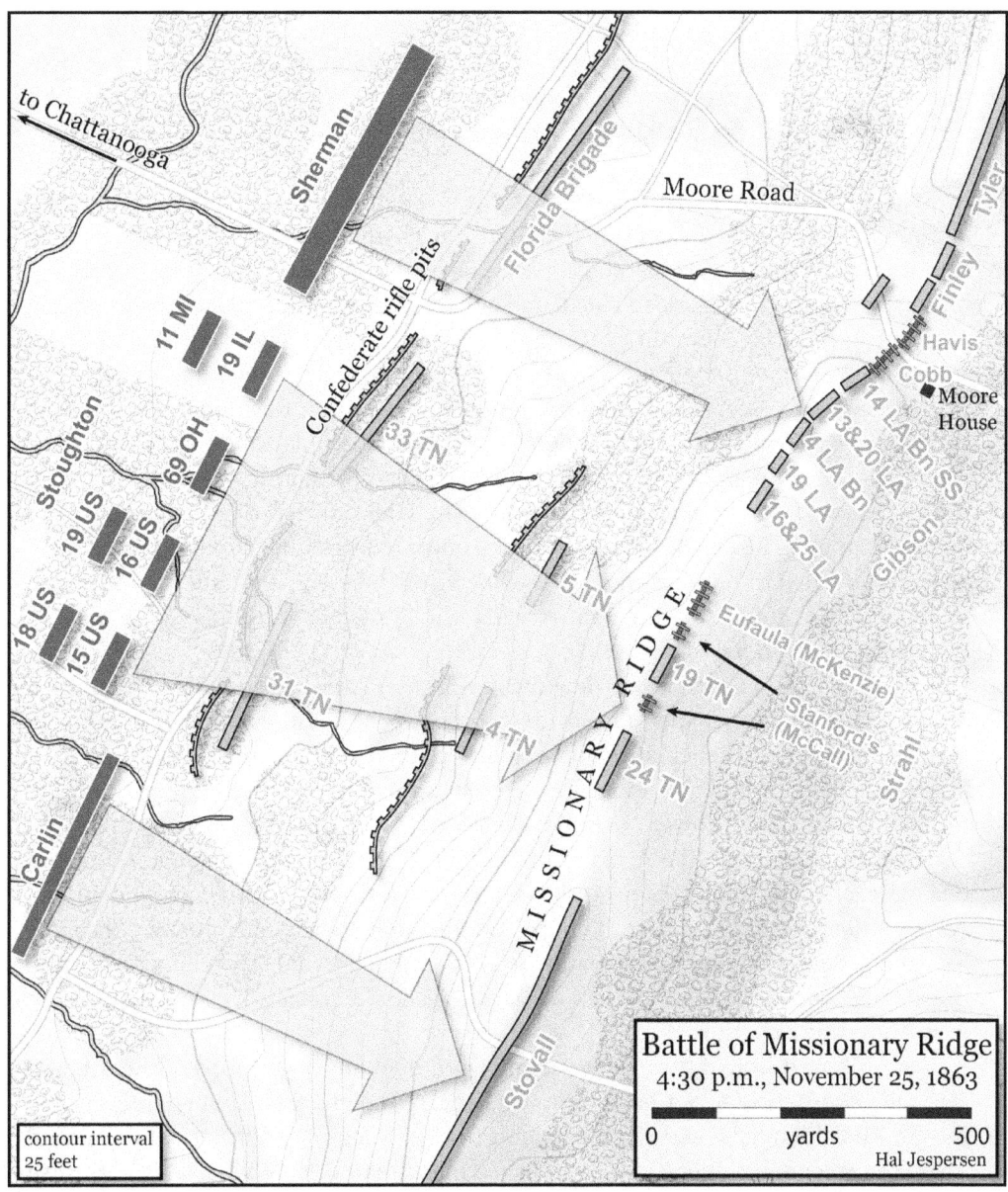

From *Conspicuous Gallantry: The Civil War and Reconstruction Letters of James W. King, 11th Michigan Volunteer Infantry,* © 2015 by The Kent State University Press. Reproduced with permission.

demise. Overruled by Stoughton, the major helplessly watched King depart to join the picket line. Nobody expected less than a full frontal assault. Bloom recorded the distribution of three days' rations, and Rose noted that he and his comrades were issued 100 cartridges instead of the usual forty.[20]

The Army of the Cumberland's initial advance proceeded in good order. Stoughton's brigade emerged from the woods into the wide-open field, which would imminently be swept by the shot and shell of fifty artillery pieces. The colonel's voice rang out, "Forward, double quick, march!" The late afternoon peace was shattered with the sharp reports of dozens of Confederate cannon. "The top of the ridge seemed a perfect blaze," Rose declared. Federal eyes rose to trace the inbound arcs across the sky. The double quick promptly gave way to a desperate, all-out sprint for the heights. Most of the shells overshot their marks and plowed harmlessly into vacant earth. With the charge now at a dead run, the ranks transformed into a swarm, with the fastest legs and bravest hearts leading the way. Several Michiganders watched as Quartermaster Sergeant King raced ahead and surpassed the front ranks of the brigade.[21]

At the ridge base, Strahl's 31st and 33rd Tennessee volleyed into the Federals from the protection of their rifle pits. With the Rebels confronting Stoughton divided into three separate defensive lines, each individual position was undermanned. The outnumbered Rebels promptly found themselves vulnerable as the troops to their right bolted, and their scattered projectiles disappeared with little effect into the great blue wave crashing down upon them. King, who Hicks declared "among the first to leap the Confederate earthworks," was in the midst of a brief melee with those Southerners who failed to flee fast enough. Bayonets and clubbed rifles quickly settled the argument, and those surviving Tennesseans who evaded capture fled uphill under a withering fire from behind.[22]

The Federals paused in their newly won rifle pits. They had successfully occupied Grant's stated objective, and did so with stunning speed, yet the entrenchments were plainly untenable as Rebel rifles and artillery poured fire into the pits from above. Retreat seemed unthinkable to soldiers who had spent weeks penned up in humiliation. How could they cower back into Chattanooga, conceding their last hope? In that desperate moment, the Army of the Cumberland famously reacted as though of one mind, charging uphill against orders. Hicks and King remembered an unidentified voice in their brigade shouting, "On up the ridge!" followed by the same words being repeated by every soldier as they launched forward in ascent. "The closter we got to the ridge," Rose explained, "the less damage they could do us with their batteries so it was our only salvation."[23]

Strahl's next line of defense was comprised of about 300 troops of the 4th and 5th Tennessee, entrenched partway up the coarse incline. They impatiently waited for the skedaddling 31st and 33rd regiments to clear their line of fire, and then opened up on the ascending Federals. Accomplished marksman Private W.C. King of the 4th Tennessee was ordered to pick off a Federal flag bearer—possibly the 11th Michigan's John Day, who had escaped the storm at Chickamauga but ran out of luck this day— and dropped him on the first shot. A private in the 16th U.S. Infantry witnessed that the Wolverines' colors fell "but were raised at once by some strong arm. It is strange what pride men take, under such circumstances in keeping the colors up. Plenty [of] men will quickly face almost certain death rather than see the colors touch the ground." The Union advance soon overlapped the flanks of the second line of Rebel entrenchments, and again a line of panicked Tennesseans scattered uphill. As before, Stoughton's troops retaliated against the running Confederates, firing into their backs as they retreated. Nearly one-third of the Southerners did not make it to the ridge top, but the more composed soldiers among them occasionally paused to return fire. About this time, Major Bennett suffered the fatal hit he had foretold the night before. In the midst of this desperate charge, the dwindling fragment of the 11th Michigan rallied under its senior officer, Captain Keegan.[24]

Once the Michiganders overran the second line, said Martin, "We had to halt, for it was awful hard work to climb the hill." The last leg of the ascent was far and away the most arduous. Upon approach to the summit, the slope steepened and the fire intensified as the 19th and 24th Tennessee, joined by rallied remnants of the Rebel troops previously driven from the works below—about 400 troops in all—enjoyed a clear line of fire against the Union troops struggling to scale the heights. "I tell you it was a hot place," Martin insisted. "All the while that we were going up the hill we were under the heaviest kind of artillery and musketry fire." Stoughton's advance, fairly steady up to this point, alarmingly began to sputter. The Michiganders sensed that the bold assault's fate would be determined imminently, one way or the other. "The line," Hicks observed, "slackened and waited for a few moments to get breath, wondering what would be the outcome if we failed." Private Charles Webb of Company H had taken a bullet through the length of his forearm, and his counterpart Fay Mead received a mortal gunshot through the jaw and throat. Captains Keegan and Bissell, and Second Lieutenant Rossiter had all been wounded, and Hicks narrowly escaped becoming the regiment's fourth wounded officer. Standing just below six cannon supporting Strahl's right, he tried to take cover behind a tree just six inches in diameter. "We had a knack of shrinking ourselves to about the size of a match when exposed to fire," he explained, but "a Johnnie up in front thought it would be well to pick off an officer, so he blazed away at me, his bullet struck my sword, the sword struck me on the leg, making a black and blue spot." Sergeant Edward Frost of Company E declared the desperate Michigan regiment's predicament "hopeless. We were within a hundred feet of the breastworks, and to turn would be certain death."[25]

But then the Rebel line wavered. "At a time when everyone was sanguine and buoyant with hope," Confederate brigadier Strahl exclaimed, the Federals "gained the top of the ridge on my right and opened an enfilading fire upon my line." Several of Stoughton's volunteers had penetrated a gap inadvertently opened between Strahl's right and Gibson's neighboring brigade. Strahl's officers had tried to plug the hole with some Floridians retreating from Gibson's front, but these men were so spooked by their initial rout that they bolted as soon as Stoughton's troops approached. Among the first to exploit the resulting breach was a man who had no business being in the battle to begin with: James King, who was in the process of earning a nomination for the Medal of Honor. Hicks, among others, witnessed King cresting the ridge, where he dove behind a log barely 100 feet from the Rebel gun batteries and fired into Strahl's flank at short range, rolling over on his back to reload, and taking fire in return whenever he rose up to squeeze the trigger. Private Byron Liddle joined King, taking position behind a tree a short distance back. With each passing minute, additional members of Stoughton's volunteer regiments trickled into the gap and bolstered the intensifying crossfire. The most prominent among their victims was Lieutenant Colonel Beriah Moore of the 19th Tennessee, shot dead within sight of his boyhood home on the ridge.[26]

King's luck finally ran out as he hurried to reload his Springfield for the twenty-first time: a bullet tore through his right arm, just above the elbow. He rushed to Liddle and handed off his loaded rifle, waited for Liddle to shoot and then bind his mangled limb, and then exposed himself to hurry the rest of his comrades up the ridge. A short distance below, Hicks glanced to his left and saw the Michigan colors fall to the ground again, announcing another casualty in the color company. Hicks and First Lieutenant Charles Coddington of Company A scrambled simultaneously to raise the colors skyward: Hicks put his neck on the line for the regimental flag, and Coddington, for the national. The two officers led a final gallant rush uphill with the men cheering themselves hoarse, and in a moment the colors of the 11th Michigan Infantry were planted on the summit of Missionary Ridge. The flags of the 19th Illinois and 69th Ohio arrived nearby, and almost simultaneously. The Confederate regimental and brigade commanders adjacent to the gap in either direction gaped in disbelief at the cluster of Federal flags appearing smack in the middle of their division's battle line. Any remaining will to resist disintegrated, and Strahl's soldiers streamed down the east side of the ridge in retreat. Gibson's adjacent brigade, flanked on its left and slammed from ahead by Sheridan, caved in and followed suit. "The enemy," boasted a jubilant Hicks, "were fleeing down the ridge like a flock of sheep."[27]

The 11th Michigan Infantry reunited around its colors on the summit of Missionary Ridge. "At that time," Ozro Bowen declared, "we experienced one of those peculiar moments in the history of the war, when the height of exultation and the lowest depth of sorrow mingled together in the same pulsation of our hearts." Every man had charged uphill fearing a massacre, so there was no small measure of elation as the great majority of the regiment's soldiers not only survived the storm, but emerged unscathed. "Thank God I came off without a scratch," Martin sighed in relief. But Bennett and Day, the regiment's commanding officer and color bearer, had both been killed outright. Four others: Private William H. Cummings of Company B, Sergeant Alonzo H. Merrick of Company C, Private George S. Gillett of Company D, and Company G's Private Cassimer E. Mannigold, were dead, and twenty-eight others were wounded, a casualty rate of 13 percent. It was a joyously low butcher's bill for a charge against fortified veterans on high ground, and Hicks declared that "such a time of hand shaking, hugging, and kissing the Old Flag, I never saw, or expect to see again. Soon up the ridge we saw coming my servant Jim, and the Company's boy, carrying between them a camp kettle of hot coffee, these faithful colored servants had brought this from our camp in Chattanooga over two miles away, the boys were welcomed, and we made out a good meal." Stoughton's entire command had performed admirably, absorbing 161 casualties in the uphill assault, versus Strahl's loss of 259 infantry plus several artillerists. Bordner spoke for all his comrades in blue when he said, "We have struck one awful blow toward crushing this rebellion.... We have given them pay for Chickamauga." Rose added that "Bragg has been thoroughly routed from as strong a position as he ever had and it is a complete victory." The siege of Chattanooga was broken, and the Confederate army, so recently the besieger, suddenly found itself engaged in a demoralizing retreat.[28]

Stoughton's brigade bivouacked on the newly won heights and joined in the pursuit of Bragg the next day. A cheering victory, bloodless for the Federals this time, came that night when Johnson's division pressed the retreating Rebels after dark. Following orders received directly from 14th Corps commander John Palmer, Stoughton formed his brigade in line of battle south of Graysville, Georgia, and commanded his soldiers to tramp through thick forest to intercept Confederates crossing the intersection of the roads to Ringgold and La Fayette. "We could not see where we was going, or what we were to find ahead, but we did not care," a confident Bordner explained. About 9:00 p.m., just as the Union soldiers reached the thoroughfare, Thomas B. Ferguson's hapless South Carolina Battery was heard approaching. "We came so still," Martin related, "that we got within ten rods of them before they knew we were there." The 11th Michigan fired blindly into the Rebels, who assumed themselves to be victims of friendly fire and yelled for their assailants to cease fire. "Col. Stoughton," Martin continued, "gave the command to charge and we went in double quick

This stone monument on the crest of Missionary Ridge marks the approximate location where the 11th Michigan breached the Confederate defenses on the summit (photograph by the author).

... and didnt lose a man. Don't you think that we done it up nice?" They had indeed "done it up nice." The 11th Michigan and 69th Ohio participated in the charge and took sixty prisoners, the battery's colors, three cannon, and two caissons. "Pretty nice troph[ies]," Bordner quipped. After sunrise they discovered the battery's remaining gun and caissons, all abandoned in retreat, and the Michiganders were dispatched to escort the captured Confederates and their armaments back to Chattanooga. Rose believed his regiment was selected for this escort duty because it was out of rations, and remarked, "Lucky for us, [because] the rest [of the brigade] kept on the advance." The balance of Stoughton's brigade marched on Ringgold, but was ordered back to Chattanooga on November 29.[29]

On December 2 the 11th regiment was ordered into winter quarters at Rossville, which Hicks described as existing "in name only, it being the home of a Mr. Ross, who had quite a palatial house, which was made use of for a hospital." Martin considered it a "splendid camping ground, with good water and plenty of wood. We have all got shantys, made either of boards or logs, and have very comfortable times. John Bennett and I have got us a log house about as large as our old hog pen, and have a fire place in it, and it would be nice if it didnt smoke so like the D__l." Bordner thanked the past Rebel occupants tongue-in-cheek for leaving building materials behind, saving him and his comrades a great deal of labor in constructing their winter shelters. This uneventful outpost duty offered a time of desperately needed recuperation. The 11th Michigan ended the year of 1863 with 275 men and officers present for duty, just over half the strength it had mustered prior to Stones River a year earlier. Rose sum-

Linus T. Squire (far right) and his comrades pose on Lookout Mountain sometime after the Battle of Missionary Ridge (Mollus Mass Civil War Collection, United States Army Heritage and Education Center, Military History Institute).

marized the Army of the Cumberland's 1863 campaign in a letter to his mother: "Our army here has gone a long distance the last year[,] if the other armies had done as much I think the war would be nearer a close but still they get the praise and we do the work." Linus Squire on December 22 reported to Adjutant General John Robertson the regimental losses and gains in personnel from November 1, 1862, through November 1, 1863 (thus omitting Missionary Ridge): fifty-three killed or mortally wounded, thirty-seven disease fatalities, eighty-seven discharged for disability, two discharged for other causes, two deserters, ninety wounded, twenty-five missing in action, and forty-two captured, versus just forty-four new recruits. Such a rate of loss rendered the regiment a mere skeleton of its former strength.[30]

On December 12, Keegan was detailed to lead a dozen Wolverines back to scattered points in Michigan to recruit for the regiment. Stoughton also returned home for a time and toured St. Joseph County, probably in hopes of boosting Keegan's success. Five additional recruiters were designated on March 9. Their efforts bore fruit: thirty-two recruits (described by Rose as "quite a rugged set") reported to the regiment in January, thirty-seven in March, and another eighteen in April. This influx was augmented in February with the transfer of seventy-four enlisted men from the 9th Michigan—men who elected not to reenlist when their regiment as a whole opted for veteran reenlistment. All told, more than 150 troops thus joined the 11th in time for the 1864 campaign. The next time the regiment went into battle, it would do so with replenished numbers, but also with many of its muskets toted by men who had never seen battle. The regiment's character had irrevocably changed, a dilemma shared by many units in 1864. Only time would tell whether the raw recruits could uphold the 11th Michigan's hard-won reputation. Rose offered a glimmer of hope on February 1 when he reported the newcomers "getting quite soldierized." Even the hardened veterans who enlisted with the regiment in 1861, however, would spend 1864 with one eye on the calendar, daydreaming of the approaching conclusion of their three-year enlistments.[31]

Efforts were initiated in late 1863 and early 1864 to convince the veteran Wolverines to reenlist. With initial three-year enlistments due to expire during 1864, the Federal government enticed its soldiers to renew their commitment to the war by offering bounties and furloughs in return. "Many of the old regiments," remarked Rose, "are enlisting in the vetteran service and going home on thirty day furloughs but I dont begrudge them their happiness for thirty days with the prospects of another three years misery." Rose's two brothers had also enlisted, leaving their widowed mother home alone, and he considered it his duty to return to her. Further, he had developed no love for military life. "We are governed entirely," he groused, "by circumstances and officers, when and where they say go or what they say to do that is our duty so we are sworn to obey our officers no matter how unjust. Mother you must know that it has been hard for me to be a slave for nearly three years." King and Wells were pressured by their sweetheart and wife, respectively, to return home. Melissa Wells went so far as to threaten—joking or not—to "hunt up another man" if her husband reenlisted. But such influences must have been commonplace throughout the army, and cannot explain the indifference to reenlistment evidenced in this

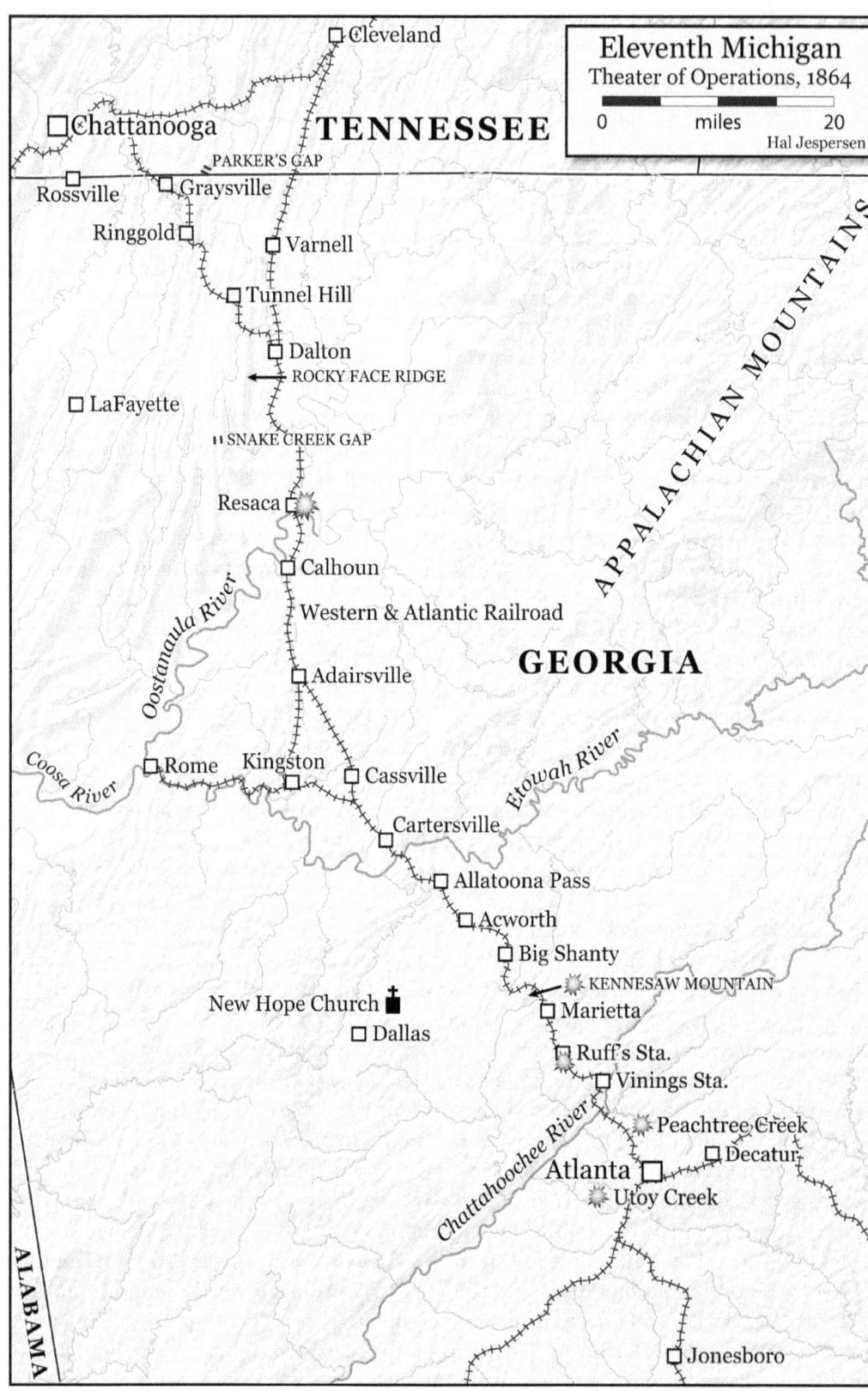

regiment. The majority of all Union soldiers qualifying for veteran reenlistment seized the offer, and many of Michigan's infantry regiments exceeded a 75 percent reenlistment rate, yet in Stoughton's regiment merely sixteen men elected to see the war to its conclusion. Nonetheless, Bloom's diary indicates that discussions and unsubstantiated rumors had persisted for months about the regiment reenlisting as heavy artillery.[32]

Scattered resignations took place in January as a consequence of the past year's rigorous campaign. Captain Fisher and Second Lieutenant Whallon resigned their commissions due to disability (Fisher had never fully recovered from contracting measles in early 1862, and additionally suffered from liver disease by August 1863—Rose mourned his departure, calling it a great loss for Company A). Captain Briggs, wounded at Chickamauga, followed suit on the twenty-fourth. Lieutenant Colonel Mudge, facing a long recovery for his own Chickamauga wound, stayed in the service but was detailed on general court martial duty in Chattanooga, and he was still months away from resuming his regular duties. The unit gained a solemn sense of closure with regard to turnover among its officer corps when Captain Newberry's body was finally retrieved from Chickamauga on the afternoon of January 20. He was buried the next day.[33]

On January 27 Stoughton was assigned to a Nashville-based examination board to judge the merits of prospective white officers for the U.S. Colored Troops (USCT), and was appointed president of that commission on March 11. Several such boards were in operation by that time. The desire to transfer to the USCT could be driven by a number of factors, including altruistic motives, but it was also an easy road to promotion: corporals, and even privates, could instantly land a commission in this manner. But Stoughton's board took its job seriously, interviewing candidates to ascertain not only their military competence, but their educational background as well—stiffer criteria than were applied to the officers of volunteer white regiments. The Nashville board spent an average of about three hours considering each applicant, and rejected more than 60 percent of the 1864 candidates, including a sergeant and private from the 22nd Michigan who interviewed on March 26. The USCT impacted the 11th Michigan in other ways as well. Rose had noted a related loss to the regiment in mid–January. "Tomorrow," he recorded, "our negro man leaves us for a colored regiment. He has been with us nearly two years and has learned to read, he is to be sergeant ... there is several darkies going with him he is as good a negro as ever I saw and we hate to part with him." Attitudes toward the colored troops ran the gamut in Stoughton's regiment. Bordner dismissively noted the colonel's absence to "examine men for Niggers commissions," but King related in a somewhat more positive tone a conversation he had with an officer of a company of black soldiers, saying, "He said he never saw men so easily controlled and who would do their duty better than they." Four soldiers from the 11th Michigan would ultimately serve as officers in USCT units:

Opposite: From Conspicuous Gallantry: The Civil War and Reconstruction Letters of James W. King, 11th Michigan Volunteer Infantry, © 2015 by The Kent State University Press. **Reproduced with permission.**

Private Daniel A. Bennett, Corporal James T. Elliott, Assistant Surgeon Wesley Vincent, and Private Martin V. Wilcox. Bennett and Wilcox would pass their examinations together on August 18 and join the 15th U.S. Colored Infantry. Vincent, unlike the others, did not enter the USCT directly from the 11th Michigan. He had resigned from the regiment in April 1863, and joined the 1st U.S. Colored Infantry in February 1864.[34]

Captain Ephraim Hall assumed command of the 11th Michigan in Stoughton's absence, and Keegan would take over upon returning from recruiting duty in Michigan on April 20. Stoughton was finally released from his board duties on April 24, and returned to the regiment by May 1.[35]

Limited obligations allowed ample time for leisure, correspondence, and general relaxation at Rossville. "We are having fine times here," Bordner exclaimed, "plenty of every thing to eat and drink and not a great deal to do." "We are living first rate now," Rose agreed, "since we draw flour and do our own baking and cooking we are all or nearly all good cooks by experience.... We had a good chicken pot-pie new years." He also reported "an occasional game of ball" among his activities, and related the story of a shindig with eight local girls (who were shared among sixty Federal dance partners) near camp one evening. Battlefield visits also helped break the monotony of camp life. Squire and Adams were among several soldiers who had their pictures taken on Lookout Mountain. Rose noted that "one of the boys got a bush from [Missionary Ridge] where our regiment charged up in the last fight we had.... It had twenty-six bullet marks in it so you can imagine how the missells of death flew around us, an other little tree has thirty-one bullet marks." Stephen Marsh paid a visit to the Chickamauga battlefield on March 3, and Bloom headed to Missionary Ridge the same day to relive past traumas and glory.[36]

On March 15, the 11th toiled through what Rose considered "a very tiresome but short march" eight miles east to rejoin the brigade at Graysville. "This is quite a pleasant place for a military station," he commented, "among the hills the country around here so very rough. the 16th was occupied in fixing our camp we had it quite comfortable." The regiment provided pickets for a railroad repair detail on the eighteenth, and then on the nineteenth, the unit uprooted camp to shift half a mile closer to its sister regiments. King appreciated the "very warm and pleasant" Southern weather, but four days later the regiment was buried under ten inches of snow, "the most we have seen since we crossed the Ohio River," according to Rose. "Of course," said Hicks, who shivered the morning away on picket duty, "it was all gone before night." The regiment guarded Parker Gap from March 31 through April 5. The weather took a turn for the worse, but the Wolverines enjoyed visiting with the Unionists of the valley. "Good Times," Bloom exclaimed. "Plenty to Eat & to Drink." That was about as strenuous a duty as the Michiganders performed during their stay at Graysville.[37]

After four months of quiet recuperation, some expected that the Army of the Cumberland would see less action in 1864. "I do not think we shall make a movement far south from this quarter," wrote King, recently returned from medical furlough for his Missionary Ridge wound. "True, there are troops coming in, but not an army large enough to fight on the offensive. If a movement is made on the Potomac we shall probably hold our line here, and may advance as far south as Dalton," where the Confederates had settled in under the leadership of Joseph E. Johnston, the replacement for Braxton Bragg. (Bragg had resigned his army command following the debacle at Missionary Ridge.) Rose flip-flopped in his predictions about the amount of fighting ahead, but others were more sanguine about the 1864 campaign. New recruit Private Eleazer J. Covey of Company A insisted that "we do not expect to remain here long; we shall go to the front and fight! The regiment was never in better spirits than now and are anxious to be on the move, for we are tired of inaction.... [We] are ready for the rebels in any shape they may see fit to present themselves." Bordner expected to "drive them into the gulf," while Martin noted that "deserters are coming in daily.... I think that the bogus Confederacy begins to tremble," and went so far as to insist that "the Potomac Army are back to their hole again, without accomplishing a thing. I guess that the western army will have to do what fighting there is to be done, for we are the only ones that have accomplished any thing as yet."[38]

Certain of the Michiganders passed the duller moments at Graysville entertaining themselves at the expense of their brigade mates in the U.S. regulars. Bloom witnessed on April 21 that "one of the Regulars Got Drumed out of The United States Servis Fore Steeling, & They March Him Threw the Camp With a Board on His Back Writen on it a Thief." To the volunteers, the regulars' strictness was a source of hilarity. The 15th U.S. Infantry's Major Edie wrote in protest to Captain Keegan on April 23. The commanding officer of the 15th's Company D had reported that "whilst engaged in drilling his co. this, and previous, mornings he and his command were much annoyed by some of your men, who, standing in the edge of your camp amused themselves, by shouting a repetition of the orders given, and by applying opprobrious epithets to the men drilling." Keegan evidently brought the hecklers under control, as the complaint did not recur, but it remained to be seen whether the volunteers and regulars could ever gel as a cohesive unit.[39]

Bloom reported a notable increase in bayonet drill, mock skirmishing, and target practice as the spring progressed. "Solomon Shirey," Bloom smirked on April 15, put "a double Load in his Gun & noct Him Over." The stir-crazy soldiers would see their boredom completely cured early in May. With the arrival of fairer weather, the time for the 1864 campaign in Georgia had come. "This morning firing was heard in the direction of Ringold," Rose informed his mother. "We are ready for it." King observed that "preparations have been going busily forward for an early move. All our surplus baggage has been sent to the rear, and the army put in trim for a long march." Imminent marching orders would inaugurate the final campaign of the 11th Michigan Infantry. The end of the original three year enlistments was tantalizingly close, and every one of the veterans dreaded being the last man to fall.[40]

CHAPTER 8

"Sick and tired of fighting"
May–October 1864

Grant had gone east to accept the rank of lieutenant general, and to supplant Henry Halleck as general in chief. Filling Grant's vacancy, William Tecumseh Sherman now commanded three cooperating armies: Thomas's Army of the Cumberland, the Army of the Tennessee under James B. McPherson, and John M. Schofield's Army of the Ohio.

The 11th Michigan struck tents at 5:00 a.m. on May 2 and departed three hours later for Ringgold, arriving at 2:00 in the afternoon. Soldiers unfit for the march had been sent to the rear, prompting Rose to speculate that "I expect they will never be with us again while in the service." Illustrating the confidence pervading the regiment, he boasted to his mother regarding the Rebels that "we will rout them out of there in about two weeks, we have got plenty force to whip them I think."[1] On the night of May 6, with everyone cognizant of the next day's advance against the Confederates, Downey was just one of many soldiers who recorded an unforgettable scene:

> Some soldier, who thought the occasion worthy of some sort of demonstration, concluded that he would illuminate; so he lighted all his candles and stuck them on top of his tent. The next soldier liked the spirit of that and put his candles out, and then the next and the next, until all the tents in the company had lighted candles upon them. The other companies of the regiment followed. It went from regiment to regiment, from brigade to brigade, from corps to corps, until that whole great army was brilliantly illuminated. We were encamped on an eminence where we could overlook nearly the entire valley where the Army of the Cumberland lay, and it was a magnificent sight. There were thousands of tents in view and each had upon it from two to a dozen candles. There were that broad valley and those hill tops and those gentle slopes, stretching away in the distance as far as the eye could reach, all brilliantly decked with those twinkling lights. Why, it looked as if the stars had been translated from the heavens to the earth.[2]

Bloom, equally enthralled but habitually less verbose, declared it "the Best Sight I Ever Saw a Scare For the Rebels."[3]

The familiar call of the bugle prodded the Michiganders to consciousness early in the morning of May 7. Brigadier General John H. King was back in command of the 11th Michigan's brigade. The 19th Illinois had just transferred to Baird's division, ending its long and close brotherhood with the 11th Michigan, and the 69th Ohio would not return from veteran furlough until May 11, leaving the Michiganders the sole volunteers among a force of regulars in the meantime. Even with the departure of the Illinoisans, the replenished brigade marshaled 2,937 soldiers, including the Ohioans—nearly double the number it had thrown at Missionary Ridge. The 11th Michigan counted sixteen officers and 428 men present for duty—almost exactly the number it had fielded against the Rebels at Stones River nearly a year and a half before. The Union host marched with the usual starts and stops of a large army. "[We] shift about one side of the road," Marsh complained, "& then the other Stop[ping] often." At one point the Michiganders formed into line of battle in support of a battery, but nothing came of it. They proceeded through an abandoned Rebel camp and bivouacked a couple miles outside of Tunnel Hill that night.[4] The wide-eyed, raw recruit Downey promptly discovered something the old veterans had learned two and a half years prior.

> A new soldier could be distinguished almost invariably by his load. He would put into his knapsack his tent, his woolen blanket, a rubber poncho, two or three pairs of socks, an extra shirt, a vest, a portfolio, a couple of towels, his girl's picture, and a euchre deck. He would roll up his overcoat and strap it on the outside, and then strap the whole thing on his back, the load causing him to lean some thirty degrees to the front of the perpendicular and making a hump bigger than that on any camel that ever lived. It is laughable to see him dispose of these articles, one after another, after marching a few miles.... At the first halt he seemed to realize that winter was over and that he was in a southern climate, and he would unstrap his overcoat and leave it reluctantly by the wayside. At the second halt he would leave his vest. At the third he would unstrap his knapsack, look wistfully at its contents, and wonder what else he would spare. Before being able to make up his mind the bugles would sound the assembly, and then he would throw out his extra shirt and a pair of socks, hastily strap up, and fall in. Thus they went one after another, until the road was completely lined with over-coats, tents, blankets, vests, shirts, socks, old letters, and [finally,] knapsacks, themselves.[5]

The regiment approached Buzzard Roost Gap in Rocky Face Ridge the next day, and filed into line of battle one mile from the ridge. "Had our division been consulted regarding its position in the line," Downey remarked, "it would not have chosen it in front of that gap, nor, being in front of it, would it have chosen to go nearer than it was." There they waited until the next afternoon, when they were pushed forward to demonstrate against imposing Confederate positions on the high ground while McPherson struck out for Resaca in the Rebel rear. Light skirmishing broke out as the Federals pressed ahead. Before long, the 11th was subjected to long-range artillery fire. The incoming shells overshot their marks initially, much to the relief of the regiment's new recruits. But the same naive fellows were caught by surprise when the gunners compensated. "Those things dropped right down there where we were stopping," Downey exclaimed. "I didn't want to stay there, and I asked [Captain Hicks] whether he didn't want me to get him a canteen of water, or post a letter for him, or something." Luck shielded the Michiganders from harm, but other Federal units were not so lucky, and the advance only proved the defenses impregnable. Hicks called the

Rebel position "a veritable hornets nest, and we were very glad that we were not required to knock the nest down."⁶

After McPherson's effort came up short at Resaca, Sherman threw the bulk of his army around Johnston's left. The 14th Corps, 11th Michigan included, set out at dawn on May 12. The Wolverines paused at Snake Creek Gap, which Marsh described as long and muddy, with a bitter, cold wind. The men were ordered to leave their knapsacks behind, "and havent had anything but our rubber blankets since," Martin complained. "Each man has to carry three days rations all the while and sixty rounds of cartridges." They encamped beyond the gap in Sugar Valley. Martin at least enjoyed the scenery, calling it "as nice a country as I ever saw." The soldiers proceeded toward Resaca the next morning. By sunset they were at the front, again eyeing formidable Confederate defenses.⁷

On May 14 Sherman vigorously tested Johnston's lines. The 11th grabbed breakfast at 7:00 a.m. and was actively skirmishing two hours later, forging ahead in line of battle. Charles Powers of Company A became the first casualty of the campaign for the 11th, surviving a bullet to his right cheekbone that Marsh labeled "a chance shot." "It was our good fortune not to be actively engaged in this battle," Hicks noted, as the regiment was spared from the balance of that day's considerable bloodshed. The unit dug in 800 yards from the main Confederate line and remained there the next day, trading long-range fire the entire time. "We keep them down in their works," Marsh boasted as the heavy skirmishing continued unabated. Corporal James Bolton received a contusion from a shell fragment, and Isaac Knapp, who had just joined the regiment in January, suffered a flesh wound to his right leg. William Lemunyon of Company A was wounded severely in his right side and soon died. "It is hard telling who will be the lucky ones," Bordner wrote, "where so many fall." The thought of perishing so far from home and so close to the end of a three-year enlistment struck a chord for many. "No loved one was near to plant flowers over your graves or water them with the tears of affection," remembered Ozro Bowen. "Many a brave man gave up his life on the skirmish line, with no name upon our colors to mark the spot where he fell; but his death was just as noble, and the sacrifice just as great, as though he had fallen amid ten thousand."

William Tecumseh Sherman led three cooperating armies to victory in the crucial Atlanta Campaign. He earned his troops' respect with his knack for turning the Confederates out of eminently defensible positions without the need for costly frontal assaults (Library of Congress).

One Michigander determined during this day at Resaca not to risk becoming one of those brave dead: Captain Frank Lane of Company D deserted. He would be "cashiered for cowardice & c." as of June 21, leaving Lieutenant Benjamin F. Hart in command of the company.[8]

That evening, Johnston learned that Sherman was again on the cusp of turning the Rebel left, and withdrew. King's brigade entered Resaca the next morning and took a number of prisoners. "On passing through the town," Downey observed, "we noticed that houses, barns, stores, churches and other buildings were very badly riddled by shell and solid shot. Johnston had left in such haste that he had not buried his dead, and the ghastly, mutilated corpses lay everywhere." Marsh observed a burnt railroad bridge on the Oostanaula River. The Michiganders and their comrades pursued the Army of Tennessee the day after. The line of march passed through Calhoun and Adairsville, and reached Kingston the following day.[9]

The Rebel army remained perfectly intact, but Sherman had pushed the Confederates halfway from Dalton to Atlanta without fighting a full-scale engagement. Morale ran high in the 11th. "The thing of it is," Benjamin Bordner exclaimed, "we have men enough to walk right along.... They have left all their best fighting grounds, and now we have them on level country." But at the same time, the Wolverines had "been marching and fighting for fourteen days," Martin wrote on the twentieth, "and expect to for some time longer." Such constant activity was draining. "We are in line of battle," Martin continued, "and have been busy throwing up breastworks nearly all day, but expect to move at any minute." With little more than three months remaining in their enlistments, the Wolverines kept one eye on the calendar. "The boys call themselves 100 day men Mich. Militia," Martin laughed.[10]

In the meantime, two of the Michiganders were off on a separate adventure of their own. Commissary Sergeant Lindley R. Harkness and Private William Clarence Iddings had been detailed as scouts for Thomas. Their task was a daring one: they were called on to dress as Confederate soldiers or civilians and go behind enemy lines to gather information about Johnston's army and its movements. Being captured as spies would surely have ended in execution. Rose said of Iddings on May 22, "He has some pretty hard times but he likes it."[11]

Johnston concentrated at Cassville, but his position was immediately proven untenable, and the Confederates backpedaled again. Sherman paused the fatiguing advance at this point, but Marsh and his comrades knew the respite would be short-lived. Orders were received on May 21 to send the regiment's wagon and trunks to the rear "& get ready for 20 days hard fiting & start the 23d." Tents were left behind as well. The Rebels were promptly turned out of their next fallback point at Allatoona Pass, but they shifted quickly enough to take up a line between Dallas and New Hope Church, barring Sherman's path. On the twenty-seventh, King's brigade was held in reserve but drew artillery fire during a failed Federal attempt to turn Johnston's flank near Picket's Mill. Division commander Richard Johnson was wounded, elevating King in his stead. Stoughton resumed brigade command, and Keegan took charge of the 11th Michigan. At Picket's Mill, Downey experienced perhaps his first up close and personal view of the human wreckage of an assault as he exposed himself to help a wounded Ohioan captain off the field. "I shall never forget," he wrote, "the frightful appearance of one poor fellow whom I saw coming out of that gap. His whole under jaw was shot off, clear back to the throat. The front of his body was completely covered with blood, and his tongue was hanging down and dangling as he walked."[12]

That night, the 11th entrenched in the field, an act that was part and parcel of the new reality of warfare. "After felling a tree," Downey described,

> we would haggle off a long log and roll it into position. Next we would place upon this log, near the end, a couple of skids, the other end of the skids resting on the ground on the rebel side. Then we would place upon these skids another log immediately over the first, the skids being notched to receive it. We would now dig a ditch on our side of these logs and bank the dirt on the rebel side, giving us a combination of earth and timber works. Lastly, if the material at hand permitted, we would place upon this wall two other skids with one end of each resting on the ground on our side, and notch into them over the wall a "head log," or parapet, leaving only a narrow crack for firing through. The skids were inclined on our side so that, in case of the head log's being struck by a cannon ball or shell, it would roll down the skids and not fall on the men in the ditch.[13]

The regiment held its position under fire through June 5, tasting the misery of trench warfare. The constant sniping all too often found a target. "I cant imagine what is going to be done," Marsh fretted. The regiment lost Spencer Blanchard, who was hit outside of the trench. His possessions couldn't be recovered owing to the eternal vigilance of the Rebel sharpshooters. Thomas Pixley and Thomas Hodgins were also killed, yet morale remained buoyant. Hicks was confident that his comrades got the better end of the contest. "This place went into history," he asserted, "as the one position where more of the enemy were slaughtered, than we could get any record of, for we spent our days in slaying every able bodied Gray Back, that showed his head." By now, even the newer recruits were desensitized enough to find occasional humor in their predicament. Downey looked on as one of the regular regiments took charge of the skirmish line, led by a strict West Pointer. When one private deviated from the mandated interval between the skirmishers in order to enjoy the protection of a tree, the officer handled the offense without missing a beat: "Forward—double time—guide center—get out from behind that tree you son of a gun—march!" Downey wryly noted that "this officer himself was not only behind the breast works, but behind a big tree just in rear of the works." Another regular officer—or perhaps the same one—while in a drunken stupor took advantage of a brief absence by Colonel Stoughton to order a suicidal charge on the Rebel works. When the men refused outright, this fearless leader attempted the assault alone, but was promptly compelled to abort the operation under fire. Stoughton returned and arrested the man. In addition to making light of the regular officers, the Wolverines managed to laugh even at their own wretched earthworks, with Hicks declaring that they were shared with "an army of knits, so we gave this place the euphonious name of 'Lousey Ditch,' and ever after if any one said to us Lousey Ditch! we replied 'Nit.'" Rose considered picking lice from his clothes the best available way to pass the long, disagreeable hours in the trench.[14]

The weather allied with the Rebels for the month of June, with incessant rains plaguing the Union advance. "Yesterday we had a very heavy shower," Rose informed his mother on June 2, "with heavy thunder and lightening. one stroke of lightening shocked our whole company." And that was only the beginning. On June 21 Sherman would complain of the nineteenth consecutive day of rain, describing the roads as impassable.[15]

Sherman gradually extended the Union left back to the railroad, culminating in Johnston's withdrawal toward Kennesaw Mountain. Rose, among others, shared a popular joke that the Rebels believed Sherman's troops so numerous that he needed only to shout the commands, "Attention creation right or left wheel march," and the Rebels would be flanked. When the Michiganders arose at last from their trenches and stretched out their weary limbs, they were fascinated by the sheer number of bullet impacts to be seen. Marsh compared one nearby house, riddled with ball holes, to a skimmer. Downey thought it more akin to a honeycomb, and studied an oak tree that "for forty feet from the ground, did not have a place as large as one's thumb that was not marked by a bullet." Rose declared it "a great relief to be where we can stand up straight without having a bullet whiz past our heads." The brigade footed its way northeast, reaching the railroad at Acworth the next day, and four days later resumed the advance southward.[16]

The journey toward Kennesaw Mountain proceeded by fits and starts through the eighteenth. Along the way, shortly after the Rebels were dislodged from Pine Mountain, some of the Wolverines were detailed to gather materials for breastworks to be erected on a hill the regiment occupied. They headed downhill to a fence in an adjacent field to gather rails, but in the midst of scooping up the planks they came under ranged fire from the woods. Providentially, the few bullets directed with true aim struck the rails in the Michiganders' arms, causing injuries more psychological than physical. The soldiers fled uphill with their arms full of fencing, and watched with a powerful sense of justice as a Union battery unlimbered and returned fire. "If you ever happen to be in a forest of dead trees," Downey smirked, "when bomb shells are being thrown among them, I can assure you that you will be the worst scared fellow that you ever were in your life. The way those shells crashed among those dead trunks, knocked off those dead limbs, and scattered smoke, iron, timber, and thunder was enough to frighten men out of their wits; the promptness with which those rebels scampered out of there was gratifying to behold."[17]

On June 19 Stoughton's brigade partook in Federal efforts to press the Confederate positions on Kennesaw Mountain, where Johnston had taken up a superior defensive position on the high ground. As the unit rushed in, according to Downey, "it seemed as if the before quiet mountain had suddenly burst into a volcano ... such thunder and smoke and screeching of iron and bursting of bombs we had not dreamed of." As at Buzzard Roost, most of the incoming fire harmlessly overshot its mark. On the twentieth, the unit advanced to the cover of woods to act as a reserve, and on the night of the twenty-second, Stoughton relieved Walter C. Whitaker's brigade from the front line. Here his Wolverines were separated from the Rebel works by just 100 yards, with a Confederate battery emplaced straight ahead, only 250 yards away. Another protracted contest of attrition ensued, with the threat of sudden death at the hands of a sharpshooter or the blast of a shell forming a harsh and unrelenting reality. "If one wanted to die," Downey suggested dryly, "all he had to do was to put his head above the works; he would very soon be accommodated." Such skirmishing dragged on until June 27, when Sherman launched a frontal assault against Kennesaw. The 11th was not engaged, but its troops passed the day in suspense. "We stood and waited nearly all day long," wrote Hicks, "for the command to charge, the works in our front were not over four rods apart, and we knew it meant death to the charging column. It was the most trying day that we experienced in our whole term of service." The sense of relief must have been palpable when the regiment was relieved from the front line, removing a half mile to the rear that night.[18]

By this point in the campaign, inconsistent mail delivery was quite possibly dimming Federal spirits more than anything Johnston's army was doing. King defended himself to his sweetheart, who complained bitterly of the lack of mail, writing, "You think I am making a trial of your faith. Far from it Jenny, and you do me a great injustice to let such a thought enter your mind." Rose complained of a lack of letters from home, and Benjamin Wells's wife reacted much as King did when her soldier-husband griped about the lack of correspondence, saying of her delayed letters, "What can I do I certainly can do no more than write them and mail them." The trickle of mail that did get through in either direction was evidently just enough to convince everyone that mail service was adequate, and that their inattentive correspondents were the real problem.[19]

The almost daily skirmishing and rainfall, on the other hand, failed to sour the Michiganders' moods. Rose told his mother that "Atlanta is our destination and we are bound to go there." King on June 20 predicted the fall of Atlanta by July 4, and four days later added, "I think ere long the Confederates will acknowledge another defeat. This war cannot always last. Even now, I think I can see the final end." Even in the aftermath of Sherman's bloody, failed charge against the mountain defenses, King assured his sweetheart that "everything is working well."[20]

With the armies in almost constant contact, logistics were a nuisance. The men had received no soap since the beginning of the campaign, the daily ration was reduced to limited quantities of hardtack with beef or bacon, and uniforms grew increasingly tattered and filthy. Nevertheless, Rose assured his mother, "I am fat, ragged and saucy, tough lazy & lousey, so you can judge that I feel pretty well considering the circumstances." Downey noted along these lines that the men were thrilled at the arrival of one camp kettle per company, which was handed around according to a daily schedule for use in preparing coffee, cooking beans, and boiling water to delouse clothing.[21]

Johnston's position was turned yet again, and the Rebels evacuated on the night of July 2. "Before sunrise," Rose exclaimed, "our flag was floating on the top of Kennesaw Mountain then what a cheer went up along our lines." Stoughton's brigade advanced over the Rebel works (which Rose found "badly torn to pieces") at 8:00 a.m. in pursuit. The Union troops enjoyed tramping through Marietta, which King considered "the pleasantest little village I have seen in all the sunny South"—a welcome contrast after hunkering down and wallowing in the muck of the trenches for two weeks straight. "There was a few families left in town," Rose observed, that "seemed to be pleased at our advance." The brigade overtook the Rebel rear guard and skirmished a good part of the day, approaching Ruff's Station toward nightfall. That night Stoughton's men constructed works. "We could easily see that we were preparing for serious business," Downey commented ominously.[22]

July 4, 1864, dawned with a beautiful blue sky. Sherman ordered Thomas to keep the Confederates occupied at Ruff's Station to give the balance of the Federals a chance to turn the Rebel position. With artillery fire brisk in both directions, Stoughton advanced to reconnoiter the enemy works and ran afoul of the cannonade. Soon after, Downey recorded, "the colonel's orderly came riding back at full speed and called out, 'Bring a stretcher: quick, Colonel Stoughton is terribly wounded.' I well remember the effect as word passed along the line that our colonel had been wounded.... There were many sad hearts and not a few moist eyes as ... he was carried on a stretcher along the regiment, his pale face turned toward his men." Yet the Confederates still had to be dealt with. A reinforced skirmish line, consisting of four companies from the 18th U.S. Infantry, three from the 19th U.S. Infantry, and five (A, C, D, E, and F) from the 11th Michigan, was placed under Captain G.W. Smith of the 18th regiment and ordered to charge stout Rebel defenses near the railroad. Impressively, the Federals drove the Rebels from their fortified position—a rare success of that nature by now, as both sides had fairly perfected the art of constructing works—but at a steep cost. Three Wolverines were killed, including Byron Liddle (numbered among the few who had reenlisted), Edward White, and William Schochenbarger. Ten more were wounded in the charge, and another four during the balance of the day. Amputations ensued: Stoughton lost his shattered leg, First Lieutenant Myron Benedict, an arm. Colonel Moore of the 69th Ohio assumed command of the brigade.[23]

The psychological impact of losing Stoughton, who was carried back to Marietta for a dicey recovery, should not be underestimated. "The regiment seems as though it had lost its father," King said twelve days later. "Col S is a great loss to the brigade and espetially to our regt," added Rose. "No one ever spoke of him but to praise." "He had led the regiment in many a battle," remarked Downey, "and, by his bravery and his many excellent qualities, he had endeared himself to his men and this was a great shock to them." With Mudge still unavailable owing to his Chickamauga wound, the regiment did not have a single officer present who had held the rank of captain or higher in 1861. With 100 percent turnover in captains and field officers, and many new recruits in the ranks, the regiment's makeup had been completely transformed.[24]

Command of the 11th remained with Keegan as the senior captain. Stoughton had put him up for major, although the promotion was never confirmed. The prospective major lacked Stoughton's reputation for valor. Downey reported Keegan's actions upon reaching the trench seized in the fateful July 4 assault:

> The major was a man who thought a good deal of his personal safety, and wishing, besides, to set a good example to his men to protect themselves, he threw himself at full length into the ditch. He was a tall man and when his great altitude was placed in a horizontal position in the bottom of that ditch, he took up so much room that two other men of our company and myself could not get in. Now I wanted dreadfully to get into that ditch—indeed, I had never before been seized with so all absorbing a desire to get into a ditch as on that occasion; but the major gave no indication of yielding any of the space which he had appropriated. The other two men, after risk-

ing themselves a while on the exposed bank, waived the courtesy ordinarily shown to an officer and crowded in on the major's legs. As for myself, ostrich like, I hid behind a little decayed stump which you could easily have kicked over with your foot.[25]

Downey, detailed as a regimental pioneer, was equipped with axe and spade, and shouted over the din to Captain Hicks, "I would not have you think that I am concerned about myself, but it strikes me that it would be a dreadful calamity to have the only axe and shovel belonging to this company knocked to shivereens by one of these cannon balls." Downey noted that he "afterward received many compliments upon the celerity with which I covered the ground between that little stump and the breast-works."[26]

Outmaneuvered again, the Confederates retreated across the Chattahoochee River on July 9. Sherman expended several days stockpiling supplies and preparing to cross the river while his army recuperated. Stephen Marsh was one of several men who took advantage of the opportunity to visit the nearby 19th Michigan, where Marsh enjoyed dinner with Major John J. Baker. Aside from staring across the river at the opposing pickets, it was a fairly quiet time. Rose reported his comrades as "getting quite well rested all of the boys begin to feel better." On July 15, the 69th Ohio was transferred out of the brigade, leaving the 11th Michigan alone with the regulars again, this time for good. The wagons and baggage were returned to the brigade the following day, evoking much rejoicing. Rose expected to stay put the remainder of July, but the forward movement against Atlanta resumed on the seventeenth, the same day that Johnston was replaced by John Bell Hood—a far more aggressive commander. By 6:00 a.m. that morning, the 11th was preparing to march again, and the brigade, back under the command of General King as of July 13, crossed the Chattahoochee. The next two days witnessed modest advances, with the Federals in line of battle at times.[27]

Hood went right to work with an attempt on July 20 to catch Thomas's army at a vulnerable moment, with Sherman having sent Schofield and McPherson marching off to the east to approach Atlanta via Decatur while Thomas crossed Peachtree Creek. King's brigade crossed the creek early that morning and was held in reserve while the battle raged, ducking and dodging a thunderous bombardment until late in the day, when they were ordered to rush to the far left to bolster the dangerously exposed flank of John Newton's 4th Corps division. The Michiganders arrived too late to be of much account, but Hicks conveyed the bright side of his unit's harrowing quick-time march. "The importance of this position," he said, "was such that we were moved by the shortest line, which led us just in rear of our men ... who were resisting the massed columns of General Hood, who were trying to break our line, this gap in our line proved to be in a blackberry patch or field, it was doubly welcome to us, not only as food, but on account of their well known medicinal qualities as an astringent." In the end, Hood's assault was more aggressive than coordinated, and ended in failure.[28]

The brigade remained stationary until the morning of July 22, when the enemy was found to have abandoned their works to fall back on Atlanta's outer defenses. The Michigan soldiers pursued their adversaries closely, arriving at the Rebel defenses two miles outside the city around 3:00 p.m. The 11th was not involved in the Battle of

Atlanta that day, but entrenched in tight proximity to the Confederates. They settled in under renewed musketry and artillery fire, taking turns on picket and skirmishing duty. With the regiment's term of service nearing expiration, Rose commented that "an application has been made to relieve us from the front soon and I hope it may be done." He noted the mortal wounding of Addison McComb, Company G, and expressed regret over the news of General McPherson's death in battle. Rose's friend and Company A comrade, Aaron White, told his parents that "we may have considerable hard fighting before we get in to the city, but I feel confident in the final success of our army."[29]

On July 23 the Michiganders enjoyed a pleasant surprise when fate returned to the regiment a man long thought to be lost. Around dusk on September 20, 1863, near the end of the legendary stand on Horseshoe Ridge, Private Henry C. Damon of Company A had escorted his wounded messmate, Jesse Carpenter, back to a log cabin behind the battle line, where the regiment's wounded were being treated. Lieutenant Marsh ordered Damon to stay and care for the casualties until morning, and the subsequent Union withdrawal left Damon and his patients in the hands of the enemy. Damon was imprisoned in Danville, Virginia, for a time before being removed to Andersonville, Georgia. The dangerously deprived inmates of Andersonville bartered frequently. With cunning and patience, Damon managed to assemble, piece by piece, a passable Confederate uniform. On June 28, 1864, Damon donned this garb and nonchalantly marched out the prison gate with a formation of departing Rebel guards. Another prisoner, William Smith of the 14th Pennsylvania Cavalry, escaped about the same time, and he and Damon cautiously made their way across the countryside, seeking the Union line.[30]

The escapees traveled primarily under cover of darkness, and their trip home constituted a real-life Odyssey. The first night, seeking shelter from a thunderstorm, they forced their way into a cabin, only to have an elderly slave discover them and alert his master. Damon and Smith narrowly escaped pursuing bloodhounds. After four days without a bite to eat, they passed themselves off to the women of another household as Confederate soldiers, and gratefully devoured an offering of bread before continuing on their way. On July 9, out in the countryside, they stumbled across a Union man who happily replenished their haversacks with food. Four days later they came to the shanty of a friendly slave who slaughtered a pig for them, and pointed them toward Sherman's position. Proceeding on their way, the ex-prisoners narrowly eluded capture again when three Rebels passed within ten feet of their hiding place. On July 21 the lucky pair reached Marietta, and two days later Damon stunned his comrades by rejoining the 11th Michigan. "He was the happiest mortal," James King recalled, "I ever expect to see this side of paradise. All he wanted was a Union pair of pants which the Qr. Sergt. of the 11th Mich. Inft. supplied." Aaron White recorded that Damon told "some pretty hard stories of the way in which our prisoners are used by the rebels. It seems as though no government could prosper who use such barbarity as they do." The day after Damon's arrival, another welcome face returned to the regiment. The respected and missed Lieutenant Colonel Mudge returned at last from his convalescence, which he had spent on general court martial duty. He had taken chronically ill and remained unable to perform his duties, but his mere presence sparked a considerable boost to morale.[31]

The Michiganders constructed an abatis by the twenty-fifth, in addition to strong earthworks. "The whole Southern army combined cant drive us from behind it," Martin insisted. He reported that the Federal guns were throwing a shell into Atlanta every five minutes. Rebel artillery returned the favor periodically. James King was wounded in the shoulder by a shell burst on July 30, sending him to the rear for medical care and effectively terminating his military career. On August 3 the brigade marched toward the extreme right of the army and entered the line of battle the next day, participating in Sherman's attempt to extend his line and sever Atlanta's railroad lifeline to East Point. The Michiganders reconnoitered on August 5, returning after sunset to encamp near a rivulet known as Utoy Creek. Their brigade was back in the line of battle on August 6, confronting strongly held Confederate entrenchments and listening to the clatter of a doomed Federal assault a short distance to the right. 14th Corps commander John Palmer resigned that day, raising Richard Johnson to corps command. General King resumed division command, and this time, Major John R. Edie of the 15th U.S. Infantry, as the senior officer present and available, assumed leadership of the brigade. The ill Lieutenant Colonel Mudge resumed his duties the next day, though his health would limit his active involvement with the regiment to just two days. His brief return, however, was fortuitously timed.[32]

Downey described August 7, 1864, as "a warm and sultry day, the sun pouring his heat out an almost insufferable degree. All nature seemed to droop beneath his power. The leaves upon the trees were almost motionless, so little air was there astir." The armies themselves seemed to grow listless, lying all but inactive, despite their close proximity. The Federals off to the right, after being bloodily fended off the day before, showed little inclination to renew their offensive. The Michiganders peeked out over the breastworks, down the gentle slope to Utoy Creek and up the gradual rise on the other side, where their Southern counterparts quietly populated two lines of breastworks at the edge of some woods. The morning passed away in relative peace. The Wolverines could not possibly have imagined that this was fated to be the second deadliest day in their regiment's history.[33]

Orders arrived about 1:00 p.m. for the brigade to prepare an assault, and the men were ordered to fall in. The 18th Regulars moved out as skirmishers and the 15th Regulars comprised the left half of the line of battle, with the 11th Michigan on their right. A murmur of disbelief arose from the Wolverine enlistees of 1861 as they gaped at the ominous Rebel fortifications in the distance. These Michiganders were just weeks shy of returning home safely after enduring and surviving three years in the service. Now they would be asked to charge across a quarter mile of open field. On the way, they would experience a helpless pause to cross the creek, and then charge uphill against entrenched, veteran Confederate infantry with ample artillery support. If that wasn't daunting enough, a steep, fifteen-foot-tall embankment immediately preceded the first line of Rebel works. And anyone taking even a casual glance to the right realized that the attack was to be made by King's division alone. Baird's neighboring division was hunkered down, apparently with no orders to advance. Furthermore, half of Edie's regulars, the 16th and 19th regiments, were to remain behind to hold the line. With no support on the right, Edie's attack force would be subject to enfilade fire from the Confederates manning the line in that direction. "We well knew what was to come," Downey groaned. "Our boys dreaded it worse than any duty that had ever been assigned them." King's other brigade, under William P. Carlin, provided the only other troops involved: just two additional regiments. Edie's men faced terrible odds, and they knew it.[34]

The moment came, and the regulars rushed forward, under fire straightaway—one captain took a bullet through the mouth before he even exited the trench. But the volunteers of the 11th Michigan stayed put. These same men had fought valiantly on the bloodstained fields at Stones River, and had thrice charged bayonets and scattered the Confederates at Chickamauga. They had scaled the 500-foot heights of Missionary Ridge and driven Bragg's defenders headlong from the crest. But now, after weeks without a field officer to command the regiment, and just weeks shy of returning home to safety and loved ones, they refused to budge one inch under orders. Their predicament was one shared by many units with enlistment terms on the verge of expiration. "They had now come to feel that they would be permitted to return home," explained Downey, "and now ... to be thrown against the enemy's fortified lines seemed too cruel. Many of them said they would not go and a mutiny seemed imminent." The two regular regiments launched across the naked field under a barrage unleashed from multiples of their own number in Confederates, leaving a trail of bodies behind in what was rapidly evolving into a quest for martyrdom. Mudge, lame from his old wound and still too sick for duty, drew his sword, stood atop the breastworks in clear view of the Rebels, and harangued his disgruntled soldiers. "Men, you have always done well," he began. "For almost three years you have stood nobly at your posts and have performed every duty that has been required of you. Yonder are the Rebels. You are again called on to meet them in battle. The regulars on your left have already gone and there they are, nobly struggling with the foe. Do you see that gap to their right? Do as well as they are doing; go as far as they have gone—aye, and go farther. Let not a man shirk from duty." With uncanny timing, General King came riding down the line shouting, "Move right forward, every man!" to which Mudge added, "11th Michigan—forward—double time—guide center—march!" For the last time ever, the 11th Michigan Volunteer Infantry charged the Confederates. "It was like an electric thrill," exclaimed Downey, "with one impulse every man leaped the works." Mudge thus triggered a charge he was too incapacitated to join in himself.[35]

The sprint across the field did nothing to lessen adrenaline levels. The regulars had taken cover in the creek in an attempt to reform their ranks before striking the Rebel line, and although they were still drawing plenty of fire, the Confederates promptly took note of the second (and even more laughably small) wave of Federal soldiers inbound. The 11th Michigan went into the fight with less than 300 men present for duty. Shells, soon accompanied with volleys of musketry from both Stovall's troops and Holtzclaw's neighboring brigade, menaced the small Wolverine regiment as it traversed the field alone. The 11th reached Utoy Creek and finally assumed its role as the diminutive assault's right flank. Edie charged the brigade forward up the

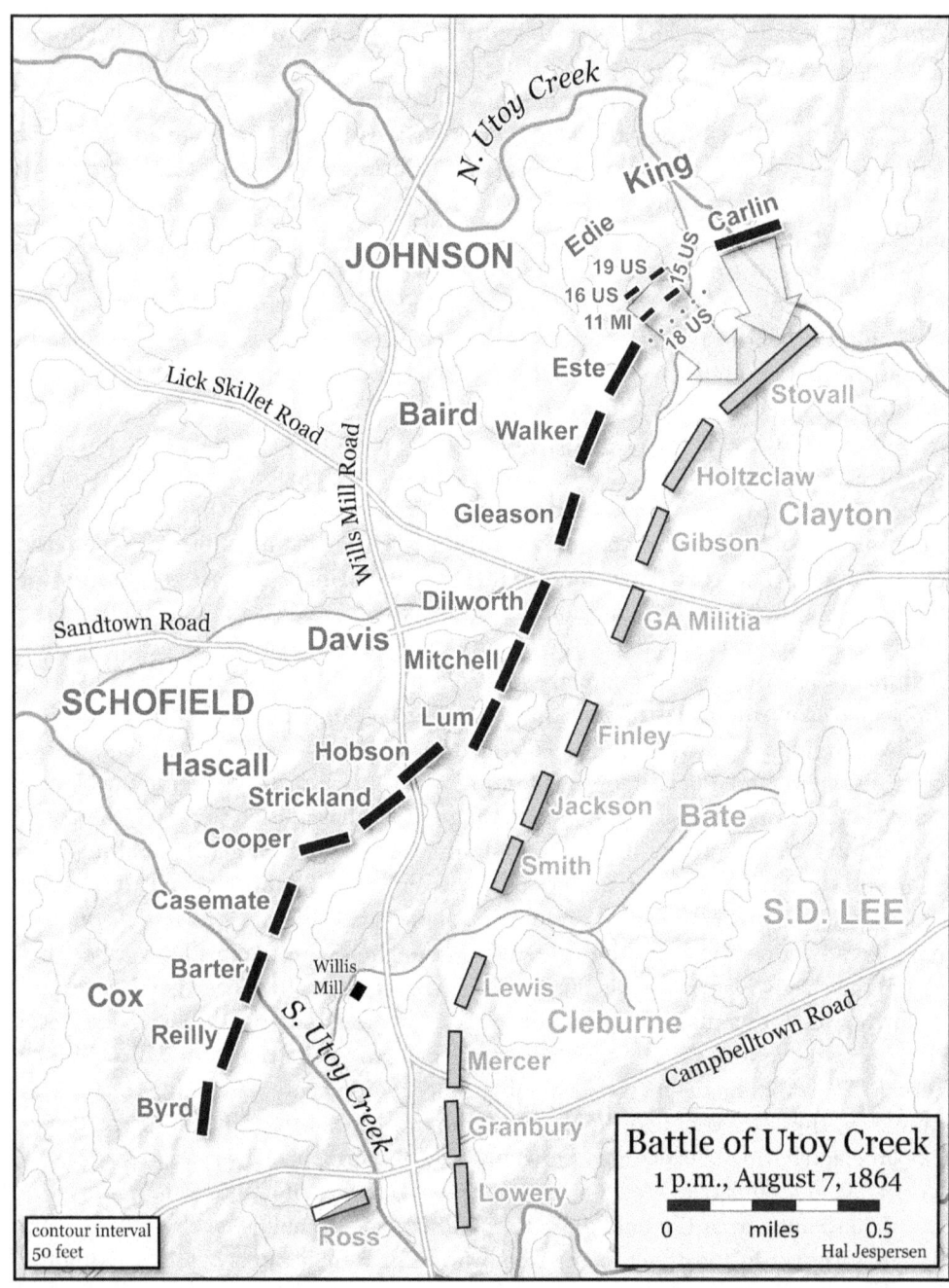

slope and toward the woods, where the Rebels of Stovall's brigade awaited. More and more fallen Union troops dotted the hill, but the attackers had their blood up now and would not be stopped. The 11th Michigan and its brigade mates clambered up the steep final rise with little semblance of unit order remaining, and spilled into the Rebel trench, overrunning hundreds of Confederates. Hicks was startled to realize at that moment that the Michigan regiment was his to command: evidently Keegan was unimpressed with Lieutenant Colonel Mudge's speech, and never left the breastworks. Hicks regrouped his men and rushed the 11th through the captured works by its right flank to meet a Rebel column attempting to gain a foothold in the trench. The Wolverines won the race and repulsed the enemy. The Confederate prisoners were sent to the rear, and Edie then charged the brigade against the second, main Confederate line: another 150 yards under fire. The blue wave's high water mark lapped within fifty feet of the second Rebel trench, with a few Federals advancing so far as to encounter the abatis. But the Confederate artillery responded with a hailstorm of grape and canister, and retreat proved imperative. The Federals fell back on the first entrenchment and frantically set about strengthening their position, which had been designed to face the opposite direction.[36]

The regulars' casualties were severe: 149 total, with the 15th U.S. Infantry taking the brunt of the butcher's bill, a loss of 15 killed, 100 wounded, and 8 missing. The 11th Michigan, with its late start across the field, counted only 30 casualties in comparison, yet the Wolverines matched the 15th Regulars in death toll, with 15 fatalities. The cause of this abnormally high ratio of dead to wounded Michiganders might be explained by Hicks's account of the fighting: dangerously wounded private William Weinberg had warned Hicks of a Rebel sharpshooter picking off Michiganders who occupied a particular section of the works. Hicks directed Weinberg to the field hospital, where he soon expired.[37]

The Southerners arose in their trench, and the men of the 11th steeled themselves as they heard the Confederate officers order a bayonet charge. But the Rebel ranks would not budge, and in their case, no officer succeeded in prying them forward. Both sides were witnessing an increasing frequency of troops choosing to face the wrath of their own officers—and possible mutiny charges—over the futility of charging strong field works.[38]

Downey described the deplorable toll incurred in the assault:

> Turn for a moment and view the field over which those men have passed. I had an opportunity of seeing just what it was for immediately after the charge I went to the rear to bring up ammunition for the company, and afterward, in carrying off the wounded, crossed the field many times. It was a sad, sad sight. Among the dead and wounded were many familiar faces. Men who a few moments before were strong and vigorous are now laid low in death, or, in the last agonies, they grasp the ground in convulsive energy. Here are men just in the prime of life, who had left pleasant homes and loving friends for their country's sake. For nearly three years they had served and they had been looking eagerly forward to their return home in a few days; but, alas! they are cut down at the last and all their hopes blighted. Here, too, are boys, just starting out in life, with bright anticipations of the future before them, whose eyes, but a few moments before, sparkled with health and humor, now lying on the field of battle wounded, perhaps mortally. The lustre of the eye is dimmed, an ashy paleness is cast over the features, the blood issues from an ugly wound. As he lies there looking upward toward the blue sky, thoughts of those loved ones so far away crowd themselves upon his mind, and when his comrades come to bear him away, he has some tender message to send to them.[39]

The Federal failure to exploit General King's lodgment in the Rebel line meant that the blood of good men had been spilled in vain. "It is too bad," scrawled an indignant James Martin three days later, "to make men charge when we havent only so few days to stay. We carried their rifle pits and held them and captured over four hundred prisoners.... We should be relieved to day from the front if we had justice done us but there is no prospect as I can see. I am sick and tired of fighting, there is artillery on both sides of us and musketry firing in our front and I am tired, tired of it."[40]

The brigade held its ground through the nineteenth, then shifted farther right down the Federal line for two consecutive days. The 11th Michigan teetered on the edge of mutiny again after August 24—the three year muster-in anniversary for most of the regiment's companies—passed by with no orders to relieve the unit from front-line duty. Muster out, in fact, was due when the *last* of the companies to join had served out their terms—September 10, in the case of the 11th Michigan. Some of the men knew this, some did not. Mudge in fact had followed procedure by filing an initial request on August 3 to schedule the unit's relief from the front accordingly, but this was disapproved owing to the Army of the Cumberland's difficulty in verifying the companies' muster dates. On August 26 at 8:00 p.m., the brigade pulled out of its breastworks and shifted right again. Initially, the 11th Michigan was ordered to furnish a skirmish line to secure the trench overnight, and unit morale at this time may be gauged by the fact that no less prominent a figure than Captain Hicks had determined to "refuse to go on that detail, as our term of service was up, and it meant sure capture of the skirmish line, and about that time no one was anxious to visit the South as a Prisoner of War." But as it turned out, Hicks's hand was not forced. The 15th Regulars were shouldered with that duty instead. Perhaps Edie foresaw, and elected to avoid, any further insubordination. The march that took place that night was a precursor to the decisive Battle of Jonesborough, which would trigger the fall of Atlanta and guarantee President Lincoln's reelection. But the 11th Michigan would not be there to see it. At last, on August 27, the Michiganders received orders to pull back to Chattanooga.[41]

Their ordeal wasn't quite over yet, though. At Chattanooga, the 11th was pressed into service one last time—but in contrast, on this occasion, not one man felt compelled to raise his voice in protest. Confederate cavalryman Joseph Wheeler was leading a raid behind the Federal lines, imperiling, among other things, the very railway that was needed to whisk the Michiganders home to their loved ones. With the exception of the 11th's company commanders, who were left behind to fill out the unit's final paperwork, the regiment was dispatched as part of a three-brigade force intended to capture or drive Wheeler off. The 11th's makeshift brigade, commanded by Colonel Abel D. Streight, included the 51st Indiana, the 2nd Ohio, and the 14th U.S. Colored Infantry—this was the one and only time the 11th Michigan served with black troops.[42]

The expedition left Chattanooga via rail at 7:30 a.m. on September 1 and reached Murfreesboro at 10:30 p.m., passing through Bridgeport and Stevenson en route. The next day they marched to La Vergne, where the pickets of the 18th Ohio (the Michiganders' old brigade mates) briefly made contact with the enemy before the Rebels withdrew. The Federals backtracked toward Murfreesboro and blocked an attempt by the Confederates to cross Stewart Creek the next morning. On September 4 the Union troops hitched a rail ride into Murfreesboro, and executed a brief, abortive northbound pursuit of the enemy. The railroad carried the expedition to Tullahoma the next day, stopping on the way to repair 300 feet of sabotaged track near Christiana. From Tullahoma the journey zigzagged through Huntsville, Alabama, to Pulaski, Tennessee, and then back into Alabama with stops at Athens and Rogersville. The Federals finally caught up with the Confederates, and drove their skirmishers across a creek on September 9. Wheeler withdrew across the Tennessee River soon after, aborting his venture with little to show for it. The 11th Michigan thus ended its active service much as it had inaugurated it versus John Hunt Morgan, chasing cavalry around on foot. Their expedition departed for Chattanooga late on the morning of September 12 and arrived late that night. With Wheeler driven off, the way home to the Great Lakes State was free and clear.[43]

The regiment finally entrained for home on the nineteenth (spilling out onto to the tops of the cars, for lack of space) and rolled down the tracks to Nashville. Two days later a train carried them to Louisville, where they arrived about sunset. They visited with their old colonel, William J. May, on the twenty-second, and then crossed the ferry to Jeffersonville and hopped on the cars again. They stopped briefly at Indianapolis around sunset the next day, moving out again so soon that the men had no opportunity to fill their canteens. Mudge dispatched his quartermaster ahead to Sidney, Ohio, to arrange for the regiment to receive supplies upon arrival and verify the train schedule for the next ride.[44]

After sunrise on the twenty-fourth, the troops began to notice posters alongside the tracks announcing a political rally at Sidney that day. Speeches were to be delivered by Democratic vice presiden-

Abel D. Streight commanded the 11th Michigan's final expedition: a futile chase of Joseph Wheeler's Confederate cavalry that mirrored the Michiganders' first active military assignment—the hapless pursuit of John Hunt Morgan in 1862 (Library of Congress).

tial candidate George H. Pendleton, and by an old acquaintance of the 11th Michigan—a politician who many vilified as the nation's greatest traitor, Copperhead Clement Vallandigham. Like most Federal soldiers, the Wolverines were overwhelmingly Lincoln supporters, and they still felt bitter that they had been commanded to safely transport Vallandigham through the Union lines at Murfreesboro sixteen months prior. The peace advocate had recently snuck back into the country via Canada, and Lincoln chose to look the other way to avoid stirring up controversy. The 11th Michigan's quartermaster met up with the regiment at a stop short of Sidney and broke the news to Mudge that the next train was not scheduled to depart Sidney until 4:00 p.m. The lieutenant colonel fretted that he would need to keep his men under control for hours in the presence of their detested enemy. "The 11th Michigan," he commented, "above all others should not have been at Sidney.... After crossing the Ohio at Louisville, the boys drew a long breath and felt free from military restraint, and about all the control over the men by the officers came from love and respect and very little from authority."[45]

The regiment disembarked at the depot in Sidney later that morning, and formed ranks along one side of the street with their bayonets fixed, preparing to stack arms. Just then, Vallandigham's train pulled in from Cincinnati. A throng of his devotees began firing off salutes with a small brass cannon, and some of the soldiers, considering these home front adversaries far worse than Rebels, broke formation and clamored for permission to "charge that battery." Mudge, not enticed at the thought of presiding over an act of mob violence, vaguely promised the soldiers that he would take action if they would only return to the ranks. Then a carriage conveying Vallandigham and Pendleton came rolling down the street toward them.[46] Upon the vehicle's approach, Mudge recorded,

> the men commenced snapping caps and firing squibs and blank cartridges.
> I knew the feeling of the men and I knew that if I could not stop that firing there would be some bullets put in the guns. In other words I did not think that carriage could pass the line and the occupants survive.... When the carriage reached the right of the regiment the blank cartridge firing and rattling of ramrods increased. I must do something to stop that.... I took off my hat and said: "Now boys three cheers for Lincoln. Now groans for Vallandigham...." While they were cheering and groaning, they were not using their ramrods.... The carriage had reached near the point where I was standing in the center of the street and [was] coming at a full gallop.[47]

He successfully gestured for the driver to turn off onto another street, but did not notice—or feigned ignorance—as a number of his subordinates chased their prey to a hotel. Vallandigham fled through the building and evaded the disappointed soldiers, who searched (or according to one account, ransacked) the hotel looking for him.[48]

Mudge began to march his regiment for the other depot, where they would catch their next ride, but that route took the soldiers right past Vallandigham's supporters and their still-booming cannon. Any remaining discipline disintegrated as the 11th Michigan scattered the civilians and captured their brass piece with two stands of colors. The lieutenant colonel reformed the unit and cleverly announced that he neither approved nor disapproved of this act, but reminded the men that mob-like actions against such prominent Democrats might jeopardize Lincoln's reelection. In order to steer his troops away from any further mischief, Mudge determined to keep them occupied by detailing patrols of the city until the next train arrived. Local Unionist women showed up with perfect timing, pleasantly distracting the men with a sumptuous feast. The ladies, remembered a grateful Mudge, "looked at us sweet, and seemed to look right at us and did not see our torn and soiled uniforms, and went up to our old flag, which was in shreds and bullet-riddled and petted it and stroked it, and I saw some of our weaker men, men who were not made of sterner stuff, turned away and talked of trivial matters and slyly wiped their eyes."[49]

A committee of locals called on Mudge, insisting that Pendleton and Vallandigham be allowed to deliver their speeches. He took offense at their boldness but simply replied, "The quicker you get me and my men out of town the better perhaps, for all concerned." Suddenly a train became available, and the regiment departed Sidney, Ohio, at about 1:00 p.m. The Wolverines fired a salute from their captured artillery, mounted on a freight car, as the train pulled away from the station. Vallandigham did ultimately give his speech (which consisted of a string of grossly exaggerated claims, asserting the failure of the Union war effort), but the Michiganders left Sidney in satisfaction, believing they had broken up the political rally for good.[50]

The *Three Rivers Reporter* responded by snickering that Vallandigham had recently asserted in Chicago that "all the soldiers were in favor of his peace platform." The artillery piece became a prized possession of the unit's veterans, destined to be discharged every July 4, and at the regiment's annual reunions, for many years to come. Sometime after the war, the cannon's rightful owner, Phillip Smith, journeyed to Michigan and initiated legal action to recover the piece. According to the *Shelby County* (Ohio) *Democrat*, the editor of which remained bitter about the gun theft almost thirty years later, Smith "came near being mobbed by the Michiganders when the business was made known." Some of the ex-soldiers rowed the gun out on a lake and dumped it in the water (later arranging for its recovery) as Smith looked on, thus foiling his efforts and sending him packing for Ohio. The cannon finally met its fate at the 1891 regimental reunion, when some citizens of Colon, site of that year's gathering, "borrowed" the gun for a wedding and attempted to fire off an excessive load of gravel, causing the piece to burst. Its shattered remnants were snatched up as relics of the war, and one larger fragment was placed on display in a store window.[51]

Back to 1864: The regiment proceeded by rail to Toledo, where the troops switched cars and finally turned homebound for Michigan. Many of the men had not seen their home state since the regiment departed for the South almost three years before. The 11th Michigan finally arrived in Sturgis, Michigan, around sunrise on September 25. The soldiers marched straight to the home of Colonel Stoughton, who had recovered nicely from his amputation, and paid him a social call. The colonel, said Mudge, "hobbled out on his one leg and crutches, and the cannon was in due form turned over to him as the last capture of his regiment." While awaiting formal muster out, members of the unit remained publicly active. On September 26, a Republican rally took place at White Pigeon, drawing a crowd of 2,000 people. Stoughton was among the speakers. It was an overwhelmingly patriotic crowd, but the *Reporter* noted that "two or three attempts were made by drunken copperhead peace sneaks to interrupt the meeting and raise a cheer for little Mac [George B. McClellan, who was running against Lincoln for president]. A delegation of the Michigan 11th being present, Cops [Copperheads] were ordered to dry up or leave; and considering discretion the better part of valor, and, in imitation of the chief of Mackerels [McClellan] in his famous skedaddle before Richmond, wisely took to their heels, which probably had never served them so well before." The paper went on to point out that the soldiers, after all they had been through during the past three years, were unlikely to stand idle among people criticizing the cause for which they had sacrificed so much—something they had already proven at Sidney. But the loyal citizens more than made up for the vocal minority, holding a grand reception dinner the next day to celebrate the return of their local heroes.[52]

The 11th Michigan Volunteer Infantry had seen a total enrollment of 1,323 men, 279 of whom would never return home. Another 265 had been discharged for disability. Those who reenlisted, and those who enlisted after the regiment's initial organization—152 men in all—stayed behind in Chattanooga. Other unfortunate souls were in no condition to make the trip home with the regiment. Of the 1,004 men who departed Michigan in December 1861 with the unit, only 340 were present to muster out together on October 11.[53]

Three long years had passed since enlistment. It was a time for goodbyes, and a time for reflection. Years later, speaking at a regimental reunion, James King shared his impressions of the war.

> The marches by day and by night; the supperless bivouacs on beds of snow and ice; the lonely picket duty, watching the enemy while comrades slept; swamps hitherto

Left: One of the regiment's silk national flags, with battle honors (courtesy and copyright, Michigan Capitol Committee and photographer Peter Glendinning). *Right:* Silk national flag with the regiment's designation (courtesy and copyright, Michigan Capitol Committee and photographer Peter Glendinning).

unknown to the tread of hoof, "corduroyed" at midnight by the light of blazing forests, and passed by an army with cannon; days of service on the deadly skirmish line, where comrade after comrade fell a prey to the bullet of the lurking enemy; the mingling clash of mighty armies, where cannon belched forth grape and canister, and musket balls numbered their victims by thousands; where masses of human beings swayed to and fro like waves of ocean, until the shout of victory went up from the victors, and the dying and wounded—the blue and the gray—lay heaped upon the field of strife. These were scenes which bound true men together as with hands of steel, and the fruit of that cowardly midnight shot hurled at Fort Sumter by traitor hands.[54]

Epilogue

Another 11th Michigan Infantry would be raised before the Civil War ended, but it was the 11th in name only. That unit, referred to as the reorganized 11th Michigan, was raised with help from Colonel Stoughton and was led by Patrick Keegan. Keegan's regiment was destined only to reside in relative peace in Tennessee for a few months. The losses it suffered were due to disease rather than Confederates.

The original 11th Michigan established a battle record worthy of recognition. Indeed, its exploits rank it among the Army of the Cumberland's finest units. At Stones River, the Wolverines, having hardly witnessed a rifle being fired in anger beforehand, were subject to a converging barrage of artillery and musketry of rare intensity. Having never before seen the elephant, they found themselves at the very epicenter of one of the war's deadliest battles. Yet they held their ground and poured one volley after another into the Rebels until ordered to withdraw. Many green regiments—and many veteran units—could not say the same at nightfall on New Year's Eve, 1862. After the war, when Colonel Stoughton enumerated the 11th's four greatest exploits, two of them were from the first day at Stones River: the rush to defend Schultz's battery, and the counterattack into the cedars to blunt the subsequent Confederate pursuit.[1] It was common practice in after-action reports for officers to shower self-serving praise on the units under their own command, but in the case of the fight in the cedars, the 11th garnered glowing recognition from Major General Lovell Rousseau as well.

But the 11th's finest hour surely came at Chickamauga. In such a great and terrible battle, there are always pivotal moments, but the 11th Michigan encountered two such situations in a matter of hours, and twice rose above and beyond what could possibly have been expected from the number of men remaining in its dwindling ranks. It was the 11th that captured the only Confederate general taken in that battle, Daniel W. Adams, and it was the 11th's colonel who took the initiative in concealing Stanley's entire brigade for that ambush. With the survival of Thomas's flanked corps possibly hanging in the balance, it was one of those intriguing instances in the war when the actions of one astute regimental commander notably impacted the course of a major engagement. Just hours later, the 11th Michigan engaged three times its own number on Horseshoe Ridge, in one of the war's most desperate, last-ditch defenses. Their Confederate counterparts fought viciously, triggering hand-to-hand combat, and gained part of the Michiganders' breastworks for a time. But a careful approximation of the casualties taken and received at this point on the battlefield puts the Michiganders' losses on Horseshoe in the neighborhood of just twenty-five to thirty men. In the process of inflicting those few casualties, Gracie's troops of the 2nd Alabama Battalion and the 43rd Alabama Infantry suffered an astoundingly disproportionate loss of approximately 150 soldiers—nearly equaling the entire number of Wolverines opposing them.

The regiment's role at Missionary Ridge is almost completely lost in modern treatments of that battle, which have invariably omitted key primary sources not only from the 11th Michigan, but overwhelmingly from its adversaries as well. Firsthand accounts from several of the Wolverines, combined with the official reports of the Confederates opposing them, prove that the rout of Alexander P. Stewart's Rebel division was triggered by leading elements of the Michigan regiment, along with its Illinoisan and Ohioan counterparts—men who pried open a gap mistakenly created between the Rebel brigades of Otho P. Strahl and Randall L. Gibson.

By the time of the Atlanta Campaign, the opposing armies had virtually perfected the art of constructing field works. Headlong assaults against entrenched troops consistently ended in a bloodbath, and rarely seized the objective. Yet the Wolverines were twice called upon to charge Rebel works, at Ruff's Station and Utoy Creek, and on both occasions overran the Confederate defenses after charging across open field under concentrated fire. Ironically, the fact that this accomplishment was possible even at Utoy Creek, where the regiment teetered on the verge of open mutiny, might be said to speak more of the unit's potency in battle than some of its ostensibly braver actions earlier in the war.

Outside of combat, the unit's record was less inspiring. Company C stole whiskey from citizens in both the North and South, and harassed slaves and other innocents after deploying to Kentucky. The regiment looted the town of Gallatin in August 1862, and threatened Clement Vallandigham and George H. Pendleton in Sidney, Ohio—and "captured" their cannon—in an incident that could easily have escalated into a national scandal. No regret was publicly expressed over any of these escapades. Indeed, a strong sense of pride accompanies the surviving comments regarding the treatment of Vallandigham, while the balance of the aforementioned incidents were recorded with a tone of indifference toward the victims. In fairness, the Michiganders' attitudes toward enemy civilians and Copperheads were not at all out of the ordinary. Nonetheless, it cannot be said that the 11th Michigan Infantry was a model of military discipline.

Of course, the thousand men who survived service in the 11th regiment did not disappear from the face of the Earth when the unit mustered out. The United States looked to the same generation that fought the war to provide the leadership the country needed as its economy, population, and territory expanded so dramatically in the ensuing decades. Many of the Michigan soldiers made names for themselves in the postwar years.

Unsurprisingly, above all others, it was Colonel Stoughton who had the most profound impact on his home state after the war. The loss of a leg did nothing to slow him down. He resumed his legal practice, was brevetted major general for his Civil War heroics, served as a delegate to Michigan's 1867 constitutional convention, and secured election to the U.S. House of Representatives in 1868 and 1870. Stoughton passed away in 1888. Seven years later, his admiring wartime subordinates gathered at the opening of the Chickamauga and Chattanooga National Military Park to dedicate a towering statue of their colonel, sword in hand, gazing in the same direction Gracie's troops had scaled the slope, to their doom, thirty-two years before.[2]

Nathaniel Eldridge also resumed legal practice after the war. He was elected mayor of Adrian in 1870, and ran for Congress the same year. Failing in that, he secured election as sheriff of Lenawee County four years later.[3]

Sylvester B. Smith, whose military career was cut short by his jaw wound at Stones River, thrived in civilian life as well. He preceded Eldridge as sheriff of Lenawee County in 1864 and 1866, followed by election to county treasurer in 1870 and 1872. He then went into the hardware business, followed by banking, and served four years on the county Republican committee.[4]

Calvin C. Hood relocated to Emporia, Kansas, and engaged in the cattle trade with Senator Preston B. Plumb, spending fourteen years in the saddle among fellow cowboys. Their company, Plumb & Hood, became a powerhouse of western commerce, with involvement in a myriad of business interests including mines, banks, and real estate. Hood went on to become president of Emporia National Bank, a role he served in from 1880–1905. He ran, unsuccessfully, for governor in 1898. Hood was remembered as a dedicated family man whose immense wealth was readily shared with the less fortunate.[5]

Others left their marks on the world in different ways. Lewis W. Heath joined the staff of Governor Crosswell, became inspector general of Michigan's military, and served on the national Republican committee. Ephraim G. Hall took the helm of the *Cincinnati Gazette*. Several others returned south to run cotton plantations after the war, including William N. Elliott, William C. Iddings, James W. King, Melvin B. Mudge and Linus T. Squire.[6]

King and Squire raised cotton together in Thompson's Station, Tennessee, in 1866. They got along swimmingly with the locals—even receiving a social call from Confederate lieutenant general Richard S. Ewell, who visited one day from his expansive plantation at nearby Spring Hill. But King and Squire, like so many transplanted

William Lewis Stoughton was brevetted major general in 1865 in recognition of his wartime gallantry (Library of Congress).

The 11th Michigan's monument on Horseshoe Ridge, pictured here in the 1890s, is surmounted with a statue of William Lewis Stoughton. This depiction of the revered Stoughton has since suffered the severing of its forearms and sword (Belknap, *History of the Michigan Organizations at Chickamauga, Chattanooga, and Missionary Ridge*).

Yankees, suffered crop failure and earned no profit. King made another attempt at an Alabama plantation in 1867, only to experience the worst of the Reconstruction South and be driven off by the Ku Klux Klan. He returned to Michigan, landed a clerk job with the auditor general, and eventually built a career in journalism that culminated with his rise to chief editor of the *Lansing Republican*, one of the state's premier political newspapers. There, King asserted views on racial equality that were a century ahead of his time. Squire served in the Freedmen's Bureau in Tennessee for a time, then returned to Michigan and joined King at the auditor general's office. Squire and his wife later earned medical degrees and went off to Washington, where he served many years in the federal government's post office and pension departments.[7]

Perhaps the longest lived friendship was that of Downey and Hicks, who evidently hit it off from the moment they met. Hicks vividly recalled the scene more than forty years later. Downey, he related, upon arriving to join the regiment in Georgia, had

> asked which one of the officers was Captain Hicks? The man pointed me out to him, when John had sized me up, his face took on a disappointed look, for he had pictured to himself, a good looking, tall, robust, fully developed man, one with the stern commanding look of a War God, whose every motion and aspect was of one dying for a fight, one who at least ought to be able to support a mustache. The contrast was too much for John, and he says what? that young, smooth faced, green looking boy Captain Hicks!...
>
> I got even with John for his poor opinion of my military appearance, by detailing him to the Regimental Pioneer Corps, arming him with an ax and spade. John made a good soldier, one who was always ready for duty, and never dodged danger, he could cut more logs, and make the dirt fly faster, than any man in the corps, he was discharged at the end of the war with the rank of high Private in the rear rank.
>
> I have always patted myself on the back, for the brilliant success John has made in mathematical lines, for I took great pains in coaching him on applied mathematics, explaining the difference in the velocity of a minne ball, and six pound solid shot, the horse power with which he would have to wield the ax, when cutting logs for a breast work to defend his Captain.[8]

Indeed, Downey proved quite the scholar, obtaining a master's degree from Hillsdale College, which opened the door to a professorship of mathematics at Pennsylvania State College (today's Penn State University). He later moved on to University of Minnesota, where he became professor of mathematics and astronomy, and eventually rose to dean. He authored books including *Higher Algebra*, published in 1900, *Elements of Differentiation* in 1902, and *The New Revelation through the Spectroscope and the Telescope* in 1914. Hicks also moved to Minneapolis, and his younger daughter was counted among Downey's students. Downey retired from the university in 1914, only to pack his bags for China two years later. He landed professorships in mathematics at University of Nanking in 1916 and then at Peking University in 1919, at the age of seventy-three.[9]

For most of the regiment, it was the annual reunions that kept everyone in touch. These inaugurated shortly after the war, and were destined to run continuously, every August 24, for more than sixty years. They were festive occasions, held in a different town each year and drawing attendance figures that easily reached into the thousands, counting family, friends, and onlookers. Local organizations would feed the veterans, typically sparing no expense, and a handful of ex-soldiers would address the crowd to discuss and relive the tumult of the early 1860s—more often than not with a healthy dose of humor thrown in. Naturally, as the years passed, reunion turnouts gradually diminished. Some, like Downey and Hicks, moved out of state, and others could not come due to the kinds of infirmities that increase with age. Inevitably—particularly toward the end of the century—more and more invitation cards came back with sad tidings of soldiers who had answered the final roll call. But the 11th Michigan's gatherings continued going strong through the 1900s and 1910s, even as the number of survivors diminished. Even throughout the 1920s there remained enough of Stoughton's men alive and well to congregate and reminisce about old times every August 24. The end finally came in the early 1930s. With only a few dozen veterans left alive, and but a small fraction of them capable of even a short

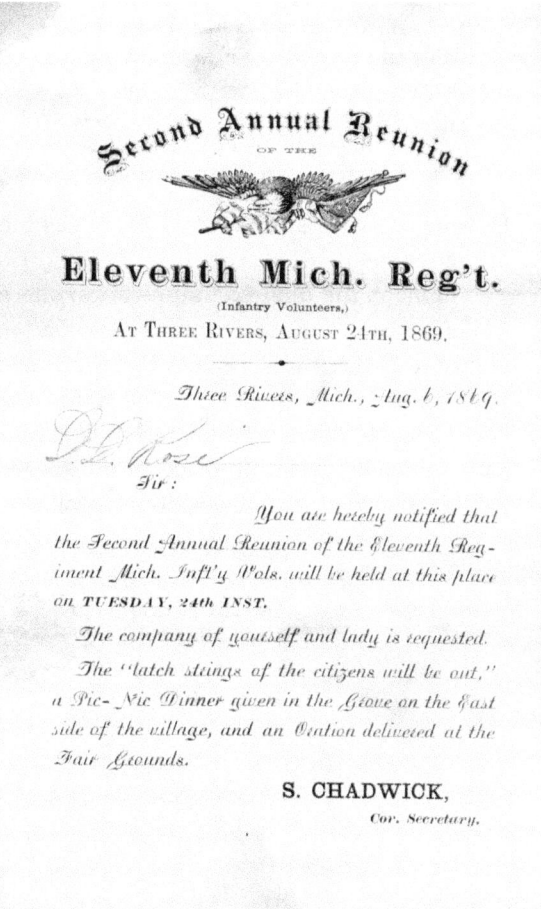

Left: A medal prepared in honor of the 1911 regimental reunion, graced with an image of William Stoughton (photograph by the author). *Right:* Daniel Rose's second reunion invitation. The regiment's festive annual reunions inaugurated shortly after the war and carried on until the early 1930s, when the infirmities of the few surviving soldiers finally rendered the gatherings impractical (courtesy Western Michigan University Archives and Regional History Collections).

journey, the 1932 reunion was cancelled for lack of turnout.[10] John Downey, having retired to California, replied to his invitation on August 17 of that year, unaware of the cancellation:

> I wish to send ... greetings to my comrades of the 11th Michigan Infantry and express my regret that I am not to be with you at this reunion. While war is what our revered General Sherman characterized it, we as participants in the Civil War, had many interesting experiences together and most pleasing associations. I often recall these and I count that period one of the most important in my life.... It is always a joy to meet one of my comrades these days. This leads me to say that I saw dear Captain Hicks when in Minneapolis last autumn.... We indulged in many pleasant reminiscences and talked much of those with whom we had been associated in the 11th. A few weeks after my return to Pasadena, where I now live, I received from his elder daughter the sad news of the dear Captains death, which occurred Dec. 12, 1931. You all remember him, and, I am sure, honored him. His men all esteemed him highly and loved him for his many good qualities and pleasing personality. We few survivors of his company—there are only four or five of us now—will sadly miss the letter of greeting he was accustomed to send to each of us at Christmastime.
>
> I am with you in my heart, comrades, and wishing for you a very enjoyable reunion and for each of you much happiness through life.[11]

Downey would pass away in 1939 at age ninety-three, one of the last living veterans of the regiment.

Perhaps the final communication shared among the last remnant of the 11th Michigan was the 1933 reunion's cancellation notice, which announced the ultimate failure to gather the survivors together one last time. The flip side of the card was graced with a poetry excerpt. The stanza was carefully selected by the wise old veterans, men who had volunteered to fight and suffer for their ideals when they could have remained home in peace, comfort, and security. The words they chose offer parting advice for the generations to follow.

> Mourn not the dead
> But rather mourn the apathetic throng,
> The cowed and the meek,
> Who see the world's great anguish and its wrong
> And dare not speak
> —Ralph Chaplin[12]

APPENDIX A

A POW Poem

At least eighty-two soldiers from the 11th Michigan suffered capture at some point during the war, mostly at Stones River and Chickamauga. Most of the POWs lived to tell the tale, with about 80 percent of the imprisoned Wolverines surviving their ordeal. Henry Damon's remarkable escape from Andersonville, retold in Chapter 8, is the most striking example of a happy ending. But approximately 20 percent of those who surrendered lost their lives. The prison at Andersonville claimed the most victims by far—at least ten of the 11th Michigan's soldiers were destined for interment there.[1]

Among the 11th's POWs was William W. Wilson of Monroe County, who enlisted as a private in Company I at the age of 19 on August 24, 1861. Wilson, like Damon, was captured at Chickamauga on September 20, 1863. Also like Damon, he was first taken to the Confederate prison at Danville, Virginia, and was later transferred to Andersonville in Georgia. The sole artifact of his imprisonment is a poem he penned in Danville on January 31, 1864:

> I wish that Stanton, Edwin M., and Gen. Halleck too,
> Were in this place that they might see how prisoners live and do;
> That they might feel the woes of want, and live on prison fare,
> That they might eat of prison bread and breathe the prison air;
> That they might lay upon a prison floor, in winter-time so cold,
> Without a blanket, bed or fire, their garments thin and old;
> No converse with the world outside, or word from friends at home,
> By pale disease and scanty fare reduced to skin and bone;
> No hopeful ray of "Liberty," no gleam of "Freedom's" light,
> To penetrate their prison gloom or cheer the dismal night.
> Have we no friends in "northern homes," who pity our sad lot?
> Or are all kindly feelings gone, and mercy's claims forgot?
> Must we within these prison walls remain from day to day,
> Until by death's relentless hand we're swept from earth away?
> Where are our many brethren, are they all dead and gone?
> Are we, of all a numerous race, left on this earth alone?[2]

Wilson passed away at Andersonville on June 17, 1864.

APPENDIX B

The 11th Michigan by the Numbers

The statistical data in this section is drawn primarily from the unit roster presented in Appendix C. That data is imperfect—containing both omissions and errors—owing to the Union army's lax standards for recordkeeping. The large sample size, however, facilitates an informative snapshot of the regiment's demographics.

For the purpose of this study, the term "officer" is used to refer only to men who entered service as commissioned officers—a necessary concession to the limited granularity of the data. Enlisted men and noncommissioned officers are labeled as rank and file for statistical purposes, including those who eventually obtained promotion to a commissioned rank. All ages are given as of the subject's last birthday at the time of their entry into service. The "killed" category includes those mortally wounded, and non-fatal wound statistics are omitted due to frequent failures to record the identities of the soldiers involved. "Reserve Corps" is used to denote transfer to the Invalid Corps, later known as the Veteran Reserve Corps.

Most of the categorized statistical breakdowns yield intuitive results, a comfort to the statistician. For example, young men were more likely to be counted as battle casualties—an apparent side effect of the recklessness of youth. Older men were more likely, under the rigors of campaign, to suffer from disease and disability. Officers, who enjoyed a cushier existence, were rather less likely to succumb to illness.

But anomalies are potentially more rewarding to study, as they may point to unexpected facts and hidden truths. Two demographics defied this researcher's expectations: soldiers in their thirties, and men who enlisted later in the war—in 1863 and 1864. In the casualty categories, the overall trend, as mentioned, was for younger men to be in graver danger in battle, and the older soldiers, at greater risk of health issues. The data consistently back these expectations, with the exception of battle deaths for soldiers in their thirties. Interestingly, the thirty-something soldier was at much greater risk of combat death than men in their twenties. And that was not the only surprise hiding among the numbers. One might well assume that men who enlisted later in the war were more likely to escape death or disability—after all, they spent less time in the service. The data fully support this expectation for 1861 versus 1862 recruits, yet the 1863 man proved far less likely to suffer disability, or to die from disease, than his 1864 peer. With only 38 recruits from 1863 identified in the roster, this may be more the illusion of a small sample size than anything else. But similarly, the 1864 enlistee, a commoner creature, was very nearly as likely to perish by bullet or germ during his brief army stint as a man who joined in 1862. This is quite stunning when one considers that the 1862 recruit endured the regiment's three great battles: Stones River, Chickamauga, and Missionary Ridge, and had far more opportunity to sicken. Perhaps trench warfare, as occurred during 1864's Atlanta Campaign, tended to claim inexperienced soldiers at an extraordinary rate. Or it could be that 1864 recruits, many of whom were induced to enlist by the carrot and stick approach of bounties and the draft—and who held a reputation as inferior specimens of the Northern population—tended to be less hardy.

Figure 2 exhibits a discrepancy in the recruits' ages that is hardly specific to the 11th Michigan among Civil War units. There are impressive spikes at ages eighteen and twenty-one. A non-musician recruit was supposed to be eighteen in order to enlist (though recruiters, as time passed, became ever more willing to shrug and accept enlistees who admitted to being younger). Age twenty-one was another milestone: the recruit no longer needed parental consent to join the army. The high frequency of eighteen and twenty-one-year-old enlistees serves as a striking indicator of the prevalence of soldiers lying about their ages at the time of enlistment.

COMMISSIONED OFFICER AGES

Oldest: William N. Elliot, 54
Youngest: Borden M. Hicks, 18
Mean: 32.4 (Union mean 29.5), standard deviation 8.4[1]

RANK AND FILE AGES

Oldest: Richard M. Hines, 55
Youngest: John Q.A. McFarlan, 13
Mean: 24.1 (Union mean 25.3; Michigan mean 25.0), standard deviation 6.7[2]

TABLE 1. DEATHS, BY INITIAL RANK

Initial Rank	# of Recruits	Died of Disease		Killed		Total Deaths	
		Abs.	Pct.	Abs.	Pct.	Abs.	Pct.
Commissioned officer	40	3	7.5%	1	2.5%	4	10%
Rank and file	1,238	177	14.3%	96	7.8%	273	22.1%
Totals	1,278	180	14.1%	97	7.6%	277	21.7%

TABLE 2. DEATH AND DISABILITY, BY YEAR OF ENTRY INTO SERVICE

Year of Entry	# of Recruits	Died of Disease		Disabled		Killed		Reserve Corps		Totals	
		Abs.	Pct.	Abs.	Pct.	Abs.	Pct.	Abs.	Pct.	Abs.	Pct.
1861	1,088	164	15.1%	231	21.2%	87	8.0%	28	2.6%	510	46.9%
1862	59	5	8.5%	8	13.6%	3	5.1%	6	10.2%	22	37.3%
1863	38	2	5.3%	1	2.6%	2	5.3%	0	0.0%	5	13.2%

Year of Entry	# of Recruits	Died of Disease		Disabled		Killed		Reserve Corps		Totals	
		Abs.	Pct.	Abs.	Pct.	Abs.	Pct.	Abs.	Pct.	Abs.	Pct.
1864	83	6	7.2%	4	4.8%	4	4.8%	0	0.0%	14	16.9%
1865	2	2	100.0%	0	0.0%	0	0.0%	0	0.0%	2	100.0%
Unknown	8	1	12.5%	1	12.5%	1	12.5%	0	0.0%	3	37.5%
Totals	1,278	180	14.1%	245	19.2%	97	7.6%	34	2.7%	556	43.5%

Table 3. Death and Disability, by Age Category

Age	# of Recruits	Died of Disease		Disabled		Killed		Reserve Corps		Totals	
		Abs.	Pct.	Abs.	Pct.	Abs.	Pct.	Abs.	Pct.	Abs.	Pct.
<21	418	61	14.6%	59	14.1%	43	10.3%	5	1.2%	168	40.2%
21–29	553	74	13.4%	100	18.1%	34	6.2%	15	2.7%	223	40.3%
30–39	137	20	14.6%	33	24.1%	12	8.8%	3	2.2%	68	49.6%
40+	70	16	22.9%	25	35.7%	3	4.3%	7	10%	51	72.9%
Unknown	100	9	9.0%	28	28.0%	5	5.0%	4	4.0%	46	46.0%
Totals	1,278	180	14.1%	245	19.2%	97	7.6%	34	2.7%	556	43.5%

Table 4. Recruits by Company and County, for Counties Providing 5 or More Men to the Company

Company	Recruits by County
A	St. Joseph, 108; Calhoun, 6
B	Branch, 80; Hillsdale, 28; Calhoun, 5
C	St. Joseph, 84; Branch, 9
D	St. Joseph, 58; Branch, 51
E	St. Joseph, 71; Cass, 25
F	Lenawee, 52; Hillsdale, 38
G	St. Joseph, 48; Hillsdale, 13; Kalamazoo, 11; Cass, 9; Lenawee, 8
H	Branch, 89
I	Monroe, 64; Wayne, 24; Washtenaw, 10
K	Lenawee, 54; Monroe, 27; Hillsdale 14; St. Joseph, 5

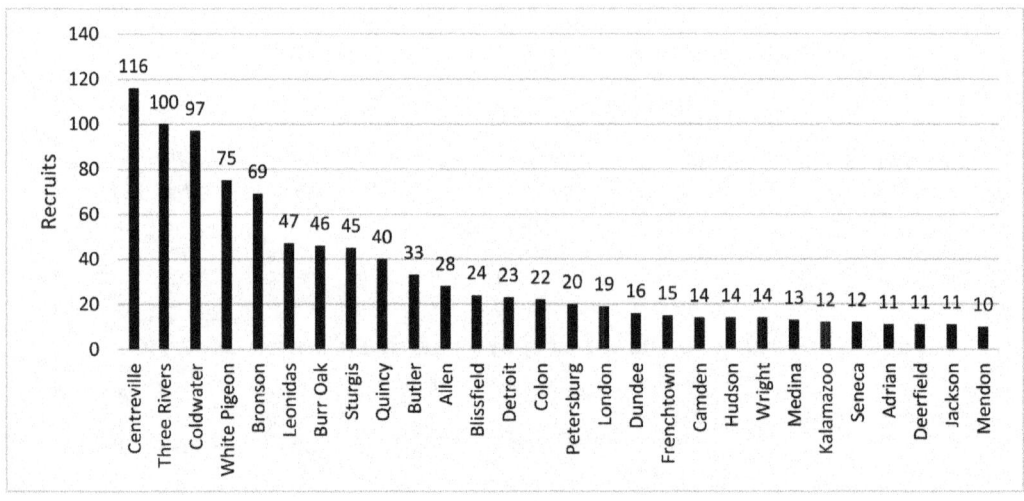

Figure 1. Recruits by town, for towns providing ten or more men to the regiment.

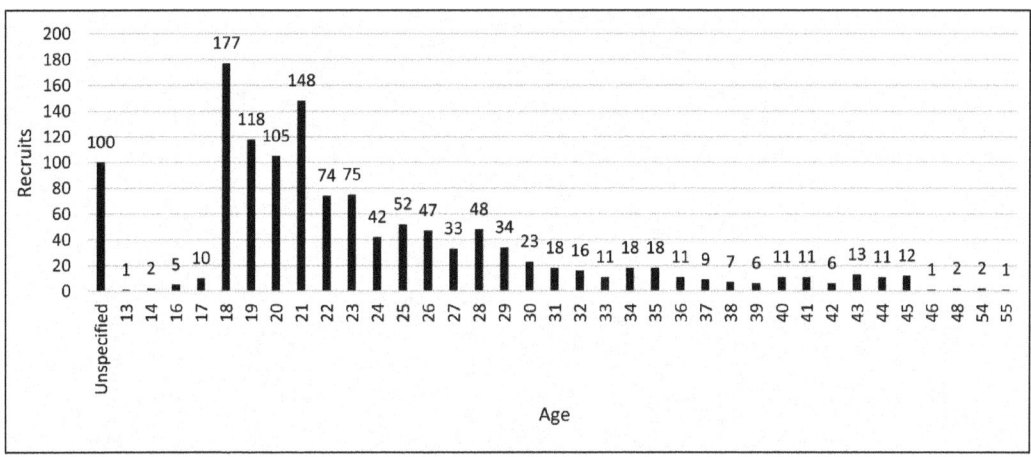

Figure 2. Number of recruits by age.

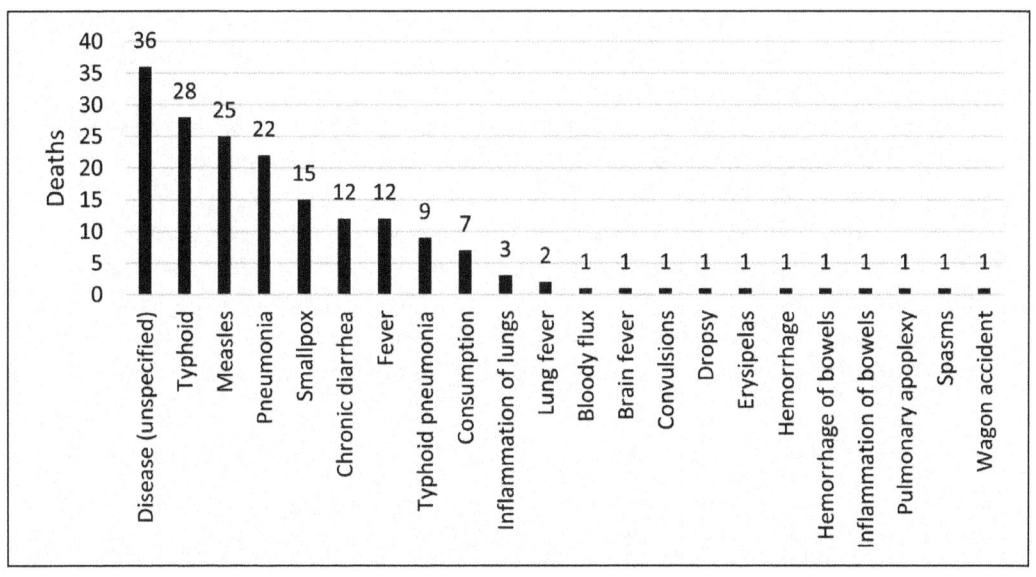

Figure 3. Causes of noncombat deaths.

APPENDIX C

Unit Roster

Record of Service of Michigan Volunteers in the Civil War, 1861–1865, volume 11, which was published circa 1905, served as the basis of this unit roster. As mentioned in Appendix B, the Union army had low standards for recordkeeping. *Record of Service* compounded this sin with frequent lapses in alphabetization. Corrections and additions have been applied to 476 of the following 1,278 entries, based on a mix of sources including regimental papers, compiled service records, and pension files. Undoubtedly, some errors and omissions remain.

Examples of data known to be missing include 100 soldiers with unlisted ages, 150 with no place of residence, 76 omitting their place of enlistment, and 36 with "no further record" specified.

All places mentioned are located in Michigan unless otherwise noted, with the exception of major cities (e.g., Chattanooga, Louisville, and Nashville). It should be noted that many initial muster dates were backdated, and this was true of the companies as well as the individual soldiers. All of the unit's companies were considered to have mustered in between August 24 and September 11, 1861.

* * *

Abram, George. Enlisted and mustered, company unassigned, Sept. 13, 1864, at Adrian, age 25. No further record.

Adams, Daniel B. St. Joseph County. Enlisted and mustered in Co. D, Aug. 24, 1861, at Colon, age 27. Discharged for disability Jan. 17, 1863, at Nashville.

Adams, Herman or Harman C. Branch County. Enlisted and mustered in Co. B, Aug. 24, 1861. Wounded at Stones River. Transferred to Invalid Corps Aug. 1, 1863.

Adams, Ira R. St. Joseph County. Enlisted and mustered in Co. D, Aug. 24, 1861, at Hillsdale, age 18. Discharged for disability Jan. 24, 1864, at Nashville.

Adams, Nathan. Branch County. Enlisted in Co. H, Aug. 24, 1861, at Coldwater, age 22. Mustered Aug. 28, 1861. Corporal Aug. 9, 1862.

Sergeant Feb. 22, 1864. Mustered out Sept. 30, 1864, at Sturgis.

Adee, William. Ridgeway. Enlisted and mustered in Co. I, Oct. 10, 1861, at Dundee, age 23. Died of disease May 22, 1862, at Nashville. Buried in national cemetery in Nashville.

Agan or Agen or Agern, William. Enlisted in Co. G at Detroit, age 22. Mustered Sept. 4, 1861. Mustered out Sept. 30, 1864, at Sturgis.

Akey, Henry. Enlisted in Co. A, Dec. 23, 1863, at Mendon, age 20. Mustered Jan. 4, 1864. Joined regiment Jan. 28, 1864, at Rossville, GA. Transferred Apr. 15, 1865, to Company A, reorganized 11th Michigan Infantry. Mustered out Sept. 16, 1865, at Nashville.

Alcock, John B. Enlisted in Co. E, Feb. 25, 1864,

at Fabius, age 44. Mustered Mar. 1, 1864. Joined regiment Mar. 15, 1864, at Rossville, GA. Died of disease July 4, 1864, at Nashville. Buried in national cemetery in Nashville.

Allard, Gabriel. Detroit. Enlisted and mustered in Co. I, Aug. 24, 1861, at Detroit, age 44. Died of pneumonia May 10, 1862, at Louisville. Buried in national cemetery in Cave Hill, KY.

Allen, Albert S. St. Joseph County. Enlisted and mustered in Co. C, Aug. 24, 1861, at Norwalk, age 19. Served in Pioneer Brigade. Reenlisted Jan. 30, 1864, at Chattanooga. Mustered Mar. 31, 1864. Transferred July 20, 1864, to 1st U.S. Engineers. Mustered out Sept. 26, 1865, at Nashville.

Allen, Harrison D. Enlisted, company unassigned, Sept. 20, 1864, at Jackson for 1 year, age 21. Mustered Sept. 26, 1864. No further record.

Allen, Jerome. Sylvania, OH. Enlisted and mustered in Co. C, Aug. 24, 1861, at Sylvania, OH, age 21. Died of typhoid fever Apr. 18, 1862, at Belmont, KY. Buried in national cemetery in Cave Hill, KY.

Alsdurf, Henry or John H. Branch County. Enlisted in Co. H as Corporal, Aug. 24, 1861, at Coldwater, age 19. Mustered Aug. 28, 1861. Sergeant Dec. 16, 1863. Mustered out Sept. 30, 1864, at Sturgis.

Alsdurf, Solomon. Branch County. Enlisted and mustered in Co. H, Sept. 1, 1861, at Coldwater, age 34. Corporal Nov. 26, 1862. Mustered out Sept. 30, 1864, at Sturgis.

Alverson, David. Lenawee County. Enlisted and mustered in Co. F, Sept. 11, 1861, at Hudson, age 20. Died of disease Sept. 25, 1864, at Chattanooga. Buried in national cemetery in Chattanooga.

Anderson, Robert. Wayne County. Enlisted and mustered in Co. I, Aug. 24, 1861, at Northville, age 45. Corporal Aug. 1862. Discharged for disability Sept. 13, 1862, at Louisville.

Andrews, Stephen M. Prairie Ronde. Enlisted in Co. G, Aug. 24, 1861, at Prairie Ronde, age 41. Mustered Sept. 4, 1861. Wounded Dec. 31, 1862, at Stones River. Died of wounds Jan. 20, 1863, at Murfreesboro, TN.

Angel, Oscar *see* Angle, Oscar.

Angle, John A. Wayne Twp. Enlisted and mustered in Co. C, Aug. 24, 1861, at Wayne Twp., age 29. Died of pneumonia Mar. 20, 1862, at Bardstown, KY. Buried in national cemetery in Lebanon, KY, Grave No. 304.

Angle, Oscar. Flowerfield. Enlisted in Co. G, Aug. 24, 1861, at White Pigeon, age 19. Mustered Sept. 4, 1861. Killed Dec. 31, 1862, at Stones River.

Annis, Joseph. Allegan County. Enlisted in Co. G at Pine Grove, age 18. Mustered Sept. 1, 1861. Mustered out Sept. 30, 1864, at Sturgis.

Anthony, Worthington. St. Joseph County. Enlisted and mustered in Co. G, Aug. 24, 1861, at Three Rivers, age 17. Captured Dec. 31, 1862, at Stones River. Paroled Apr. 1863. Mustered out Sept. 30, 1864, at Sturgis.

Armstrong, James. St. Joseph County. Enlisted in Co. G at Centreville, age 25. Mustered Sept. 4, 1861. Mustered out Sept. 30, 1864, at Sturgis. Resided c. 1905 at Muskegon.

Austin, Ephraim W. Enlisted in Co. G, Feb. 4, 1864, at Nottawa, age 26. Mustered Feb. 22, 1864. Joined regiment Mar. 15, 1864, at Rossville, GA. Transferred Apr. 15, 1865, to Company G, reorganized 11th Michigan Infantry. Died of disease at Nashville, June 1865. Buried in national cemetery in Nashville.

Austin, John P. Schoolcraft. Enlisted in Co. G at Schoolcraft, age 20. Mustered Sept. 4, 1861. Wounded Dec. 31, 1862, at Stones River. Died of wounds Jan. 20, 1863, at Murfreesboro, TN.

Austin, Levi. Schoolcraft. Enlisted in Co. G at Prairie Ronde, age 23. Mustered Sept. 4, 1861. Died of chronic diarrhea Mar. 1, 1863, at Nashville. Buried in national cemetery in Nashville.

Auten, Harrison. Mendon. Enlisted and mustered in Co. C, Aug. 24, 1861, at Mendon, age 21. Died of typhoid fever May 2, 1862, at Belmont, KY.

Auten, William H. St. Joseph County. Enlisted and mustered in Co. C, Aug. 24, 1861, at Mendon, age 18. Transferred to Invalid Corps Nov. 13, 1863. Discharged Aug. 31, 1864, at Indianapolis.

Avery, Dexter C. Allen. Enlisted in Co. B, Oct. 24, 1862, at Allen, age 18. Joined regiment Dec. 9, 1862, at Nashville. Captured Jan. 2, 1863, at Stones River. Discharged for disability Apr. 16, 1863, at Camp Chase, OH.

Avery, Dillason S. Hillsdale County. Enlisted and mustered in Co. B, Aug. 24, 1861, at Allen, age 18. Mustered out Sept. 30, 1864, at Sturgis.

Avery, James. Lenawee County. Enlisted in Co. K, Aug. 24, 1861, at Deerfield, age 34. Mustered Sept. 1, 1861. Mustered out Sept. 30, 1864, at Sturgis.

Avery, Oscar F. Hillsdale County. Enlisted and mustered in Co. B, Aug. 24, 1861, at Allen, age 20. Wounded Sept. 20, 1863, at Chickamauga. Corporal July 17, 1864. Mustered out Sept. 30, 1864, at Sturgis. Resided c. 1905 at Logansport, IN.

Babbitt, Elkins. Trowbridge. Enlisted in Co. G at Pine Grove, age 25. Mustered Sept. 4, 1861. Died of typhoid pneumonia Mar. 18, 1862, at Bardstown, KY.

Babbitt, Franklin. Allegan County. Enlisted in Co. G at Pine Grove, age 41. Mustered Sept. 4, 1861. Discharged for disability Feb. 24, 1862. Died Dec. 14, 1890.

Bacon, Nelson. St. Joseph County. Enlisted and mustered in Co. C, Aug. 24, 1861, at Sturgis, age 18. Wounded July 4, 1864, at Ruff's Station. Mustered out Sept. 30, 1864, at Sturgis.

Bagley, Frederick. Washtenaw County. Enlisted and mustered in Co. I as Corporal, Aug. 24, 1861, at Belleville, age 18. Died of measles Jan. 26, 1862, at Bardstown, KY.

Bair, Andrew. Branch County. Enlisted and mustered in Co. C, Aug. 24, 1861, at Bethel, age 25. Discharged for disability Dec. 9, 1861, at White Pigeon, due to blindness.

Baird, Charles W. St. Joseph. Enlisted and mustered in Co. A, Aug. 24, 1861, at Centreville, age 19. Discharged for disability Feb. 3, 1863, at Bowling Green, KY.

Baker, Edward. Monroe County. Enlisted and mustered in Co. I, Aug. 24, 1861, at Frenchtown, age 19. Sergeant October 1863. Mustered out Sept. 30, 1864, at Sturgis. Resided c. 1905 at Carleton.

Baker, George. Hillsdale County. Enlisted and mustered in Co. F, Sept. 11, 1861, at Wright, age 18. Discharged for disability Oct. 26, 1861.

Baker, Ira. Lenawee County. Enlisted and mustered in Co. F, Sept. 11, 1861, at Medina, age 24. Corporal. Deserted Oct. 13, 1862, near Nashville.

Baker, Marcus D. Monroe County. Enlisted and mustered in Co. I, Aug. 24, 1861, at Frenchtown, age 31. Wounded at Stones River. Sergeant Apr. 25, 1863. Mustered out Sept. 30, 1864, at Sturgis. Resided c. 1905 at Sturgis.

Baker, Robert. St. Joseph County. Enlisted and mustered in Co. A, Aug. 24, 1861, at Centreville, age 20. Discharged for disability Aug. 1863 at Nashville.

Baker, Solomon M. Monroe County. Enlisted and mustered in Co. I, Aug. 24, 1861, at Frenchtown, age 33. Discharged Aug. 5, 1862, at Nashville.

Balderry, Felix C. Colon. Enlisted in Co. A, Dec. 7, 1863, at Leonidas, age 21. Mustered Jan. 4, 1864. Joined regiment Jan. 28, 1864, at Rossville, GA. Transferred Mar. 30, 1864, to Company F. Transferred Apr. 15, 1865, to Company F, reorganized 11th Michigan Infantry. Mustered out Sept. 16, 1865, at Nashville. Resided c. 1905 at Colon.

Baldwin, Daniel. Cass County. Enlisted and mustered in Co. E, Aug. 24, 1861, at Three Rivers, age 22. Killed Aug. 7, 1864, at Utoy Creek.

Banter, Frank see Bauter, Frank.

Banter, John W. see Bauter, John W.

Barber, Edward T. Enlisted in Co. B, Aug. 30, 1864, at Adrian for 1 year, age 17. Mustered Sept. 1, 1864. Joined regiment Jan. 7, 1865, at Chattanooga. Transferred Apr. 15, 1865, to reorganized 11th Michigan Infantry.

Barber, George A. Monroe County. Enlisted and mustered in Co. I as Corporal, Aug. 24, 1861, at London, age 40. Discharged for disability June 8, 1862.

Barber, Josiah A. Wayne County. Enlisted and mustered in Co. I, Aug. 26, 1861, at Detroit, age 18. Captured Dec. 31, 1862, at Stones River. Paroled Aug. 1863. Mustered out Sept. 30, 1864, at Sturgis.

Barclay, Kindle or Kendall. St. Joseph County. Enlisted in Co. G at Three Rivers, age 21. Mustered Sept. 11, 1861. Transferred Nov. 26, 1862, at Nashville to 4th U.S. Cavalry.

Bargerow, Augustus J. Branch County. Enlisted and mustered in Co. B, Aug. 24, 1861, at Quincy, age 18. Transferred Nov. 25, 1862, at Nashville to 4th U.S. Cavalry. Resided c. 1905 at California, MI.

Bargerow, Timothy C. Branch County. Enlisted in Co. H, Aug. 24, 1861, at Coldwater, age 43. Mustered Aug. 28, 1861. Discharged Jan. 1, 1862.

Barker, Byron V. St. Joseph County. Enlisted and mustered in Co. A, Aug. 24, 1861, at Centreville, age 21. Wounded at Stones River. Discharged for disability June 24, 1863, at Louisville. Reentered service. Commissioned 2nd Lieutenant, Co. E, in reorganized 11th Michigan Infantry, Mar. 1, 1865, mustered Mar. 16, 1865. Mustered out Sept. 16, 1865, at Nashville.

Barker, Henry C. Leonidas. Enlisted and mustered in Co. A, Aug. 14, 1862, at Leonidas, age 18. Joined regiment Feb. 1, 1863, at Murfreesboro, TN. Transferred Apr. 15, 1865, to Company A, reorganized 11th Michigan Infantry. Discharged June 16, 1865, at Chattanooga.

Barker, Jonas N. Enlisted in Co. A, Feb. 8, 1864, at Leonidas, age 25. Mustered Feb. 27, 1864. Joined regiment Mar. 15, 1864, at Rossville, GA. Transferred Apr. 15, 1865, to Company A, reorganized 11th Michigan Infantry. Corporal Aug. 28, 1865. Mustered out Sept. 16, 1865, at Nashville.

Barker, Myron H. Enlisted in Co. A, Feb. 8, 1864, at Leonidas, age 23. Mustered Feb. 27, 1864. Joined regiment Mar. 15, 1864, at Rossville, GA. Transferred Apr. 15, 1865, to Company A, reorganized 11th Michigan Infantry. Discharged for disability June 8, 1865, at Chicago.

Barker, William J. Burr Oak. Enlisted in Co. A, Aug. 11, 1862, at Leonidas, age 22. Mustered Sept. 11, 1862. Transferred to Veteran Reserve Corps Apr. 30, 1864. Discharged June 30, 1865, at Nashville, from 154th Company, 2nd Btn., VRC. Resided c. 1905 at Belding.

Barnes, Charles E. Sturgis. Enlisted and mustered in Co. C, Aug. 24, 1861, at White Pigeon, age 18. Corporal. Died of measles Dec. 4, 1863, at Chattanooga. Buried in national cemetery in Chattanooga.

Barnes, George C. Cambria. Enlisted and mustered in Co. F, Sept. 11, 1861, at Cambria, age 40. Died of disease 1863 at Nashville. Buried in national cemetery in Chattanooga.

Barnes, Linn or Lynn. Monroe County. Enlisted and mustered in Co. I, Aug. 24, 1861, at London, age 20. Wounded at Stones River. Mustered out Sept. 30, 1864, at Sturgis. Resided c. 1905 at Milan.

Barnes, Rockwell. Enlisted in Co. A, Dec. 3, 1863, at Colon, age 16. Mustered Dec. 9, 1863. Joined regiment Mar. 15, 1864, at Rossville, GA. Transferred Mar. 30, 1864, to Company F. Wounded July 4, 1864, at Ruff's Station. Transferred Apr. 15, 1865, to Company F, reorganized 11th Michigan Infantry. Discharged July 13, 1865, at Detroit.

Barnes, Warren F. St. Joseph County. Enlisted and mustered in Co. C, Aug. 24, 1861, at White Pigeon, age 23. Wounded June 18, 1864, near Kennesaw Mountain. Mustered out Sept. 30, 1864, at Sturgis.

Barrett, David. Lenawee County. Enlisted in Co. G at White Pigeon, age 19. Mustered Sept. 4, 1861. Wounded at Stones River. Mustered out Sept. 30, 1864, at Sturgis.

Barton, Eugene. Branch County. Enlisted in Co. H, Sept. 1, 1861, at Coldwater, age 18. Mustered Aug. 28, 1861. Discharged Sept. 27, 1861, at White Pigeon, on writ of habeas corpus as a minor enlisted without parental permission.

Barton, George. St. Joseph County. Enlisted and mustered in Co. K, Sept. 1, 1861, at Three Rivers, age 37. Mustered out Sept. 30, 1864, at Sturgis.

Bascom, Charles. St. Joseph County. Enlisted and mustered in Co. C, Aug. 24, 1861, at Sturgis, age 36. Discharged for disability Feb. 25, 1863, at Nashville.

Bates, Chester. Branch County. Enlisted in Co. H, Aug. 24, 1861, at Coldwater, age 39. Mustered Aug. 28, 1861. Mustered out Sept. 30, 1864, at Sturgis.

Bates, Harvey J. Mendon. Enlisted and mustered in Co. H, Sept. 1, 1862, at Mendon, age 18. Transferred Apr. 15, 1865, to Company H, reorganized 11th Michigan Infantry. Discharged June 16, 1865, at Chattanooga. Resided c. 1905 at Mecosta.

Baum, George S. St. Joseph County. Enlisted and mustered in Co. E, Aug. 24, 1861, at Three Rivers, age 19. Mustered out Sept. 30, 1864, at Sturgis.

Bauter, Frank. St. Joseph County. Enlisted and mustered in Co. E, Aug. 24, 1861, at Three Rivers, age 18. Captured Dec. 31, 1862, at Stones River. Discharged for disability Apr. 11, 1863, at Murfreesboro, TN, due to wounds.

Bauter, John W. St. Joseph County. Enlisted and mustered in Co. E as Corporal, Aug. 24, 1861, at Three Rivers, age 19. Sergeant Jan. 22, 1863. Wounded Nov. 1863. Mustered out Sept. 30, 1864, at Sturgis.

Beard, Dexter. Enlisted in Co. F, Feb. 15, 1864, at Leonidas, age 21. Mustered Feb. 27, 1864. Joined regiment Mar. 15, 1864, at Rossville, GA. Died Oct. 10, 1864. Buried in national cemetery in Chattanooga.

Beardsley, Elisha L. Cass County. Enlisted and mustered in Co. C, Nov. 22, 1861, at White Pigeon, age 18. Died of smallpox Jan. 31, 1862, at Bardstown, KY.

Beck, James W. St. Joseph County. Enlisted and mustered in Co. E, Aug. 24, 1861, at Three Rivers, age 24. Captured Dec. 31, 1862, at Stones River. Paroled Apr. 1863. Mustered out Sept. 30, 1864, at Sturgis.

Belcher, Jesse M. Branch County. Enlisted and mustered in Co. B, Aug. 24, 1861, at Quincy, age 18. Transferred to Company K, 16th Michigan Infantry. No further record.

Benedict, James M. Enlisted in Co. A, Feb. 20, 1864, at Leonidas, age 27. Mustered Feb. 27, 1864. Joined regiment Mar. 15, 1864, at Rossville, GA. Transferred Apr. 15, 1865, to Company A, reorganized 11th Michigan Infantry. Discharged May 16, 1865, at Nashville.

Benedict, Myron A. Leonidas. Entered service in Co. A as 2nd Lieutenant. Commissioned Jan. 5, 1864. Mustered Jan. 23, 1864. Commissioned 1st Lieutenant Jan. 23, 1864, mustered Mar. 29, 1864. Wounded July 4, 1864, at Ruff's Station. Mustered out Sept. 30, 1864, at Sturgis.

Benedict, Smith A. St. Joseph County. Enlisted and mustered in Co. C as Sergeant, Aug. 24, 1861, at Sturgis, age 29. 1st Sergeant June 10, 1862. Commissioned 2nd Lieutenant Jan. 15, 1864. Not mustered. Mustered out Sept. 30, 1864, at Sturgis.

Beneway, Wilber. Lenawee County. Enlisted in

Co. K as Corporal, Aug. 24, 1861, at Deerfield, age 23. Mustered Sept. 1, 1861. Mustered out Sept. 30, 1864, at Sturgis.

Bennett, Benjamin Grove. Burr Oak. Enlisted in Co. G as 1st Sergeant, 1st Michigan Infantry, Apr. 24, 1861, at Burr Oak for 3 months, age 38. Mustered May 1, 1861. Mustered out Aug. 7, 1861, at Detroit. Reentered service. Commissioned and mustered as Captain, Co. D, 11th Michigan Infantry, Aug. 24, 1861. Commissioned Major Jan. 7, 1863, mustered Aug. 4, 1863. Killed Nov. 25, 1863, at Missionary Ridge.

Bennett, Clarence E. St. Joseph County. Enlisted and mustered in Co. D, Aug. 24, 1861, at Burr Oak, age 18. Discharged Dec. 25, 1862, at Nashville.

Bennett, Daniel A. Morenci. Enlisted and mustered in Co. F, Sept. 11, 1861, at Hudson, age 20. Transferred Nov. 18, 1863, to 15th USCT as 2nd Lieutenant.

Bennett, Franklin. Mattison. Enlisted in Co. H, Aug. 24, 1861, at Coldwater, age 19. Mustered Oct. 11, 1861. Died of typhoid fever Dec. 25, 1862, at Nashville.

Bennett, Henry C. Branch County. Enlisted and mustered in Co. B, Aug. 24, 1861, at Litchfield, age 21. Discharged for disability June 4, 1862, at Columbia, TN.

Bennett, John. Branch County. Enlisted in Co. H, Aug. 24, 1861, at Coldwater. Mustered Aug. 28, 1861. Mustered out Sept. 30, 1864, at Sturgis.

Bennett, Moses D. Lenawee County. Enlisted and mustered in Co. F, Sept. 23, 1861. Discharged Nov. 1862 at Bardstown, KY.

Berdett, Charles. Enlisted in Co. K as Corporal, Aug. 24, 1861, at Macon, age 21. Mustered Sept. 1, 1861. Deserted Oct. 1, 1861, at White Pigeon.

Biddle, Roderick P. Belleville. Enlisted and mustered in Co. I, Aug. 24, 1861, at Belleville, age 19. Died of chronic diarrhea Oct. 31, 1862, at Nashville.

Billings, John D. St. Joseph County. Enlisted and mustered in Co. A, Aug. 24, 1861, at Centreville, age 21. Discharged for disability July 1862 at Nashville. Died Apr. 24, 1896. Buried at Nottawa.

Birdsall, John W. Morenci. Enlisted and mustered in Co. F as Sergeant, Sept. 11, 1861, at Morenci, age 28. 1st Sergeant Mar. 1, 1862. Commissioned 2nd Lieutenant Jan. 2, 1863, mustered May 6, 1863. Commissioned 1st Lieutenant May 29, 1863, mustered Aug. 3, 1863. Commissioned Captain Jan. 1, 1864, mustered Feb. 17, 1864. Mustered out Sept. 30, 1864, at Sturgis.

Birdzell, John C. Cass County. Enlisted and mustered in Co. C, Aug. 24, 1861, at Pavilion, age 25. Discharged for disability Sept. 15, 1862, at Detroit.

Bishop, Aristus O. Enlisted in Co. G, Feb. 1, 1864, at Centreville, age 27. Mustered Feb. 22, 1864. Joined regiment Mar. 15, 1864, at Rossville, GA. Discharged for disability Feb. 5, 1865, at Camp Douglas, IL.

Bishop, Charles W. Sturgis. Enlisted and mustered in Co. C as 1st Sergeant, Aug. 24, 1861, at Sturgis, age 24. Died of typhoid fever May 30, 1862, at Sturgis.

Bishop, Olney. St. Joseph County. Enlisted and mustered in Co. A, Aug. 24, 1861, at Centreville, age 19. Discharged for disability June 24, 1863.

Bissell, Francis M. Quincy. Enlisted and mustered in Co. B as 1st Sergeant, Aug. 24, 1861, at Butler, age 28. Commissioned 2nd Lieutenant Feb. 19, 1862, mustered Mar. 20, 1862. Commissioned 1st Lieutenant Nov. 26, 1862, mustered Jan. 21, 1863. Commissioned Captain Jan. 7, 1863, mustered Aug. 3, 1863. Wounded Nov. 25, 1863, at Missionary Ridge. Discharged for disability June 4, 1864, due to wounds.

Bissell, Marcus. Butler. Enlisted and mustered in Co. B, Aug. 24, 1861, at Butler, age 19. Died of consumption Mar. 16, 1862, at Bardstown, KY. Buried in national cemetery in Lebanon, KY.

Black, William. Ovid. Enlisted in Co. H, Aug. 24, 1861, at Coldwater, age 18. Mustered Aug. 28, 1861. Died of pneumonia Feb. 9, 1862, at Bardstown, KY.

Blair, George. Branch County. Enlisted and mustered in Co. H, Sept. 1, 1861. Discharged May 14, 1862.

Blakeley, Thomas L. Cass County. Enlisted and mustered in Co. E, Aug. 24, 1861, at Three Rivers, age 21. Discharged for disability June 18, 1862, at Louisville.

Blanchard, Spencer M. Enlisted in Co. C, Jan. 29, 1864, at Burlington, age 33. Mustered Feb. 4, 1864. Joined regiment Mar. 15, 1864, at Rossville, GA. Killed May 30, 1864, near Dallas, GA. Buried in national cemetery in Atlanta, section G grave 7663.

Bland, General V. Enlisted and mustered in Co. I, Dec. 29, 1863, at Mendon, age 38. Transferred Apr. 15, 1865, to Company I, reorganized 11th Michigan Infantry. Mustered out Sept. 16, 1865, at Nashville.

Blood, Augustus W. Enlisted and mustered in Co. I, Aug. 24, 1861, at Augusta, age 18. Transferred Nov. 28, 1862, at Nashville to 4th U.S. Cavalry.

Bloom, John J. St. Joseph County. Enlisted and mustered in Co. E as Corporal, Aug. 24, 1861, at Three Rivers, age 21. Sergeant May 23, 1864. Mustered out Sept. 30, 1864, at Sturgis.

Boardman, Charles. Petersburg. Enlisted in Co. K, Aug. 24, 1861, at Petersburg, age 20. Mustered Sept. 1, 1861. Died of typhoid Apr. 8, 1862, at Belmont, KY.

Bockes, Egbert B. Enlisted in Co. A, Dec. 5, 1863, at Waukeshma, age 29. Mustered Jan. 4, 1864. Joined regiment Jan. 28, 1864, at Graysville, GA. Transferred Mar. 30, 1864, to Company F. Transferred Apr. 15, 1865, to Company F, reorganized 11th Michigan Infantry. Discharged Aug. 21, 1865, at Cleveland, TN. Died May 16, 1890.

Bogart, Cornelius E. Enlisted and mustered in Co. D, Aug. 24, 1861. No further record.

Bolton, Daniel. Lenawee County. Enlisted and mustered in Co. K, Aug. 24, 1861. Discharged for disability July 4, 1862.

Bolton, James. Lenawee County. Enlisted in Co. K as Corporal, Aug. 24, 1861, at Ogden, age 20. Mustered Sept. 1, 1861. Wounded at Stones River. Wounded May 15, 1864, at Resaca. Mustered out Sept. 30, 1864, at Sturgis.

Booth, Wesley. Lenawee County. Enlisted in Co. K, Aug. 24, 1861, at Ogden. Mustered Sept. 1, 1861. Deserted Oct. 1, 1861, at White Pigeon.

Booth, Zeevala or Zavala V. Cass County. Enlisted and mustered in Co. E, Aug. 24, 1861, at Three Rivers, age 19. Corporal Dec. 1, 1863. Mustered out Sept. 30, 1864, at Sturgis.

Bordner, Benjamin F. St. Joseph County. Enlisted and mustered in Co. D, Aug. 24, 1861, at Bronson. Sergeant. Wounded at Stones River. Mustered out Sept. 30, 1864, at Sturgis.

Bordner, Henry. St. Joseph County. Enlisted and mustered in Co. D, Aug. 24, 1861, at Bronson, age 22. Discharged Oct. 30, 1862, at Nashville.

Boughton, James *see* Bouton, James.

Boughton, Levi L. Athens. Enlisted and mustered in Co. A, Aug. 24, 1861, at Centreville, age 28. Discharged for disability Oct. 30, 1862, at Nashville. Died of chronic diarrhea Nov. 16, 1862, at Nashville. Buried in national cemetery in Nashville.

Bournes, William. St. Joseph County. Enlisted and mustered in Co. C, Aug. 24, 1861, at Three Rivers, age 18. Mustered out Sept. 30, 1864, at Sturgis.

Bouton, James. St. Joseph County. Enlisted in Co. B as Sergeant at Schoolcraft, age 26. Mustered Sept. 4, 1861. Wounded at Stones River. Mustered out Sept. 30, 1864, at Sturgis.

Bowen, Jerome. Quincy. Entered service in Co. B as 1st Lieutenant, Aug. 24, 1861, at Butler, age 22. Commissioned Aug. 24, 1861. Resigned Nov. 27, 1862, due to disability. Resided c. 1905 at Lansing.

Bowen, Joesph A. Branch County. Enlisted and mustered in Co. B, Aug. 24, 1861. Wounded at Stones River. Captured Sept. 20, 1863, at Chickamauga. Released at N.E. Bridge, NC. Transferred Apr. 15, 1865, to Company B, reorganized 11th Michigan Infantry. Discharged at Detroit. Resided c. 1905 at Lansing.

Bowen, Ozro A. Branch County. Enlisted and mustered in Co. B as Corporal, Aug. 24, 1861, at Butler, age 19. Captured Apr. 1863. Paroled. Sergeant. 1st Sergeant Mar. 1864. Mustered out Sept. 30, 1864, at Sturgis.

Bowers, Cyrus A. St. Joseph County. Enlisted and mustered in Co. C, Aug. 24, 1861, at Burr Oak, age 20. Mustered out Sept. 30, 1864, at Sturgis. Resided c. 1905 at Trinidad, CO.

Bowers, George L. St. Joseph County. Enlisted and mustered in Co. E, Aug. 24, 1861, at Three Rivers, age 22. Mustered out Sept. 30, 1864, at Sturgis.

Bowers, Jacob. Three Rivers. Enlisted and mustered in Co. E, Aug. 24, 1861, at Three Rivers, age 22. Died of lung fever Feb. 22, 1862, at Bardstown, KY. Buried in national cemetery in Lebanon, KY, grave 295.

Boyce, Henry. Wayne County. Enlisted and mustered in Co. I, Aug. 26, 1861, at Detroit, age 19. Mustered out Sept. 30, 1864, at Sturgis.

Boyer, Phillip V. Indiana. Enlisted and mustered in Co. D, Aug. 24, 1861, at Rome, IN, age 19. Discharged for disability Feb. 7, 1864, at Nashville.

Bradley, Elmer. Lenawee County. Enlisted in Co. K as Sergeant, Aug. 24, 1861, at Ogden, age 22. Mustered Sept. 1, 1861. Wounded at Stones River. 1st Sergeant Apr. 20, 1863. Captured Sept. 11, 1863, at Davis's Crossroads. Died Sept. 11, 1864. Buried in national cemetery in Andersonville, GA.

Bradley, Kendal *see* Barclay, Kindle.

Bradshaw, Stephen. Allen. Enlisted and mustered in Co. B, Aug. 24, 1861, at Allen, age 44. Died of pneumonia Jan. 23, 1862, at Bardstown, KY. Buried in national cemetery in Lebanon, KY, grave 302.

Bragg, Myron. Monroe County. Enlisted in Co. K, Aug. 24, 1861, at Petersburg, age 19. Mustered Sept. 1, 1861. Wounded Jan. 2, 1863, at Stones River. Wounded Sept. 20, 1863, at Chickamauga. Mustered out Sept. 30, 1864, at Sturgis.

Bragg, Nelson Clifford. Petersburg. Enlisted in Co. K, Aug. 24, 1861, at Petersburg, age 21. Mustered Sept. 1, 1861. Died of disease Jan. 16, 1863, at Nashville. Buried in national cemetery in Nashville.

Branshaw, Joseph. Monroe County. Enlisted and mustered in Co. I, Aug. 24, 1861, at Frenchtown, age 21. Mustered out Sept. 30, 1864, at Sturgis.

Brayman, Richard. St. Joseph County. Enlisted and mustered in Co. E, Aug. 24, 1861, at Three Rivers, age 21. Corporal Mar. 1, 1864. Mustered out Sept. 30, 1864, at Sturgis.

Briggs, Thomas H. Schoolcraft. Entered service in Co. G as 1st Lieutenant at White Pigeon, age 22. Commissioned Aug. 24, 1861. Mustered Sept. 4, 1861. Commissioned Captain Nov. 14, 1862, mustered Jan. 22, 1863. Wounded at Stones River. Wounded Sept. 20, 1863, at Chickamauga. Discharged for disability Jan. 24, 1864. Died Apr. 7, 1899. Buried at Battle Creek.

Brighty, Thomas. Blissfield. Enlisted in Co. K, Aug. 24, 1861, at Blissfield, age 35. Mustered Sept. 1, 1861. Wounded Dec. 31, 1862, at Stones River. Died of wounds Jan. 2, 1863, at Murfreesboro, TN.

Britton, Joseph L. La Grange County, IN. Enlisted and mustered in Co. D, Aug. 24, 1861, age 25. Captured Sept. 20, 1863, at Chickamauga. Wounded Oct. 1863. Mustered out Sept. 30, 1864, at Sturgis.

Britton, Lewis. Hillsdale County. Enlisted in Co. G at Jefferson, age 36. Mustered Sept. 4, 1861. Discharged for disability Feb. 13, 1862.

Britton, Samuel H. La Grange County, IN. Enlisted and mustered in Co. D, Aug. 24, 1861, at Bronson, age 22. Mustered out Sept. 30, 1864, at Sturgis.

Brockway, Oliver W. Lenawee County. Enlisted in Co. K, Aug. 24, 1861, at Ogden, age 28. Mustered Sept. 1, 1861. Corporal Sept. 1863. Captured Sept. 11, 1863, at Davis's Crossroads. Died June 27, 1864. Buried in national cemetery in Andersonville, GA.

Bronson, Byron C. St. Joseph County. Enlisted and mustered in Co. D, Aug. 24, 1861, at Colon, age 18. Died of fever May 16, 1862, at Colon.

Bronson, Elisha C. South Haven. Enlisted in Co. G, Aug. 24, 1861, at Flowerfield, age 22. Mustered Sept. 4, 1861. Died of typhoid pneumonia Jan. 30, 1862, at Bardstown, KY.

Bronson, Marcenus A. St. Joseph County. Enlisted and mustered in Co. D as Corporal, Aug. 24, 1861, at Coldwater, age 20. Discharged for disability June 26, 1862, at Nashville.

Brooks, Luzern G. St. Joseph County. Enlisted and mustered in Co. C, Aug. 24, 1861, at Constantine, age 28. Discharged for disability Oct. 7, 1862, at Nashville.

Brown, Alfred Q. Branch County. Enlisted in Co. H, Aug. 24, 1861, at Coldwater, age 18. Mustered Aug. 28, 1861. Corporal Nov. 1, 1863. Mustered out Sept. 30, 1864, at Sturgis.

Brown, George T. Enlisted in Co. K, Mar. 18, 1864, at Blissfield, age 39. Mustered Mar. 31, 1864. Joined regiment Apr. 8, 1864, at Graysville, GA. Transferred Apr. 15, 1865, to Company K, reorganized 11th Michigan Infantry. Mustered out Sept. 16, 1865, at Nashville.

Brown, John W. Enlisted in Co. B, Aug. 31, 1864, at Blissfield for 1 year, age 23. Mustered Sept. 1, 1864. Joined regiment Jan. 7, 1865, at Chattanooga. Transferred Apr. 15, 1865, to Company B, reorganized 11th Michigan Infantry. Discharged June 16, 1865, at Chattanooga.

Brown, Joseph S. St. Joseph County. Enlisted in Co. E, Feb. 23, 1864, at Lockport, age 22. Mustered Feb. 29, 1864. Joined regiment Apr. 10, 1864, at Graysville, GA. Transferred Apr. 15, 1865, to Company E, reorganized 11th Michigan Infantry. Mustered out Sept. 16, 1865, at Nashville. Resided c. 1905 at Marcellus.

Brown, Lewis. Lenawee County. Enlisted and mustered in Co. C, Aug. 24, 1861, at Hudson, age 41. Discharged June 26, 1862, at Louisville.

Brown, Loren W. Van Buren County. Enlisted in Co. G at Flowerfield, age 19. Mustered Sept. 4, 1861. Discharged for disability Jan. 24, 1863, at Bowling Green, KY.

Brown, Neri H. Enlisted in Co. C, Jan. 15, 1864, at Burlington, age 33. Mustered Feb. 3, 1864. Joined regiment Mar. 15, 1864, at Rossville, GA. Transferred Apr. 15, 1865, to Company B, reorganized 11th Michigan Infantry. Corporal. Mustered out Sept. 16, 1865, at Nashville.

Brown, Oscar A. St. Joseph. Enlisted in Co. H, Aug. 24, 1861, at Coldwater, age 18. Mustered Aug. 28, 1861. Deserted Apr. 5, 1862, at Belmont, KY.

Brown, Peter F. Monroe County. Enlisted and mustered in Co. I, Aug. 24, 1861, at Raisinville, age 21. Corporal Mar. 1, 1863. Mustered out Sept. 30, 1864, at Sturgis.

Brown, William. Branch County. Enlisted in Co. H, Aug. 24, 1861, at Coldwater, age 24. Mustered Aug. 28, 1861. Corporal Feb. 5, 1862. Sergeant Nov. 13, 1862. Captured Sept. 20, 1863, at Chickamauga. Buried in national cemetery in Wilmington, NC.

Brundage, Stephen D. Ypsilanti. Enlisted and mustered in Co. I as Corporal, Aug. 24, 1861, at Augusta, age 20. Discharged for disability Nov. 3, 1863, at Detroit.

Brunson, Byron C. *see* Bronson, Byron C.

Bryan, James K.P. Cass County. Enlisted in Co. G, age 18. Mustered Sept. 4, 1861. Mustered out Sept. 30, 1864, at Sturgis.

Bryan, Moses. Cass County. Enlisted in Co. G at Cass County, age 45. Mustered Sept. 4, 1861. Wounded Aug. 7, 1864, at Utoy Creek. Died Sept. 6, 1864, at Chattanooga. Buried in national cemetery in Chattanooga.

Buck, Benjamin. Lenawee County. Enlisted in Co. K, Aug. 24, 1861, at Adrian, age 20. Mustered Sept. 1, 1861. Served in Pioneer Corps. Reenlisted Jan. 30, 1864, at Chattanooga. Mustered Mar. 31, 1864. Transferred July 15, 1864, to 1st U.S. Engineers. Mustered out Sept. 26, 1865, at Nashville.

Buckingham, Charles E. Camden. Enlisted, company unassigned. Substitute for Hiram Alward of Camden, drafted Feb. 10, 1863, for 9 months. Joined regiment Mar. 11, 1863. No further record.

Buffham, Hubbard F. Branch County. Enlisted and mustered in Co. D, Aug. 24, 1861, at Bethel, age 23. Corporal. Discharged for disability July 2, 1862, at Nashville.

Buischlen, John F. St. Joseph County. Enlisted and mustered in Co. C as Corporal, Aug. 24, 1861, at White Pigeon, age 24. Sergeant Nov. 26, 1863. Mustered out Sept. 30, 1864, at Sturgis. Died of disease Jan. 13, 1866, at Stark County, OH.

Burch, Nathaniel E. Butler. Enlisted and mustered in Co. B, Aug. 24, 1861, at Butler, age 19. Died of pneumonia Feb. 11, 1862, at Bardstown, KY. Buried in national cemetery in Lebanon, KY.

Burch, Wallace. Branch County. Enlisted and mustered in Co. H, Sept. 11, 1861. Deserted May 12, 1862, at Nashville.

Burchard, Solomon. Burr Oak. Enlisted and mustered in Co. C, Aug. 24, 1861, at Burr Oak, age 23. Died Feb. 6, 1862, at Bardstown, KY.

Burdeaux, Alexander. Monroe County. Enlisted and mustered in Co. I, Aug. 24, 1861, at Monroe, age 23. Transferred to Veteran Reserve Corps Apr. 30, 1864. Discharged Aug. 24, 1864, at Nashville.

Burke, Robert. Lenawee County. Enlisted in Co. G at White Pigeon, age 19. Mustered Sept. 4, 1861. Mustered out Sept. 30, 1864, at Sturgis. Resided c. 1905 at Detroit.

Burkholder, Joseph. Burr Oak. Enlisted in Co. D, Aug. 15, 1862, at Burr Oak, age 24. Joined regiment Feb. 25, 1863, at Murfreesboro, TN. Corporal. Killed Aug. 7, 1864, at Utoy Creek. Buried in national cemetery in Atlanta, grave 6172.

Burkson, Henry *see* Burleson, Henry.

Burleson, David G. Branch County. Enlisted and mustered in Co. D, Aug. 24, 1861, at Bronson, age 18. 1st Sergeant July 1, 1864. Wounded Aug. 7, 1864, at Utoy Creek. Mustered out Sept. 30, 1864, at Sturgis.

Burleson, Henry. Branch County. Enlisted and mustered in Co. D, Aug. 24, 1861, at Bronson, age 16. Killed Dec. 31, 1862, at Stones River.

Burleson, Jerry M. Branch County. Enlisted and mustered in Co. B, Aug. 24, 1861, at Quincy, age 22. Mustered out Sept. 30, 1864, at Sturgis. Died Nov. 30, 1894. Buried at Macon.

Burleson, Silas. Quincy. Enlisted and mustered in Co. F, Sept. 11, 1861, at Quincy, age 18. Died of fever at Belmont, KY. Buried in national cemetery in Louisville.

Burleson, Stephen. Branch County. Enlisted in Co. H, Aug. 24, 1861, at Coldwater, age 29. Mustered Aug. 28, 1861. Mustered out Sept. 30, 1864, at Sturgis.

Burnham, Abner. Lenawee County. Enlisted in Co. K, Aug. 24, 1861, at Blissfield, age 18. Mustered Sept. 1, 1861. Wounded Aug. 7, 1864, at Utoy Creek. Mustered out Sept. 30, 1864, at Sturgis.

Burnham, Charles. Enlisted in Co. F, Feb. 23, 1864, at Waukeshma, age 30. Mustered Feb. 27, 1864. Joined regiment Mar. 15, 1864, at Rossville, GA. Corporal Mar. 16, 1865. Transferred Apr. 15, 1865, to Company F, reorganized 11th Michigan Infantry. Sergeant July 12, 1865. Mustered out Sept. 16, 1865, at Nashville.

Burns, George C. *see* Barnes, George C.

Burrows, William. Quincy. Enlisted and mustered in Co. H, Sept. 15, 1861. Discharged for disability July 1863 at Detroit.

Burton, David. Lenawee County. Enlisted and mustered in Co. F, Sept. 11, 1861, at Medina, age 23. Corporal Apr. 9, 1864. Mustered out Sept. 30, 1864, at Sturgis.

Bush, Arthur M. St. Joseph County. Enlisted and mustered in Co. E, Aug. 24, 1861, at Three Rivers. Discharged for disability Aug. 4, 1862, at Nashville.

Busley, Levi. Branch County. Enlisted and mustered in Co. B, Aug. 24, 1861, at Butler, age 19. Discharged for disability July 6, 1862.

Busley, Oliver. Butler. Enlisted and mustered in Co. B, Aug. 24, 1861, at Butler, age 18. Killed Dec. 31, 1862, at Stones River.

Butts, Simeon G. Burr Oak. Enlisted in Co. D, Aug. 15, 1862, at Burr Oak, age 27. Transferred to Invalid Corps June 30, 1863, at Quincy, IL.

Byrnes, David L. Burr Oak. Enlisted in Co. D at Bronson, age 21. Mustered Aug. 24, 1861. Wounded Dec. 31, 1862, at Stones River. Died of wounds Jan. 29, 1863, at Murfreesboro, TN.

Cady, Henry G. Branch County. Enlisted and mustered in Co. D, Aug. 24, 1861, at Bronson, age 22. Transferred Apr. 1, 1862, to Medical Department at Bardstown, KY.

Caldwell, John. Hillsdale County. Enlisted and mustered in Co. B, Aug. 24, 1861, at Litchfield, age 45. Discharged for disability May 23, 1863, at Nashville.

Calhoon, Alvin. London. Enlisted and mustered in Co. I, Aug. 24, 1861, at London, age 18. Died of measles Jan. 9, 1862, at Bardstown, KY.

Caner, Stephen A. Hillsdale County. Enlisted and mustered in Co. C, Mar. 20, 1862. Reenlisted Mar. 24, 1864, at Graysville, GA. Mustered Apr. 11, 1864. Transferred to Veteran Reserve Corps Jan. 4, 1865. Discharged Sept. 26, 1865, at Detroit from Co. C, 2nd Regiment VRC.

Canfield, Charles H. Branch County. Enlisted and mustered in Co. H, Oct. 1, 1861. Discharged at expiration of term of service Oct. 1, 1864, at Chattanooga. Died Apr. 24, 1897. Buried at Battle Creek.

Carkenord, Leonard F. Mendon. Enlisted and mustered in Co. A, Aug. 24, 1861, at Centreville, age 22. Captured Aug. 13, 1862, at Gallatin, TN. Paroled by Sept. 6, 1862. Died of fever Oct. 15, 1863, at Stevenson, AL.

Carkenord, Nicholas C. St. Joseph County. Enlisted and mustered in Co. A, Aug. 24, 1861, at Centreville, age 20. Discharged for disability Dec. 2, 1862, at Louisville.

Carlisle, Royal M. Centreville. Enlisted and mustered in Co. A, Aug. 24, 1861, at Centreville, age 23. Died of measles Jan. 21, 1862, at Bardstown, KY. Buried in national cemetery in Lebanon, KY, grave no. 303.

Carlton, George W. Quincy. Enlisted in Co. H, Aug. 24, 1861, at Coldwater, age 32. Mustered Aug. 28, 1861. Died of disease May 13, 1862, at Columbia, TN.

Carnes, David. Enlisted in Co. F, Feb. 19, 1864, at Waukeshma, age 18. Mustered Feb. 27, 1864. Joined regiment Mar. 15, 1864, at Rossville, GA. Transferred Apr. 15, 1865, to Company F, reorganized 11th Michigan Infantry. Mustered out Sept. 16, 1865, at Nashville.

Carney, John H. Monroe County. Enlisted and mustered in Co. I, Aug. 24, 1861, at Dundee, age 24. Mustered out Sept. 30, 1864, at Sturgis.

Carney, Robert B. Monroe County. Enlisted and mustered in Co. I as Sergeant, Aug. 24, 1861, at Dundee, age 21. Discharged for disability Feb. 22, 1863, at Nashville.

Carpenter, Calvin L. Jr. Calhoun County. Enlisted and mustered in Co. A, Aug. 24, 1861, at Centreville, age 28. Transferred to Invalid Corps Nov. 28, 1863. Discharged Aug. 25, 1864, at Lexington, KY, from 61st company, 2nd Battalion Veteran Reserve Corps. Died July 19, 1894. Buried at Prairieville.

Carpenter, Eugene. St. Joseph County. Enlisted and mustered in Co. A, Aug. 24, 1861, at Centreville, age 24. Discharged for disability Sept. 30, 1863, at Louisville.

Carpenter, Jessie N. Kalamazoo County. Enlisted and mustered in Co. A, Aug. 24, 1861, at Centreville, age 21. Wounded and captured Sept. 20, 1863, at Chickamauga. Paroled Sept. 1863 at Camp Chase, OH. Mustered out Sept. 30, 1864, at Sturgis.

Carpenter, Joseph Rollin. Blissfield. Enlisted in Co. K, Aug. 24, 1861, at Blissfield, age 19. Mustered Sept. 1, 1861. Commissioned 1st Lieutenant Nov. 3, 1863, mustered May 23, 1864. Mustered out Sept. 30, 1864, at Sturgis. Resided c. 1905 at Washington, D.C.

Carpenter, Robert. Calhoun County. Enlisted and mustered in Co. A, Aug. 24, 1861, at Centreville, age 22. Wounded at Stones River. Mustered out Sept. 30, 1864, at Sturgis.

Carr, Thomas. Enlisted in Co. F, Feb. 15, 1864, at Leonidas, age 24. Mustered Feb. 27, 1864. Joined regiment Mar. 15, 1864, at Rossville, GA. Transferred Apr. 15, 1865, to Co. F, reorganized 11th Michigan Infantry. Mustered out Sept. 16, 1865, at Nashville.

Cary, Martin L. Lenawee County. Enlisted and mustered in Co. H, Sept. 11, 1861, at Medina, age 25. Discharged for disability Nov. 20, 1861.

Cary, Willard E. Burr Oak. Enlisted and mustered in Co. D, Oct. 1, 1862, at Burr Oak, age 37. Transferred Apr. 15, 1865, to Co. D, reorganized 11th Michigan Infantry. Corporal May 11, 1865. Discharged June 16, 1865, at Chattanooga. Died Feb. 15, 1892, at Decatur.

Case, Daniel. Monroe County. Enlisted in Co. I. No further record.

Castle or Cassel, George. Lenawee County. Enlisted in Co. K, Aug. 24, 1861, at Adrian, age

23. Mustered Sept. 1, 1861. Deserted Dec. 5, 1861.

Catlin, Edward N. Algansee. Enlisted in Co. C, 1st Michigan Infantry, Apr. 24, 1861, at Coldwater for 3 months, age 21. Mustered May 1, 1861. Mustered out Aug. 7, 1861, at Detroit. Reentered service. Sergeant, Co. H, 11th Michigan Infantry, Aug. 24, 1861, mustered Aug. 28, 1861. 1st Sergeant. Commissioned 2nd Lieutenant, Co. E, June 23, 1862, mustered Nov. 13, 1862. Commissioned 1st Lieutenant Jan. 1, 1863, mustered Mar. 21, 1863. Acting Assistant Quartermaster of Contraband Camp from May to July 1863. Assigned to duty in Co. H from Aug. 1863 to Mar. 1, 1864. Commanded Co. H from March to July 1864. Wounded Aug. 7, 1864, at Utoy Creek. Died of wounds Aug. 8, 1864. Buried in national cemetery in Marietta, GA, section H, grave 9173.

Catlin, George W. Branch County. Enlisted and mustered in Co. B, Aug. 24, 1861, at Quincy, age 20. Transferred Sept. 20, 1862, to Co. C, 16th Michigan Infantry. Died of disease Oct. 26, 1862, near Sharpsburg, MD.

Caton, George. Lenawee County. Enlisted and mustered in Co. K, Sept. 1, 1861, at Deerfield, age 18. Mustered out Sept. 30, 1864, at Sturgis.

Cauchie, James. Monroe County. Enlisted and mustered in Co. I, Aug. 24, 1861, at Raisinville, age 22. Transferred to Veteran Reserve Corps Apr. 10, 1864. Served in 11th Regiment VRC.

Cay, Benjamin F. Cambria. Enlisted and mustered in Co. F, Sept. 11, 1861, at Quincy. Died of measles Feb. 4, 1862, at Bardstown, KY.

Chadwick, Jabez. Enlisted in Co. G for 1 year. Mustered Feb. 22, 1865. Died of disease May 15, 1865, at Chattanooga.

Chadwick, Samuel. Three Rivers. Entered service as Adjutant, age 43. Resigned Feb. 13, 1863. Commissioned and mustered as Captain, Co. H, 28th Michigan, Oct. 1864.

Chamberlain, Lewis C. Frenchtown. Enlisted and mustered in Co. I, Aug. 24, 1861, at Frenchtown, age 32. Died of consumption Feb. 15, 1862, at Bardstown, KY.

Chamberlain, Nelson. London. Entered service in Co. I as Captain, Aug. 24, 1861, at London, age 37. Commissioned Aug. 24, 1861. Resigned Feb. 19, 1863, due to disability.

Chamberlain, Richard. Branch County. Enlisted in Co. H, Aug. 24, 1861, at Coldwater, age 43. Mustered Aug. 28, 1861. Discharged for disability Apr. 29, 1862.

Chamberlain, William E. Mattison. Enlisted in Co. H, Aug. 24, 1861, at Coldwater, age 21. Mustered Oct. 1, 1861. Killed Dec. 31, 1862, at Stones River.

Chamberlain, William L. Cass County. Enlisted in Co. E at Three Rivers, age 20. Mustered Aug. 24, 1861. Corporal Aug. 22, 1862. Mustered out Sept. 30, 1864, at Sturgis.

Champlin, William G. St. Joseph County. Enlisted in Co. C at Kinderhook, age 34. Mustered Aug. 24, 1861. Discharged for disability Feb. 13, 1862, at Bardstown, KY.

Chandler, George. Branch County. Enlisted and mustered in Co. C, Aug. 24, 1861, at Clarendon, age 46. Discharged for disability Feb. 13, 1862, at Bardstown, KY.

Chandler, Thomas G. Enlisted and mustered in Co. K, Sept. 17, 1864, at Jackson for 1 year, age 27. Transferred Apr. 15, 1865, to Co. K, reorganized 11th Michigan Infantry. Discharged June 16, 1865, at Chattanooga.

Chapin, William A. Lenawee County. Enlisted in Co. G at Huron County, age 18. Mustered Sept. 4, 1861. Deserted Dec. 6, 1861, at White Pigeon.

Chapman, Samuel or Stephen. St. Joseph County. Enlisted and mustered in Co. D, Aug. 24, 1861, at Bronson, age 20. Discharged Aug. 19, 1862, at Louisville.

Cheney, Alphreus or Alpheus. Lenawee County. Enlisted in Co. K, Aug. 24, 1861, at Fairfield, age 22. Mustered Sept. 1, 1861. Wounded Jan. 2, 1863, at Stones River. Mustered out Sept. 30, 1864, at Sturgis.

Cheney, Cullen T. Lenawee County. Enlisted in Co. K, Aug. 24, 1861, at Fairfield, age 20. Mustered Sept. 1, 1861. Corporal Dec. 3, 1862. Mustered out Sept. 30, 1864, at Sturgis.

Cheney, Edward S. Lenawee County. Enlisted in Co. K as Corporal, Aug. 24, 1861, at Adrian, age 32. Mustered Sept. 1, 1861. Discharged for disability Aug. 27, 1862, at Nashville.

Childs, Lewis E. Ypsilanti. Entered service in Co. I as 1st Lieutenant, Aug. 24, 1861, at Augusta, age 25. Commissioned Aug. 24, 1861. Commissioned Captain Mar. 12, 1862, mustered Apr. 27, 1863. Wounded and captured Sept. 20, 1863, at Chickamauga. Exchanged. Mustered out Sept. 30, 1864, at Sturgis. Died Feb. 1, 1889.

Chittendon, Orville A. St. Joseph County. Enlisted and mustered in Co. A, Aug. 24, 1861, at Centreville, age 18. Discharged for disability Nov. 9, 1861, at White Pigeon.

Christy, Jesse J. Branch County. Enlisted and mustered in Co. D as Corporal, Aug. 24, 1861, at Bronson, age 23. Captured Dec. 31, 1862, at Stones River. Paroled Mar. 1863 at Camp

Chase, OH. Mustered out Sept. 30, 1864, at Sturgis.

Church, Thelisimar A. St. Joseph County. Enlisted and mustered in Co. A, Aug. 24, 1861, at Centreville, age 26. Mustered out Sept. 30, 1864, at Sturgis.

Clark, Allen W. *see* Clark, William A.

Clark, Andrew. Butler. Enlisted and mustered in Co. B, Aug. 24, 1861, at Butler, age 22. Died of chronic diarrhea Apr. 13, 1862, at Belmont, KY. Buried in national cemetery in Louisville.

Clark, Andrew J. Lenawee County. Enlisted and mustered in Co. F, Sept. 11, 1861, at Morenci, age 25. Mustered out Sept. 30, 1864, at Sturgis.

Clark, George D. St. Joseph County. Enlisted as Musician, Aug. 24, 1861, at White Pigeon, age 21. Mustered Sept. 24, 1861. Mustered out Aug. 22, 1862, at Nashville.

Clark, George L. Enlisted and mustered in Co. E, Aug. 24, 1861, at Three Rivers, age 21. Mustered out Sept. 30, 1864, at Sturgis.

Clark, Henry H. St. Joseph County. Enlisted and mustered in Co. A, Aug. 24, 1861, at Centreville, age 20. Wounded at Stones River. Captured September 1863. Mustered out Sept. 30, 1864, at Sturgis.

Clark, Jason. St. Joseph County. Enlisted as Musician, Aug. 24, 1861, at White Pigeon, age 19. Mustered Sept. 24, 1861. Mustered out Aug. 22, 1862, at Nashville.

Clark, John. Berrien County. Enlisted and mustered in Co. A, Aug. 24, 1861, at Centreville, age 23. Wounded and captured. Paroled Sept. 1863. Mustered out Sept. 30, 1864, at Sturgis. Resided c. 1905 at Benton Harbor.

Clark, Martin V.B. St. Joseph County. Enlisted and mustered in Co. A, Aug. 24, 1861, at Centreville, age 22. Mustered out Sept. 30, 1864, at Sturgis. Reentered service. Private, Co. I, in 30th Michigan Infantry, for 1 year, Dec. 5, 1864, mustered Dec. 14, 1864. Corporal Jan. 9, 1865. Mustered out June 24, 1865, at Detroit. Resided c. 1905 at Traverse City.

Clark, Norman L. Lenawee County. Enlisted in Co. K, Feb. 26, 1864, at Franklin, age 26. Mustered Feb. 27, 1864. Joined regiment June 10, 1864, at Chattanooga. Sergeant Mar. 16, 1865. Transferred Apr. 15, 1865, to Co. K, reorganized 11th Michigan Infantry. Mustered out Sept. 16, 1865, at Nashville. Resided c. 1905 at Milford.

Clark, Samuel A. Branch County. Enlisted and mustered in Co. D, Aug. 24, 1861, at White Pigeon, age 20. Died of measles Apr. 1, 1862, at Bardstown, KY. Buried in national cemetery in Lebanon, KY, grave 354.

Clark, Thomas. Branch County. Enlisted and mustered in Co. B, Aug. 24, 1861, at Butler, age 18. Discharged for disability Sept. 15, 1861, at White Pigeon.

Clark, William A. Noble. Enlisted in Co. D, Aug. 15, 1862, at Bronson, age 21. Mustered Sept. 1, 1862. Died of measles Jan. 5, 1863, at Nashville. Buried in national cemetery in Nashville.

Clark, William O. Hillsdale County. Enlisted and mustered in Co. F, Sept. 11, 1861, at Ransom, age 18. Wounded Nov. 1863 near Chattanooga. Wounded July 30, 1864, near Atlanta. Mustered out Sept. 30, 1864, at Sturgis.

Clase, David. Vandalia. Enlisted in Co. E, age 37. Mustered Aug. 24, 1861. Corporal Jan. 28, 1862. Wounded Sept. 20, 1863, at Chickamauga. Died of wounds Oct. 16, 1863, at Chattanooga.

Clase, Henry. St. Joseph County. Enlisted and mustered in Co. E, Aug. 24, 1861, at Three Rivers, age 21. Captured Sept. 20, 1863, at Chickamauga. Paroled May 8, 1864. Mustered out Sept. 30, 1864, at Sturgis.

Clemens, Warren. Hillsdale County. Enlisted and mustered in Co. B, Aug. 24, 1861, at Allen, age 22. Discharged for disability Feb. 1, 1863, at Nashville. Resided c. 1905 at Allen.

Clemens, William. Enlisted and mustered in Co. D, Aug. 5, 1862, at Burr Oak, age 44. Transferred to Invalid Corps Nov. 1, 1863.

Cleveland, Elijah. Lenawee County. Enlisted in Co. K, Aug. 24, 1861, at Adrian, age 18. Mustered Sept. 1, 1861. Mustered out Sept. 30, 1864, at Sturgis.

Clingelman, Daniel. St. Joseph County. Enlisted and mustered in Co. E, Aug. 24, 1861, at Three Rivers, age 22. Mustered out Sept. 30, 1864, at Sturgis.

Clipfell, Henry F. St. Joseph County. Enlisted as Musician, Aug. 24, 1861, at White Pigeon, age 21. Mustered Sept. 24, 1861. Mustered out Aug. 22, 1862, at Nashville.

Clubine, Benjamin F. Barry County. Enlisted in Co. E at Three Rivers, age 20. Mustered Aug. 24, 1861. Wounded Dec. 31, 1862, at Stones River. Mustered out Sept. 30, 1864, at Sturgis.

Coats, Leroy. Lenawee County. Enlisted and mustered in Co. F, Sept. 11, 1861, at Medina, age 19. Corporal Apr. 9, 1864. Mustered out Sept. 30, 1864, at Sturgis.

Coberley, Isaac. Hillsdale County. Enlisted and mustered in Co. F, Sept. 11, 1861, age 31. Discharged Nov. 21, 1861.

Coddington, Charles. Leonidas. Enlisted and mustered in Co. A as Sergeant, Aug. 24, 1861, at Centreville, age 19. 1st Sergeant Feb. 7, 1862. Commissioned 1st Lieutenant Jan. 30,

1863, mustered Mar. 31, 1863. Commissioned Captain Jan. 6, 1864, mustered Apr. 22, 1864. Mustered out Sept. 30, 1864, at Sturgis.

Coe, John W. Branch County. Enlisted and mustered in Co. D, Aug. 24, 1861, at Bronson, age 29. Served in Pioneer Corps. Mustered out Sept. 30, 1864, at Sturgis.

Cole, Henry D. Enlisted in Co. D, Feb. 11, 1865, at Franklin for 1 year. Mustered Feb. 14, 1865. Died of disease Mar. 15, 1865, at Louisville.

Cole, John F. Branch County. Enlisted and mustered in Co. B, Aug. 24, 1861, at Quincy, age 18. Corporal Jan. 22, 1863. Sergeant July 17, 1864. Mustered out Sept. 30, 1864, at Sturgis.

Cole, Lyman L. Branch County. Enlisted and mustered in Co. B, Aug. 24, 1861, at Quincy, age 18. Mustered out Sept. 30, 1864, at Sturgis.

Colyer, William H. Blissfield. Enlisted in Co. B, Aug. 31, 1864, at Blissfield for 1 year, age 21. Mustered Sept. 1, 1864. Joined regiment Feb. 20, 1865, at Chattanooga. Transferred Apr. 15, 1865, to Co. B, reorganized 11th Michigan Infantry. Discharged June 16, 1865, at Chattanooga. Resided c. 1905 at Blissfield.

Combs, Eber M. Enlisted in Co. D at Bronson, age 20. Mustered Aug. 24, 1861. Died of chronic diarrhea June 5, 1863, at Nashville. Buried in national cemetery in Nashville.

Comstock, Myron M. Hillsdale County. Enlisted and mustered in Co. F, Sept. 11, 1861, at Wheatland, age 21. Corporal Aug. 27, 1862. Wounded and captured Dec. 31, 1862, at Stones River. Mustered out Sept. 30, 1864, at Sturgis.

Comstock, Silas G. Three Rivers. Entered service in Co. G as 2nd Lieutenant at White Pigeon, age 28. Commissioned Aug. 24, 1861. Mustered Sept. 4, 1861. Resigned July 20, 1862.

Condick, Daniel. Enlisted and mustered in Co. G, Jan. 4, 1864, at Flowerfield, age 35. Joined regiment Jan. 28, 1864, at Rossville, GA. Transferred Apr. 15, 1865, to Co. G, reorganized 11th Michigan Infantry. Discharged Sept. 26, 1865, at Detroit.

Cone, Reuben. Hillsdale County. Enlisted and mustered in Co. F, Sept. 11, 1861, at Hillsdale, age 18. Deserted Nov. 2, 1861, at White Pigeon.

Coney, Eleazor J. *see* Covey, Eleazor J.

Conley, Christopher. Branch County. Enlisted and mustered in Co. B as Corporal, Aug. 24, 1861, at Quincy, age 43. Discharged for disability Oct. 18, 1862, at Nashville. Died Mar. 10, 1895. Buried at Quincy.

Converse, James O. Medina. Enlisted and mustered in Co. F as Sergeant, Sept. 11, 1861, at Medina, age 23. Discharged for disability July 27, 1862, at Detroit.

Coon, Abel. Branch County. Enlisted in Co. H as Fifer, Aug. 24, 1861, at Coldwater, age 38. Mustered Aug. 28, 1861. Captured Dec. 31, 1862, at Stones River. Mustered out Sept. 30, 1864, at Sturgis.

Cooney, Thomas E.A. Hillsdale County. Enlisted in Co. K, Aug. 24, 1861, at Camden, age 21. Mustered Sept. 1, 1861. Discharged for disability Feb. 18, 1863, at Murfreesboro, TN.

Coplin, William. Hillsdale County. Enlisted and mustered in Co. B, Aug. 24, 1861, at Allen, age 20. Transferred Sept. 20, 1861 to Co. F, 16th Michigan Infantry. Discharged Oct. 24, 1862, at Washington, D.C.

Cornwell, Anson. Branch County. Enlisted in Co. K, Aug. 24, 1861, at Petersburg, age 29. Mustered Sept. 1, 1861. Discharged for disability Apr. 6, 1862.

Corwin, Aretus. Branch County. Enlisted in Co. H, Aug. 24, 1861, at Coldwater, age 18. Mustered Aug. 28, 1861. Discharged for disability June 26, 1862.

Courtright, Constant. Enlisted and mustered, company unassigned, Sept. 1, 1864, at Jackson for 1 year, age 21. No further record.

Covey, Eleazor J. Leonidas. Enlisted in Co. A, Dec. 30, 1863, at Leonidas, age 21. Mustered Jan. 4, 1864. Joined regiment Jan. 28, 1864, at Rossville, GA. Transferred Mar. 30, 1864, to Co. F. Transferred Apr. 15, 1865, to Co. F, reorganized 11th Michigan Infantry. Discharged May 22, 1865, at Nashville.

Cowen, Daman. Monroe County. Enlisted in Co. K, Aug. 24, 1861, at Dundee, age 23. Mustered Sept. 1, 1861. Mustered out Sept. 30, 1864, at Sturgis.

Coy, Benjamin F. *see* Cay, Benjamin F.

Craig, Edwin. St. Joseph County. Enlisted and mustered in Co. E, Aug. 24, 1861, at Three Rivers, age 18. Discharged for disability Oct. 20, 1862, at Nashville.

Cramer, George H. or W. Enlisted in Co. A, Dec. 11, 1863, at Leonidas, age 19. Mustered Jan. 4, 1864. Joined regiment Jan. 28, 1864, at Rossville, GA. Wounded Aug. 7, 1864, at Utoy Creek. Transferred Apr. 15, 1865, to Co. A, reorganized 11th Michigan Infantry. Mustered out Sept. 16, 1865, at Nashville.

Crane, Joseph B. Monroe County. Enlisted and mustered in Co. I, Aug. 24, 1861, at Ash, age 35. Discharged for disability Aug. 14, 1862, at Nashville. Resided c. 1905 at Carleton.

Crocker, James A. Hillsdale County. Enlisted in Co. G as Corporal at Jefferson, age 26. Mustered Sept. 4, 1861. Mustered out Sept. 30, 1864, at Sturgis. Resided c. 1905 at Stanton.

Cronering, Uriah. Monroe. Enlisted and mustered in Co. I, Aug. 24, 1861, at Exeter, age 22. Discharged for disability May 25, 1863, at Detroit.

Crow, Thomas. St. Joseph County. Enlisted in Co. G at Centreville, age 35. Mustered Sept. 4, 1861. Discharged for disability at Louisville.

Crull, Henry. Branch County. Enlisted in Co. H, Aug. 24, 1861, at Coldwater, age 19. Mustered Aug. 28, 1861. Died of pneumonia Feb. 9, 1862, at Bardstown, KY.

Crull, Horace. Ovid. Enlisted in Co. H, Aug. 24, 1861, at Coldwater, age 18. Mustered Aug. 28, 1861. Discharged for disability Apr. 9, 1862.

Cummings, William H. Quincy. Enlisted and mustered in Co. B, Aug. 24, 1861, at Quincy, age 21. Killed Nov. 25, 1863, at Missionary Ridge. Buried in national cemetery in Chattanooga.

Curn, James. St. Joseph County. Enlisted in Co. G at White Pigeon, age 22. Mustered Sept. 4, 1861. Mustered out Sept. 30, 1864, at Sturgis.

Currien or Currier, Almeenen or Almerin C. St. Joseph County. Enlisted in Co. G at Centreville, age 22. Mustered Sept. 4, 1861. Corporal June 1, 1862. Captured Dec. 31, 1862, at Stones River. Paroled Apr. 1863. Mustered out Sept. 30, 1864, at Sturgis.

Curtis, Thomas B. Augusta. Enlisted and mustered in Co. I, Aug. 24, 1861, at Augusta, age 24. Died of hemorrhage of bowels Dec. 17, 1861, at Louisville. Buried in national cemetery in Louisville, section A3, grave 5.

Cushman, James M. Bronson. Enlisted in Co. F, 1st Michigan Infantry, Apr. 20, 1861, at Detroit for 3 months, age 21. Mustered May 1, 1861. Mustered out Aug. 7, 1861, at Detroit. Reentered service. Sergeant, Co. H, 11th Michigan Infantry, Aug. 24, 1861, mustered Aug. 28, 1861. 1st Sergeant Aug. 9, 1862. Commissioned 1st Lieutenant Aug. 3, 1863, mustered Aug. 31, 1863. Mustered out Sept. 30, 1864, at Sturgis.

Cusick or Cusic, Hiram. Quincy. Enlisted in Co. H, Aug. 24, 1861, at Coldwater, age 21. Mustered Aug. 28, 1861. Died of chronic diarrhea Aug. 10, 1863, at Nashville. Buried in national cemetery in Nashville.

Cutler, Abel A. Washtenaw County. Enlisted and mustered in Co. I, Aug. 24, 1861, at Sumpter, age 22. Discharged for disability June 30, 1862.

Daggat, James B. Branch County. Enlisted and mustered in Co. B, Aug. 24, 1861, at Quincy, age 23. Transferred Sept. 20, 1861, to 16th Michigan Infantry. Reenlisted Dec. 21, 1863, at Rappahannock Station, VA. Mustered Dec. 24, 1863. Corporal, Co. G, in 16th Michigan Infantry, May 1, 1865. Mustered out July 8, 1865, near Jeffersonville, IN.

Dailey, Alva P. Three Rivers. Enlisted and mustered in Co. E, Aug. 24, 1861, at Three Rivers, age 22. Died of smallpox Dec. 8, 1861, at White Pigeon.

Dakin, Colman. Lenawee County. Enlisted in Co. K as Sergeant, Aug. 24, 1861, at Ogden, age 26. Mustered Sept. 1, 1861. Captured Jan. 2, 1863, at Stones River. Discharged for disability Oct. 2, 1863, at Camp Chase, OH.

Damon, Charles A. Leonidas. Enlisted in Co. A, Dec. 5, 1863, at Leonidas, age 19. Mustered Jan. 4, 1864. Joined regiment Jan. 28, 1864, at Rossville, GA. Transferred Apr. 15, 1865, to Co. F, reorganized 11th Michigan Infantry. Mustered out Sept. 16, 1865, at Nashville. Resided c. 1905 at Leonidas.

Damon, Henry C. St. Joseph County. Enlisted and mustered in Co. A, Aug. 24, 1861, at Centreville, age 30. Captured Sept. 20, 1863, at Chickamauga. Escaped June 28, 1864, from Andersonville, GA. Rejoined regiment July 23, 1864. Mustered out Sept. 30, 1864, at Sturgis. Resided c. 1905 at Leonidas.

Daniel, Charles *see* David, Charles.

Danks, Henry S. Branch County. Enlisted and mustered in Co. B, Aug. 24, 1861, at Butler, age 35. Mustered out Sept. 30, 1864, at Sturgis.

Dates, William J. Algansee. Enlisted in Co. H, Aug. 24, 1861, at Coldwater, age 20. Mustered Aug. 28, 1861. Died of typhoid fever Mar. 22, 1862, at Bardstown, KY. Buried in national cemetery in Lebanon, KY, grave 309.

David, Charles. St. Joseph County. Enlisted and mustered in Co. E, Aug. 24, 1861, at Three Rivers, age 25. Served in Pioneer Brigade. Mustered out Sept. 30, 1864, at Sturgis. Resided c. 1905 at East Gilead.

Davis, David. Wayne County. Enlisted and mustered in Co. I, Aug. 26, 1861, at Detroit, age 44. Discharged for disability Mar. 12, 1863, at Louisville.

Davis, Henry M. Enlisted in Co. A, Dec. 30, 1863, at Colon, age 24. Mustered Jan. 4, 1864. Joined regiment Jan. 28, 1864, at Rossville, GA. Transferred Mar. 30, 1864, to Co. F. Died of disease June 22, 1864, at Nashville. Buried in national cemetery in Nashville.

Davis, William. St. Joseph County. Enlisted and mustered in Co. A, Aug. 24, 1861, at Centreville, age 21. Mustered out Sept. 30, 1864, at Sturgis.

Day, James. Kalamazoo County. Enlisted in Co.

G as Sergeant at Schoolcraft, age 27. Mustered Sept. 4, 1861. 1st Sergeant Jan. 22, 1863. Wounded Aug. 7, 1864, at Utoy Creek. Mustered out Sept. 30, 1864, at Sturgis.

Day, John M. Parkville. Enlisted and mustered in Co. E as Corporal, Aug. 24, 1861, at Three Rivers, age 35. Color Bearer June 1863. Killed Nov. 25, 1863, at Missionary Ridge. Buried in national cemetery in Chattanooga.

Day, Robert S. Burr Oak. Enlisted and mustered in Co. E, Aug. 5, 1862, at Centreville, age 27. Joined regiment Jan. 1863 at Murfreesboro, TN. Transferred Apr. 15, 1865, to Co. E, reorganized 11th Michigan Infantry. Discharged June 16, 1865, at Chattanooga. Resided c. 1905 at Empire.

De Bois, Eugene. Branch County. Enlisted and mustered in Co. B, Aug. 24, 1861, at Algansee, age 18. Discharged for disability Nov. 20, 1861, at White Pigeon.

De Bois, Harvey. Branch County. Enlisted in Co. B, Jan. 4, 1864, at Kalamazoo, age 20. Mustered Feb. 15, 1864. Joined regiment Mar. 15, 1864, at Rossville, GA. Corporal. Transferred Apr. 15, 1865, to Co. B, reorganized 11th Michigan Infantry. Mustered out Sept. 16, 1865, at Nashville. Resided c. 1905 at McLean.

De Forrest, Perry. Prairie Ronde. Enlisted in Co. G at White Pigeon, age 19. Mustered Sept. 4, 1861. Killed Dec. 31, 1862, at Stones River.

Dean, William. Monroe County. Enlisted and mustered in Co. I as Corporal, Aug. 24, 1861, at Frenchtown, age 42. Discharged for disability May 28, 1862.

Demott, Levi. Lenawee County. Enlisted in Co. K, Aug. 24, 1861, at Macon, age 19. Mustered Sept. 1, 1861. Deserted Oct. 1, 1861, at White Pigeon.

Denis, Dwight V. St. Joseph County. Enlisted and mustered in Co. C, Aug. 24, 1861, at Sturgis, age 18. Reenlisted Feb. 27, 1864, at Rossville, GA. Mustered Mar. 31, 1864. Transferred Apr. 15, 1865, to Co. C, reorganized 11th Michigan Infantry. Mustered out Sept. 16, 1865, at Nashville.

Derry, Orlando. Branch County. Enlisted and mustered in Co. H, Aug. 24, 1861, at Coldwater, age 19. Mustered out Sept. 30, 1864, at Sturgis.

Devee, Jacob J. Monroe County. Enlisted and mustered in Co. I, Aug. 24, 1861, at Monroe, age 18. Mustered out Sept. 30, 1864, at Sturgis. Resided c. 1905 at London.

Dewey, Cyrus J. Enlisted in Co. K, Feb. 26, 1864, at Wright, age 18. Mustered Mar. 1, 1864. Joined regiment June 10, 1864. Transferred Apr. 15, 1865, to Co. K, reorganized 11th Michigan Infantry. Corporal May 8, 1865. Mustered out Sept. 16, 1865, at Nashville.

Dewsenberry, Alba M. Branch County. Enlisted and mustered in Co. D, Aug. 24, 1861, at Bronson, age 36. Died of measles Feb. 16, 1862, at Bardstown, KY.

Dickinson or Dickerson, Alfred H. Branch County. Enlisted and mustered in Co. B, Aug. 24, 1861, at Butler, age 18. Discharged to date June 30, 1862.

Dickinson, Augustus E. St. Joseph County. Enlisted in Co. G at Leonidas, age 19. Mustered Sept. 4, 1861. Wounded at Stones River. Mustered out Sept. 30, 1864, at Sturgis.

Dickinson, Darius C. St. Joseph County. Enlisted in Co. G as Corporal at Leonidas, age 42. Mustered Sept. 4, 1861. Transferred Oct. 19, 1862, to Band. Returned to Company Dec. 1, 1862. Wounded Sept. 1863. Mustered out Sept. 30, 1864, at Sturgis.

Dickinson, George W. St. Joseph County. Enlisted and mustered in Co. A, Aug. 24, 1861, at Centreville, age 23. Corporal May 5, 1863. Wounded July 26, 1864, near Atlanta. Mustered out Sept. 30, 1864, at Sturgis.

Dickinson, Jay. Burr Oak. Enlisted and mustered in Co. A, Aug. 29, 1862, at Burr Oak, age 22. Joined regiment Jan. 18, 1863, at Murfreesboro, TN. Died of disease Jan. 4, 1864, at Louisville.

Dickinson, Samuel C. Leonidas. Enlisted and mustered in Co. G, Dec. 17, 1862, at Detroit, age 29. Joined regiment Feb. 20, 1863, at Murfreesboro, TN. Captured Aug. 26, 1864, at East Point, GA. Transferred Apr. 15, 1865, to Co. G, reorganized 11th Michigan Infantry. Admitted to Harper Hospital, Sept. 6, 1865. Discharged Sept. 22, 1865, at Detroit.

Dingman, John. Monroe County. Enlisted in Co. K, Aug. 24, 1861, at Petersburg, age 30. Mustered Sept. 1, 1861. Mustered out Sept. 30, 1864, at Sturgis.

Dinsmore, Rufus. Lenawee County. Enlisted and mustered in Co. F, Sept. 11, 1861, at Pittsford, age 24. Discharged for disability Feb. 18, 1862.

Dir, Peter S. Enlisted in Co. F, Feb. 19, 1864, at Waukeshma, age 29. Mustered Feb. 27, 1864. Joined regiment Mar. 15, 1864, at Rossville, GA. Transferred Apr. 15, 1865, to Co. F, reorganized 11th Michigan Infantry. Mustered out Sept. 16, 1865, at Nashville.

Dixon, Alonzo. Dundee. Enlisted in Co. K, Aug. 24, 1861, at Dundee, age 20. Mustered Sept. 1, 1861. Died of measles Jan. 27, 1862, at Bardstown, KY. Buried in national cemetery in Lebanon, KY, grave 500.

Dixon, Cuthbert. St. Joseph County. Enlisted

and mustered in Co. A as Sergeant, Aug. 24, 1861, at Centreville, age 19. 1st Sergeant Mar. 21, 1863. Commissioned 2nd Lieutenant Apr. 19, 1864. Wounded May 27, 1864, near Dallas, GA. Mustered out Sept. 30, 1864, at Sturgis.

Dodd, Wesley. Lenawee County. Enlisted and mustered in Co. F, Sept. 11, 1861, at Seneca, age 18. Wounded July 4, 1864, at Ruff's Station. Died of wounds Aug. 9, 1864. Buried in national cemetery in Chattanooga.

Dodd, William H. Lenawee County. Enlisted and mustered in Co. F, Sept. 11, 1861, at Seneca, age 22. Corporal Mar. 1, 1862. Sergeant Jan. 1, 1863. Wounded July 4, 1864, at Ruff's Station. Mustered out Sept. 30, 1864, at Sturgis.

Dolbee, Peter V. Enlisted and mustered in Co. E, Aug. 24, 1861, at Three Rivers. Wounded Dec. 31, 1862, at Stones River. Discharged for disability Mar. 27, 1863, at Louisville. Died of wounds Aug. 29, 1866.

Dolton, Charles H. Enlisted in Co. E, Feb. 25, 1864, at Three Rivers, age 21. Mustered Feb. 29, 1864. Joined regiment Apr. 10, 1864, at Graysville, GA. Wounded Aug. 7, 1864, at Utoy Creek. Transferred Apr. 15, 1865, to Co. E, reorganized 11th Michigan Infantry. Discharged for disability June 14, 1865, at Jeffersonville, IN, on account of wounds.

Donkin, Charles W. St. Joseph County. Enlisted and mustered in Co. A, Aug. 24, 1861, at Centreville, age 21. Mustered out Sept. 30, 1864, at Sturgis.

Doran, Edward. Monroe County. Enlisted and mustered in Co. I, Aug. 24, 1861, at Dundee, age 35. Discharged for disability Jan. 15, 1863, at Nashville.

Dorn, James. Burr Oak. Enlisted and mustered in Co. D, Aug. 20, 1862, at Burr Oak, age 18. Transferred Apr. 15, 1865, to Co. D, reorganized 11th Michigan Infantry. Discharged June 16, 1865, at Chattanooga.

Doughty, Benjamin F. Entered service as Major, Aug. 24, 1861. Commissioned Aug. 24, 1861. Resigned Aug. 18, 1862.

Doughty, Courtland W. St. Joseph County. Enlisted and mustered in Co. C as Corporal, Aug. 24, 1861, at Colon, age 30. Discharged for disability Jan. 1, 1863, at Nashville.

Downey, John Florian. Enlisted in Co. E, Feb. 22, 1864, at Kalamazoo, age 18. Mustered Feb. 23, 1864. Joined regiment Apr. 10, 1864, at Graysville, GA. Transferred Apr. 15, 1865, to Co. E, reorganized 11th Michigan Infantry. Drum Major July 1865. Mustered out Sept. 16, 1865, at Nashville.

Doyle, Peter. St. Joseph County. Enlisted and mustered in Co. C, Aug. 24, 1861, at Sturgis, age 26. Discharged for disability June 27, 1862, at Nashville.

Drake, Addison T. Sturgis. Entered service as Quartermaster, Aug. 24, 1861, at White Pigeon. Commissioned Aug. 24, 1861. Mustered Sept. 24, 1861. Served as Acting Quartermaster at the brigade, division, and corps levels from February 1863 through muster out. Commissioned Captain, Co. K, June 17, 1864. Mustered out Sept. 30, 1864, at Sturgis.

Drake, Foster. St. Joseph County. Enlisted in Co. G at Three Rivers, age 19. Mustered Sept. 4, 1861. Mustered out Sept. 30, 1864, at Sturgis.

Drake, John C. Sturgis. Enlisted and mustered in Co. C, Aug. 9, 1862, at Sturgis, age 26. Transferred Apr. 15, 1865, to Co. C, reorganized 11th Michigan Infantry. Discharged June 16, 1865, at Chattanooga. Died Nov. 5, 1895.

Drake, Thomas. Palmyra. Enlisted in Co. K, Aug. 24, 1861, at Palmyra, age 20. Mustered Sept. 1, 1861. Died of typhoid Apr. 16, 1862, at Belmont, KY. Buried in national cemetery in Louisville.

Drake, William A. Enlisted and mustered in Co. G, Jan. 14, 1864, at Kalamazoo, age 18. Transferred Apr. 15, 1865, to Co. G, reorganized 11th Michigan Infantry. Mustered out Sept. 16, 1865, at Nashville.

Draper, Stephen S. Washtenaw County. Enlisted and mustered in Co. I, Aug. 24, 1861, at Ypsilanti, age 22. Mustered out Sept. 30, 1864, at Sturgis. Resided c. 1905 at Ypsilanti.

Dresher, George. St. Joseph County. Enlisted and mustered in Co. E, Aug. 24, 1861, at Three Rivers, age 20. Mustered out Sept. 30, 1864, at Sturgis.

Driggs, Jehiel D. Branch County. Enlisted and mustered in Co. D as Corporal, Aug. 24, 1861, at Bronson, age 20. Discharged for disability May 19, 1862, at Louisville.

Du Bois, Eugene *see* De Bois, Eugene.

Duffy, John. Sparta. Enlisted in Co. G at Jefferson, age 33. Mustered Sept. 4, 1861. Died of typhoid fever Mar. 9, 1863, at Nashville. Buried in national cemetery in Nashville.

Dunn, Michael. Bethel. Enlisted and mustered in Co. D, Nov. 25, 1862, at Bronson, age 41. Transferred Apr. 15, 1865, to Co. D, reorganized 11th Michigan Infantry. Mustered out Sept. 16, 1865, at Nashville.

Dunn, Sylvester. Detroit. Enlisted and mustered in Co. I, Aug. 26, 1861, at Detroit, age 26. Died of pneumonia Dec. 24, 1861, at White Pigeon.

Dunning, Leroy. St. Joseph County. Enlisted and

mustered in Co. C, Aug. 24, 1861, at Leonidas, age 20. Corporal Dec. 22, 1863. Mustered out Sept. 30, 1864, at Sturgis.

Durfee, George. Hillsdale County. Enlisted in Co. F, Aug. 24, 1861. Mustered Nov. 19, 1861. Discharged at Bardstown, KY.

Durfee, Sidney A. St. Joseph County. Enlisted and mustered in Co. A, Aug. 24, 1861, at Centreville, age 19. Mustered out Sept. 30, 1864, at Sturgis.

Dusenberry, Seth L. Branch County. Enlisted in Co. H as Sergeant, Aug. 24, 1861, at Coldwater, age 20. Mustered Aug. 28, 1861. Mustered out Sept. 30, 1864, at Sturgis.

Earl, Brazillai or Barzillia, M. St. Joseph County. Enlisted and mustered in Co. A, Aug. 24, 1861, at Centreville, age 26. Corporal Jan. 11, 1864. Mustered out Sept. 30, 1864, at Sturgis. Resided c. 1905 at Ithaca.

Early, Henry T. St. Joseph County. Enlisted and mustered in Co. D, Aug. 24, 1861, at White Pigeon, age 18. Mustered out Sept. 30, 1864, at Sturgis.

Eastman, Benjamin F. Coldwater. Enlisted in Co. H, Aug. 24, 1861, at Coldwater, age 18. Mustered Aug. 28, 1861. Reenlisted Mar. 27, 1864, at Graysville, GA. Mustered Apr. 11, 1864. Wounded Aug. 7, 1864, at Utoy Creek. Died of wounds Aug. 1864, Aug. 12 or 16. Buried in national cemetery in Marietta, GA, section H, grave 9096.

Eaton, Rollin or Rolland O. St. Joseph County. Enlisted and mustered in Co. A, Aug. 24, 1861, at Centreville, age 20. Captured Dec. 31, 1862, at Stones River. Mustered out Sept. 30, 1864, at Sturgis.

Eaton, Tacitus E. Nottawa. Enlisted in Co. A, Dec. 16, 1862, at Nottawa, age 44. Mustered Dec. 24, 1862. Joined regiment Feb. 1, 1863, at Murfreesboro, TN. Transferred Apr. 15, 1865, to Co. A, reorganized 11th Michigan Infantry. Mustered out Sept. 16, 1865, at Nashville.

Eberhard, James. St. Joseph County. Enlisted and mustered in Co. D, Aug. 24, 1861, at Bronson, age 19. Captured Dec. 31, 1862, at Stones River. Paroled Apr. 1863. Discharged for disability Jan. 10, 1864, at Louisville.

Eckenberger, Jacob. Bronson. Enlisted and mustered in Co. D, Aug. 25, 1861, at Bronson, age 28. Captured Sept. 20, 1863, at Chickamauga. Paroled. Transferred Apr. 15, 1865, to Co. D, reorganized 11th Michigan Infantry. Discharged June 20, 1865, at Detroit. Buried at Decatur.

Edmonds, Melvin T. Branch County. Enlisted and mustered in Co. B as Sergeant, Aug. 24, 1861, at Quincy, age 23. Wounded May 28, 1864, near Dallas, GA. Mustered out Sept. 30, 1864, at Sturgis.

Edson, David. St. Joseph County. Enlisted and mustered in Co. B, Aug. 24, 1861, at Sherman, age 33. Mustered out Sept. 30, 1864, at Sturgis.

Edwards, Andrew. St. Joseph County. Enlisted in Co. K, Aug. 24, 1861, at White Pigeon, age 31. Mustered Sept. 1, 1861. Deserted Oct. 1, 1861.

Edwards, David. Medina. Enlisted and mustered in Co. F as Corporal, Sept. 11, 1861, at Morenci, age 30. Sergeant. Wounded Sept. 11, 1863, at Davis's Crossroads. Died Sept. 24, 1863.

Edwards, William H. Branch County. Enlisted and mustered in Co. D, Aug. 24, 1861, at Bronson, age 28. Discharged Aug. 14, 1862, at Nashville.

Eggleshoffer or Egelshofer, John. St. Joseph County. Enlisted and mustered in Co. E, Aug. 24, 1861, at Three Rivers, age 21. Wounded Sept. 1863. Mustered out Sept. 30, 1864, at Sturgis.

Eggleston, Bruce H. *see* Eggleston, Henry B.

Eggleston, Charles W. St. Joseph County. Enlisted and mustered in Co. D, Aug. 24, 1861, at Bronson, age 18. Mustered out Sept. 30, 1864, at Sturgis.

Eggleston, George. St. Joseph County. Enlisted and mustered in Co. E, Aug. 24, 1861, at Three Rivers, age 21. Mustered out Sept. 30, 1864, at Sturgis. Resided c. 1905 at Marcellus.

Eggleston, Henry B. Bronson. Enlisted and mustered in Co. D as 1st Sergeant, Aug. 24, 1861, at Bronson, age 20. Commissioned 2nd Lieutenant Mar. 12, 1862, mustered May 29, 1862. Commissioned 1st Lieutenant Dec. 20, 1862, mustered Jan. 21, 1863. Detached for duty in Pioneer Brigade, Jan. 23, 1863. Dismissed Jan. 9, 1864, for conduct prejudicial to good order and military propriety.

Eichoff, Francis. Ft. Wayne, IN. Enlisted and mustered in Co. F as Corporal, Sept. 11, 1861, at Fairfield, age 19. Transferred Dec. 5, 1862, to 4th U.S. Cavalry.

Eldridge, Nathaniel B. Lapeer. Entered service as Major, 7th Michigan Infantry, Aug. 7, 1861, age 48. Commissioned Aug. 7, 1861. Mustered Aug. 22, 1861. Resigned Dec. 18, 1861. Reentered service. Commissioned Lt. Colonel 11th Michigan Infantry, Apr. 1, 1862. Resigned Jan. 7, 1863, at Murfreesboro, TN.

Elliott, James T. Three Rivers. Enlisted and mustered in Co. E as Corporal, Aug. 24, 1861, at Three Rivers, age 21. Discharged July 1, 1864, to accept promotion as 1st Lieutenant and Quartermaster in 9th U.S. Colored Heavy Artillery. Relieved of duty Feb. 15, 1865. Arrested March 1, 1865, and court-martialed for drunkenness and misconduct. Pled guilty to misconduct; sentenced to forfeit one month's pay. Resigned June 17, 1865.

Elliott, Justin C. St. Joseph County. Entered service as Asst. Surgeon, Aug. 24, 1861, at White Pigeon, age 35. Mustered with regiment, but never commissioned.

Elliott, William N. White Pigeon. Entered service as Surgeon, Aug. 24, 1861, at White Pigeon, age 54. Commissioned Aug. 24, 1861. Acting Brigade Surgeon July 1863. Mustered out Sept. 30, 1864, at Sturgis.

Ellis, Elisha D. St. Joseph County. Enlisted and mustered in Co. C, Aug. 24, 1861, at White Pigeon, age 21. Transferred to Invalid Corps Sept. 30, 1863. Discharged Aug. 26, 1864, at Chicago. Resided c. 1905 at White Pigeon.

Elmer, Caleb U. Constantine. Enlisted and mustered in Co. E, Aug. 24, 1861, at Three Rivers, age 32. Died of disease May 6, 1862, at Louisville. Buried in national cemetery in Louisville.

Emmons, William H. Branch County. Enlisted and mustered in Co. B, Aug. 24, 1861, at Quincy, age 19. Discharged for disability Apr. 19, 1863, at Murfreesboro, TN. Resided c. 1905 at Algansee.

Engle, Nelson B. St. Joseph County. Enlisted and mustered in Co. C, Aug. 24, 1861, at Sturgis, age 20. Sergeant June 10, 1862. Mustered out Sept. 30, 1864, at Sturgis.

Ennis, Alexander. St. Joseph County. Enlisted and mustered in Co. E, Aug. 24, 1861, at Three Rivers, age 17. Mustered out Sept. 30, 1864, at Sturgis.

Ennis, Augustus. St. Joseph County. Enlisted and mustered in Co. E, Aug. 24, 1861, at Three Rivers, age 21. Mustered out Sept. 30, 1864, at Sturgis.

Ennis, James. Nottawa. Enlisted in Co. A, Dec. 16, 1862, at Nottawa, age 24. Mustered Dec. 24, 1862. Joined regiment Feb. 1, 1863, at Murfreesboro, TN. Transferred Apr. 15, 1865, to Co. A, reorganized 11th Michigan Infantry. Mustered out Sept. 16, 1865, at Nashville. Resided c. 1905 at Centreville.

Ennis, Robert D. Enlisted in Co. G, Feb. 1, 1864, at Centreville, age 24. Mustered Feb. 22, 1864. Joined regiment Mar. 15, 1864, at Rossville, GA. Killed Aug. 7, 1864, at Utoy Creek. Buried in national cemetery in Marietta, GA, section E, grave 6167.

Ensign, James H. Branch County. Enlisted and mustered in Co. A, Aug. 24, 1861, at Centreville, age 21. Captured Sept. 11, 1863, at Davis's Crossroads. Died July 2, 1864. Buried in national cemetery in Andersonville, GA.

Etheridge, John T. *see* Ethridge, John T.

Ethridge, Henry. Enlisted in Co. A, Dec. 22, 1863, at Leonidas, age 23. Mustered Jan. 4, 1864. Joined regiment Jan. 28, 1864, at Rossville, GA. Transferred Mar. 30, 1864, to Co. F. Wounded July 4, 1864, at Ruff's Station. Transferred Apr. 15, 1865, to Co. F, reorganized 11th Michigan Infantry. Mustered out Sept. 16, 1865, at Nashville.

Ethridge, John T. Enlisted in Co. A, Feb. 24, 1864, at Leonidas, age 22. Mustered Feb. 27, 1864. Joined regiment Mar. 15, 1864, at Rossville, GA. Transferred Mar. 30, 1864, to Company F. Transferred Apr. 15, 1865, to Co. F, reorganized 11th Michigan Infantry. Mustered out Sept. 16, 1865, at Nashville.

Evans, Lyman. Branch County. Enlisted and mustered in Co. D, Aug. 24, 1861, at Bronson, age 18. Wounded July 26, 1864, near Atlanta. Mustered out Sept. 30, 1864, at Sturgis. Buried in national cemetery in New Albany, IN, grave 657.

Evans, Oliver. Bethel. Enlisted and mustered in Co. D, Aug. 24, 1861, at Bronson, age 22. Died of typhoid fever Mar. 28, 1863, at Nashville. Buried in national cemetery in Nashville.

Evans, Richard. Monroe County. Enlisted in Co. K, Aug. 24, 1861, at Petersburg, age 35. Mustered Sept. 1, 1861. Captured Jan. 2, 1863, at Stones River. Mustered out Sept. 30, 1864, at Sturgis.

Evans, Robert. Hillsdale County. Enlisted in Co. H, Aug. 24, 1861, at Coldwater, age 26. Mustered Aug. 28, 1861. Deserted Nov. 6, 1861, at White Pigeon.

Everett, Hiram J. Three Rivers. Enlisted and mustered in Co. E, Aug. 24, 1861, at Three Rivers, age 17. Killed Dec. 31, 1862, at Stones River.

Everhard, James *see* Eberhard, James.

Evert, Hiram J. *see* Everett, Hiram J.

Everton, James. St. Joseph County. Enlisted and mustered in Co. A, Aug. 24, 1861, at Centreville, age 22. Mustered out Sept. 30, 1864, at Sturgis.

Everton, William H. St. Joseph County. Enlisted and mustered in Co. D, Aug. 24, 1861, at Bronson, age 42. Blacksmith Jan. 1862. Transferred to Invalid Corps Jan. 1, 1863.

Farmer, Anson. Lenawee County. Enlisted in Co. K, Aug. 24, 1861, at Palmyra, age 20. Mustered Sept. 1, 1861. Wounded and captured Jan. 2, 1863, at Stones River. Corporal May 1, 1864. Mustered out Sept. 30, 1864, at Sturgis.

Farnham, Alvin E. Enlisted in Co. A, Dec. 23,

1863, at Leonidas, age 16. Mustered Jan. 4, 1864. Joined regiment Jan. 28, 1864, at Rossville, GA. Wounded July 4, 1864, at Ruff's Station. Transferred Apr. 15, 1865, to Co. A, reorganized 11th Michigan Infantry. Discharged July 26, 1865, at Detroit.

Farnham, Charles H. Leonidas. Enlisted in Co. A, Feb. 22, 1864, at Leonidas, age 29. Mustered Feb. 27, 1864. Joined regiment Mar. 15, 1864, at Rossville, GA. Transferred Mar. 30, 1864, to Co. F. Transferred Apr. 15, 1865, to Co. F, reorganized 11th Michigan Infantry. Corporal July 12, 1865. Mustered out Sept. 16, 1865, at Nashville. Resided c. 1905 at White Pigeon.

Farnham, John B. Edwardsburg. Enlisted and mustered in Co. C, Aug. 24, 1861, at Edwardsburg, age 28. Died of measles Feb. 6, 1862, at Bardstown, KY.

Farrand, James W. St. Joseph County. Enlisted and mustered in Co. D as Corporal, Aug. 24, 1861, at Bronson, age 22. Discharged for disability Apr. 9, 1863, at Murfreesboro, TN. Resided c. 1905 at Sherwood.

Farrand or Farren, Joseph P. Burr Oak. Enlisted in Co. D, Aug. 21, 1862, at Burr Oak, age 29. Mustered Sept. 1, 1862. Transferred to Veteran Reserve Corps July 1, 1864. Discharged Sept. 1, 1865, at Detroit, from 25th Co., 2nd Battalion, VRC.

Faulknor, Mathias M. Sturgis. Entered service in Co. C as 1st Lieutenant, Aug. 24, 1861, at Sturgis, age 27. Commissioned Aug. 24, 1861. Captured Dec. 31, 1862, at Stones River. Released by Jan. 3, 1863. Commissioned Captain Jan. 7, 1863, mustered Apr. 8, 1863. Resigned Oct. 2, 1863.

Fearnley or Fearnly, Joseph W. Amboy. Enlisted and mustered in Co. F, Sept. 11, 1861, at Amboy, age 31. Died of convulsions Apr. 6, 1862, at Belmont, KY. Buried in national cemetery in Cave Hill, KY.

Fell, William W. Branch County. Enlisted in Co. H, Aug. 24, 1861, at Coldwater, age 19. Mustered Aug. 28, 1861. Discharged for disability Jan. 26, 1864.

Fellinger, Michael. St. Joseph County. Enlisted and mustered in Co. E, Aug. 24, 1861, at Three Rivers, age 31. Discharged for disability Feb. 16, 1863, at Murfreesboro, TN.

Fellows, Samuel H. Hillsdale County. Enlisted and mustered in Co. B, Aug. 24, 1861, at Litchfield, age 33. Discharged for disability Oct. 18, 1862, at Nashville. Resided c. 1905 at Litchfield.

Ferguson, Hugh J. Enlisted and mustered in Co. H, Sept. 13, 1864, at Coldwater for 1 year, age 22. Transferred Apr. 15, 1865, to Co. H, reorganized 11th Michigan Infantry. Discharged June 16, 1865, at Chattanooga.

Ferguson, Jonathan. Monroe County. Enlisted and mustered in Co. I, Aug. 24, 1861, at Milan, age 34. Discharged for disability Oct. 30, 1862, at Nashville.

Ferguson, William. Enlisted and mustered in Co. H, Sept. 14, 1864, at Jackson for 1 year, age 27. Joined regiment Jan. 7, 1865, at Chattanooga. Transferred Apr. 15, 1865, to Co. H, reorganized 11th Michigan Infantry. Discharged June 16, 1865, at Chattanooga.

Fields, James. Hillsdale County. Enlisted and mustered in Co. B, Aug. 24, 1861, at Allen, age 21. Served in Pioneer Corps. Reenlisted Jan. 30, 1864, at Chattanooga. Mustered Mar. 31, 1864. Transferred June 20, 1864, to 1st U.S. Engineers. Discharged Sept. 26, 1865, at Nashville from Co. E, 1st U.S. Engineers.

Fields, Myron A.A. Monroe County. Enlisted and mustered in Co. I, Aug. 24, 1861, at Ida, age 18. Discharged Feb. 1, 1865, at Detroit.

Filson, Thomas C. Hillsdale County. Enlisted and mustered in Co. F, Sept. 11, 1861, at Amboy, age 30. Captured Dec. 7, 1862, at Hartsville, TN. Discharged Jan. 15, 1865, at Chattanooga.

Finch, Edward C. Lenawee County. Enlisted and mustered in Co. K, Sept. 1, 1861, at Adrian, age 18. Wounded at Stones River. Corporal May 1, 1864. Mustered out Sept. 30, 1864, at Sturgis.

Findley, James. St. Joseph County. Enlisted and mustered in Co. C, Aug. 24, 1861, at Centreville, age 30. Transferred Oct. 26, 1861, to U.S. Engineers.

Fisher, Calvin B. Enlisted in Co. H, Aug. 3, 1864, at Fairfield for 1 year, age 38. Mustered Sept. 1, 1864. Joined regiment Jan. 7, 1865, at Chattanooga. Transferred Apr. 15, 1865, to Co. H, reorganized 11th Michigan Infantry. Discharged June 16, 1865, at Chattanooga.

Fisher, Charles. St. Joseph County. Enlisted and mustered in Co. A, Aug. 24, 1861, at Centreville, age 29. Mustered out Sept. 30, 1864, at Sturgis.

Fisher, Henry S. Mendon. Entered service in Co. A as 2nd Lieutenant, Aug. 24, 1861, at Centreville, age 23. Commissioned Aug. 24, 1861. Commissioned 1st Lieutenant Feb. 7, 1862, mustered Mar. 5, 1862. Commissioned Captain Jan. 30, 1863, mustered Mar. 21, 1863. Discharged for disability Jan. 6, 1864. Died July 6, 1866, at East Pembroke, NY.

Fisher, James. White Pigeon. Enlisted and mustered in Co. C, Aug. 24, 1861, at Hanover, age 20. Killed Dec. 31, 1862, at Stones River.

Fisher, John. St. Joseph County. Enlisted and

mustered in Co. C, Aug. 24, 1861, at White Pigeon, age 36. Mustered out Sept. 30, 1864, at Sturgis.

Fletcher, Samuel. Washtenaw County. Enlisted and mustered in Co. I, Aug. 24, 1861, at Ypsilanti, age 19. Mustered out Sept. 30, 1864, at Sturgis. Resided c. 1905 at Ypsilanti.

Flynn, Thomas. Three Rivers. Enlisted in Co. G, 1st Michigan Infantry, Apr. 24, 1861, at Burr Oak, age 20. Mustered May 1, 1861. Mustered out Aug. 7, 1861, at Detroit. Reentered service. Commissioned and mustered as 1st Lieutenant, Co. E, 11th Michigan Infantry, Aug. 24, 1861. Commissioned Captain Nov. 15, 1862. Killed Dec. 31, 1862, at Stones River.

Fonda, Cornelius J. Three Rivers. Enlisted and mustered in Co. E, Aug. 24, 1861, at Three Rivers, age 20. Died of typhoid fever Aug. 10, 1862, at Nashville. Buried in national cemetery in Nashville.

Forbes, Charles V. St. Joseph County. Enlisted and mustered in Co. C, Aug. 24, 1861, at Centreville, age 21. Corporal Oct. 6, 1862. Wounded Mar. 1864. Mustered out Sept. 30, 1864, at Sturgis.

Forbes, Daniel or David. Enlisted in Co. A, Dec. 21, 1863, at Leonidas, age 30. Mustered Jan. 4, 1864. Joined regiment Jan. 28, 1864, at Rossville, GA. Transferred Mar. 30, 1864, to Co. F. Transferred Apr. 15, 1865, to Co. F, reorganized 11th Michigan Infantry. Mustered out Sept. 16, 1865, at Nashville.

Forbes, Elias P. Lenawee County. Enlisted and mustered in Co. F, Sept. 11, 1861, at Medina, age 24. Sergeant Oct. 19, 1861. Discharged for disability Oct. 29, 1862, at Nashville.

Force, Isaac. Lenawee County. Enlisted in Co. K, Aug. 24, 1861, at Adrian, age 29. Mustered Sept. 1, 1861. Transferred to Invalid Corps Feb. 15, 1864.

Ford, Oren or Orin J. Hillsdale County. Enlisted and mustered in Co. B as Sergeant, Aug. 24, 1861, at Allen, age 24. Mustered out Sept. 30, 1864, at Sturgis.

Foreman, Burke or Burk. St. Joseph County. Enlisted and mustered as Musician, Aug. 24, 1861, at White Pigeon, age 25. Died of disease July 11, 1862, at Nashville.

Fosdick, Ira or James P. St. Joseph County. Enlisted and mustered in Co. E, Aug. 24, 1861, at Three Rivers. Discharged for disability Nov. 24, 1862, at Nashville.

Francisco, Charles. Leonidas. Enlisted and mustered in Co. A, Aug. 24, 1861, at Centreville, age 22. Discharged for disability July 1, 1862, at Detroit.

Francisco, George W. Monroe County. Enlisted and mustered in Co. I, Aug. 24, 1861, at London, age 18. Wounded at Stones River. Mustered out Sept. 30, 1864, at Sturgis.

Frankish, William. St. Joseph County. Enlisted and mustered in Co. E, Aug. 24, 1861, at Three Rivers, age 20. Corporal. Sergeant Major Oct. 6, 1863. Mustered out Sept. 30, 1864.

Franklin, Charles E. St. Joseph. Enlisted and mustered as Drum Major, Aug. 24, 1861, at White Pigeon. Discharged for disability Feb. 6, 1862, at Bardstown, KY.

Franklin, George. Enlisted in Co. H, Sept. 15, 1862, at White Pigeon, age 18. Transferred to Invalid Corps Sept. 1, 1863. Discharged Nov. 12, 1865, at Springfield, IL.

Franklin, John. St. Joseph. Enlisted and mustered in Co. H, Aug. 24, 1861. Transferred Dec. 8, 1862, at Nashville to 4th U.S. Cavalry.

Franklin, Joseph. Enlisted in Co. A, Feb. 15, 1864, at Leonidas, age 19. Mustered Feb. 22, 1864. Joined regiment Apr. 7, 1864, at Graysville, GA. Transferred Apr. 15, 1865, to Co. A, reorganized 11th Michigan Infantry. Mustered out Sept. 16, 1865, at Nashville.

Frederick, Edwin S. Branch County. Enlisted in Co. H, Aug. 24, 1861, at Coldwater, age 34. Mustered Aug. 28, 1861. Corporal Feb. 22, 1864. Mustered out Sept. 30, 1864, at Sturgis. Resided c. 1905 at Batavia.

Freeman, A. I. Van Buren County. Enlisted in Co. G at Waverly, age 18. Mustered Sept. 4, 1861. Mustered out Sept. 30, 1864, at Sturgis.

Frell, William W. *see* Fell, William W.

French, Ephraim. Adrian. Entered service in Co. K as 2nd Lieutenant, Aug. 24, 1861, at Adrian, age 21. Commissioned Aug. 24, 1861. Mustered Sept. 1, 1861. Commissioned 1st Lieutenant Jan. 1, 1863, mustered Mar. 21, 1863. Resigned Nov. 3, 1863, due to disability.

Friedt, Jacob. Enlisted in Co. K, Jan. 4, 1864, at Deerfield, age 21. Mustered Jan. 9, 1864. Joined regiment Mar. 15, 1864, at Rossville, GA. Transferred Apr. 15, 1865, to Co. K, reorganized 11th Michigan Infantry. Mustered out Sept. 16, 1865, at Nashville. Resided c. 1905 at Petersburg.

Frost, Edward M. St. Joseph County. Enlisted and mustered in Co. E as Sergeant, Aug. 24, 1861, at Three Rivers, age 23. Commissioned 2nd Lieutenant Feb. 17, 1864. Mustered out Sept. 30, 1864, at Sturgis.

Fulkerson, Loriston Alden. Three Rivers. Enlisted and mustered in Co. A, Aug. 24, 1861, at Centreville, age 26. Died of measles Feb. 15, 1862, at Bardstown, KY. Buried in national cemetery in Lebanon, KY.

Fuller, Cash D. Lenawee County. Enlisted and mustered in Co. F, Sept. 11, 1861, at Seneca, age 18. Sergeant Mar. 14, 1864. Mustered out Sept. 30, 1864, at Sturgis.

Fullmer or Fulmer, Charles W. Calhoun County. Enlisted and mustered in Co. A, Aug. 24, 1861, at Centreville, age 24. Mustered out Sept. 30, 1864, at Sturgis.

Furguson, William *see* Ferguson, William.

Gardner, Abraham. Monroe County. Enlisted in Co. K, Aug. 24, 1861, at Petersburg, age 28. Mustered Sept. 1, 1861. Served in Pioneer Brigade. Mustered out Sept. 30, 1864, at Sturgis.

Gardner, Ira A. or R. St. Joseph County. Enlisted and mustered in Co. D, Aug. 24, 1861. Discharged for disability Dec. 7, 1861.

Gary, John A. Branch County. Enlisted and mustered in Co. C, Aug. 24, 1861, at Clarendon, age 19. Killed Aug. 7, 1864, at Utoy Creek. Buried in national cemetery in Marietta, GA, grave 6171.

George, John. Branch County. Enlisted and mustered in Co. D, Aug. 24, 1861, at Burr Oak, age 22. Wounded and captured Dec. 31, 1862, at Stones River. Paroled. Mustered out Sept. 30, 1864, at Sturgis.

German, Samuel. Hillsdale County. Enlisted in Co. G at Hillsdale, age 21. Mustered Sept. 4, 1861. Served in Pioneer Brigade. Reenlisted Jan. 30, 1864, at Chattanooga. Mustered Mar. 31, 1864. Transferred July 20, 1864, at Chattanooga to 1st U.S. Engineers. Discharged Sept. 26, 1865, at Detroit from Co. E, 1st U.S. Engineers. Resided c. 1905 at East Gilead.

Gibson, Ephraim G. Mendon. Enlisted and mustered in Co. A, Aug. 24, 1861, at Centreville, age 21. Died of typhoid fever Apr. 19, 1862, at Elizabethtown, KY.

Gilbert, Amos T. St. Joseph County. Enlisted and mustered in Co. D, Aug. 24, 1861, at Burr Oak, age 18. Mustered out Sept. 30, 1864, at Sturgis. Resided c. 1905 at Colon.

Gilbert, Cyrus W. Leonidas. Enlisted in Co. G, Aug. 24, 1861, at White Pigeon, age 20. Mustered Sept. 4, 1861. Killed Dec. 31, 1862, at Stones River.

Gilbert, Martin W. St. Joseph County. Enlisted and mustered in Co. C as Corporal, Aug. 24, 1861, at Burr Oak, age 21. Discharged for disability Feb. 4, 1862, at Bardstown, KY.

Giles, William A. Lenawee County. Enlisted in Co. K, Aug. 24, 1861, at Blissfield, age 19. Mustered Sept. 1, 1861. Corporal Mar. 1, 1862. Mustered out Sept. 30, 1864, at Sturgis. Died Apr. 7, 1890. Buried at Blissfield.

Gilkinson, Steven W. Enlisted and mustered in Co. G, Feb. 20, 1864, at Leonidas, age 21. Joined regiment Mar. 15, 1864, at Rossville, GA. Transferred Apr. 15, 1865, to Co. G, reorganized 11th Michigan Infantry. Mustered out Sept. 16, 1865, at Nashville.

Gilkirson or Gilkison, Simeon B. St. Joseph County. Enlisted and mustered in Co. C, Aug. 24, 1861, at Sherman, age 23. Missing Sept. 20, 1863, at Chickamauga. Returned to regiment, June 1, 1864. Mustered out Sept. 30, 1864, at Sturgis.

Gilkison, Steven W. *see* Gilkinson, Steven W.

Gillaspie, Enoch J. St. Joseph County. Enlisted and mustered in Co. C, Aug. 24, 1861, at Sturgis, age 19. Deserted Dec. 26, 1861, at Bardstown, KY.

Gillaspie, Ira Myron Bailey. St. Joseph County. Enlisted and mustered in Co. C, Aug. 24, 1861, at Sturgis, age 24. Corporal Aug. 10, 1862. Mustered out Sept. 30, 1864, at Sturgis. Died Nov. 13, 1897.

Gillaspie, Martin V. St. Joseph County. Enlisted and mustered in Co. C, Dec. 9, 1861. Musician May 1864. Discharged Dec. 9, 1864, at Chattanooga. Resided c. 1905 at South Haven.

Gillet, George S. Burr Oak. Enlisted and mustered in Co. D, Aug. 24, 1861, at Burr Oak, age 20. Killed Nov. 25, 1863, at Missionary Ridge.

Glavin, Morris. St. Joseph County. Enlisted and mustered in Co. C, Aug. 24, 1861, at White Pigeon, age 28. Discharged for disability Mar. 17, 1863, at Nashville.

Gliddon or Glidden, Wilder B. St. Joseph County. Enlisted and mustered in Co. A, Aug. 24, 1861, at Centreville, age 26. Discharged for disability Feb. 18, 1862, at Bardstown, KY.

Glover, Martin H. Enlisted in Co. A, Feb. 24, 1864, at Leonidas, age 18. Mustered Feb. 27, 1864. Joined regiment Mar. 15, 1864, at Rossville, GA. Transferred Apr. 15, 1865, to Co. A, reorganized 11th Michigan Infantry. Mustered out Sept. 16, 1865, at Nashville.

Goff, Nelson W. Lenawee County. Enlisted in Co. K, Aug. 24, 1861, at Blissfield, age 23. Mustered Sept. 1, 1861. Transferred to Veteran Reserve Corps Apr. 10, 1864.

Goodale, Homer. Deerfield. Enlisted in Co. K, Aug. 24, 1861, at Deerfield, age 19. Mustered Sept. 1, 1861. Wounded Dec. 31, 1862, at Stones River. Died of wounds Jan. 22, 1863.

Goodle, John. White Pigeon. Enlisted and mustered in Co. C, Aug. 24, 1861, at White Pigeon, age 45. Died of bloody flux Jan. 19, 1863, at Nashville.

Goodrich, Enoch H. Hillsdale County. Enlisted and mustered in Co. F, Sept. 11, 1861, at Hudson. Fifer. Discharged for disability June 7, 1862.

Goodrich, Marcus. Lenawee County. Enlisted

and mustered in Co. F, Sept. 11, 1861, at Rollin, age 23. Wounded and captured Sept. 19, 1863, at Chickamauga. No further record.

Gould, James. Seneca. Enlisted and mustered in Co. F, Sept. 11, 1861, at Seneca, age 20. Died of typhoid fever Apr. 25, 1862, at Belmont, KY.

Gould, John L. St. Joseph County. Enlisted and mustered in Co. A, Aug. 24, 1861, at Centreville, age 28. Discharged for disability May 2, 1863, at Nashville.

Gould, Sylvanus. Leonidas. Enlisted and mustered in Co. A, Aug. 24, 1861, at Centreville, age 19. Died of consumption Apr. 1, 1862, at Bardstown, KY. Buried in national cemetery in Lebanon, KY.

Gould, William H. Girard. Enlisted in Co. H, Aug. 24, 1861, at Coldwater, age 25. Mustered Aug. 28, 1861. Died of inflammation of lungs Feb. 1, 1862, at Bardstown, KY.

Graham, Arthur S. Enlisted and mustered in Co. C, Aug. 25, 1862, at Bronson, age 26. Transferred Apr. 15, 1865, to Co. C, reorganized 11th Michigan Infantry. Discharged June 16, 1865, at Chattanooga.

Graham, Irving S. Kalamazoo County. Enlisted and mustered in Co. B, Aug. 24, 1861, at Richland, age 19. Corporal. Sergeant Jan. 22, 1863. Wounded Nov. 1863. Mustered out Sept. 30, 1864, at Sturgis.

Graham, John. Three Rivers. Enlisted and mustered in Co. E as Sergeant, Aug. 24, 1861, at Three Rivers, age 25. 1st Sergeant Aug. 22, 1862. Commissioned 1st Lieutenant Feb. 17, 1864, mustered May 23, 1864. Commissioned Captain, Co. C, Mar. 1, 1865, mustered Apr. 11, 1865. Transferred Apr. 15, 1865, to Co. C, reorganized 11th Michigan Infantry. Mustered out Sept. 16, 1865, at Nashville.

Granger, Chauncey M. or W. Cass County. Enlisted in Co. G at Cass County, age 34. Mustered Sept. 4, 1861. Captured Dec. 31, 1862, at Stones River. Paroled Apr. 1863. Corporal May 1864. Discharged for disability June 8, 1864, at Louisville.

Grather, George F. Centreville. Enlisted and mustered in Co. A, Aug. 24, 1861, at Centreville, age 25. Died of typhoid Oct. 19, 1861, at White Pigeon.

Graves, Charles F. St. Joseph County. Enlisted and mustered in Co. C, Aug. 24, 1861, at Sturgis, age 28. Discharged for disability Apr. 8, 1863, at Nashville. Later served as Private in the 10th and 19th Michigan regiments.

Graves, Harrison. St. Joseph County. Enlisted and mustered in Co. C as Sergeant, Aug. 24, 1861, at Sturgis, age 21. Discharged Oct. 1, 1862, at Nashville.

Graves, John L. Coldwater. Enlisted and mustered in Co. H, Aug. 24, 1861, age 20. Reenlisted Mar. 27, 1864, at Rossville, GA. Mustered Apr. 11, 1864. Corporal July 1, 1864. Transferred Apr. 15, 1865, to Co. H, reorganized 11th Michigan Infantry. Sergeant Aug. 1, 1865. Deserted Aug. 1, 1865 at Cleveland, TN.

Graves, Samuel L. St. Joseph County. Enlisted and mustered in Co. C as Corporal, Aug. 24, 1861, at Sturgis, age 29. Discharged for disability June 12, 1862, at Nashville.

Graves, Walter M *see* Groves, Walter M.

Gray, Elliott S. Enlisted and mustered in Co. C, Nov. 28, 1861. Discharged Nov. 29, 1864. Resided c. 1905 at Constantine.

Gray, Henry. Enlisted in Co. D, Aug. 31, 1864, at Blissfield for 1 year, age 37. Mustered Sept. 1, 1864. Joined regiment Feb. 20, 1865, at Chattanooga. Transferred Apr. 15, 1865, to Co. D, reorganized 11th Michigan Infantry. Discharged June 16, 1865, at Chattanooga.

Greeley, Charles E. Morenci. Enlisted and mustered in Co. F, Sept. 11, 1861, at Seneca, age 23. 1st Sergeant Nov. 1862. Commissioned and mustered as 2nd Lieutenant May 29, 1863. Transferred Nov. 18, 1863, to 15th USCT as 2nd Lieutenant. Discharged Jan. 17, 1864.

Green, Chauncey B. Batavia. Enlisted in Co. H, Aug. 24, 1861, at Coldwater, age 25. Mustered Aug. 28, 1861. Killed Dec. 31, 1862, at Stones River.

Green, Edwin A. Branch County. Enlisted in Co. H, Aug. 24, 1861, at Coldwater, age 38. Mustered Aug. 28, 1861. Wounded and captured Dec. 31, 1862, at Stones River. Died July 29, 1864, at Andersonville, GA. Buried in national cemetery in Andersonville, GA.

Green, George. Branch County. Enlisted in Co. H, Aug. 24, 1861, at Coldwater, age 31. Mustered Aug. 28, 1861. Deserted Sept. 26, 1861, at White Pigeon.

Green, John. Branch County. Enlisted and mustered in Co. H, Aug. 24, 1861, at Coldwater, age 41. Discharged Sept. 16, 1861.

Green, John O. Enlisted in Co. F, Feb. 8, 1864, at Leonidas, age 21. Mustered Feb. 27, 1864. Joined regiment Mar. 15, 1864, at Rossville, GA. Wounded May 1864 near Dallas, GA. Died of wounds July 14, 1864. Buried in national cemetery in Louisville.

Green, Lorenzo D. Branch County. Enlisted in Co. H, Aug. 24, 1861, at Coldwater, age 19. Mustered Aug. 28, 1861. Deserted Oct. 24, 1861, at White Pigeon.

Green, Seneca. Monroe County. Enlisted and mustered in Co. I, Aug. 24, 1861, at Dundee, age 18. Corporal Apr. 25, 1863. Mustered out Sept. 30, 1864, at Sturgis.

Greenwood, Milton. Enlisted in Co. A, Dec. 4, 1863, at Leonidas, age 19. Mustered Jan. 4, 1864. Joined regiment Jan. 28, 1864, at Rossville, GA. Transferred Mar. 30, 1864, to Co. F. Corporal Mar. 16, 1865. Transferred Apr. 15, 1865, to Co. F, reorganized 11th Michigan Infantry. Mustered out Sept. 16, 1865, at Nashville.

Grey, Henry *see* Gray, Henry.

Gribben or Gribbin, George W. Branch County. Enlisted and mustered in Co. D, Aug. 24, 1861, at Brandon, age 22. Discharged for disability Mar. 6, 1863, at Nashville.

Griffin, George S. Branch County. Enlisted in Co. H, Aug. 24, 1861, at Coldwater, age 21. Mustered Aug. 28, 1861. Captured Sept. 20, 1863, at Chickamauga. Died July 27, 1864, at Andersonville, GA. Buried in national cemetery in Andersonville, GA, grave 4092.

Griffin, James H. Ovid. Enlisted in Co. H, Aug. 24, 1861, at Coldwater, age 18. Mustered Aug. 28, 1861. Died of measles Jan. 28, 1862, at Bardstown, KY. Buried in national cemetery in Lebanon, KY, grave 307.

Griffith, Lorenzo H. St. Joseph County. Enlisted and mustered in Co. C, Aug. 24, 1861, at White Pigeon, age 20. Mustered out Sept. 30, 1864, at Sturgis.

Griggs, Reuben. Enlisted in Co. F, Feb. 23, 1864, at Waukeshma, age 25. Mustered Feb. 27, 1864. Joined regiment Mar. 15, 1864, at Rossville, GA. Died of disease Mar. 27, 1864, at Chattanooga. Buried in national cemetery in Chattanooga.

Grinnell, Amos A. St. Joseph County. Enlisted as Musician, Aug. 24, 1861, at White Pigeon, age 19. Mustered Sept. 24, 1861. Mustered out Aug. 22, 1862, at Nashville.

Griswold, Daniel. Blissfield. Enlisted in Co. K, Aug. 24, 1861, at Blissfield, age 21. Mustered Sept. 1, 1861. Captured Jan. 2, 1863, at Stones River. Discharged for disability May 20, 1863, at Detroit. Resided c. 1905 at Toledo, OH.

Griswold, Hiram S. Flint. Entered service as Asst. Surgeon, May 7, 1863. Commissioned May 7, 1863. Mustered June 8, 1863. Captured Sept. 18, 1863, at Chickamauga. Rejoined regiment Feb. 8, 1864. Mustered out Sept. 30, 1864, at Sturgis.

Groves, Walter M. Hillsdale County. Enlisted in Co. H, Aug. 24, 1861, at Coldwater, age 43. Mustered Aug. 28, 1861. Reenlisted Mar. 27, 1864, at Graysville, GA. Mustered Apr. 11, 1864. Killed Aug. 7, 1864, at Utoy Creek.

Gruber, Jacob. Enlisted in Co. G, 19th Michigan Infantry, Jan. 19, 1864, at Kalamazoo, age 41. Mustered Jan. 20, 1864. Transferred to Co. G, 11th Michigan Infantry. Joined regiment Mar. 15, 1864, at Rossville, GA. Transferred Apr. 15, 1865, to Co. G, reorganized 11th Michigan Infantry. Discharged Sept. 28, 1865, at Detroit.

Guyer, George W. Burlington. Enlisted and mustered in Co. H as Corporal, Aug. 24, 1861, at Coldwater, age 25. Killed Dec. 31, 1862, at Stones River.

Guyer, James. Calhoun County. Enlisted in Co. H, Aug. 24, 1861, at Coldwater, age 20. Mustered Aug. 28, 1861. Discharged for disability Nov. 4, 1862, at Nashville.

Hackenberg or Hackenburg, Henry H. *see* Hackenburgh, Henry H.

Hackenburg, Jacob *see* Hackenburgh, Jacob.

Hackenburgh, Henry H. St. Joseph County. Enlisted as Musician, Aug. 24, 1861, at White Pigeon. Mustered Sept. 24, 1861. Mustered out Aug. 22, 1862, at Nashville. Resided c. 1905 at White Pigeon.

Hackenburgh, Jacob. Cincinnati, OH. Enlisted and mustered in Co. C, Aug. 24, 1861, at La Grange, IN, age 18. Wounded at Stones River. Reenlisted Feb. 27, 1864, at Rossville, GA. Mustered Mar. 31, 1864. Transferred Apr. 15, 1865, to Co. C, reorganized 11th Michigan Infantry. Mustered out Sept. 16, 1865, at Nashville.

Hackstaff, John L. Coldwater. Entered service in Co. H as Captain, Aug. 24, 1861, at Coldwater, age 41. Commissioned Aug. 24, 1861. Resigned Mar. 11, 1862, due to disability. Died of disease May 22, 1862, in Michigan. Buried at Coldwater.

Haight, Christopher. Leonidas. Entered service in Co. A as 1st Lieutenant, Aug. 24, 1861, at Centreville, age 28. Commissioned Aug. 24, 1861. Resigned Feb. 1, 1862, at Bardstown, KY, due to disability. Died of typhoid Feb. 5, 1862, at Bardstown, KY.

Haight, Marvel G. Lenawee County. Enlisted in Co. K as Drummer, Aug. 24, 1861, at Petersburg, age 29. Mustered Sept. 1, 1861. Principal Musician Jan. 28, 1864. Mustered out Sept. 30, 1864, at Sturgis.

Haines, James L. Cass County. Enlisted and mustered in Co. E, Aug. 24, 1861, at Three Rivers, age 18. Mustered out Sept. 30, 1864, at Sturgis.

Hale, Charles. Burr Oak. Enlisted and mustered in Co. D, Aug. 15, 1862, at Burr Oak, age 23. Sergeant Mar. 4, 1865. Transferred Apr. 15, 1865, to Co. D, reorganized 11th Michigan Infantry. Discharged June 16, 1865, at Chattanooga. Resided c. 1905 at Constantine.

Hale, John. Three Rivers. Enlisted and mustered

in Co. E, Aug. 24, 1861, at London, age 20. Died of consumption Jan. 27, 1862, at Bardstown, KY. Buried in national cemetery in Lebanon, KY.

Hall, Ephraim Gaylord. London. Enlisted and mustered in Co. I as 1st Sergeant, Aug. 24, 1861, at London, age 21. Commissioned 2nd Lieutenant, Co. F, Apr. 1, 1862, mustered Apr. 12, 1862. Commissioned 1st Lieutenant Aug. 18, 1862, mustered May 6, 1863. Wounded and captured Dec. 31, 1862, at Stones River. Commissioned Captain Feb. 19, 1863, mustered Aug. 3, 1863. Acting assistant adjutant general, 2nd Brigade, June 17, 1864. Mustered out Sept. 30, 1864, at Sturgis.

Hall, Henry. St. Joseph County. Enlisted and mustered in Co. A, Aug. 24, 1861, at Centreville, age 23. Mustered out Sept. 30, 1864, at Sturgis.

Hall, John *see* Hale, John.

Hall, John N. Monroe County. Enlisted and mustered in Co. I, Aug. 24, 1861, at La Salle, age 23. Corporal Mar. 25, 1863. Mustered out Sept. 30, 1864, at Sturgis.

Hall, John W. St. Joseph County. Enlisted and mustered in Co. A as Corporal, Aug. 24, 1861, at Centreville, age 24. Discharged for disability July 1, 1862. Resided c. 1905 at Colon.

Hall, Judson A. Enlisted in Co. A, Dec. 25, 1863, at Leonidas, age 18. Mustered Jan. 21, 1864. Joined regiment Jan. 28, 1864, at Rossville, GA. Transferred Mar. 30, 1864, to Co. F. Transferred Apr. 15, 1865, to Co. F, reorganized 11th Michigan Infantry. Admitted Sept. 5, 1865, to Harper Hospital. Discharged Sept. 8, 1865, at Detroit.

Hall, Richard W. Monroe County. Enlisted and mustered in Co. I, Aug. 24, 1861, at La Salle, age 25. Transferred to Invalid Corps Aug. 1, 1863. Discharged Aug. 24, 1864, at Washington, D.C., from Co. H, 12th Regiment, VRC. Resided c. 1905 at Chelsea.

Halleck, Walter F. Enlisted in Co. I, July 25, 1862, at Nashville. Captured Dec. 31, 1862, at Stones River. Discharged for disability Aug. 13, 1863, at Cowan, TN. Commissioned and mustered as 2nd Lieutenant in Veteran Reserve Corps, Apr. 14, 1864. Resigned Sept. 6, 1865.

Hallroner, Henry E. Enlisted and mustered in Co. C, Aug. 24, 1861, at Brandon, age 18. Mustered out Sept. 30, 1864, at Sturgis.

Hamilton, Charles. Branch County. Enlisted and mustered in Co. D, Aug. 24, 1861, at Bronson, age 17. Transferred to Invalid Corps Feb. 15, 1864.

Hamilton, Harry N. Branch County. Enlisted and mustered in Co. D, Aug. 24, 1861, at Colon, age 21. Discharged for disability Dec. 4, 1863, at Louisville.

Hamilton, John H. Frenchtown. Enlisted in Co. I, Aug. 24, 1861, at Frenchtown, age 22. Mustered Sept. 1, 1861. Died of pneumonia Feb. 1862 at Bardstown, KY.

Hamilton, Simon. Blissfield. Enlisted in Co. K, Aug. 24, 1861, at Blissfield, age 20. Mustered Sept. 1, 1861. Wounded Dec. 31, 1862, at Stones River. Died of wounds Jan. 2, 1863, at Murfreesboro, TN.

Hamlin, John R. St. Joseph County. Enlisted and mustered in Co. A, Aug. 24, 1861, at Centreville, age 30. Mustered out Sept. 30, 1864, at Sturgis. Resided c. 1905 at Traverse City.

Hammer, Charles D. Branch County. Enlisted and mustered in Co. D, Aug. 24, 1861, at Bronson, age 26. Mustered out Sept. 30, 1864, at Sturgis.

Hammond, James. Enlisted and mustered, company unassigned, Sept. 23, 1864, at Jackson, age 21. No further record.

Harding, Thomas D. St. Joseph County. Enlisted and mustered in Co. C, Aug. 24, 1861, at Sherman, age 45. Discharged for disability June 4, 1862.

Harding, Wilber S. Branch County. Enlisted and mustered in Co. B, Aug. 24, 1861, at Quincy, age 19. Discharged for disability May 14, 1863, at Nashville.

Hare, Daniel. Hillsdale County. Enlisted in Co. G at Hillsdale, age 41. Mustered Sept. 4, 1861. Died of smallpox Jan. 8, 1862, at Bardstown, KY. Buried in national cemetery in Lebanon, KY.

Harker, John. Lenawee County. Enlisted in Co. K, Aug. 24, 1861, at Dover, age 21. Mustered Sept. 1, 1861. Killed Aug. 7, 1864, at Utoy Creek. Buried in national cemetery in Marietta, GA, section E, grave 6169.

Harkness, Lindley R. Hudson. Enlisted in Co. E, Aug. 9, 1862, at Burr Oak, age 20. Mustered Aug. 29, 1862. Commissary Sergeant Mar. 1863. Commissioned and mustered as 1st Lieutenant Mar. 16, 1865. Transferred Apr. 15, 1865, to reorganized 11th Michigan Infantry. Discharged Aug. 1, 1865.

Harper, Abraham. Lenawee County. Entered service in Co. F as 2nd Lieutenant at Hudson, age 26. Mustered Sept. 11, 1861. Resigned Oct. 23, 1861.

Harrington, Melvin. Lenawee County. Enlisted in Co. K, Aug. 24, 1861, at Deerfield, age 25. Mustered Sept. 1, 1861. Corporal. Sergeant Apr. 20, 1863. Mustered out Sept. 30, 1864, at Sturgis.

Harrington, William H. Enlisted in Co. E, Feb. 22, 1864, at Kalamazoo, age 18. Mustered

Feb. 23, 1864. Joined regiment Apr. 10, 1864, at Graysville, GA. Transferred Apr. 15, 1865, to Co. E, reorganized 11th Michigan Infantry. Mustered out Sept. 16, 1865, at Nashville.

Harris, James M. Branch County. Enlisted in Co. H, Aug. 24, 1861, at Coldwater, age 32. Mustered Aug. 28, 1861. Served in Pioneer Brigade. Mustered out Sept. 30, 1864, at Sturgis.

Harris, Jeremiah. Enlisted in Co. C, Jan. 15, 1864, at Burlington, age 30. Mustered Feb. 3, 1864. Joined regiment Mar. 15, 1864, at Rossville, GA. Transferred Apr. 15, 1865, to Co. C, reorganized 11th Michigan Infantry. Discharged May 18, 1865, at Nashville.

Harris, Joel. Cass County. Enlisted and mustered in Co. E, Aug. 24, 1861, at Three Rivers, age 41. Deserted July 11, 1862, at Cave City, KY.

Harris, William. Monroe County. Enlisted in Co. K, Aug. 24, 1861, at Petersburg, age 22. Mustered Sept. 1, 1861. Wounded Jan. 1863. Mustered out Sept. 30, 1864, at Sturgis.

Hart, Benjamin F. Bronson. Enlisted and mustered in Co. D, Aug. 24, 1861, at Bronson, age 22. 1st Sergeant. Served in Pioneer Corps. Commissioned 1st Lieutenant Jan. 9, 1864, mustered June 20, 1864. Mustered out Sept. 30, 1864, at Sturgis. Died Sept. 1, 1901. Buried at White Pigeon.

Hart, Urban. Amboy. Enlisted and mustered in Co. D, Aug. 15, 1862, at Bronson, age 28. Joined regiment Feb. 25, 1863, at Murfreesboro, TN. Wounded June 25, 1864, near Kennesaw Mtn., GA. Sergeant Mar. 4, 1865. Transferred Apr. 15, 1865, to Co. D, reorganized 11th Michigan Infantry. Discharged June 16, 1865, at Chattanooga.

Hart, William A. St. Joseph County. Enlisted and mustered in Co. A, Aug. 24, 1861, at Centreville, age 21. Transferred Nov. 30, 1861, to Co. K. No further record.

Harvey, Andrew. Enlisted and mustered in Co. I, Aug. 24, 1861, at Ash, age 26. No further record.

Harwood, Daniel. St. Joseph County. Enlisted in Co. G, Aug. 24, 1861, at Three Rivers, age 35. Mustered Sept. 4, 1861. Deceased.

Harwood, Edwin. Monroe. Enlisted in Co. K, Aug. 24, 1861, at Dundee, age 18. Mustered Sept. 1, 1861. Wounded Sept. 1863. Mustered out Sept. 30, 1864, at Sturgis.

Hass, James R. St. Joseph County. Enlisted in Co. G at Prairie Ronde, age 22. Mustered Sept. 4, 1861. Wounded at Stones River. Mustered out Sept. 30, 1864, at Sturgis.

Hass, Samuel B. St. Joseph County. Enlisted in Co. G at Mottville, age 18. Corporal June 6, 1862. Died of disease Apr. 5, 1864, at Graysville, GA. Buried in national cemetery in Chattanooga.

Hathaway, Henry C. Cass County. Enlisted and mustered in Co. D, Aug. 24, 1861. Sick at Chattanooga, May 1864. No further record.

Hawker, George W. Dundee. Enlisted and mustered in Co. I as Corporal, Aug. 24, 1861, at Augusta, age 29. Sergeant. Commissioned 2nd Lieutenant Dec. 10, 1862, mustered Mar. 21, 1863. Resigned Jan. 14, 1864.

Hawse, Andrew J. Branch County. Enlisted and mustered in Co. B, Aug. 24, 1861, at Butler, age 18. Discharged Nov. 15, 1861, at White Pigeon, as a minor enlisted without parental consent.

Hayes, Horace. London. Enlisted and mustered in Co. I, Aug. 24, 1861, at London, age 42. Discharged for disability July 1, 1862, at Detroit.

Haynes, Daniel. Quincy. Enlisted and mustered in Co. B, Aug. 24, 1861, at Quincy, age 18. Wounded at Stones River. Died of wounds Jan. 2, 1863, at Murfreesboro, TN. Buried in national cemetery in Murfreesboro, TN, grave 1755.

Haynes, Horace *see* Hayes, Horace.

Haynes, Solomon. Branch County. Enlisted in Co. H, Aug. 24, 1861, at Coldwater, age 34. Mustered Aug. 28, 1861. Discharged for disability Nov. 9, 1863, at Chattanooga.

Hazard, Melvin D. St. Joseph County. Enlisted and mustered in Co. C, Aug. 24, 1861, at Centreville, age 29. Deserted Nov. 11, 1862, at Nashville.

Heath, Lewis W. Medina. Enlisted in Co. K, 1st Michigan Infantry, Apr. 18, 1861, at Adrian for 3 months, age 24. Mustered May 1, 1861. Mustered out Aug. 7, 1861, at Detroit. Reentered service. Commissioned 2nd Lieutenant, Co. K, 11th Michigan Infantry, Aug. 24, 1861. Commissioned Captain Apr. 1, 1862. Transferred Jan. 1, 1863, to Co. F. Resigned Apr. 29, 1863, due to disability.

Hedge, Samuel K. Quincy. Enlisted and mustered as Musician, Aug. 24, 1861, at Quincy, age 44. Died of chronic diarrhea Jan. 28, 1863, at Nashville. Buried in national cemetery in Nashville.

Hedge, Stillman. Allen. Enlisted and mustered as Musician, Aug. 24, 1861, at Allen, age 45. Transferred to Co. H. Captured Dec. 31, 1862, at Stones River. Died of fever Mar. 3, 1863, at Annapolis, MD. Buried in national cemetery in Annapolis, MD.

Hemingway or Hemenway, Richard R. Enlisted in Co. A, Jan. 4, 1864, at Sherwood, age 31. Mustered Jan. 11, 1864. Joined regiment Jan.

28, 1864, at Rossville, GA. Transferred Apr. 15, 1865, to Co. A, reorganized 11th Michigan Infantry. Discharged May 31, 1865, at Chattanooga.

Hendershot, James. Lenawee County. Enlisted in Co. K, Aug. 24, 1861, at Macon, age 21. Mustered Sept. 1, 1861. Deserted Oct. 1, 1861.

Henderson, John W. Branch County. Enlisted and mustered in Co. D, Aug. 24, 1861, at Bronson, age 26. Discharged for disability June 10, 1862, at Louisville.

Henderson, Samuel. St. Joseph County. Enlisted and mustered in Co. C, Aug. 24, 1861, at Novi, age 26. Corporal Aug. 22, 1863. Mustered out Sept. 30, 1864, at Sturgis.

Henderson, Wellington. Branch County. Enlisted and mustered in Co. D, Aug. 24, 1861, at Bronson, age 18. Mustered out Sept. 30, 1864, at Sturgis.

Henigan, John. Branch County. Enlisted and mustered in Co. D, Aug. 24, 1861, at Bronson, age 19. Died of fever Mar. 28, 1862, at Nolin, KY. Buried in national cemetery in Louisville.

Henry, Howard. Kalamazoo County. Enlisted in Co. G at Mottville, age 24. Mustered Sept. 4, 1861. Discharged for disability Oct. 23, 1862, at Nashville.

Herington or Herrington, Melvin see Harrington, Melvin.

Herrington, William. Detroit. Enlisted and mustered in Co. I, Aug. 26, 1861, at Detroit, age 45. Died of pneumonia May 28, 1862, at Columbia, TN.

Herrington, William H. see Harrington, William H.

Hewes, Albert. Branch County. Enlisted in Co. H, Aug. 24, 1861, at Coldwater, age 23. Mustered Aug. 28, 1861. Corporal Apr. 14, 1863. Mustered out Sept. 30, 1864, at Sturgis.

Hibberelee, Samuel. St. Joseph County. Enlisted and mustered in Co. C, Aug. 24, 1861, at Sturgis, age 35. Discharged for disability Feb. 13, 1862.

Hicks, Borden Mills. Fabius. Enlisted and mustered in Co. E as Sergeant, Aug. 24, 1861, age 17. Commissioned 2nd Lieutenant Nov. 15, 1862, mustered Jan. 22, 1863. Commissioned Captain Sept. 20, 1863, mustered Feb. 17, 1864. Mustered out Sept. 30, 1864, at Sturgis.

Higgins, Edwin A. Branch County. Enlisted in Co. H as Bugler, Aug. 24, 1861, at Coldwater, age 20. Mustered Aug. 28, 1861. Chief Bugler Dec. 1, 1861. Transferred Dec. 1, 1862, to Co. H. Discharged at Nashville. No further record.

Higgins, Thomas William. Marcellus. Enlisted in Co. G at Cass County, age 27. Mustered Sept. 4, 1861. Died of typhoid fever Mar. 19, 1862, at Wilson's Creek, KY.

Hill or Hile, Henry J. St. Joseph County. Enlisted and mustered in Co. A, Aug. 24, 1861, at Centreville, age 18. Mustered out Sept. 30, 1864, at Sturgis.

Hinds, Richard M. see Hines, Richard M.

Hinds, Wilson E. Bronson. Enlisted and mustered in Co. A, Aug. 24, 1861, at Centreville, age 18. Died of measles Feb. 1, 1862, at Bardstown, KY. Buried in national cemetery in Lebanon, KY.

Hines, Richard M. Branch County. Enlisted and mustered in Co. D, Aug. 24, 1861, at Bronson, age 55. Died of smallpox Jan. 1862 at Bardstown, KY.

Hines, Wilson E. see Hinds, Wilson E.

Hix, Henry. St. Joseph County. Enlisted and mustered in Co. E, Aug. 24, 1861, at Three Rivers, age 36. Served in Pioneer Brigade. Discharged for disability Feb. 23, 1863, at Murfreesboro, TN. Resided c. 1905 at Grand Rapids.

Hodge, Henry E. Enlisted and mustered in Co. E, Sept. 23, 1864, at Jackson for 1 year, age 18. Joined regiment Jan. 7, 1865, at Chattanooga. Transferred Apr. 15, 1865, to Co. K, reorganized 11th Michigan Infantry. Discharged June 16, 1865, at Chattanooga.

Hodgins, Thomas R. St. Joseph County. Enlisted and mustered in Co. D, Aug. 24, 1861, at Burr Oak, age 21. Killed May 31, 1864, near New Hope Church.

Hogaboom, Isaac. St. Joseph County. Enlisted and mustered in Co. C, Aug. 24, 1861, at Constantine, age 27. Mustered out Sept. 30, 1864, at Sturgis.

Hogan, James H. Enlisted, company unassigned, Sept. 21, 1864, at Jackson for 1 year, age 20. Mustered Sept. 23, 1864. No further record.

Hoisington, Abisha. St. Joseph County. Enlisted in Co. G, Aug. 24, 1861, at Three Rivers, age 45. Mustered Sept. 4, 1861. Drum Major Feb. 6, 1862. Discharged for disability Aug. 27, 1862, at Nashville.

Hoisington, William W. Three Rivers. Enlisted and mustered in Co. E as 1st Sergeant, Aug. 24, 1861, at Three Rivers, age 25. Died of typhoid fever Aug. 15, 1862, at Nashville. Buried in national cemetery in Nashville.

Holbrook, Daniel Webster. Branch County. Enlisted and mustered in Co. A, Aug. 24, 1861, at Centreville, age 28. Wounded Jan. 23, 1863, at Murfreesboro, TN. Discharged for disability Oct. 28, 1863, at Chattanooga.

Holdridge or Holdredge or Holdrich, Heman or Herman C. Seneca. Enlisted and mustered in Co. F, Sept. 11, 1861, at Morenci, age 18.

Died of measles Jan. 31, 1862, at Bardstown, KY.

Holland, Isaac. Hillsdale County. Enlisted and mustered in Co. B, Aug. 24, 1861, at Allen, age 21. Deserted Aug. 25, 1861, at White Pigeon.

Holly, Coe. St. Joseph County. Enlisted and mustered in Co. C, Aug. 24, 1861, at Sturgis, age 27. Mustered out Sept. 30, 1864, at Sturgis.

Hood, Calvin. Sturgis. Entered service in Co. C as Captain, Aug. 24, 1861, at Sturgis, age 28. Commissioned Aug. 24, 1861. Detached to Pioneer Brigade, Nov. 22, 1862. Commissioned Major Jan. 7, 1863. Resigned Mar. 17, 1863.

Hopkins, Edward B. Lenawee County. Enlisted and mustered in Co. F, Sept. 11, 1861, at Hudson, age 19. Captured Dec. 31, 1862, at Stones River. Mustered out Sept. 30, 1864, at Sturgis.

Hor, William. Enlisted in Co. G, Aug. 24, 1861, at Prairie Ronde, age 35. Mustered Sept. 4, 1861. Musician. Transferred Nov. 1, 1861, to Co. B. Died of disease Feb. 13, 1863, at Murfreesboro, TN.

Hosley, Richard F. St. Joseph County. Enlisted and mustered in Co. A, Aug. 24, 1861, at Centreville, age 27. Discharged for disability Mar. 16, 1863, at Murfreesboro, TN.

Houghton, Jerome M. Milan. Enlisted and mustered in Co. I, Aug. 24, 1861, at Milan, age 36. Died of disease Feb. 28, 1863, at Nashville.

Howard, Loren H. Fawn River. Entered service in Co. C as 2nd Lieutenant, Aug. 24, 1861, at Sturgis, age 34. Commissioned Aug. 24, 1861. Wounded at Stones River. Commissioned 1st Lieutenant Jan. 7, 1863, mustered Apr. 8, 1863. Commissioned Captain Oct. 2, 1863, mustered Feb. 17, 1864. Mustered out Sept. 30, 1864, at Sturgis.

Howard, Oliver P. Monroe County. Enlisted and mustered in Co. I, Aug. 24, 1861, at London, age 20. Discharged for disability Aug. 5, 1862, at Nashville.

Howe, Thomas J. Enlisted and mustered in Co. E, Feb. 23, 1864, at Kalamazoo, age 18. Joined regiment Mar. 15, 1864, at Rossville, GA. Transferred Apr. 15, 1865, to Co. E, reorganized 11th Michigan Infantry. Mustered out Sept. 16, 1865, at Nashville.

Howes, Alfred B. Lenawee County. Enlisted in Co. K, Aug. 24, 1861, at Cambridge, age 18. Mustered Sept. 1, 1861. Mustered out Sept. 30, 1864, at Sturgis. Resided c. 1905 at Benton Harbor.

Hoxie, Hiram L. Branch County. Enlisted and mustered in Co. D, Aug. 24, 1861, at Bronson, age 19. Killed Sept. 11, 1863, at Davis's Crossroads. Buried in cemetery at Covington, GA.

Hoyt, Eli. Algansee. Enlisted and mustered in Co. H, Aug. 24, 1861, at Coldwater, age 30. Reenlisted Mar. 27, 1864, at Graysville, GA. Mustered Apr. 11, 1864. Corporal July 1, 1864. Transferred Apr. 15, 1865, to Co. H, reorganized 11th Michigan Infantry. Mustered out Sept. 16, 1865, at Nashville. Resided c. 1905 at Quincy.

Hoyt, Philo. Colon. Enlisted and mustered in Co. A as Corporal, Aug. 24, 1861, at Coldwater, age 30. Died of chronic diarrhea Dec. 26, 1862, at Nashville. Buried in national cemetery in Nashville.

Hudson, Henry A. Enlisted as Musician, Aug. 24, 1861, at White Pigeon, age 24. Mustered Sept. 24, 1861. Deserted Dec. 1861 at White Pigeon.

Hull, Charles. Wright. Enlisted and mustered in Co. F, Sept. 11, 1861, at Wright, age 21. Died Nov. 23, 1863, drowned in Sequatchie River in TN.

Hull, Edwin J. Branch County. Enlisted and mustered in Co. B, Aug. 24, 1861, at Centreville, age 20. Discharged Sept. 10, 1861, at White Pigeon, as a minor enlisted without parental consent.

Hunt, Hiram R. Belleville. Enlisted and mustered in Co. I, Aug. 24, 1861, at Sumpter, age 28. Died of disease Jan. 25, 1863, at Murfreesboro, TN. Buried in national cemetery in Murfreesboro, TN, grave 62.

Huxley, Stephen. Calhoun County. Enlisted and mustered in Co. A, Aug. 24, 1861, at Centreville, age 26. Wounded at Stones River. Mustered out Sept. 30, 1864, at Sturgis.

Hyde, Pelatiah. Pittsford. Enlisted in Co. G at Pittsford, age 44. Mustered Sept. 4, 1861. Died of smallpox Jan. 8, 1862, at Bardstown, KY. Buried in national cemetery in Lebanon, KY, grave 364.

Iddings, William Clarence. St. Joseph County. Enlisted and mustered in Co. A, Aug. 24, 1861, at Centreville, age 19. Mustered out Sept. 30, 1864, at Sturgis.

Ingraham or Inghram, Charles W. Kalamazoo County. Enlisted and mustered in Co. A, Aug. 24, 1861, at Centreville, age 21. Missing Sept. 20, 1863, at Chickamauga. No further record.

Isabel, James. Monroe County. Enlisted in Co. K, Aug. 24, 1861, at Ida, age 23. Mustered Sept. 1, 1861. Killed Sept. 20, 1863, at Chickamauga.

Jacob, Neil. St. Joseph County. Enlisted and mustered in Co. C, Aug. 24, 1861, at Sturgis, age 25. Mustered out Sept. 30, 1864, at Sturgis.

James, Peter. Branch County. Enlisted and mustered in Co. D, Aug. 24, 1861, at Bronson, age 43. Discharged for disability Dec. 24, 1862, at Nashville. Died of disease Jan. 27, 1863.

Janson, Carlos B. *see* Johnson, Carlos B.

Jarmain, Henry. Enlisted and mustered in Co. I, Aug. 26, 1861, at Detroit, age 37. Deserted Oct. 20, 1861, at White Pigeon.

Jenkins, Lorenzo. Jefferson. Enlisted in Co. G at Jefferson, age 18. Mustered Sept. 4, 1861. Died of typhoid pneumonia Feb. 4, 1862, at Bardstown, KY. Buried in national cemetery in Lebanon, KY, grave 301.

Jennings, William E. Clarendon. Enlisted and mustered in Co. B, Aug. 24, 1861, at Quincy, age 32. Died of pneumonia Mar. 19, 1862, at Belmont, KY. Buried in national cemetery in Louisville.

Jerome, Francis. Branch County. Enlisted and mustered in Co. B, Aug. 24, 1861, at Butler, age 22. Discharged for disability Feb. 11, 1863, at Nashville.

Jewett, George E. Belleville. Enlisted and mustered in Co. I, Aug. 24, 1861, at Belleville, age 18. Killed Dec. 31, 1862, at Stones River.

Jibb, Matthew. Medina. Enlisted and mustered in Co. F, Nov. 8, 1861, at White Pigeon, age 25. Killed Sept. 20, 1863, at Chickamauga.

Jibb, William. Medina. Enlisted and mustered in Co. F, Sept. 11, 1861, at Hudson, age 18. Mustered out Sept. 30, 1864, at Sturgis.

Johnson, Alfred P. Enlisted and mustered in Co. I, Aug. 24, 1861, at Exeter, age 20. Discharged for disability.

Johnson, Carlos B. Hillsdale County. Enlisted in Co. K, Aug. 24, 1861, at Camden, age 20. Mustered Sept. 1, 1861. Mustered out Sept. 30, 1864, at Sturgis. Resided c. 1905 at Grayling.

Johnson, Jasper or Jesper. Dundee. Enlisted and mustered in Co. I, Aug. 24, 1861, at Dundee, age 18. Died of disease Aug. 1, 1863, at Decherd, TN. Buried in national cemetery in Murfreesboro, TN, grave 6129.

Johnson, John H. Adrian. Enlisted in Co. K as 1st Sergeant, Aug. 24, 1861, at Fairfield, age 26. Mustered Sept. 1, 1861. Wounded at Stones River. Commissioned 2nd Lieutenant Jan. 1, 1863, mustered Mar. 20, 1863. Resigned Dec. 4, 1863, due to disability.

Johnson, Walter W. Centreville. Enlisted and mustered in Co. A as Sergeant, Aug. 24, 1861, at Centreville, age 23. Died of typhoid Jan. 12, 1862, at Centreville.

Johnson, William C. Hillsdale County. Enlisted in Co. K, Aug. 24, 1861, at Camden, age 26. Mustered Sept. 1, 1861. Corporal. Sergeant July 2, 1863. Mustered out Sept. 30, 1864, at Sturgis.

Johnson, William W. Quincy. Enlisted and mustered in Co. B, Aug. 24, 1861, at Quincy, age 19. Killed Dec. 31, 1862, at Stones River.

Jones, Charles E. Enlisted in Co. E, Feb. 8, 1864, at Lockport, age 18. Mustered Feb. 9, 1864. Joined regiment Mar. 15, 1864, at Rossville, GA. Transferred Apr. 15, 1865, to Co. E, reorganized 11th Michigan Infantry. Mustered out Sept. 16, 1865, at Nashville.

Jones, James M. Medina. Enlisted and mustered in Co. F, Nov. 30, 1861, at White Pigeon. Died of pneumonia Feb. 13, 1862, at Bardstown, KY. Buried in national cemetery in Lebanon, KY, grave 355.

Jones, Philip. St. Joseph County. Enlisted and mustered in Co. E, Aug. 24, 1861, at Three Rivers, age 28. Corporal Apr. 9, 1864. Mustered out Sept. 30, 1864, at Sturgis.

Jordan or Jorden, John C. St. Joseph County. Enlisted and mustered in Co. C, Aug. 24, 1861, at Sturgis, age 18. Corporal. Discharged for disability Nov. 17, 1863, at Louisville. Reentered service. Private, Co. G, in 10th Michigan Cavalry, for 1 year, Feb. 15, 1865, mustered Feb. 21, 1865. Joined regiment Mar. 16, 1865, at Knoxville, TN. Corporal. Mustered out Nov. 11, 1865, at Memphis, TN.

Jubenville, Henry E. Wayne County. Enlisted and mustered in Co. I, Aug. 26, 1861, at Detroit, age 21. Sergeant Jan. 1863. Captured Dec. 18, 1864. Discharged Jan. 21, 1865, at Chattanooga.

Jubenville or Jubinville or Juvenville, John. Hillsdale County. Enlisted and mustered in Co. F, Sept. 11, 1861, at Wright, age 21. Wounded Nov. 1863 at Chattanooga. Mustered out Sept. 30, 1864, at Sturgis.

Juvenville, John D. Deerfield. Enlisted and mustered in Co. F, Sept. 11, 1861, at Hudson. Discharged for disability Oct. 26, 1861.

Keegan, John D. Deerfield. Enlisted in Co. K as Sergeant, Aug. 24, 1861, at Deerfield, age 25. Mustered Sept. 1, 1861. Wounded Dec. 31, 1862, at Stones River. Died of wounds Jan. 30, 1863. Buried in national cemetery in Murfreesboro, TN, grave 6013.

Keegan, Patrick H. Deerfield. Entered service in Co. K as 1st Lieutenant, Aug. 24, 1861, at Deerfield, age 21. Commissioned Aug. 24, 1861. Wounded at Stones River. Commissioned Captain Jan. 1, 1863, mustered Mar. 21, 1863. Mustered out Sept. 30, 1864, at Sturgis. Reentered service. Commissioned Lt. Colonel in reorganized 11th Michigan Infantry, Mar. 1, 1865, mustered Mar. 4, 1865. Commissioned Colonel Mar. 16, 1865, mustered June 16, 1865. Mustered out Sept. 16, 1865, at Nashville.

Keeler, John R. Burr Oak. Entered service in Co. D as 1st Lieutenant, Aug. 24, 1861, at Burr Oak, age 36. Commissioned Aug. 24, 1861. Resigned Dec. 10, 1862, at Nashville.

Kellam, William T.H. Branch County. Enlisted and mustered in Co. D as Corporal, Aug. 24, 1861, at Bronson, age 19. Mustered out Sept. 30, 1864, at Sturgis.

Kelley, Simon. Hillsdale County. Enlisted and mustered in Co. F, Sept. 11, 1861, at Hudson. Discharged for disability Apr. 25, 1862, at Louisville.

Kelly, Silas M. Jefferson. Enlisted in Co. G at Leonidas, age 20. Mustered Sept. 4, 1861. Killed Dec. 31, 1862, at Stones River.

Kemberling, Isaac. Burr Oak. Enlisted in Co. D, Aug. 15, 1862, at Burr Oak, age 23. Joined regiment Apr. 12, 1863, at Murfreesboro, TN. Transferred Apr. 15, 1865, to Co. D, reorganized 11th Michigan Infantry. Discharged June 16, 1865, at Chattanooga.

Kemberling or Kemerling, James. Colon. Enlisted in Co. A, Dec. 30, 1863, at Colon, age 27. Mustered Jan. 4, 1864. Joined regiment Jan. 28, 1864, at Rossville, GA. Transferred Mar. 30, 1864, to Co. F. Wounded Aug. 7, 1864, at Utoy Creek. Transferred Apr. 15, 1865, to Co. F, reorganized 11th Michigan Infantry. Mustered out Sept. 16, 1865, at Nashville. Resided c. 1905 at Colon.

Kenfield, Sylvanus. Kalamazoo County. Enlisted in Co. G, age 21. Mustered Sept. 4, 1861. Wounded May 27, 1864, near Dallas, GA. Mustered out Sept. 30, 1864, at Sturgis.

Kent, George W. St. Joseph County. Enlisted and mustered in Co. A as Fifer, Aug. 24, 1861, at Centreville, age 40. Discharged Sept. 4, 1862, at Nashville.

Kerschner, Andrew. St. Joseph County. Enlisted in Co. G at White Pigeon, age 24. Mustered Sept. 4, 1861. Wounded at Stones River. Mustered out Sept. 30, 1864, at Sturgis.

Kesler, Jacob. Lenawee County. Enlisted in Co. G at Blissfield, age 26. Mustered Sept. 4, 1861. Captured Sept. 20, 1863, at Chickamauga. Died Sept. 9, 1864, at Andersonville, GA. Buried in national cemetery in Andersonville, GA.

Kesler, John. Wayne. Enlisted and mustered in Co. H, Aug. 24, 1861. Transferred Dec. 8, 1862, at Nashville to 4th U.S. Cavalry.

Kesler, Theodore P. Bronson. Entered service in Co. D as 2nd Lieutenant, Aug. 24, 1861, at Bronson, age 23. Commissioned Aug. 24, 1861. Resigned Feb. 12, 1862.

Keyes, Rowdon or Rawdon. St. Joseph County. Enlisted and mustered in Co. D, Aug. 24, 1861, at Bronson, age 22. Discharged for disability Mar. 15, 1863, at Nashville. Resided c. 1905 at Colon.

King, James Wood. Fabius. Enlisted and mustered in Co. A, Aug. 24, 1861, at Centreville, age 19. Corporal Feb. 7, 1862. Quartermaster Sergeant Mar. 1, 1863. Wounded Nov. 25, 1863, at Missionary Ridge. Wounded July 30, 1864, near Atlanta. Mustered out Sept. 30, 1864, at Sturgis. Died Oct. 9, 1903, at Coldwater. Buried in Riverside Cemetery, Three Rivers.

Kinne, Alonzo H. Lenawee County. Enlisted and mustered in Co. F, Nov. 28, 1861. Discharged Nov. 25, 1864, at Chattanooga. Resided c. 1905 at Williamston.

Kinne, Newton I. Wayne County. Enlisted and mustered in Co. I, Aug. 24, 1861, at Belleville, age 22. Served in Pioneer Brigade. Mustered out Sept. 30, 1864, at Sturgis. Resided c. 1905 at Scottville.

Kinney, Alonzo H. see Kinne, Alonzo H.

Kinnie, Newton I. see Kinne, Newton I.

Kittelinger or Kittinger or Kittlinger, Joseph. Flushing. Enlisted in Co. G at Jefferson, age 28. Mustered Sept. 4, 1861. Killed Dec. 31, 1862, at Stones River.

Klady, Francisco. St. Joseph County. Enlisted and mustered in Co. A, Aug. 24, 1861, at Centreville, age 20. Mustered out Sept. 30, 1864, at Sturgis. Resided c. 1905 at Nottawa.

Klase, Henry see Clase, Henry.

Kline, George. St. Joseph County. Enlisted and mustered in Co. C, Aug. 24, 1861, at Sturgis, age 21. Corporal. Discharged for disability June 12, 1862, at Nashville.

Knapp, Andrew. St. Joseph County. Enlisted and mustered in Co. E, Aug. 24, 1861, at Three Rivers, age 19. Wounded at Stones River. Mustered out Sept. 30, 1864, at Sturgis.

Knapp, Isaac. Enlisted in Co. A, Dec. 30, 1863, at Colon, age 18. Mustered Jan. 4, 1864. Joined regiment Jan. 28, 1864, at Rossville, GA. Wounded May 15, 1864, at Resaca. Transferred Apr. 15, 1865, to Co. A, reorganized 11th Michigan Infantry. Discharged for disability June 8, 1865, at Camp Douglas, IL.

Knappen, Albert S. Batavia. Enlisted and mustered in Co. H, Aug. 24, 1861, at Coldwater, age 19. Died of typhoid fever May 16, 1862, at Louisville.

Knappen, Edward S. Batavia. Enlisted in Co. C, 1st Michigan Infantry, Apr. 24, 1861, at Coldwater for 3 months, age 18. Mustered May 1, 1861. Mustered out Aug. 7, 1861, at Detroit. Reentered service. Sergeant, Co. H, 11th

Michigan Infantry, Aug. 24, 1861. Transferred Nov. 28, 1862, at Nashville to 4th U.S. Cavalry.

Knappin, Albert S. *see* Knappen, Albert S.

Knevels, James A. St. Joseph County. Enlisted as Musician, Aug. 24, 1861, at White Pigeon, age 21. Mustered Sept. 24, 1861. Mustered out Aug. 22, 1862, at Nashville.

Knevels, John H. Enlisted in Co. E, Feb. 22, 1864, at Kalamazoo, age 18. Mustered Feb. 23, 1864. Joined regiment Apr. 10, 1864, at Graysville, GA. Corporal Mar. 16, 1865. Transferred Apr. 15, 1865, to Co. E, reorganized 11th Michigan Infantry. Mustered out Sept. 16, 1865, at Nashville.

Knickerbocker, Bert. St. Joseph County. Enlisted and mustered in Co. A, Aug. 24, 1861, at Centreville, age 18. Mustered out Sept. 30, 1864, at Sturgis.

Knoll, William N. or M. St. Joseph. Enlisted and mustered in Co. H, Aug. 24, 1861, at Coldwater, age 29. Discharged for disability Oct. 4, 1863, at Nashville.

Koon, Chauncey E. Allen. Enlisted and mustered in Co. E as Sergeant, Aug. 24, 1861, at Allen, age 19. 1st Sergeant Feb. 19, 1862. Commissioned 2nd Lieutenant Nov. 26, 1862, mustered Nov. 27, 1862. Commissioned 1st Lieutenant Jan. 7, 1863, mustered Mar. 19, 1863. Commissioned Captain June 17, 1864, mustered July 25, 1864. Mustered out Sept. 30, 1864, at Sturgis. Resided c. 1905 at Grand Rapids.

Koon, Sherman J. Enlisted as Hospital Steward, Aug. 24, 1861, at White Pigeon. Mustered Sept. 1, 1861. Discharged Mar. 1, 1862.

Krents, John H. *see* Knevels, John H.

Kullman, Louis A. St. Joseph County. Enlisted and mustered in Co. E, Aug. 24, 1861, at Three Rivers, age 25. Discharged for disability Aug. 18, 1862, at Nashville.

Lacy, Thomas J. Blissfield. Enlisted in Co. K as Sergeant, Aug. 24, 1861, at Deerfield, age 34. Mustered Sept. 1, 1861. Wounded Sept. 1863. Discharged for disability Nov. 19, 1863, at Detroit.

Ladow, Jasper D. St. Joseph County. Enlisted and mustered in Co. C as Corporal, Aug. 24, 1861, at Sturgis, age 21. Discharged for disability June 12, 1862, at Nashville.

Lamkin or Lampkins, Elijah M. Monroe County. Enlisted and mustered in Co. I, Aug. 24, 1861, at London, age 31. Wounded at Stones River. Mustered out Sept. 30, 1864, at Sturgis.

Lampman, Moses. Branch County. Enlisted in Co. B, Nov. 10, 1861, age 31. Served in Pioneer Corps. Discharged Nov. 10, 1864, at Chattanooga. Resided c. 1905 at Quincy.

Landon, Frederick. Monroe County. Enlisted and mustered in Co. I as Corporal, Aug. 24, 1861, at Milan, age 34. Discharged for disability Feb. 14, 1862.

Landon, Theodore E. St. Joseph County. Enlisted and mustered in Co. C, Aug. 24, 1861, at Grand Rapids, age 20. Mustered out Sept. 30, 1864, at Sturgis.

Lane, Alfred *see* Lantz, Alfred.

Lane, Bradley L. St. Joseph County. Enlisted and mustered in Co. E, Aug. 24, 1861, at Three Rivers, age 18. Wounded at Stones River. Corporal Apr. 9, 1864. Mustered out Sept. 30, 1864, at Sturgis.

Lane, Frank H. Bronson. Enlisted and mustered in Co. D as Sergeant, Aug. 24, 1861, at Bronson, age 20. 1st Sergeant May 1, 1862. Commissioned 2nd Lieutenant Dec. 20, 1862, mustered Jan. 22, 1863. Commissioned Captain Jan. 7, 1863, mustered Aug. 3, 1863. Cashiered June 29, 1864.

Lantz, Alfred. St. Joseph County. Enlisted as Musician, Aug. 24, 1861, at White Pigeon, age 22. Mustered Sept. 24, 1861. Discharged for disability May 31, 1862, at Columbia, TN.

Latham, Kneeland. Cass County. Enlisted and mustered in Co. E, Aug. 24, 1861, at Three Rivers. Transferred to Invalid Corps July 1, 1863.

Latta, Alonzo B. Branch County. Enlisted and mustered in Co. H, Oct. 1, 1861. Left at Chattanooga Sept. 1864. No further record.

Lautenschlager, Henry. Monroe County. Enlisted and mustered in Co. I, Aug. 24, 1861, at Exeter, age 19. Mustered out Sept. 30, 1864, at Sturgis. Died Feb. 2, 1902, at Flat Rock.

Le Meyer, Jacob. Enlisted in Co. A, Feb. 24, 1864, at Leonidas, age 40. Mustered Feb. 27, 1864. Joined regiment Mar. 15, 1864, at Rossville, GA. Transferred Mar. 30, 1865, to Co. F. Transferred Apr. 15, 1865, to Co. K, reorganized 11th Michigan Infantry. Mustered out Sept. 16, 1865, at Nashville.

Leach, Charles. Lenawee County. Enlisted in Co. K, Aug. 24, 1861, at Blissfield, age 18. Mustered Sept. 1, 1861. Corporal Jan. 30, 1862. Mustered out Sept. 30, 1864, at Sturgis.

Lear, Adam *see* Lehr, Adam.

Lechner or Lechmer, George F. Enlisted and mustered, company unassigned, Sept. 14, 1864, at Jackson for 1 year, age 24. Discharged Sept. 15, 1865, at Detroit.

Lee, Jay. Lenawee County. Enlisted in Co. K, Aug. 24, 1861, at Ogden, age 19. Mustered Sept. 1, 1861. Mustered out Sept. 30, 1864, at Sturgis.

Legg, Charles H. Lenawee County. Enlisted in Co. G, Aug. 1, 1862, at Nashville. Died of typhoid pneumonia Jan. 21, 1863, at Nashville. Buried in national cemetery in Nashville.

Legg, Nathan H. St. Joseph County. Enlisted in Co. G at Sturgis, age 32. Mustered Sept. 4, 1861. Discharged for disability Sept. 16, 1862, at Nashville.

Lehr, Adam. Monroe County. Enlisted in Co. K, Aug. 24, 1861, at Ida, age 19. Mustered Sept. 1, 1861. Wounded Jan. 2, 1863, at Stones River. Mustered out Sept. 30, 1864, at Sturgis.

Leigh, Charles W. Branch County. Enlisted and mustered in Co. A, Aug. 24, 1861, at Centreville, age 21. Transferred Oct. 1863 at Chattanooga to Signal Corps. Died Feb. 27, 1899. Buried at Sebewa.

Lemunyon, William S. St. Joseph County. Enlisted and mustered in Co. A, Aug. 24, 1861, at Centreville, age 19. Wounded at Stones River. Killed May 15, 1864, at Resaca.

Leonard, Charles. St. Joseph County. Enlisted and mustered in Co. C, Aug. 24, 1861, at Sturgis, age 18. Wounded at Stones River. Died June 24, 1864, at Sturgis.

Leonard, Daniel C. Sturgis. Enlisted and mustered in Co. C, Aug. 24, 1861, at Sturgis, age 18. Killed Dec. 31, 1862, at Stones River.

Leonard, Mort. St. Joseph County. Enlisted in Co. K, Aug. 24, 1861, at White Pigeon, age 23. Mustered Sept. 1, 1861. Discharged for disability Aug. 27, 1862, at Nashville.

Leonard, William. Hillsdale County. Enlisted in Co. G at Jefferson, age 40. Mustered Sept. 4, 1861. Discharged for disability May 28, 1862, at Detroit.

Letson, Perry. St. Joseph County. Enlisted and mustered in Co. C, Aug. 24, 1861, at White Pigeon, age 23. Discharged for disability Feb. 13, 1862.

Letson, Timothy. Medina. Enlisted and mustered in Co. F, Nov. 25, 1861, at White Pigeon. Died of fever Apr. 9, 1862, at Belmont, KY.

Leversee or Leverse, Anthony. Branch County. Enlisted in Co. H, Aug. 24, 1861, at Coldwater, age 19. Mustered Aug. 28, 1861.

Lewis, Charles. Deerfield. Enlisted in Co. I, Sept. 2, 1864, for 1 year, age 18. Mustered Sept. 3, 1864. Transferred Apr. 15, 1865, to Co. I, reorganized 11th Michigan Infantry. Discharged June 19, 1865, at Camp Chase, OH.

Lewis, George M.D. Lenawee County. Enlisted and mustered in Co. F as Corporal, Sept. 11, 1861, at Morenci, age 19. Deserted Aug. 27, 1862, at Louisville.

Lewis, Jerome C. Enlisted in Co. F, Feb. 10, 1864, at Leonidas, age 22. Mustered Feb. 27, 1864. Joined regiment Mar. 15, 1864, at Rossville, GA. Transferred Apr. 15, 1865, to Co. K, reorganized 11th Michigan Infantry. Discharged Aug. 21, 1865, at Detroit.

Lewis, Lyman. Lenawee County. Enlisted in Co. K as Corporal, Aug. 24, 1861, at Macon, age 21. Mustered Sept. 1, 1861. Deserted.

Liddle, Byron J. St. Joseph County. Enlisted and mustered in Co. D, Aug. 24, 1861, at White Pigeon. Captured Aug. 13, 1862, at Gallatin, TN. Reenlisted Feb. 27, 1864, at Rossville, GA. Mustered Mar. 31, 1864. Killed July 4, 1864, at Ruff's Station. Buried in national cemetery in Marietta, GA, grave 5033.

Liscomb, John. Medina. Enlisted and mustered in Co. F, Sept. 11, 1861, at Medina, age 45. Died of chronic diarrhea Dec. 9, 1862, at Nashville.

Liverson, Anthony *see* Leversee, Anthony.

Lockwood, Adelbert E. Branch County. Enlisted and mustered in Co. B, Aug. 24, 1861, at Butler, age 19. Discharged for disability June 4, 1862, at Columbia, TN. Resided c. 1905 at Coldwater.

Lockwood, George W. Monroe County. Enlisted and mustered in Co. I, Aug. 24, 1861, at Dundee, age 31. Corporal. Wounded Aug. 7, 1864, at Utoy Creek. Died of wounds Aug. 23, 1864, at Chattanooga. Buried in national cemetery in Chattanooga.

Lockwood, Harvey or Henry. St. Joseph County. Enlisted and mustered in Co. E as Corporal, Aug. 24, 1861, at Three Rivers, age 21. Sergeant Aug. 22, 1862. 1st Sergeant May 23, 1864. Mustered out Sept. 30, 1864, at Sturgis.

Loffland, William. Enlisted and mustered in Co. D, Aug. 24, 1861, at Burr Oak. No further record.

Long, James. Wright. Enlisted in Co. F, Aug. 15, 1862, at Hillsdale, age 23. Mustered Sept. 17, 1862. Wounded July 23, 1864, near Atlanta. Corporal Oct. 31, 1864. Transferred Apr. 15, 1865, to Co. K, reorganized 11th Michigan Infantry. Discharged June 16, 1865, at Chattanooga. Resided c. 1905 at Kalkaska.

Long, Simeon D. St. Joseph County. Enlisted and mustered in Co. D as Corporal, Aug. 24, 1861, at Colon, age 18. Captured Dec. 31, 1862, at Stones River. Paroled Mar. 1863. Mustered out Sept. 30, 1864, at Sturgis. Resided c. 1905 at Coldwater.

Lords, William L. St. Joseph County. Enlisted and mustered in Co. C, Aug. 24, 1861, at South Bend, IN, age 19. Mustered out Sept. 30, 1864, at Sturgis.

Lovett, James T. Centreville. Enlisted and mustered in Co. A as Sergeant, Aug. 24, 1861, at Centreville, age 20. Killed Sept. 11, 1863, at Davis's Crossroads. Buried in national cemetery in Chattanooga.

Lowder or Lowden, Isaac. Burr Oak. Enlisted and mustered in Co. D, Aug. 24, 1861, at Burr Oak, age 21. Transferred Apr. 15, 1865, to Co. C, reorganized 11th Michigan Infantry. Discharged June 15, 1865, at Chattanooga.

Lowry or Lowery, Samuel W. Enlisted and mustered in Co. D, Aug. 24, 1861, at Burr Oak, age 19. Mustered out Sept. 30, 1864, at Sturgis.

Lucus or Lucas, William H. Cass County. Enlisted and mustered in Co. D, Aug. 24, 1861, at Bronson, age 20. Killed Dec. 31, 1862, at Stones River.

Ludwig, Charles P. Enlisted in Co. E, Feb. 22, 1864, at Kalamazoo, age 19. Mustered Feb. 23, 1864. Joined regiment Apr. 10, 1864, at Graysville, GA. Musician Dec. 1864. Transferred Apr. 15, 1865, to Co. E, reorganized 11th Michigan Infantry. Mustered out Sept. 16, 1865, at Nashville. Resided c. 1905 at Holland.

Ludwig, John. St. Joseph County. Enlisted as Musician, Aug. 24, 1861, at White Pigeon, age 19. Mustered Sept. 24, 1861. Mustered out Aug. 22, 1862, at Nashville. Reentered service. Musician in Band, 2nd Brigade, 2nd Division, 14th AC. Resided c. 1905 at South Haven.

Lynch, Gordon R. Branch County. Enlisted and mustered in Co. C, Aug. 24, 1861, at Clarendon, age 19. Discharged Nov. 6, 1861, at White Pigeon by writ of habeas corpus as a minor enlisted without parental consent.

Lyon, Isaac B. St. Joseph County. Enlisted in Co. G at Leonidas, age 21. Mustered Sept. 4, 1861. Served in Pioneer Brigade. Mustered out Sept. 30, 1864, at Sturgis. Reentered service. Private, Co. E, in 49th Wisconsin Infantry.

Lyon, Melvin J. St. Joseph. Enlisted and mustered in Co. D, Aug. 24, 1861, at Bronson, age 18. Mustered out Sept. 30, 1864, at Sturgis. Died Mar. 30, 1899. Buried at Galien.

Lytle, Martin V. St. Joseph County. Enlisted and mustered in Co. D, Aug. 24, 1861, at Bronson, age 21. Died of measles Feb. 13, 1862, at Bardstown, KY.

Machin, Robert. Algansee. Enlisted in Co. H, Aug. 24, 1861, at Coldwater, age 33. Mustered Aug. 28, 1861. Reenlisted Feb. 27, 1864, at Rossville, GA, mustered Mar. 31, 1864. Wounded Aug. 7, 1864, at Utoy Creek. Corporal Sept. 1864. Died of wounds Sept. 11, 1864, at Chattanooga. Buried in national cemetery in Chattanooga.

Malalivly or Malalively, Joseph. Three Rivers. Enlisted and mustered in Co. E, Aug. 24, 1861, at Three Rivers, age 26. Died of disease July 12, 1863, at Tullahoma, TN. Buried in national cemetery in Murfreesboro, TN.

Malleson, Joseph C. Branch County. Enlisted and mustered in Co. H, Dec. 1, 1861. Discharged Nov. 7, 1864, at Chattanooga. Resided c. 1905 at Perry.

Malleson, Marion. Algansee. Enlisted in Co. H, Aug. 24, 1861, at Coldwater, age 18. Mustered Aug. 28, 1861. Died of spasms Sept. 24, 1862, at Nashville. Buried in national cemetery in Nashville.

Mallison, Joseph C. *see* Malleson, Joseph C.

Mallison, Marion *see* Malleson, Marion.

Mallory, William. Enlisted in Co. H, Aug. 31, 1864, at Blissfield for 1 year, age 35. Mustered Sept. 1, 1864. Joined regiment Feb. 16, 1865, at Chattanooga. Transferred Apr. 15, 1865, to Co. H, reorganized 11th Michigan Infantry. Discharged June 16, 1865, at Chattanooga.

Maltman, Frederick. Branch County. Enlisted and mustered in Co. B, Aug. 24, 1861, at Butler, age 21. Wounded and captured Jan. 2, 1863, at Stones River. Paroled Mar. 1863. Mustered out Sept. 30, 1864, at Sturgis.

Manigold, Cassimer E. *see* Mannigold, Cassimer E.

Manley, Jason W. Three Rivers. Enlisted and mustered in Co. E, Aug. 24, 1861, at Three Rivers, age 18. Died of typhoid fever Sept. 24, 1862, at Nashville. Buried in national cemetery in Nashville.

Manley, Reuben. Three Rivers. Enlisted and mustered in Co. E, Aug. 24, 1861, at Three Rivers, age 19. Died of smallpox Dec. 20, 1861, at White Pigeon.

Mann, Eli. St. Joseph County. Enlisted in Co. G at Mottville, age 18. Mustered Sept. 4, 1861. Mustered out Sept. 30, 1864, at Sturgis.

Mannigold, Cassimer E. St. Joseph County. Enlisted in Co. G at White Pigeon, age 18. Mustered Sept. 4, 1861. Killed Nov. 25, 1863, at Missionary Ridge.

Manning, Levi L. Lenawee County. Enlisted and mustered in Co. F, Sept. 11, 1861, at Medina, age 23. Discharged for disability Jan. 31, 1862. Resided c. 1905 at Fowlerville.

Manning, Thomas. Marcellus. Enlisted and mustered in Co. E, Aug. 24, 1861, at Three Rivers, age 22. Killed Dec. 31, 1862, at Stones River.

Mansion, William. Enlisted in Co. G at Detroit, age 22. Mustered Sept. 4, 1861. Wounded June 29, 1864, near Kennesaw Mtn. Died of wounds June 30, 1864. Buried in national cemetery in Marietta, GA, section A, grave 956.

Marsh, Clark. Enlisted and mustered in Co. B, July 1, 1862, at Nashville, age 21. Corporal Dec. 2, 1863. Sergeant Dec. 9, 1864. 1st Sergeant Mar. 16, 1865. Transferred Apr. 15, 1865, to Co. C, reorganized 11th Michigan Infantry. Discharged June 16, 1865, at Chattanooga.

Marsh, Frederick A. Sturgis. Enlisted in Co. G, Aug. 11, 1862, at Sturgis, age 21. Joined regiment Jan. 10, 1863, at Murfreesboro, TN. Died of typhoid pneumonia Feb. 12, 1863, at Murfreesboro, TN. Buried in national cemetery in Nashville.

Marsh, Stephen P. Leonidas. Enlisted and mustered in Co. A as Corporal, Aug. 24, 1861, at Centreville, age 28. Sergeant Jan. 24, 1862. Commissioned 2nd Lieutenant Feb. 13, 1863, mustered Mar. 21, 1863. Commissioned 1st Lieutenant Jan. 6, 1864, mustered Apr. 20, 1864. Transferred Jan. 23, 1864, to Co. E. Mustered out Sept. 30, 1864, at Sturgis.

Martin, James. Branch County. Enlisted in Co. H as Corporal, Aug. 24, 1861, at Coldwater, age 19. Mustered Aug. 28, 1861. Sergeant Nov. 13, 1862. 1st Sergeant Sept. 1, 1863. Mustered out Sept. 30, 1864, at Sturgis. Resided c. 1905 at Geneva.

Marvin, Dudley C. Colon. Enlisted and mustered in Co. A, Aug. 24, 1861, at Centreville, age 18. Joined regiment Nov. 27, 1862. Died of chronic diarrhea Mar. 4, 1863, at Murfreesboro, TN.

Mason, Elisha C. Enlisted in Co. G at Detroit, age 26. Mustered Sept. 4, 1861. Deserted Nov. 20, 1861, at White Pigeon.

Masser, Edward C. Enlisted in Co. E, Feb. 22, 1864, at Kalamazoo, age 20. Mustered Feb. 23, 1864. Joined regiment Apr. 10, 1864, at Graysville, GA. Wounded Aug. 7, 1864, at Utoy Creek. Died of wounds Aug. 7, 1864. Buried in national cemetery in Chattanooga.

Masters, Daniel. Burr Oak. Enlisted and mustered in Co. H, Aug. 11, 1862, at Burr Oak, age 22. Joined regiment Dec. 18, 1862, at Nashville. Transferred Apr. 15, 1865, to Co. H, reorganized 11th Michigan Infantry. Discharged June 16, 1865, at Chattanooga. Resided c. 1905 at Bangor.

Masters, John. Amboy. Enlisted and mustered in Co. F, Sept. 11, 1861, at Amboy, age 21. Died of pulmonary apoplexy May 28, 1862, at Nashville. Buried in national cemetery in Nashville.

Matheson, Alcibiades or Archibald. Enlisted in Co. F, Jan. 15, 1864, at Colon, age 18. Mustered Jan. 16, 1864. Joined regiment Apr. 8, 1864, at Graysville, GA. Died of disease June 23, 1864, at Nashville. Buried in national cemetery in Nashville.

Matthew, William R. St. Joseph County. Enlisted and mustered in Co. C, Aug. 24, 1861, at Fawn River, age 19. Discharged Jan. 18, 1865, at Chattanooga.

Matthews, Amos. La Grange, IN. Enlisted and mustered in Co. C, Aug. 24, 1861, at Metz, IN, age 24. Discharged to date Mar. 17, 1862.

Matthews, Henry. La Grange, IN. Enlisted and mustered in Co. C, Aug. 24, 1861, at Metz, IN, age 19. Died of measles Feb. 20, 1862, at Bardstown, KY. Buried in national cemetery in Lebanon, KY, grave 353.

Matthews, William R. *see* Matthew, William R.

Maxon, Ambrose. Jackson. Enlisted in Co. A, Nov. 19, 1862, at Mendon, age 22. Mustered Dec. 21, 1862. Transferred Apr. 15, 1865, to Co. A, reorganized 11th Michigan Infantry. Corporal Aug. 28, 1865. Mustered out Sept. 16, 1865, at Nashville.

May, David C. St. Joseph County. Enlisted and mustered in Co. D, Aug. 24, 1861, at Bronson, age 22. Corporal. Color guard Jan. 1864. Mustered out Sept. 30, 1864, at Sturgis. Resided c. 1905 at Gilead.

May, William J. White Pigeon. Entered service as Colonel, Aug. 24, 1861, at White Pigeon, age 38. Commissioned Oct. 11, 1861. Mustered to date Sept. 24, 1861. Resigned Apr. 1, 1862.

McCarty, William N. Lenawee County. Enlisted and mustered in Co. F, Sept. 11, 1861, at Medina, age 24. Discharged for disability Feb. 13, 1863, at Nashville. Reentered service. Private, Co. F, in 18th Michigan Infantry.

McComb or McCombs, Addison. Enlisted in Co. G. Joined regiment Apr. 1, 1863, at Murfreesboro, TN. Wounded July 23, 1864, near Atlanta. Died of wounds Sept. 15, 1864, at Chattanooga.

McCormick, Hugh. St. Joseph County. Enlisted and mustered in Co. A, Aug. 24, 1861, at Centreville, age 28. Discharged for disability July 1862 at Nashville.

McDonald, Edward C. Branch County. Enlisted and mustered in Co. B, Aug. 24, 1861, at Butler, age 25. Corporal Nov. 24, 1861. Discharged for disability Oct. 4, 1862.

McFarlan, John Q.A. Wayne County. Enlisted and mustered in Co. I as Drummer, Oct. 10, 1861, at Brownstown, age 13. Discharged Oct. 12, 1864, at Detroit.

McGiness, James Levi. Quincy. Enlisted and mustered in Co. B, Aug. 24, 1861, at Quincy, age 23. Wounded Dec. 31, 1862, at Stones River. Died of wounds Feb. 4, 1863, at Murfreesboro, TN.

McGiness, John. Branch County. Enlisted and mustered in Co. B, Aug. 24, 1861, at Quincy, age 25. Discharged for disability Oct. 15, 1861, at White Pigeon.

McGinnis, James Levi *see* McGiness, James Levi.

McGinnis, John *see* McGiness, John.

McGuire, John. Monroe County. Enlisted and mustered in Co. I as Sergeant, Aug. 24, 1861, at Dundee, age 44. Discharged for disability Aug. 17, 1862, at Nashville.

McIlvain or McIlvaine or McIlwain, Robert. St. Joseph County. Enlisted and mustered in Co. E, Aug. 24, 1861, at Three Rivers, age 18. Killed Dec. 31, 1862, at Stones River.

McKenney, Barnum *see* McKinney, Barney.

McKenny, Barney *see* McKinney, Barney.

McKenzie, John *see* McKinzie, John.

McKinney or McKinna, Barney. Burr Oak. Enlisted and mustered in Co. D, Aug. 12, 1862, at Burr Oak, age 30. Transferred Apr. 15, 1865, to Co. D, reorganized 11th Michigan Infantry. Discharged June 16, 1865, at Chattanooga.

McKinney, Joseph. Branch County. Enlisted in Co. H, Aug. 24, 1861, at Coldwater, age 23. Mustered Aug. 28, 1861. Reentered service. Private in 1st Michigan Artillery, Battery F, Dec. 13, 1861, mustered Jan. 9, 1862. Reenlisted and mustered Feb. 20, 1864, at Knoxville, TN. Bugler May 1, 1865. Mustered out July 1, 1865, at Jackson.

McKinzie, John. St. Joseph County. Enlisted and mustered in Co. E, Aug. 24, 1861, at Three Rivers. Discharged for disability Nov. 27, 1862, at Nashville.

McKnight, George S. Branch County. Enlisted in Co. H, Aug. 24, 1861, at Coldwater, age 28. Mustered Aug. 28, 1861. Mustered out Sept. 30, 1864, at Sturgis.

McLathlin, Nathan. Monroe County. Enlisted in Co. K, Aug. 24, 1861, at Petersburg, age 20. Mustered Sept. 1, 1861. AWOL June 6, 1864. No further record.

McLaughlin, Thomas. Branch County. Enlisted and mustered in Co. D, Aug. 24, 1861, at Bronson, age 32. Discharged Oct. 30, 1862, at Nashville.

McNair, Samuel T. Lenawee County. Enlisted in Co. K, Aug. 24, 1861, at Deerfield, age 21. Mustered Sept. 1, 1861. Corporal Dec. 1862. Mustered out Sept. 30, 1864, at Sturgis. Resided c. 1905 at Deerfield.

McNamee or McNames, Abram. Lenawee County. Enlisted in Co. K, Aug. 24, 1861, at Fairfield, age 23. Mustered Sept. 1, 1861. Mustered out Sept. 30, 1864, at Sturgis.

Mead, Fay. Branch County. Enlisted in Co. H, Aug. 24, 1861, at Coldwater, age 21. Mustered Aug. 28, 1861. Wounded Nov. 25, 1863, at Missionary Ridge. Died of wounds Jan. 27, 1864, at Chattanooga. Buried in national cemetery in Chattanooga.

Mead, Henry E. St. Joseph County. Enlisted and mustered in Co. C, Aug. 24, 1861, at Constantine, age 19. Mustered out Sept. 30, 1864, at Sturgis.

Merrick, Alonzo Howard. Sturgis. Enlisted and mustered in Co. C as Corporal, Aug. 24, 1861, at Sturgis, age 35. Sergeant Apr. 1, 1862. Killed Nov. 25, 1863, at Missionary Ridge. Buried in national cemetery in Chattanooga.

Merrill, William H. Hillsdale County. Enlisted in Co. K, Aug. 24, 1861, at Camden, age 26. Mustered Sept. 1, 1861. Mustered out Sept. 30, 1864, at Sturgis.

Metcalf, Irving J. St. Joseph County. Enlisted and mustered in Co. D, Aug. 24, 1861, at Burr Oak, age 22. Discharged for disability Apr. 18, 1863, at Murfreesboro, TN.

Metcalf, John. Hillsdale County. Enlisted and mustered in Co. F as Corporal, Sept. 11, 1861, at Amboy, age 37. Transferred to Veteran Reserve Corps Apr. 10, 1864.

Miles, John. Lenawee County. Enlisted and mustered in Co. F, Sept. 11, 1861, at Dover, age 22. Mustered out Sept. 30, 1864, at Sturgis.

Miles, Nilo D. Branch County. Enlisted and mustered in Co. B, Aug. 24, 1861, at Quincy, age 21. Mustered out Sept. 30, 1864, at Sturgis.

Millard, Charles. Enlisted in Co. A, Dec. 21, 1863, at Leonidas, age 22. Mustered Jan. 4, 1864. Joined regiment Jan. 28, 1864, at Rossville, GA. Corporal Mar. 4, 1865. Transferred Apr. 15, 1865, to Co. A, reorganized 11th Michigan Infantry. Mustered out Sept. 16, 1865, at Nashville.

Miller, Arthur W. Branch County. Enlisted and mustered in Co. D, Aug. 24, 1861, at Bronson, age 28. Died of consumption Feb. 10, 1862, at Bardstown, KY. Buried in national cemetery in Lebanon, KY, grave 361.

Miller, David Nelson. Branch County. Enlisted and mustered in Co. D, Aug. 24, 1861, at Branch County, age 20. Mustered out Sept. 30, 1864, at Sturgis.

Miller, Edmund. Branch County. Enlisted and mustered in Co. D, Aug. 24, 1861, at Bronson, age 26. Discharged for disability Jan. 18, 1863, at Nashville.

Miller, Halsey. Branch County. Enlisted and mustered in Co. B, Aug. 24, 1861, at Quincy, age 21. Corporal Mar. 1, 1862. Captured Jan. 2, 1863, at Stones River. Paroled Mar. 1863. Mustered out Sept. 30, 1864, at Sturgis.

Miller, Joseph. Camden. Enlisted in Co. K, Aug.

24, 1861, at Camden, age 22. Mustered Sept. 1, 1861. Wounded Dec. 31, 1862, at Stones River. Died of wounds Jan. 2, 1863, at Murfreesboro, TN.

Miller, William. Enlisted in Co. A, Dec. 28, 1863, at Leonidas, age 20. Mustered Jan. 4, 1864. Joined regiment Jan. 28, 1864, at Rossville, GA. Transferred Mar. 30, 1864, to Co. F. Transferred Apr. 15, 1865, to Co. K, reorganized 11th Michigan Infantry. Corporal May 15, 1865. Mustered out Sept. 16, 1865, at Nashville.

Milliman, Bryant. Cass County. Enlisted and mustered in Co. E, Aug. 24, 1861, age 28. Mustered out Sept. 30, 1864, at Sturgis. Resided c. 1905 at Covert.

Milliman, Jerome B. Branch County. Enlisted and mustered in Co. D, Aug. 24, 1861, at Bronson, age 24. Discharged for disability Mar. 5, 1863, at Nashville.

Mills, Halley M. Hillsdale County. Enlisted and mustered in Co. B, Aug. 24, 1861, at Allen, age 28. Mustered out Sept. 30, 1864, at Sturgis.

Mills, John A. St. Joseph County. Enlisted and mustered in Co. A, Aug. 24, 1861, at Centreville, age 26. Transferred to Veteran Reserve Corps Apr. 30, 1864.

Mills, Leonidas E. Coldwater. Entered service in Co. H as 2nd Lieutenant, Aug. 24, 1861, at Coldwater, age 31. Commissioned Aug. 24, 1861. Mustered Aug. 28, 1861. Resigned June 23, 1863. Reentered service. Commissioned and mustered as 2nd Lieutenant, Co. H, Jan. 19, 1864. Joined regiment Mar. 15, 1864, at Rossville, GA. Commissioned 1st Lieutenant, Co. A, Mar. 1, 1865, mustered Mar. 4, 1865. Commissioned Captain Mar. 16, 1865, mustered June 16, 1865. Transferred Apr. 15, 1865, to Co. A, reorganized 11th Michigan Infantry. Mustered out Sept. 16, 1865, at Nashville.

Mills, Samuel Cartiss. Coldwater. Enlisted in Co. C as Corporal, 1st Michigan Infantry, Apr. 24, 1861, at Coldwater for 3 months, age 25. Mustered May 1, 1861. Mustered out Aug. 7, 1861, at Detroit. Reentered service. Commissioned 1st Lieutenant, Co. H, 11th Michigan Infantry, Aug. 24, 1861, mustered Aug. 28, 1861. Resigned June 24, 1862.

Mitchell, Newton. Branch County. Enlisted in Co. H, Aug. 24, 1861, at Coldwater, age 18. Mustered Aug. 28, 1861. Corporal Aug. 9, 1862. Wounded and captured. Paroled May 1864. Mustered out Sept. 30, 1864, at Sturgis.

Moase, Charles. Bronson. Entered service in Co. G as 2nd Lieutenant, 1st Michigan Infantry, Apr. 24, 1861, at Burr Oak, age 26. Commissioned May 1, 1861. Mustered out Aug. 7, 1861, at Detroit. Reentered service. Commissioned Captain, Co. G, 11th Michigan Infantry, Aug. 24, 1861, mustered Sept. 4, 1861. Resigned Nov. 14, 1862. Resided c. 1905 at Tampa Bay, FL.

Molter, Daniel *see* Moyer, Daniel.

Montgomery, John H. St. Joseph County. Enlisted and mustered in Co. D as Sergeant, Aug. 24, 1861, at Colon, age 23. Deserted Feb. 1, 1863, at Murfreesboro, TN.

Moore, Henry. Lenawee County. Enlisted in Co. K, Aug. 24, 1861, at Palmyra, age 18. Mustered Sept. 1, 1861. Mustered out Sept. 30, 1864, at Sturgis.

Moore, William or Wilson B. Hillsdale County. Enlisted and mustered in Co. F, Sept. 11, 1861, at Wright, age 19. Wounded June 3, 1864, near Dallas, GA. Mustered out Sept. 30, 1864, at Sturgis.

More, Henry *see* Moore, Henry.

Morehouse, Jerome. St. Joseph County. Enlisted and mustered in Co. C, Dec. 9, 1861. Discharged Dec. 9, 1864, at Chattanooga.

Morgan, William E. Mendon. Enlisted and mustered in Co. A, Oct. 27, 1862, at Mendon, age 19. Joined regiment Dec. 8, 1862, at Nashville. Corporal Mar. 4, 1865. Transferred Apr. 15, 1865, to Co. A, reorganized 11th Michigan Infantry. Mustered out Sept. 16, 1865, at Nashville.

Mosher, Bradley. Hillsdale County. Enlisted and mustered in Co. B, Aug. 24, 1861, at Allen, age 20. Captured Jan. 2, 1863, at Stones River. Paroled Apr. 1863. Corporal June 11, 1863. Mustered out Sept. 30, 1864, at Sturgis.

Mosher, Isaac C. Hillsdale County. Enlisted and mustered in Co. B, Aug. 24, 1861, at Allen, age 19. Wounded and captured Sept. 20, 1863, at Chickamauga. Died of wounds Dec. 22, 1863, at POW camp in Danville, VA. Buried in cemetery in Danville, VA.

Moulton, John F. London. Enlisted and mustered in Co. I, Aug. 24, 1861, at London, age 18. Died of pneumonia Oct. 29, 1862, at Nashville. Buried in national cemetery in Nashville.

Moyer, Daniel. Enlisted in Co. E, Feb. 22, 1864, at Kalamazoo, age 21. Mustered Feb. 23, 1864. Joined regiment Apr. 10, 1864, at Graysville, GA. Transferred Apr. 15, 1865, to Co. E, reorganized 11th Michigan Infantry. Mustered out Sept. 16, 1865, at Nashville.

Moyer, John. Enlisted, company unassigned, Feb. 22, 1864, at Kalamazoo, age 27. Mustered Feb. 23, 1864. Discharged for disability Apr. 12, 1864, at Grand Rapids.

Mudge, Melvin. Quincy. Entered service in Co.

B as Captain, Aug. 24, 1861, at Quincy, age 27. Mustered Aug. 24, 1861. Commissioned Lt. Colonel Jan. 7, 1863, mustered Apr. 25, 1863. Wounded Sept. 20, 1863, at Chickamauga. Mustered out Sept. 30, 1864, at Sturgis. Resided c. 1905 at Los Angeles, CA.

Mudge, William H. Branch County. Enlisted in Co. H, Aug. 24, 1861, at Coldwater, age 40. Mustered Aug. 28, 1861. Discharged for disability Aug. 24, 1862, at Nashville.

Mullen, Sidney S. Cass County. Enlisted and mustered in Co. E, Aug. 24, 1861, age 22. Mustered out Sept. 30, 1864, at Sturgis.

Mulliman, Jerome B. *see* Milliman, Jerome B.

Mullin, Sidney S. *see* Mullen, Sidney S.

Murphy, Charles M. St. Joseph County. Enlisted in Co. G at York, age 21. Mustered Sept. 4, 1861. Corporal Feb. 13, 1862. Mustered out Sept. 30, 1864, at Sturgis.

Murphy, Martin T. Lenawee County. Enlisted and mustered in Co. F, Sept. 11, 1861, at Morenci, age 18. Mustered out Sept. 30, 1864, at Sturgis.

Musgrove, William. Enlisted in Co. G, Aug. 24, 1861, at Hillsdale, age 28. Mustered Sept. 4, 1861. Deserted Nov. 25, 1861, at White Pigeon.

Myers, Walter. Hillsdale County. Enlisted in Co. K, Aug. 24, 1861, at Camden, age 18. Mustered Sept. 1, 1864. Mustered out Sept. 30, 1864, at Sturgis.

Myrick, Albert. Monroe County. Enlisted and mustered in Co. K, Sept. 1, 1861, at Petersburg, age 20. Discharged for disability June 1, 1863, at Detroit.

Nash, Jesse M. Bristol, IN. Enlisted in Co. G, Aug. 24, 1861, at York, IN, age 21. Mustered Sept. 4, 1861. Wounded Jan. 2, 1863, at Stones River. Died of wounds Jan. 1863.

Naughton, Thomas B. Jackson. Enlisted and mustered in Co. A, Aug. 24, 1861, at Centreville, age 21. Died of brain fever Apr. 17, 1862, at Belmont, KY. Buried in national cemetery in Louisville.

Naughton, William H. Calhoun County. Enlisted and mustered in Co. A, Aug. 24, 1861, at Centreville, age 19. Died July 12, 1864, at Louisville. Buried in national cemetery in Louisville.

Newberry, Charles W. Three Rivers. Enlisted in Co. G, 1st Michigan Infantry, Apr. 24, 1861, at Burr Oak for 3 months, age 32. Mustered May 1, 1861. Mustered out Aug. 7, 1861, at Detroit. Reentered service. Commissioned and mustered as 2nd Lieutenant, Co. E, 11th Michigan Infantry, Aug. 24, 1861. Commissioned and mustered as 1st Lieutenant, Co. H, June 24, 1862. Commissioned Captain, Co. E, Jan. 1, 1863, mustered Mar. 21, 1863. Killed Sept. 20, 1863, at Chickamauga. Buried in national cemetery in Chattanooga.

Newberry, Warren H. Quincy. Enlisted in Co. H as Corporal, Aug. 24, 1861, at Coldwater, age 22. Mustered Aug. 28, 1861. Sergeant June 1863. Died of fever June 30, 1863, at Nashville. Buried in national cemetery in Nashville.

Newell, Nathaniel. Enlisted in Co. B, Aug. 31, 1864, at Blissfield for 1 year, age 18. Mustered Sept. 1, 1864. Joined regiment Jan. 7, 1865, at Chattanooga. Transferred Apr. 15, 1865, to Co. B, reorganized 11th Michigan Infantry. Discharged June 16, 1865, at Chattanooga. Resided c. 1905 at Dundee.

Neygus, George. Lenawee County. Enlisted and mustered in Co. F, Sept. 11, 1861, at Seneca, age 28. Discharged for disability May 23, 1862.

Neygus, John. Lenawee County. Enlisted and mustered in Co. F, Sept. 11, 1861, at Seneca, age 23. Deserted Sept. 15, 1861, at White Pigeon.

Nichols, Charles N. Cass County. Enlisted in Co. G at Pittsford, age 27. Mustered Sept. 4, 1861. Wounded at Stones River. Mustered out Sept. 30, 1864, at Sturgis. Died Feb. 11, 1902.

Nichols, Dorry or Darry. Branch County. Enlisted and mustered in Co. B, Aug. 24, 1861, at California, MI, age 22. Wounded at Stones River. Mustered out Sept. 30, 1864, at Sturgis.

Nichols, George W. Calhoun County. Enlisted and mustered in Co. B, Aug. 24, 1861, at Clarendon, age 41. Discharged for disability Mar. 19, 1863, at Louisville.

Nichols, James O. Cass County. Enlisted in Co. G, age 21. Mustered Sept. 4, 1861. Killed Sept. 20, 1863, at Chickamauga.

Nichols, John. Branch County. Enlisted in Co. H as 1st Sergeant, Aug. 24, 1861, at Coldwater, age 33. Mustered Aug. 28, 1861. Discharged for disability Aug. 9, 1862, at Nashville.

Nichols, John W. Calhoun County. Enlisted and mustered in Co. B, Aug. 24, 1861, at Clarendon, age 33. Discharged for disability Feb. 24, 1862, at Bardstown, KY.

Nichols, Orin P. Quincy. Enlisted and mustered in Co. B, Aug. 24, 1861, at Quincy, age 21. Killed Dec. 31, 1862, at Stones River.

Nichols, Sylvester. Cass County. Enlisted in Co. G at White Pigeon, age 19. Mustered Sept. 4, 1861. Wounded at Stones River. Died of wounds Jan. 2, 1863, at Murfreesboro, TN.

Noble, Peter S. St. Joseph County. Enlisted and mustered in Co. E, Aug. 24, 1861, at Three

Rivers, age 18. Mustered out Sept. 30, 1864, at Sturgis.

Norris, David H. Detroit. Enlisted and mustered in Co. I, Aug. 19, 1862, at Detroit, age 28. Transferred Apr. 15, 1865, to Co. E, reorganized 11th Michigan Infantry. Discharged June 16, 1865, at Chattanooga.

Norris, Everett W. La Salle. Enlisted and mustered in Co. E, Aug. 19, 1862, at Detroit, age 18. Transferred Apr. 15, 1865, to Co. E, reorganized 11th Michigan Infantry. Discharged June 16, 1865, at Chattanooga.

Norton, George H. Fawn River. Enlisted and mustered in Co. C, Aug. 24, 1861, at Fawn River, age 20. Died of smallpox Jan. 2, 1862, at Bardstown, KY. Buried in national cemetery in Lebanon, KY, grave 363.

Nottage, Charles. Gorham, OH. Enlisted and mustered in Co. F, Sept. 11, 1861, at Medina, age 26. Died of measles Jan. 28, 1862, at Bardstown, KY.

Nottingham, Judson. Cass County. Enlisted in Co. E, age 20. Mustered Aug. 24, 1861. Mustered out Sept. 30, 1864, at Sturgis.

Nyce, George. St. Joseph County. Enlisted and mustered in Co. E, Aug. 24, 1861, at Three Rivers. Discharged for disability June 23, 1862.

O'Brien, Thomas. Wayne County. Enlisted and mustered in Co. I, Aug. 26, 1861, at Detroit, age 26. Deserted Dec. 8, 1861, at White Pigeon. Reentered service. Private in 8th Michigan Cavalry.

O'Connor, Cyrus W. Cass County. Enlisted and mustered in Co. D, Aug. 24, 1861, at Bronson, age 20. Captured Nov. 13, 1862. Wounded July 4, 1864, at Ruff's Station. Mustered out Sept. 30, 1864, at Sturgis.

O'Doud, Peter. St. Joseph County. Enlisted in Co. G at White Pigeon, age 35. Mustered Sept. 4, 1861. Mustered out Sept. 30, 1864, at Sturgis. Died Aug. 21, 1886. Buried at White Pigeon.

Oakes, David Jr. Centreville. Entered service in Co. A as Captain, Aug. 24, 1861, at Centreville, age 31. Mustered Aug. 24, 1861. Wounded Dec. 31, 1862, at Stones River. Died of typhoid Jan. 30, 1863, at Murfreesboro, TN.

Oaldfield, Samuel A. Hillsdale County. Enlisted and mustered in Co. F, Sept. 11, 1861, at Amboy, age 40. Mustered out Sept. 30, 1864, at Sturgis. Resided c. 1905 at Amboy.

Olds, Charles B. St. Joseph County. Enlisted in Co. G at York, IN, age 31. Mustered Sept. 4, 1861. Transferred to Veteran Reserve Corps Mar. 20, 1864.

Oppliger, Fritz. Enlisted in Co. G, Feb. 4, 1864, at Nottawa, age 28. Mustered Feb. 22, 1864.

Died of disease Oct. 9, 1864, at Chattanooga. Buried in national cemetery in Chattanooga.

Orcutt, Mark W. Enlisted in Co. A, Dec. 11, 1863, at Leonidas, age 23. Mustered Jan. 4, 1864. Joined regiment at Rossville, GA. Transferred Mar. 30, 1864, to Co. F. Wounded July 4, 1864, at Ruff's Station. Transferred Apr. 15, 1865, to Co. K, reorganized 11th Michigan Infantry. Discharged to date Aug. 29, 1865.

Ormsby, Albert A. Enlisted, company unassigned, Sept. 2, 1864, at Blissfield for 1 year, age 18. Mustered Sept. 3, 1864. Captured. Died Apr. 6, 1865, near Flint River, GA, in captivity.

Osborn, George. Enlisted in Co. K, Aug. 24, 1861, at Petersburg, age 18. Mustered Sept. 1, 1861. Discharged for disability Nov. 4, 1861.

Osmer, Albert. St. Joseph County. Enlisted and mustered in Co. E, Aug. 24, 1861, at Three Rivers, age 19. Mustered out Sept. 30, 1864, at Sturgis.

Otto, Harmon. Branch County. Enlisted and mustered in Co. D, Aug. 24, 1861, at Bronson, age 20. Mustered out Sept. 30, 1864, at Sturgis.

Owens, Owen. Wayne County. Enlisted and mustered in Co. I, Aug. 24, 1861, at Belleville, age 25. Mustered out Sept. 30, 1864, at Sturgis.

Packard, Nelson I. Sturgis. Entered service as Asst. Surgeon, Oct. 28, 1862, at Detroit. Commissioned Oct. 28, 1862. Mustered out Sept. 30, 1864, at Sturgis.

Palmer, Ansyl. London. Enlisted in Co. I as Sergeant, Aug. 24, 1861, at London, age 36. Mustered Sept. 1, 1861. Wounded at Stones River. Died of wounds Jan. 2, 1863, at Murfreesboro, TN. Buried in national cemetery in Murfreesboro, TN, grave 1402.

Palmer, John J. Lenawee County. Enlisted in Co. G at Blissfield, age 26. Mustered Sept. 4, 1861. Mustered out Sept. 30, 1864, at Sturgis.

Palmer, Myron C. Leonidas. Enlisted in Co. I at Leonidas, age 18. Mustered Sept. 4, 1861. Died of typhoid fever Mar. 19, 1862, at Jeffersonville, IN.

Palmer, Orvil. Enlisted and mustered in Co. F, Sept. 11, 1861, at Wright, age 18. Discharged for disability Oct. 26, 1861.

Palmer, Robert. St. Joseph County. Enlisted in Co. G at Leonidas, age 42. Mustered Sept. 4, 1861. Transferred to Invalid Corps July 18, 1863. No further record.

Palmiter, Albert. Hillsdale County. Enlisted and mustered in Co. K, Sept. 1, 1861, at Camden, age 19. Discharged for disability Mar. 1, 1863, at Murfreesboro, TN.

Palmiter, Henry. Hillsdale County. Enlisted in Co. K as Corporal, Aug. 24, 1861, at Camden, age 38. Mustered Sept. 1, 1861. Discharged for disability Dec. 3, 1862, at Nashville.

Palten, William *see* Patten, William.

Papin or Papine, Frank. Camden. Enlisted in Co. K as Corporal, Aug. 24, 1861, at Blissfield, age 21. Mustered Sept. 1, 1861. Wounded Jan. 2, 1863, at Stones River. Died of wounds Jan. 3, 1863. Buried in national cemetery in Murfreesboro, TN, grave 1728.

Parkhurst, David D. Branch County. Enlisted and mustered in Co. H, Dec. 1, 1861. Deserted July 14, 1862, at Louisville. No further record.

Parsons, Aaron J. Branch County. Enlisted and mustered in Co. B, Aug. 24, 1861, at Butler, age 28. Mustered out Sept. 30, 1864, at Sturgis.

Patten, Henry. Branch County. Enlisted and mustered in Co. C, Aug. 24, 1861, at Clarendon, age 21. Mustered out Sept. 30, 1864, at Sturgis.

Patten, William. Branch County. Enlisted and mustered in Co. C, Oct. 1, 1861. Wounded at Stones River. Discharged for disability Mar. 17, 1863, at Nashville.

Patterson, Charles V. Branch County. Enlisted and mustered in Co. B, Aug. 24, 1861, at Butler, age 21. Wounded Sept. 20, 1863, at Chickamauga. Wounded Aug. 12, 1864, near Atlanta. Died of wounds Aug. 24, 1864, at Kingston, GA. Buried in national cemetery in Marietta, GA, grave 689.

Patterson, David. Lenawee County. Enlisted in Co. K, Aug. 24, 1861, at Palmyra, age 18. Mustered Sept. 1, 1861. Wounded at Stones River. Wounded Sept. 1863. Mustered out Sept. 30, 1864, at Sturgis. Resided c. 1905 at Jackson.

Patterson, William F. St. Joseph County. Enlisted and mustered in Co. A, Aug. 24, 1861, at Centreville, age 18. Mustered out Sept. 30, 1864, at Sturgis. Resided c. 1905 at Mendon.

Pattison, Holmes A. Colon. Entered service as Chaplain, Aug. 24, 1861, at White Pigeon, age 34. Commissioned Aug. 24, 1861. Mustered out Sept. 30, 1864, at Sturgis.

Peck, Jeremiah C. Hudson. Enlisted and mustered in Co. F as Corporal, Sept. 11, 1861, at Hudson, age 28. Sergeant Mar. 1, 1862. Killed Dec. 31, 1862, at Stones River.

Peeler, Jacob. Branch County. Enlisted and mustered in Co. D, Aug. 24, 1861, at Bronson, age 43. Transferred to Invalid Corps Dec. 10, 1863. Discharged for disability Mar. 15, 1864, at Camp Dennison, OH, from Co. K, 21st Regiment VRC.

Pence, Samuel D. Monroe County. Enlisted in Co. K, Aug. 24, 1861, at Petersburg, age 18. Mustered Sept. 1, 1861. Transferred Dec. 3, 1862, to 4th U.S. Cavalry.

Perkins, Joseph W. Butler. Enlisted and mustered in Co. B, Aug. 24, 1861, at Butler, age 19. Died of pneumonia Feb. 8, 1862, at Bardstown, KY. Buried in national cemetery in Lebanon, KY.

Perret, Edward. Three Rivers. Enlisted and mustered in Co. A, Aug. 24, 1861, at Centreville, age 23. Died of fever Sept. 7, 1863, at Nashville. Buried in national cemetery in Nashville.

Pettit, Abraham. Hudson. Enlisted and mustered in Co. F, Sept. 11, 1861, at Hudson. Died of chronic diarrhea Oct. 1862 at Nashville. Buried in national cemetery in Nashville.

Phelps, Samuel B. Branch County. Enlisted in Co. H as Corporal, Aug. 24, 1861, at Coldwater, age 24. Mustered Aug. 28, 1861. Discharged for disability June 23, 1862.

Philips, Charles *see* Phillips, Charles.

Philips, Francis S. *see* Phillips, Francis S.

Phillips, Abe or Abel. Hillsdale County. Enlisted in Co. G as Fifer at Blissfield, age 34. Mustered Sept. 4, 1861. Discharged for disability Feb. 24, 1862.

Phillips, Charles. Enlisted and mustered, company unassigned, Dec. 26, 1863, at Allen, age 26. No further record.

Phillips, Francis S. Mendon. Enlisted, company unassigned, Dec. 16, 1863, at Mendon, age 23. Mustered Jan. 4, 1864. Admitted to Harper Hospital, Oct. 14, 1864. Discharged May 17, 1865, at Detroit. Resided c. 1905 at Cedar Springs.

Phillips, Halsey C. Branch County. Enlisted and mustered in Co. B, Aug. 24, 1861, at Quincy, age 20. Discharged for disability Nov. 21, 1861, at White Pigeon.

Phillips, Menzo. Branch County. Enlisted and mustered in Co. B, Aug. 24, 1861. Discharged Dec. 9, 1864, at Chattanooga.

Phillips, Ogden B. Branch County. Enlisted and mustered in Co. B as Corporal, Aug. 24, 1861, at Quincy, age 23. Mustered out Sept. 30, 1864, at Sturgis.

Phillips, William J. Cass County. Enlisted and mustered in Co. D, Aug. 24, 1861, at Bronson, age 18. Mustered out Sept. 30, 1864, at Sturgis.

Phillips, William W. Adrian. Entered service in Co. K as Captain, Aug. 24, 1861, at Adrian, age 35. Commissioned Aug. 24, 1861. Mustered Sept. 1, 1861. Resigned Feb. 19, 1862.

Pickering, Byron. St. Joseph County. Enlisted and mustered in Co. A, Aug. 24, 1861, at Centreville, age 20. Wounded Nov. 1863. Discharged Aug. 25, 1864, at Detroit.

Pierce, Cyrus E. St. Joseph County. Enlisted and mustered in Co. A, Aug. 24, 1861, at Centreville, age 18. Discharged for disability July 1862 at Nashville.

Pierce, Elvah F. St. Joseph County. Enlisted and mustered in Co. A, Aug. 24, 1861, at Centreville, age 43. Transferred to Invalid Corps July 1, 1863. Died May 10, 1887. Buried at Centreville.

Pierce, James. Allen. Enlisted in Co. B, Aug. 16, 1862, at Allen, age 18. Mustered Aug. 23, 1862. Died of typhoid fever Dec. 21, 1862, at Nashville.

Pierce, Joel. Flowerfield. Enlisted in Co. G at Flowerfield, age 23. Mustered Sept. 4, 1861. Died of smallpox Jan. 11, 1862, at Bardstown, KY.

Pierce, Laban. Flowerfield. Enlisted in Co. G as Corporal at Schoolcraft, age 25. Mustered Sept. 4, 1861. Died of smallpox Feb. 11, 1862, at Bardstown, KY. Buried in national cemetery in Lebanon, KY, grave 308.

Pierce, Lemuel Packard. St. Joseph County. Enlisted and mustered in Co. A as Corporal, Aug. 24, 1861, at Centreville, age 21. Discharged for disability May 2, 1864, at Ringgold, GA. Died Mar. 3, 1904, at Three Rivers.

Pigler, George. Monroe County. Enlisted and mustered in Co. I, Aug. 24, 1861, at Frenchtown, age 27. Died of disease Feb. 21, 1863, at Nashville.

Pippinger, Lewis. Enlisted and mustered in Co. H, Sept. 23, 1864, at Jackson for 1 year, age 19. Joined regiment Jan. 7, 1865, at Chattanooga. Transferred Apr. 15, 1865, to Co. H, reorganized 11th Michigan Infantry. Corporal May 5, 1865. Discharged June 16, 1865, at Chattanooga.

Pixley, Alvin F. Hillsdale. Enlisted and mustered in Co. F, Nov. 8, 1861. No further record.

Pixley, Thomas. Hillsdale County. Enlisted and mustered in Co. F, Sept. 11, 1861, at Wright, age 18. Killed May 31, 1864, near Dallas, GA. Buried in national cemetery in Marietta, GA, grave 7669.

Platt, Henry S. Jr. St. Joseph County. Enlisted and mustered in Co. C, Aug. 24, 1861, at Sturgis, age 27. Sergeant Major Oct. 16, 1861. Commissioned 2nd Lieutenant, Co. I, Mar. 12, 1862, mustered Apr. 12, 1862. Aide-de-Camp to Colonel Timothy R. Stanley, Oct 6, 1862. Commissioned 1st Lieutenant Dec. 10, 1862, mustered Mar. 21, 1863. Captured July 1, 1863, near Elk River. Exchanged. Commissioned Captain, Co. D, July 13, 1864, mustered July 14, 1864. Mustered out Sept. 30, 1864, at Sturgis.

Platt, Hiram G. St. Joseph County. Enlisted and mustered in Co. A as Corporal, Aug. 24, 1861, at Centreville, age 29. Sergeant Feb. 7, 1862. Mustered out Sept. 30, 1864, at Sturgis.

Platt, William H. St. Joseph County. Enlisted and mustered in Co. A as Drummer, Aug. 24, 1861, at Centreville, age 21. Wounded and captured Dec. 31, 1862, at Stones River. Mustered out Sept. 30, 1864, at Sturgis.

Plumb, Carlos. Burr Oak. Enlisted and mustered in Co. C, Aug. 24, 1861, at Burr Oak, age 19. Died of smallpox Feb. 5, 1862, at Bardstown, KY.

Plumb, Henry S. St. Joseph County. Enlisted and mustered in Co. F, Dec. 6, 1861. Transferred Dec. 5, 1862, at Nashville to 4th U.S. Cavalry. Discharged Dec. 2, 1865, at San Antonio, TX, from Troop G.

Pool, Hiram or Heman A. Enlisted in Co. K, Mar. 30, 1864, at Blissfield, age 21. Mustered Mar. 31, 1864. Joined regiment Apr. 8, 1864, at Graysville, GA. Transferred Apr. 15, 1865, to Co. K, reorganized 11th Michigan Infantry. Mustered out Sept. 16, 1865, at Nashville. Resided c. 1905 at Deerfield.

Poorman, John. Cass County. Enlisted and mustered in Co. E, Aug. 24, 1861, at Three Rivers, age 23. Corporal Mar. 1, 1864. Mustered out Sept. 30, 1864, at Sturgis. Died Aug. 20, 1891.

Porter, Leander M. Enlisted in Co. K, Dec. 19, 1863, at Leonidas, age 29. Mustered Jan. 4, 1864. Transferred Apr. 15, 1865, to Co. K, reorganized 11th Michigan Infantry. Mustered out Sept. 16, 1865, at Nashville.

Portors, William. Enlisted and mustered in Co. H, Aug. 24, 1861, at Coldwater, age 18. Mustered out Sept. 30, 1864, at Sturgis.

Post, John D. Branch County. Enlisted and mustered in Co. H, Oct. 10, 1861. Deserted Dec. 9, 1861, at White Pigeon.

Potts, Benjamin F. Noble County, IN. Enlisted and mustered in Co. C, Aug. 24, 1861, at Jefferson, age 22. Died of hemorrhage Feb. 13, 1862, at Bardstown, KY.

Pound, Jacob M. Camden. Enlisted in Co. K, Aug. 24, 1861, at Camden, age 31. Mustered Sept. 1, 1861. Served in Pionieer Brigade. Wounded and captured Dec. 31, 1862, at Stones River. Died of wounds Feb. 16, 1863, at Atlanta, GA.

Powell, Henry. Lenawee County. Enlisted and mustered in Co. F, Sept. 11, 1861, at Seneca, age 18. Discharged for disability Mar. 12, 1863, at Nashville.

Powers, Charles E. Burr Oak. Enlisted and mustered in Co. A, Aug. 29, 1862, at Burr Oak, age 24. Joined regiment Jan. 18, 1863, at Murfreesboro, TN. Wounded May 14, 1864, at Resaca. Transferred Apr. 15, 1865, to Co.

A, reorganized 11th Michigan Infantry. Discharged June 16, 1865, at Chattanooga. Died June 16, 1889.

Powers, Reuben. St. Joseph County. Enlisted and mustered in Co. D, Aug. 24, 1861, at Burr Oak, age 22. Mustered out Sept. 30, 1864, at Sturgis.

Poyns, Edward. Branch County. Enlisted and mustered in Co. B, Aug. 24, 1861, at Quincy, age 18. Musician Apr. 1863. Wounded July 22, 1864, near Atlanta. Mustered out Sept. 30, 1864, at Sturgis.

Poyns, Thomas C. Branch County. Enlisted and mustered in Co. B, Aug. 24, 1861, at Quincy. Discharged for disability Dec. 2, 1862, at Nashville.

Pratt, John W. Lenawee County. Enlisted in Co. K, Aug. 24, 1861, at Blissfield, age 24. Mustered Sept. 1, 1861. Discharged for disability Feb. 13, 1863, at Murfreesboro, TN.

Price, Charles O. Calhoun County. Enlisted and mustered in Co. B, Aug. 24, 1861, at Butler, age 19. Transferred Sept. 20, 1861, to Co. G, 16th Michigan Infantry. Deserted Aug. 28, 1862.

Probert, George W.L. Lenawee County. Enlisted in Co. G at White Pigeon, age 21. Mustered Sept. 4, 1861. Transferred Nov. 26, 1862, to 4th U.S. Cavalry.

Purchase, Charles B. Leonidas. Enlisted and mustered in Co. A, Aug. 24, 1861, at Centreville, age 18. Killed Sept. 4, 1862, at LaVergne, TN, in a wagon accident.

Purdy, Charles E. Branch County. Enlisted and mustered in Co. D, Aug. 24, 1861, at Bronson, age 29. Mustered out Sept. 30, 1864, at Sturgis.

Purdy, John W. Branch County. Enlisted and mustered in Co. D, Aug. 24, 1861, at Bronson. Paroled Mar. 1863. Wounded July 4, 1864, at Ruff's Station. Captured Aug. 7, 1864, at Utoy Creek. Mustered out Sept. 30, 1864, at Sturgis.

Quaco, Samuel M. St. Joseph County. Enlisted and mustered in Co. E, Aug. 24, 1861, at Three Rivers, age 18. Captured at Stones River. Paroled Apr. 1863. Mustered out Sept. 30, 1864, at Sturgis.

Quay, George W. Cass County. Enlisted and mustered in Co. E, Aug. 24, 1861, at Three Rivers. Wounded Dec. 31, 1862, at Stones River. Killed Aug. 7, 1864, at Utoy Creek.

Quillhot or Quilhot, James. Hillsdale County. Enlisted in Co. G at Pittsford, age 36. Mustered Sept. 4, 1861. Mustered out Sept. 30, 1864, at Sturgis.

Rapp, John. St. Joseph County. Enlisted and mustered in Co. C, Aug. 24, 1861, at Sturgis, age 27. Discharged for disability Nov. 8, 1861, at White Pigeon.

Rapp, Thomas. Sturgis. Enlisted and mustered in Co. C, Aug. 24, 1861, at Sturgis, age 19. Died of measles Jan. 29, 1862, at Bardstown, KY.

Rapps, Daniel. Dundee. Enlisted in Co. K, Aug. 24, 1861, at Dundee, age 18. Mustered Sept. 1, 1861. Wounded Dec. 31, 1862, at Stones River. Died of wounds Jan. 26, 1863, at Murfreesboro, TN. Buried in national cemetery in Murfreesboro, TN, grave 1861.

Rasler, Phillip N. La Grange, IN. Enlisted and mustered in Co. C, Aug. 24, 1861, at Sturgis, age 21. Mustered out Sept. 30, 1864, at Sturgis.

Rathbun or Rathburn, Daniel. St. Joseph County. Enlisted and mustered in Co. C, Aug. 24, 1861, at Sturgis, age 54. Mustered out Sept. 30, 1864, at Sturgis.

Raymond, George. Wayne County. Enlisted and mustered in Co. C, Aug. 24, 1861, at Detroit, age 23. Deserted Dec. 17, 1861, at Louisville.

Raymond, John M. Enlisted in Co. H as Drummer. Discharged Dec. 5, 1864, at Chattanooga.

Raymond, William E. St. Joseph County. Enlisted and mustered in Co. F, Dec. 6, 1861. Hospital Steward Dec. 25, 1863. Discharged Dec. 9, 1864, at Chattanooga.

Rayner, Charles B. Hillsdale County. Enlisted and mustered in Co. B as Corporal, Aug. 24, 1861, at Allen, age 25. Discharged June 4, 1862, at Columbia, TN.

Rayner, James S. Hillsdale County. Enlisted and mustered in Co. B, Aug. 24, 1861, at Allen, age 23. Mustered out Sept. 30, 1864, at Sturgis.

Raynolds, William P. Branch County. Enlisted and mustered in Co. H, Oct. 1, 1861. Captured Sept. 20, 1863, at Chickamauga. Discharged Apr. 15, 1865, at Detroit.

Reber, Daniel J. St. Joseph County. Enlisted and mustered in Co. C, Aug. 24, 1861, at Sturgis, age 27. Discharged for disability Feb. 13, 1862.

Reed, Charles A. Branch County. Enlisted and mustered in Co. B, Aug. 24, 1861, at Butler, age 20. Mustered out Sept. 30, 1864, at Sturgis.

Reed, Ezekiel. Cass County. Enlisted and mustered in Co. E, Aug. 24, 1861, age 23. Mustered out Sept. 30, 1864, at Sturgis.

Reed, John H. Monroe County. Enlisted in Co. K, Aug. 24, 1861, at Ida, age 26. Mustered Sept. 1, 1861. Deserted Nov. 11, 1861.

Reeves, Charles L. Monroe County. Enlisted and mustered in Co. I, Aug. 24, 1861, at London, age 23. Discharged for disability Feb. 26, 1863, at Nashville.

Regal, Ibrahim. Monroe County. Enlisted in Co. K, Aug. 24, 1861, at Ida, age 21. Mustered Sept. 1, 1861. Mustered out Sept. 30, 1864, at Sturgis.

Reglow, Martin. Lenawee County. Enlisted in Co. G at Blissfield, age 21. Mustered Sept. 4, 1861. Mustered out Sept. 30, 1864, at Sturgis.

Reilly, John. St. Joseph County. Enlisted and mustered in Co. B, Dec. 6, 1861. Discharged for disability Feb. 28, 1862, at Bardstown, KY.

Reisdorff, Benjamin. Monroe County. Entered service in Co. I as 2nd Lieutenant, Aug. 24, 1861, at Monroe, age 39. Commissioned Aug. 24, 1861. Commissioned 1st Lieutenant Mar. 12, 1862. Resigned Dec. 16, 1862, due to disability.

Renner, Robert. St. Joseph County. Enlisted and mustered in Co. A, Aug. 24, 1861, at Centreville, age 23. Wounded Nov. 1863. Mustered out Sept. 30, 1864, at Sturgis.

Renner, William T. St. Joseph County. Enlisted and mustered in Co. A, Aug. 24, 1861, at Centreville, age 23. Mustered out Sept. 30, 1864, at Sturgis. Resided c. 1905 at Colon.

Reynolds, Corwin. Monroe County. Enlisted in Co. K as Corporal, Aug. 24, 1861, at Petersburg, age 19. Mustered Sept. 1, 1861. Discharged for disability Apr. 6, 1862.

Reynolds, Lorenzo D. Branch County. Enlisted in Co. H, Aug. 24, 1861, at Coldwater, age 27. Mustered Aug. 28, 1861. Corporal Aug. 9, 1862. Discharged for disability Mar. 14, 1863, at Murfreesboro, TN. Resided c. 1905 at Algansee.

Reynolds, William P. *see* Raynolds, William P.

Rhoades, Bartholemew or Barthomer. Lenawee County. Enlisted in Co. K, Aug. 24, 1861, at Blissfield, age 19. Mustered Sept. 1, 1861. Captured Jan. 2, 1863, at Stones River. Mustered out Sept. 30, 1864, at Sturgis.

Rhoades, David. St. Joseph County. Enlisted and mustered in Co. K, Sept. 1, 1861. Sick at White Pigeon, Dec. 9, 1861. No further record.

Rhoades or Rhoads, John M. Hillsdale County. Enlisted and mustered in Co. F, Sept. 11, 1861, at Amboy, age 20. Corporal Aug. 27, 1862. Mustered out Sept. 30, 1864, at Sturgis.

Rhodes, Albert *see* Rhoades, David.

Rhodes, John M. *see* Rhoades, John M.

Rice, Ancel G. Lenawee County. Enlisted and mustered in Co. F, Sept. 11, 1861, at Dover, age 19. Mustered out Sept. 30, 1864, at Sturgis.

Rice, Charles. Three Rivers. Enlisted as Musician, Aug. 24, 1861, at White Pigeon, age 28. Mustered Sept. 24, 1861. Mustered out Aug. 22, 1862, at Nashville. Reentered service. Musician in 1st Brigade, 3rd Division, 14th A.C., Aug. 4, 1863. Wounded July 26, 1864, near Atlanta. Discharged for disability May 31, 1865, at Jeffersonville, IN, due to wounds.

Rice, Rufus. Lenawee County. Enlisted and mustered in Co. F, Sept. 11, 1861, at Seneca, age 21. Transferred Dec. 5, 1862, to 4th U.S. Cavalry.

Rich, Ansel. Branch County. Enlisted and mustered in Co. B as Corporal, Aug. 24, 1861, at Quincy, age 22. Captured Sept. 20, 1863, at Chickamauga. Died Sept. 6, 1864, at Andersonville, GA. Buried in national cemetery in Andersonville, GA.

Rich, Lyman. Monroe County. Enlisted and mustered in Co. I, Aug. 24, 1861, at Milan, age 25. Discharged for disability Feb. 14, 1862. Resided c. 1905 at Grand Ledge.

Richardson, Perry. Burr Oak. Enlisted in Co. D, Aug. 15, 1862, at Bronson, age 25. Mustered Sept. 1, 1862. Wounded Sept. 20, 1863, at Chickamauga. Died of wounds Oct. 11, 1863, at Chattanooga.

Robard or Robart, Franklin. Branch County. Enlisted in Co. H as Corporal, Aug. 24, 1861, at Coldwater, age 19. Mustered Aug. 28, 1861. Deserted Oct. 20, 1861, at White Pigeon.

Roberts, Anthony. Monroe County. Enlisted and mustered in Co. I, Aug. 24, 1861, at La Salle, age 23. Sergeant Apr. 25, 1863. Mustered out Sept. 30, 1864, at Sturgis.

Roberts, Frederick A. Enlisted in Co. A, Feb. 24, 1864, at Leonidas, age 21. Mustered Feb. 27, 1864. Joined regiment Mar. 15, 1864, at Rossville, GA. Transferred Apr. 15, 1865, to Co. K, reorganized 11th Michigan Infantry. Mustered out Sept. 16, 1865, at Nashville. Resided c. 1905 at Leonidas.

Roberts, Hillery. Monroe County. Enlisted and mustered in Co. I, Aug. 24, 1861, at Exeter, age 18. Mustered out Sept. 30, 1864, at Sturgis. Died Mar. 1, 1896.

Robinson, Clarkson. Branch County. Enlisted and mustered in Co. D, Aug. 24, 1861, at Bronson, age 43. Discharged Oct. 30, 1862, at Nashville.

Robinson, Stillman R. St. Joseph County. Enlisted and mustered in Co. D, Aug. 24, 1861, at Burr Oak, age 20. Died of smallpox Jan. 2, 1862, at Bardstown, KY.

Robinson, William. St. Joseph County. Enlisted and mustered in Co. D, Aug. 24, 1861, at White Pigeon, age 21. Sergeant June 1, 1862. Wounded at Stones River. Mustered out Sept. 30, 1864, at Sturgis.

Rockwell, David. St. Joseph County. Enlisted and mustered in Co. A, Aug. 24, 1861, at Centreville, age 48. Wounded at Stones River.

Wounded Feb. 1863. Transferred to Invalid Corps July 1, 1863.

Roemine, Homer F. St. Joseph County. Enlisted and mustered in Co. D as Corporal, Aug. 24, 1861, at Colon, age 19. Discharged for disability June 15, 1862, at Nashville.

Rogers, James H. Quincy. Enlisted and mustered in Co. B, Aug. 24, 1861, at Butler, age 28. Discharged for disability Sept. 24, 1862, at Detroit. Resided c. 1905 at Litchfield.

Rogers, William. Hillsdale County. Enlisted in Co. K, Aug. 24, 1861, at Camden, age 23. Mustered Sept. 1, 1861. Discharged for disability June 3, 1862.

Rogers, William J. Branch County. Enlisted and mustered in Co. B, Aug. 24, 1861, at Allen, age 21. Transferred to Invalid Corps Jan. 15, 1864.

Rolson, William *see* Robinson, William.

Rose, Daniel D.V. St. Joseph County. Enlisted and mustered in Co. A, Aug. 24, 1861, at Centreville, age 18. Wounded at Stones River. Mustered out Sept. 30, 1864, at Sturgis.

Ross, John. Enlisted and mustered in Co. I, Aug. 24, 1861, at Frenchtown, age 18. Mustered out Sept. 30, 1864, at Sturgis.

Ross, William G. Monroe County. Enlisted and mustered in Co. I as Sergeant, Aug. 24, 1861, at Exeter, age 24. 1st Sergeant Mar. 1, 1863. Commissioned 1st Lieutenant July 13, 1864, mustered July 14, 1864. Mustered out Sept. 30, 1864, at Sturgis.

Rossiter, Albert C. Morris, IL. Enlisted in Co. G as 1st Sergeant at Schoolcraft, age 25. Mustered Sept. 4, 1861. Commissioned 2nd Lieutenant July 22, 1863. Wounded Nov. 25, 1863, at Missionary Ridge. Commissioned Captain Jan. 24, 1864, mustered Feb. 17, 1864. Mustered out Sept. 30, 1864, at Sturgis.

Rouse, German M. St. Joseph County. Enlisted and mustered in Co. D, Aug. 24, 1861, at Colon, age 18. Captured Nov. 15, 1862. Mustered out Sept. 30, 1864, at Sturgis.

Roy, Joseph L. St. Joseph County. Enlisted and mustered in Co. E, Aug. 24, 1861, at Three Rivers. Wounded and captured Dec. 31, 1862, at Stones River. Exchanged. Wounded Nov. 25, 1863, at Missionary Ridge. Discharged Aug. 25, 1864, at Detroit. Resided c. 1905 at Marcellus.

Rumsey, John. St. Joseph County. Enlisted and mustered in Co. E, Aug. 24, 1861, at Three Rivers. Discharged for disability July 1, 1862.

Runyan, George N. Branch County. Enlisted and mustered in Co. B, Aug. 24, 1861, at Bronson, age 43. Mustered out Sept. 30, 1864, at Sturgis. Resided c. 1905 at Quincy.

Runyan, Seth C. Belleville. Enlisted and mustered in Co. I, Oct. 10, 1861, at Belleville, age 20. Died of pneumonia Feb. 7, 1862, at Bardstown, KY.

Rush, Alfonzo or Alphonzo. Branch County. Enlisted and mustered in Co. H, Aug. 24, 1861, at Coldwater, age 19. Mustered out Sept. 30, 1864, at Sturgis.

Russell, Henry V. St. Joseph County. Enlisted and mustered in Co. C, Aug. 24, 1861, at Sturgis, age 39. Discharged for disability Feb. 25, 1863, at Nashville.

Russell, John. Hillsdale County. Enlisted and mustered in Co. B, Aug. 24, 1861, at Jefferson, age 40. Discharged for disability Oct. 10, 1862, at Nashville.

Russey, Atticus S. St. Joseph County. Enlisted as Musician, Aug. 24, 1861, at White Pigeon, age 25. Mustered Sept. 24, 1861. Mustered out Aug. 22, 1862, at Nashville.

Russey, Charles W. St. Joseph County. Enlisted as Musician, Aug. 24, 1861, at White Pigeon, age 26. Mustered Sept. 24, 1861. Discharged for disability Feb. 15, 1862, at Bardstown, KY.

Russey, James H. St. Joseph County. Enlisted as Musician, Aug. 24, 1861, at White Pigeon, age 16. Mustered Sept. 24, 1861. Mustered out Aug. 22, 1862, at Nashville.

Ryan, James N.C. Cass County. Enlisted and mustered in Co. E, Aug. 24, 1861, age 43. Mustered out Sept. 30, 1864, at Sturgis.

Ryan or Ryon, John L. La Grange, IN. Enlisted and mustered in Co. C, Aug. 24, 1861, at Kendalville, IN, age 20. Wounded Sept. 20, 1863, at Chickamauga. Discharged for disability Apr. 26, 1864, at Detroit, due to wounds.

St. George, Michael. Lenawee County. Enlisted in Co. K, Aug. 24, 1861, at Macon, age 20. Mustered Sept. 1, 1861. Deserted Oct. 1, 1861.

Salmon, John. Centreville. Enlisted in Co. G, Feb. 3, 1864, at Centreville, age 29. Mustered Feb. 22, 1864. Joined regiment Apr. 8, 1864, at Graysville, GA. Transferred Apr. 15, 1865, to Co. G, reorganized 11th Michigan Infantry. Discharged July 16, 1865, at Chattanooga.

Salter, John. St. Joseph County. Enlisted and mustered in Co. E, Aug. 24, 1861, at Three Rivers, age 41. Mustered out Sept. 30, 1864, at Sturgis.

Sampson, Samuel W. Lenawee County. Enlisted and mustered in Co. F as Drummer, Sept. 11, 1861, at Morenci, age 30. Died of disease Nov. 10, 1864, at Chattanooga. Buried in national cemetery in Chattanooga.

Sanburn, Hiram. Sturgis. Enlisted and mustered in Co. C, Aug. 24, 1861, at Sturgis, age 30. Died of smallpox Mar. 12, 1862, at Bardstown, KY.

Sandford, Jesse *see* Sanford, Jesse.

Sanford, Henry. Enlisted in Co. H at Coldwater, age 18. Mustered Aug. 28, 1861. No further record.

Sanford, Jesse. Lenawee County. Enlisted and mustered in Co. E, Sept. 11, 1861, at Seneca, age 23. Wounded Dec. 1863 at Chattanooga. Mustered out Sept. 30, 1864, at Sturgis.

Savage, George. Cass County. Enlisted and mustered in Co. E, Aug. 24, 1861, at Three Rivers. Deserted Mar. 13, 1862.

Savage, George W. Lenawee County. Enlisted and mustered in Co. F, Nov. 26, 1861. Wounded Nov. 1863. Corporal Dec. 1863. No further record.

Savage, George W. St. Joseph County. Enlisted in Co. G, age 28. Mustered Sept. 4, 1861. Mustered out Sept. 30, 1864, at Sturgis.

Savage, John. St. Joseph County. Enlisted in Co. G at White Pigeon, age 26. Mustered Sept. 4, 1861. Corporal Dec. 15, 1862. Mustered out Sept. 30, 1864, at Sturgis.

Sayles, Charles W. St. Joseph County. Enlisted and mustered in Co. D, Aug. 24, 1861, at Bronson, age 18. Mustered out Sept. 30, 1864, at Sturgis.

Schochenbarger, William. St. Joseph County. Enlisted and mustered in Co. C, Aug. 24, 1861, at Bronson, age 23. Wounded Dec. 9, 1861, by accidental discharge of pistol. Wounded July 4, 1864, at Ruff's Station. Died of wounds July 4, 1864. Buried in national cemetery in Atlanta, GA.

Schock, Aaron A. Monroe County. Enlisted and mustered in Co. I, Aug. 24, 1861, at Frenchtown, age 28. Captured Sept. 20, 1863, at Chickamauga. Died of disease Mar. 2, 1864, at Danville, VA. Buried in national cemetery in Danville, GA.

Schock, Flavius J. Monroe County. Enlisted and mustered in Co. I, Aug. 24, 1861, at Frenchtown, age 32. Mustered out Sept. 30, 1864, at Sturgis.

Schock, William. Monroe County. Enlisted and mustered in Co. I, Aug. 24, 1861, at Frenchtown, age 26. Mustered out Sept. 30, 1864, at Sturgis.

Schofield, Alanson. Branch County. Enlisted in Co. H, Aug. 24, 1861, at Coldwater, age 18. Mustered Aug. 28, 1861. Deserted Oct. 23, 1861, at White Pigeon.

Schug, Emanuel. Cass County. Enlisted and mustered in Co. E, Aug. 24, 1861, age 20. Mustered out Sept. 30, 1864, at Sturgis. Resided c. 1905 at Marcellus.

Schug, William H. Cass County. Enlisted and mustered in Co. E, Aug. 24, 1861, at Three Rivers. Transferred to Invalid Corps Nov. 15, 1863.

Scofield, Alanson *see* Schofield, Alanson.

Scott, Abram or Abraham. Monroe County. Enlisted in Co. I. Mustered Oct. 10, 1861. Transferred Nov. 28, 1862, at Nashville to 4th U.S. Cavalry.

Scott, Lorenzo H. Cass County. Enlisted in Co. G at Three Rivers, age 18. Mustered Sept. 4, 1861. Wounded Sept. 1863 near Chattanooga. Mustered out Sept. 30, 1864, at Sturgis.

Scoville, Milo. Hillsdale County. Enlisted and mustered in Co. F, Sept. 11, 1861, at Amboy, age 45. Corporal May 1, 1862. Discharged for disability Aug. 27, 1862, at Nashville.

Scripture, John G. Branch County. Enlisted and mustered in Co. E, Aug. 24, 1861, at Butler, age 19. Mustered out Sept. 30, 1864, at Sturgis.

Seabury, Edwin. Branch County. Enlisted and mustered in Co. H, Sept. 20, 1861. Wounded Mar. 1864. Discharged for disability July 14, 1864, at Detroit.

Seekell, Charles Leslie. St. Joseph County. Enlisted and mustered in Co. E as Fifer, Aug. 24, 1861, at Three Rivers, age 14. Discharged Feb. 4, 1863.

Seekell, James Wesley. St. Joseph County. Enlisted and mustered in Co. E as Drummer, Aug. 24, 1861, at Three Rivers, age 14. Discharged Feb. 4, 1863, at Murfreesboro, TN.

Seekell, William H. Flowerfield. Enlisted and mustered in Co. E, Aug. 24, 1861, at Three Rivers, age 40. Died of typhoid fever Oct. 20, 1862, at Nashville. Buried in national cemetery in Nashville.

Seeley, Edward M. Enlisted and mustered in Co. C, Sept. 20, 1864, at Jackson for 1 year, age 30. Sergeant Mar. 16, 1865. Transferred Apr. 15, 1865, to Co. C, reorganized 11th Michigan Infantry. Discharged June 16, 1865, at Chattanooga.

Seeley, James M. Camden. Enlisted in Co. K, Aug. 24, 1861, at Camden, age 25. Mustered Sept. 1, 1861. Died of chronic diarrhea Mar. 1865 at Nashville. Buried in national cemetery in Nashville.

Seeley, Joseph. Hillsdale County. Enlisted in Co. G at Hillsdale, age 44. Mustered Sept. 4, 1861. Discharged for disability Oct. 15, 1862, at Nashville.

Seeley, Peter. Hillsdale County. Enlisted in Co. K, Aug. 24, 1861, at Camden, age 22. Mustered Sept. 1, 1861. Captured Dec. 31, 1862, at Stones River. Mustered out Sept. 30, 1864, at Sturgis.

Sewick, Dennis *see* Usewick, Dennis.

Seymour, Henry. Enlisted and mustered in Co. I, Jan. 18, 1863, at Detroit, age 23. Joined regiment Feb. 10, 1863, at Murfreesboro, TN. Wounded Aug. 7, 1864, at Utoy Creek. Transferred Apr. 15, 1865, to Co. H, reorganized 11th Michigan Infantry. No further record.

Shaffer or Shafer, Albert C. Enlisted in Co. A, Dec. 23, 1863, at Leonidas, age 31. Mustered Jan. 4, 1864. Joined regiment Jan. 28, 1864, at Rossville, GA. Transferred Mar. 30, 1864, to Co. F. Wounded July 4, 1864, at Ruff's Station. Transferred Apr. 15, 1865, to Co. K, reorganized 11th Michigan Infantry. Discharged Aug. 10, 1865, at Cleveland, TN.

Shaffer, Charles. St. Joseph County. Enlisted in Co. G at White Pigeon, age 45. Mustered Sept. 4, 1861. Discharged for disability Nov. 20, 1863, at Chattanooga.

Shanger, Joseph *see* Shranger, Joseph.

Shay, George. Wayne County. Enlisted and mustered in Co. I, Aug. 24, 1861, at Detroit, age 26. Mustered out Sept. 30, 1864, at Sturgis. Resided c. 1905 at Detroit.

Shear, Melvin. Branch County. Enlisted and mustered in Co. B, Aug. 24, 1861, at Quincy, age 20. Mustered out Sept. 30, 1864, at Sturgis.

Sheffield, George S. St. Joseph County. Enlisted and mustered in Co. A, Aug. 24, 1861, at Centreville, age 29. Mustered out Sept. 30, 1864, at Sturgis.

Sheldon, Irwin A. Batavia. Enlisted in Co. H, Aug. 24, 1861, at Coldwater, age 19. Mustered Aug. 28, 1861. Died of lung fever Jan. 18, 1863, at Murfreesboro, TN. Buried in national cemetery in Murfreesboro, TN.

Sheldon, Thaddeus. Hillsdale County. Enlisted in Co. G as Corporal at Schoolcraft, age 24. Mustered Sept. 4, 1861. Deserted Dec. 6, 1861, at White Pigeon.

Shenavarre or Shenevarre, Jule. Monroe County. Enlisted and mustered in Co. I, Aug. 24, 1861, at Frenchtown, age 19. Mustered out Sept. 30, 1864, at Sturgis.

Shepard or Sheperd, William R. Calhoun County. Enlisted and mustered in Co. B, Aug. 24, 1861, at Clarendon, age 18. Corporal July 17, 1864. Mustered out Sept. 30, 1864, at Sturgis. Resided c. 1905 at Litchfield.

Sherman, Cyrus. Hillsdale County. Enlisted and mustered in Co. C, Dec. 9, 1861. Sergeant Dec. 1862. Captured Dec. 31, 1862, at Stones River. Paroled Mar. 1863. Discharged Dec. 9, 1864, at Chattanooga. Resided c. 1905 at Ovid.

Sherman, Edward C. Allen. Enlisted and mustered in Co. B, Aug. 24, 1861, at Allen, age 34. Died of pneumonia Mar. 8, 1862, at Bardstown, KY. Buried in national cemetery in Lebanon, KY.

Sherman, Watts. Enlisted and mustered in Co. C as Fifer, Aug. 24, 1861, at Allen, age 24. Reenlisted Feb. 27, 1864, at Rossville, GA. Mustered Mar. 31, 1864. Transferred Apr. 15, 1865, to Co. C, reorganized 11th Michigan Infantry. Fife Major Apr. 20, 1865. Mustered out Sept. 16, 1865, at Nashville.

Sherman, William M. St. Joseph County. Enlisted and mustered in Co. E, Aug. 24, 1861, at Three Rivers, age 20. Wounded Dec. 31, 1862, at Stones River. Died of wounds Mar. 1863 at Nashville. Buried in national cemetery in Nashville.

Shipman, John. St. Joseph County. Enlisted in Co. G at White Pigeon, age 29. Mustered Sept. 4, 1861. Transferred to Invalid Corps Oct. 10, 1863.

Shippy, Daniel A. Branch County. Enlisted and mustered in Co. D, Aug. 24, 1861, at Bronson, age 21. Mustered out Sept. 30, 1864, at Sturgis. Resided c. 1905 at Newaygo.

Shippy, Stephen. Branch County. Enlisted and mustered in Co. D, Aug. 24, 1861, at Bronson, age 19. Died of measles Feb. 8, 1862, at Bardstown, KY.

Shirey, Solomon. St. Joseph County. Enlisted and mustered in Co. E, Aug. 24, 1861, at Three Rivers, age 27. Captured Oct. 2, 1863, near Chattanooga. Returned to regiment Nov. 10, 1863. Mustered out Sept. 30, 1864, at Sturgis.

Shoemaker, Adam J. Enlisted in Co. E, Feb. 27, 1864, at Three Rivers, age 18. Mustered Feb. 29, 1864. Joined regiment Apr. 10, 1864, at Graysville, GA. Transferred Apr. 15, 1865, to Co. E, reorganized 11th Michigan Infantry. Mustered out Sept. 16, 1865, at Nashville.

Shoemaker, Samuel S. Vandalia. Enlisted and mustered in Co. E, Aug. 24, 1861, at Three Rivers. Discharged for disability July 19, 1862, at Detroit.

Shranger, Joseph. Parkville. Enlisted and mustered in Co. E, Aug. 24, 1861, at Three Rivers, age 21. Served in Pioneer Corps. Died Aug. 29, 1863, near Stevenson, AL.

Sidley, David. Branch County. Enlisted and mustered in Co. B, Aug. 24, 1861, at Butler, age 29. Discharged for disability July 1, 1862.

Silliman, John B. St. Joseph County. Enlisted as Musician, Aug. 24, 1861, at White Pigeon, age 23. Mustered Sept. 24, 1861. Discharged for disability Mar. 1, 1862, at Bardstown, KY.

Silverwood, Andrew J. Allen. Enlisted and mustered in Co. B, Aug. 24, 1861, at Reading, age 19. Wounded at Stones River. Died of wounds Jan. 2, 1863, at Murfreesboro, TN.

Simeon, Rollin H. Enlisted, company unassigned, Dec. 30, 1863, at Sherwood, age 17. Mustered Jan. 11, 1864. No further record.

Simmons, Orrin. Hillsdale County. Enlisted and mustered in Co. B, Aug. 24, 1861, at Allen, age 21. Deserted Aug. 25, 1861, at White Pigeon.

Sisk, Jonas. St. Joseph County. Enlisted in Co. G, Apr. 5, 1862. Transferred Nov. 26, 1862, at Nashville to 4th U.S. Cavalry.

Skinner, Harrison H. Cass County. Enlisted in Co. G as Corporal, age 34. Mustered Sept. 4, 1861. Discharged for disability Feb. 15, 1862. Reentered service. Corporal Sept. 7, 1863, mustered Sept. 23, 1863. Sergeant Nov. 1864. Discharged for disability Dec. 6, 1864, at Ft. Carroll, D.C.

Slayton, George. Branch County. Enlisted and mustered in Co. B, Aug. 24, 1861, at Butler, age 26. Transferred Nov. 25, 1862, at Nashville to 4th U.S. Cavalry.

Slayton, Morris. Allen. Enlisted and mustered in Co. B, Aug. 24, 1861, at Allen, age 32. Died of fever Apr. 19, 1862, at Bardstown, KY. Buried in national cemetery in Lebanon, KY, grave 358.

Sloan, David. Amboy. Enlisted and mustered in Co. F, Sept. 11, 1861, at Amboy, age 20. Wounded Nov. 25, 1863, at Missionary Ridge. Died of wounds Dec. 22, 1863, at Chattanooga. Buried in national cemetery in Chattanooga.

Sloan, Elias. Amboy. Enlisted and mustered in Co. F, Sept. 11, 1861, at Amboy, age 30. Died of pneumonia Feb. 16, 1862, at Bardstown, KY.

Slote, James. Enlisted in Co. E, Feb. 22, 1864, at Kalamazoo, age 21. Mustered Feb. 23, 1864. Joined regiment Apr. 10, 1864, at Graysville, GA. Corporal Mar. 16, 1865. Transferred Apr. 15, 1865, to Co. E, reorganized 11th Michigan Infantry. Mustered out Sept. 16, 1865, at Nashville.

Smetts, Bennett. Hillsdale County. Enlisted and mustered in Co. C, Mar. 27, 1862, at Sparta, age 20. Served in Pioneer Brigade. Killed Dec. 31, 1862, at Stones River.

Smith, Albion. St. Joseph County. Enlisted and mustered in Co. C, Aug. 24, 1861, at Constantine, age 30. Mustered out Sept. 30, 1864, at Sturgis.

Smith, Charles. Enlisted in Co. A, Feb. 20, 1864, at Leonidas, age 18. Mustered Feb. 27, 1864. Joined regiment Mar. 15, 1864, at Rossville, GA. Transferred Apr. 15, 1865, to Co. K, reorganized 11th Michigan Infantry. Mustered out Sept. 16, 1865, at Nashville.

Smith, Cyrus. Cass County. Enlisted and mustered in Co. E, Aug. 24, 1861, at Three Rivers, age 18. Mustered out Sept. 30, 1864, at Sturgis.

Smith, David R. Branch County. Enlisted and mustered in Co. D as Corporal, Aug. 24, 1861, at Bronson, age 23. Mustered out Sept. 30, 1864, at Sturgis.

Smith, Edward W. Enlisted in Co. G, Feb. 13, 1864, at Nottawa, age 20. Mustered Feb. 22, 1864. Joined regiment Mar. 15, 1864, at Rossville, GA. Transferred Apr. 15, 1865, to Co. G, reorganized 11th Michigan Infantry. Corporal May 1, 1865. Mustered out Sept. 16, 1865, at Nashville.

Smith, Emanuel. St. Joseph County. Enlisted and mustered in Co. D, Aug. 24, 1861, at Colon, age 21. Mustered out Sept. 30, 1864, at Sturgis. Resided c. 1905 at Colon.

Smith, George L. Branch County. Enlisted and mustered in Co. D, Aug. 24, 1861, at Bronson, age 21. Discharged for disability Feb. 20, 1862, at Bardstown, KY.

Smith, George W. London. Enlisted and mustered in Co. I, Oct. 10, 1861, at Monroe, age 29. Corporal Nov. 1862. Killed Nov. 13, 1862, at Nashville, by accidental gunshot.

Smith, Henry B. Three Rivers. Enlisted and mustered in Co. E, Aug. 24, 1861, at Three Rivers, age 32. Died of disease Jan. 19, 1863, at Murfreesboro, TN.

Smith, Homer C. Branch County. Enlisted and mustered in Co. D, Aug. 24, 1861, at Bronson, age 18. Bugler May 1864. Mustered out Sept. 30, 1864, at Sturgis.

Smith, John C. St. Joseph County. Enlisted and mustered in Co. E, Aug. 24, 1861, at Three Rivers. Discharged for disability Sept. 26, 1862, at Nashville.

Smith, Joseph W. Enlisted in Co. A, Dec. 5, 1863, at Waukeshma, age 29. Mustered Jan. 4, 1864. Joined regiment Jan. 28, 1864, at Rossville, GA. Transferred Mar. 30, 1864, to Co. F. Killed Aug. 7, 1864, at Utoy Creek. Buried in national cemetery in Marietta, GA, section E, grave 6170.

Smith, Oliver. Petersburg. Enlisted in Co. K, Aug. 24, 1861, at Petersburg, age 19. Mustered Sept. 1, 1861. Died of measles Jan. 30, 1862, at Bardstown, KY.

Smith, Sylvester B. Morenci. Entered service in Co. F as Captain, Aug. 24, 1861, age 28. Commissioned Aug. 24, 1861. Mustered Sept. 11, 1861. Commissioned Major Aug. 18, 1862. Wounded Dec. 31, 1862, at Stones River. Commissioned Lt. Colonel Jan. 7, 1863, mustered Jan. 8, 1863. Resigned Mar. 19, 1863, due to disability.

Smith, Thomas. St. Joseph County. Enlisted and mustered in Co. D, Aug. 24, 1861, at Bronson, age 26. Discharged for disability Nov. 20, 1862, at Nashville.

Smith, Thomas. St. Joseph County. Enlisted in Co. G at Colon, age 27. Mustered Sept. 4, 1861. Sergeant Feb. 1, 1862. Mustered out Sept. 30, 1864, at Sturgis.

Smith, William H. Allegan County. Enlisted in Co. G at Allegan, age 21. Mustered Sept. 4, 1861. Died of typhoid pneumonia Feb. 5, 1862, at Bardstown, KY.

Smyth or Smythe, Charles. Lenawee County. Enlisted in Co. G at Camden, age 19. Mustered Sept. 4, 1861. Deserted July 14, 1862, at Louisville.

Snook, William. Enlisted in Co. E, Dec. 30, 1863, at Colon, age 21. Mustered Jan. 4, 1864. Joined regiment Jan. 28, 1864, at Rossville, GA. Transferred Mar. 30, 1864, to Co. F. Transferred Apr. 15, 1865, to Co. K, reorganized 11th Michigan Infantry. Mustered out Sept. 16, 1865, at Nashville.

Snyder, Washington Irving. Three Rivers. Enlisted and mustered in Co. E as Corporal, Aug. 24, 1861, at Three Rivers, age 18. Sergeant Jan. 1, 1863. Sergeant Major Apr. 7, 1863. Wounded Sept. 20, 1863, at Chickamauga. Died of wounds Oct. 5, 1863, at Chattanooga. Buried in national cemetery in Chattanooga.

Somer or Somers or Somes, Roscoe or Rosco. Branch County. Enlisted and mustered in Co. B, Aug. 24, 1861, at Quincy, age 27.

Southerley or Southerly, Sylvester. St. Joseph County. Enlisted and mustered in Co. E, Aug. 24, 1861, at Three Rivers, age 28. Corporal Jan. 1, 1862. Mustered out Sept. 30, 1864, at Sturgis.

Spafford, William. Amboy. Enlisted in Co. F, Sept. 11, 1861, at Hudson, age 20. Mustered Oct. 27, 1861. Wounded Dec. 31, 1862, at Stones River. Died of wounds Jan. 15, 1863, at Nashville. Buried in national cemetery in Nashville.

Spalding, Charles H. Monroe County. Enlisted and mustered in Co. I, Aug. 24, 1861, at Monroe, age 18. Discharged for disability Dec. 9, 1862, at Nashville. Died Dec. 25, 1862. Buried at Lambertville.

Spalding, Samuel. Monroe County. Enlisted and mustered in Co. C as Drummer, Aug. 24, 1861, at Dundee, age 20. Discharged for disability Jan. 1863 at Nashville.

Spaulding, Charles H. *see* Spalding, Charles H.

Spaulding, Samuel *see* Spalding, Samuel.

Spawn, James. Wayne County. Enlisted and mustered in Co. I, Aug. 24, 1861, at Belleville, age 18. Transferred Nov. 28, 1862, at Nashville to 4th U.S. Cavalry. Discharged Nov. 25, 1865, from Co. G, 4th U.S. Cavalry.

Spear, Melvin. Enlisted and mustered in Co. F, Sept. 11, 1861, at Gorham, OH, age 19. Mustered out Sept. 30, 1864, at Sturgis.

Spence, William. Hillsdale County. Enlisted and mustered in Co. B, Aug. 24, 1861, at Allen, age 25. Corporal. Mustered out Sept. 30, 1864, at Sturgis. Buried at Indianapolis, IN.

Spencer, Anson. St. Joseph County. Enlisted and mustered in Co. A, Aug. 24, 1861, at Centreville, age 18. Wounded Dec. 31, 1862, at Stones River. Discharged for disability June 24, 1863, at Louisville.

Spencer, Ezra. Three Rivers. Enlisted and mustered in Co. E as Corporal, Aug. 24, 1861, at Three Rivers, age 26. Sergeant. Killed Dec. 31, 1862, at Stones River.

Spencer, George W. St. Joseph County. Enlisted and mustered in Co. E, Aug. 24, 1861, at Three Rivers, age 18. Mustered out Sept. 30, 1864, at Sturgis.

Spencer, Henry N. Three Rivers. Entered service in Co. E as Captain, Aug. 24, 1861, at Three Rivers, age 43. Commissioned Aug. 24, 1861. Resigned Nov. 15, 1862, due to disability.

Spencer, John. Frenchtown. Enlisted and mustered in Co. I, Aug. 24, 1861, at Frenchtown, age 40. Wounded Oct. 1863. Died of disease Dec. 4, 1863, at Chattanooga. Buried in national cemetery in Chattanooga.

Spencer, William *see* Spence, William.

Spitler, John H. St. Joseph County. Enlisted and mustered in Co. D, Aug. 24, 1861, at Burr Oak, age 22. Discharged Aug. 25, 1864, at Detroit.

Sprague, Darius or James. Allegan County. Enlisted in Co. G as Corporal at Schoolcraft, age 39. Mustered Sept. 4, 1861. Wounded Nov. 25, 1863, at Missionary Ridge. No further record.

Sprague, Napolean B. Wayne County. Enlisted and mustered in Co. I, Aug. 26, 1861. Missing Dec. 31, 1862, at Stones River. Captured Sept. 20, 1863, at Chickamauga. Died July 31, 1864, at Andersonville, GA.

Spring, James H. Lenawee County. Enlisted and mustered in Co. F, Sept. 11, 1861, at Medina, age 18. Sergeant Apr. 9, 1864. Mustered out Sept. 30, 1864, at Sturgis. Resided c. 1905 at DeWitt.

Spristers, Henry B. St. Joseph County. Enlisted and mustered in Co. C, Aug. 24, 1861, at Sturgis, age 21. Reenlisted Jan. 30, 1864, at Chattanooga. Mustered Mar. 31, 1864. Transferred July 20, 1864, to 1st U.S. Engineers. Mustered out Sept. 26, 1865, at Detroit from Co. E, 1st U.S. Engineers.

Squire, Linus Truman. Quincy. Enlisted in Co. H as Sergeant, Aug. 24, 1861, at Coldwater.

Mustered Aug. 28, 1861. Commissioned 2nd Lieutenant June 24, 1862. Commissioned 1st Lieutenant Jan. 1, 1863. Acting adjutant Feb. to July 1863. Commissioned and mustered as Adjutant Aug. 3, 1863. Mustered out Sept. 30, 1864, at Sturgis.

Staunton, Francis E. Flowerfield. Enlisted in Co. G at White Pigeon, age 26. Mustered Sept. 4, 1861. Died of typhoid pneumonia Mar. 6, 1862, at Bardstown, KY. Buried in national cemetery in Lebanon, KY, grave 356.

Staunton, Lyman. St. Joseph County. Enlisted in Co. G at White Pigeon, age 27. Mustered Sept. 4, 1861. Discharged for disability Feb. 27, 1863, at Nashville.

Sterne, Franklin E. Batavia. Enlisted in Co. H, Aug. 24, 1861, at Coldwater, age 19. Mustered Sept. 1, 1861. Died of pneumonia Mar. 10, 1862, at Bardstown, KY. Buried in national cemetery in Lebanon, KY, grave 305.

Stevenson, Anthony. Batavia. Enlisted and mustered in Co. H, Aug. 24, 1861, at Coldwater, age 20. Died of pneumonia Feb. 10, 1862, at Bardstown, KY.

Stewart, Alonzo B. Monroe County. Enlisted and mustered in Co. I, Aug. 24, 1861, at London, age 18. Discharged for disability Dec. 9, 1862, at Nashville.

Stewart, Duncan. Centreville. Enlisted and mustered in Co. E, Aug. 24, 1861, at Three Rivers, age 21. Died of typhoid fever June 30, 1862, at Columbia, TN.

Stitt, Charles D. Washtenaw County. Enlisted and mustered in Co. I, Aug. 24, 1861, at Augusta, age 27. Discharged for disability July 5, 1862, at Detroit.

Stone, Richard E. Allen. Enlisted and mustered in Co. B, Aug. 24, 1861, at Allen, age 21. Died of pneumonia Apr. 10, 1862, at Bardstown, KY. Buried in national cemetery in Lebanon, KY.

Stoner, Nathaniel. Enlisted and mustered in Co. K, Sept. 17, 1864, at Riga for 1 year, age 21. Joined regiment Jan. 7, 1865, at Chattanooga. Transferred Apr. 15, 1865, to Co. K, reorganized 11th Michigan Infantry. Corporal May 1, 1865. Discharged June 16, 1865, at Chattanooga.

Storer, Lewis H. Hillsdale County. Enlisted in Co. K, Aug. 24, 1861, at Camden, age 24. Mustered Sept. 1, 1861. Discharged for disability July 11, 1862, at Nashville.

Stoughton, William Lewis. Sturgis. Entered service as Lt. Colonel, Aug. 24, 1861, at White Pigeon, age 34. Commissioned Oct. 11, 1861. Mustered to date Sept. 24, 1861. Commissioned and mustered as Colonel Apr. 1, 1862. Commanded brigade at Chickamauga, Sept. 20, 1863. Commanded brigade at Missionary Ridge, Nov. 25, 1863. President of Board of Examination for USCT officers, Nashville, March–April 1864. Wounded July 4, 1864, at Ruff's Station, causing amputation of right leg. Brevetted major general March 13, 1865, for meritorious services during the war. Died June 6, 1888. Buried in Oak Lawn Cemetery, Sturgis.

Stowell, Abram E. Branch County. Enlisted in Co. H as Corporal, Aug. 24, 1861, at Coldwater, age 18. Mustered Aug. 28, 1861. Transferred Oct. 20, 1861, to Battery F, 1st Michigan Light Artillery. Discharged for disability Oct. 14, 1862.

Stowell, Hazard L. Mendon. Enlisted in Co. K, Oct. 17, 1862, at Mendon, age 29. Mustered Dec. 2, 1862. Transferred to Co. K, reorganized 11th Michigan Infantry. Discharged for disability Mar. 8, 1865, at Nashville.

Straight, Luther W. Mendon. Enlisted and mustered in Co. A, Aug. 24, 1861, at Centreville, age 26. Died of disease Oct. 27, 1862, at Louisville. Buried in national cemetery in Louisville, section A 10, grave 29.

Straw, George F. St. Joseph County. Enlisted in Co. G as Corporal at Schoolcraft, age 21. Mustered Sept. 4, 1861. Deserted Aug. 27, 1862, at Louisville.

Straw, Thomas E. Flowerfield. Enlisted in Co. G at Flowerfield, age 24. Mustered Sept. 4, 1861. Died of typhoid pneumonia Feb. 20, 1862, at Bardstown, KY.

Stroud, David W. Hillsdale County. Enlisted and mustered in Co. F, Sept. 11, 1861, at Wright, age 18. Discharged for disability Mar. 17, 1862.

Stuart, Alonzo B. *see* Stewart, Alonzo B.

Stults, James M. St. Joseph County. Enlisted and mustered in Co. D, Aug. 24, 1861, at White Pigeon, age 21. Deserted Dec. 31, 1862, at Stones River.

Sturges, Aaron B. Sturgis. Enlisted and mustered in Co. A as 1st Sergeant, Aug. 24, 1861, at Centreville, age 23. Detached to Pioneer Brigade, Nov. 22, 1862. Commissioned 2nd Lieutenant Feb. 7, 1863. Resigned Feb. 13, 1863, due to disability. Died Mar. 1, 1863.

Surdam, Elmer or Elmar. St. Joseph County. Enlisted and mustered in Co. A, Aug. 24, 1861, at Centreville, age 22. Mustered out Sept. 30, 1864, at Sturgis.

Surdam or Surdem, Harrison. Lockport. Enlisted and mustered in Co. A, Aug. 25, 1862, at Leonidas, age 21. Joined regiment Jan. 18, 1863, at Murfreesboro, TN. Transferred Apr. 15, 1865, to Co. B, reorganized 11th Michigan Infantry. Discharged June 16, 1865, at Chattanooga.

Sutter, Alonzo B. *see* Latta, Alonzo B.

Sutton, Harvey. Lenawee County. Enlisted and mustered in Co. F, Sept. 11, 1861, at Morenci, age 18. Transferred to Invalid Corps Jan. 15, 1864. Discharged Sept. 12, 1864.

Sutton, William. Medina. Enlisted and mustered in Co. F, Nov. 26, 1861, at White Pigeon. Died of measles Jan. 21, 1862, at Bardstown, KY.

Swart, George. Branch County. Enlisted and mustered in Co. B, Aug. 24, 1861, at Butler, age 18. Mustered out Sept. 30, 1864, at Sturgis.

Swart, Martin. Branch County. Enlisted and mustered in Co. B as Corporal, Aug. 24, 1861, at Butler, age 30. Color Bearer Mar. 1863. Died of disease Feb. 5, 1864, at Litchfield.

Swart, Oliver. Branch County. Enlisted and mustered in Co. B, Aug. 24, 1861. Captured Jan. 2, 1863, at Stones River. Paroled Apr. 1863. Wounded Sept. 20, 1863, at Chickamauga. Discharged Nov. 16, 1864, at Chattanooga.

Swart, Peter L. Branch County. Enlisted and mustered in Co. B, Aug. 24, 1861, at Butler, age 24. Transferred Nov. 25, 1862, to 4th U.S. Cavalry.

Sweezy or Sweezey, James. Branch County. Enlisted and mustered in Co. B, Aug. 24, 1861, at Quincy, age 28. Mustered out Sept. 30, 1864, at Sturgis.

Sylvester, Charles. Hillsdale County. Enlisted and mustered in Co. B, Aug. 24, 1861, at Allen, age 28. Discharged for disability Oct. 11, 1862, at Nashville. Died Sept. 28, 1890. Buried at Litchfield.

Taft, Thomas. Monroe County. Enlisted and mustered in Co. I, Aug. 24, 1861, at London, age 34. Discharged for disability Feb. 14, 1862.

Taggart, Horatio G. St. Joseph County. Enlisted as Musician, Aug. 24, 1861, at White Pigeon, age 25. Mustered Sept. 24, 1861. Mustered out Aug. 22, 1862, at Nashville.

Tanner, Martin. St. Joseph County. Enlisted in Co. G at Three Rivers, age 21. Mustered Sept. 4, 1861. Wounded Dec. 31, 1862, at Stones River. Discharged for disability May 7, 1863, at Louisville, due to wounds.

Taylor, George. Marcellus. Enlisted and mustered in Co. E, Aug. 24, 1861, at Three Rivers, age 20. Died of inflammation of bowels Feb. 5, 1862, at Bardstown, KY. Buried in national cemetery in Lebanon, KY.

Taylor, George W. Branch County. Enlisted and mustered in Co. B, Aug. 24, 1861, at Butler, age 21. Transferred to Invalid Corps Feb. 15, 1864. Discharged Sept. 3, 1864, at Indianapolis, IN, from Co. H, 5th Regiment, VRC. Died Jan. 1903. Buried at Fayette, ID.

Taylor, James. Enlisted in Co. G, Aug. 19, 1863, at Stevenson, AL, age 28. Mustered Aug. 20, 1863. Transferred Apr. 15, 1865, to Co. H, reorganized 11th Michigan Infantry. Ordered dropped from company roll, May 15, 1865.

Taylor, Jared M. Burr Oak. Enlisted in Co. A, Aug. 29, 1862, at Burr Oak, age 25. Mustered Sept. 20, 1862. Joined regiment Jan. 18, 1863, at Murfreesboro, TN. Captured Sept. 20, 1863, at Chickamauga. Died Oct. 18, 1864, at Andersonville, GA. Buried in national cemetery in Andersonville, GA.

Taylor, John O. Hillsdale County. Enlisted and mustered in Co. F, Sept. 11, 1861, at Wright, age 23. Mustered out Sept. 30, 1864, at Sturgis. Died Dec. 26, 1891. Buried at Union City.

Taylor, John S. Enlisted in Co. A, Dec. 30, 1863, at Colon, age 29. Mustered Jan. 4, 1864. Joined regiment Jan. 28, 1864, at Rossville, GA. Transferred Mar. 30, 1864, to Co. F. Corporal Mar. 16, 1865. Transferred Apr. 15, 1865, to Co. K, reorganized 11th Michigan Infantry. Discharged Sept. 28, 1865, at Detroit.

Taylor, Royal M. St. Joseph County. Enlisted and mustered in Co. A, Aug. 24, 1861, at Centreville, age 27. Mustered out Sept. 30, 1864, at Sturgis.

Taylor, William H. St. Joseph County. Enlisted and mustered in Co. D, Aug. 24, 1861, at White Pigeon, age 19. Died of measles Jan. 29, 1862, at Bardstown, KY. Buried in national cemetery in Lebanon, KY, grave 370.

Teach, Charles *see* Leach, Charles.

Teal, Charles. Monroe County. Enlisted in Co. K, Aug. 24, 1861, at Petersburg, age 20. Mustered Sept. 1, 1861. Corporal Jan. 30, 1862. Mustered out Sept. 30, 1864, at Sturgis.

Teal, George. Monroe County. Enlisted in Co. K, Aug. 24, 1861, at Petersburg, age 25. Mustered Sept. 1, 1861. Deserted Nov. 10, 1861.

Teal, Stephen V. Monroe County. Enlisted in Co. K, Aug. 24, 1861, at Petersburg, age 29. Mustered Sept. 1, 1861. Sergeant June 1, 1863. Mustered out Sept. 30, 1864, at Sturgis.

Tenant or Tennant, Danford. Lenawee County. Enlisted in Co. K, Aug. 24, 1861, at Deerfield, age 21. Mustered Sept. 1, 1861. Corporal May 1, 1864. Mustered out Sept. 30, 1864, at Sturgis. Resided c. 1905 at Deerfield.

Terry, Walker or Walter S. Enlisted in Co. A, Dec. 22, 1863, at Leonidas, age 27. Mustered Jan. 4, 1864. Joined regiment Jan. 28, 1864, at Rossville, GA. Transferred Mar. 30, 1864, to Co. F. Transferred Apr. 15, 1865, to Co. K, reorganized 11th Michigan Infantry. Corporal May 8, 1865. Mustered out Sept. 16, 1865, at Nashville.

Thayer, Andrew J. Enlisted and mustered in Co. K, Feb. 27, 1864, at Franklin, age 39. Joined regiment Apr. 8, 1864, at Graysville, GA. Transferred Apr. 15, 1865, to Co. K, reorganized 11th Michigan Infantry. Mustered out Sept. 16, 1865, at Nashville.

Thayer, Samuel N. Monroe. Enlisted and mustered in Co. I, Nov. 2, 1861, at Monroe, age 19. Corporal Sept. 1863. Killed Sept. 20, 1863, at Chickamauga.

Thomas, Byron. St. Joseph County. Enlisted and mustered in Co. A, Aug. 24, 1861, at Centreville, age 21. Missing Jan. 2, 1863, at Stones River. No further record.

Thomas, Robert W. St. Joseph County. Enlisted in Co. A at White Pigeon, age 18. Mustered Sept. 19, 1861. Transferred Nov. 23, 1861, to Co. B. Captured Jan. 2, 1863, at Stones River. Escaped from Atlanta, GA, and rejoined regiment Sept. 10, 1863. Discharged Nov. 24, 1864, at Chattanooga. Resided c. 1905 at Eagle Grove, IA.

Thomas, William P. Enlisted in Co. A, Dec. 22, 1863, at Leonidas, age 28. Mustered Jan. 4, 1864. Joined regiment Jan. 28, 1864, at Rossville, GA. Died of disease Feb. 10, 1864, at Rossville, GA.

Thompson, Joseph E. St. Joseph County. Enlisted and mustered in Co. E, Aug. 24, 1861, at Three Rivers. Discharged for disability July 1, 1862, at Bardstown, KY.

Thompson, Leman or Leaman O. Monroe County. Enlisted in Co. I as Corporal, Aug. 24, 1861, at London, age 30. Mustered out Sept. 30, 1864, at Sturgis.

Thompson, Smith. Cass County. Enlisted and mustered in Co. E, Aug. 24, 1861, at Three Rivers. Discharged for disability Dec. 7, 1861.

Thorn, Wray. Hillsdale County. Enlisted in Co. G at Hillsdale, age 21. Mustered Sept. 4, 1861. Mustered out Sept. 30, 1864, at Sturgis.

Thornton, William E. Burr Oak. Enlisted in Co. D, Apr. 13, 1862, at Burr Oak, age 25. Mustered Aug. 15, 1862. Transferred Apr. 15, 1865, to Co. D, reorganized 11th Michigan Infantry. Corporal. Discharged June 16, 1865, at Chattanooga. Resided c. 1905 at Grand Rapids.

Thornton, William L. Enlisted in Co. A, Dec. 30, 1863, at Colon, age 25. Mustered Jan. 4, 1864. Joined regiment Jan. 28, 1864, at Rossville, GA. Transferred Mar. 30, 1864, to Co. F. Transferred Apr. 15, 1865, to Co. K, reorganized 11th Michigan Infantry. Corporal June 16, 1865. Mustered out Sept. 16, 1865, at Nashville.

Thorp, James. Hillsdale County. Enlisted and mustered in Co. F, Sept. 11, 1861, at Hudson, age 29. Discharged for disability.

Thrasher, William R. St. Joseph County. Enlisted and mustered in Co. A, Aug. 24, 1861, at Centreville, age 34. Discharged for disability Aug. 3, 1862, at Nashville.

Thurston, Miltiades A. Enlisted in Co. F, Jan. 15, 1864, at Colon, age 18. Mustered Jan. 16, 1864. Joined regiment Mar. 15, 1864, at Rossville, GA. Transferred Apr. 15, 1865, to Co. K, reorganized 11th Michigan Infantry. Mustered out Sept. 16, 1865, at Nashville.

Tice, George H. Burr Oak. Enlisted in Co. H, Aug. 13, 1862, at Burr Oak, age 31. Joined regiment Feb. 26, 1863, at Murfreesboro, TN. Discharged for disability May 14, 1863, at Murfreesboro, TN.

Tice, Perry. Burr Oak. Enlisted, company unassigned, Aug. 15, 1862, age 35. Died Dec. 1, 1862.

Tice, William. Bronson. Enlisted in Co. D, Aug. 15, 1862, at Burr Oak, age 25. Discharged for disability Feb. 28, 1863, at Detroit.

Tifft, William *see* Tift, William.

Tift, Alson A. Branch County. Enlisted in Co. H, Aug. 24, 1861, at Coldwater, age 20. Mustered Aug. 28, 1861. Discharged for disability Nov. 21, 1863, at Nashville.

Tift, William. Lenawee County. Enlisted in Co. K, Aug. 24, 1861, at Tecumseh, age 25. Mustered Sept. 1, 1861. Discharged for disability May 20, 1863, at Nashville. Resided c. 1905 at Scottville.

Timm, Edward. Centreville. Enlisted and mustered in Co. A, Aug. 24, 1861, at Centreville, age 16. Wounded Jan. 2, 1863, at Stones River. Died of wounds Jan. 4, 1863, at Murfreesboro, TN.

Timm, Frederick P. St. Joseph County. Enlisted and mustered in Co. A, Aug. 24, 1861, at Centreville, age 20. Discharged for disability at Nashville.

Timm, Lewis. St. Joseph County. Enlisted and mustered in Co. A, Aug. 24, 1861, at Centreville, age 17. Wounded Aug. 7, 1864, at Utoy Creek. Mustered out Sept. 30, 1864, at Sturgis.

Tindall, Jonathan S. Branch County. Enlisted and mustered in Co. B, Aug. 24, 1861, at Algansee, age 25. Mustered out Sept. 30, 1864, at Sturgis. Died Jan. 27, 1903. Buried at Holton.

Tindall, Joseph H. Branch County. Enlisted and mustered in Co. B, Aug. 24, 1861, at Algansee, age 27. Discharged for disability Oct. 28, 1862, at Nashville.

Tindall, William H. Branch County. Enlisted

and mustered in Co. B, Aug. 24, 1861, at Algansee, age 20. Corporal Apr. 29, 1863. Captured Sept. 20, 1863, at Chickamauga. No further record.

Todd, James A. St. Joseph County. Enlisted and mustered in Co. A, Aug. 24, 1861, at Centreville, age 23. Discharged for disability Feb. 21, 1863, at Murfreesboro, TN.

Tompkins, Julius H. St. Joseph County. Enlisted and mustered in Co. A, Aug. 24, 1861, at Centreville, age 18. Wounded at Stones River. Wounded Aug. 3, 1864. Mustered out Sept. 30, 1864, at Sturgis. Died 1899. Buried at Colon.

Townsend, Charles. Lenawee County. Enlisted and mustered in Co. F, Sept. 11, 1861, at Medina, age 19. Mustered out Sept. 30, 1864, at Sturgis.

Trim, Zabina G. Branch County. Enlisted in Co. H, Aug. 24, 1861, at Coldwater, age 33. Mustered Aug. 28, 1861. Mustered out Sept. 30, 1864, at Sturgis.

Trussell or Trussle, William W. St. Joseph County. Enlisted and mustered in Co. D, Aug. 24, 1861, at Burr Oak, age 28. Transferred to Veteran Reserve Corps Apr. 10, 1864.

Tubbs, Joseph. Branch County. Enlisted and mustered in Co. D, Aug. 24, 1861, at Bronson, age 18. Discharged for disability June 28, 1862, at Nashville.

Turner, Andrew M. Branch County. Enlisted in Co. H, Aug. 24, 1861, at Coldwater, age 21. Mustered Aug. 28, 1861. Mustered out Sept. 30, 1864, at Sturgis. Resided c. 1905 at Quincy.

Turner, Edmond or Edmund or Edwin A. Branch County. Enlisted in Co. H, Aug. 24, 1861, at Coldwater, age 18. Mustered Aug. 28, 1861. Mustered out Sept. 30, 1864, at Sturgis. Resided c. 1905 at California, MI.

Turner, Joseph E. Quincy. Enlisted in Co. H as Corporal, Aug. 24, 1861, at Coldwater, age 23. Mustered Aug. 28, 1861. Died of smallpox Dec. 1861 at White Pigeon.

Turpin, George M. Branch County. Enlisted and mustered in Co. B, Aug. 24, 1861, at Quincy, age 18. Musician Apr. 1863. Mustered out Sept. 30, 1864, at Sturgis.

Tutewiler or Tutewiller, Sydnor or Sidnor. Enlisted in Co. A, Dec. 18, 1863, at Leonidas, age 19. Mustered Jan. 4, 1864. Joined regiment Jan. 28, 1864, at Rossville, GA. Transferred Mar. 30, 1864, to Co. F. Wounded May 27, 1864, near Dallas, GA. Transferred Apr. 15, 1865, to Co. K, reorganized 11th Michigan Infantry. Corporal June 15, 1865. Mustered out Sept. 16, 1865, at Nashville.

Tuttle, Benjamin. St. Joseph County. Enlisted and mustered in Co. D as Fifer, Aug. 24, 1861, at Bronson, age 44. Discharged for disability Mar. 18, 1862, at Bardstown, KY.

Twichell, Enos M. St. Joseph County. Enlisted and mustered in Co. C as Sergeant, Aug. 24, 1861, at Sturgis, age 29. Mustered out Sept. 30, 1864, at Sturgis. Buried at Centreville.

Twiford, Henry. St. Joseph County. Enlisted and mustered in Co. D, Aug. 24, 1861, at White Pigeon, age 19. Discharged for disability Nov. 29, 1862.

Twist, Charles O. Branch County. Enlisted and mustered in Co. H, Sept. 1, 1861, at Coldwater. Discharged.

Tyler, Grove M. Batavia. Enlisted in Co. H, Aug. 24, 1861, at Coldwater, age 21. Mustered Aug. 28, 1861. Corporal 1862. Died of consumption Mar. 10, 1862, at Bardstown, KY.

Ulam, Jacob or John. Leonidas. Enlisted in Co. D. Discharged for disability Apr. 17, 1862.

Unar or Unas, Alexander. Monroe County. Enlisted in Co. K, Aug. 24, 1861, at Petersburg, age 20. Mustered Sept. 1, 1861. Discharged for disability Jan. 22, 1863, at Bowling Green, KY.

Underwood, John H. Adrian. Enlisted and mustered as Quartermaster Sergeant, Sept. 1, 1861. Commissioned 1st Lieutenant, Co. G, Nov. 14, 1862, mustered Jan. 22, 1863. Acting Quartermaster Feb. 1863 to Sept. 1864. Mustered out Sept. 30, 1864, at Sturgis. Reentered service. Commissioned and mustered as Quartermaster in reorganized 11th Michigan Infantry, Mar. 1, 1865. Acting Assistant Quartermaster, 3rd Brigade, July 1865. Discharged Sept. 28, 1865, at Detroit.

Underwood, Zenas H. St. Joseph County. Enlisted and mustered in Co. C, Aug. 24, 1861, at Sturgis, age 40. Discharged for disability Feb. 14, 1863, at Nashville.

Upell, Moses. Monroe County. Enlisted in Co. K, Aug. 24, 1861, at Petersburg, age 19. Mustered Sept. 1, 1861. Wounded Nov. 1863. Mustered out Sept. 30, 1864, at Sturgis. Resided c. 1905 at Petersburg.

Upton, George. Quincy. Enlisted and mustered in Co. B, Aug. 24, 1861, at Quincy, age 18. Died of typhoid fever May 23, 1862, at Nashville. Buried in national cemetery in Nashville.

Usewick, Dennis. Branch County. Enlisted in Co. H at Coldwater, age 28. Mustered Aug. 28, 1861. Wounded at Stones River. Mustered out Sept. 30, 1864, at Sturgis.

Vale, John W. Enlisted in Co. A, Feb. 9, 1864, at Leonidas, age 22. Mustered Feb. 27, 1864. Joined regiment Mar. 15, 1864, at Rossville, GA. Transferred Mar. 30, 1864, to Co. F. Died of disease June 22, 1864. Buried in national cemetery in New Albany, IN, grave 829.

Van Camp, James M. Branch County. Enlisted and mustered in Co. B, Aug. 24, 1861, at Quincy, age 18. Transferred Jan. 31, 1863, to Mississippi Marine Brigade. Discharged Feb. 1, 1865, at Vicksburg, MS, from Marine Corps.

Van Fleet, Jared. Kalamazoo County. Enlisted in Co. G at Prairie Ronde, age 28. Mustered Sept. 4, 1861. Discharged for disability Mar. 20, 1864, at Murfreesboro, TN.

Van Valkenburg, Benjamin. Cass County. Enlisted in Co. E, age 24. Mustered Aug. 24, 1861. Mustered out Sept. 30, 1864, at Sturgis.

Van Valkenburg, George W. Quincy. Enlisted and mustered in Co. B, Aug. 24, 1861, at Quincy, age 18. Captured Jan. 2, 1863, at Stones River. Died of erysipelas Feb. 5, 1863, at Annapolis, MD. Buried in national cemetery in Annapolis, MD.

Van Valkenburgh, Benjamin see Van Valkenburg, Benjamin.

Van Volkenburgh, George W. see Van Valkenburg, George W.

Vance, John. Hillsdale County. Enlisted in Co. F, Aug. 24, 1861, at White Pigeon. Mustered Sept. 11, 1861. Died of disease Jan. 18, 1863, at Murfreesboro, TN.

Vanderhoof, Harvey. Coldwater. Enlisted in Co. H, Aug. 24, 1861, at Coldwater, age 20. Mustered Aug. 28, 1861. Wounded Dec. 31, 1862, at Stones River. Died of wounds Feb. 4, 1863, at Murfreesboro, TN.

Vanderhoof, Martin. Branch County. Enlisted in Co. H, Aug. 24, 1861, at Coldwater, age 21. Mustered Aug. 28, 1861. Deserted Dec. 9, 1861, at White Pigeon.

Vandyne, George. Enlisted and mustered in Co. H, Sept. 12, 1864, at Blissfield for 1 year, age 27. Joined regiment Jan. 7, 1865, at Chattanooga. Transferred Apr. 15, 1865, to Co. H, reorganized 11th Michigan Infantry. Discharged June 16, 1865, at Chattanooga.

Vanlieu or Vanliew, Henry J. Dundee. Enlisted in Co. K, Aug. 24, 1861, at Dundee, age 26. Mustered Sept. 1, 1861. Died of typhoid June 13, 1862, at Columbia, TN.

Vanmiller, Numan. Dundee. Enlisted in Co. K, Aug. 24, 1861, at Dundee, age 21. Mustered Sept. 1, 1861. Died of measles Feb. 15, 1862, at Bardstown, KY.

Vannordstrand, Jerome. Cass County. Enlisted in Co. E, age 18. Mustered Aug. 24, 1861. Corporal Nov. 8, 1862. Sergeant Nov. 1, 1863. Mustered out Sept. 30, 1864, at Sturgis.

Vannordstrand, John. Cass County. Enlisted and mustered in Co. E, Aug. 24, 1861, at Three Rivers, age 29. Mustered out Sept. 30, 1864, at Sturgis.

Vanordstrant, Jerome see Vannordstrand, Jerome.

Vanordstrant, John see Vannordstrand, John.

Vanschaick, Abram see Vanschoick, Abraham.

Vanschaick, Cornelius H. see Vanschaik, Cornelius H.

Vanschaick, Franklin. Enlisted in Co. F, Feb. 29, 1864, at Hudson, age 20. Mustered Mar. 1, 1864. Joined regiment Apr. 20, 1864, at Graysville, GA. Transferred Apr. 15, 1865, to Co. K, reorganized 11th Michigan Infantry. Mustered out Sept. 16, 1865, at Nashville.

Vanschaik, Cornelius H. Wright. Enlisted and mustered in Co. F, Sept. 11, 1861, at Wright, age 26. Died of pneumonia Feb. 28, 1862, at Bardstown, KY.

Vanschaik, Franklin see Vanschaick, Franklin.

Vanschick, Franklin see Vanschaick, Franklin.

Vanschoick, Abraham. Milan. Enlisted and mustered in Co. I, Aug. 24, 1861, at Milan, age 35. Died of dropsy Dec. 13, 1862, at Nashville. Buried in national cemetery in Nashville.

Vanvalkenburg, Benjamin see Van Valkenburg, Benjamin.

Vanvalkenburg, George W. see Van Valkenburg, George W.

Veilie or Velie, Timothy. Fawn River. Enlisted and mustered in Co. C, Aug. 24, 1861, at Fawn River, age 26. Died of smallpox Mar. 9, 1862, at Bardstown, KY.

Verclet, Charles. Lenawee County. Enlisted and mustered in Co. K, Sept. 1, 1861. Deserted.

Vetie, Timothy see Veilie, Timothy.

Vincent, Wesley. Entered service as Asst. Surgeon, Dec. 29, 1862. Commissioned Dec. 29, 1862. Resigned Apr. 12, 1863. Reentered service. Commissioned Surgeon in 1st MI Colored Infantry/102nd U.S. Colored, Feb. 3, 1864. Mustered out Sept. 30, 1865, at Charleston, SC from 102nd U.S. Colored Infantry.

Vorce, George P. Kalamazoo County. Enlisted in Co. G at Prairie Ronde, age 36. Mustered Sept. 4, 1861. Discharged for disability July 3, 1862. Resided c. 1905 at Leroy.

Vosburgh or Vosburg, James. Enlisted and mustered in Co. H, Sept. 20, 1864, at Jackson for 1 year, age 25. Joined regiment Jan. 7, 1865, at Chattanooga. Transferred Apr. 15, 1865, to Co. H, reorganized 11th Michigan Infantry. Discharged June 16, 1865, at Chattanooga.

Wait, James W. London. Enlisted and mustered in Co. I, Aug. 24, 1861, at London, age 22. Killed Dec. 31, 1862, at Stones River.

Wakefield, Alphonzo. Lenawee County. Enlisted and mustered in Co. B, Aug. 24, 1861, at Quincy, age 21. Transferred Sept. 20, 1861, to Co. C, 16th Michigan Infantry. Discharged for disability Dec. 29, 1861.

Walker, James. St. Joseph County. Enlisted in Co. G, Aug. 9, 1862, at Flowerfield, age 18. Mustered Sept. 4, 1862. Mustered out Sept. 30, 1864, at Sturgis.

Waltman, Frederick *see* Maltman, Frederick.

Ward, Elias. Centreville. Enlisted in Co. A, Aug. 22, 1862, at Burr Oak, age 24. Discharged for disability Mar. 28, 1863, at Detroit.

Ward, Lorenzo. Enlisted and mustered in Co. I, Aug. 24, 1861, at Bellevue, age 29. No further record.

Warren, David. Hillsdale County. Enlisted and mustered in Co. F, Sept. 11, 1861, at White Pigeon. Discharged for disability Mar. 17, 1862.

Warren, Ezra. Colon. Enlisted and mustered in Co. C, Aug. 24, 1861, at Colon, age 27. Died of pneumonia Apr. 12, 1862, at Belmont, KY. Buried in national cemetery in Louisville.

Warren, Harvey E. Algansee. Enlisted in Co. H, Aug. 24, 1861, at Coldwater, age 21. Mustered Aug. 28, 1861. Died of measles Jan. 31, 1862, at Bardstown, KY. Buried in national cemetery in Lebanon, KY.

Warren, Henry. St. Joseph County. Enlisted in Co. G at Leonidas, age 21. Mustered Sept. 4, 1861. Corporal Jan. 22, 1863. Mustered out Sept. 30, 1864, at Sturgis. Resided c. 1905 at Leonidas.

Warren, Matthew H. St. Joseph County. Enlisted and mustered in Co. C, Aug. 24, 1861, at Sturgis, age 32. Mustered out Sept. 30, 1864, at Sturgis.

Warren, Miles. Quincy. Entered service in Co. B as 2nd Lieutenant, Aug. 24, 1861, at Butler, age 36. Commissioned Aug. 24, 1861. Resigned Feb. 18, 1862, due to disability.

Warren, Samuel E. Branch County. Enlisted in Co. H, Aug. 24, 1861, at Coldwater, age 18. Mustered Aug. 28, 1861. Discharged for disability June 24, 1862.

Warren, Stephen V. Branch County. Enlisted and mustered in Co. B, Aug. 24, 1861, at Butler, age 43. Transferred Oct. 15, 1861, to Co. H. Served in Pioneer Corps. Transferred to Invalid Corps Sept. 1, 1863. No further record.

Washburn, Wallace. Centreville. Enlisted and mustered in Co. A, Aug. 24, 1861, at Centreville, age 19. Died of measles Jan. 29, 1862, at Bardstown, KY. Buried in national cemetery in Lebanon, KY.

Waters, Henry. Monroe County. Enlisted and mustered in Co. I, Aug. 24, 1861, at Monroe, age 22. Sergeant Mar. 1, 1863. Mustered out Sept. 30, 1864, at Sturgis.

Watkins, Albert O. St. Joseph County. Enlisted and mustered in Co. A, Aug. 24, 1861, at Centreville, age 19. Mustered out Sept. 30, 1864, at Sturgis.

Watkins, Daniel B. St. Joseph County. Enlisted and mustered in Co. C, Aug. 24, 1861, at Sturgis, age 21. Served in Pioneer Brigade. Mustered out Sept. 30, 1864, at Sturgis.

Watkins, Edward W. Enlisted in Co. A, Nov. 30, 1863, at Leonidas, age 20. Mustered Jan. 4, 1864. Joined regiment Jan. 28, 1864, at Rossville, GA. Transferred Mar. 30, 1864, to Co. F. Corporal Mar. 16, 1865. Transferred Apr. 15, 1865, to Co. K, reorganized 11th Michigan Infantry. Sergeant May 8, 1865. Mustered out Sept. 16, 1865, at Nashville. Resided c. 1905 at Sherwood.

Watson, Clark. Monroe County. Enlisted and mustered in Co. I, Aug. 24, 1861, at Frenchtown, age 42. Discharged for disability Aug. 17, 1862, at Nashville.

Weach, Adolph. Washtenaw County. Enlisted and mustered in Co. I, Aug. 24, 1861, at Augusta, age 21. Mustered out Sept. 30, 1864, at Sturgis.

Weaver, Alexander. Hillsdale County. Enlisted and mustered in Co. F, Sept. 11, 1861, at Wright, age 24. Mustered out Sept. 30, 1864, at Sturgis.

Weaver, Horace. Hillsdale County. Enlisted and mustered in Co. F, Sept. 11, 1861, at Wright, age 30. Captured Sept. 20, 1863, at Chickamauga. Paroled May 8, 1864. Mustered out Sept. 30, 1864, at Sturgis.

Webb, Charles. Branch County. Enlisted in Co. H, Aug. 24, 1861, at Coldwater, age 19. Mustered Aug. 28, 1861. Mustered out Sept. 30, 1864, at Sturgis.

Weeks, William H. Wayne. Enlisted and mustered in Co. E, Aug. 24, 1861, at Three Rivers, age 23. Mustered out Sept. 30, 1864, at Sturgis.

Weigle, Ezron or Ezrom J. Erie, PA. Enlisted and mustered in Co. C, Aug. 24, 1861, at Fairview, PA, age 23. Discharged for disability Sept. 21, 1863, at Nashville.

Weinberg, Reuben G. St. Joseph County. Enlisted and mustered in Co. E, Aug. 24, 1861, at Three Rivers, age 34. Captured Sept. 1863. Paroled Oct. 1863. Mustered out Sept. 30, 1864, at Sturgis.

Weinberg, William H. St. Joseph County. Enlisted and mustered in Co. E, Aug. 24, 1861, at Three Rivers. Wounded Aug. 7, 1864, at Utoy Creek. Died of wounds. Buried in national cemetery in Atlanta, GA, Section H, grave 9117.

Weinburg, Reuben G. *see* Weinberg, Reuben G.

Welch, Andrew J. Lenawee County. Enlisted and mustered in Co. F, Sept. 11, 1861, at Seneca, age 21. Corporal Apr. 9, 1864. Mustered out Sept. 30, 1864, at Sturgis.

Welch, John H. Quincy. Enlisted in Co. B, Aug. 15, 1862, at Quincy, age 18. Discharged for disability Apr. 17, 1863, at Murfreesboro, TN.

Welch, Richard H. Mendon. Enlisted in Co. A, Oct. 20, 1862, at Mendon, age 24. Mustered Nov. 24, 1862. Joined regiment Dec. 8, 1862, at Nashville. Transferred Apr. 15, 1865, to Co. B, reorganized 11th Michigan Infantry. Mustered out Sept. 16, 1865, at Nashville.

Weller, John C. Branch County. Enlisted and mustered in Co. B, Aug. 24, 1861, at Butler, age 22. Discharged for disability Aug. 10, 1862, at Nashville. Resided c. 1905 at Union City.

Wellesley, Edwin P. St. Joseph County. Enlisted and mustered in Co. D as Sergeant, Aug. 24, 1861, at Colon, age 20. 1st Sergeant. Discharged for disability May 18, 1863, at Murfreesboro, TN. Resided c. 1905 at Colon.

Wellman, Augustus Milo. Enlisted in Co. A, Jan. 18, 1864, at Nottawa, age 21. Mustered Feb. 9, 1864. Joined regiment Apr. 7, 1864, at Graysville, GA. Wounded Aug. 7, 1864, at Utoy Creek. Transferred Apr. 15, 1865, to Co. B, reorganized 11th Michigan Infantry. Mustered out Sept. 16, 1865, at Nashville.

Wells, Benjamin Franklin. St. Joseph County. Enlisted and mustered in Co. A, Aug. 24, 1861, at Centreville, age 23. Corporal Jan. 24, 1862. Sergeant Mar. 21, 1863. Mustered out Sept. 30, 1864, at Sturgis.

Wescott or Wescot, Hiram D. St. Joseph County. Enlisted and mustered in Co. A, Aug. 24, 1861, at Centreville, age 18. Mustered out Sept. 30, 1864, at Sturgis. Resided c. 1905 at Centreville.

West, Randall C. Hillsdale County. Enlisted and mustered in Co. B as Corporal, Aug. 24, 1861, at Litchfield, age 23. Mustered out Sept. 30, 1864, at Sturgis.

Weston, William. Enlisted in Co. B, Aug. 13, 1862, at Detroit, age 23. Captured Sept. 20, 1863, at Chickamauga. No further record.

Whallon, James M. Fawn River. Enlisted and mustered in Co. C as Sergeant, Aug. 24, 1861, at Sturgis, age 21. Sergeant Major Mar. 12, 1862. Commissioned 2nd Lieutenant, Co. C, Jan. 7, 1863, mustered Apr. 8, 1863. Resigned Jan. 15, 1864, due to disability.

Wheeler, Hiram M. St. Joseph County. Enlisted as Musician, Aug. 24, 1861, at White Pigeon, age 23. Mustered Sept. 24, 1861. Mustered out Aug. 22, 1862, at Nashville.

Wheeler, Lewis or Louis. St. Joseph County. Enlisted and mustered in Co. C, Aug. 24, 1861, at Fawn River, age 18. Mustered out Sept. 30, 1864, at Sturgis.

Wheeler, Milo L.G. St. Joseph County. Enlisted and mustered in Co. A, Aug. 24, 1861, at Centreville, age 21. Corporal Mar. 21, 1863. Sergeant Jan. 15, 1864. Mustered out Sept. 30, 1864, at Sturgis.

Wheeler, Rufus C. Branch County. Enlisted in Co. H, Aug. 24, 1861, at Coldwater, age 18. Mustered Aug. 28, 1861. Discharged for disability Feb. 3, 1863, at Nashville.

Wheeler, William A. Branch County. Enlisted and mustered in Co. B, Aug. 24, 1861, at Quincy, age 18. Transferred to Invalid Corps Nov. 1863. Discharged Aug. 25, 1864, at Chicago, IL, from Co. I, 15th Regiment VRC. Resided c. 1905 at Delta, CO.

Wheeler, William F. Batavia. Enlisted in Co. H, Aug. 24, 1861, at Coldwater, age 23. Mustered Aug. 28, 1861. Died of inflammation of lungs Dec. 7, 1861, at White Pigeon.

Wheeling, John. Kalamazoo County. Enlisted in Co. G at Prairie Ronde, age 24. Mustered Sept. 4, 1861. Corporal Dec. 15, 1862. Mustered out Sept. 30, 1864, at Sturgis.

Whelan, Arvin F. Entered service as Asst. Surgeon. Commissioned Nov. 12, 1861. Resigned Oct. 13, 1862. Reentered service. Commissioned Surgeon in 1st Michigan Sharpshooters, Jan. 1, 1863, mustered Jan. 3, 1863.

Whipple, Ezra S. Wayne County. Enlisted and mustered in Co. I, Aug. 24, 1861, at Belleville, age 33. Transferred to Invalid Corps Jan. 15, 1864.

White, Aaron B. St. Joseph County. Enlisted and mustered in Co. A as Corporal, Aug. 24, 1861, at Centreville, age 23. Captured Dec. 31, 1862, at Stones River. Sergeant Jan. 15, 1864. Mustered out Sept. 30, 1864, at Sturgis.

White, Charles A. St. Joseph County. Enlisted and mustered in Co. D, Aug. 24, 1861, at Burr Oak, age 22. Died of fever Apr. 22, 1862, at Belmont, KY.

White, Daniel A. Enlisted and mustered in Co. D as Drummer, Aug. 24, 1861, at White Pigeon. No further record.

White, Edward. Enlisted in Co. A, Dec. 25, 1863, at Leonidas, age 17. Mustered Jan. 4, 1864. Joined regiment Jan. 28, 1864, at Rossville, GA. Transferred Mar. 30, 1864, to Co. F. Wounded July 4, 1864, at Ruff's Station. Died of wounds. Buried in national cemetery in Marietta, GA, Section F, grave 5034.

White, Edwin. Enlisted in Co. A, Dec. 24, 1863, at Colon, age 18. Mustered Jan. 4, 1864. Joined regiment Jan. 28, 1864, at Rossville, GA. Transferred Mar. 30, 1864, to Co. F. Wounded July 4, 1864, at Ruff's Station. No further record.

White, Edwin D. St. Joseph County. Enlisted and mustered in Co. A as Corporal, Aug. 24, 1861, at Centreville, age 25. Wounded at Stones River. Wounded Feb. 1863. Mustered out Sept. 30, 1864, at Sturgis.

White, Levi E. Monroe County. Enlisted and mustered in Co. I, Aug. 24, 1861, at London, age 31. Discharged for disability Dec. 13, 1862, at Nashville. Reentered service. Private, Co. G, in 6th Michigan Heavy Artillery, Jan. 26, 1864, mustered Feb. 3, 1864. Mustered out Aug. 20, 1865, at New Orleans, LA.

White, Thomas A. St. Joseph County. Enlisted and mustered in Co. A, Aug. 24, 1861, at Centreville, age 32. Discharged for disability May 6, 1862, at Louisville.

White, Thomas N. St. Joseph County. Enlisted and mustered in Co. D, Aug. 24, 1861, at Burr Oak, age 22. Captured Dec. 31, 1862, at Stones River. Paroled. Mustered out Sept. 30, 1864, at Sturgis.

Whitehead, Charles. Branch County. Enlisted in Co. H, Aug. 24, 1861, at Coldwater, age 25. Mustered Aug. 28, 1861. Discharged for disability June 26, 1862.

Whitehead, Henry V. Hillsdale County. Enlisted and mustered in Co. B, Aug. 24, 1861, at Allen, age 21. Mustered out Sept. 30, 1864, at Sturgis.

Whitney, Washington. Quincy. Enlisted in Co. B, Aug. 15, 1862, at Quincy, age 25. Joined regiment Feb. 2, 1863, at Murfreesboro, TN. Sergeant Dec. 9, 1864. 1st Sergeant Mar. 16, 1865. Transferred Apr. 15, 1865, to Co. B, reorganized 11th Michigan Infantry. Discharged June 16, 1865, at Chattanooga.

Whitney, William G. Allen. Enlisted and mustered in Co. B as Sergeant, Aug. 24, 1861, at Allen, age 21. Commissioned 2nd Lieutenant Jan. 7, 1863. Wounded Sept. 20, 1863, at Chickamauga. Commissioned 1st Lieutenant June 17, 1864, mustered July 25, 1864. Commissioned Captain Mar. 1, 1865. Transferred Apr. 15, 1865, to Co. B, reorganized 11th Michigan Infantry. Mustered out Sept. 16, 1865, at Nashville. Received Medal of Honor for gallantry at Chickamauga. Resided c. 1905 at Allen.

Wicoff, Joseph. Williams County, OH. Enlisted in Co. K, Aug. 24, 1861, at OH, age 21. Mustered Sept. 1, 1861. Transferred Sept. 20, 1862, to Mississippi Marine Brigade.

Wilber, Charles. Branch County. Enlisted and mustered in Co. D, Aug. 24, 1861, at Bronson, age 32. Corporal Aug. 1862. Mustered out Sept. 30, 1864, at Sturgis.

Wilber, Wallace. Branch County. Enlisted and mustered in Co. D, Aug. 24, 1861, at Bronson, age 23. Mustered out Sept. 30, 1864, at Sturgis.

Wilbur, Charles see Wilber, Charles.

Wilbur, Wallace see Wilber, Wallace.

Wilcox, Abner V. Leonidas. Enlisted and mustered in Co. A as Corporal, Aug. 24, 1861, at Centreville, age 20. Captured. Paroled Sept. 1863. Wounded Sept. 20, 1863, at Chickamauga. Died of wounds Oct. 29, 1863, at Chattanooga.

Wilcox, Levi or Lewis. Sturgis. Enlisted and mustered in Co. C, Aug. 24, 1861, at Sturgis, age 19. Died of fever June 28, 1863, at Murfreesboro, TN. Buried in national cemetery in Murfreesboro, TN.

Wilcox, Martin V. St. Joseph County. Enlisted and mustered in Co. A, Aug. 24, 1861, at Centreville, age 30. Transferred Aug. 18, 1863, to 15th USCT as 2nd Lieutenant.

Wilcox, Warren. Batavia. Enlisted in Co. H, Aug. 24, 1861, at Coldwater, age 21. Mustered Aug. 28, 1861. Died of inflammation of lungs Jan. 15, 1862, at Bardstown, KY. Buried in national cemetery in Lebanon, KY.

Wilder, Marion. Enlisted in Co. A, Dec. 23, 1863, at Leonidas, age 21. Mustered Jan. 4, 1864. Joined regiment Jan. 28, 1864, at Rossville, GA. Transferred Mar. 30, 1864, to Co. F. Transferred Apr. 15, 1865, to Co. K, reorganized 11th Michigan Infantry. Discharged Aug. 10, 1865, at Cleveland, TN.

Wilhelm, Aaron. St. Joseph County. Enlisted and mustered in Co. E, Aug. 24, 1861, at Three Rivers. Discharged for disability Dec. 7, 1861.

Wilkins, Levi P. Lenawee County. Enlisted and mustered in Co. F, Sept. 11, 1861, at Medina, age 31. Corporal Jan. 31, 1862. Sergeant May 1863. Wounded Aug. 7, 1864, at Utoy Creek. Died of wounds Aug. 16, 1864, at Vinings, GA. Buried in national cemetery in Marietta, GA, Section 1, grave 9597.

Willard, Calvin. St. Joseph County. Enlisted in Co. G at Porter, age 21. Mustered Sept. 4, 1861. Mustered out Sept. 30, 1864, at Sturgis.

Willard, Edward P. St. Joseph County. Enlisted and mustered in Co. C, Aug. 24, 1861, at Sturgis, age 22. Discharged for disability Dec. 24, 1862, at Nashville. Resided c. 1905 at Petoskey.

Willard, Eugene P. St. Joseph County. Enlisted

and mustered in Co. C, Aug. 24, 1861, at Sturgis, age 18. Mustered out Sept. 30, 1864, at Sturgis. Resided c. 1905 at Luther.

Willcox, Warner *see* Wilcox, Warren.

Williams, Evans. St. Joseph County. Enlisted and mustered in Co. C, Aug. 24, 1861, at Sturgis, age 21. Wounded June 23, 1864, near Kennesaw Mtn. Mustered out Sept. 30, 1864, at Sturgis.

Williams, Harvey S. Burr Oak. Enlisted in Co. C, Aug. 11, 1862, at Burr Oak, age 21. Mustered Sept. 1, 1862. Joined regiment Dec. 20, 1862, at Murfreesboro, TN. Transferred Apr. 15, 1865, to Co. C, reorganized 11th Michigan Infantry. Discharged June 16, 1865, at Chattanooga.

Williams, John. Butler. Enlisted and mustered in Co. B, Aug. 24, 1861, at Butler, age 25. Died of pneumonia Mar. 22, 1862, at Bardstown, KY. Buried in national cemetery in Lebanon, KY.

Williams, Martin V.B. St. Joseph County. Enlisted in Co. G at Porter, age 19. Mustered Sept. 4, 1861. Wounded at Stones River. Mustered out Sept. 30, 1864, at Sturgis. Resided c. 1905 at Grand Ledge.

Williams, Orlando B. Flowerfield. Enlisted in Co. G at Schoolcraft, age 20. Mustered Sept. 4, 1861. Died of typhoid pneumonia Feb. 1, 1862, at Bardstown, KY.

Williard, Calvin *see* Willard, Calvin.

Willsey, Charles. St. Joseph County. Enlisted as Musician, Aug. 24, 1861, at White Pigeon, age 26. Mustered Sept. 24, 1861. Mustered out Aug. 22, 1862, at Nashville.

Wilson, Charles. Wright. Enlisted in Co. F, Aug. 30, 1862, at Hillsdale, age 19. Discharged for disability Apr. 20, 1863, at Murfreesboro, TN.

Wilson, Charles. Branch County. Enlisted in Co. H, Aug. 24, 1861, at Coldwater, age 25. Mustered Aug. 28, 1861. Mustered out Sept. 30, 1864, at Sturgis. Resided c. 1905 at Coldwater.

Wilson, Edward. St. Joseph County. Enlisted in Co. F at White Pigeon. Mustered Sept. 11, 1861. Hospital Steward Mar. 1, 1862. Discharged for disability Jan. 9, 1863, at Nashville. Resided c. 1905 at Elm Hall.

Wilson, John. Wayne County. Enlisted and mustered in Co. I, Aug. 24, 1861, at Detroit, age 20. Mustered out Sept. 30, 1864, at Sturgis.

Wilson, Johnson. Branch County. Enlisted in Co. H, Aug. 24, 1861, at Coldwater, age 20. Mustered Aug. 28, 1861. Discharged for disability Oct. 21, 1862, at Nashville.

Wilson, Joseph F. Wright. Entered service in Co. F as 1st Lieutenant, Aug. 24, 1861, age 45. Commissioned Aug. 24, 1861. Mustered Sept. 11, 1861. Commissioned Captain Aug. 18, 1862. Killed Dec. 30, 1862, at Stones River. Buried in national cemetery in Murfreesboro, TN, grave 2787.

Wilson, Reuben. Hillsdale County. Enlisted and mustered in Co. F as Corporal, Sept. 11, 1861, at Wright, age 20. Mustered out Sept. 30, 1864, at Sturgis.

Wilson, William W. Monroe County. Enlisted and mustered in Co. I, Aug. 24, 1861, at Monroe, age 19. Captured Sept. 20, 1863, at Chickamauga. Died June 17, 1864, at Andersonville, GA. Buried in national cemetery in Andersonville, GA.

Winters, Lewis. Monroe County. Enlisted and mustered in Co. I, Aug. 24, 1861, at Dundee, age 37. Wounded Aug. 1864 near Atlanta. Died Oct. 27, 1864. Buried in national cemetery in Nashville.

Wisdom, Amos. Wayne County. Enlisted and mustered in Co. I, Aug. 24, 1861, at Belleville, age 32. Discharged for disability Apr. 26, 1862. Resided c. 1905 at Milan.

Wisner, John W. Wheatland. Enlisted and mustered in Co. F, Sept. 11, 1861, at Wright, age 20. Died of typhoid fever Apr. 15, 1862, at Belmont, KY. Buried in national cemetery in Louisville.

Wixom, Joseph. St. Joseph County. Enlisted and mustered in Co. D, Aug. 24, 1861, at Burr Oak, age 29. Sergeant May 1864. Mustered out Sept. 30, 1864, at Sturgis. Resided c. 1905 at North Muskegon.

Wood, Ammon. Branch County. Enlisted in Co. H, Aug. 24, 1861, at Coldwater, age 24. Mustered Aug. 28, 1861. Discharged for disability Apr. 25, 1862, at Nashville.

Wood, Andrew J.M. Hillsdale County. Enlisted and mustered in Co. C, Dec. 9, 1861, at White Pigeon, age 37. Died of consumption Jan. 24, 1862, at Louisville. Buried in national cemetery in Louisville, Section A, grave 11.

Wood, Marvin S. Lenawee County. Enlisted and mustered in Co. F, Dec. 6, 1861. Wounded Sept. 1863 at Chattanooga. Discharged for disability Jan. 19, 1864, at Louisville.

Wood, Smoloff H. St. Joseph County. Enlisted and mustered in Co. A, Aug. 24, 1861, at Centreville, age 21. Discharged for disability Aug. 23, 1862, at Nashville.

Wood, William W. St. Joseph County. Enlisted and mustered in Co. A, Aug. 24, 1861, at Centreville, age 17. Wounded and captured Dec. 31, 1862, at Stones River. Discharged for disability Mar. 12, 1863, at Louisville.

Woodard, Henry M. Sherman. Enlisted and mustered in Co. C, Aug. 24, 1861, at Sherman, age 22. Died of typhoid fever Apr. 16, 1862, at Belmont, KY. Buried in national cemetery in Louisville.

Woodhouse, Thomas E. St. Joseph County. Enlisted and mustered in Co. A, Aug. 24, 1861, at Centreville, age 28. Mustered out Sept. 30, 1864, at Sturgis.

Woodward, William D. Lenawee County. Enlisted and mustered in Co. F, Sept. 11, 1862, at Seneca, age 28. Mustered out Sept. 30, 1864, at Sturgis.

Woodworth, Lott T. St. Joseph County. Enlisted and mustered in Co. E as Corporal, Aug. 24, 1861, at Three Rivers. Discharged for disability May 30, 1862.

Woolcott, Charles. Wayne County. Enlisted in Co. G at Jefferson, age 18. Mustered Sept. 4, 1861. Deserted Nov. 25, 1861, at White Pigeon.

Worden, Ephraim. Branch County. Enlisted and mustered in Co. D, Aug. 24, 1861, at Bronson, age 25. Served in Pioneer Corps. Mustered out Sept. 30, 1864, at Sturgis. Resided c. 1905 at Orland, IN.

Worden, Eugene. Hillsdale County. Enlisted and mustered in Co. F, Sept. 11, 1861, at Pittsford, age 18. Discharged for disability July 6, 1862.

Wright, Alfred G. Van Buren County. Enlisted and mustered in Co. E, Aug. 24, 1861, at Three Rivers, age 20. Mustered out Sept. 30, 1864, at Sturgis.

Wyant, Abraham H. Colon. Enlisted and mustered in Co. D, Aug. 24, 1861, at Burr Oak, age 30. Discharged for disability Jan. 15, 1864, at Detroit.

Wyant, William M. St. Joseph County. Enlisted and mustered in Co. D, Aug. 24, 1861, at Burr Oak, age 18. Discharged Aug. 14, 1862, at Nashville.

Young, Peter. Wayne County. Enlisted and mustered in Co. I, Aug. 26, 1861, at Detroit, age 27. Killed June 23, 1864, near Kennesaw Mtn. Buried in national cemetery in Marietta, GA, Section G, grave 8028.

Youngs, Jackson. Enlisted and mustered in Co. D, Aug. 24, 1861, at White Pigeon. No further record.

Youngs, James. Medina. Enlisted and mustered in Co. F, Sept. 11, 1861, at Morenci, age 20. Sergeant. Died of fever Dec. 18, 1863, at Chattanooga.

Chapter Notes

Preface

1. Guelzo, *Gettysburg: The Last Invasion*, xiv.

Chapter 1

1. "Enthusiastic Union Meeting in Three Rivers," *Three Rivers* (MI) *Reporter*, 18 April 1861, hereafter cited as *Reporter*.
2. *History of St. Joseph County*, 32; Robertson, *Michigan in the War*, 10, 37.
3. "Volunteers from St. Joseph County," *Three Rivers* (MI) *Western Chronicle*, 18 April 1861, hereafter cited as *Chronicle*; "History of the Michigan Eleventh Regiment," *Reporter*, 21 August 1869; Samuel Chadwick to John Robertson, 22 April 1861, in Regimental Service Records, 11th Michigan Infantry, Archives of Michigan, hereafter cited as Regimental Service Records.
4. "History of the Michigan Eleventh Regiment," *Reporter*, 21 August 1869; *Reporter*, 2 May 1861, p. 3; "Corporation Election," *Chronicle*, 8 May 1861; *Constantine* (MI) *Weekly Mercury*, 23 May 1861, p. 2, hereafter cited as *Mercury*; "Large and Enthusiastic Meeting at Centreville," *Reporter*, 9 May 1861.
5. 1860 United States Census, Schedule 1, Sturgis Village, St. Joseph County, Michigan, dwelling 1852, family 1848, August 1860; Fitch, *Army of the Cumberland*, 238; William L. Stoughton to John Robertson, 25 and 26 April 1861, in Regimental Service Records; Robertson, *Michigan in the War*, 23, 222; "Peninsular Guards," *Chronicle*, 8 May 1861; *Reporter*, 13 June 1861, p. 3.
6. 1860 United States Census, Schedule 1, Quincy Village, Branch County, Michigan, dwelling 880, family 902, 23 June 1860; Melvin Mudge to John Robertson, 12 June, 23 July, and 29 July 1861, in Regimental Service Records.
7. Whitney and Bonner, *History of Lenawee County*, 1:241–42; 1860 United States Census, Schedule 1, Morenci Village, Lenawee County, Michigan, dwelling 2123, family 2198, 14 August 1860; Sylvester B. Smith to John Robertson, 3 June, 18 June, 24 June, and 6 July 1861, in Regimental Service Records; Sylvester B. Smith to Austin Blair, 31 July 1861, in Regimental Service Records.
8. *History of St. Joseph County*, 33; David Oakes, Jr. to John Robertson, 20 April and 31 July 1861, in Regimental Service Records; "Centreville Home Guards," *Chronicle*, 2 May 1861; *Reporter*, 13 June 1861, p. 3; "Jeff Davis at Centreville!" *Chronicle*, 12 June 1861; "Grand Union Meeting," *Chronicle*, 31 July 1861; *Reporter*, 1 August 1861, p. 2; *Reporter*, 25 July 1861, p. 3.
9. May's dining hall had gone out of business due to changes in the railroad schedule. Sydney Herrick was ultimately appointed as assistant surgeon of the 1st New York Cavalry. "History of the Michigan Eleventh Regiment," *Reporter*, 21 August 1869; "Corporation Election," *Chronicle*, 8 May 1861; *Record of Michigan Volunteers*, 11:64; 1860 United States Census, Schedule 1, White Pigeon Township, St. Joseph County, Michigan, dwelling 412, family 415, 16 and 18 June 1860; "St. Jo. Independent Regiment," *Mercury*, 19 September 1861; 1860 United States Census, Schedule 1, Lockport Township, St. Joseph County, Michigan, dwelling 1556, family 1572, 8 August 1860; "Army Surgeons from This County," *Chronicle*, 14 August 1861; *Reporter*, 11 July 1861, p. 2.
10. Smith's company combined with Joseph Wilson's Hudson Riflemen. "Recruiting Offices," *Mercury*, 22 August 1861; *Reporter*, 8 August 1861, p. 3; *Reporter*, 17 August 1861, p. 3; "A Regiment from St. Joseph County," *Chronicle*, 14 August 1861; Thornton, *When Gallantry Was Commonplace*, 38–39.
11. *Reporter*, 17 August 1861, p. 3.
12. *History of St. Joseph County*, 54; "Meeting at Parkville," *Chronicle*, 21 August 1861; "Three Rivers Military Company," *Chronicle*, 28 August 1861; *Mercury*, 29 August 1861, p. 3.
13. Gillaspie was hardly the only soldier who enlisted for the money. See Wiley, *Life of Billy Yank*, 37–38. *Kansas*, 2:1049; 1870 United States Census, Schedule 1, Sturgis Township, St. Joseph County, Michigan, dwelling 470, family 471, 10 June 1870; *Diary of Ira Gillaspie*, 7.
14. "An Editor in the Ranks," *Chronicle*, 8 May 1861; "From the First Regiment," *Mercury*, 20 June 1861; "The Brave Michigan Boys," *Chronicle*, 31 July 1861; "Wanted," *Chronicle*, 11 September 1861.
15. 1860 United States Census, Schedule 1, Lockport Township, St. Joseph County, Michigan, dwelling 1461, family 1477, 6 August 1860; *History of St. Joseph County*, 139, 145, 147; "Three Rivers Company Mustered In," *Chronicle*, 4 September 1861; "Three Rivers Light Guard," *Chronicle*, 4 September 1861; "Departure of the Three Rivers Light Guard," *Chronicle*, 11 September 1861.

16. Briggs's men for a time turned their hopes to joining Stockton's Independent Regiment, which is discussed in more detail later. *Reporter*, 11 July 1861, p. 3; "Col. May's St. Jo. Regiment," *Chronicle*, 11 September 1861; *Record of Michigan Volunteers*, 11:14, 11:66; *Chronicle*, 1 August 1861, p. 3; 1860 United States Census, Schedule 1, Schoolcraft Township, Kalamazoo County, Michigan, dwelling 639, family 634, 12 July 1860; *History of St. Joseph County*, 54; 1860 United States Census, Schedule 1, Bronson, Branch County, Michigan, dwelling 425, family 424, 16 June 1860; 1900 United States Census, Schedule 1, Precinct 3, Hillsborough County, Florida, dwelling 683, family 683, 27 June 1900; Robertson, *Michigan in the War*, 890; "May's Independent Regiment," *Mercury*, 22 August 1861; "Recruiting Offices," *Mercury*, 22 August 1861.

17. John L. Hackstaff's Pension Application, Application No. 7530, Certificate No. 12678, National Archives, Washington, D.C.; 1860 United States Census, Schedule 1, Coldwater Village, Branch County, Michigan, dwelling 494, family 508, 9 June 1860; *History of St. Joseph County*, 45; Turner, *Gazetteer of St. Joseph*, 24, 28; *History of Branch County 1979*, 66.

18. Paddock, *History of Texas*, 1:623; Nelson Chamberlain to John Robertson, 23 September, 1 October, and 5 October 1861, in Regimental Service Records; 1860 United States Census, Schedule 1, 2nd Ward City of Monroe, Monroe County, Michigan, dwelling 524, family 524, 18 June 1860.

19. 1860 United States Census, Schedule 1, 4th Ward City of Adrian, Lenawee County, Michigan, dwelling 1147, family 1177, 9 July 1860; *Record of Michigan Volunteers*, 11:73; "Col. May's Independent Regiment," *Chronicle*, 25 September 1861.

20. James W. King to Sarah J. Babcock, 18 October 1861 and 23 March 1862, James W. King Collection, 1861–1903, Western Michigan University Archives and Regional History Collections, hereafter cited as King Collection; *Diary of Ira Gillaspie*, 7; Hicks, "Personal Recollections," 520.

21. "Col. May's St. Jo. Regiment," *Chronicle*, 11 September 1861; "Presentation," *Chronicle*, 23 October 1861; "Sword Presentation to Captain Hood," *Journal*, 10 October 1861; "Eleventh Regt. Mich. Infantry," *Reporter*, 30 November 1861; Nelson Clifford Bragg to unidentified recipient, 27 November 1861, Bragg Papers, U.S. Army Military History Institute; "From the Independent Regiment," *Reporter*, 28 September 1861.

22. "The Independent Regiment," *Reporter*, 14 September 1861.

23. "The Independent Regiment," *Reporter*, 14 September 1861.

24. James W. King, "Truth Is Stranger Than Fiction," n.d., pp. 1–2, King Collection; Harvey Tilden to John Robertson, 4 November 1861, in Regimental Service Records.

25. "Reunion of Michigan Veterans," unidentified newspaper, 25 August 1873.

26. *War of the Rebellion*, series 3, vol. 1, pt. 1, pp. 489–90, hereafter cited as *OR*. Subsequent references are to series 1, unless otherwise indicated.

27. "Condensed News Items," *Reporter*, 8 August 1861; Robertson, *Michigan in the War*, 940–41; "Col. May's St. Jo. Regiment," *Chronicle*, 11 September 1861.

28. William J. May to Austin Blair, 15 September 1861, in Regimental Service Records; David Oakes, Jr. to William J. May, 16 September 1861, in Regimental Service Records; *OR*, series 3, vol. 1, pt. 1, pp. 518–19.

29. "Col. May's Independent Regiment," *Chronicle*, 18 September 1861; James W. King to Sarah J. Babcock, 17 September 1861, King Collection; Daniel Rose to unidentified recipient, 18 September 1861, Carroll Masterson Collection, 1861–1865, Western Michigan University Archives and Regional History Collections, hereafter cited as Masterson Collection.

30. Drake and Elliott were married to the McKinney sisters, Catherine and Sarah. The customary election of volunteer officers is discussed in Wiley, *Life of Billy Yank*, 24. "Col. May's St. Jo. Regiment," *Chronicle*, 11 September 1861; *History of St. Joseph County*, 15, 42–43, 66, 69, 78–79, 105, 146; "St. Jo. Independent Regiment," *Mercury*, 19 September 1861; "Unfounded Reports of Small Pox!" *Chronicle*, 20 November 1861.

31. May likely had cause to question Chadwick's loyalty to the regiment. A surviving letter suggests Chadwick recommended that the governor break May's unit up to fill the other regiments currently forming. It seems odd that Chadwick would endanger the regiment he helped create, but perhaps his loyalties were divided: he had served under Colonel Stockton in the Mexican War. 1860 United States Census, Schedule 1, Village of Colon, St. Joseph County, Michigan, dwelling 713, family 709, 30 June 1860; "Lieut. Col. Stoughton—A Mistake," *Chronicle*, 11 September 1861; "The Lieutenant Colonelcy," *Reporter*, 21 September 1861; Thornton, *When Gallantry Was Commonplace*, 23.

32. The artillerists ultimately joined the 4th Michigan Light Artillery. "Col. May's St. Jo. Regiment," *Chronicle*, 11 September 1861; "Col. May's Independent Regiment," *Chronicle*, 25 September 1861.

33. "Col. May's Independent Regiment," *Chronicle*, 9 October 1861; "The Governor's Visit," *Reporter*, 12 October 1861; *Mercury*, 10 October 1861, p. 3; "Review of Col. May's Regiment by Gov. Blair," *Sturgis (MI) Journal*, 10 October 1861, hereafter cited as *Journal*.

34. "The Picnic at White Pigeon," *Chronicle*, 16 October 1861; "May's Regiment the Eleventh," *Chronicle*, 16 October 1861.

35. Civil War units had no Company J. Note that Mudge's company had been renamed from the Rifles to the Wolverines. *History of St. Joseph County*, 54; *Record of Michigan Volunteers*, 11:1; Robertson, *Michigan in the War*, 313; "Col. May's Independent Regiment," *Chronicle*, 25 September 1861.

36. "Col. May's Regiment," *Mercury*, 26 September 1861.

37. "Col. May's Regiment," *Mercury*, 26 September 1861; "Col. May's Independent Regiment," *Chronicle*, 9 October 1861; *Reporter*, 26 October 1861, p. 3; James W. King to Sarah J. Babcock, 18 October 1861, King Collection; "At White Pigeon," *Chronicle*, 13 November 1861; "Col. May's Regiment," *Chronicle*, 27 November 1861.

38. Camp vices are discussed in Wiley, "Evil and Goodness," chap. 10 in *Life of Billy Yank*. James W. King to Sarah J. Babcock, 29 September and 6 December 1861, King Collection.

39. William W. Hoisington also went by "Wallace" or "Walter." "Col. May's Independent Regiment," *Chronicle*, 2 October 1861; *Record of Michigan Volunteers*, 11:49; *Diary of Ira Gillaspie*, 8–12; Hicks, "Personal Recollections," 522.

40. "The Eleventh Regiment," *Reporter*, 19 October 1861.

41. *Record of Michigan Volunteers*, 11:4–106 passim.

42. Twiford's service would end a year later with a discharge for disability. *Record of Michigan Volunteers*, 11:9, 11:47, 11:51, 11:60, 11:96; Hicks, "Personal Recollections," 521; Benjamin G. Bennett to John Robertson, 9 November 1861, in Regimental Service Records.

43. Benjamin F. Wells to Susan M. Wells, 2 November 1861, Wells Family Papers, 1857–1902, Bentley Historical Library, hereafter cited as Wells Papers.
44. Hicks, "Personal Recollections," 522.
45. Aaron White mentioned that the regiment's flank companies received rifles—not an uncommon practice early in the war—but were required to exchange them for smoothbore muskets before the end of December. Most likely this was done for logistical purposes, to use the same ammunition for the entire unit. *Diary of Ira Gillaspie*, 11; "Col. May's Independent Regiment," *Chronicle*, 4 December 1861; "Our Army Correspondence," *Journal*, 16 January 1862; "Our Army Correspondence," *Journal*, 6 February 1862; "Reunion of Michigan Veterans," unidentified newspaper, 25 August 1873; Hicks, "Personal Recollections," 522; Aaron B. White to Daniel Rose, 26 December 1861, Masterson Collection.
46. "Eleventh Regt. Mich. Infantry," *Reporter*, 30 November 1861.
47. This was a fairly typical flag ceremony. See Wiley, *Life of Billy Yank*, 28–30. "Eleventh Regt. Mich. Infantry," *Reporter*, 30 November 1861; "Reunion of Michigan Veterans," unidentified newspaper, 25 August 1873.
48. Don Carlos Buell to Austin Blair, 26 November 1861, Regimental Service Records; "Col. May's Regiment," *Chronicle*, 27 November 1861; "Reunion of Michigan Veterans," unidentified newspaper, 25 August 1873.

Chapter 2

1. *Mercury*, 28 November 1861, p. 2; *Reporter*, 7 December 1861, p. 2.
2. Union soldiers were supposed to take their pay every other month, but compensation was often delayed significantly. "Paying the 11th Regt.," *Reporter*, 7 December 1861; Wiley, *Life of Billy Yank*, 48–49.
3. James W. King to Sarah J. Babcock, 6 December 1861, King Collection; *Diary of Ira Gillaspie*, 12; *Record of Michigan Volunteers*, 11:58; Bingham, *Early History of Michigan*, 681.
4. Joseph E. Turner's Pension Application, Application No. 7621, Certificate No. 12497, National Archives; *Diary of Ira Gillaspie*, 12; "List of Deaths in Co. A," Regimental Service Records; "Unfounded Reports of Small Pox!" *Chronicle*, 20 November 1861; "Col. May's Independent Regiment," *Chronicle*, 4 December 1861.
5. *Diary of Ira Gillaspie*, 12; "Reunion of Michigan Veterans," unidentified newspaper, 25 August 1873; *Reporter*, 7 December 1861, p. 2.
6. "From the 11th Michigan Regiment," *Chronicle*, 25 December 1861; *Diary of Ira Gillaspie*, 13.
7. *Diary of Ira Gillaspie*, 13.
8. "From the 11th Michigan Regiment," *Chronicle*, 25 December 1861; "Army Intelligence," *Reporter*, 21 December 1861; "From the 11th Michigan Regiment," *Chronicle*, 8 January 1862, "Our Army Correspondence," *Journal*, 26 December 1861.
9. "Army Intelligence," *Reporter*, 21 December 1861; James W. King to Sarah J. Babcock, 11 December 1861, King Collection; "Reunion of Michigan Veterans," unidentified newspaper, 25 August 1873.
10. "Our Army Correspondence," *Journal*, 26 December 1861; James W. King to Sarah J. Babcock, 11 December 1861, King Collection; *Diary of Ira Gillaspie*, 13; *Reporter*, 21 December 1861, p. 3; "Army Intelligence," *Reporter*, 21 December 1861.
11. The troubled relationship between Union soldiers and their rations is described in Wiley, "Hardtack, Salt Horse and Coffee," chap. 9 in *Life of Billy Yank*. Hicks, "Personal Recollections," 522–23; James Martin to his parents, 13 December 1861, James Martin Letters, 1861–1864, Bentley Historical Library, hereafter cited as Martin Letters; "Reunion of Michigan Veterans," unidentified newspaper, 25 August 1873; *Diary of Ira Gillaspie*, 13; James W. King to Sarah J. Babcock, 13 December 1861, King Collection; "Our Army Correspondence," *Chronicle*, 19 February 1862; "Army Intelligence," *Reporter*, 15 February 1862; "Letter from Adjutant Chadwick," *Reporter*, 25 January 1862.
12. James W. King to Sarah J. Babcock, 16 April 1865, King Collection; "From the 11th Michigan Regiment," *Chronicle*, 8 January 1862; "Letter from Adjutant Chadwick," *Reporter*, 11 January 1862.
13. James W. King to Sarah J. Babcock, 13 December 1861, King Collection.
14. *Diary of Ira Gillaspie*, 13.
15. "Army Intelligence," *Reporter*, 25 January 1862; *Diary of Ira Gillaspie*, 13–14; *Proceedings of Eighth Reunion*, 5; Hicks, "Personal Recollections," 523; "Letter from Adjutant Chadwick," *Reporter*, 11 January 1862.
16. "Letter from Adjutant Chadwick," *Reporter*, 11 January 1862; "From the 11th Regiment," *Chronicle*, 25 December 1861; James W. King to Sarah J. Babcock, 13 December 1861, King Collection; "Head Quarters 11th Mich. Inf.," *Reporter*, 1 February 1862.
17. "Letter from Adjutant Chadwick," *Reporter*, 11 January 1862.
18. "Army Correspondence," *Mercury*, 3 April 1862.
19. *Diary of Ira Gillaspie*, 23.
20. "Letter from Adjutant Chadwick," *Reporter*, 11 January 1862; "Reunion of Michigan Veterans," unidentified newspaper, 25 August 1873; James W. King to Sarah J. Babcock, 22 December 1861, King Collection.
21. *Diary of Ira Gillaspie*, 14; "From the Regimental Band," *Chronicle*, 15 January 1862; "Letter from Rev. H.A. Pattison," *Chronicle*, 22 January 1862; "Our Army Correspondence," *Journal*, 9 January 1862; "Our Army Correspondence," *Chronicle*, 19 March 1862.
22. It was commonplace for newly deployed units to suffer dramatically from disease—even more so for units like the 11th Michigan that were recruited from lightly settled areas. See Wiley, *Life of Billy Yank*, 132–33. *Diary of Ira Gillaspie*, 14; "List of Deaths in Co. C," Regimental Service Records; "Reunion of Michigan Veterans," unidentified newspaper, 25 August 1873; Daniel Rose to friends, 11 December 1861, Masterson Collection; *Proceedings of Eighth Reunion*, 6.
23. James W. King to Sarah J. Babcock, 22 December 1861, King Collection; Nathan Adams to Emily Parsons, 26 December 1861, Civil War Letters of Nathan Adams, 1861–1865, Library of Michigan, an agency of the Michigan Department of Education, hereafter cited as Adams Letters.
24. Target practice was performed with striking infrequence in the Union Army. See Wiley, *Life of Billy Yank*, 26–27. Nelson Clifford Bragg to Myron Bragg, 8 January 1862, Bragg Papers; "From the 11th Michigan Regiment," *Chronicle*, 5 March 1862; *Diary of Ira Gillaspie*, 14; James W. King to Sarah J. Babcock, 26 December 1861, King Collection.
25. James W. King to Sarah J. Babcock, 26 December 1861, King Collection.
26. *Diary of Ira Gillaspie*, 14; "From the 11th Michigan Regiment," *Chronicle*, 5 March 1862.
27. *Diary of Ira Gillaspie*, 14–16; "From the 11th Michigan Regiment," *Chronicle*, 5 March 1862.
28. Bennett claimed that smallpox was used as an excuse to push the regiment aside for some ulterior mo-

tive, but said it would be improper for him to discuss it publicly. "From the 11th Michigan Regiment," *Chronicle*, 5 March 1862; Benjamin F. Bordner to his brother, 15 January 1862, Benjamin F. Bordner Papers, 1862–1864, Bentley Historical Library, hereafter cited as Bordner Papers; "From the Eleventh Regiment," *Mercury*, 13 March 1862; James W. King to Sarah J. Babcock, 12 January 1862, King Collection; *Diary of Ira Gillaspie*, 15–16; "Letter from Adjutant Chadwick," *Reporter*, 18 January 1862; *Mercury*, 13 March 1862, p. 3, "Our Army Correspondence," *Journal*, 6 February 1862.

29. Benjamin F. Bordner to his brother, 15 January 1862, Bordner Papers.

30. "List of Deaths," all companies, Regimental Service Records; James Martin to his parents, 11 January 1862, Martin Letters; *Diary of Ira Gillaspie*, 16–17.

31. The role of unsanitary conditions in causing and spreading disease is discussed in Wiley, *Life of Billy Yank*, 125–28.

32. "Letter from Michigan 11th," *Reporter*, 5 April 1862.

33. Nathan Adams to Emily Parsons, February 1862, Adams Letters; "Our Army Correspondence," *Chronicle*, 19 February 1862; "Our Army Correspondence," *Journal*, 6 February 1862; "Letter from Michigan 11th," *Reporter*, 5 April 1862; "List of Deaths," all companies, Regimental Service Records.

34. Regimental Papers, Box 1999, Michigan—11th Infantry, National Archives, hereafter cited as Regimental Papers; *Record of Michigan Volunteers*, 11:47, 11:73; "List of Officers and Enlisted Men Who Have Been Enrolled in Company K," Regimental Service Records; "Note from Adjutant Chadwick," *Chronicle*, 19 March 1862; Nelson Clifford Bragg to his parents, 17 October 1861, Bragg Papers; Myron Bragg to his family, 12 May 1862, Bragg Papers.

35. "List of Deaths," all companies, Regimental Service Records; "Our Army Correspondence," *Chronicle*, 5 February 1862; "Our Army Correspondence," *Chronicle*, 19 February 1862; "Army Intelligence," *Reporter*, 15 February 1862; James Martin to his parents, 24 January 1862, Martin Letters; Irving Metcalf to his parents, 9 February 1862, Doris L. King Family Papers, 1822–1877, Clarke Historical Library, hereafter cited as Doris King Papers.

36. Susan M. Wells to Benjamin F. Wells, 7 March 1862, Wells Papers.

37. *Diary of Ira Gillaspie*, 16–17; James W. King to Sarah J. Babcock, 21 January 1862, King Collection.

38. *Record of Michigan Volunteers*, 11:44, 11:54, 11:66, 11:99; "Col. May Arrested!" *Reporter*, 22 February 1862; "From the 11th Michigan Regiment," *Chronicle*, 26 February 1862; "Head Quarters 11th Mich. Inf.," *Reporter*, 1 February 1862; "Reply to Captain Oakes," *Chronicle*, 26 February 1862; "Army Correspondence," *Mercury*, 3 April 1862; "Note from Adjutant Chadwick," *Chronicle*, 19 March 1862; "Letter from Captain Oakes," *Reporter*, 12 April 1862; "Our Army Correspondence," *Journal*, 16 January 1862; John L. Hackstaff's Pension Application, Application No. 7530, Certificate No. 12678, National Archives.

39. Union soldiers shared their Southern counterparts' prejudices toward the black race. The mentioned mistreatment of slaves was nothing uncommon. See Wiley, "Along Freedom Road," chap. 5 in *Life of Billy Yank*. *Diary of Ira Gillaspie*, 12–13, 17, 19, 23–25.

40. Benjamin F. Bordner to his brother, 15 January 1862, Bordner Papers; "Letter from Company A," *Chronicle*, 26 February 1862; James W. King to Sarah J. Babcock, 21 and 25 January 1862, King Collection; James Martin to his parents, 24 January 1862, Martin Letters; Irving Metcalf to his parents, 6 April 1862, Doris King Papers; "Letter from Adjutant Chadwick," *Reporter*, 25 January 1862; "Our Army Correspondence," *Journal*, 27 February 1862.

41. "Army Intelligence," *Reporter*, 15 March 1862.

42. Calhoun was the subject of an 1862 book, *The Life, Trial, Death and Confession of Samuel H. Calhoun, the Soldier-Murderer*, by Captain Jonathan Harrington Green, an experienced author and crusader against his own former pastime of gambling. Green in his volume purported to present Calhoun's confession, but the text is not so much a confession as a biography, approaching 20,000 words, and so eloquent, vivid, and polished, that it clearly was not dictated extemporaneously by Calhoun as Green implied. Apparently the captain turned his literary talents loose and took liberties with Calhoun's account for the purpose of crafting a memorable story for the purpose Green set forth in his preface: "for its moral effect upon the Army, and indeed the general reader." "Army Intelligence," *Reporter*, 22 February 1862; Irving Metcalf to his parents, 9 February 1862, Doris King Papers; "Our Army Correspondence," *Journal*, 27 February 1862; Daniel Rose to his brother, 6 February 1862, Masterson Collection.

43. The *Gazette* was quoted in the Constantine *Mercury*. *Diary of Ira Gillaspie*, 18–19; "From the 11th Michigan Regiment," *Chronicle*, 26 February 1862; "Our Army Correspondence," *Journal*, 20 March 1862; "Army Intelligence," *Reporter*, 15 March 1862; James W. King to Sarah J. Babcock, 28 February 1862, King Collection; *Mercury*, 13 March 1862, p. 3; *Life of James Jackson*, 13; "Our Army Correspondence," *Journal*, 27 February 1862.

44. Wickliffe's mansion still stands. James W. King to Sarah J. Babcock, 28 February 1862, King Collection.

45. John C. Walker to James B. Fry, 24 February 1862, in Regimental Papers, Box 1998; *OR*, vol. 52, pt. 1, p. 217; "Our Army Correspondence," *Chronicle*, 19 March 1862; "Our Army Correspondence," *Journal*, 20 March 1862.

46. *Diary of Ira Gillaspie*, 18, 20; *Proceedings of Eighth Reunion*, 6; "Army Intelligence," *Reporter*, 15 March 1862.

47. "Army Correspondence," *Mercury*, 3 April 1862; Benjamin F. Bordner to his brother and sister, 23 March 1862, Bordner Papers.

48. "Army Correspondence," *Mercury*, 3 April 1862.

49. "Army Correspondence," *Mercury*, 3 April 1862.

50. James W. King to Sarah J. Babcock, 14 March 1862, King Collection.

51. *Diary of Ira Gillaspie*, 21; James W. King to Sarah J. Babcock, 14 March 1862, King Collection.

52. "Army Correspondence," *Mercury*, 3 April 1862; James Martin to his parents, 7 April 1862, Martin Letters; Benjamin F. Bordner to his brother and sister, 23 March 1862, Bordner Papers; Benjamin F. Wells to Susan M. Wells, 18 April 1862, Wells Papers.

53. James W. King to Sarah J. Babcock, 11 March 1862, King Collection; "Our Army Correspondence," *Chronicle*, 2 April 1862; Benjamin F. Wells to Susan M. Wells, 18 April 1862, Wells Papers; James Martin to his parents, 7 April 1862, Martin Letters; *Diary of Ira Gillaspie*, 23.

54. James W. King to Sarah J. Babcock, 14 March 1862, King Collection; "Our Army Correspondence," *Chronicle*, 29 January 1862; "Col. May Arrested!" *Reporter*, 22 February 1862; "Resignation of Col. May!" *Chronicle*, 26 March 1862; "Army Correspondence," *Mercury*, 3 April 1862; William J. May to Austin Blair, 29 March 1862, in Regimental Service Records.

55. James W. King to Sarah J. Babcock, 6 April 1862,

Chapter 3

1. *Diary of Ira Gillaspie*, 25–26; "Army Intelligence," *Reporter*, 24 May 1862; "Our Army Correspondence," *Chronicle*, 28 May 1862; Benjamin F. Wells to Susan M. Wells, 2 May 1862, Wells Papers.
2. Benjamin F. Wells to Susan M. Wells, 2 May 1862, Wells Papers; James Martin to his parents, 6 May 1862, Martin Letters; Irvin Metcalf to his parents, 4 May 1862, Doris King Papers; *Diary of Ira Gillaspie*, 26; James W. King to Sarah J. Babcock, 3 May 1862, King Collection; "Army Intelligence," *Reporter*, 24 May 1862; "Our Army Correspondence," *Chronicle*, 21 May 1862; "Our Army Correspondence," *Chronicle*, 28 May 1862.
3. Benjamin F. Wells to Susan M. Wells, 2 May 1862, Wells Papers; James W. King to Sarah J. Babcock, 3 May 1862, King Collection; *Diary of Ira Gillaspie*, 26; Irving Metcalf to his parents, 4 May 1862, Doris King Papers.
4. Benjamin F. Wells to Susan M. Wells, 2 May 1862, Wells Papers; James W. King to Sarah J. Babcock, 3 May 1862, King Collection; "Our Army Correspondence," *Chronicle*, 21 May 1862; Daniel Rose to his mother, 2 June 1862, Masterson Collection; "Army Intelligence," *Reporter*, 24 May 1862.
5. Benjamin F. Wells to Susan M. Wells, 18 April 1862, Wells Papers; Daniel Rose to his mother, 2 June 1862, Masterson Collection; Rollin Eaton to Edgar, 15 April 1862, Watkins Collection.
6. Benjamin F. Wells to Susan M. Wells, 2 May 1862, Wells Papers; "Army Intelligence," *Reporter*, 24 May 1862; Daniel Rose to his mother, 2 June 1862, Masterson Collection; "Our Army Correspondence," *Chronicle*, 21 May 1862; James W. King to Sarah J. Babcock, 3 May 1862, King Collection.
7. "Our Army Correspondence," *Chronicle*, 28 May 1862; *OR*, vol. 10, pt. 2, p. 161; Daniel Rose to his mother, 9 May 1862, Masterson Collection; *Diary of Ira Gillaspie*, 27.
8. "History of the Michigan Eleventh Regiment," *Reporter*, 21 August 1869.
9. "Communicated," *Reporter*, 7 June 1862; "Our Army Correspondence," *Chronicle*, 21 May 1862; "Our Army Correspondence," *Chronicle*, 28 May 1862; Nathan Adams to Emily Parsons, 12 May 1862, Adams Letters; Benjamin F. Wells to Susan M. Wells, 9 May 1862, Wells Papers; Daniel Rose to his mother, 9 May 1862, Masterson Collection; *Diary of Ira Gillaspie*, 27–28.
10. Gillaspie is the only source for this incident, and he does not name the victim. *Diary of Ira Gillaspie*, 28.
11. "Communicated," *Reporter*, 7 June 1862; James Martin to his parents, 19 May 1862, Martin Letters; *Diary of Ira Gillaspie*, 28; Benjamin F. Wells to Susan M. Wells, 23 May 1862, Wells Papers.
12. "Communicated," *Reporter*, 7 June 1862; Knapp and Bonner, *Illustrated History of Lenawee*, 233–34; Officers of the 11th Michigan to Austin Blair, 10 April 1862, in Regimental Service Records; Nathaniel B. Eldridge to John Robertson, 17 April and 7 May 1862, in Regimental Service Records.
13. Presumably it was Major Doughty who was passed over for promotion due to the clique Chadwick refers to. (It is striking how rarely Doughty was mentioned by his comrades in their writings.) "Communicated," *Reporter*, 7 June 1862; *Mercury*, 27 March 1862, p. 3; *Diary of Ira Gillaspie*, 24; Benjamin F. Wells to Susan M. Wells, 23 May 1862, Wells Papers.
14. "Army Intelligence," *Reporter*, 21 June 1862; "Our Army Correspondence," *Journal*, 19 June 1862.
15. "Army Intelligence," *Reporter*, 21 June 1862.
16. "Army Intelligence," *Reporter*, 21 June 1862; Monthly Return for July 1862, Regimental Service Records.
17. "Army Intelligence," *Reporter*, 21 June 1862; James W. King to Sarah J. Babcock, 2 June 1862, King Collection; "Unionism in Tennessee," *New York Times*, 9 June 1862; "Our Army Correspondence," *Journal*, 19 June 1862; Nathan Adams to Emily Parsons, 3 June 1862, Adams Letters; Savage, *Life of Andrew Johnson*, 264; *Diary of Ira Gillaspie*, 29.
18. Savage, *Life of Andrew Johnson*, 255, 264–66.
19. "Army Intelligence," *Reporter*, 21 June 1862; James W. King to Sarah J. Babcock, 2 June 1862, King Collection; "Unionism in Tennessee," *New York Times*, 9 June 1862; Savage, *Life of Andrew Johnson*, 266; *Diary of Ira Gillaspie*, 29.
20. Benjamin F. Wells to Susan M. Wells, 10 June 1862, Wells Papers; *Diary of Ira Gillaspie*, 29; "Our Army Correspondence," *Journal*, 10 July 1862; *Minnesota in the Wars*, 2:111–12; *OR*, vol. 16, pt. 1, p. 852.
21. Benjamin F. Wells to Susan M. Wells, 20 June 1862, Wells Papers; *Diary of Ira Gillaspie*, 29–30; *Minnesota in the Wars*, 2:111–12; Daniel Rose to his brother, 25 June 1862, Masterson Collection; *OR*, vol. 16, pt. 1, p. 852; Vale, *Minty and the Cavalry*, 72–74; Furoughi, *Go If Your Duty*, 103. (Wells's letter of June 20 is mistakenly transcribed as June 26 in the typed transcription provided in the Wells Papers.)
22. Benjamin F. Wells to Susan M. Wells, 20 June 1862, Wells Papers; *Diary of Ira Gillaspie*, 29–30; *Minnesota in the Wars*, 2:111–12; Daniel Rose to his brother, 25 June 1862, Masterson Collection; *OR*, vol. 16, pt. 1, p. 852; Vale, *Minty and the Cavalry*, 72–74; Furoughi, *Go If Your Duty*, 103; Nathan Adams to Emily Parsons, 19 June 1862, Adams Letters.
23. For further discussion regarding the importance of mail to Union soldiers, see McPherson, *For Cause and Comrades*, 132–34. "Our Army Correspondence," *Journal*, 10 July 1862.
24. Benjamin F. Wells to Susan M. Wells, 23 and 28 June 1862, Wells Papers; *Diary of Ira Gillaspie*, 30–31; *Reporter*, 12 July 1862, p. 3.
25. *OR*, vol. 16, pt. 1, pp. 753–56; James Martin to his parents, 16 July 1862, Martin Letters; "The Eleventh Michigan After Morgan," *Chronicle*, 23 July 1862.
26. James Martin to his parents, 16 July 1862, Martin Letters; *Diary of Ira Gillaspie*, 31; "Our Army Correspondence," *Journal*, 24 July 1862; Duke, *History of Morgan's Cavalry*, 184; *OR*, vol. 16, pt. 1, pp. 732, 762; *OR*, vol. 16, pt. 2, pp. 132–33; Benjamin F. Wells to Susan M. Wells, 22 July 1862, Wells Papers.
27. *Diary of Ira Gillaspie*, 31–32; "Our Army Correspondence," *Journal*, 24 July 1862; Duke, *History of Morgan's Cavalry*, 184; *OR*, vol. 16, pt. 1, pp. 732, 762; *OR*, vol. 16, pt. 2, pp. 132–33.
28. The quoted *Louisville Journal* article was reprinted in the *Chronicle*. "The Eleventh Michigan After Morgan," *Chronicle*, 23 July 1862; "From the Eleventh Michigan Regiment," *Chronicle*, 30 July 1862; "Important from the Southwest; Capture of Murfreesboro, Tenn., by the Rebels," *New York Times*, 14 July 1862; *OR*, vol. 16, pt. 2, pp. 87–88, 132–33; *Reporter*, 19 July 1862, p. 3; "Our Army Correspondence," *Journal*, 24 July 1862.

King Collection; *Diary of Ira Gillaspie*, 24–25; Rollin Eaton to Edgar, 15 April 1862, Bertha Watkins Collection, 1841–1919, Western Michigan University Archives and Regional History Collections, hereafter cited as Watkins Collection.

29. *OR*, vol. 16, pt. 1, pp. 759–60, 762; Duke, *History of Morgan's Cavalry*, 199; *Diary of Ira Gillaspie*, 32; James Martin to his parents, 25 July 1862, Martin Letters.

30. Wells, in his quote of Stoughton, was surely mistaken as he claimed his colonel was confronting General Smith. The 11th Michigan and Smith were out of contact that early in the day. Stoughton's dispute can only have been with Maxwell, and this much was confirmed by Sergeant Major Platt in a letter to the *Sturgis Journal*. Wells was not present, so his version of events was secondhand. On the other hand, Martin, who was present with the unit, also blamed Smith for not driving the Rebels into Maxwell's inanimate line. *OR*, vol. 16, pt. 1, pp. 762–63; Duke, *History of Morgan's Cavalry*, 203; *Diary of Ira Gillaspie*, 32; 1860 United States Census, Schedule 1, Paris, Bourbon County, Kentucky, dwelling 493, family 497, 4 August 1860; Benjamin F. Wells to Susan M. Wells, 1 August 1862, Wells Papers; *Journal*, "Our Army Correspondence," 21 July 1862; James Martin to his parents, 25 July 1862, Martin Letters.

31. *OR*, vol. 16, pt. 1, pp. 761–63; *Diary of Ira Gillaspie*, 32–33; Duke, *History of Morgan's Cavalry*, 204; James Martin to his parents, 25 July 1862, Martin Letters.

32. Monthly Return for July 1862, Regimental Service Records; *OR*, vol. 16, pt. 1, pp. 751–52, 854; *OR*, vol. 16, pt. 2, p. 220; *Diary of Ira Gillaspie*, 33; "Our Army Correspondence," *Chronicle*, 3 September 1862; *History of Branch County 1879*, 66–67.

33. James King and Colonel Miller stated that Morgan's three cornfield casualties included two captains, but Miller incorrectly identified one of them as William Campbell Preston Breckinridge (a cousin of John C. Breckinridge who survived the war). Duke, on the contrary (who was not present), stated that a Lieutenant Manly was killed, and was the ranking officer present. The Federals' confusion might be explained by the differences between Union and Confederate rank insignias. Duke, *History of Morgan's Cavalry*, 210–15; *OR*, vol. 16, pt. 2, pp. 318–19; "Our Army Correspondence," *Chronicle*, 3 September 1862; "Our Army Correspondence," *Journal*, 28 August 1862; James Martin to his parents, 18 August 1862, Martin Letters; *Diary of Ira Gillaspie*, 33–34; James W. King to Sarah J. Babcock, 15 August 1862, King Collection; *OR*, vol. 16, pt. 1, pp. 843–44.

34. "Our Army Correspondence," *Chronicle*, 3 September 1862; "Our Army Correspondence," *Journal*, 28 August 1862; Duke, *History of Morgan's Cavalry*, 214–15; James Martin to his parents, 18 August 1862, Martin Letters; *Diary of Ira Gillaspie*, 34; James W. King to Sarah J. Babcock, 15 August 1862, King Collection; "Army Intelligence," *Reporter*, 15 March 1862; *OR*, vol. 16, pt. 1, pp. 843–44.

35. Basil Duke, who was not present, placed the attack on the train-boarding Federals a day later, claimed only sixteen Rebels were involved, and that none were hurt. Sturges stated that only part of the 11th Michigan was present at Gallatin: Companies C, E, H, I, and parts of A and D. No other source mentions the unit having split up at this time. Carkenard's entry in *Record of Michigan Volunteers* wrongly implies that he remained a prisoner from August 13, 1862, until his death. By September 6, Daniel Rose heard that Carkenard was paroled and sent to Camp Chase. A regimental return lists him in September 1863 sick at Stevenson, Alabama, where he died of fever on October 15 of that year. "Our Army Correspondence," *Chronicle*, 3 September 1862; "Our Army Correspondence," *Journal*, 28 August 1862; James Martin to his parents, 18 August 1862, Martin Letters; *Diary of Ira Gillaspie*, 34; James W. King to Sarah J. Babcock, 15 August 1862, King Collection; Robertson, *Michigan in the War*, 314; Monthly Returns for August 1862, September 1863, and October 1863, Regimental Service Records; *Record of Michigan Volunteers*, 11:18, 11:59; "List of Deaths in Co. A," Regimental Service Records; Daniel Rose to his brother, 6 September 1862, Masterson Collection; Duke, *History of Morgan's Cavalry*, 215.

36. Ramage, *Rebel Raider*, 113–15; "Our Army Correspondence," *Journal*, 28 August 1862.

37. *Diary of Ira Gillaspie*, 34–35; Benjamin F. Wells to Susan M. Wells, 29 August 1862, Wells Papers; *Proceedings of Eighth Reunion*, 6; James Martin to his parents, 6 September 1862, Martin Letters.

38. *OR*, vol. 16, pt. 2, pp. 430–32; *Diary of Ira Gillaspie*, 35–36; James Martin to his parents, 6 September 1862, Martin Letters.

39. *Diary of Ira Gillaspie*, 36–37; "List of Deaths in Co. A," Regimental Service Records.

40. Linus T. Squire to John Robertson, 28 May 1863, in Regimental Service Records.

41. As usual, Doughty's comrades hardly mentioned him, even when he resigned. *Record of Michigan Volunteers*, 11:78, 11:87; Monthly Return for September 1862, Regimental Service Records.

42. *Reporter*, 21 August 1869; "Special Order No. 26," 25 July 1862, Regimental Papers; Monthly Return for September 1862, Regimental Service Records; "From Adjutant Chadwick," *Reporter*, 30 August 1862; "The Michigan Eleventh," *Chronicle*, 10 September 1862.

43. *Diary of Ira Gillaspie*, 37–38; Benjamin F. Wells to Susan M. Wells, 8 September 1862, Wells Papers.

44. *Proceedings of Eighth Reunion*, 6; James Martin to his parents, 6 September 1862, Martin Letters; *Diary of Ira Gillaspie*, 38; James W. King to Sarah J. Babcock, 10 September and 29 November 1862, King Collection; "A Voice from Camp," *Reporter*, 25 October 1862; Benjamin F. Wells to Susan M. Wells, 8 September 1862, Wells Papers.

45. James W. King to Sarah J. Babcock, 29 October 1862, King Collection; Linus T. Squire to John Robertson, 28 May 1863, in Regimental Service Records; Robertson, *Michigan in the War*, 314; Fitch, *Army of the Cumberland*, 238–39; Nathan Adams to Emily Parsons, October 1862, Adams Letters.

46. Benjamin F. Wells to Susan M. Wells, 12 November 1862, Wells Papers.

47. Monthly Return for October 1862, Regimental Service Records; William H. Seekell's Pension Application, Application No. 13405, Certificate No. 13388, National Archives; Muster-In Roll, Company E, Regimental Service Records; citizens of Three Rivers to William L. Stoughton, 17 November 1862, in Regimental Papers, Box 1999; *Record of Michigan Volunteers*, 11:82.

48. James W. King to Sarah J. Babcock, 29 October and 29 November 1862, King Collection.

49. *OR*, vol. 20, pt. 2, pp. 6–7; *Diary of Ira Gillaspie*, 40; *Index to Executive Documents*, 572–73.

50. *Diary of Ira Gillaspie*, 40; Daniel Rose to his mother, 22 December 1862, Masterson Collection; James W. King to Sarah J. Babcock, 14 and 24 December 1862, King Collection.

Chapter 4

1. The name Army of the Cumberland did not become an official designation until January 9, but the sol-

diers were already using this name to describe Rosecrans's host. Cozzens, *No Better Place*, 14–15; James W. King to Sarah J. Babcock, 24 December 1862, King Collection.

2. *OR*, vol. 20, pt. 1, p. 372.

3. *Diary of Ira Gillaspie*, 41.

4. "Reunion of Michigan Veterans," unidentified newspaper, 25 August 1873; *Proceedings of Eighth Reunion*, 7.

5. *Diary of Ira Gillaspie*, 42; Hicks, "Personal Recollections," 525; James W. King to Sarah J. Babcock, 3 January 1863, King Collection; Joseph Wilson's Pension Application, Application No. 85407, Certificate No. 49877, National Archives.

6. *Diary of Ira Gillaspie*, 42–43; James W. King to Sarah J. Babcock, 3 January 1863, King Collection.

7. "From the Eleventh Regiment," *Reporter*, 17 January 1863; Haynie, *Nineteenth Illinois*, 186.

8. James W. King to Sarah J. Babcock, 3 January 1863, King Collection; James Martin to his parents, 12 January 1863, Martin Letters; William E. Raymond to Marmaduke, 28 February 1863, William E. Raymond Papers, 1863–1864, Bentley Historical Library, hereafter cited as Raymond Papers.

9. Ira Gillaspie's account of the fighting on December 31, though highly detailed, is chronologically inaccurate. "From the 11th Regiment," *Mercury*, 29 January 1863; "From the Eleventh Regiment," *Reporter*, 17 January 1863; James W. King, "11th Michigan Infantry," *Lansing* (MI) *Weekly State Republican*, 11 January 1901, hereafter cited as *Republican*; *OR*, vol. 20, pt. 1, p. 426; Bickham, *Rosecrans' Campaign*, 201; *Diary of Ira Gillaspie*, 43–44; Hicks, "Personal Recollections," 525; Cozzens, *No Better Place*, 125; Jim Lewis, "Battle of Stones River," *Blue & Gray* 28, no. 6 (2012): 16, 25–26, 54; "Our Army Correspondence," *Journal*, 5 February 1863.

10. "From the 11th Regiment," *Mercury*, 29 January 1863; "From the Eleventh Regiment," *Reporter*, 17 January 1863; James W. King, "11th Michigan Infantry," *Lansing* (MI) *Weekly State Republican*, 11 January 1901, hereafter cited as *Republican*; *OR*, vol. 20, pt. 1, pp. 426, 688; Cozzens, *No Better Place*, 125–27; Jim Lewis, "Battle of Stones River," *Blue & Gray* 28, no. 6 (2012): 25–26, 54; "Our Army Correspondence," *Journal*, 5 February 1863.

11. The 11th's stand against Anderson's and Stewart's superior numbers did not go unnoticed: the *Cincinnati Commercial*'s well-known correspondent Joseph McCullagh credited the 11th Michigan and 19th Illinois with driving back a full Confederate division (actually Stewart's and Anderson's brigades). *Proceedings of Eighth Reunion*, 7; *OR*, vol. 20, pt. 1, p. 426; "From the Eleventh Regiment," *Reporter*, 17 January 1863; James W. King, "11th Michigan Infantry," *Republican*, 11 January 1901; *Diary of Ira Gillaspie*, 43; Haynie, *Nineteenth Illinois*, 186–88; William L. Stoughton to James W. King, 20 December 1879, in Regimental Service Records; "Our Army Correspondence," *Journal*, 5 February 1863; Cozzens, *No Better Place*, 141; Jim Lewis, "Battle of Stones River," *Blue & Gray* 28, no. 6 (2012): 25–26, 54; *Michigan in the War*, 316.

12. Lieutenant Faulknor secured his release from captivity by January 3 by passing himself off as a surgeon. *Proceedings of Eighth Reunion*, 7; *OR*, vol. 20, pt. 1, pp. 426, 677, 764; "From the Eleventh Regiment," *Reporter*, 17 January 1863; James W. King, "11th Michigan Infantry," *Republican*, 11 January 1901; *Diary of Ira Gillaspie*, 43; Haynie, *Nineteenth Illinois*, 186–88; "Our Army Correspondence," *Journal*, 5 February 1863; Coz-

zens, *No Better Place*, 142; Jim Lewis, "Battle of Stones River," *Blue & Gray* 28, no. 6 (2012): 25–26, 54.

13. Cozzens, *No Better Place*, 142; *Diary of Ira Gillaspie*, 44; Jim Lewis, "Battle of Stones River," *Blue & Gray* 28, no. 6 (2012): 55.

14. *OR*, vol. 20, pt. 1, pp. 424, 426; Cozzens, *No Better Place*, 155; "Capt. E. G. Hall," 3; *Diary of Ira Gillaspie*, 44; "From the Eleventh Regiment," *Reporter*, 17 January 1863.

15. Johnson, *Body of Brave Men*, 285–291; Cozzens, *No Better Place*, 155–56; *OR*, vol. 20, pt. 1, pp. 421, 426, 429; "Our Army Correspondence," *Journal*, 5 February 1863; Hicks, "Personal Recollections," 526.

16. Jim Lewis, "Battle of Stones River," *Blue & Gray* 28, no. 6 (2012): 43, 45, 56; Cozzens, *No Better Place*, 144–48; *OR*, vol. 20, pt. 1, pp. 243, 247–48.

17. *OR*, vol. 20, pt. 1, pp. 380, 424–25; "From the Eleventh Regiment," *Reporter*, 17 January 1863; *Diary of Ira Gillaspie*, 42–43.

18. The December 31 casualties may be extrapolated by taking the loss report in Linus Squire's December 1863 letter to Robertson, which listed 140 casualties for the entire battle, and subtracting one man killed on December 30 along with nine January 2 casualties reported by Chadwick in a letter to the *Reporter*. The regiment's monthly returns are less helpful since January's report apparently enumerates a number of losses incurred December 31. James W. King to Sarah J. Babcock, 3 January 1863, King Collection; *Diary of Ira Gillaspie*, 44–45; Linus Squire to John Robertson, 22 December 1863, in Regimental Service Records; "From the Eleventh Regiment," *Reporter*, 17 January 1863; Monthly Returns for December 1862 and January 1863, Regimental Service Records; Daniel Rose to his mother, 7 January 1863, Masterson Collection; "Our Army Correspondence," *Journal*, 5 February 1863; *Proceedings of Eighth Reunion*, 7; "List of Deaths," all companies, 1863, Regimental Service Records.

19. James W. King to Sarah J. Babcock, 3 January 1863, King Collection; James Martin to his parents, 12 January 1863, Martin Letters.

20. *Diary of Ira Gillaspie*, 45; James Martin to his parents, 12 January 1863, Martin Letters.

21. *OR*, vol. 20, pt. 1, pp. 422, 424–25, 427, 434–35; Stevenson, *Battle of Stone's River*, 138–39; James Martin to his parents, 12 January 1863, Martin Letters; *Diary of Ira Gillaspie*, 45; "From the Eleventh Regiment," *Reporter*, 17 January 1863; *Diary of Ira Gillaspie*, 45; Jim Lewis, "Battle of Stones River," *Blue & Gray* 28, no. 6 (2012): 48; *Proceedings of Eighth Reunion*, 7.

22. *Diary of Ira Gillaspie*, 45; Linus Squire to John Robertson, 22 December 1863, in Regimental Service Records; "From the Eleventh Regiment," *Reporter*, 17 January 1863; James Martin to his parents, 12 January 1863, Martin Letters.

23. Cozzens, *No Better Place*, 203; "From the Eleventh Regiment," *Reporter*, 17 January 1863; James W. King to Sarah J. Babcock, 14 January 1863, King Collection.

24. "From the 11th Michigan Regiment," *Chronicle*, 5 March 1862.

Chapter 5

1. Daniel Rose to his mother, 18 January 1863, Masterson Collection; "From the Eleventh Regiment," *Reporter*, 7 March 1863; Solomon Shirey to William H. Fox, 30 January 1863, William H. Fox Letters, 1862–

1863, Bentley Historical Library; *Diary of Ira Gillaspie*, 46; James Martin to his parents, 6 March 1863, Martin Letters; James W. King to Sarah J. Babcock, 8 February 1863, King Collection.

2. *Diary of Ira Gillaspie*, 46–47; Monthly Returns for January and February 1863, Regimental Service Records; James Martin to his parents, 23 January 1863, Martin Letters; James W. King to Sarah J. Babcock, 8 February 1863, King Collection; Benjamin F. Bordner to Mr. and Mrs. Hill, 3 March and 2 April 1863, Bordner Papers.

3. *Diary of Ira Gillaspie*, 46–47; *Record of Michigan Volunteers*, 11:14, 11:20, 11:63, 11:90; "History of Officers," Aaron B. Sturges, Regimental Service Records; "List of Deaths in Co. A," Regimental Service Records.

4. Chadwick resumed his legal practice, and by July was serving Three Rivers as justice of the peace. He returned to the war in October 1864 as captain of Company H in the newly organized 28th Michigan Infantry. Chadwick died in 1872 and was buried in Riverside Cemetery in Three Rivers. *Record of Michigan Volunteers*, 11:50, 11:89, 28:14; William L. Stoughton to John Robertson, 23 February 1863, in Regimental Service Records; History of Officers, Sylvester B. Smith, Regimental Service Records; Officers of the 11th Michigan to Austin Blair, 8 April 1863, in Regimental Service Records; William L. Stoughton to Austin Blair, 18 April 1863, in Regimental Service Records; Lewis Childs to James Lowry, 16 January 1863, in Regimental Papers, Box 1999; *Reporter*, 21 March 1863, p. 3; "Justice Chadwick Replies to the Reporter," *Reporter*, 11 July 1863.

5. Hicks, "Personal Recollections," 521, 526–27.

6. *Diary of Ira Gillaspie*, 47–48; Daniel Rose to his brother, 28 February 1863, Masterson Collection; *Record of Michigan Volunteers*, 11:39.

7. Daniel Rose to Mark, 1 March 1863, Masterson Collection; *Diary of Ira Gillaspie*, 48.

8. James W. King to Sarah J. Babcock, 8 February 1863, King Collection; Daniel Rose to his mother, 28 February 1863, Masterson Collection.

9. Verbal jousting between Federal soldiers and Southern women was nothing unusual. James W. King to Sarah J. Babcock, 8 February and 12 May 1863, King Collection; Ellen Snell Coleman, "The Harding House," *Rutherford County Historical Society* 23 (Summer 1984), 1–13; Wiley, *Life of Billy Yank*, 107.

10. McPherson, *For Cause and Comrades*, 143–45; "From the Eleventh," *Reporter*, 28 March 1863; "From a Soldier," *Reporter*, 28 March 1863; Myron Bragg to his parents, 11 June 1863, Bragg Papers.

11. For more about Union soldiers' attitudes toward slaves and emancipation, see McPherson, "Slavery Must Be Cleaned Out," chap. 9 in *For Cause and Comrades*. James W. King to Sarah J. Babcock, 4 March 1863, King Collection.

12. Daniel Rose to his mother, 3 March and 12 March 1863, Masterson Collection; James Martin to his parents, 6 March 1863, Martin Letters; Benjamin F. Bordner to Mr. Austin and Sarah Hill, 3 March 1863, Bordner Papers.

13. James W. King to Sarah J. Babcock, 13 March 1863, King Collection; Daniel Rose to his mother, 12 March 1863, Masterson Collection.

14. "From the Eleventh Regiment," *Reporter*, 2 May 1863; "Sword Presentation," *Reporter*, 2 May 1863; James W. King to Sarah J. Babcock, 7 April 1863, King Collection.

15. The *Reporter* reprinted these speeches from the *Nashville Union*. "Sword Presentation," *Reporter*, 2 May 1863.

16. James Martin to his parents, 10 April 1863, Martin Letters.

17. James Martin to his parents, 28 March, 29 April, and 3 May 1863, Martin Letters; James W. King to Sarah J. Babcock, 7 April and 21 May 1863, King Collection.

18. Hicks, "Personal Recollections," 527; Robertson, *Michigan in the War*, 316–17; "That Stolen Cannon Again," *Shelby County* (OH) *Democrat*, 28 July 1893; Vallandigham, *Life of Clement Vallandigham*, 297–98.

19. James W. King to Sarah J. Babcock, 5 June 1863, King Collection; Union Provost Marshal's File of Papers Relating to Individual Civilians, 1861–67, microfilm publication M345, roll 241, National Archives.

20. "Our Correspondence from Murfreesboro," *Nashville Daily Press*, 6 June 1863.

21. "Our Correspondence from Murfreesboro," *Nashville Daily Press*, 6 June 1863; "A Military Execution in Gen. Rosecrans' Army," *New York Times*, 14 June 1863; James W. King to Sarah J. Babcock, 5 June 1863, King Collection.

22. For more about Pattison and McGee, see Thomas Fox, *Drummer Boy Willie McGee, Civil War Hero and Fraud* (Jefferson, NC: McFarland, 2008). Monthly Returns for June 1863-September 1864, Regimental Service Records; Myron Bragg to his parents, 14 May and 11 June 1863, Bragg Papers.

23. Benjamin F. Wells to Susan M. Wells, 24 June 1863, Wells Papers; Myron Bragg to his parents, 6 August 1863, Bragg Papers; *OR*, vol. 23, pt. 1, p. 523.

24. *OR*, vol. 23, pt. 1, pp. 442–43, 447–48; James W. King to Sarah J. Babcock, 19 July 1863, King Collection.

25. *OR*, vol. 23, pt. 1, pp. 442–43, 447–48, 523; James W. King to Sarah J. Babcock, 19 July 1863, King Collection; James Martin to his parents, 9 July 1863, Martin Letters.

26. *OR*, vol. 23, pt. 1, p. 443.

27. Platt was later paroled, and rose to the captaincy of Company D in July 1864. *OR*, vol. 23, pt. 1, pp. 443, 448; *Record of Michigan Volunteers*, 11:74.

28. *OR*, vol. 23, pt. 1, pp. 443–44, 446–48; James W. King to Sarah J. Babcock, 19 July 1863, King Collection; James Martin to his parents, 9 and 19 July 1863, Martin Letters.

29. *OR*, vol. 23, pt. 1, pp. 424–25, 444; "Army Correspondence," *Reporter*, 29 August 1863.

30. James W. King to Sarah J. Babcock, 19 July and 12 August 1863, King Collection; James Martin to his parents, 9 July 1863, Martin Letters; Belknap, *Michigan Organizations*, 109.

31. "Army Correspondence," *Reporter*, 29 August 1863.

32. "Army Correspondence," *Reporter*, 29 August 1863; James W. King to Sarah J. Babcock, 12, 21, and 23 August 1863, King Collection; Belknap, *Michigan Organizations*, 109; Daniel Rose to his mother, 21 August 1863, Masterson Collection.

33. "Army Correspondence," *Reporter*, 29 August 1863; James W. King to Sarah J. Babcock, 12, 21, and 23 August 1863, King Collection; Belknap, *Michigan Organizations*, 109; Daniel Rose to his mother, 21 August 1863, Masterson Collection.

34. Daniel Rose to his mother, 21 August 1863, Masterson Collection; James W. King to Sarah J. Babcock, 23 August 1863, King Collection.

35. John J. Bloom Diary, 24 August and 2 September 1863, Chickamauga and Chattanooga National Military Park, hereafter cited as Bloom Diary, CCNMP; *OR*, vol. 30, pt. 1, pp. 242, 325; Belknap, *Michigan Organizations*, 109; James W. King to Sarah J. Babcock, 5 September 1863, King Collection; Daniel Rose to his mother, 5 September 1863, Masterson Collection.

36. Belknap, *Michigan Organizations*, 109–10; *OR*, vol. 30, pt. 1, pp. 246, 325, 383–84; James W. King to Sarah J. Babcock, 5 September 1863, King Collection; Daniel Rose to his mother, 5 September 1863, Masterson Collection.
37. *OR*, vol. 30, pt. 1, pp. 325–26; Belknap, *Michigan Organizations*, 110.
38. *OR*, vol. 30, pt. 1, pp. 247, 326, 378; Belknap, *Michigan Organizations*, 110–11, 243; Melvin Mudge to James W. King, 9 February 1901, King Collection; *Record of Michigan Volunteers*, 11:63.
39. *OR*, vol. 30, pt. 1, p. 326; Belknap, *Michigan Organizations*, 111, 243–44; *OR*, vol. 30, pt. 2, pp. 27–28; *OR*, vol. 30, pt. 3, pp. 484–86.
40. *OR*, vol. 30, pt. 1, pp. 247, 271, 326; *OR*, vol. 30, pt. 3, p. 485; William Glenn Robertson, "The Chickamauga Campaign," *Blue & Gray*, Spring 2007, 20–22; Bloom Diary, 9 September 1863, CCNMP.

Chapter 6

1. *OR*, vol. 30, pt. 1, pp. 293, 301–2, 326; William Glenn Robertson, "The Chickamauga Campaign," *Blue & Gray*, Spring 2007, 20, 22; *OR*, vol. 30, pt. 2, p. 138.
2. *OR*, vol. 30, pt. 1, pp. 271–72, 327, 384; William Glenn Robertson, "The Chickamauga Campaign," *Blue & Gray*, Spring 2007, 19, 44.
3. Belknap, *Michigan Organizations*, 111, 244; *OR*, vol. 30, pt. 1, pp. 271–73, 284, 294–96, 327–28, 367, 384; *OR*, vol. 30, pt. 2, p. 138; William Glenn Robertson, "The Chickamauga Campaign," *Blue & Gray*, Spring 2007, 44–45.
4. *OR*, vol. 30, pt. 1, pp. 272–73, 284–85, 296, 327–28, 376–77; *OR*, vol. 30, pt. 2, p. 139; Belknap, *Michigan Organizations*, 244; Myron Bragg to his family, 27 September 1863, Bragg Papers.
5. *OR*, vol. 30, pt. 1, pp. 376–77; *OR*, vol. 30, pt. 2, p. 139; William Glenn Robertson, "The Chickamauga Campaign," *Blue & Gray*, Spring 2007, 45; Belknap, *Michigan Organizations*, 244; Myron Bragg to his family, 27 September 1863, Bragg Papers.
6. Belknap has Beatty covering Stanley's retreat instead of Starkweather, but Beatty's brigade was back at Bailey's Crossroads with the division train by this time. *OR*, vol. 30, pt. 1, pp. 328, 377; Belknap, *Michigan Organizations*, 112, 244–45; James Martin to his parents, 15 September 1863, Martin Letters.
7. Bloom Diary, 11 September 1863, CCNMP; Hicks, "Personal Recollections," 527–28; Daniel Rose to his mother, 13 September 1863, Masterson Collection.
8. James W. King, "11th Michigan Infantry," *Republican*, 11 January 1901; *OR*, vol. 30, pt. 1, pp. 273–74, 376, 384; William Glenn Robertson, "The Chickamauga Campaign," *Blue & Gray*, Spring 2007, 46; Belknap, *Michigan Organizations*, 112; "List of Deaths in Co. A," Regimental Service Records; "List of Deaths in Co. F," Regimental Service Records; Monthly Return for September 1863, Regimental Service Records; *Record of Michigan Volunteers*, 11:13–14, 11:32–33, 11:50; *Proceedings of Eighth Reunion*, 8.
9. *OR*, vol. 30, pt. 1, pp. 247–48, 328, 378; Bloom Diary, 12–16 September 1863, CCNMP; Belknap, *Michigan Organizations*, 112–13; James Martin to his parents, 15 September 1863, Martin Letters; Daniel Rose to his mother, 13 September 1863, Masterson Collection.
10. *OR*, vol. 30, pt. 1, pp. 248–49, 328, 347, 367, 378, 384; Belknap, *Michigan Organizations*, 245–46; *Proceedings of Eighth Reunion*, 8.
11. James Martin to his parents, 24 September 1863, Martin Letters; *OR*, vol. 30, pt. 1, p. 329; James W. King to Sarah J. Babcock, 4 October 1863, King Collection; Belknap, *Michigan Organizations*, 115, 246; Monthly Return for September 1863, Regimental Service Records; Powell, *Maps of Chickamauga*, 269.
12. *OR*, vol. 30, pt. 1, p. 249.
13. *OR*, vol. 30, pt. 1, pp. 329, 367, 378; Belknap, *Michigan Organizations*, 113, 246.
14. Powell, *Maps of Chickamauga*, 124–25; *OR*, vol. 30, pt. 1, p. 329; Belknap, *Michigan Organizations*, 247; Bloom Diary, 19 September 1863, CCNMP; James W. King, "11th Michigan Infantry," *Republican*, 11 January 1901; James Martin to his parents, 24 September 1863, Martin Letters; Hicks, "Personal Recollections," 528.
15. *OR*, vol. 30, pt. 1, pp. 69–70, 251, 329–30, 338, 355, 367, 378, 385, 1014–15; James W. King, "11th Michigan Infantry," *Republican*, 11 January 1901; Hicks, "Personal Recollections," 528–29; Belknap, *Michigan Organizations*, 114, 247.
16. Beatty, *Citizen Soldier*, 336–37; *OR*, vol. 30, pt. 1, pp. 329, 367–69, 378–79; Belknap, *Michigan Organizations*, 247–48; Bloom Diary, 20 September 1863, CCNMP.
17. *OR*, vol. 30, pt. 1, p. 379; Salling, *Louisianians*, 125; Belknap, *Michigan Organizations*, 114–15, 248.
18. Corporal Simeon D. Long relieved the general of his revolver, and Private John H. Spitler seized his field glass. The number of prisoners taken is unrecorded, but Bloom offered the round figure of 100. Beatty, *Citizen Soldier*, 337–38; Belknap, *Michigan Organizations*, 115, 248; Salling, *Louisianians*, 125–28, 134; Myron Bragg to his family, 27 September 1863, Bragg Papers; James Martin to his parents, 24 September 1863, Martin Letters; *OR*, vol. 30, pt. 1, p. 379; James W. King, "11th Michigan Infantry," *Republican*, 11 January 1901; William Glenn Robertson, "The Chickamauga Campaign," *Blue & Gray*, Summer 2008, 21; Hicks, "Personal Recollections," 529; Bloom Diary, 20 September 1863, CCNMP.
19. Salling, *Louisianians*, 131; Belknap, *Michigan Organizations*, 116, 249; James Martin to his parents, 24 September 1863, Martin Letters; William Glenn Robertson, "The Chickamauga Campaign," *Blue & Gray*, Summer 2008, 21–22; Cozzens, *This Terrible Sound*, 354–55; *OR*, vol. 30, pt. 1, p. 379; "The Second Brigade at Chickamauga," *Reporter*, 27 November 1863; Powell, *Maps of Chickamauga*, 156–57, 164–65; Beatty, *Citizen Soldier*, 338–39.
20. *OR*, vol. 30, pt. 1, pp. 255, 380; Belknap, *Michigan Organizations*, 116; Myron Bragg to his family, 27 September 1863, Bragg Papers.
21. *OR*, vol. 30, pt. 1, p. 380; Belknap, *Michigan Organizations*, 116–17, 249; James W. King, "11th Michigan Infantry," *Republican*, 11 January 1901; Powell, *Maps of Chickamauga*, 209; Haynie, *Nineteenth Illinois*, 230; William L. Stoughton to James A. Lowrie, 24 September 1863, in Regimental Papers.
22. Powell, *Maps of Chickamauga*, 226–27.
23. Shaver, *History of the Sixtieth*, 16; Haynie, *Nineteenth Illinois*, 226; Belknap, *Michigan Organizations*, 117; Powell, *Maps of Chickamauga*, 226–27, 231; *OR*, vol. 30, pt. 1, p. 381; Cozzens, *Terrible Sound*, 472–74.
24. Haynie, *Nineteenth Illinois*, 226; Belknap, *Michigan Organizations*, 117; Powell, *Maps of Chickamauga*, 226–27, 231; *OR*, vol. 30, pt. 1, p. 381; *OR*, vol. 30, pt. 2, pp. 305, 416, 505; Beyer and Keydel, *Deeds of Valor*, 1:270.
25. *OR*, vol. 30, pt. 2, p. 423; Powell, *Maps of Chickamauga*, 230–31, 276; Haynie, *Nineteenth Illinois*, 227,

241; James Martin to his parents, 24 September 1863, Martin Letters; "The Second Brigade at Chickamauga," *Reporter*, 27 November 1863. The letter cited from the *Reporter*, which was reprinted from the *Nashville Union*, uses phrases lifted directly from Stoughton's official report of the battle; it is likely that he authored the submission.

26. Stoughton's losses on Horseshoe can only be estimated since his brigade had already been heavily engaged that morning, but the Michiganders stated that the lion's share of their loss for the day occurred during the fighting withdrawal that followed General Adams's capture. The 11th lost sixty-six men total at Chickamauga and the 19th Illinois, seventy-one; all things considered it seems reasonable to estimate their combined loss against Gracie around 50 men. *OR*, vol. 30, pt. 2, pp. 416, 423–26; Dedmondt, *Flags of Alabama*, 111; Belknap, *Michigan Organizations*, 116; Powell, *Maps of Chickamauga*, 276; *OR*, vol. 30, pt. 1, p. 172.

27. Hicks, "Personal Recollections," 530; *OR*, vol. 30, pt. 1, p. 381; *OR*, vol. 30, pt. 2, p. 417; James Martin to his parents, 24 September 1863, Martin Letters; Myron Bragg to his family, 27 September 1863, Bragg Papers.

28. Belknap, *Michigan Organizations*, 118–19, 250; *OR*, vol. 30, pt. 1, pp. 370, 382; "The Second Brigade at Chickamauga," *Reporter*, 27 November 1863; James W. King, "11th Michigan Infantry," *Republican*, 11 January 1901; James Martin to his parents, 24 September 1863, Martin Letters; Beatty, *Citizen Soldier*, 343; Hicks, "Personal Recollections," 530; Haynie, *Nineteenth Illinois*, 221, 242–43; Thornton, *When Gallantry Was Commonplace*, 182–83; William Glenn Robertson, "The Chickamauga Campaign," *Blue & Gray*, Summer 2008, 48–49; Cozzens, *This Terrible Sound*, 503–508; Powell, *Maps of Chickamauga*, 234–39; Linus Squire to John Robertson, 22 December 1863, in Regimental Service Records.

29. James W. King, "11th Michigan Infantry," *Republican*, 11 January 1901; Hicks, "Personal Recollections," 531; *OR*, vol. 30, pt. 1, pp. 332, 382; William L. Stoughton to John Robertson, 25 November 1868, in Regimental Service Records; Bloom Diary, 21 September 1863, CCNMP; James Martin to his parents, 24 September 1863, Martin Letters; Powell, *Maps of Chickamauga*, 252–53.

30. Bloom's use of the term jackass in reference to the Confederate battery likely refers to the use of mules for lugging the artillery around. James W. King, "11th Michigan Infantry," *Republican*, 11 January 1901; Hicks, "Personal Recollections," 530–31; *OR*, vol. 30, pt. 1, pp. 332, 382; William L. Stoughton to John Robertson, 25 November 1868, in Regimental Service Records; Bloom Diary, 21 September 1863, CCNMP; James Martin to his parents, 24 September 1863, Martin Letters; Powell, *Maps of Chickamauga*, 252–53.

31. Beatty, *Citizen Soldier*, 345; Morton, *Artillery of Forrest's Cavalry*, 127; James W. King, "11th Michigan Infantry," *Republican*, 11 January 1901.

32. Belknap, *Michigan Organizations*, 125; *OR*, vol. 30, pt. 1, p. 380.

33. Haynie, *Nineteenth Illinois*, 243; *OR*, vol. 30, pt. 1, p. 172; Daniel Rose to his mother, 27 September 1863, Masterson Collection; James Martin to his parents, 24 September 1863, Martin Letters.

Chapter 7

1. *Proceedings of Eighth Reunion*, 8; James W. King to Sarah J. Babcock, 13 October 1863, King Collection; James Martin to his parents, 24 September 1863, Martin Letters; Daniel Rose to his mother, 4 October 1863, Masterson Collection; Haynie, *Nineteenth Illinois*, 242.

2. Bloom Diary, 22 September–7 October 1863, CCNMP; Hicks, "Personal Recollections," 531; James Martin to his parents, 24 September 1863, Martin Letters; Daniel Rose to his mother, 27 September 1863, Masterson Collection; Monthly Return for October 1863, Regimental Service Records; James W. King to Sarah J. Babcock, 23 September and 13 October 1863, King Collection.

3. "Reunion of Michigan Veterans," unidentified newspaper, 25 August 1873; James Martin to his parents, 24 September 1863, Martin Letters.

4. Solomon Shirey was exchanged promptly, returning to the regiment on November 9. James W. King to Sarah J. Babcock, 4 October 1863, King Collection; Hicks, "Personal Recollections," 531; James Martin to his parents, 15 and 26 October 1863, Martin Letters; James W. King, "The Charge of Mission Ridge," *Three Rivers* (MI) *Tribune*, 1 May 1896, hereafter cited as *Tribune*; Bloom Diary, 8–9 November 1863, CCNMP.

5. Fraternization and bartering between Union and Confederate troops is discussed in Wiley, "Billy Yank and Johnny Reb," chap. 13 in *Life of Billy Yank*. James W. King to Sarah J. Babcock, 4 October 1863, King Collection; James Martin to his parents, 15 and 26 October 1863, Martin Letters; *Record of Michigan Volunteers*, 11:31.

6. *Record of Michigan Volunteers*, 11:37, 11:87; Bloom Diary, 6 October 1863, CCNMP.

7. William Frankish to Mr. Snyder, 5 October 1863, Washington Irving Snyder Collection, 1862–1898, William L. Clements Library, University of Michigan.

8. James W. King, "11th Michigan Infantry," *Republican*, 11 January 1901; Bloom Diary, 28–29 September 1863, CCNMP; *Record of Michigan Volunteers*, 11:21, 11:103; Monthly Returns for September and October 1863, and June and July 1864, Regimental Service Records; David Clase's Pension Application, Application No. 148483, Certificate No. 123428, National Archives; Daniel Rose to his mother, 8 November 1863, Masterson Collection.

9. Monthly Return for October 1863, Regimental Service Records; *Record of Michigan Volunteers*, 11:48; Bloom Diary, 18 February 1864, CCNMP.

10. James Martin to his parents, 26 October 1863, Martin Letters; James W. King, "The Charge of Mission Ridge," *Tribune*, 1 May 1896.

11. James W. King, "The Charge of Mission Ridge," *Tribune*, 1 May 1896.

12. Bloom Diary, 26–28 October 1863, CCNMP; James W. King to Sarah J. Babcock, 30 October 1863, King Collection.

13. Bloom Diary, 19 November 1863, CCNMP; James W. King to Sarah J. Babcock, 20 November 1863, King Collection.

14. James W. King, "The Charge of Mission Ridge," *Tribune*, 1 May 1896; Bloom Diary, 22–24 November 1863, CCNMP; James Martin to his parents, 28 November 1863, Martin Letters; Benjamin F. Bordner to his brother and sister, 1 December 1863, Bordner Papers; James W. King, "Truth Is Stranger Than Fiction," 2–3, King Collection; Hicks, "Personal Recollections," 532.

15. James W. King to J.C. Burrows, 17 February 1902, King Collection.

16. James W. King, "11th Michigan Infantry," *Republican*, 11 January 1901; "Letter from the Eleventh Mich.," *Reporter*, 12 December 1863; Hicks, "Personal Recollections," 532.

17. *OR*, vol. 31, pt. 2, pp. 459, 479–82.

18. James Martin to his parents, 28 November 1863, Martin Letters; James W. King, "The Charge of Mission Ridge," *Tribune*, 1 May 1896; *OR*, vol. 31, pt. 2, pp. 479–80; Benjamin F. Bordner to his brother and sister, 1 December 1863, Bordner Papers; Hewett, *Supplement to Official Records*, vol. 6, pt. 1, pp. 136, 184–85 (hereafter cited as *ORS*); Cozzens, *Shipwreck of Their Hopes*, 248.

19. James W. King, "The Charge of Mission Ridge," *Tribune*, 1 May 1896.

20. According to Captain Keegan, Bennett placed Keegan in command of the regiment prior to the charge, yet still fought in the ranks, determined to meet his own fate. However, no other source mentions this change in command, and on the contrary, other survivors explicitly referred to Bennett dying leading his regiment. James W. King to J.C. Burrows, 17 February 1902, King Collection; James W. King's Medal of Honor Nomination File, Record & Pension Office, Document Number 670252, National Archives; Bloom Diary, 25 November 1863, CCNMP; Daniel Rose to his brother, 1 December 1863, Masterson Collection.

21. James W. King, "The Charge of Mission Ridge," *Tribune*, 1 May 1896; Daniel Rose to his mother, 28 November 1863, Masterson Collection; James W. King's Medal of Honor Nomination File, Record & Pension Office, Document Number 670252, National Archives; James W. King to J.C. Burrows, 17 February 1902, King Collection.

22. James W. King's Medal of Honor Nomination File, Record & Pension Office, Document Number 670252, National Archives; James W. King to J.C. Burrows, 17 February 1902, King Collection; James W. King, "The Charge of Mission Ridge," *Tribune*, 1 May 1896; Hicks, "Personal Recollections," 532–33; Hewett, *ORS*, vol. 6, pt. 1, pp. 124, 137, 142, 150, 152; *OR*, vol. 31, pt. 2, pp. 482, 485–86, 488.

23. Hicks, "Personal Recollections," 533; James W. King, "The Charge of Mission Ridge," *Tribune*, 1 May 1896; Daniel Rose to his brother, 1 December 1863, Masterson Collection.

24. Hewett, *ORS*, vol. 6, pt. 1, p. 143; Lindsley, *Military Annals of Tennessee*, 188–89; Johnson, *Body of Brave Men*, 451; Robertson, *Michigan in the War*, 319.

25. James Martin to his parents, 28 November 1863, Martin Letters; James W. King, "The Charge of Mission Ridge," *Tribune*, 1 May 1896; Hicks, "Personal Recollections," 533; *OR*, vol. 31, pt. 2, p. 485; Belknap, *Michigan Organizations*, 122.

26. Hewett, *ORS*, vol. 6, pt. 1, pp. 107–9, 137, 147–48; Belknap, *Michigan Organizations*, 121; James W. King's Medal of Honor Nomination File, Record & Pension Office, Document Number 670252, National Archives.

27. Not surprisingly, each of the volunteer regiments insisted that theirs was the first unit on the summit. Belknap, *Michigan Organizations*, 121; James W. King's Medal of Honor Nomination File, Record & Pension Office, Document Number 670252, National Archives; Hicks, "Personal Recollections," 534; James W. King, "The Charge of Mission Ridge," *Tribune*, 1 May 1896; Hewett, *ORS*, vol. 6, pt. 1, pp. 116–17, 126, 146–47, 187–88; *OR*, vol. 31, pt. 2, pp. 480, 484, 486.

28. *Proceedings of Eighth Reunion*, 8; James Martin to his parents, 28 November 1863, Martin Letters; Monthly Return for November 1863, Regimental Service Records; Hicks, "Personal Recollections," 534; *OR*, vol. 31, pt. 2, p. 481; *ORS*, vol. 6, pt. 1, pp. 110, 183, 186; Benjamin F. Bordner to his brother and sister, 1 December 1863, Bordner Papers; Daniel Rose to his brother, 1 December 1863, Masterson Collection.

29. *OR*, vol. 31, pt. 2, pp. 460, 480; Benjamin F. Bordner to his brother and sister, 1 December 1863, Bordner Papers; James Martin to his parents, 28 November 1863, Bloom Diary, 26 November 1863, CCNMP; Martin Letters; Daniel Rose to his brother, 1 December 1863, Masterson Collection; *Annual Report Adjutant General 1864*, 148.

30. Hicks, "Personal Recollections," 536; James Martin to his father, 8 December 1863, Martin Letters; Benjamin Bordner to his sister, 8 December 1863, Bordner Papers; Monthly Returns for November 1862, and December 1863, Regimental Service Records; Ephraim G. Hall to William McMichael, 9 March 1864, in Box 1999, Regimental Papers; Linus T. Squire to John Robertson, 22 December 1863, in Box 1999, Regimental Papers; Daniel Rose to his mother, 24 December 1863, and 24 January and 1 February 1864, Masterson Collection.

31. Many of the transfers from the 9th Michigan were detailed for other duties. Bloom noted the arrival of only thirty of these men on February 12. Hicks, "Personal Recollections," 536; Monthly Returns for January-April 1864, Regimental Service Records; Ephraim G. Hall to William McMichael, 9 March 1864, in Box 1999, Regimental Papers; *Reporter*, 23 January 1864, p. 2; Daniel Rose to his mother, 24 December 1863, and 24 January and 1 February 1864, Masterson Collection; Bloom Diary, 12 February 1864, CCNMP.

32. For more about Union soldiers and reenlistment, see McPherson, *For Cause and Comrades*, 172–75. Daniel Rose to his mother, 4 January, 4 February, 28 February, and 29 April 1864, Masterson Collection; *Annual Report Adjutant General 1864*, 6, 150, 549; James W. King to Sarah J. Babcock, 12 and 21 April 1864, King Collection; Susan M. Wells to Benjamin F. Wells, 8 July 1864, Wells Papers; Bloom Diary, 9 December 1863 and 25 February 1864, CCNMP; McPherson, *For Cause and Comrades*, 172–75.

33. Fisher's wife became pregnant almost as soon as he returned to Michigan. They named the child Philip Sheridan Fisher. Henry Fisher never regained his health, and passed away on July 7, 1866, at age twenty-eight. Monthly Return for January 1864, Regimental Service Records; Henry S. Fisher's Pension File, Application No. 131445, Certificate No. 91688, National Archives; Daniel Rose to his mother, 15 January 1864, Masterson Collection; Bloom Diary, 20–21 January 1864, CCNMP.

34. For more about the USCT and the associated examination boards, see Glatthaar, *Forged in Battle: The Civil War Alliance of Black Soldiers and White Officers* (New York: Free Press, 1990). White soldiers' views regarding black troops are discussed in Wiley, *Life of Billy Yank*, 119–23. Monthly Returns for January-April 1864, Regimental Service Records; Renard, "Selection of White Officers," 162–63, 175–77; Daniel Rose to his mother, 15 January 1864, Masterson Collection; Benjamin Bordner to A. Hill, 7 February 1864, Bordner Papers; James W. King to Sarah J. Babcock, 12 April 1864, King Collection; *Record of Michigan Volunteers*, 11:10, 11:32, 11:98, 11:103.

35. Monthly Returns for January-April 1864, Regimental Service Records; "List of Changes in Commissioned Officers, 11th Michigan Vol. Infantry during the Month of May 1864," Box 1999, Regimental Papers; Bloom Diary, 29 April 1864, CCNMP.

36. Benjamin Bordner to A. Hill, 7 February 1864, Bordner Papers; Nathan Adams to Emily Parsons, 18 January 1864, Adams Letters; Daniel Rose to his mother, 4 January, 1 February, and 12 March 1864, Masterson Collection; Marsh Diary, 3 March 1864, Guy Marsh Collection, 1861–1865, Western Michigan University

Archives and Regional History Collections, hereafter cited as Marsh Collection; Bloom Diary, 3 March 1864, CCNMP.

37. *Annual Report Adjutant General 1864*, 148; Daniel Rose to his mother, 20 March 1864, Masterson Collection; Marsh Diary, 15 March, 18 March, 23 March, 31 March, and 5 April 1864, Marsh Collection; James W. King to Sarah J. Babcock, 18 March 1864, King Collection; Bloom Diary, 19 March 1864, CCNMP; Hicks, "Personal Recollections," 537.

38. Daniel Rose to his mother, 28 February, 26 March, and 5 April 1864, Masterson Collection; James W. King to Sarah J. Babcock, 12 April 1864, King Collection; Bloom Diary, 31 March–5 April 1864, CCNMP; "From the Eleventh," *Reporter*, 9 April 1864; Benjamin Bordner to A. Hill, 7 February 1864, Bordner Papers; James Martin to his father, 8 December 1863, Martin Letters.

39. Johnson, *Body of Brave Men*, 478–79.

40. Bloom Diary, 9 April–6 May 1864 passim, CCNMP; Daniel Rose to his mother, 29 April 1864, Masterson Collection; James W. King to Sarah J. Babcock, 1 May 1864, King Collection.

Chapter 8

1. Bloom Diary, 3 May 1864, CCNMP; Daniel Rose to his mother, 4 May 1864, Masterson Collection.

2. "The Atlanta Campaign," pp. 5–6, John F. Downey Papers, 1864–1936, University of Minnesota Archives, Minneapolis, hereafter cited as Downey Papers.

3. Bloom Diary, 6 May 1864, CCNMP.

4. Bloom Diary, 3 May 1864, CCNMP; *OR*, vol. 38, pt. 1, pp. 560, 570; Johnson, *Body of Brave Men*, 486, 489; Marsh Diary, 7 May 1864, Marsh Collection.

5. "The Atlanta Campaign," pp. 5–6, Downey Papers.

6. *OR*, vol. 38, pt. 1, p. 570; "The Atlanta Campaign," pp. 9–10, Downey Papers; Hicks, "Personal Recollections," 538.

7. *OR*, vol. 38, pt. 1, pp. 560, 570; Marsh Diary, 12 May 1864, Marsh Collection; James Martin to his parents, 20 May 1864, Martin Letters.

8. William E. Raymond to Duke, 5 June 1864, Raymond Papers; Marsh Diary, 14 May 1864, Marsh Collection; Hicks, "Personal Recollections," 538; *OR*, vol. 38, pt. 1, pp. 560, 570; *Record of Michigan Volunteers*, 11:12, 11:56, 11:58; Benjamin F. Bordner to his brother George, 22 May 1864, Bordner Papers; *Proceedings of Eighth Reunion*, 9; "List of Changes in Commissioned Officers," May 1864, Regimental Papers, Box 1999; Monthly Return for June 1864, Regimental Service Records.

9. *OR*, vol. 38, pt. 1, p. 560; "The Atlanta Campaign," p. 16, Downey Papers; Marsh Diary, 16 May 1864, Marsh Collection.

10. Hundred Days Men were soldiers who volunteered in 1864 to serve for 100 days. Benjamin F. Bordner to his brother George, 22 May 1864, Bordner Papers; James Martin to his parents, 20 May 1864, Martin Letters.

11. Belknap, *Michigan Organizations*, 125; Daniel Rose to his mother, 22 May 1864, Masterson Collection.

12. Marsh Diary, 21 May 1864, Marsh Collection; *OR*, vol. 38, pt. 1, pp. 561, 570; "The Atlanta Campaign," pp. 21–22, Downey Papers.

13. "The Atlanta Campaign," pp. 21–22, Downey Papers.

14. *OR*, vol. 38, pt. 1, pp. 561, 567, 570–71; Marsh Diary, 30 May 1864, Marsh Collection; *Record of Michigan Volunteers*, 11:12, 11:49, 11:73; "The Atlanta Campaign," pp. 23–24, 29–30, Downey Papers; Daniel Rose to his mother, 2 June 1864, Masterson Collection.

15. Daniel Rose to his mother, 2 June 1864, Masterson Collection; Sherman, *Memoirs*, 56–57.

16. Daniel Rose to his mother, 9 June 1864, Masterson Collection; Marsh Diary, 5 June 1864, Marsh Collection; "The Atlanta Campaign," p. 23, Downey Papers; Daniel Rose to his mother, 9 June 1864, Masterson Collection; *OR*, vol. 38, pt. 1, p. 571.

17. *OR*, vol. 38, pt. 1, p. 571; "The Atlanta Campaign," pp. 26–27, Downey Papers.

18. *OR*, vol. 38, pt. 1, pp. 561, 571; "The Atlanta Campaign," p. 29, Downey Papers; Hicks, "Personal Recollections," 540.

19. For more discussion about the importance of mail to morale, see McPherson, *For Cause and Comrades*, 132–33. James W. King to Sarah J. Babcock, 20 and 25 June 1864, King Collection; Daniel Rose to his mother, 9 June 1864, Masterson Collection; Susan M. Wells to Benjamin F. Wells, 22 July 1864, Wells Papers.

20. Daniel Rose to his mother, 9 June 1864, Masterson Collection; James W. King to Sarah J. Babcock, 20 June, 24 June, and 1 July 1864, King Collection.

21. Daniel Rose to his mother, 26 June 1864, Masterson Collection; "The Atlanta Campaign," pp. 31–33, Downey Papers.

22. Daniel Rose to his mother, 6 July 1864, Masterson Collection; James W. King to Sarah J. Babcock, 7 July 1864, King Collection; *OR*, vol. 38, pt. 1, p. 561; "The Atlanta Campaign," p. 42, Downey Papers.

23. James W. King to Sarah J. Babcock, 7 July 1864, King Collection; "The Atlanta Campaign," p. 42, Downey Papers; Daniel Rose to his mother, 6 July 1864, Masterson Collection; *OR*, vol. 38, pt. 1, pp. 561, 578; Johnson, *Body of Brave Men*, 511; *Record of Michigan Volunteers*, 11:6, 11:8, 11:10, 11:29, 11:34, 11:59, 11:69, 11:70, 11:76, 11:81, 11:83, 11:102; Robertson, *Michigan in the War*, 321.

24. James W. King to Sarah J. Babcock, 16 July 1864, King Collection; Daniel Rose to his mother, 6 July 1864, Masterson Collection; "The Atlanta Campaign," p. 42, Downey Papers.

25. Later comments by Hicks lend credence to Downey's claim regarding Keegan, and indicate that this was not an isolated incident. Both men delicately referred to Keegan not by name, but as major—a rank that had been vacant in the regiment since Bennett's death on Missionary Ridge. Keegan was never mustered as major, but he was the senior captain, and the only other individual Downey and Hicks could have referred to as major was John R. Edie of the regulars, who was not involved in the July 4 charge. Hicks's later negative comments about the unnamed major, regarding the Battle of Utoy Creek on August 7, also cannot refer to Edie since Hicks assumed command of the 11th Michigan as a direct result of the major's absence. This could have been the case only with Keegan; Edie was commanding the entire brigade. *Record of Michigan Volunteers* lists Keegan as receiving a major's commission effective November 25, 1863, but regimental papers and his compiled service record show that he remained a captain through muster out. "The Atlanta Campaign," p. 43, Downey Papers; Hicks, "Personal Recollections," 541–42; Monthly Returns for May-August 1864, Regimental Service Records; *Record of Michigan Volunteers*, 11:53; Patrick H. Keegan's Compiled Military Service File, National Archives.

26. "The Atlanta Campaign," p. 45, Downey Papers.
27. Marsh Diary, 10–16 July 1864, Marsh Collection; Daniel Rose to his mother, 13 July 1864, Masterson Collection; *OR*, vol. 38, pt. 1, pp. 562, 571.
28. Stoughton penned an undated letter sometime after the war to the adjutant general (presumably Robertson) in which he put the regimental loss at Peachtree Creek at two killed and nine wounded. Robertson's *Michigan in the War* gives the same numbers. But other regimental records, and *Record of Michigan Volunteers*, indicate a bloodless engagement for the 11th Michigan. *OR*, vol. 38, pt. 1, p. 562; William L. Stoughton to adjutant general, undated, in Regimental Service Records; Monthly Return for July 1864, Regimental Service Records; Robertson, *Michigan in the War*, 321.
29. *OR*, vol. 38, pt. 1, pp. 562, 572; Daniel Rose to his mother, 23 July 1864, Masterson Collection; Aaron B. White to his parents, 24 July 1864, Aaron B. White Papers, 1863–1864, Bentley Historical Library, hereafter cited as White Papers.
30. James W. King, "Truth Is Stranger Than Fiction," 7–10, King Collection; Daniel Rose to his mother, 29 July 1864, Masterson Collection; Aaron B. White to his parents, 24 July 1864, White Papers.
31. James W. King, "Truth Is Stranger Than Fiction," 7–10, King Collection; Daniel Rose to his mother, 29 July 1864, Masterson Collection; Aaron B. White to his parents, 24 July 1864, White Papers; Monthly Return for July 1864, Regimental Service Records; *OR*, vol. 38, pt. 1, p. 562.
32. James Martin to his parents, 25 July 1864, Martin Letters; *OR*, vol. 38, pt. 1, p. 562; "The Atlanta Campaign," pp. 58–59, Downey Papers.
33. "The Atlanta Campaign," p. 57, Downey Papers.
34. "The Atlanta Campaign," pp. 57–58, Downey Papers; *OR*, vol. 38, pt. 1, pp. 533, 562, 572, 579.
35. *OR*, vol. 38, pt. 1, p. 563; McPherson, *For Cause and Comrades*, 81; "The Atlanta Campaign," pp. 58–59, Downey Papers.
36. Oddly, Keegan was noted in the regiment's monthly report as being sent on August 7 for recruiting duty in Michigan, just weeks before the regiment was due to return home. Possibly this was Mudge's way of tactfully removing Keegan from the regiment after this charge—or it could be a clerical error, since *OR* does not indicate that anyone replaced Keegan in command of the 11th. Hicks mentions that Keegan was with the regiment on August 26. It is unlikely that Keegan would have returned from recruiting in the Great Lakes State so soon. *OR*, vol. 38, pt. 1, pp. 94, 510, 562, 572, 579–80; Monthly Returns for July-August 1864, Regimental Service Records; "The Atlanta Campaign," pp. 59–60, Downey Papers; Hicks, "Personal Recollections," 541–42.
37. *OR*, vol. 38, pt. 1, pp. 562, 567, 572; Hicks, "Personal Recollections," 541.
38. "The Atlanta Campaign," p. 60, Downey Papers.
39. "The Atlanta Campaign," pp. 61–62, Downey Papers.
40. James Martin to his father, 10 August 1864, Martin Letters.
41. *OR*, vol. 38, pt. 1, pp. 563, 572–73; Hicks "Personal Recollections," 541–42; Melvin B. Mudge to William D. Whipple, 3 August 1864, in Regimental Papers, Box 1999.
42. Hicks, "Personal Recollections," 542; *OR*, vol. 38, pt. 5, pp. 854–56; Rose Diary, 9 and 12 September 1864, Masterson Collection.
43. Hicks, "Personal Recollections," 542; *OR*, vol. 38, pt. 5, pp. 854–56; Rose Diary, 9 and 12 September 1864, Masterson Collection.

44. Rose Diary, 19–23 September 1864, Masterson Collection; "That Stolen Cannon Again," *Shelby County* (OH) *Democrat*, 28 July 1893.
45. "That Stolen Cannon Again," *Shelby County* (OH) *Democrat*, 28 July 1893.
46. "That Stolen Cannon Again," *Shelby County* (OH) *Democrat*, 28 July 1893; Robertson, *Michigan in the War*, 317.
47. "That Stolen Cannon Again," *Shelby County* (OH) *Democrat*, 28 July 1893. Key parts of Mudge's account are supported by Hicks, "Personal Recollections," 542; Rose Diary, 24 September 1864, Masterson Collection; and Robertson, *Michigan in the War*, 317. The cited newspaper article, containing Mudge's account, also discussed locals' recollections of this event and did not dispute the details of Mudge's story, which is far and away the most detailed source for this occasion.
48. "That Stolen Cannon Again," *Shelby County* (OH) *Democrat*, 28 July 1893; Hicks, "Personal Recollections," 542; Robertson, *Michigan in the War*, 317; "Veteran Reunion at Colon," *Tribune*, 25 August 1891.
49. "That Stolen Cannon Again," *Shelby County* (OH) *Democrat*, 28 July 1893; Hicks, "Personal Recollections," 542; Rose Diary, 24 September 1864, Masterson Collection; Robertson, *Michigan in the War*, 317; "Veteran Reunion at Colon," *Tribune*, 25 August 1891.
50. "That Stolen Cannon Again," *Shelby County* (OH) *Democrat*, 28 July 1893; Howard, *Life of Rutherford Hayes*, 182–83; Hicks, "Personal Recollections," 542.
51. Hicks, "Personal Recollections," 542; "Last Victory of the Eleventh Regiment Over the Rebels," *Reporter*, 1 October 1864; Rose Diary, 24 September 1864, Masterson Collection; "Veteran Reunion at Colon," *Tribune*, 25 August 1891; "Report of a Gun After Twenty-Eight Years," *Shelby County* (OH) *Democrat*, 26 May 1893.
52. "That Stolen Cannon Again," *Shelby County* (OH) *Democrat*, 28 July 1893; "The Grand Republican Rally at White Pigeon," *Reporter*, 1 October 1864; Rose Diary, 24–25 September 1864, Masterson Collection.
53. There are minor discrepancies between the casualty numbers given in the referenced sources. *Record of Michigan Volunteers*, 11:3; Robertson, *Michigan in the War*, 321–22; *Annual Report Adjutant General 1864*, 149–50; James W. King, "11th Michigan Infantry," *Republican*, 11 January 1901.
54. James W. King, "Reunion of Michigan Veterans," unidentified newspaper, 25 August 1873.

Epilogue

1. The other two events Stoughton listed were the ambush of Daniel Weisiger Adams's brigade at Chickamauga, and the regiment's charge up Missionary Ridge (the colonel, like many of his soldiers, asserted that the 11th Michigan was first to the summit). William L. Stoughton to James W. King, 20 December 1879, in Regimental Service Records.
2. The arms and sword from Stoughton's statue have since been broken off. Other monuments to the regiment were constructed at the location of General Adams's capture, and at the site where the 11th surmounted Missionary Ridge. The unit's only representation on the Stones River battlefield is a marker honoring all Michigan soldiers present at that battle. *Annual Report Attorney General 1883*, 79; Lord and Brown, *Debates and Proceedings*, 1:1.

3. Knapp and Bonner, *Illustrated History of Lenawee*, 234.
4. Whitney and Bonner, *History of Lenawee County*, 1:242–43.
5. *Kansas*, 2:1049–51.
6. *Grand Rapids* (MI) *Press*, 2 October 1911; *History of St. Joseph County, Michigan*, 44; "Death of Captain E.G. Hall," *Lansing Republican*, 14 April 1881; James W. King to Sarah J. Babcock, 4 February 1865, King Collection.
7. James W. King to Sarah J. King, 6 October 1866, 18 April 1869, and 16 May 1869, King Collection; "Opinions of James W. King," *Three Rivers* (MI) *News Reporter*, 15 October 1903; Washington, *Records of Field Offices*, 8, 10; "Local News Brevities: At the Capital," *Lansing Republican*, 2 July 1881; *History of Branch County 1979*, 441.
8. Hicks, "Personal Recollections," 536–37.
9. Downey Papers.
10. James W. King, "Reunion of Michigan Veterans," unidentified newspaper, 25 August 1873; "Veteran Reunion at Colon," *Three Rivers* (MI) *Tribune*, 25 August 1891; "Re-Union of the 11th. Mich.," *Mendon* (MI) *Weekly Globe*, 25 August 1893; Regimental Reunion Records, Kalamazoo Valley Museum.
11. John F. Downey to Edward Coats, 17 August 1932, in Regimental Reunion Records.
12. Regimental Reunion Records.

Appendix A

1. *Record of Michigan Volunteers*, 11:4–106 passim.
2. *Fifth Annual Report*, 717.

Appendix B

1. Gould, *Investigations*, 58.
2. In order to compare apples to apples, the Union and Michigan means in Gould are adjusted to reflect the soldiers' ages as of their last birthdays upon enlistment. Gould, *Investigations*, 39, 53.

Bibliography

Archives

Archives of Michigan, Lansing
Records of the Michigan Military Establishment. Record Group 59-14.
Bentley Historical Library, University of Michigan, Ann Arbor
Bordner, Benjamin F., Papers, 1862–1864.
Fox, William H., Letters, 1862–1863.
Martin, James. Letters, 1861–1864.
Raymond, William E., Papers, 1863–1864.
Wells Family Papers, 1857–1902.
White, Aaron B., Papers, 1863–1864.
Chickamauga and Chattanooga National Military Park, Fort Oglethorpe, GA
John J. Bloom Diary.
Clarke Historical Library, Central Michigan University, Mt. Pleasant
King, Doris L., Collection, 1822–1877.
Kalamazoo Valley Museum, Kalamazoo, MI
Civil War Reunion Records, 11th Michigan Volunteer Infantry.
Library of Michigan, Lansing
Adams, Nathan. Civil War Letters, 1861–1865.
National Archives and Records Administration, Washington, D.C.
Records of the Adjutant General's Office, 1780s–1917. Record Group 94.
Records of the Department of Veterans Affairs. Record Group 15.
University Archives & Historical Collections, Michigan State University, East Lansing
Wilson Family Papers, 1863–1925.
University of Minnesota Archives, Minneapolis
John F. Downey Papers, 1864–1936.
U.S. Army Military History Institute, Carlisle, PA
Bragg Family Papers, 1861–1864.
Western Michigan University Archives and Regional History Collections, Kalamazoo
King, James W., Collection, 1861–1903.
Marsh, Guy. Collection, 1864.
Masterson, Carroll. Collection, 1861–1865.
Watkins, Bertha. Collection, 1841–1919.
William L. Clements Library, University of Michigan, Ann Arbor
Snyder, Washington Irving. Collection, 1862–1898.

Newspapers

Constantine (MI) *Weekly Mercury & St. Joseph County Advertiser*
Grand Rapids (MI) *Press*
Lansing (MI) *Republican*
Lansing (MI) *Weekly State Republican*
Nashville Daily Press
New York Times
Shelby County (OH) *Democrat*
Sturgis (MI) *Journal*
Three Rivers (MI) *News Reporter*
Three Rivers (MI) *Reporter*
Three Rivers (MI) *Tribune*
Three Rivers (MI) *Western Chronicle*

Books and Articles

Annual Report of the Adjutant General of the State of Michigan for the Year 1864. Lansing, MI: John A. Kerr, 1865.
Beatty, John. *The Citizen-Soldier; Or, Memoirs of a Volunteer*. Cincinnati: Wilstach, Baldwin & Co., 1897.
Belknap, Charles E. *History of the Michigan Organizations at Chickamauga, Chattanooga, and Missionary Ridge*, 2d ed. Lansing, MI: Robert Smith, 1899.
Beyer, Walter H., and Oscar F. Keydel, eds. *Deeds of Valor...*, Vol. 1. Detroit: Perrien-Keydel, 1907.
Bickham, W.D. *Rosecrans' Campaign with the Fourteenth Army Corps, or the Army of the Cumberland: A Narrative of Personal Observations, with an Appendix, Consisting of Official Reports of the*

Battle of Stone River. Cincinnati: Moore, Wilstach, Keys, 1863.

Bingham, S.D. *Early History of Michigan with Biographies of State Officers, Members of Congress, Judges and Legislators*. Lansing: Thorp and Godfrey, 1888.

Boatner, Mark Mayo. *The Civil War Dictionary*, rev. ed. New York: Vintage, 1991.

"Capt. E.G. Hall." *Student's Journal* 10, no. 5 (May 1881): 3–4.

Castel, Albert. *Decision in the West: The Atlanta Campaign of 1864*. Lawrence: University Press of Kansas, 1992.

Coleman, Ellen Snell. "The Harding House." *Rutherford County Historical Society* 23 (Summer 1984): 1–13.

Connelly, Thomas Lawrence. *Autumn of Glory: The Army of Tennessee, 1862–1865*. Baton Rouge: Louisiana State University Press, 2001.

Cozzens, Peter. *No Better Place to Die: The Battle of Stones River*. Urbana: University of Illinois Press, 1991.

Cozzens, Peter. *The Shipwreck of Their Hopes: The Battles for Chattanooga*. Urbana: University of Illinois Press, 1996.

Cozzens, Peter. *This Terrible Sound: The Battle of Chickamauga*. Urbana: University of Illinois Press, 1992.

Daniel, Larry J. *Battle of Stones River: The Forgotten Conflict Between the Confederate Army of Tennessee and the Union Army of the Cumberland*. Baton Rouge: Louisiana State University Press, 2012.

Dedmondt, Glenn. *The Flags of Civil War Alabama*. Gretna, LA: Pelican, 2001.

Duke, Basil W. *History of Morgan's Cavalry*. Cincinnati: Miami Printing, 1867.

Evans, E. Raymond. *The Battle of Davis' Crossroads: September 10–11, 1863*. Signal Mountain, TN: CASI, 2008.

Faust, Patricia L., ed. *Historical Times Illustrated Encyclopedia of the Civil War*. New York: Harper Perennial, 1991.

Fifth Annual Report of the Chief of the Bureau of Military Statistics, with Appendices. Albany: C. Van Benthuysen & Sons, 1868.

Fitch, John. *Annals of the Army of the Cumberland: Comprising Biographies, Descriptions of Departments, Accounts of Expeditions, Skirmishes, and Battles...*, 5th ed. Philadelphia: J.B. Lippincott, 1864.

Fox, Thomas. *Drummer Boy Willie McGee, Civil War Hero and Fraud*. Jefferson, NC: McFarland, 2008.

Furoughi, Andrea R. *Go If You Think It Your Duty: A Minnesota Couple's Civil War Letters*. St. Paul: Minnesota Historical Society, 2008.

Gillaspie, Ira. *The Diary of Ira Gillaspie of the Eleventh Michigan Infantry*. Edited by Daniel B. Weber. Mount Pleasant: Central Michigan University Press, 1965.

Glatthaar, Joseph T. *Forged in Battle: The Civil War Alliance of Black Soldiers and White Officers*. New York: Free Press, 1990.

Gould, Benjamin Apthorp. *Investigations in the Military and Anthropological Statistics of American Soldiers*. New York: Hurd and Houghton, 1869.

Gracie, Archibald. *The Truth about Chickamauga*. Boston: Houghton Mifflin, 1911.

Greene, Jonathan H. *A Desperado in Arizona 1858–1860*. Santa Fe: Stagecoach Press, 1964.

Guelzo, Allen C. *Gettysburg: The Last Invasion*. New York: Vintage, 2013.

Guernsey, Alfred H., and Henry Mills Alden. *Harper's Pictorial History of the Great Rebellion*, 2 vols. New York: Harper, 1866–68.

Haynie, J. Henry, ed. *The Nineteenth Illinois: A Memoir of a Regiment of Volunteer Infantry Famous in the Civil War of Fifty Years Ago for Its Drill, Bravery, and Distinguished Services*. Chicago: M.A. Donahue, 1912.

Hewett, Janet B., et al., eds. *Supplement to the Official Records of the Union and Confederate Armies*, Vol. 6, Part 1. Wilmington, NC: Broadfoot, 1996.

Hicks, Borden M. "Personal Recollections of the War of the Rebellion." In *Glimpses of the Nation's Struggle, Sixth Series: Papers Read Before the Minnesota Commandery of the Military Order of the Loyal Legion of the United States, January 1903–1908*, 519–44. Minneapolis: Aug. Davis, 1909.

History of Branch County, Michigan. Coldwater, MI: Branch County Historical Society, 1979.

History of Branch County, Michigan, with Illustrations and Biographical Sketches of Some of Its Prominent Men and Pioneers. Philadelphia: Everts and Abbott, 1879.

History of Hillsdale County, Michigan, with Illustrations and Biographical Sketches of Some of Its Prominent Men and Pioneers. Philadelphia: Everts and Abbott, 1879.

History of St. Joseph County, Michigan, with Illustrations Descriptive of Its Scenery, Palatial Residences, Public Buildings, Fine Blocks, and Important Manufactories, from Original Sketches by Artists of the Highest Ability. Philadelphia: L.H. Everts, 1877.

Howard, J.Q. *The Life, Public Services and Select Speeches of Rutherford B. Hayes*. Cincinnati: Robert Clarke, 1876.

Index to the Executive Documents of the Senate of the United States at the Special Session of March, 1863. Washington, D.C.: Government Printing Office, 1863.

Johnson, Mark W. *That Body of Brave Men: The U.S. Regular Infantry and the Civil War in the West*. Cambridge, MA: Da Capo, 2003.

Kansas: A Cyclopedia of State History, Embracing Events, Institutions, Industries, Counties, Cities, Towns, Prominent Persons, Etc., Vol. 2. Chicago: Standard, 1912.

Knapp, John I., and R.I. Bonner. *Illustrated History and Biographical Record of Lenawee County, Mich., Containing an Accurate Epitomized History from the First Settlement in 1824 to the Present Time*. Adrian, MI: Times Printing, 1903.

Leslie, Frank. *Frank Leslie's Illustrated History of the Civil War: The Most Important Events of the Conflict Between the States....* Edited by Louis Shepheard Moat. New York: Mrs. Frank Leslie, 1895.

Lewis, Jim. "The Battle of Stones River." *Blue & Gray* 28, no. 6 (2012): 6–50.

Life of James W. Jackson: The Alexandria Hero, the Slayer of Ellsworth, the First Martyr in the Cause of Southern Independence.... Richmond: West & Johnson, 1862.

Lindsley, John Berrien, Ed. *The Military Annals of Tennessee, Confederate....* Nashville: J.M. Lindsley, 1886.

Lord, William Blair, and David Wolfe Brown. *The Debates and Proceedings of the Constitutional Convention of the State of Michigan, Convened at the City of Lansing, Wednesday, May 15th, 1867*, Vol. 1. Lansing: John A. Kerr, 1867.

Mann, Wayne C. "The Road to Murfreesboro: The Eleventh Michigan Volunteer Infantry from Organization through Its First Battle." Master's thesis, Western Michigan University, 1963.

McPherson, James M. *For Cause and Comrades: Why Men Fought in the Civil War.* New York: Oxford University Press, 1997.

Minnesota in the Civil and Indian Wars, 1861–1865, Vol. 2, 2d ed. St. Paul, MN: Pioneer, 1899.

Morton, John Watson. *The Artillery of Nathan Bedford Forrest's Cavalry.* Nashville: M.E. Church, South Smith & Lamar, 1909.

Paddock, B.B., ed. *A Twentieth Century History and Biographical Record of North and West Texas*, Vol. 1. Chicago: Lewis Publishing, 1906.

Powell, David A. *The Chickamauga Campaign: A Mad Irregular Battle: From the Crossing of the Tennessee River Through the Second Day, August 22–September 19, 1863.* El Dorado Hills, CA: Savas Beatie, 2014.

Powell, David A. *The Maps of Chickamauga: An Atlas of the Chickamauga Campaign, Including the Tullahoma Operations, June 22–September 23, 1863.* Cartography by David A. Friedrichs. New York: Savas Beatie, 2009.

Proceedings of the Eighth Annual Reunion of the Eleventh Michigan Infantry and Fourth Michigan Battery, Held at Centreville, Mich., August 24, 1875. Three Rivers, MI: W.H. Clute, [1875].

Ramage, James A. *Rebel Raider: The Life of General John Hunt Morgan.* Lexington: University Press of Kentucky, 1986.

Record of Service of Michigan Volunteers in the Civil War, 1861–1865. 46 vols. Kalamazoo: Ihling Bros. and Everard [c. 1905].

Report on the Battle of Murfreesboro,' Tenn. by Major Gen. W.S. Rosecrans, U.S.A. Washington, D.C.: Government Printing Office, 1863.

Renard, Paul D. "The Selection and Preparation of White Officers for the Command of Black Troops in the American Civil War: A Study of the 41st and 100th U.S. Colored Infantry." Ph.D. thesis, Virginia Polytechnic Institute and State University, 2006.

Robertson, John, comp. *Michigan in the War*, rev. ed. Lansing, MI: W.S. George, 1882.

Robertson, William Glenn. "The Chickamauga Campaign, McLemore's Cove: Rosecrans' Gamble, Bragg's Lost Opportunity." *Blue & Gray* (Spring 2007): 6–50.

Robertson, William Glenn. "The Chickamauga Campaign, The Battle of Chickamauga: Day 2, September 20, 1863." *Blue & Gray* (Summer 2008): 6–50.

Salling, Stuart. *Louisianians in the Western Confederacy: The Adams-Gibson Brigade in the Civil War.* Jefferson, NC: McFarland, 2010.

Savage, John. *The Life and Public Services of Andrew Johnson, Seventeenth President of the United States, Including His State Papers, Speeches and Addresses.* New York: Derby and Miller, 1866.

Shaver, Lewellyn A. *A History of the Sixtieth Alabama Regiment, Gracie's Alabama Brigade.* Montgomery, AL: Barrett & Brown, 1867.

Sherman, William Tecumseh. *Memoirs of General William T. Sherman*, Vol. 2. New York: D. Appleton, 1875.

Shively, Carol A., ed. *Asian and Pacific Islanders and the Civil War.* Fort Washington, PA: Eastern National, 2015.

Stevenson, Alexander F. *The Battle of Stone's River Near Murfreesboro,' Tenn., December 30, 1862 to January 3, 1863.* Boston: James R. Osgood, 1884.

Thornton, Leland W. *When Gallantry Was Commonplace: The History of the Michigan Eleventh Volunteer Infantry, 1861–1864.* New York: Peter Lang, 1991.

Turner, T. G. *Gazetteer of the St. Joseph Valley, Michigan and Indiana, With a View of Its Hydraulic and Business Capacities.* Chicago: Hazlett & Reed, 1867.

Vale, Joseph G. *Minty and the Cavalry: A History of Cavalry Campaigns in the Western Armies.* Harrisburg, PA: Edwin K. Meyers, 1886.

Vallandigham, James L. *A Life of Clement L. Vallandigham.* Baltimore: Turnbull Bros., 1872.

The War of the Rebellion: A Compilation of the Official Records of the Union and Confederate Armies. 128 vols. Washington, D.C.: Government Printing Office, 1880–1901.

Washington, Reginald. *M1911: Records of the Field Offices for the State of Tennessee, Bureau of Refugees, Freedmen, and Abandoned Lands, 1865–1872.* Edited by Benjamin Guterman. Washington, D.C.: United States Congress and National Archives and Records Administration, 2005.

Whitney, W.A., and R.I. Bonner. *History and Biographical Record of Lenawee County, Michigan...*, Vol. 1. Adrian, MI: W. Stearns, 1879.

Wiley, Bell Irvin. *The Life of Billy Yank: The Common Soldier of the Union.* Baton Rouge: Louisiana State University Press, 1971.

Index

Numbers in ***bold italics*** refer to pages with photographs.

Acworth, Georgia 137
Adairsville, Georgia 135
Adams, Daniel Weisiger 102–3, 107, 112–13, 115–16, 120, 152
Adams, Nathan 33, 36, 50, 53, 130
Adrian, Michigan 8, 9, 11, 13, 20, 36, 154, 162
alcohol 20, 27, 38–39, 44, 71, 87, 114, 136, 150, 153; *see also* temperance
Allatoona Pass 135
Allen, Michigan 162
Anderson, Patton 69, 71, 96
Andersonville 99, 141, 159
Andrews, Norman S. 45
Antietam 66
antiwar movement 67, 83, 86; *see also* Copperheads; Vallandigham, Clement Laird
arms 7, 21, 23, 43, 45, 107
Army of Northern Virginia 105
Army of the Ohio 61, 132
Army of the Potomac 85, 114, 130–31
Army of the Tennessee 132
Athens, Alabama 61, 147
Atlanta, Georgia 90, 135, 138, 140–42, 146, 153, 161
Atlanta Campaign 132–46, 153, 161
Autocrat 53

Bailey's Crossroads 94–95, 97, 99–100
Baird, Absalom 94–97, 99, 133, 142
Baker, John J. 140
band 25, 29, 31–33, 40, 42, 45, 50; disbanded 61
Bardstown, Kentucky 30–42, 77
Bardstown Gazette 40
Barton, Eugene 22
bayonets 2, 31, 72, 103, 107–8, 110, 120, 122, 131, 143, 145, 148
Beatty, John 88–89, 93, 96–97, 100–3, 105, 107, 111–12
Beatty, Samuel 74
Beauregard, P.G.T. 44
Belmont Furnace 41–42
Benedict, Myron 139
Bennett, Benjamin Grove 12, 19, 22–23, 27, 30, 32, 37, 40, 44–46, 57, 61, 81, 84, 90, 94, 110, 116, 119–20; death 123–24
Bennett, Daniel A. 130
Bennett, John 125
Bennett, Smetts 73
Bissell, Francis M. 123
Blair, Austin 5, 7–9, 15, 19, 20, 25, 48–49, 73
Blanchard, Spencer 136
Blissfield, Michigan 162
Bloom, John J. 91, 99–100, 111, 114, 116–17, 121, 129–32
Bobo's Crossroads 88
Boone, William P. 61
Booth, John Wilkes 30
Bordner, Benjamin 35, 38, 41, 79, 83, 118, 120, 124–25, 129–31, 134–35
bounties 12–13, 127, 161
Bowen, Ozro 30, 33, 41, 59, 62, 67, 71, 74–75, 99–100, 113, 124, 134
Bowers, Jacob 37
Bowling Green, Kentucky 40, 42, 54–55, 57, 61
Bowman farm 35
Boyle, Jeremiah T. 57
Bradley, Elmer 99
Bragg, Braxton 57, 60, 63, 66–68, 74, 76–78, 85, 87–90, 93–95, 101, 111–12, 114, 117, 119–20, 124–25, 131, 143
Bragg, Myron 79, 83, 87–88, 97, 105, 110
Bragg, Nelson Clifford 33, 36, 79
Branch County, Michigan 8, 12, 19–20, 162
Brannan, John M. 111–12
Breckinridge, John C. 74–75, 95
Bremner, David 113
Brentwood, Tennessee 66
Briggs, Thomas H. 12, 105, 129
Brockway, Oliver W. 99
Bronson, Michigan 12, 19, 162
Bronson Guards 12, 19
Brotherton Field 102
Brown, Neill S. 49–51
Brown Ferry 116
Brown's Hotel 11
Brown's Spring 93
Buchanan, James 26, 45
Buckner, Simon B. 95
Buell, Don Carlos 25, 29, 36, 40, 43–44, 53–55, 57, 59–63
Buell, Frank Wolford 59
Bull Run 8–10, 12
Burnside, Ambrose 67, 78, 116–17
Burr Oak, Michigan 12, 162
Burr Oak Guards 12
Butler, Michigan 162
Buzzard Roost Gap 133

Cairo, Illinois 29, 53
Calhoun, Alvin 35
Calhoun, Georgia 135
Calhoun, Samuel H. 39
Calhoun County, Michigan 162
Camden, Michigan 162
Cameron, Simon 7, 15
Camp May 33
Camp Morton 35, 41
Camp Stoughton 34, 41
Camp Tilden 15, 19–20
Caperton's Ferry 91
Carkenard, Leonard F. 59
Carlin, William P. 143
Carpenter, Jesse 141
carpetbaggers 154–55
Carthage, Tennessee 59
Cass County 162
Cassville, Georgia 135
casualties 57–58, 63, 114–16, 127, 129, 134–36, 141, 153, 160–63; at Chickamauga 102–3, 105,

237

107–8, 110, 112; at Davis's Crossroads 99–100; at Missionary Ridge 122–24; at Ruff's Station 139; at Stones River 67–69, 71–74, 76, 79, 89–90; at Utoy Creek 145
Cave City, Kentucky 54
Centreville, Michigan 7, 9, 13–14, 19, 27, 162
Centreville Home Guards 9
Chadwick, Samuel 2, 7, 10–11, 13, 16, 19, 30–31, 35, 38–39, 41, 43, 45–51, 61, 68, 71, 73, 76, 81
Chamberlain, Nelson 12–13, 20, 48–49, 79
Chancellorsville 85
Chandler Guards 12, 20
Charleston, South Carolina 90–91
Chattahoochee River 140
Chattanooga, Tennessee 53, 62, 90, 94, 96, 100–1, 107, 111–17, 122, 124–25, 129, 146–47, 150
Chickamauga 2, 97, 99–117, 119, 122, 124, 129–30, 139, 143, 152, 159, 161
Chickamauga and Chattanooga National Military Park 154
Childs, Lewis E. 79, 105, 116
Christiana, Tennessee 147
Christmas 33, 35, 158
Cincinnati, Ohio 84, 148
civilians 1–2, 29, 31–32, 41, 94–95, 141, 148–150; hostility toward soldiers 45, 82; mistreated by soldiers 20–21, 34, 38, 46, 58–59, 153; socializing with soldiers 38–39, 82, 130
Clarksville, Tennessee 45
Clase, David 116
Clayton, Henry 102
Cleburne, Patrick 89, 96–97
Coddington, Charles 124
Coldwater, Michigan 12, 20, 162
Coldwater Democratic Union 12
Coldwater Tigers 12, 20
Colon, Michigan 162
Columbia, Tennessee 47, 49
Confederate Memorial Hall Museum 115–16
Constantine, Michigan 7, 9, 11
Constantine Mercury 16, 20, 26, 31, 41
Copperheads 83–84, 86, 148, 150, 153; *see also* antiwar movement; Vallandigham, Clement Laird
Corinth, Mississippi 44, 53, 63
Covey, Eleazer J. 131
Cowan, Tennessee 90
Cracker Line 117
Crawfish Spring 100
Crittenden, Thomas Leonidas 64, 66, 88, 101, 105
Cumberland Gap 29
Cumberland Mountains 90
Cumberland River 45, 63
Cummings, William H. 124

Dallas, Georgia 135

Dalton, Georgia 95, 131, 135
Damon, Henry C. 141, 159
Danville, Virginia 141, 159
Davis, Billy 69, 73–74, 114
Davis, Garrett 56
Davis, Jefferson 9, 66
Davis, Jefferson C. 68, 108, 113, 117
Davis's Crossroads 2, 95–100, 102
Day, John 122
Decatur, Georgia 140
Decherd, Tennessee 89–90
Deerfield, Michigan 162
desertion 21, 34, 61, 127, 131, 135
Detroit, Michigan 13, 15, 17, 162
Detroit Free Press 17, 83
discharges 13, 21–22, 36, 63, 79, 127, 150
disease 1, 20, 26–27, 32–33, 35–39, 41–42, 48–49, 63, 79, 81, 88, 127, 129, 143, 152, 160–63; *see also* measles; pneumonia; smallpox; typhoid
Dixon, Cuthbert 82
Donelson, Daniel 72–73
Doughty, Benjamin F. 16, 61
Downey, John Florian 132–33, 135–40, 142–43, 145, 156–58
draft 83, 161
Drake, Addison T. *16*, 20, 47, 61, 114
Duck River 47
Duffield, William W. 36
Dug Gap 95–96
Duke, Basil 56
Dumont, Ebenezer 46, 51–53
Dundee, Michigan 162
Dusenberry, Seth 115

East Point, Georgia 142
Eaton, Rollin 46
Ector, Mathew 73
Edie, John R. 119, 131, 142–46
Edwards, David 99
E.H. Fairchild 45–46
18th Ohio Infantry 61, 67–68, 72, 89, 94, 97, 101–3, 107, 110, 119, 146
18th U.S. Infantry 119, 139, 142
8th Kentucky Infantry 52
8th Michigan Infantry 8–9
89th Ohio Infantry 110
Eldridge, Nathaniel B. 2, 48–49, *50*, 62, 79, 154
Elizabethtown, Kentucky 42
Elk River 89
Elliott, James T. 130
Elliott, William N. 16, *17*, 35–36, 154, 161
Ellsworth, Elmer 40
Emancipation Proclamation 67, 83
Ensign, James H. 99
Ewell, Richard S. 154
Ewing, Andrew 46
examination boards 36, 116, 129–30
executions 39, 42, 86–87, 135

Fabius, Michigan 13

Fairfield, Tennessee 88
Farragut, David Glasgow 46
Faulknor, Mathias 76
Ferguson, Jonathan 48
Ferguson, Thomas B. 125
Ferguson's Battery 2, 125
15th Kentucky Infantry 111
15th U.S. Colored Infantry 130
15th U.S. Infantry 119, 131, 142, 145–46
5th Michigan Light Artillery 63
5th Tennessee Cavalry 59
5th Tennessee Infantry 122
55th Indiana Infantry 55, 57
51st Indiana Infantry 146
1st Alabama Battalion 107
1st Kentucky Cavalry 59
1st Michigan Engineers 47, 91
1st Michigan Infantry (Civil War) 12, 36
1st Michigan Infantry (Mexican War) 7, 15
1st Michigan Light Artillery 45
1st U.S. Colored Infantry 130
Fisher, Henry S. 129
flags 7, 23, 25, 32, 45, 52, 71, 75, 85, 101, 103, 108, 110, 114–15, 118, 122, 124–25, 134, 138, 148–49, **150**
Flynn, Thomas 72
foraging 32, 38, 60, 62–63, 93, 100, 114–15
Forrest, Nathan Bedford 53, 55, 59, 66, 87, 111–12
Fort Donelson 40, 45
Fort Negley 57, 114–15, 118
Fort Riley 63
Fort Sumter 5, 9, 151
Fort Wood 118
Fort Zollicoffer 45
43rd Alabama Infantry 108, 153
14th Pennsylvania Cavalry 141
14th U.S. Colored Infantry 146
4th Corps 140
4th Indiana Light Artillery 57, 99
4th Kentucky Cavalry 52, 59
4th Michigan Infantry 8–9
4th Tennessee Infantry 122
Frankfort, Kentucky 54–55, 57
Frankish, William 115
Franklin Pike 65–66
Fredericksburg 67, 78
Freedmen's Bureau 156
French, Ephraim 36, 55
Frenchtown, Michigan 162
Frey, J.W. 23
Frost, Edward M. 57–58, 118, 123
Fry, James B. 54

Gallatin, Tennessee 2, 57–59, 61, 153
gambling 20
Garfield, James Abram 84
Georgetown, Kentucky 55
Gettysburg 90, 105, 108
Gibson, Randall L. 120, 123–24, 153
Gillaspie, Enoch 34
Gillaspie, Ira 11–13, 21, 23, 27,

29–35, 37–38, 40, 42–44, 48, 52–53, 55–56, 60, 62, 67–69, 72–76, 79, 82
Gillet, George S. 124
Glasgow, Kentucky 54
Glenn, Samuel 50–51
Goodwin, Major 14
Gordon, Lynch 22
Govan, Daniel 103, 105
Gracie, Archibald 89, 107–8, 110, 112–13, 153
Grant, Ulysses S. 40, 43–44, 67, 78, 85, 87, 90–91, 114, 116–18, 120, 122, 132
Grather, George F. 27
Graysville, Georgia 125, 130–31
Green, Oliver 55
Green River 54
Guelzo, Allen C. 1
guerrillas 47–48, 55, 57, 59, 62–63

Hackstaff, John L. 12, 20, 22–23, 26–27, 38
Haight, Christopher 37
Hale's Mill 89
Hall, Ephraim Gaylord 53, 61, 72, 82, 130, 154
Hall, Henry 44–45
Halleck, Henry H. 29, 40, 44, 53, 66, 85, 116, 132, 159
Harding, Giles 82
Harding, Mary 82
Harkness, Lindley R. 135
Hart, Benjamin F. 135
Harwood, Daniel 35–36
Hawse, Andrew 22
Haynie, J. Henry 68, 71, 107
Hazen, William 100
Heath, Lewis Wadsworth 36, 84, 154
Herrick, Sydney L. 10
Hibberlee, Samuel 34
Hicks, Borden Mills 13, 21–23, *24*, 30–31, 67–69, 73, 81, 86, 99, 102–3, 107, 110–11, 115–16, 118, 122–25, 130, 133–34, 136, 138, 140, 144–46, 156–58, 161
Hiett, Robert 108
Hill, Daniel Harvey 95–96
Hillsborough Pike 88
Hillsdale College 156
Hillsdale County 162
Hindman, Thomas C. 96–97, 99, 108
Hines, Richard M. 161
Hodgins, Thomas 136
Hoisington, William W. *21*, 27, 31, 37, 42
Holland, Isaac 21
Holly, Coe 42
Holtzclaw, James T. 143
Hood, Calvin C. 11–13, 19, 38, 53, 62, 65, 73, 79–80, 154
Hood, John Bell 140
Hooker, Joseph 85, 114, 117–18
Hoover's Gap 88
Horseshoe Ridge 105–8, *109*, 110, 112–13, 115, 141, 152–53, *155*;

see also Snodgrass Hill
hospitals 35–37, 41, 77, 79, 82, 87–88, 115–16, 125, 145
Howard, Loren 69, 72–73
Hoxie, Hiram L. 99
Hudson, Michigan 20, 162
Hudson Riflemen 20
Hull, Edwin J. 22
Huntsville, Alabama 44, 48, 147

Iddings, William Clarence 135, 154
independent units 10, 15–16
Indianapolis, Indiana 27
Invalid Corps 88, 160; *see also* Veteran Reserve Corps

Jackson, James 40
Jackson, John 40
Jackson, Michigan 162
Jackson, Mississippi 85
Jacob's Store 88
Jeffersonville, Indiana 27, 147
Jerome, Francis 52
Johnson, Andrew 49–50, *51*
Johnson, Richard W. 68, *119*, 125, 135, 142
Johnston, Albert Sidney 29
Johnston, Joseph E. 131, 134–35, 137–38, 140
Jonesborough, Georgia 146
Jubenville, Henry 48

Kalamazoo, Michigan 162
Kalamazoo County, Michigan 12, 20, 162
Keegan, Patrick H. 57, 116, 123, 127, 130–31, 135, 139–40, 144–45, 152
Kelly Field 107, 110
Kennesaw Mountain 137–38
Kershaw, Joseph B. 105, 107–8, 112–13
King, James Wood 1, 13, *14*, 15, 20–21, 23, 26–33, 37–38, 40–46, 50, 58, 62–67, 69, 73–74, 77–79, 82–91, 93–94, 97, 99–101, 111–18, 127, 129–31, 138–39, 141–42, 150–51, 154–56; Medal of Honor nomination 123; at Missionary Ridge 120–24
King, John Haskell 119, 132, 135, 140, 142–43, 145
King, W.C. 122
Kingston, Georgia 135
Knapp, Isaac 134
Kneeland, Latham 48
Knoxville, Tennessee 117
Ku Klux Klan 156

La Fayette, Georgia 94–95, 125
La Porte, Indiana 13
La Vergne, Tennessee 60, 74, 146
Ladies Aid Society of Centreville 27
The Ladies of St. Joseph County 23
Lane, Frank 135
Lansing Republican 156

Lapeer, Michigan 48–49
Lebanon, Tennessee 59
Lee, Robert E. 85, 90, 105
Lemunyon, William 134
Lenawee County, Michigan 8–9, 13, 20, 154, 162
Lenawee Lions 13, 20
Leonard, Charles 26
Leonidas, Michigan 162
Lester, Henry C. 53
Lexington, Kentucky 55–57
Liberty, Tennessee 59
Liberty Gap 88
Liddle, Byron 59, 123–24, 139
light brigade 59–60
lightning 137
Lincoln, Abraham 5, 7–8, 84–86, 114, 146, 148–50
London, Michigan 162
Longstreet, James 105, 107, 117
Lookout Mountain 93, 113, 117–18, *126*, 130
Lookout Valley 93, 100, 118
Louisville, Kentucky 25, 27, 29–30, 32, 40, 43–44, 53–54, 147–48
Louisville and Nashville Railroad 42, 57
Louisville Journal 29, 55
Lovett, James T. 99
lunar eclipse 52, 118
Lytle, William Haines 39–40, 58

Macon Iron Works 93
mail 12, 33, 53, 55, 59, 63, 79, 83, 93, 111, 115, 130, 138
Mammoth Cave 38
Manchester, Tennessee 88
Maney, George 72
Manigault, Arthur 72
Mannigold, Cassimer E. 124
Marietta, Georgia 138–39, 141
Marsh, Frederick 79
Marsh, Stephen 94, 96–97, 130, 133–37, 140–41
Martin, James 29, 35, 38, 42, 48, 54, 56, 58–59, 62, 69, 74–76, 78–79, 83, 85, 88–90, 99–100, 101–3, 108, 110, 112, 114–16, 118–20, 123–25, 131, 134–35, 142, 146
Mason, Germain 19
Masonic Society 16
Maxwell, Cicero 55–56
May, William J. 11, 13–17, 19, 25, 30–31, 34, 36, 40–43, 49, 147
McClellan, George Brinton 46, 66, 150
McComb, Addison 141
McCook, Alexander McDowell 64, 66–68, 72, 88, 90, 105
McCown, John P. 73
McFarlan, John Q.A. 161
McGee, William Henry 87
McGuire, John 48
McLemore's Cove 94, 111
McMinnville, Tennessee 52
McNair, Evander 73
McPherson, James B. 132–34, 140–41

Mead, Fay 123
measles 35, 37, 129, 163
Medal of Honor 87, 99, 108, 123
medical staff 16, 35–36, 130, 154; *see also* Elliott, William N.; Vincent, Wesley
Mendon, Michigan 162
Merrick, Alonzo H. 124
Metcalf, Irving 37–39, 45
Mexican War 7, 12, 15, 30
Michigan Southern Railroad 12, 14, 19
Military Division of the Mississippi 116
Miller, John Franklin *54*, 57–59, 64, 66, 71
Missionary Ridge 2, 105, 111, 113, 117–24, 127, 130–31, 133, 143, 153
Mitchel, Ormsby M. 44, 48, 53
Moase, Charles 12, 20
Moccasin Point 118
Monroe, Michigan 12, 20
Monroe County, Michigan 12, 20, 159, 162
monuments *105*, *125*, 154, *155*
Moore, Beriah 123
Moore, Marshall 119–20, 139
Moore's Spring 91
Morenci, Michigan 8
Morenci Guards 8–9, 20
Morgan, John Hunt *47*, 48, 51, 53–59, 61, 66, 86, 147
Mudge, Melvin B. 2, 8, 10–11, 19, 22, 49–50, 57, 61, 81, 84, 90, 94, 110, 116, 129, 139, 141–143, 145, 147–49, 154
Munfordville, Kentucky 40, 54–55
Murfreesboro, Tennessee 50–53, 55, 59, 66–67, 74, 76, 78, 81–83, 85–88, 146–48
mutiny 27, 143, 145–46, 153

Nashville, Tennessee 43–47, 50, 53–55, 57–63, 65–66, 73–74, 77, 84, 116, 119, 129, 147
Nashville and Chattanooga Railroad 89
Nashville Daily Press 86–87
Nashville Pike 73
Nashville Union 84
Negley, James Scott 47–48, *60*, 64, 66–69, 72–74, 84, 88–91, 93–97, 99–102, 105, 111–12, 119
Nelson House 50
New Haven, Kentucky 54
New Hope Church 135
New Orleans, Louisiana 46, 115
New York Herald 50–51
New York Times 50, 55
Newberry, Charles W. 58, 107, 116, 129
Newton, John 140
19th Illinois Infantry 59–62, 67–68, 71, 89, 94, 97, 102–3, 107, 113, 117, 119, 124, 133
19th Michigan Infantry 140
19th Tennessee Infantry 123
19th U.S. Infantry 119, 139, 143

9th Indiana Infantry 110
9th Michigan Infantry 36, 55, 59, 127
9th Pennsylvania Cavalry 54–55
Nolensville, Tennessee 66
Nolin River 42
Norris, Charles 36
Norton, George Henry 32, 35

Oakes, David, Jr. 9, *10*, 11, 13–14, 19, 22, 30, 32, 37–38, 49, 73–74, 79
"The Oath" 84
officer elections 9, 11–12, 16–17, 19, 22
Ohio River 44, 130
Oostanaula River 135
Orchard Knob 118, 120
Overton, John 65
Owen's Ford 100
Owen's Store 66

Palmer, John 100, 125, 142
Paris, Kentucky 56
Parker Gap 130
Parkville, Michigan 11
Pattison, Holmes A. 16, *18*, 32, 87
pay 26, 40, 61, 82, 117; *see also* bounties
Peachtree Creek 140
Peking University 156
Pendleton, George H. 2, 148–49, 153
Peninsular Guards 7–8
Penn State University 156
Pennsylvania State College 156
Perryville 63
Petersburg, Michigan 162
Phillips, William W. 13, 20, 36
Picket's Mill 135
Pierce, Lemuel Packard 114
Pikeville, Tennessee 52–53
pillaging 58, 61
Pine Mountain 137
Pioneer Brigade 64–65, 73, 79
Pixley, Thomas 136
Platt, Henry 12, 29, 32, 38–40, 54–55, 57, 89
Plumb, Preston B. 154
pneumonia 37, 163
Polk, Leonidas 69, 95, 97
pontoon bridges 47, 91, *93*
Port Hudson 90
Powers, Charles 134
Preston, William 107
prisoners of war 48, 58–59, 72, 78, 82, 89–90, 93, 99–100, 105, 114, 116, 125, 141, 146, 152, 159
prostitution 38
provost guard 39, 49, 51, 78–79, 83, 85–86
provost marshal 49, 78–79
Pulaski, Tennessee 48, 147
Purchase, Charles B. 59

Quincy, Michigan 8, 19, 162
Quincy Rifles 8; *see also* Quincy Wolverines
Quincy Wolverines 19; *see also* Quincy Rifles

Raymond, William E. 69
Read, Thomas Buchanan 84–85
Ready, Charles, Jr. 86
recruiting 2, 5–13, 26, 49, 57, 61, 81, 127, 130
reenlistment 127–29, 139, 150
regulars 14, 56, 72, 83, 87, 119–20, 131, 133, 136, 140, 143, 145; *see also* 18th U.S. Infantry; 15th U.S. Infantry; 19th U.S. Infantry; 16th U.S. Infantry
Renner, Robert 32
reunions 149–50, 156–158
Rice, Charles 32–33, 61, 77
Richardson, Perry 116
Richmond, Kentucky 56
Richmond, Virginia 46, 74, 150
Roberts, George W. 69
Robertson, John 7–10, 13, 19, 22, 49, 127
Rocky Face Ridge 133
Rogersville, Alabama 147
Rose, Daniel 38–39, 46, 48, 65–66, 73, 78, 82, 83, 91, 93, 99–100, 113–16, 121–22, 124–27, 129–32, 135–41
Rosecrans, William Starke 63, *64*, 65–69, 72–74, 78, 83–91, 93–94, 100–2, 105, 111, 113–14, 116
Rossiter, Albert C. 35–36, 123
Rossville, Georgia 111, 125, 130
Rossville Gap 111
Rousseau, Lovell 69, 72–73, 87–88, 152
Ruff's Station 139, 153
Russellville, Kentucky 57

St. Joseph County, Michigan 5, 7, 9, 11–17, 19–20, 127, 162
St. Joseph County Guards 9, 11, 19
Sand Mountain 91
Schochenbarger, William 139
Schofield, John M. 132, 140
Schoolcraft, Michigan 12, 20
Schoolcraft Rifle Rangers 12, 20
Schultz's Battery 69, 71, 101, 152
Scribner, Benjamin 96–97
2nd Alabama Battalion 107–8, *109*, 110, 153
2nd Indiana Cavalry 36, 59
2nd Kentucky Infantry 39
2nd Ohio Infantry 146
2nd Pioneer Battalion 73
Seekell family 63
Selkirk, William A. 86–87
Semple's Battery 97
Seneca, Michigan 8, 162
Sequatchie Valley 114–15
Seven Days Battles 66
7th Michigan Infantry 8, 48
7th Pennsylvania Cavalry 52
7th South Carolina Infantry 107, 115
78th Pennsylvania Infantry 93
74th Ohio Infantry 52, 63, 71
Shaver, Lewellyn A. 107
Shawneetown, Illinois 44
Shelby County Democrat 149

Shelbyville, Tennessee 78, 88–89
Shepherdsville, Kentucky 42, 54
Sheridan, Philip 68–69, 71–73, 120, 124
Sherman, Francis 120
Sherman, William Tecumseh 114, 117, 119–20, 132, **134**, 135, 137–42, 158
Shiloh 43–44, 46
Shippy, Daniel 53
Shirey, Solomon 114, 131
Shorty 31, 41–42
Sibley tents 29–30, 33, 78
Sidney, Ohio 147–50, 153
Simmons, Orrin 21
Sirwell, William 88, 93, 95–97, 99–100, 102, 105, 112
16th/25th Louisiana Infantry 103
16th U.S. Infantry 14, 55, 119, 122, 143
69th Ohio Infantry 50, 52, 57–58, 61, 67, 71, 78, 94, 101, 119, 124–25, 133, 139–40
slaughter pen 71
slaves 1–2, 13, 29, 31, 38, 46, 141
Slocomb's Battery 103
smallpox 26–27, 32–35, 39–40, 163
Smetts, Bennett 73
Smith, Green Clay 55–56
Smith, G.W. 139
Smith, Phillip 149
Smith, Sylvester B. 8, **9**, 10–11, 20, 61, 71, 79, 81, 154
Smith, William 141
Smithville, Tennessee 59
Snake Creek Gap 134
Snodgrass Hill 105, 117; *see also* Horseshoe Ridge
Snyder, Washington Irving 103, 107, 115
Spears James G. 64, 66
Spencer, Henry N. 12–13, 20, 31, 40, 42–43, 47, 50, 58
spies 135
Squire, Linus Truman *81*, 87, ***126***, 127, 130, 154, 156
Stanley, Timothy Robbins 61, 64, 66–67, 69, 71–73, 75–76, 84, 88, 90, 93–94, 96–97, 99–103, 105, 108, 112–13, 119, 152
Stanton, Edwin M. 159
Starkweather, John 96–97, 99
State Military Board 49
Stevens's Gap 93–94, 99
Stevenson, Alabama 146
Steward, Tom 2, 31–32
Stewart, Alexander P. 2, 71–72, 89, 96, 101, 153
Stewart Creek 146
Stewartsboro, Tennessee 66
Stockton, Thomas B.W. 15–16
Stockton's Independent Regiment 15–16
Stone, Charles P. 49
Stones River 1–2, 67–75, **76**, 77–79, 81–82, 102, 108, 125, 133, 143, 152, 154, 159, 161
Stoughton, William Lewis 1, 2, 7, **8**, 9–11, 16–17, 19, 23–24, 38, 43–44, 46, 48–49, 53–59, 61–63, 68–69, 71–73, 75, 78–79, 81–82, 84–86, 88–91, 94, 96, 100, 102–3, 105, 107–8, 110–13, 116, 119–25, 127, 129–30, 135–39, 149, 152–53, ***154, 155, 157***
Stovall, Marcellus 102, 143–44
Strahl, Otho P. 120, 122–24, 153
Streight, Abel D. 146, ***147***
Sturges, Aaron 33, 49–51, 53, 59, 79
Sturgis, Michigan 7, 9, 11, 13, 16, 19, 149, 162
Sturgis Journal 38, 55
Sturgis Light Guards 11, 19
Sugar Valley 134
Sutherland, William 39

target practice 33, 131
Taylor's Store 91
temperance 16, 20–21, 38; *see also* alcohol
Tennessee River 91, 147
3rd Minnesota Infantry 41, 52–53
30th Mississippi Infantry 69
35th Indiana Infantry 40
35th Ohio Infantry 110
31st Tennessee Infantry 122
37th Indiana Infantry 63
33rd New Jersey Infantry 87
33rd Tennessee Infantry 122
Thomas, George Henry ***64***, 66–67, 72, 88–91, 94–95, 99–103, 105, 107, 110, 112, 116–18, 120, 132, 135, 139–40, 152
Three Rivers, Michigan 5, 7, 9, 12–13, 20, 35, 45, 61, 63, 76, 81, 103, 115, 162
Three Rivers Bass Band 12
Three Rivers Light Guard 12–13, 20
Three Rivers Reporter 9–11, 14, 17, 19, 26–27, 35, 38–39, 41, 43, 49, 55, 62, 83, 149–50
Three Rivers Western Chronicle 11- 12, 15–17, 38, 42, 55
Three Rivers Wide Awakes 7
Tilden, Harvey 14–16, 19–20, 22
Toledo, Ohio 149
trench warfare 134–46, 153, 161
Trenton, Georgia 93
Tullahoma, Tennessee 78, 147
Tullahoma Campaign 89–90
Tunnel Hill, Georgia 133
Turchin, John Basil 61–62
Turner, Eugene 26–27
20th Corps 88
28th Kentucky Infantry 52, 57–58
21st Corps 88
21st Kentucky Infantry 52
21st Ohio Infantry 110
24th Illinois Infantry 97
24th Tennessee Infantry 123
22nd Michigan Infantry 110, 129
26th Kentucky Infantry 55
26th Tennessee Infantry 75
Twiford, Henry 22
typhoid 27, 37, 63, 79, 87, 163

underage enlistees 22, 161, 163
uniforms 13, 19–23, 25–26, 78, 138, 141, 149
Union Guard 7
Union meetings 7, 9, 11, 83–85
U.S. Colored Troops 2, 129–30, 146
U.S. Congress 8, 36, 40, 46, 51, 84, 86–87, 99, 154
University of Minnesota 156
University of Nanking 156
Utoy Creek 2, 142–46, 153

Vallandigham, Clement Laird 2, **86**, 148–49, 153; *see also* anti-war movement; Copperheads
Veteran Reserve Corps 160; *see also* Invalid Corps
Vicksburg 114
Vincent, Wesley 130

Walker, John C. 40
War Department 7, 11, 15–16, 25, 61, 87, 116
Ward, Marcus 87
Warren's Mill 91
Wartrace, Tennessee 78
Washington, D.C. 7, 10, 11, 16, 51, 61, 63–64, 66, 73, 87, 116, 156
Washtenaw County 162
Wauhatchie 117
Wayne County 162
Weaver, Adam 86
Webb, Charles 123
Weinberg, William 145
Wells, Benjamin Franklin 22, **23**, 37–38, 42, 44–46, 49, 52–53, 56, 62–63, 88, 127, 138
Wells, Marshall M. 26
Wells, Susan Melissa 37, 127
Western Michigan University 1
Whallon, James M. 103, 129
Wheeler, Joseph 67, 69, 114, 146–47
Wheeler, Milo 32
Whitaker, Walter C. 137
White, Aaron B. 23, 141
White, Edward 139
White Pigeon, Michigan 11–16, 19–22, 27, 31–32, 38–39, 43, 149, 162
White Pigeon Railroad Dining Hall 11, 14, 20
Whitney, William G. 108
Wickliffe, Charles Anderson 40
Widow Glenn house 101
Wilcox, Abner 116
Wilcox, Martin V. 130
Wilder, John T. 88
Wiles, William M. 86–87
Wilson, Joseph 67–68
Wilson, William W. 159
Wilson Pike 66
Winchester, Kentucky 56
Winchester Pike 88
Wood, Sterling A.M. 96
Wood, Thomas John 33, ***34***, 35, 39, 102, 105, 118
Woodbury, Tennessee 52, 59

www.ingramcontent.com/pod-product-compliance
Lightning Source LLC
Chambersburg PA
CBHW081551300426
44116CB00015B/2833